GAIL E. TOMPKINS

California State University, Fresno

LITERACY *for the* TWENTY-FIRST CENTURY

A Balanced Approach

**Merrill, an imprint of
Prentice Hall**
Upper Saddle River, New Jersey   *Columbus, Ohio*

Library of Congress Cataloging-in-Publication Data
Tompkins, Gail E.
    Literacy for the twenty-first century: a balanced approach / Gail
E. Tompkins
        p.   cm.
    Includes bibliographical references and index.
    ISBN 0-02-420651-2 (pbk.)
    1. Language arts (Elementary)   2. Literature—Study and teaching
(Elementary)   3. Reading (Elementary)   4. Literacy.   I. Title.
LB1576.T657   1997
372.6—dc20   96-22788
                                                                              CIP

Editor: Bradley J. Potthoff
Developmental Editor: Linda Scharp McElhiney
Production Editor: Patricia S. Kelly
Copyeditor: Jonathan Lawrence
Design Coordinator: Jill E. Bonar
Text Designer: Anne Flanagan
Cover Designer: Brian Deep
Production Manager: Patricia A. Tonneman
Director of Marketing: Kevin Flanagan
Advertising/Marketing Coordinator: Julie Shough

This book was set in ITC Galliard and Helvetica by The Clarinda Company and was printed and
bound by R.R. Donnelley & Sons Company. The cover was printed by Phoenix Color Corp.

 © 1997 by Prentice-Hall, Inc.
Simon & Schuster/A Viacom Company
Upper Saddle River, New Jersey 07458

Photo credits: All photos supplied by Gail E. Tompkins

Printed in the United States of America

10 9 8 7 6 5 4 3

ISBN: 0-02-420651-2

Prentice-Hall International (UK) Limited, *London*
Prentice-Hall of Australia Pty. Limited, *Sydney*
Prentice-Hall of Canada, Inc., *Toronto*
Prentice-Hall Hispanoamericana, S. A., *Mexico*
Prentice-Hall of India Private Limited, *New Delhi*
Prentice-Hall of Japan, Inc., *Tokyo*
Simon & Schuster Asia Pte. Ltd., *Singapore*
Editora Prentice-Hall do Brasil, Ltda., *Rio de Janeiro*

With love to my husband,

Dick

ABOUT THE AUTHOR

Gail E. Tompkins is a Professor at California State University, Fresno, in the Department of Literacy and Early Education, where she teaches courses in language arts, reading, and writing for preservice and inservice teachers. She co-directs the San Joaquin Valley Writing Project and works regularly with teachers, both by teaching model lessons in classrooms and by leading inservice workshops. Previously, Dr. Tompkins taught at Miami University in Ohio and at the University of Oklahoma, where she received the prestigious Regent's Award for Superior Teaching. She was also an elementary teacher in Virginia for eight years.

Dr. Tompkins is also the author of *Teaching Writing: Balancing Process and Product*, 2nd ed., (Merrill, 1994); co-author, with Kenneth Hoskisson, of *Language Arts: Content and Teaching Strategies*, 3rd ed., (Merrill, 1995); and co-author, with Lea McGee, of *Teaching Reading with Literature* (Merrill, 1993). She has written numerous articles related to language arts that have appeared in *Language Arts, The Reading Teacher, Journal of Reading*, and other professional journals.

PREFACE

FACING THE CHALLENGE: How do today's teachers chart a course to create competent, literate citizens for tomorrow?

Helping children become literate is one of the greatest challenges facing teachers today. Literacy has become a controversial topic, and one that can be confusing for students, parents, and teachers as some teachers and researchers jump on the bandwagon touting and defending one approach after another. Parents are frightened that the new instructional methods aren't getting the job done, and the news media have fueled the controversy with reports lamenting falling test scores and criticizing schools for failing to produce literate citizens who can function competently today and in the twenty-first century. I have written this textbook to blaze a pathway toward implementing a thoughtful, balanced approach to teaching reading and writing—a pathway that incorporates the best of both traditional and holistic practices.

Literacy for the Twenty-First Century: A Balanced Approach presents several sound, research-based approaches to literacy instruction and incorporates the teaching of both skills and strategies within a literature-based reading perspective. This comprehensive textbook is both reader-friendly and practical in that it includes many descriptions of how *real* teachers teach reading and writing effectively every day. The text has been designed with preservice teachers in mind, and it can be used as the core text in traditional introductions to reading methods courses as well as in the newer literacy "block" courses.

THE PURPOSE OF THIS TEXTBOOK

My goal in this text is to show beginning teachers how to teach reading and writing effectively, how to create a classroom climate where literacy flourishes, and how to empower the diverse array of students in today's classrooms to function competently as literate adults in the twenty-first century. To that end, I have based the text on four contemporary theories of literacy learning—namely, constructivist, interactive, sociolinguistic, and reader response theories.

Readers will learn how to implement a literature-based reading program with skills and strategies taught in context using a whole-part-whole organizational approach. The approach I take can, I believe, best be described as "balanced." Literature provides the major focus for reading instruction and for integrating the language arts. You will learn how to teach vital skills and useful strategies within the context of authentic reading and writing experiences.

I have carefully selected the principles, skills, strategies, and examples of literature that will empower the beginning teacher to get "up and running" quickly. In creating this textbook, I used knowledge I gleaned from a host of teachers who have been students in my beginning reading course over the years, and I also sifted through the array of practices and procedures proven effective in today's classrooms with today's diverse student populations. Although there are many other useful ideas and strategies that can accomplish the goal of producing literate students, I have deliberately and painstakingly chosen research-based, classroom-tested ideas—"the best of the best"—as the focus of this textbook.

It is widely recognized that today's teachers need as many approaches and strategies in their repertoire as possible. However, I have carefully culled out a critical path for *beginning* teachers to follow. Why? Because it is important for beginning teachers of reading and writing to learn a few things well at the outset so that they are prepared to "hit the ground running" as they confidently implement effective methods. If you know how to be effective from the first day, you will have the confidence necessary to add to your "bag of tricks" as your experience guides you.

So, could it be argued that there are many more principles for effective teaching of reading and writing than the ten I outline in Chapter 1? Sure. But I am certain that the ten principles I present there will be memorable, useful, helpful, and effective. Does this textbook cover every permutation of every practice option? No. But I am sure that the thirty-six procedures outlined in detail in the Compendium at the back of the text constitute a memorable, useful, helpful, and effective critical mass of practice options upon which you can build.

This textbook is neither an encyclopedia of reading methods nor a comprehensive history of reading. Rather, it is intended as a practical application of knowledge obtained from these encyclopedias and histories, and more importantly, from the experiences of hundreds of teachers across the country. Not only is the focus on practical application the reason professors will *adopt* this book, but that focus is also the reason beginning teachers will *keep* this book.

HOW THE TEXTBOOK IS ORGANIZED

The book is organized into three sections. The two chapters in the first section address the question "What is literacy?" Chapter 1 sets out ten basic instructional principles on which to build balanced literacy instruction. These ten principles describe how effective teachers teach reading and writing. The second chapter explains how teachers create a community of learners in their classrooms and stresses the importance of building and maintaining an active partnership among students, teachers, and parents.

The second section examines the question "How do readers and writers construct meaning?" Chapters 3 through 6 focus on teaching the basic components of reading and writing: graphophonics, skills and strategies, word identification, vocabulary, and the structure of text.

Answering the question "How do teachers organize literacy instruction?" is the focus of the six chapters in the third section of the book. Chapter 7 presents the reading and writing processes and provides the foundation for the chapters that follow. Chapters on literature focus units, reading and writing workshop, and across-the-curriculum themes show teachers how to set up their instructional programs based on the processes described in Chapter 7. Chapter 10 is devoted to the special needs of emergent readers and writers (kindergartners and first graders), and the final chapter describes both traditional and authentic assessment procedures.

SPECIAL FEATURES

I have included nine special features to increase the effectiveness of the text and to address the most current resources in the field of literacy.

Principles of Effective Reading Instruction

I set out a list of ten principles of effective reading instruction in Chapter 1, and these principles provide the foundation for the entire textbook. Near the end of each chapter (except Chapter 1), the Review section includes a figure in which I contrast effective and ineffective instructional practices related to the chapter topic. Instructors and students alike will find these figures very interesting.

Vignettes

Starting with Chapter 2, I begin each chapter with a vignette in which you will see how a real teacher teaches the topic addressed in the chapter. These vignettes are rich and detailed, with chapter-opener photos, dialogue, student writing samples, and illustrations. Readers will be drawn into the story of literacy instruction in a real classroom as they build background and activate prior knowledge about the chapter's topic. Throughout the chapter and in some activities, I refer readers back to the vignette so that they can apply the concepts they are reading about and make connections to the world of practice.

Technology Links

Readers will learn about innovative uses of technology in teaching reading and writing through the Technology Links. Among the topics I present in these special features are screen reading using captioned text on television, electronic dialoguing to write back and forth to a reading buddy, videotape portfolios, and interactive electronic books on CD-ROM.

Chapter on "Breaking the Code"

Chapter 3 focuses on the phonological system: phonemic awareness, phonics instruction, and invented spelling. Phonics is a controversial topic in reading, and the position I take in this chapter is that phonics and related topics are part of a complete literacy program and are best taught in the context of real literature using a whole-part-whole approach.

Chapter on Skills and Strategies

In Chapter 4 I explain the difference between skills and strategies and set out twelve strategies that readers and writers use. In this chapter I recommend minilessons as the best way to teach skills and strategies. To emphasize the importance of helping children become strategic readers and writers, I compare more capable readers with less capable readers and writers and conclude that more capable students have both more skills and more strategies, but what really separates the two groups is that more capable readers and writers are more strategic.

Chapter on the Reading and Writing Processes

In Chapter 7 I describe the reading and writing processes. These two processes provide the foundation for the chapters on how to organize the instructional programs—literature focus units (Chapter 8), reading and writing workshop (Chapter 9), and theme studies (Chapter 11)—that follow.

Chapter on Literature Focus Units

In Chapter 8 I focus on how to develop literature focus units—reading units that focus on one piece of literature, with integrated listening, talking, and writing components—whether the featured selection is a trade book or a selection from a basal reader. I describe the steps in developing a unit, and I've included a number of sample units with lesson plans.

Chapter on Reading and Writing Workshop

Chapter 9 shows how to set up a workshop program in an elementary or middle-school classroom. I present the components of both reading and writing workshop and explain the guidelines for putting the programs into practice. Book clubs (also called literature study groups) are also explained.

Compendium of Instructional Procedures

For your ready reference, the Compendium at the back of the book provides a comprehensive review of thirty-six instructional procedures used in literature-based reading classrooms, with step-by-step directions and student samples. These procedures are highlighted when they are mentioned in the text to cue readers to consult the Compendium for more detailed information.

ACKNOWLEDGMENTS

Many people helped and encouraged me during the development of this text. My heartfelt thanks goes to each of them. First, I want to thank my students at California State University, Fresno, who taught me as I taught them, and the teacher-consultants in the San Joaquin Valley Writing Project, who shared their expertise with me. Their insightful questions challenged and broadened my thinking.

Thanks, too, go to the teachers who welcomed me into their classrooms, showed me how they used literature in innovative ways, and allowed me to learn from them and their students. In particular, I want to express my appreciation to the teachers and students who appear in the vignettes: Jessica Bradshaw, Rocky Hill Elementary School, Exeter, CA; Roberta Dillon, Armona Elementary School, Armona, CA; Whitney Donnelly, Williams Ranch School, Penn Valley, CA; Laurie Goodman, Parkview Middle School, Armona, CA; Judy Hoddy, Hennessey School, Grass Valley, CA; Sally Mast, Thomas Elementary School, Fresno, CA; Jill Peterson, Mickey Cox

Elementary School, Clovis, CA; Judy Roberts, Lincoln Elementary School, Madera, CA; and Camilla Simmons, Charles Wright School, Merced, CA. Sonja Wiens, Leavenworth Elementary School, Fresno, CA; Lisa Coronado and Wendy Magill, Lincoln Elementary School, Madera, CA; Bob Dickinson, Williams Ranch School, Penn Valley, CA; Judith Salzberg and Mr. Lee, Charles Wright School, Merced, CA; and Kim Ransdell, Armona Elementary School, Armona, CA, and their students also appeared in photos in the book. I also want to acknowledge Jenny Reno and the teachers and students at Western Hills Elementary School, Lawton, OK, and Carol Ochs, Jackson Elementary School, Norman, OK, who have been a part of each of the books I have written.

Finally, I am indebted to Jeff Johnston and his team at Merrill/Prentice Hall in Columbus, Ohio, who produce so many high-quality publications. I am honored to be a Merrill author. Linda Scharp McElhiney continues to be the guiding force behind my work. I want to express my appreciation to Patty Kelly, who supervised the production of this book, and to Jonathan Lawrence, who has again dealt so expertly with production details and copyediting.

BRIEF CONTENTS

CONTENTS

ROSie is home saf.

4 *Developing Strategic Readers and Writers* 124

5 *Identifying and Understanding Words* 158

PART III
How Do Teachers Organize for Literacy Instruction?   240

PART IV
Compendium of Instructional Procedures   470

SPECIAL FEATURES

Technology Link

How Effective Teachers . . .

PART I
What Is Literacy?

Mrs. Hoddy collects a text set of books related to *Rosie's Walk* to use in this literature focus unit.

Students take turns dramatizing the story using puppets and other props. Through drama, first graders internalize the structure of the story.

watch out for the fox!

Mrs. Hoddy's first graders listen as their teacher reads aloud Pat Hutchins's *Rosie's Walk*; students follow along in their own copies as she reads.

Rosie's Walk

Students use story boards to retell the story and sequence the events.

Debra and Caitlin reread the story together. Rereading provides valuable reading practice, and students model reading strategies for each other.

A fox is a mamle. It has red fer.

Mark writes an "All About Foxes" book with a fact on each page.

Mrs. Hoddy reads a book about foxes and helps students find answers to their questions about this animal. Later Mrs. Hoddy writes facts that students dictate on sentence strips. Students read the sentence strips and examine words in each sentence.

ROSie is home saf.

CHAPTER 1

Becoming an Effective Teacher of Reading

*T*he children of the twenty-first century will face many challenges that will require them to use reading and writing in different forms, and as the millennium approaches, teachers are learning new ways to teach reading and writing that will prepare their students for the future. Teachers *can* make a difference in children's lives, and this book is designed to help you become an effective reading teacher. Researchers have examined many teaching practices and have drawn some important conclusions about the most effective ones. We must teach students the processes of reading and writing, as well as how to use reading and writing as learning tools. Bill Teale (1995) challenges us to teach students to think with and through reading and writing, to use reading and writing to get a wide variety of things done in their lives, and to use reading and writing for pleasure and insight.

Let's start with some definitions. "Literacy" used to mean knowing how to read, but the term has been broadened to encompass both reading and writing, so that literacy now means the competence "to carry out the complex tasks using reading and writing related to the world of work and to life outside the school" (*Cases in Literacy,* 1989, p. 36). Educators are also identifying other literacies that they believe will be needed in the twenty-first century. Our reliance on radio and television for conveying ideas has awakened us to the importance of "oracy," the ability to express and understand spoken language. Visual literacy, the ability to create meaning from illustrations, is also receiving a great deal of attention.

The term "literacy" is being used in other ways as well. Teachers are introducing even very young children to computers and developing their "computer literacy." Similarly, math and science educators speak of mathematical and scientific literacies. Hirsch (1987) called for another type of literacy, "cultural literacy," as a way to introduce children "to the major ideas and ideals from past cultures that have defined and shaped today's society" (p. 10). Literacy, however, is not a prescription of certain books to read or concepts to define. Rather, literacy is a tool, a way to come to learn about the world and a means to participate more fully in society.

Both reading and writing are processes of constructing meaning. Sometimes children describe reading as "saying all the words right," or writing as "making all your letters neatly," but when they do they are focusing only on the surface features of reading and writing. In actuality, readers create meaning for the words in the book based on their own knowledge and experiences. Similarly, writers take ideas and organize them using their knowledge of spelling and grammar to transcribe their ideas onto paper or computer screens. Phonics, decoding, and reading aloud are all part of reading, but the essence of reading is the creation of meaning. By the same token, spelling, handwriting, and using capital letters correctly are parts of writing, but without important ideas to communicate, neat handwriting isn't very important.

In this chapter, I introduce the ten principles of a balanced reading program. Each principle is stated in terms of what an effective reading teacher does. Ernest Boyer, in his book *The Basic School* (1995), explains that we really *do* know what works in elementary schools. From the research that has been conducted in the last 25 years and the effective practices used in good schools today, we can identify the characteristics of a quality literacy program and incorporate them in our own teaching. As you read, think about these questions:

■ What is an effective teacher of reading?

■ Which instructional practices are most effective for teaching reading and writing?

1. Effective Teachers of Reading Create a Community of Learners in Their Classrooms

Literature-based reading classrooms are social settings in which students read, discuss, and write about literature. Together, students and their teachers create the classroom community, and the type of community they create strongly influences students' learning. Effective teachers of reading establish a community of learners in which students are motivated to learn and are actively involved in reading and writing activities. Teachers and students work collaboratively and purposefully. Perhaps the most striking quality of classroom communities is the partnership that the teacher and students create. Students are a "family" in which all the members respect one another and support each other's learning. Students value culturally and linguistically diverse classmates and recognize that all students can make important contributions to the classroom (Wells & Chang-Wells, 1992).

Students and the teacher work together for the common good of the community. Consider the differences between renting and owning a home. In a classroom community, students and the teacher are joint owners of the classroom. Students assume responsibility for their own learning and behavior, work collaboratively with classmates, complete assignments, and care for the classroom. In contrast, in traditional classrooms, the classroom is the teacher's and students are simply renters for the school year. This doesn't mean that, in a classroom community, teachers abdicate their responsibility to the students. Teachers retain all of their roles as guide, instructor, monitor, coach, mentor, and grader. Sometimes these roles are shared with students, but the ultimate responsibility remains with the teacher.

Classroom communities have certain characteristics that are conducive to learning and which support students' interactions with literature. Ten of the characteristics are:

1. **Responsibility.** Students are responsible for their learning, their behavior, and the contributions they make in the classroom. They see themselves as valued and contributing members of the classroom community.

2. **Opportunities.** Students have opportunities to read and write for genuine and meaningful purposes. They read real books and write for real audiences—their classmates, their parents and grandparents, members of their community. They rarely use workbooks or drill-and-practice sheets.

3. **Engagement.** Students are motivated to learn and to be actively involved in reading and writing activities. In a student-centered classroom, the literacy activities are interesting, and students sometimes choose which books to read, how they will respond to a book, and which reading and writing projects they will pursue.

4. **Demonstration.** Teachers provide demonstrations of reading and writing skills and strategies, and students observe and take part in the demonstrations in order to learn what more capable readers and writers do.

5. **Risk-taking.** Students are encouraged to explore topics, make guesses, and take risks. Rather than having students focus on correct answers, teachers promote students' experimentation with new skills and strategies.

6. **Instruction.** Teachers are expert readers and writers, and they provide instruction through **minilessons** (see the Compendium for more information about this and all other highlighted terms in this chapter) on procedures, skills, and

strategies related to reading and writing. These minilessons are planned and taught to small groups, the whole class, or individual students so that students can apply what they are learning in meaningful reading and writing projects.

7. *Response.* Students have opportunities to respond after reading and to share their interpretations of stories. Through writing in **reading logs** and participating in **grand conversations,** students share personal connections to the story, make predictions, ask questions, and deepen their comprehension. When they write, students share their rough drafts in **writing groups** to get feedback on how well they are communicating, and they celebrate their published books by sharing them with classmates and other "real" audiences.

8. *Choice.* Students often make choices about the books they read and the writing they do. They also choose what projects to create after reading a book. Students make choices within the parameters set by the teacher. When they are given the opportunity to make choices, students are often more highly motivated to do the reading or writing, and they value their learning experience more. It is more meaningful to them.

9. *Time.* Students need large chunks of time to pursue reading and writing activities. It doesn't work well for teachers to break the classroom schedule into many small time blocks. Students need two to three hours of uninterrupted time each day for reading and writing instruction. It is important to minimize disruptions during the time set aside for literacy instruction, and administrators should schedule computer, music, art, and other pull-out programs so that they do not interfere. This is especially important in the primary grades.

10. *Assessment.* Teachers and students work together to establish guidelines for assessment, and students monitor their own work and participate in the evaluation. Rather than imposing assessment on students, teachers share with their students the responsibility for monitoring and evaluating their progress.

These ten characteristics are reviewed in Figure 1–1.

Susan Hepler (1991) writes that "the real challenge to teachers . . . is to set up the kind of classroom community where children pick their own ways to literacy and continue to learn to read" (p. 179). Frank Smith (1988) calls these classrooms "literacy clubs" in which all students feel a sense of acceptance and belonging and no one is left out because he or she doesn't read as well as the others. All students are welcome and treated with respect, and teachers expect excellence. Students read literature and make choices about books they will read and the activities they will engage in, and from these experiences they become responsible, independent learners (Calkins, 1994; Hansen, 1987). Donald Graves (1994) identifies similar characteristics for writing classrooms. He says that students need opportunities, demonstrations, choice, time, and engagement.

The classroom community also extends beyond the walls of the classroom to include the entire school and the wider community. Within the school, students become buddies with students in other classes and get together to read and write in pairs (Morrice & Simmons, 1991). When parents and other community members come into the school, they demonstrate the value they place on education by working as tutors and aides, sharing their cultures, and demonstrating other types of expertise. A parent who writes for the local newspaper might help students start their own school newspaper, or a parent who is an artist might demonstrate artistic techniques that students can use in illustrations they add to books they are writing.

FIGURE 1–1   Characteristics of a Community of Learners

Characteristic	Student's Role	Teacher's Role
Responsibility	Students are responsible for their full participation in the classroom. They are responsible for completing assignments and other tasks, for participating in groups, and for cooperating with classmates.	Teachers set guidelines and have the expectation that students will be responsible. Teachers also model responsible behavior.
Opportunities	Students take advantage of learning opportunities provided in class. They read independently during reading workshop, and they share their writing during sharing time.	Teachers provide opportunities for students to read and write in genuine and meaningful activities, not contrived practice activities.
Engagement	Students are actively involved in reading and writing activities. They are motivated and industrious because they are reading real literature and are involved in activities they find meaningful.	Teachers make it possible for students to be engaged by the literature and activities they provide for students. Also, by planning units with students and allowing them to make choices, students are more motivated to complete assignments.
Demonstration	Students observe teacher's demonstrations of skills and strategies that readers and writers use.	Teachers provide demonstrations of what readers and writers do. They also use think-alouds to explain what they are thinking during the demonstrations.
Risk-taking	Students explore what they are learning, take risks as they ask questions, and make guesses. They expect not to be laughed at or made fun of. They view learning as a process of exploration.	Teachers encourage students to take risks, make guesses, and explore their thinking. They deemphasize students' need to get things "right."
Instruction	Students look to the teacher to provide instruction on procedures, concepts, strategies, and skills related to reading and writing. Students participate in minilessons and then apply what they have learned in their own reading and writing.	Teachers provide instruction through minilessons. During minilessons, teachers provide information and make connections to the reading and writing in which students are involved. Some instruction takes place with the whole class and other with small groups and individual students.
Response	Students respond to books they are reading by writing in reading logs and participating in grand conversations. They share their writing in writing groups and get feedback from classmates. They also share projects they have completed.	Teachers provide opportunities for students to share and respond to reading and activities. Students are a supportive audience for classmates.
Choice	Students make choices about some books they read, some writing activities, and some projects they develop. Students make choices within parameters set by the teacher.	Teachers encourage students to choose some of the books they read and some of the writing activities and projects they develop. Teachers also allow students to participate in making other decisions about classroom life.

FIGURE 1–1   *continued*

Characteristic	Student's Role	Teacher's Role
Time	Students have large chunks of time for reading and writing activities. They also work on projects over days and weeks. They have an understanding of deadlines and when assignments are due.	Teachers organize the class schedule so that students have large chunks of time for reading and writing activities. Teachers plan units with students, and together they set deadlines for reading and writing projects.
Assessment	Students understand how they will be assessed and graded, and they participate in their assessment. They collect their work in progress in folders and choose which work they will place in portfolios.	Teachers involve students in assessment and set grading plans with students before beginning each unit. Teachers meet with students in assessment conferences and assist students in collecting work to place in their portfolios.

Children go out into the community to conduct research, to experience firsthand what they are learning about in social studies and science, and to learn about their communities (Graves, 1995). For example, after reading *Number the Stars* (Lowry, 1989), a story about the Holocaust, fifth graders interview older members of the community about their memories of World War II. Or, second graders visit their pen pals at the local senior citizen center. Students apply what they are learning about reading and writing through each of these projects.

As you begin teaching, you will want to continue to learn about reading and writing instruction and ways to become a more effective teacher. Through professional organizations, you can stay abreast of the newest research and ways to implement the research in your classroom. Two organizations dedicated to improving literacy instruction are the International Reading Association (IRA) and the National Council of Teachers of English (NCTE). Both organizations publish journals for classroom teachers, and both also organize yearly conferences that are held in major cities around the United States. In addition, these organizations have state and local affiliate groups that you can join. Through these local groups, you can meet other teachers with similar interests and concerns and form support networks.

In addition, teachers learn more about teaching writing by participating in workshops sponsored by the National Writing Project (NWP). More than 20 years ago, the NWP began at the University of California at Berkeley, and it has spread to more than 150 sites located in almost every state. For example, the Gateway Writing Project serves the St. Louis area, the Capital Writing Project serves the Washington, DC, area, and the Oklahoma Writing Project serves the state of Oklahoma. You may be able to attend inservice workshops that are scheduled in school districts near each affiliate group. After you have a few years' teaching experience, you might be interested in applying to participate in a special summer institute. Figure 1–2 provides information about ways to continue learning about teaching reading and writing.

2. *Effective Teachers of Reading Use Instructional Approaches Based on How Children Learn*

Understanding how children learn, and particularly how they learn to read, influences the instructional approaches that effective teachers use. A generation ago,

FIGURE 1–2 Ways to Learn More About Teaching Reading and Writing

- Join these literacy organizations:

International Reading
   Association (IRA)
800 Barksdale Road
P.O. Box 8139
Newark, DE 19711

National Council of
   Teachers of English (NCTE)
1111 Kenyon Road
Urbana, IL 61801

- Attend conferences sponsored by local professional organizations, IRA and NCTE affiliate groups, and national organizations.
- Subscribe to one or more of these journals and magazines about reading, children's literature, and writing:

Book Links
P.O. Box 1347
Elmhurst, IL 60126

CBC Features
Children's Book Council, Inc.
350 Scotland Rd.
Orange, NJ 07050

The Horn Book
Park Square Building
31 Saint James Avenue
Boston, MA 02116

*Journal of Adolescent and
   Adult Literacy*
International Reading
   Association
800 Barksdale Road
P.O. Box 8139
Newark, DE 19711

Language Arts
National Council of Teachers
   of English
1111 Kenyon Road
Urbana, IL 61801

The New Advocate
480 Washington Street
Norwood, MA 02062

Primary Voices K–6
National Council of Teachers
   of English
1111 Kenyon Road
Urbana, IL 61801

The Reading Teacher
International Reading
   Association
800 Barksdale Road
P.O. Box 8139
Newark, DE 19711

Teaching K–8
P.O. Box 54808
Boulder, CO 80322

Voices From the Middle
National Council of Teachers
   of English
1111 Kenyon Road
Urbana, IL 61801

Writing Teacher
P.O. Box 791437
San Antonio, TX 78279

- Attend staff development programs offered by your school district or regional educational agencies on topics related to reading and writing.
- Visit local children's bookstores and libraries to preview newly published children's books and meet children's authors when they visit.
- Attend writing workshops sponsored by the local affiliate of the National Writing Project (NWP) or apply to participate in a summer invitational institute. To learn the location of the NWP affiliate group nearest you, contact the National Writing Project, School of Education, University of California, Berkeley, CA 94720.

behaviorists influenced how teachers taught reading. According to behavioral theory, students learn to read by learning a series of discrete, sequenced skills (Skinner, 1968). Students were grouped according to reading development, often into three reading groups. Teachers introduced vocabulary words, and students practiced them by reading flash cards. The textbooks students used contained simplistic stories written to rehearse newly introduced vocabulary words, phonetic principles, and other skills. Students often took turns reading aloud in round-robin fashion, and teachers corrected words students did not pronounce correctly. Teachers drilled students on skills, and students practiced skills by completing worksheets.

Reading instruction has changed considerably in the past 25 years, thanks to four intertwining theories of learning, language, and literacy. These theories are called the constructivist, interactive, sociolinguistic, and reader response theories. They are overviewed in Figure 1–3. In the figure, the theories are drawn as though they were parts of a jigsaw puzzle in order to show how they are linked. First are the constructivist learning theories. Piaget's (1969) theoretical framework differed substantially from behaviorist theories. Piaget described learning as the modification of students' cognitive structures, or schemata, as they interact with and adapt to their environ-

FIGURE 1–3   Overview of the Four Learning Theories

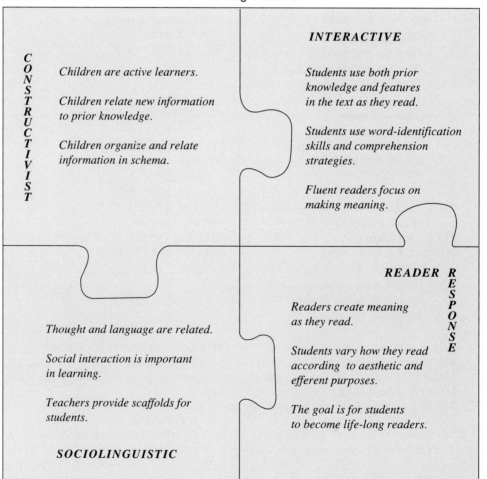

ment. Schemata are like mental filing cabinets, and new information is organized with prior knowledge in the filing system. Piaget also posited that children are active and motivated thinkers and learners. This definition of learning and children's role in learning requires a reexamination of the teacher's role. Instead of being dispensers of knowledge, teachers engage students with experiences so that they modify their schemata and construct their own knowledge. The key concepts are:

■ Children are active learners.
■ Children relate new information to prior knowledge.
■ Children organize and integrate information in schemata.

Next, the interactive theories describe what readers do as they read. These theories emphasize that readers focus on comprehension, or making meaning, as they read (Rumelhart, 1977; Stanovich, 1980). Readers construct meaning using a combination of information from the text and their backgrounds of knowledge, or schemata. These theories echo the importance of schemata described in the constructivist theories. In the past educators have argued whether children's attention during reading moves from noticing the letters on the page and grouping them into words to making meaning in the brain, or the other way around, from activating background knowledge in the brain to examining letters and words on the page. Now, educators agree that the two processes take place interactively, at the same time.

The interactive model of reading includes an executive function, or decision maker. Fluent readers identify words automatically and use word-identification skills when they come across unfamiliar words so that they can focus their attention on comprehension. The decision maker monitors the reading process and the skills and strategies that readers use. Teachers focus on reading as a comprehension process and teach word-identification skills and comprehension strategies. The key concepts are:

■ Students use both their prior knowledge and features in the text as they read.
■ Students use word-identification skills and comprehension strategies to understand what they read.
■ Teachers help students become fluent readers.

Third, the sociolinguists contribute a cultural dimension to our consideration of how children learn. They view reading and writing as social activities that reflect the culture and community in which students live (Heath, 1983; Vygotsky, 1978, 1986). According to Vygotsky, language helps to organize thought, and children use language to learn as well as to communicate and share experiences with others. Understanding that children use language for social purposes allows teachers to plan instructional activities that incorporate a social component, such as having students talk about books they are reading or share their writing with classmates. And, because children's language and concepts of literacy reflect their cultures and home communities, teachers must respect students' language and appreciate cultural differences in their attitudes toward learning and becoming literate.

Social interaction enhances learning in two other ways: scaffolding and the zone of proximal development. Scaffolding is a support mechanism that teachers and parents use to assist students. Vygotsky suggests that children can accomplish more difficult things in collaboration with adults than they can on their own. For example, when teachers assist students to read a book they could not read independently or help students revise a piece of writing, they are scaffolding. Vygotsky also suggests that children learn very little when they perform tasks that they can already do independently. He recommends the zone of proximal development, the range of tasks between students' actual developmental level and their potential development. More challenging tasks done with the teacher's scaffolding are more conducive to learning. As students learn, teachers gradually withdraw their support so that eventually students perform the task independently. Then the cycle begins again. Key concepts are:

- Thought and language are interrelated.
- Social interaction is important in learning.
- Teachers provide scaffolds for students.
- Teachers plan instruction based on students' zone of proximal development.

Fourth, reader response theories consider how students create meaning as they read (Rosenblatt, 1978, 1983). These theories extend the constructivist theories about schemata and making meaning in the brain, not the eyes. According to reader response theorists, students do not try to figure out the author's meaning as they read. Instead, they negotiate or create a meaning that makes sense based on the words they are reading and their own background knowledge. Reader response theorists agree with Piaget that readers are active and responsible for their learning.

Louise Rosenblatt (1991) explains that there are two stances or purposes for reading. When readers read for enjoyment or pleasure, they assume an aesthetic stance, and when they read to locate and remember information, they read efferently. Rosenblatt suggests that these two stances represent the ends of a continuum and that readers often use a combination of the two stances when they read, whether they are reading stories or informational books. For example, when students read *A Penguin Year* (Bonners, 1981), an informational book about the life cycle of penguins, they may read efferently to locate information about penguin chick "kindergartens." Or they may read aesthetically, carried off—in their minds, at least—on a expedition to Antarctica. When students read a novel such as *Sarah, Plain and Tall* (MacLachlan, 1983), a story about a mail-order bride, they usually read aesthetically as they relive life on the prairie nearly a century ago. Students are encouraged to step into the story and become a character and to "live" the story. This conflicts with more traditional approaches in which teachers ask students to recall specific information from the story, thus forcing students to read efferently, to take away information. Reader response theory suggests that when students read efferently rather than aesthetically, they do not learn to love reading and they do not become lifelong readers. Key concepts are:

- Readers create meaning as they read.
- Students vary how they read depending on whether they are reading for aesthetic or efferent purposes.
- The goal of literacy instruction is for students to become lifelong readers.

Effective teachers put literature at the center of their instructional programs and use components of two instructional approaches for their literature-based reading programs: literature focus units and reading and writing workshop. The literature focus unit approach involves all students in the class or small heterogeneous groups of students reading and responding to the same book. In reading workshop, students choose what book they will read and then read independently; in writing workshop, students choose their own topics for writing and move through the writing process at their own speed as they write and publish books. These two approaches are used at all grade levels, from kindergarten through eighth grade. Effective teachers use a combination of these approaches. Some teachers alternate literature focus units with reading and writing workshop, while others use some components from each approach throughout the school year. Figure 1–4 presents an overview of literature focus units and reading and writing workshop.

FIGURE 1–4   Two Instructional Approaches

Features	Literature Focus Units	Reading and Writing Workshop
Description	Teacher and students read and respond to one text together as a class or in small groups. Teachers choose texts that are high-quality literature, either trade books or from a basal reader textbook. After reading, students explore the text and extend their reading by creating projects.	Students choose books and read and respond to them independently during reading workshop and write books on self-selected topics during writing workshop. Teachers monitor students' work through conferences. Students share the books they read and the books they write with classmates during a sharing period.
Variations	Author and illustrator units focus on books written by an author or illustrated by an illustrator. Students learn about the person's life and sometimes write letters to the author/illustrator. In genre units students read several books in the same genre (e.g., folktales) and learn about the genre.	In book clubs, students choose one of five or six books to read and respond to in a small group. Students may use writing workshop to write stories, reports, or other compositions as part of theme studies.
Strengths	Teachers develop units using the reading process. Teachers can select picture books or chapter books or use textbooks for units. Teachers guide reading instruction as they read with the whole class or small groups. Teachers teach minilessons on reading skills and strategies. Students explore vocabulary and literary language. Students develop projects to extend their reading.	Students read books appropriate for their reading levels. Students are more strongly motivated because they choose the books they read. Students work through the stages of the writing process during writing workshop. Teachers teach minilessons on reading skills and strategies. Activities are student-directed and students work at their own pace. Teachers have opportunities to work individually with students during conferences.
Drawbacks	Students all read the same book whether they like it or not or whether it is at their reading level or not. Many of the activities are teacher-directed.	Teachers often feel a loss of control since students are reading different books and working at different stages of the writing process. Students must learn to be task-oriented and use time wisely in order to be successful.

3.   *Effective Teachers of Reading Support Students' Use of the Four Cueing Systems*

Language is a complex system for creating meaning through socially shared conventions (Halliday, 1978). English, like other languages, involves four cueing systems:

- the phonological or sound system
- the syntactic or structural system
- the semantic or meaning system
- the pragmatic or social and cultural use system

Together these four systems make communication possible, and children and adults use all four systems simultaneously as they read, write, listen, and talk. Information about the four cueing systems is summarized in Figure 1–5.

The Phonological System

There are approximately 44 speech sounds in English. Students learn to pronounce these sounds as they learn to talk, and they learn to associate the sounds with letters as they learn to read and write. Sounds are called phonemes, and they are represented in print with diagonal lines to differentiate them from graphemes (letter or letter combinations). Thus, the first letter in *mother* is written *m,* while the phoneme is written /m/. The phoneme in *soap* that is represented by the graphemes *oa* is called long *o* and written /ō/.

The phonological system is important for both oral and written language. Regional and cultural differences exist in the way people pronounce phonemes. For example, Jimmy Carter's speech is characteristic of the southeastern United States, while John F. Kennedy's is typical of New England. Similarly, the English spoken in Australia is different from American English. Children who are learning English as a second language must learn to pronounce English sounds, and sounds that are different from those in their native language are particularly difficult for students to learn. For example, Spanish does not have /th/, and children who have immigrated to the United States from Mexico and other Spanish-speaking countries have difficulty pronouncing this sound. They often substitute /d/ for /th/ because both sounds are articulated in similar ways (Nathenson-Mejia, 1989). Younger children usually learn to pronounce the difficult sounds more easily than older children and adults.

Children use their knowledge of the phonological system as they learn to read and write. In a purely phonetic language, there would be a one-to-one correspondence between letters and sounds, and teaching students to sound out words would be a simple process. But English is not a purely phonetic language because there are 26 letters and 44 sounds and many ways to combine the letters to spell some of the sounds, especially vowels. Consider these ways to spell long *e: sea, green, Pete, me,* and *people.* And sometimes the patterns used to spell long *e* don't work, as in *head* and *great.* Phonics, which describes the phoneme-grapheme correspondences and related spelling rules, is an important part of reading instruction. Students use phonics information to decode words; however, because not all words can easily be decoded, and because good readers do much more than just decode words when they read, phonics instruction cannot be an entire reading program, even though the advertisements for some commercial phonics programs claim that they are complete programs.

FIGURE 1–5 The Four Cueing Systems

Type	Terms	Uses in the Elementary Grades
Phonological System The sound system of English with approximately 44 sounds and more than 500 ways to spell the 44 sounds	• Phoneme (the smallest unit of sound) • Grapheme (the written representation of a phoneme using one or more letters) • Phonics (teaching sound-symbol correspondences and spelling rules)	• Pronouncing words • Detecting regional and other dialects • Decoding words when reading • Using invented spelling • Reading and writing alliterations and onomatopoeia • Noticing rhyming words • Dividing words into syllables
Syntactic System The structural system of English that governs how words are combined into sentences	• Syntax (the structure or grammar of a sentence) • Morpheme (the smallest meaningful unit of langauge) • Free morpheme (a morpheme that can stand alone as a word) • Bound morpheme (a morpheme that must be attached to a free morpheme)	• Adding inflectional endings to words • Combining words to form compound words • Adding prefixes and suffixes to root words • Using capitalization and punctuation to indicate beginnings and ends of sentences • Writing simple, compound, and complex sentences • Combining sentences
Semantic System The meaning system of English that focuses on vocabulary	• Semantics (meaning)	• Learning the meanings of words • Discovering that some words have multiple meanings • Studying synonyms, antonyms, and homonyms • Using a dictionary and thesaurus • Reading and writing comparisons (metaphors and similes)
Pragmatic System The system of English that varies language according to social and cultural uses	• Function (the purpose for which a person uses language) • Standard English (the form of English used in textbooks and by television newscasters) • Nonstandard English (other forms of English)	• Varying language to fit specific purposes • Reading and writing dialogue in dialects • Comparing standard and nonstandard forms of English

Students in the primary grades also use their understanding of the phonological system to create invented or temporary spellings. First graders might, for example, spell *home* as *hm* or *hom,* and second graders might spell *school* as *skule,* based on their knowledge of phoneme-grapheme relationships and the English spelling patterns. As students learn more phonics and gain more experience reading and writing, their spellings become more sophisticated and finally become conventional. For students who are learning English as a second language, their spellings often reflect their pronunciations of words (Nathenson-Mejia, 1989).

The Syntactic System

The syntactic system is the structural organization of English. This system is the grammar that regulates how words are combined into sentences. The word *grammar* here means the rules governing how words are combined in sentences, not the grammar of English textbooks or the conventional etiquette of language. Children use the syntactic system as they combine words to form sentences. Word order is important in English, and English speakers must arrange words into a sequence that makes sense. Young Spanish-speaking children who are learning English as a second language, for example, learn to say "This is my red sweater," not "This is my sweater red," which is the literal translation from Spanish. Children also learn to comprehend and produce statements, questions, and other types of sentences during the preschool years.

Students use their knowledge of the syntactic system as they read. They anticipate that the words they are reading have been strung together into sentences. When they come to an unfamiliar word, they recognize its role in the sentence even if they don't know the terms for parts of speech. In the sentence "The horses galloped through the gate and out into the field," students may not be able to decode the word *through,* but they can easily substitute a reasonable word or phrase, such as *out of* or *past.* Many of the capitalization and punctuation rules that elementary students learn reflect the syntactic system of language. Similarly, when students learn about simple, compound, and complex sentences they are learning about the syntactic system.

Another component of syntax is word forms. Words such as *dog* and *play* are morphemes, the smallest meaningful units in language. Word parts that change the meaning of a word are also morphemes. When the plural marker *-s* is added to *dog* to make *dogs,* for instance, or the past-tense marker *-ed* is added to *play* to make *played,* these words now have two morphemes because the inflectional endings change the meaning of the words. The words *dog* and *play* are free morphemes because they convey meaning while standing alone. The endings *-s* and *-ed* are bound morphemes because they must be attached to free morphemes to convey meaning. Compound words are two or more morphemes combined to create a new word. *Birthday,* for example, is a compound word made up of two free morphemes.

During the elementary grades, students learn to add affixes to words. Affixes that are added at the beginning of a word are prefixes, and affixes added at the end are suffixes. Both kinds of affixes are bound morphemes. The prefix *un-* in *unhappy* is a bound morpheme, and *happy* is a free morpheme because it can stand alone as a word.

The Semantic System

The third language system is the semantic or meaning system. Vocabulary is the key component of this system. As children learn to talk, they acquire a vocabulary that is continually increasing through the preschool years and the elementary grades. Researchers estimate that children have a vocabulary of 5,000 words by the time they enter school, and they continue to acquire 3,000 or more words each year during the elementary grades (Lindfors, 1987; Nagy, 1988). Considering how many words students learn each year, it is unreasonable to assume that they learn words only through formal instruction. Students learn many, many words informally through reading and through social studies, science, and other content-area classes. Students probably learn 8 to 10 words a day. A remarkable achievement! As students learn a word, they move from a general understanding to a better-developed understanding, and they learn these words through real reading, not through practice reading flash cards. Vocabulary activities must be devised so that students learn to identify a word, understand its meaning, and use the word in reading and writing. Researchers have estimated that students need to read a word 4 to 14 times to make it their own, and this is only possible when students read and reread books and write about what they are reading in reading logs.

The Pragmatic System

The fourth language system is pragmatics, which deals with the social and cultural aspects of language use. People use language for many different purposes, and how they talk or write varies according to their purpose and audience. Language use also varies among social classes, cultural and ethnic groups, and geographic regions. These varieties are known as dialects. School is one cultural community, and the language of school is Standard English. This register, or style, is formal—the one used in textbooks, newspapers, and magazines and by television newscasters. Other forms, including those spoken in urban ghettos, in Appalachia, and by Mexican Americans in the Southwest, are generally classified as nonstandard English. These nonstandard forms of English are alternatives in which the phonology, syntax, and semantics differ from those of Standard English. These forms are neither inferior nor substandard. They reflect the communities of speakers, and the speakers communicate as effectively as those who use Standard English in their communities. The goal is for students to add Standard English to their repertoire of language registers, not to replace their home dialect with Standard English.

As students who speak nonstandard English read texts written in Standard English, they often translate what they read into their own dialect. Sometimes this occurs when they are reading aloud. For example, a sentence that is written "They are going to school" might be read aloud this way: "They be goin' to school." Emergent or beginning readers are not usually corrected when they translate words into nonstandard dialects without changing the meaning, but older, more fluent readers should be directed to read the words as they are printed in the book.

Many reading materials include dialogue written in nonstandard English. *Shiloh* (Naylor, 1991), for example, is set in West Virginia, and some of the characters speak nonstandard English. *Mirandy and Brother Wind* (McKissack, 1988) is an African-American folktale, and some of the characters speak Black English. *White Dynamite and Curly Kidd* (Martin & Archambault, 1986) is a rodeo story, rich with the vocabulary, rhyme, and sentence structure of this truly American institution. As students read these books, they learn about the richness and variety of English dialects in the United States.

Effective teachers of reading understand that students use all four cueing systems as they read and write. For example, when students read the sentence "Jimmy is playing ball with his father" correctly, they are probably using information from all four systems. When a child substitutes *dad* for *father* and reads "Jimmy is playing ball with his dad," he might be focusing on the semantic system rather than the phonological system. When a child substitutes *basketball* for *ball* and reads "Jimmy is playing basketball with his father," he might be relying on an illustration or his own experience in choosing a more specific word than *ball*. Because both *basketball* and *ball* begin with *b*, he might have used the beginning sound as an aid in decoding, but he apparently did not notice how long the word *basketball* is compared with the word *ball*. When the child changes the syntax, as in "Jimmy, he play ball with his father," he may speak a nonstandard dialect. Sometimes a child reads the sentence as "Jump is play boat with his father," so that it doesn't make sense. The child chooses words with the correct beginning sound and uses appropriate parts of speech for at least some of the words, but there is no comprehension. This is a serious problem because the child doesn't seem to understand that what he reads must make sense.

4. *Effective Teachers Integrate the Four Language Arts in Teaching Reading*

Reading is one language art, and the other three are listening, talking, and writing. Sometimes thinking is referred to as the fifth language art, but, more accurately, it permeates all four language arts. Effective teachers integrate reading with the other language arts; they do not teach reading in isolation.

Students use the four language arts as they read and respond to literature.

Listening

Students use listening for genuine and meaningful communication purposes in literature-based reading classrooms. They listen to the teacher read books and poems aloud, listen to monitor their understanding in book discussions, listen to the information teachers provide in minilessons, and listen when their classmates give **book talks** and present oral reports and other projects. In these activities, students are listening for aesthetic and efferent purposes (Tompkins & Hoskisson, 1995). Aesthetic listening is at the heart of literature-based reading. Students use aesthetic listening as they listen for enjoyment and engage in aesthetic experience. Students listen for aesthetic purposes when they listen to teachers read a book aloud or to other students as they perform a puppet show or a **readers theatre** presentation of a story.

Listening instruction is often neglected in elementary classrooms because teachers feel that students have already learned to listen and that instructional time should be devoted to reading. Teachers need to know that there are two types of listening that are parallel to the types of reading, and that the strategies used in both reading and listening can be more effectively taught through listening. Actually, teachers can share literature with students orally, and children can learn to use a variety of reading strategies, such as predicting and connecting to personal experiences, more easily as they listen to the teacher read books aloud than when they are reading independently and trying to deal with both decoding and comprehension.

Efferent listening is listening to remember; students determine their purpose for listening and may use strategies such as noting the speaker's organization or keeping track of main points as an aid to recall. Students are listening for comprehension purposes when they listen to an informational book being read aloud in order to note specific details to use in a project they are working on, or when they listen to a story being read aloud a second time to check their sequencing of story details.

Talking

Talk is a cornerstone of literacy experiences and an essential part of learning in a classroom community (Heath, 1983; Hepler, 1991). Too often, quiet classrooms are considered the most conducive to learning, even though research shows that talk is a necessary ingredient for learning. In literature-based reading classrooms, teachers create a classroom community that encourages students to talk to each other and to take a more active role in their own learning (Staab, 1991). Sometimes students talk to a partner or in small groups. At other times, the whole class talks together. Children use talk in many ways during reading instruction—to make predictions about stories they are reading, discuss stories they have read in grand conversations, reflect on their experiences, ask questions, retell and dramatize stories, and give book talks to share books they have read, to name only a few ways.

The teacher's role shifts in literature-based reading programs. Teachers encourage talk because they understand its value and importance in learning. Teachers become one source of information, but not the only source. It is not a matter of having control or losing control; instead, the teacher and students share responsibility for learning. Reardon (1988) describes her role in reading group meetings in her classroom:

> Reading groups meet around a table. The children have notes they have made in response to the discussion questions and their "reading books" are filled with paper slips to mark

important passages. The discussion begins. It is a conversation. Children do not raise their hands but respond to what the previous speaker has said. I sit in for part of the meeting, but the children control the discussion. I rarely give my ideas. I listen, question, and help make connections. It is an exciting and thoughtful time as the children explain their ideas. They read passages to substantiate points, laugh and argue with each other, with the author, and with characters. They make discoveries. (p. 59)

Drama is a special type of talk activity; it plays a central role in language learning because students use drama as a tool for learning (Kardash & Wright, 1987; Wagner, 1988). Students participate in dramatic activities to explore what they are reading and to respond to that reading. These activities can be classified as informal drama, interpretive drama, and dramatic productions.

In informal drama, students participate in spontaneous and unrehearsed dramatic activities, such as role-playing. They assume roles in a story and act out the events together to understand the plot and the characters. Interpretive drama is slightly more formal; students use their voices, facial expressions, and gestures to dramatize a story or an event from an informational book. Some rehearsal is needed, and there is usually an audience—often a small group of children. **Choral reading** and readers theatre are two types of interpretive drama. In dramatic productions, students interpret stories through storytelling, puppet shows, and plays. Dramatic productions are the most formal type of drama and involve rehearsal, collecting props, and more elaborate planning and rehearsal. Sometimes students write their own scripts for stories or sequels of stories. These dramatic productions can also be videotaped.

Reading

In the elementary grades, teachers plan instructional activities using five types of reading: shared reading, guided reading, independent reading, buddy reading, and reading aloud to students. The type of reading that students use depends on the teacher's purpose, the availability of reading materials, and students' reading proficiencies. In some classrooms all five types of reading take place daily; in others, teachers and students use two or three types. Over a school year, however, all five types are used in most classrooms.

Shared Reading.   In shared reading, the teacher or another fluent reader reads aloud while students follow along in the text and often join in the reading (Holdaway, 1979). Students who want to read either read in unison with the teacher or they take turns, with each student reading a sentence, a paragraph, or more, if they choose. Primary-grade students often follow along by looking at a big book (an enlarged version of the story) or at a chart of a song or poem that the teacher has made. Choral reading of poems is another example of shared reading. Older students usually follow along in individual books. The shared reading experience is relaxed and social, and the teacher accepts and encourages all efforts and approximations that students make. Shared reading is a good way to immerse students in literature without worrying about the reading level of the text. Beginning readers, linguistically and culturally diverse readers, and reluctant readers feel more successful through shared reading than when they struggle to read the text by themselves (Trachtenburg & Ferruggia, 1989; Wicklund, 1989).

Guided Reading.   In guided reading, students and the teacher read, think, and talk their way through the reading of a text together. This approach is "guided" in that the teacher directs students' reading by asking them to make predictions and by focusing on vocabulary words, comprehension, and reading skills and strategies. Teachers usually guide students to make predictions, read and discuss a section of the text, and then repeat the process. As students talk about their reading, teachers gauge students' comprehension or understanding of their reading. This approach can be used when students are reading individual copies of a book or when teachers read aloud to students, and it can be used with the whole class or with small groups of students. One example of guided reading is the **Directed Reading-Thinking Activity** (DRTA) (Stauffer, 1975).

Independent Reading.   In independent reading, students are in charge of their own reading (Hornsby, Sukarna, & Parry, 1986). Students read books by themselves and at their own pace. They often choose the books they will read from the class library, or they bring a book from home. Sometimes teachers ask students to read particular types of books—biographies, for example, or books written by Beverly Cleary—but students choose individual books to read. Young children often tell a story by looking at the pictures or from memory rather than by reading the text conventionally. However young children approach reading, it is important that they spend time looking at books and thinking about literature regardless of whether they can read every word in a book. At the primary-grade level, students may read independently for only 10 to 20 minutes each day. Older students should be encouraged to read independently up to 45 minutes daily.

Buddy Reading.   Students often read and reread books with a "reading buddy" or partner. As students read with classmates, they have someone to help them with unfamiliar words and to encourage them to continue reading. Students talk together about their reading, making connections to their own lives and favorite books. Many students often choose to buddy-read because they say it's more fun to read with a classmate than to read alone. Sometimes teachers try to pair capable and less-capable readers together so that the better readers can assist their less-proficient classmates, and other teachers allow students to choose friends with whom to read. No matter how they are paired together, students gain valuable reading practice and become more fluent readers through buddy reading.

Reading Aloud to Students.   Teachers read aloud to students to share literature students cannot read themselves. Reading aloud is not an "extra" or a reward for good behavior; it is an important component of the literacy program. As they read aloud, teachers introduce students to a wide variety of books, nurture a love of literature, and model what capable readers do. Teachers read aloud to students at all grade levels, kindergarten through eighth grade, not just to young children who do not read independently yet. Teachers use reading aloud for a variety of instructional purposes. They read aloud to share literature with students when the book is appropriate for their interests but too difficult for them to read on their own. They might also read aloud when there is only one copy of the book available. Teachers usually read an entire picture book or short story aloud in one sitting, but for longer chapter books they read one or two chapters aloud each day until the book is finished.

Writing

Elementary students learn to do two types of writing. They write informally to explore what they are learning, and they use the writing process to share what they have learned (Tompkins, 1994). Students use informal writing when they use **quickwrites** and **clusters** to clarify their understanding of a book or story they have read. Another way they make personal connections with books is by writing in response journals. These journals go by many names, including reading logs and **literature logs.** No matter what they are called, students at all grade levels use them to focus and sharpen their understanding of what they read (Atwell, 1987; Barone, 1990; Five, 1986). At other times, students' writing is more polished, written to share learning, as in these examples:

- writing a prequel (story to precede) or sequel (story to follow) to a favorite story
- writing a report as part of a theme study
- writing an essay to compare a book with its film version
- writing a letter to an author or illustrator
- writing a poem to describe a favorite character

For more polished writing, students use a process approach involving a series of steps in which they draft, revise, and edit their writing. They come to view spelling and handwriting as tools that writers use to communicate effectively with their readers. When students are making final copies of their compositions, they take care to use conventional spelling and neat handwriting to make their compositions more readable.

All four language arts are used in literature-based reading programs for an important reason: Developing fluency and competence in one language art supports the growth of fluency and competence in the others. More capable readers are more capable talkers, listeners, and writers. Over a 13-year period, researcher Walter Loban (1976) documented the interrelationships among the language arts by tracking the language growth and development of a group of 338 students from kindergarten through twelfth grade. He examined the differences between students who used language effectively and those who did not. Three of Loban's conclusions are especially noteworthy to our discussion of the relationships among the four language arts. First, Loban reported positive correlations among the four language arts. Second, he found that students with less effective oral language (listening and talking) abilities tended to have less effective written language (reading and writing) abilities. And third, he found a strong correlation between students' oral language ability and their overall academic ability. Loban's seminal study demonstrates clear relationships among the language arts and emphasizes the need to broaden the subject traditionally called "reading" to include all four language arts.

5.   Effective Teachers of Reading View Reading and Writing as Related Processes and Teach Students to Use Them

Both reading and writing are complex cognitive processes, not simplistic, one-step acts. Effective teachers are familiar with the steps in the reading and writing processes, and they teach students how to use the processes. The reading process involves five steps:

1. ***Preparing to read.***   Teachers help students activate prior knowledge about the topic, the genre, the author, or something else related to the book.
2. ***Reading.***   Students read the book using one of several approaches, such as independent reading, guided reading, shared reading, buddy reading, or reading aloud to students.
3. ***Responding.***   Students react to the book, ask questions, and express their feelings through reading logs, grand conversations, and dramatizations.
4. ***Exploring.***   Teachers focus on vocabulary, teach minilessons on skills and strategies, and teach students about genre and author.
5. ***Extending.***   Students go beyond the book to create projects in reading, writing, oral language, or the arts.

In recent years, the emphasis in writing instruction has shifted from the finished product that students have written to the process they use as they gather and organize ideas, draft their ideas, and refine and polish their compositions. The teacher's role has changed from merely assigning and grading the finished product to work-

During an author unit on Beverly Cleary, students create puppets and present puppet shows for their classmates.

ing with students through the writing process. The writing process also includes five steps:

1. *Prewriting.*   Students gather and organize ideas for writing.
2. *Drafting.*   Students pour out their ideas in a rough draft.
3. *Revising.*   Students share their rough drafts, get feedback from classmates about how well they are creating meaning, and then make revisions based on the feedback they receive.
4. *Editing.*   Students proofread to identify mechanical errors and then correct spelling, capitalization, punctuation, and grammar errors.
5. *Publishing.*   Students put their papers into final form and share their final copies with real audiences.

Reading and writing are both meaning-making processes, and readers and writers are involved in many similar activities (Butler & Turbill, 1984). Even though these processes are described step by step, they are not lockstep sequential processes. Students do not always proceed through them in the same order; instead, they work in recurring cycles. The labeling of the stages is an aid to introducing and discussing the activities that represent each stage. In the classroom, the stages merge and repeat. It is important that teachers plan literacy activities so that students can connect reading and writing. Figure 1–6 overviews the steps in the reading and writing processes.

Research shows that students learn to read and write better when the two processes are connected. Shanahan (1988) identified seven instructional principles for relating reading and writing:

1. Teachers provide daily opportunities for students to read literature and write in response to their reading.
2. Teachers introduce reading and writing in kindergarten and provide opportunities for these students to read and write for genuine purposes.
3. Teachers understand that students' reading and writing reflect the developmental nature of the reading-writing relationship.
4. Teachers make the reading-writing connection explicit to students by providing opportunities for them to share their writing with classmates, publish their own books, and learn about authors.
5. Teachers emphasize that the quality of the reading and writing products students produce depends on the processes they have used. For example, as students reread and talk about literature they clarify interpretations, and they revise their writing to communicate more effectively.
6. Teachers emphasize the communicative functions of reading and writing and involve students in reading and writing for genuine communication purposes.
7. Teachers teach reading and writing in meaningful contexts with literature.

The grouping of language arts into listening, talking, reading, and writing activities, while convenient for discussion, is both arbitrary and artificial. This arrangement wrongly implies that the four language arts develop separately or that children use different mental processes for listening, talking, reading, and writing (Smith, 1979). It

FIGURE 1–6   Overview of the Reading and Writing Processes

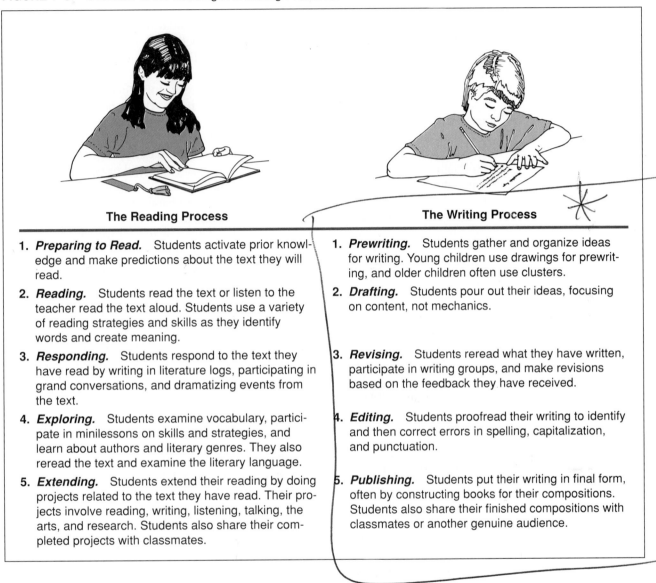

The Reading Process

1. ***Preparing to Read.***   Students activate prior knowledge and make predictions about the text they will read.

2. ***Reading.***   Students read the text or listen to the teacher read the text aloud. Students use a variety of reading strategies and skills as they identify words and create meaning.

3. ***Responding.***   Students respond to the text they have read by writing in literature logs, participating in grand conversations, and dramatizing events from the text.

4. ***Exploring.***   Students examine vocabulary, participate in minilessons on skills and strategies, and learn about authors and literary genres. They also reread the text and examine the literary language.

5. ***Extending.***   Students extend their reading by doing projects related to the text they have read. Their projects involve reading, writing, listening, talking, the arts, and research. Students also share their completed projects with classmates.

The Writing Process

1. ***Prewriting.***   Students gather and organize ideas for writing. Young children use drawings for prewriting, and older children often use clusters.

2. ***Drafting.***   Students pour out their ideas, focusing on content, not mechanics.

3. ***Revising.***   Students reread what they have written, participate in writing groups, and make revisions based on the feedback they have received.

4. ***Editing.***   Students proofread their writing to identify and then correct errors in spelling, capitalization, and punctuation.

5. ***Publishing.***   Students put their writing in final form, often by constructing books for their compositions. Students also share their finished compositions with classmates or another genuine audience.

has generally been assumed that children learn to use the language arts in sequence—from listening to talking before they come to school, to reading in the elementary grades, and then to writing in middle school and high school. Although listening is the first language mode to develop, with talking beginning soon after, parents and preschool teachers have recently documented children's early interest in both reading and writing (Bagban, 1984; Bissex, 1980). Carol Chomsky (1971) and other researchers have observed young children experimenting with writing earlier than with reading. On the basis of reports from parents, teachers, and researchers, we can no longer assume that there is a definite sequence in learning and using the four language modes.

6. *Effective Teachers Use Literature to Teach Reading*

One of the biggest questions facing reading teachers today is whether to use literature or published reading programs for reading instruction. A decade ago, almost all teachers used basal readers and relied on them for their entire reading program (Anderson, Hiebert, Scott, & Wilkinson, 1985; Shannon, 1989). Often the students were divided into small groups by ability, and they read stories and practiced reading skills with the teacher. They completed workbook pages when not reading with the teacher, and they did little writing except filling in the blanks on worksheets.

Basal reading programs have been a staple of American reading instruction for generations, and they have several advantages. They have been judged as successful, especially as measured by students' achievement on standardized tests, and teachers— especially beginning teachers—feel secure using the step-by-step guidance provided by teacher's manuals. Traditionally, the stories used in basals were developed around a hierarchy of skills and contained a tightly controlled vocabulary. The stories were used to provide students with practice on the skills, not for enjoyment. The short, contrived stories designed for skills practice and the abundance of accompanying skill-based workbook activities were probably the greatest drawbacks of these programs because they limited students' aesthetic responses. Today, many published reading programs have replaced most of the contrived stories with "real" literature.

In the past ten years, there has been a proliferation of literature for children published as hardcover and paperback trade books, and teachers have begun using literature in place of textbooks, with remarkable results (Dekker, 1991; Egawa, 1990; O'Brien, 1991; Swift, 1993). As teachers gain experience using literature as the core of their literacy programs, they are becoming convinced that exposing children to the best in literature and helping them make choices about their literacy experiences will ensure that children become not only expert readers but also lifelong readers (Cullinan, 1992; Danielson & LaBonty, 1994; Goodman, Shannon, Freeman, & Murphy, 1988; Zarrillo, 1991).

The position in this book is that effective teachers of reading use literature, whether published as trade books or contained in published reading programs, to teach reading. Literature is the core of the literacy program because of its universal appeal. It enriches children's personal lives and contributes to their educational development. Reading is enjoyable, and as they read, students meet characters they can relate to and heroes who grapple with all of life's tragedies, joys, and triumphs. Students learn about the world around them as they read and are vicariously transported to other lands or back or forward in time to experience lives very different from their own. Literature can also help children understand how they are affected by the institutions of society and the forces of nature. Through reading, students learn about the power of language to narrate a story or to persuade. Literature is our cultural heritage and should be central to our curriculum. Dorothy Strickland (1994–1995) reports that "textbooks continue to be important classroom resources, but they are no longer the dominant materials" (p. 295) for reading and writing instruction or for learning in social studies, science, or other content areas. She recommends that elementary students have opportunities to read and respond to literature.

In response to teachers' move to literature, the companies that publish basal readers began including more stories in their textbooks. Initially, however, the stories were often simplified and rewritten so that the vocabulary and reading difficulty were controlled. The abundance of activities and workbooks focusing on skills continued.

In 1988, Ken Goodman argued persuasively against the "basalization" of children's literature, and the latest editions of basal readers incorporate much more high-quality literature than earlier series. These literature-based reading programs no longer contain a series of isolated, disconnected stories designed to emphasize a particular skill or to teach a list of vocabulary words.

It is encouraging to see that high-quality stories, poetry, and informational articles are included in newer literature-based basal programs, but Goodman continues to warn that the instructional materials that accompany them are problematic (Goodman, Maras, & Birdeye, 1994; Noll & Goodman, 1995). Teachers should also make sure that all text from original versions is included and that all pictures from picture books are included. If some have been deleted due to space limitations, teachers must consider what the impact of the deletions will be on students' reading. The skills activities, vocabulary activities, and other activities should never overwhelm the literature, and workbook materials should be used judiciously. There are, however, older and more traditional basals still being used in schools and still available for purchase today. These textbooks are not recommended for teaching literature-based reading as it is described in this book. Teachers should carefully examine reading textbooks they are considering adopting or using in their classrooms to make sure that they contain high-quality literature that has not been abridged.

Effective teachers of reading use good literature in trade books if they can arrange to get class sets of the books, and when effective teachers use literature selections from basals, they make decisions about how to teach the story and don't follow all directions in the teacher's manual slavishly. In this book you will learn how to develop a literature focus unit using a trade book or a literature selection from a basal textbook. You will learn how to use a model of the reading process to organize for instruction and how to involve students in responding, exploring, and extending activities after reading. You will learn how and when to focus on vocabulary, what reading skills and strategies to teach, and how to teach them through minilessons. Teachers should not fall into the trap of purchasing unit plans, often complete with worksheets, that are advertised in professional magazines and available at reading conferences. Often they are no better than the preplanned basal reading programs.

Teachers choose three types of literature to include in their reading programs: stories, poems, and informational books or articles. Students need opportunities to read all three types and then apply what they have learned in writing all three types of literature. The whole class will read some books together. These books represent the finest in children's literature and are called featured books. Often they have won prestigious awards, such as the Caldecott Medal, which is given each year for the best illustrated picture book for children, and the Newbery Medal, which is given each year for the book deemed the best written for children. These awards are given by the American Library Association. A list of award winners and runners-up (called Honor Books) for each year since 1960 is presented in Appendix A at the back of this book.

It is also important that teachers incorporate multicultural literature in their reading programs. Multicultural literature helps students appreciate diversity and become more tolerant of members of minority groups and more aware of other cultures (Edwards, Beasley, & Thompson, 1991; May, 1993). Reading multicultural literature presents students with the opportunity to "walk a mile" in an African American's shoes in books like *Roll of Thunder, Hear My Cry* (Taylor, 1976), or in a recent immigrant's shoes through *How Many Days to America? A Thanksgiving Story* (Bunting, 1988) or *Angel Child, Dragon Child* (Surat, 1983).

7.   *Effective Teachers of Reading Balance Direct Instruction of Skills and Strategies With Authentic Reading and Writing Experiences*

Readers and writers use both skills and strategies when they read and write. They use skills automatically, such as sounding out an unfamiliar word when reading, or capitalizing the first letter of a name when writing. In contrast, strategies are problem-solving procedures that students choose and use consciously. Readers, for example, use fix-up strategies when they're reading and realize that they don't understand something. Writers use clustering to organize ideas before writing, and use proofreading to identify mechanical errors. The behavioristic theories of the past suggested that the heart of reading instruction was teaching a fixed sequence of discrete skills. Newer theories of learning and language development suggest that skills continue to play a role in learning to read and write. However, they suggest that strategies are even more useful to readers and writers. Dorothy Strickland (1994–1995) suggests that "we must redefine what is basic to becoming literate" (p. 296). Theorists and researchers emphasize that through skills instruction alone children do not become readers and writers. Children construct knowledge through instruction together with daily opportunities to apply what they have learned about skills and strategies in authentic reading and writing experiences. When reading and writing are segmented into discrete skills, children no longer have an authentic activity or understand the context for using the skill. *This change is not an abandonment of the skills, but a different view of the role of skills in reading and writing.*

Students learn to sequence the events of a story using story boards made by cutting apart two paperback copies of the book.

Researchers recommend using a whole-part-whole organization for teaching skills and strategies (Flood & Lapp, 1994; Trachtenburg, 1990). Students read and respond to a piece of literature—this is the whole; then teachers focus on a skill or strategy and teach a minilesson using examples from the piece of literature—this is the part. Finally, students return to the literature to use what they have learned by doing more reading or writing or doing a project—this is the whole again. In the past, the skills approach to reading was described as part-to-whole, and sometimes holistic approaches are described as whole-to-part. This approach takes both into account. Isolated drill-and-practice activities are often meaningless to students. Workbooks and practice sheets are not recommended for skills instruction—except, perhaps, as extra practice.

Effective teachers of reading use a variety of grouping practices, both for skill and strategy instruction and for other literacy activities: the whole class, small groups, partners, and individual assignments. They also make assignment to small groups flexible and changing (Berghoff & Egawa, 1991). Wiggins (1994) suggests that literature first be shared with the whole class, followed by lessons planned for small groups. The makeup of the groups changes according to students' needs. Teachers often arrange students into small groups for skill and strategy instruction so that the instruction is directed to students who do not know the skill or strategy, not to everyone in the class. These groupings also work when students are reading and writing as part of theme studies in social studies and science (Pardo & Raphael, 1991).

8. *Effective Teachers of Reading Help Students Become Fluent, Strategic Readers*

The goal of reading instruction is comprehension, and in order for students to focus on using strategies for comprehending or making meaning, they must become fluent readers, capable of identifying words automatically. Reading has been described as involving two components: decoding and comprehension. Neither component is equivalent to reading by itself, and both are necessary for reading (Adams, 1990).

Decoding is the translation of written words into verbal speech for oral reading or mental speech for silent reading. Decoding includes both word recognition, a fast translation process for familiar words, and word identification, slower processes of figuring out unknown words (Eldredge, 1995). Beginning readers must use the slower word-identification processes most of the time because they don't know many words, but capable readers use the quicker word-recognition process because they are familiar with most words they read.

Comprehension is the construction of meaning, and it is the goal of reading. Readers construct meaning by making connections—by integrating what they are reading with what they already know about the topic (Rumelhart, 1981). As they construct meaning, readers use their knowledge about the structure of the text they are reading (for example, folk tales and biographies have different kinds of structures). They also use problem-solving strategies to elaborate and monitor their understanding as well as to make repairs when comprehension breaks down (Collins & Smith, 1980).

According to the automaticity theory described by LaBerge and Samuels (1974), some readers have difficulty comprehending because they spend too much time and attention on word identification, while fluent readers identify words automatically without paying much attention to decoding. Fluent readers are in control of their reading and, as a result, are able to focus on making meaning. They find it easier to comprehend text than poor decoders because fluency releases the energy necessary for students to utilize their comprehension strategies. In other words, if readers use all their energy for decoding words, they don't have enough energy left for thinking about the structure of text and using their comprehension strategies. Therefore, effective teachers of reading help their students become fluent readers so that they are better able to focus on comprehending.

9. Effective Teachers Use Reading and Writing as Tools for Learning Across the Curriculum

Language is a powerful learning tool, and reading and writing are valuable ways to learn in all content areas. Effective teachers encourage students to use reading and writing in meaningful ways in theme studies so that they learn information better and refine their literacy competencies. Thaiss (1986) identified three benefits students gain from studying across the curriculum:

1. Students understand and remember better when they use reading and writing to explore what they are learning.
2. Students' literacy learning is reinforced when they read and write about what they are learning.
3. Students learn best through active involvement, collaborative projects, and interaction with classmates, the teacher, and the world.

Theme studies are a relatively new way of developing a curriculum in which students use language to learn (Altwerger & Flores, 1994; Farough, 1994). Social studies and science topics are often integrated for themes. For example, students might study ways people and animals communicate, life in the oceans, or World War II. In theme studies, students work with the teacher to plan for the theme by suggesting topics they want to learn about. They also ask questions. During the theme, students use listening, talking, reading, and writing as they learn, and they share what they have learned through books they write, presentations they give, and displays they create.

Teachers collect informational books, stories, and poems for a text set related to a theme. Books of children's literature are very useful in teaching social studies and science concepts (Farris & Fuhler, 1994; Freeman & Person, 1992; Tunnell & Ammon, 1993). For example, students learn about ecosystems when they read *Cactus Hotel* (Guiberson, 1991), the human body through *The Magic School Bus Inside the Human Body* (Cole, 1989), and oviparous (egg-laying) animals in *Chickens Aren't the Only Ones* (Heller, 1981). Students read the books to learn about the concepts being studied. They often take notes or write in **learning logs,** and then they use the information in creating reports, murals, and other displays and projects. As students read informational books, they also learn about expository text—how it is organized, how to read charts and diagrams, and how to use an index.

At some elementary schools, all classes participate in schoolwide themes. At their elementary school in Halifax, Nova Scotia, students participate in a large-scale theme focusing on houses. Students at different grade levels study different aspects of hous-

Students use reading and writing during an across-the-curriculum theme on immigration.

ing, but all students focus on houses. One class of primary students, for example, studies homes around the world; a class of middle-grade students investigates how homes have changed throughout history; and a class of upper-grade students learns about building a house. During this theme, students use reading and writing as tools for learning about houses. Other broad themes include world cultures, inventions that have changed our lives, traveling back in time, American landmarks, and the world's resources.

Theme studies are successful with all students because the students are involved in the planning, take responsibility for their own learning, and cooperate with class-mates on projects. They discipline themselves because they want to be a part of the learning community in the classroom. One of the most important outcomes of theme studies is that students gain self-confidence because they are motivated to learn and apply what they are learning, and this confidence breeds success.

10. *Effective Teachers of Reading Use a Variety of Authentic Assessment Procedures to Plan for and Document Student Learning*

Assessment is more than testing; it is an integral part of teaching and learning (Good-man, Goodman, & Hood, 1989). Teachers learn about their students, about them-selves as teachers, and about the impact of instructional programs through assess-ment. Similarly, students learn about themselves as learners and about their learning. Effective teachers use a variety of authentic assessment techniques to plan for and document students' learning, including **running records** and story retellings. The key word is *authentic* (Moffett, 1992; Valencia, Hiebert, & Afflerbach, 1994). Authentic assessment procedures involve documenting students' accomplishments in reading and writing activities using genuine materials for real-life purposes. Tests can also be used to assess students' learning, but they are often not as effective because they are artificial and ask students to recall bits of knowledge, not authentic and require application of knowledge. These authentic procedures are used to monitor students' progress and collect students' work in portfolios as well as to assign grades.

Literacy assessment is beginning to catch up with the dramatic changes in teaching that have occurred over the past 10 years. Teachers now understand that students learn to read and write by doing lots of authentic reading and writing, not by doing exercises on isolated literacy skills. Students learn best when they learn skills and strategies in the context of real reading and writing. These changes affect the way we assess students. No longer does it seem enough to grade students' vocabulary exercises or ask them to answer multiple-choice comprehension questions on reading passages that have no point beyond the exercise. Similarly, it no longer seems appropriate to measure success in writing by means of spelling and grammar tests. Instead, teachers need assessment information that tells about the complex achievements that students are making in real reading and writing.

Effective teachers of reading plan for assessment at the same time they plan for instruction. Teachers identify what they are going to teach during a literature focus unit or reading and writing workshop, and they develop their assessment plan then. They have a variety of authentic assessment procedures available to monitor students' achievements in reading and writing. Many teachers develop an assignment sheet for students to use as they read and respond during a literature focus unit. In this way students understand how they will be assessed, and they can take more responsibility for their own learning. Students participate in assessment conferences with the teacher and talk about what they are reading and writing, the strategies and skills they are learning to use, and problem areas. They reflect on what they do well as readers and writers and on what they need to learn next. They also write reflective letters in which they analyze their accomplishments, their uses of reading strategies and skills, and their goals for the next unit (Atwell, 1987). Here is a list of authentic assessment techniques:

■ *Activity*

Make a list of recommended practices that effective teachers of reading use, such as reading aloud to students every day, and another list of practices that are not recommended. Then, to help you think about how you will become an effective teacher of reading, highlight the recommended practices that you want to learn more about.

- Students audiotape or videotape their oral reading and oral language projects, such as puppet shows, oral reports, and story retellings.
- Students demonstrate their comprehension by writing in reading logs.
- Students analyze stories by making charts, dioramas, murals, Venn diagrams, and other **story maps.**
- Students keep lists of books they have read.
- Students do projects to demonstrate their understanding of a book.
- Students complete the **cloze procedure,** in which they fill in the words that have been deleted from a story.
- Students keep all drafts of their writing to document their use of the writing process.
- Teachers observe students and write anecdotal notes.
- Teachers listen to students read aloud and make running records of their oral-reading "miscues" or errors.
- Teachers keep lists of skills and strategies they have taught during minilessons.

■ Teachers keep records of reading and writing conferences.

■ Teachers analyze students' invented spellings and spelling errors.

Effective teachers also assist students as they create portfolios to showcase their reading and writing projects and demonstrate how they have grown as readers and writers. Portfolios are systematic and meaningful collections of artifacts documenting students' reading and writing, compiled over a period of time (D'Aoust, 1992; De Fina, 1992). These collections are dynamic and reflect students' day-to-day learning activities in reading and writing and across the curriculum. Students not only select pieces to be placed in their portfolios but also learn to establish criteria for their selections. Because of students' involvement in selecting pieces for their portfolios and their reflections on them, portfolio assessment is a way of demonstrating respect for students and their abilities.

Review

This chapter set out 10 principles of effective teaching of reading:

1. Effective teachers of reading create a community of learners in their classrooms.

2. Effective teachers of reading use instructional approaches based on how children learn.

3. Effective teachers of reading support students' use of the four cueing systems.

4. Effective teachers integrate the four language arts in teaching reading.

5. Effective teachers of reading view reading and writing as related processes and teach students to use them.

6. Effective teachers use literature to teach reading.

7. Effective teachers of reading balance direct instruction of skills with authentic reading and writing experiences.

8. Effective teachers of reading help students become fluent, strategic readers.

9. Effective teachers use reading and writing as tools for learning across the curriculum.

10. Effective teachers of reading use a variety of authentic assessment procedures to plan for and document student learning.

These principles were drawn from research over the past 25 years about how children learn to read and the "best teaching practices" used in successful elementary schools. These principles suggest a balanced reading program with literature at the center. In the chapters that follow, you will learn how to develop and implement a literature-based reading program for kindergarten through eighth grade.

References

Adams, M. J. (1990). *Beginning to read: Thinking and learning about print.* Cambridge, MA: MIT Press.

Altwerger, B., & Flores, B. (1994). Theme cycles: Creating communities of learners. *Primary Voices, K–6, 2,* 2–6.

Anderson, R. C., Hiebert, E. H., Scott, J. A., & Wilkinson, I. A. G. (1985). *Becoming a nation of readers.* Washington, DC: National Institute of Education.

Atwell, N. (1987). *In the middle: Writing, reading, and thinking with adolescents.* Portsmouth, NH: Heinemann.

Bagban, M. (1984). *Our daughter learns to read and write: A case study from birth to three.* Newark, DE: International Reading Association.

Barone, D. (1990). The written responses of young children: Beyond comprehension to story understanding. *The New Advocate, 3,* 49–56.

Berghoff, B., & Egawa, K. (1991). No more "rocks": Grouping to give students control of their learning. *The Reading Teacher, 44,* 536–541.

Bissex, G. L. (1980). *Gnys at wrk: A child learns to write and read.* Cambridge, MA: Harvard University Press.

Boyer, E. (1995). *The basic school: A community for learning.* Princeton, NJ: Carnegie Foundation for the Advancement of Teaching.

Butler, A., & Turbill, J. (1984). *Towards a reading-writing classroom.* Portsmouth, NH: Heinemann.

Calkins, L. M. (1994). *The art of teaching writing* (2nd ed.). Portsmouth, NH: Heinemann.

Cases in literacy: An agenda for discussion. (1989). Newark, DE: International Reading Association and the National Council of Teachers of English.

Chomsky, C. (1971). Write now, read later. *Childhood Education, 47,* 296–299.

Collins, A., & Smith, E. (1980). *Teaching the process of reading comprehension* (Technical Report #182). Urbana, IL: University of Illinois, Center for the Study of Reading.

Cullinan, B. E. (Ed.). (1992). *Invitation to read: More children's literature in the reading program.* Newark, DE: International Reading Association.

Danielson, K. E., & LaBonty, J. (1994). *Integrating reading and writing through children's literature.* Boston: Allyn & Bacon.

D'Aoust, C. (1992). Portfolios: Process for students and teachers. In K. B. Yancy (Ed.), *Portfolios in the writing classroom* (pp. 39–48). Urbana, IL: National Council of Teachers of English.

De Fina, A. A. (1992). *Portfolio assessment: Getting started.* New York: Scholastic.

Dekker, M. M. (1991). Books, reading, and response: A teacher-researcher tells a story. *The New Advocate, 4,* 37–45.

Edwards, P. A., Beasley, K., & Thompson, J. (1991). Teachers in transition: Accommodating reading curriculum to cultural diversity. *The Reading Teacher, 44,* 436–437.

Egawa, K. (1990). Harnessing the power of language: First graders' literature engagement with *Owl Moon. Language Arts, 67,* 582–588.

Eldredge, J. L. (1995). *Teaching decoding in holistic classrooms.* Englewood Cliffs, NJ: Merrill/Prentice Hall.

Farough, D. (1994). Launching ships. *The Reading Teacher, 47,* 626–631.

Farris, P. J., & Fuhler, C. J. (1994). Developing social studies concepts through picture books. *The Reading Teacher, 47,* 380–391.

Five, C. L. (1986). Fifth graders respond to a changed reading program. *Harvard Educational Review, 56,* 395–405.

Flood, J., & Lapp, D. (1994). Developing literary appreciation and literacy skills: A blueprint for success. *The Reading Teacher, 48,* 76–79.

Freeman, E. B., & Person, D. G. (Eds.). (1992). *Using nonfiction trade books in the elementary classroom: From ants to zeppelins.* Urbana, IL: National Council of Teachers of English.

Goodman, K. S. (1988). Look what they've done to Judy Blume!: The "basalization" of children's literature. *The New Advocate, 1,* 29–41.

Goodman, K. S., Goodman, Y. M., & Hood, W. J. (Eds.). (1989). *The whole language evaluation book.* Portsmouth, NH: Heinemann.

Goodman, K., Maras, L., & Birdeye, D. (1994). Look! Look! Who stole the pictures form the picture book? The basalization of picture books. *The New Advocate, 7,* 1–24.

Goodman, K. S., Shannon, P., Freeman, Y. S., & Murphy, S. (1988). *Report card on basal readers.* Katonah, NY: Richard C. Owen.

Graves, D. H. (1994). *A fresh look at writing.* Portsmouth, NH: Heinemann.

Graves, D. H. (1995). A tour of Segovia School in the year 2005. *Language Arts, 72,* 12–18.

Halliday, M. A. K. (1978). *Language as social semiotic: The social interpretation of language and meaning.* Baltimore: University Park Press.

Hansen, J. (1987). *When writers read.* Portsmouth, NH: Heinemann.

Heath, S. B. (1983). Research currents: A lot of talk about nothing. *Language Arts, 60,* 999–1007.

Hepler, S. (1991). Talking our way to literacy in the classroom community. *The New Advocate, 4,* 179–191.

Hirsch, E. D., Jr. (1987). *Cultural literacy: What every American needs to know.* Boston: Houghton Mifflin.

Holdaway, D. (1979). *The foundations of literacy.* Portsmouth, NH: Heinemann.

Hornsby, D., Sukarna, D., & Parry, J. (1986). *Read on: A conference approach to reading.* Portsmouth, NH: Heinemann.

Kardash, C. A. M., & Wright, L. (1987, Winter). Does creative drama benefit elementary school students? A meta-analysis. *Youth Theater Journal, 29,* 11–18.

LaBerge, D., & Samuels, S. J. (1974). Toward a theory of automatic information processing in reading. *Cognitive Psychology, 6,* 293–323.

Lindfors, J. W. (1987). *Children's language and learning* (2nd ed.). Englewood Cliffs, NJ: Prentice Hall.

Loban, W. (1976). *Language development: Kindergarten through grade twelve* (Research Report No. 18). Urbana, IL: National Council of Teachers of English.

May, S. A. (1993). Redeeming multicultural education. *Language Arts, 70,* 364–372.

Moffett, J. (1992). *Detecting growth in language.* Portsmouth, NH: Boynton/Cook.

Morrice, C., & Simmons, M. (1991). Beyond reading buddies: A whole language cross-age program. *The Reading Teacher, 44,* 572–578.

Nagy, W. E. (1988). *Teaching vocabulary to improve reading comprehension.* Urbana, IL: ERIC Clearinghouse on Reading and Communication Skills and the National Council of Teachers of English and the International Reading Association.

Nathenson-Mejia, S. (1989). Writing in a second language: Negotiating meaning through invented spelling. *Language Arts, 66,* 516–526.

Noll, E., & Goodman, K. (1995). "Using a howitzer to kill a butterfly": Teaching literature with basals. *The New Advocate, 8,* 243–254.

O'Brien, K. L. (1991). A look at one successful literature program. *The New Advocate, 4,* 113–123.

Pardo, L. S., & Raphael, T. E. (1991). Classroom organization for instruction in content areas. *The Reading Teacher, 44,* 556–565.

Piaget, J. (1969). *The psychology of intelligence.* Paterson, NJ: Littlefield, Adams.

Reardon, S. J. (1988). The development of critical readers: A look into the classroom. *The New Advocate, 1,* 52–61.

Rosenblatt, L. (1978). *The reader, the text, the poem: The transactional theory of the literary work.* Carbondale, IL: Southern Illinois University Press.

Rosenblatt, L. (1983). *Literature as exploration* (4th ed.). New York: Modern Language Association.

Rosenblatt, L. (1991). Literature—S.O.S.! *Language Arts, 68,* 444–448.

Rumelhart, D. E. (1977). Toward an interactive model of reading. In S. Dornic (Ed.), *Attention and performance* (Vol. 6). Hillsdale, NJ: Erlbaum.

Rumelhart, D. E. (1981). Schemata: The building blocks of cognition. In J. T. Guthrie (Ed.), *Comprehension and teaching: Research reviews* (pp. 3–26). Newark, DE: International Reading Association.

Shanahan, T. (1988). The reading-writing relationship: Seven instructional principles. *The Reading Teacher, 41,* 636–647.

Shannon, P. (1989). *Broken promises: Reading instruction in twentieth-century America.* New York: Bergin & Garvey.

Skinner, B. F. (1968). *The technology of teaching.* New York: Appleton-Century-Crofts.

Smith, F. (1979). The language arts and the learner's mind. *Language Arts, 56,* 118–125.

Smith, F. (1988). *Joining the literacy club: Further essays into education.* Portsmouth, NH: Heinemann.

Staab, C. (1991). Talk in whole-language classrooms. In V. Froese (Ed.), *Whole-language practice and theory* (pp. 17–49). Needham Heights, MA: Allyn & Bacon.

Stanovich, K. (1980). Toward an interactive-compensatory model of individual differences in the development of reading fluency. *Reading Research Quarterly, 16,* 32–71.

Stauffer, R. G. (1975). *Directing the reading-thinking process.* New York: Harper & Row.

Strickland, D. S. (1994–1995). Reinventing our literacy programs: Books, basics, balance. *The Reading Teacher, 48,* 294–301.

Swift, K. (1993). Try reading workshop in your classroom. *The Reading Teacher, 46,* 366–371.

Teale, B. (1995). Dear readers. *Language Arts, 72,* 8–9.

Thaiss, C. (1986). *Language across the curriculum in the elementary grades.* Urbana, IL: ERIC Clearinghouse on Reading and Communication Skills and the National Council of Teachers of English.

Tompkins, G. E. (1994). *Teaching writing: Balancing process and product* (2nd ed.). Englewood Cliffs, NJ: Merrill/Prentice Hall.

Tompkins, G. E., & Hoskisson, K. (1995). *Language arts: Content and teaching strategies* (3rd ed.). Englewood Cliffs, NJ: Merrill/Prentice Hall.

Trachtenburg, P. (1990). Using children's literature to enhance phonics instruction. *The Reading Teacher, 43,* 648–654.

Trachtenburg, P., & Ferruggia, A. (1989). Big books from little voices: Reaching high-risk beginning readers. *The Reading Teacher, 42,* 284–289.

Tunnell, M. O., & Ammon, R. (Eds.). *The story of ourselves: Teaching history through children's literature.* Portsmouth, NH: Heinemann.

Valencia, S. W., Hiebert, E. H., & Afflerbach, P. P. (Eds.). (1994). *Authentic reading assessment: Practices and possibilities.* Newark, DE: International Reading Association.

Vygotsky, L. S. (1978). *Mind in society.* Cambridge, MA: Harvard University Press.

Vygotsky, L. S. (1986). *Thought and language.* Cambridge, MA: MIT Press.

Wagner, B. J. (1988). Research currents: Does classroom drama affect the arts of language? *Language Arts, 65,* 46–55.

Wells, G., & Chang-Wells, G. L. (1992). *Constructing knowledge together: Classrooms as centers of inquiry and literacy.* Portsmouth, NH: Heinemann.

Wicklund, L. K. (1989). Shared poetry: A whole language experience adapted for remedial readers. *The Reading Teacher, 42,* 478–481.

Wiggins, R. A. (1994). Large group lesson/small group follow-up: Flexible grouping in a basal reading program. *The Reading Teacher, 47,* 450–460.

Zarrillo, J. (1991). Theory becomes practice: Aesthetic teaching with literature. *The New Advocate, 4,* 221–233.

Children's Book References

Bonners, S. (1981). *A penguin year.* New York: Dell.

Bunting, E. (1988). *How many days to America? A Thanksgiving story.* New York: Clarion.

Cole, J. (1989). *The magic school bus inside the human body.* New York: Scholastic.

Guiberson, B. Z. (1991). *Cactus hotel.* New York: Henry Holt.

Heller, R. (1981). *Chickens aren't the only ones.* New York: Grosset & Dunlap.

Lowry, L. (1989). *Number the stars.* Boston: Houghton Mifflin.

MacLachlan, P. (1983). *Sarah, plain and tall.* New York: Harper & Row.

Martin, B., Jr., & Archambault, J. (1986). *White Dynamite and Curly Kidd.* New York: Henry Holt.

McKissack, P. C. (1988). *Mirandy and Brother Wind.* New York: Knopf.

Naylor, P. R. (1991). *Shiloh.* New York: Atheneum.

Surat, M. M. (1983). *Angel child, dragon child.* Milwaukee: Raintree.

Taylor, M. D. (1976). *Roll of thunder, hear my cry.* New York: Dial.

CHAPTER 2

Students, Teachers, and Parents Working Together

The students in Mrs. Bradshaw's multi-age classroom have divided into six small-group book clubs to read and respond to these chapter books:

- *On My Honor* (Bauer, 1986), a story about a boy who breaks a promise to his father with disastrous results
- *Freckle Juice* (Blume, 1971), a humorous story about a boy who tried to rid himself of his freckles
- *Shiloh* (Naylor, 1991), a heartwarming boy-and-dog story
- *Bunnicula: A Rabbit-Tale of Mystery* (Howe & Howe, 1979), a fantasy about a bunny who just might be a vampire
- *How to Eat Fried Worms* (Rockwell, 1973), a humorously revolting story about a boy who makes a bet that he can eat 15 worms in 15 days
- *Bridge to Terabithia* (Paterson, 1977), a touching story of a friendship between two lonely children

All six of these books are good stories and popular with middle-grade students. Two have won the Newbery Award for excellence, and one is a Newbery Honor Book (runner-up for the Newbery Award). Mrs. Bradshaw chose these books after reflecting on the interests and needs of the students in the classroom, and based on requests and recommendations from her students. The reading levels of the books range from second to fifth grade.

Mrs. Bradshaw has a set of six of each of these books, and she introduced the books using a **book talk** (see the Compendium for more information about this and all other highlighted terms in this chapter). Students had a day to preview the books and sign up for one of the groups. After students get into groups, Mrs. Bradshaw holds a class meeting to set the guidelines for this unit. Students will have 75 minutes each day for five days to read and respond to the books. Students in each group set their own schedules for reading, discussing the book, and writing in **reading logs.** They decide how they will read the book, plan for at least three **grand conversations,** write at least three entries in their reading logs, and develop a presentation to share their book with the class at the end of the unit. Mrs. Bradshaw distributes a "Book Club Notes" sheet for students to use to keep track of their schedules and the assignments. A copy of this sheet is shown in Figure 2–1. Students keep this sheet and their reading logs in their book club folders.

The students in each book club talk about their books and make plans. Four of the groups decide to write their first reading log entry before beginning to read, and the other two groups begin reading right away. As the students read, write, and talk about their books, Mrs. Bradshaw moves from group to group and writes anecdotal notes about students.

Mrs. Bradshaw joins the *Bridge to Terabithia* group as they finish reading the first chapter, and one student asks about the dedication. Mrs. Bradshaw shares that she read that Katherine Paterson wrote this book after the child of a friend of hers died, and she guesses that the Lisa mentioned in the dedication is that child. Another child asks about the setting of the story, and from the information in the first chapter, the group de-

FIGURE 2–1   Mrs. Bradshaw's Schedule and Assignment Sheet

Book Club Notes

Name _____   Date _____

Book _____

Schedule

1	2	3	4	5

Requirements

☐ Read the book
☐ Discuss the book   1 ____   2 ____   3 ____
☐ Write in a reading log   1 ____   2 ____   3 ____
☐ Make a project

duces that the story is set in a rural area outside of Washington, DC. Several students comment on how vividly Paterson describes Jesse and his family. After speculating on who might be moving into the old Perkins place, they continue reading.

Next, Mrs. Bradshaw moves to the book club reading *Freckle Juice* and helps them set up their group schedule. The students in this group decide to read together. They will take turns reading aloud as the other group members follow along and help each other with unfamiliar words. Mrs. Bradshaw stays with this group as they read the first three pages. Then she encourages them to continue reading and moves on to another group.

The next day, the book club reading *Bunnicula: A Rabbit-Tale of Mystery* asks Mrs. Bradshaw to meet with them. They have a lot of questions and confusions about vampires and Dracula. Mrs. Bradshaw is prepared for their requests, and she brings with her the "V" and "D" volumes of an encyclopedia and several other books about vampires. She spends 20 minutes with the group, helping them find information and clarify confusions.

She also joins with the *How to Eat Fried Worms* book club as they read Chapter 3. The students ask Mrs. Bradshaw what "monshure" is, and she explains that Alan is pretending to speak French. As they continue reading Chapters 4 and 5, she points out similar instances. Once they finish reading, the group discusses the chapters they have read and talks about whether or not they would have made a similar bet. They compare themselves to Billy, the boy who eats the worms, and talk about how real the story seems and how they feel themselves tasting the worm as Billy eats it. Mrs. Bradshaw seizes the moment for an impromptu lesson on reading strategies, and she explains that good readers often seem to connect with or become a character in a story and can see, hear, smell, and even taste the same things the character does.

A few days later, Mrs. Bradshaw meets with the *Shiloh* book club as they are writing in their reading logs. Students in this group decided to write **double-entry journals.** They write interesting quotes from the book in one column and their reactions to the quotes in another column. Students are writing quotes and reactions from the last three chapters of the book. Todd chooses "I begin to see now I'm no better than Judd Travers—willing to look the other way to get something I want" (p. 124), and writes:

> *Marty IS better than Judd Travers. This book makes you realize that things are not just right and wrong and most of the time right and wrong and good and bad and fair and not fair get a little mixed up. Marty is keeping quiet about the doe for a real important reason. The deer is dead and that can't be helped but Marty can save Shiloh. He must save the dog. He's a much better person than he thinks even though he did do some wrong. Part of the reason you know he is a good person is that he knows he did the wrong things. He has a conscience. Judd don't have a conscience, none at all.*

Next, Mrs. Bradshaw meets with the *On My Honor* book club as they discuss the end of the book. Kara comments, "I don't think Joel should feel so guilty about Tony dying. It wasn't his fault." Mrs. Bradshaw asks, "Who's fault was it?" Several children say it was Tony's fault. Will explains, "He knew he couldn't swim and he went swimming anyway. That was just plain dumb." "What about Joel's dad?" Mrs. Bradshaw asks, "Was it his fault, too?" Brooke says, "His dad seems like he thinks he's guilty and he tells Joel he's sorry." Jered offers another opinion, "It was just an accident. I don't think it was anyone's fault. No one killed Tony on purpose. He just died." The group continues to talk about the effect of Tony's death on his own family and on Josh and his family.

Mrs. Bradshaw and the students in this multi-age classroom have created a community of learners. They have learned to work together in small groups. They are responsible for assignments and supportive of their classmates. They know the literacy routines and procedures to use during the book club unit. The classroom is arranged to facilitate their learning. They know where supplies are kept and how to use them. Mrs. Bradshaw assumes a number of roles during the unit. She chooses books, organizes the unit, provides information and encouragement, teaches lessons, monitors students' progress, and assesses their work.

On the fifth day, students in each book club share their projects with the class. The purpose of these projects is to celebrate the reading experience and bring closure to it. An added benefit is that students "advertise" the books during these sharing sessions, and then other students want to read them. Each group takes approximately 5 to 10 minutes to share their projects.

The *How to Eat Fried Worms* group goes first. They present a book commercial. Group members tell a little about the story and dare students to eat the worms—big earthworms or night crawlers—that they have brought to school. One student, Nathan, explains that it is perfectly safe to eat the worms and extols their nutritional benefits. Even so, no one volunteers.

Next, the group reading *Freckle Juice* shares two projects. Two students share a graph they have made showing how many children in the class have freckles, and the other students present a commercial to sell a bottle of guaranteed "freckle juice."

The group reading *Bunnicula: A Rabbit-Tale of Mystery* explains that they've read a mystery about vegetables turning white, and they show some vegetables they have made out of light-colored clay as evidence. They point out two tiny marks on each vegetable. One student, Bill, pretends to be Harold, the family dog who wrote the book, and he explains that their pet rabbit—Bunnicula—who seemed to be harmless at first, may be responsible for sucking the vegetable juices out of the vegetables. Dolores displays a stuffed animal bunny dressed in a black cape to look like a vampire. The group recommends that classmates read this book if they want to find out what happens to Bunnicula.

The *Shiloh* group shares information from the local ASPCA, and Angelica reads an "I Am" poem about Marty that the group has written:

> *I am a boy who knows right from wrong*
> *but I will do anything to save that dog.*
> *I know how to treat a dog.*
> *I say, "Please don't kick him like that."*
> *I am afraid of Judd Travers.*
> *But I will do anything to save Shiloh.*
> *I dream of Shiloh being mine.*
> *I have a secret hiding place for him.*
> *I catch Judd Travers killing a doe out of season.*
> *I will make mean Mr. Travers sell Shiloh to me.*
> *I work hard for 20 hours to earn $40 to buy him.*
> *I learn that nothing is as simple as it seems.*
> *I am a boy who knows right from wrong*
> *but I will do anything to save my dog.*

The group reading *Bridge to Terabithia* presents a tabletop diorama they have made of the magical kingdom of Terabithia.

Last, Hector and Carlos from the group reading *On My Honor* role-play Joel and Tony, the two boys in the story. The reenact the scene where the boys decide to go swimming. They explain that Tony drowns, and then the boy playing Joel describes what it was like to search for Tony and then pretend that he didn't know what had happened to Tony. Then the other group members ask their classmates what they would have done after Tony died if they had been Joel.

Many students trade books with classmates, and students spend the next two days independently reading any book they choose. Many students read one of the other books read during the book clubs, but some students bring other books from home to read or choose a different book from the class library.

*L*iteracy is a three-way partnership among students, teachers, and parents. Teachers can expect to have a diverse mix of students in their classes, and it is their responsibility to create a community of learners in their classrooms, as Mrs. Bradshaw did. Students bring their home cultures to school and together create a school community. Developing a classroom community is a prerequisite for learning. Teachers begin on the first day of the school year to establish the learning environment, and they nurture students' feelings of responsibility, cooperation, respect, and industry throughout the year.

Teachers organize a literature-based reading program using literature focus units and reading and writing workshop. These two instructional approaches can be integrated or alternated. Teachers assume a variety of roles during literature-based reading, ranging from model and manager to instructor and participant. Students also use reading and writing during across-the-curriculum themes.

Schools cannot be expected to foster children's literacy development alone. Parents must become active participants in their children's literacy development. In some schools, parents regularly volunteer and help out in classrooms and with special school projects. In other schools, however, parents don't realize that teachers want and need their assistance. It is up to teachers to let parents know that they are needed and to find ways for parents to help. Even parents who don't speak English can be valuable school volunteers. There are other ways parents help, too. They stimulate and support their children's reading and writing at home. When students know that their parents value learning and expect them to do well in school, they are more likely to be successful.

In this chapter, you will learn about the three-way partnership among students, teachers, and parents. As you read, think about these questions:

- How do teachers meet the needs of the diverse students in their classes?
- How do teachers create a community of learners?
- What are the teacher's roles in a literature-based reading classroom?
- What are the two instructional approaches that teachers use in literature-based reading classrooms?
- How can parents support children's literacy development?

DEVELOPING LIFELONG READERS AND WRITERS

Our ultimate task as teachers is to help students become independent learners and lifelong readers and writers. Students who become lifelong readers love books and choose to read as a leisure-time activity. They have favorite authors and genres. Lifelong writers enjoy writing and know how to use the writing process to develop and refine their writing. They have confidence that they can use writing to communicate their ideas. They may keep journals, write to pen pals, or submit stories and poems they have written to literary magazines.

In elementary classrooms today, students are increasingly diverse. They represent varied cultural and racial groups. They may be recent immigrants seeking a better life in the United States, or they may speak a language other than English. They may have physical, emotional, or learning disabilities. They may live with grandparents or foster families, or they may be homeless, staying temporarily in a community shelter.

Whether they live in rural, suburban, or urban communities, teachers will most likely work with a variety of students.

Culturally Pluralistic Classrooms

America is a culturally pluralistic society, and our ethnic, racial, and socioeconomic diversity is increasingly reflected in elementary classrooms. According to the 1990 census, 25% of the population in the United States classified themselves as non-European Americans. The percentage of culturally diverse children is even higher. In California 51% of school-age children belong to ethnic minority groups, and in New York State 40% do. Given current immigration patterns and the birthrates of minority groups, it has been estimated that by the year 2000, both Hispanic-American and Asian-American populations will have grown by more than 20%. The African-American population is estimated to grow by 12%. In fact, demographers predict that 1 in 3 Americans will be nonwhite by the year 2000 (American Council on Education and the Education Commission of the States, 1988). These changing demographic statistics will have a significant impact on elementary classrooms, as more and more students come from linguistically and culturally diverse backgrounds while teachers remain overwhelmingly white. More than ever before, all of today's students will live in a global society, and they need the skills and knowledge to live harmoniously with other cultural groups.

America is a nation of immigrants, and dealing with cultural diversity is not a new responsibility for public schools; however, the magnitude of diversity is much greater now. In the past, America was viewed as a melting pot in which language and cultural differences would be assimilated or combined to form a new, truly American culture. What actually happened, though, was that the European-American culture rose to the top because it was the dominant immigrant group, and the cultures of other groups sank (Banks, 1988). The concept of cultural pluralism has replaced assimilation. According to cultural pluralism, people have the right to retain their cultural identity within American society, and each culture contributes to and enriches the total society. This concept is an outgrowth of the Civil Rights movement of the 1960s. Other ethnic cultures were inspired by the Civil Rights movement and the pride that African Americans showed for their culture, and they have been empowered too.

Children of diverse cultures come to school with a broad range of language and literacy experiences, even if they are not the same as those of mainstream or European-American children. Minority children have already learned to communicate in at least one language, and, if they don't speak English, they want to learn English in order to make friends, learn, and communicate just like their classmates do. Teachers of culturally and linguistically diverse students must implement a language arts program that is sensitive to and reflective of these students' backgrounds and needs. In fact, all teachers must be prepared to work with this ever-growing population, and teachers who have no minority students in their classrooms still need to incorporate a multicultural perspective in their curriculum in order to prepare their students to interact effectively in the increasingly multicultural American society.

Cultural and linguistic diversity is not a problem for teachers to overcome; instead, it provides an opportunity to enhance and enrich the learning of all students. Teachers need to provide literacy experiences that reflect the multitude of backgrounds from which their students come, and multicultural literature plays an important role in filling that need (Yokota, 1993).

Culture affects the way people use reading and writing. In her study of three culturally different American communities, Shirley Brice Heath (1983) found that different lifestyles and child-rearing practices result in children coming to school with radically different literacy experiences and expectations about learning. Since the American families in the Heath study had dramatically different experiences with written language in their English-speaking homes, the diversity of experiences of children from homes where a language other than English is spoken is even greater.

Children from each cultural group bring their unique backgrounds and experiences to the process of learning, and they have difficulty with reading concepts that are outside their backgrounds and experiences. This difficulty is worse for students who are learning English as a second language. Think, for example, of the different experiences and language knowledge that children of Vietnamese refugees, Native American children, and children of Russian Jewish immigrants bring to school. No matter what ethnic group they belong to or what language they speak, all students use the same cognitive and linguistic processes to learn.

Children of diverse ethnic groups have met with varying degrees of success in schools, depending on their previous cultural experiences, expectations that students and their parents have, and expectations that teachers have for students. Often a discrepancy exists between the way classrooms operate and the ways students from various ethnic groups behave (Law & Eckes, 1990). Four common cultural behaviors that differ from mainstream behaviors are:

■ *Avoiding eye contact.*   In some Asian and Hispanic cultures, avoiding eye contact is polite and respectful behavior. Mainstream teachers sometimes mistakenly assume that when students avoid eye contact they are not paying attention or are sullen and uncooperative.

■ *Cooperation.*   Students from many Southeast Asian, Polynesian, and Native American cultures are taught to cooperate with and help each other, and in school they often assist classmates with their work. In contrast, many mainstream students are more competitive than cooperative, and sometimes mainstream teachers view cooperating on assignments as cheating.

■ *Fear of making mistakes.*   Mainstream teachers encourage students to take risks and view making mistakes as part of the learning process. In some cultures, especially the Japanese culture, correctness is valued above all else, and students are taught to not guess or take risks.

■ *Formal classroom environment.*   In European and Asian cultures, the school environment is much more formal than it is in American schools. Students from these cultures view American schools as chaotic, and they interpret the informality as permission to misbehave.

Many Asian-American students have been taught to keep a social distance between the teacher and themselves. For example, out of respect to the teacher, they look down when they are spoken to and feel more comfortable remaining in their assigned seats. Grand conversations and other informal activities can make these students feel uncomfortable because the lack of structure appears to indicate disrespect for the teacher. Asian-American parents typically equate learning and knowledge with factual information, and they expect a great deal of homework (Cheng, 1987).

Hakuta and Garcia (1989) found that the most effective classrooms for Mexican-American students have a discourse style similar to the one they know at home. Many

Mexican-American students are familiar with the give-and-take of cooperative learning, and they value working together and learning in a warm, responsive environment. These students work well in a child-centered, integrated program that is responsive to children's needs. When it is possible, Spanish-speaking children in the primary grades should have the opportunity to develop literacy in their home language first.

African-American and Native American students have special needs too. For too long schools have neglected and failed these students. Effective teachers understand and build on these students' abilities, appreciate their varied backgrounds, and cultivate their potential for learning (Brooks, 1985). Teachers must also take into account historical, economic, psychological, and linguistic barriers that have led to oppression and low expectations. One way to help raise these children's self-esteem and build pride in their cultural groups is by incorporating literature about African Americans and Native Americans into their instructional programs.

Bilingual and English as a Second Language (ESL) Speakers

Students whose native language is not English are referred to as English as a Second Language (ESL) students, and students who are not yet sufficiently fluent in English to perform academic tasks successfully are called English Language Learners (ELL). Children who speak their native language at home and speak English fluently at school are bilingual speakers.

Students learning English as a second language are a diverse group. Some speak some English, while others know little or no English. Some learn to speak English quickly, while others learn more slowly. It often takes four to seven years to become a proficient speaker of English, and the more similar the first language is to English, the easier it will be to learn (Allen, 1991).

One conflict for bilingual students is that learning to speak and write Standard English is often perceived by family and community members as a rejection of family and culture. Cultural pluralism has replaced the melting pot point of view, and people in minority ethnic groups are no longer as willing to give up their culture and language to join the mainstream culture. Often they choose to live and function in both cultures, with free access to their cultural patterns, and switch from one culture to the other as the situation demands.

Until recently, most non-English-speaking students were submerged into English-speaking classrooms and left to "sink or swim." Unfortunately, many students sank and dropped out before graduating from high school. In order to better meet the needs of linguistically diverse students, teachers now value students' native language and help them develop a high level of proficiency in their native language as well as add English as a second language. Instruction in students' native language is effective and equitable for large groups of language-minority students (Faltis, 1993). Freeman and Freeman (1993) recommend five guidelines for supporting and valuing students' native languages. Teachers can accomplish most of these guidelines using a foreign-language dictionary, even if they do not speak or write the language themselves.

1. Environmental print. Teachers post signs and other environmental print written in students' native language in the classroom, as shown in Figure 2–2. In a primary-grade classroom, posters with color words, numbers, and the days of the week should be written both in English and in students' native language. Bulletin

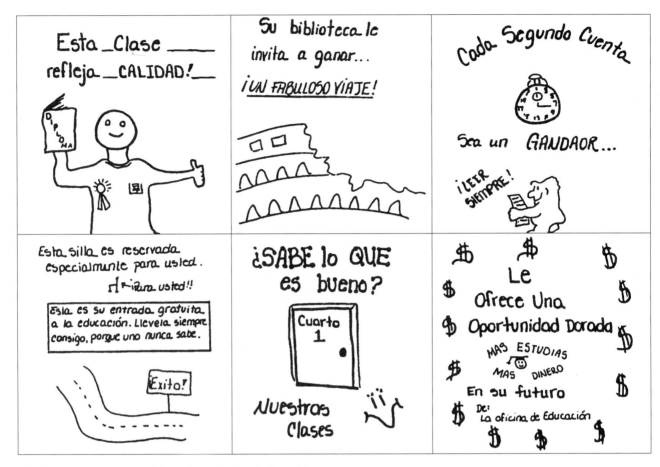

FIGURE 2–2   A Library Center Sign Written in Spanish

Note. From "Strategies for Promoting the Primary Languages of All Students," by D. E. Freeman and
Y. S. Freeman, 1993, *The Reading Teacher, 46,* p. 553. Reprinted with permission.

board titles and captions on posters can also be translated into students' native
languages.

2. Reading materials.   Teachers add books, magazines, and other reading materials written in the students' native language in the library center. Quality books for
children written in a variety of languages are becoming increasingly available in the
United States. Also, award-winning books of children's literature are being translated
into other languages, especially Spanish and Chinese. Books such as *Where the Wild
Things Are* (Sendak, 1962) have been translated for younger children and *Tuck Everlasting* (Babbitt, 1975) for older children. A list of books written in other languages
or with parallel English and other-language texts is presented in Figure 2–3. Sometimes parents and other members of the community are willing to lend books written
in a child's native language for the child to use in school. Or, sometimes parents can
translate a book being used in class for their child.

3. Writing books.   Language-minority students can write and publish books in
their native language. They use the writing process just as English-speaking students

FIGURE 2–3 Multilingual Books Available in the United States

Books Written/Translated in Other Languages

Ancona, G. (1993). *Pablo recuerda: La fiesta del dia de los muertos (Pablo remembers).* New York: Lothrop, Lee & Shepard. (Spanish) (P–M)

Ancona, G. (1995). *Fiesta U.S.A.* New York: Lodestar. (Spanish) (M–U)

Anno, M. (Ed.). (1986). *All in a day.* New York: Philomel. (Chinese). (P–M))

Armstrong, W. H. (1969). *Sounder.* New York: Harper & Row. (Chinese) (M–U)

Cleary, B. (1992). *Ramona la chinche (Ramona the pest).* New York: Morrow. (Spanish) (M)

Dorros, A. (1995). *La isla: edición en español.* New York: Dutton. (Spanish) (See other books by the same author.) (P)

Freeman, D. (1968). *Corduroy.* New York: Viking. (Chinese, Spanish) (P)

Hastings, S. (1985). *Sir Gawain and the loathly lady/Sir Gawain y la adominable dama.* Compton, CA: Santillana. (Spanish). (U)

Kellogg, S. (1992). *Paul Bunyan.* New York: Morrow. (Spanish) (M)

Lobel, A. (1970). *Frog and toad are friends.* New York: Harper & Row. (Chinese, Spanish) (P–M)

McDermott, G. (1978). *The stonecutter: A Japanese folk tale.* New York: Puffin. (Chinese). (P–M)

Rylant, C. (1985). *The relatives came.* New York: Bradbury Press. (Chinese) (M)

Sendak, M. (1963). *Where the wild things are.* New York: Harper & Row. (Chinese, Japanese, Spanish) (P)

Spier, P. (1980). *People.* New York: Doubleday. (Chinese) (P–M)

Taylor, M. D. (1976). *Roll of thunder, hear my cry.* New York: Dial Press. (Chinese) (M–U)

Williams, V. B. (1982). *Un sillón para máma (A chair for my mother).* New York: Morrow. (Spanish) (P)

Zelinsky, P. O. (1986). *Rumpelstiltskin.* New York: Dutton. (Spanish, Chinese) (M)

Books With Parallel Texts in English and Another Language

Ancona, G. (1994). *The piñata maker/El piñatero.* San Diego: Harcourt Brace. (E/Spanish) (P–M)

Garza, C. L. (1990). *Family pictures/Cuadros de familia.* Emeryville, CA: Children's Book Press. (E/Spanish) (P)

Hayes, J. (1994). *Watch out for clever women!/ ¡Cuidado con las mujeres astutas!* El Paso, TX: Cinco Puntos Press. (E/Spanish) (M–U)

Hom, N. (1987). *The little weaver of Thai-yen village.* San Francisco: Children's Book Press. (E/Vietnamese) (M)

Lucas, A. (1990). *Four champa trees.* El Monte, CA: Pacific Asia Press. (E/Lao) (M–U)

Mora, P. (1994). *The desert is my mother/El desierto es mi madre.* Houston: Pinata Books/Arte Publico Press. (E/Spanish) (M)

Nhuan, N. T. (n.d.). *Tam Cam: The Vietnamese Cinderella story.* San Diego: The Gioi Publishing. (E/Vietnamese). (M–U)

Reiser, L. (1993). *Margaret and Margarita, Margarita y Margaret.* New York: Greenwillow. (E/Spanish) (P)

Roe, E. (1991). *Con mi hermano/With my brother.* New York: Macmillan. (E/Spanish) (P)

Rohmer, H. (1989). *Uncle Nacho's hat/El sombrero del tío Nacho.* Emeryville, CA: Children's Book Press. (E/Spanish) (P)

Shea, P. D. (1995). *The whispering cloth.* Honesdale, PA: Boyds Mill Press (Hmong text is supplemental and can be ordered free of charge from the publisher.) (P–M)

Spagnoti, C. (1991). *Judge rabbit and the tree spirit: A folktale from Cambodia.* Emeryville, CA: Children's Book Press. (E/Cambodian) (M)

Vang, L. (1990). *Grandmother's path, grandfather's way.* San Francisco: Children's Book Press. (E/Hmong) (U)

Books With Other-Language Words and Sentences Inserted Into the English Text

Bunting, E. (1994). *A day's work.* New York: Clarion. (Spanish) (P–M)

Cazet, D. (1993). *Born in the gravy.* New York: Orchard Books. (Spanish) (P)

De Zutter, H. (1993). *Who says a dog does bow-wow?* New York: Doubleday. (Many languages) (P–M)

Dorros, A. (1991). *Abuela.* New York: Dutton. (Spanish) (P)

Dorros, A. (1992). *This is my house.* New York: Scholastic. (Many languages) (P)

Haskins, J. (1989). *Count your way through Russia.* Minneapolis: Carolrhoda. (Series of books including Mexico, Arab World, Korea, India, China, and Germany) (P–M)

Pomerantz, C. (1993). *If I had a paka: Poems in eleven languages.* New York: Greenwillow. (M–U)

Soto, G. (1990). *Baseball in April and other stories.* Orlando: Harcourt Brace Jovanovich (Spanish) (See other books by the same author.) (M–U)

P = primary grades (K–2); M = middle grades (3–5); U = upper grades (6–8).

These Spanish-speaking students read and responded to the Spanish version of *Leo the Late Bloomer* while their classmates read the trade book in English.

do, and they can share their published books with classmates and place them in the classroom library.

4. Bilingual tutors. Language-minority students can read and write with tutors, older students, classmates, and parents who speak their native language. Some classrooms have native-language aides who read and write with students in the native language. At other times, parents or older native-speaking students come into the classroom to work with students.

5. Native-language videotapes. Teachers can use videotapes of students reading and dramatizing stories in their native language. Or they can dramatize events in history or demonstrate how to do something in their native language. Creating and viewing these videotapes is useful for building students' native-language proficiency.

Through these activities, teachers value the language-minority students' native language. The activities also help students expand their native-language proficiency, develop greater self-confidence, and value their own language.

Three programs are being used with students who are learning English as a second language. One type is submersion, in which students are thrown into the regular classroom with no special help. A second type is immersion. The language of the classroom is English, but a teacher's aide or other classmates speak the student's native language and provide translations for the language-minority student in the classroom. A third type of program is bilingual. In this program, instruction is carried on both in English and in the student's native language. Of these three programs, researchers have found that bilingual programs are the most effective.

The preferred approach to bilingual education is preview/teach/review. In this approach, the content of the lesson is previewed in one language, the body of the lesson is taught in the second language, and then the lesson is reviewed in the first language (Scarcella, 1990). This approach is often used when two teachers—one English-speaking teacher and one fluent in Spanish or another language—team teach. Alternative approaches for bilingual education are alternating English and another language day by day, and direct translation, in which the teacher provides instant translation in the second language for everything that is said in English. These two approaches are not as effective because students learn to tune out when the unfamiliar language is being spoken.

Students are moved out of bilingual programs into English-only programs as soon as they reach a level where they can communicate in English. These programs are known as early exit programs. In other programs, students remain in bilingual programs longer and receive instruction to further develop their native-language proficiency. These programs are late exit or bilingual maintenance programs, and they are preferred (Scarcella, 1990). There is strong evidence that language-minority children do better in bilingual programs than in English-only programs because bilingual students do not fall as far behind in content-area courses, have better self-esteem, and reach higher levels of proficiency in both languages (Scarcella, 1990).

Bilingual programs, however, are not possible when students in a school speak too many different language or when there are not enough qualified bilingual teachers. For example, in a classroom with one Punjabi speaker, one Portuguese speaker, and one Arabic speaker, the teacher will not be able to help these three students learn to read and write in their native languages first. However, teachers can convey an interest in and appreciation for the students' home languages and cultures. Students can bring a native-language book from home to display or read during reading workshop. Teachers can find out about the students' home cultures and languages from parents or other sources. By finding out which aspects of the classroom environment are most alien to students' home cultures and languages, teachers can help make students and parents more at ease by modifying expectations and by working on areas of special need.

Other Students With Special Learning Needs

Some students in every classroom do not learn to read and write as well as their classmates or as well as the teacher believes they can. Reading materials may be too difficult for some students, some may have difficulty thinking about the meaning of the story and articulating responses to literature, some may not write well-developed reports or use conventional spelling, and others may be unable to work cooperatively with classmates to develop a group project. Every year teachers encounter students who are not developing into capable readers and writers like their classmates, and they need to focus on helping students develop literate behaviors as well as literacy skills and strategies. Literate behaviors are the things that students can do with reading and writing, such as choosing books to read, writing letters, presenting puppet shows to retell stories, and making **clusters** to report information from informational books.

■ *Activity*

Contact a local school district to ask about the cultural and linguistic diversity in the district. Ask how the student population of the district has changed in the past 10 years and how administrators anticipate it will change in the next 10 years.

Five types of students with special needs are:

■ students with specific learning disabilities
■ students with mental retardation
■ students with behavior disorders
■ students with language disorders
■ students with attention deficit disorder

Each type of student is discussed in Figure 2–4, and suggestions are made about how to adapt the instructional program to meet these students' needs. These labels, you may notice, reflect the difficulties students have in school—their limitations with language, difficulties with word identification, and confusions as they try to create meaning from the story—rather than what they can do. It is crucial for teachers to find ways to adapt their instructional programs so that every student can be successful (Wood, 1993).

Most students with special learning needs benefit from the same type of literature-based reading program that other students benefit from (Rhodes & Dudley-Marling, 1988). The biggest difference is that teachers provide more explicit instruction, practice, and guidance as students participate in reading and writing activities and projects (Kameenui, 1993; Sears, Carpenter, & Burstein, 1994). Kameenui (1993) makes the following recommendations for teachers:

1. Use instructional time efficiently.
2. Intervene and provide additional instruction quickly for students who are not making adequate progress.
3. Explicitly teach the most useful skills and strategies through minilessons.
4. Guide students through instructional procedures before having them work independently or in small groups.
5. Assess the effectiveness of instruction by observing students as they read and write and examining their work samples.

Through these modifications, most special-needs students can learn to read and write. It is not appropriate to focus on reading and writing skills to the exclusion of meaningful reading and writing experiences with authentic literacy materials. Substituting drill-and-practice worksheets for books is not recommended. Special-needs students also need more reading practice than other students. They can use **assisted reading, choral reading,** buddy reading, and **readers theatre** for this practice.

Children who do not learn to read and write along with their classmates fall farther and farther behind each year. For example, a fourth grader who is working at the second-grade level might make a year's progress during a school year, but then as a fifth grader the student is now only at the third-grade level. It is even more likely that this fourth grader may not make a whole year's progress and will still be reading at the second-grade level at the beginning of fifth grade. At the same time, other fourth graders make a year's progress or more during that same year, and as fifth graders they are at the fifth-grade level or above (Stanovich, 1986). Kameenui (1993) called this situation "the tyranny of time" and emphasized the importance of teachers using their instructional time efficiently and intervening quickly when students are not making expected progress.

FIGURE 2–4 Adapting the Literature-Based Reading Program for Students With Special Learning Needs

Group	Description	Instructional Guidelines
Students With Specific Learning Disabilities	Students with learning disabilities have significant difficulties in learning and using reading or writing. Even though these students can have severe learning difficulties, they have average or above-average intelligence. Students may not express themselves well, may not read fluently, and may have trouble spelling words correctly and using other written language skills. They may exhibit poor coordination and have difficulty with handwriting. In addition, they may have low self-images, exhibit socially inappropriate behaviors, and have difficulty relating to their classmates. Students can learn the academic content in their weak areas. They learn to compensate for their learning problems. The most important consideration in working with these students is that the classroom and the instruction be structured.	• Allow students to work at their own level. • Teach reading and writing strategies in small groups. • Keep assignments short. • Have students self-select books to read. • Use peer tutors and cross-age tutors. • Connect listening and reading experiences. • Have students choose projects to do after reading. • Allow students to use talk rather than writing whenever possible (e.g., dictate stories and give oral reports instead of written reports). • Try word processing for students with handwriting problems.
Students With Mental Retardation	Students with mental retardation have significantly subaverage intellectual functioning along with limitations in two or more of the following areas: communicating, self-care, home living, social skills, self-direction, health and safety, functional academics, leisure, and work. Their academic performance lags far behind that of other students, but they can learn to read and write. The focus of instruction is to develop the functional skills considered essential to living independently. The most valuable activities for these students are concrete, meaningful, and based on personal experience. When the pace of classroom activities is too fast, individualized instruction with peer tutors can be provided. This individualized instruction should involve more repetition and practice than is necessary for other students.	• Focus on functional skills for independent living. • Connect activities to students' personal experiences. • Use objects and other manipulatives with literature. • Teach decoding and spelling skills. • Provide many opportunities to practice skills and develop fluency. • Use peer tutors to reread familiar books using assisted reading. • Use the language experience approach. • Have students tell stories using wordless picture books. • Teach high-frequency words.

FIGURE 2–4   *continued*

Group	Description	Instructional Guidelines
Students With Behavior Disorders	Students with behavior disorders exhibit inappropriate behavior and feelings that interfere with learning. They may be either aggressive and disruptive or anxious and withdrawn. They are unable to have satisfactory relationships with classmates and the teacher. Often, they are unhappy or depressed. Although any student can exhibit one of these behaviors for a brief period, students with behavior disorders exhibit more than one of these behaviors to a marked degree and consistently over time. Students with behavior disorders need a structured and positive classroom environment in order to be successful. Students need to learn to control their disruptive and socially inappropriate behavior and develop interpersonal skills.	• Closely monitor students' frustration levels and help them find ways to communicate their frustration. • Involve students in grand conversations in small groups. • Have students dramatize stories. • Ask students to assume the role of a character in a story to retell the story or write in a simulated journal. • Structure assignments using checklists and a time schedule. • Have students use personal journals or letters to write their feelings and frustrations. • Use art and music as alternatives for projects.
Students With Language Disorders	Students who have grown up in an English-speaking community but have difficulty understanding or expressing language are classified as having a language disorder. Often these children talk very little, speak in childlike phrases, and lack the language to understand basic concepts. This is a very serious problem because students' limited ability to communicate has a negative impact on learning as well as social interaction with classmates and the teacher. It is important to note that students who speak their native language fluently and are learning English as a second language do not have a language disorder.	• Encourage students to participate in conversations with a classmate or in a small group. • Share books with predictable language patterns. • Invent new versions for the predictable books. • Play with rhyming words and make riddles with students. • Have students use role-playing and puppets. • Have students do choral reading. • Have students retell stories and sequence story boards. • Have students listen to books at the listening center. • Have students work with a partner to develop socialization skills.
Students With Attention Deficit Disorder	Students with attention disorder (ADD) have great difficulty attending to tasks and activities. These students display distractibility, impulsiveness, inattention, and mood fluctuations. It is crucial that students with ADD are able to be successful in the classroom, and that teachers structure their environment to minimize the effects of their distractibility.	• Allow students to move around the classroom. • Structure assignments using checklists and time schedules. • Monitor students closely as they work. • Encourage students to participate in talk and dream activities. • Provide choices for students. • Use graphic organizers for students to complete while reading or listening. • Use reading and writing workshop.

Why are some students unmotivated to read and write?

Some students, especially those in the upper grades, often say that reading is boring. They say that it takes too long and that the words are hard to understand (Robb, 1993). Unmotivated students rarely are good readers. If students are reading uninteresting books, teachers can help students find fast-paced, action-packed stories. But the word "boring" is more likely a cover for children who are not fluent readers. When children have to struggle to decode almost every word, reading truly isn't much fun. Teachers need to locate books written at children's reading levels and provide lots of reading practice so that students can become more fluent readers.

Other children answer "I don't know" when teachers ask them to talk about what they are reading and what they think about what they have read. An "I don't know" answer suggests that students may look like they are reading but actually aren't. Even if they are going to the effort of decoding the words on the page, they aren't comprehending what they are reading. Teachers can have children choose the books they want to read, build background before reading a book together as a class, or use reading buddies to read with younger children. Teachers need to look behind the "this is boring" and "I don't know" responses that less able readers try to hide behind and find ways to reach these students (Robb, 1993).

Ruddell (1995) researched influential reading and writing teachers—those who had a profound effect on students' lives—and found that these teachers stimulated students' internal motivation through the classroom community they created and through the literacy activities in which students were involved. Internal motivation is the innate curiosity within each of us that makes us want to figure things out. Internal motivation is social, too. We want to socialize, share ideas, and participate in group activities. Ruddell found that these teachers encouraged students to assume an aesthetic stance as they read and responded to books. In contrast, noninfluential teachers depended on external motivation, such as teacher praise, peer pressure, and grades. They encouraged students to assume an efferent stance during reading. These teachers asked students factual questions and judged their answers against predetermined answers, rather than exploring students' interpretations and their relationships with the characters.

The types of literacy activities also affect students' motivation for literacy. Turner and Paris (1995) compared the literacy activities in literature-based and skills-based reading classrooms and concluded that students' motivation was determined by the daily classroom activities. They found that open-ended activities and projects in which students were in control of the processes they used and the products they created were the most successful. Open-ended activities involve choice, challenge, control, collaboration, constructing meaning, and consequences, and Turner and Paris recommend that teachers consider these six C's as they develop their instructional programs.

■ *Activity*
Reread the vignette at the beginning of the chapter and consider how Mrs. Bradshaw used open-ended activities in her classroom.

THE TEACHER'S ROLE

The teacher's role in a literature-based reading classroom is complex and multidimensional. No longer are teachers simply providers of knowledge. No longer do teachers slavishly follow a teacher's manual and move story by story through a basal reader over the course of a school year. Nor do teachers assign an endless series of worksheets and "busy work." Instead, teachers understand that children's literacy develops most effectively through purposeful and meaningful social contexts. These

FIGURE 2–5   The Teacher's Ten Roles in a Literature-Based Reading Program

Role	Description
1. Organizer	• Plans literature-based reading program • Sets time schedules • Develops literature focus units • Schedules reading and writing workshop • Uses reading and writing as tools for across-the-curriculum themes
2. Facilitator	• Develops a classroom community of learners • Stimulates students' interest in literacy • Allows students to choose books to read and topics for projects • Provides opportunities for students to read and write using genuine materials for authentic purposes • Involves students in collaborative reading and writing experiences • Invites parents to become involved in classroom activities
3. Participant	• Reads and writes with students • Learns along with students • Asks questions and seeks answers to questions
4. Instructor	• Provides information about books, genres, authors, and illustrators • Explains literacy procedures • Teaches minilessons on skills and strategies • Provides background knowledge before reading • Groups students for instruction
5. Model	• Demonstrates how to perform literacy procedures, skills, and strategies • Thinks aloud how an expert reader and writer uses skills and strategies • Reads aloud to students every day

teachers create the classroom environment and a community of learners. They choose literature and plan an instructional program using that literature to meet the needs of their increasingly diverse classrooms of students. Their goal is to excite students about reading and writing and to help them consider themselves readers and writers—members of the "literacy club," as Frank Smith (1988) would say.

Teachers of literature-based reading might be compared to orchestra conductors, and effective teachers "orchestrate" the life of the classroom. They are instructors, coaches, facilitators, and managers. Figure 2–5 presents a list of some of the roles teachers assume.

Establishing a Community of Learners

Teachers begin the process of establishing a community of learners when they make deliberate decisions about the kind of classroom culture they want to create (Sumara & Walker, 1991). School is "real" life for students, and they learn best when they see a purpose for learning to read and write. The social contexts that teachers create are

FIGURE 2–5   *continued*

Role	Description
6. Manager	• Sets expectations and responsibilities • Keeps track of students' progress during literature focus units • Monitors students' work during reading and writing workshop • Keeps records • Arranges the classroom to facilitate learning • Has necessary equipment and supplies available
7. Diagnostician	• Conferences with students • Observes students in literacy activities • Assesses students' strengths and weaknesses as readers and writers • Plans instruction based on students' needs
8. Evaluator	• Assesses students' progress in reading and writing • Helps students self-assess their learning • Assigns grades • Reports students' progress to parents • Examines the effectiveness of the literacy program
9. Coordinator	• Works with resource teachers, librarians, aides, and parent volunteers • Works with other teachers for grade-level literacy projects and cross-age reading buddy programs
10. Communicator	• Expects students to do their best • Encourages students to become lifelong readers • Communicates the literacy program to parents and administrators • Shares new literacy goals and activities with parents and the community • Encourages parents to support and extend the literacy program at home

an important key. Teachers must think about their role and the kind of literacy instruction they want in their classrooms. They must decide to have a democratic classroom where students' abilities in reading and writing develop through purposeful and meaningful literacy activities.

Teachers are more successful when they take the first two weeks of the school year to establish the classroom environment (Sumara & Walker, 1991). Teachers can't assume that students will be familiar with the procedures and routines used in literature-based reading or that they will instinctively be cooperative, responsible, and respectful of classmates. Teachers explicitly explain classroom routines, such as how to get supplies out and put them away and how to work with classmates in a cooperative group, and set the expectation that students will adhere to the rou-tines. Next, they demonstrate literacy procedures, including how to use the "Goldilocks Strategy" to choose a book from the classroom library, how to provide feedback in a **writing group,** and how to participate in a grand conversation or discussion about a book. Third, teachers model ways of interacting with students, responding

Teachers create a community of learners as they establish routines for collaborating and working in small groups.

to literature, respecting classmates, and assisting classmates with reading and writing projects.

Teachers are the classroom managers or administrators. They set expectations and clearly explain to students what is expected of them and what is valued in the classroom. The classroom rules are specific and consistent, and teachers also set limits. For example, students might be allowed to talk quietly with classmates when they are working, but they are not allowed to shout across the classroom or talk when the teacher is talking or when students are making a presentation to the class. Teachers also model classroom rules themselves as they interact with students. According to Sumara and Walker (1991), the process of socialization at the beginning of the school year is planned, deliberate, and crucial to the success of the literacy program.

Not everything can be accomplished during the first two weeks, however. Teachers continue to reinforce classroom routines and literacy procedures. One way is to have student leaders model the desired routines and behaviors. When this is done, other students are likely to follow the lead. Teachers also continue to teach additional literacy procedures as students are involved in new types of activities. The classroom community evolves during the school year, but the foundation is laid during the first two weeks.

Teachers develop a predictable classroom environment with familiar routines and literacy procedures. Students feel comfortable, safe, and more willing to take risks and experiment in a predictable classroom environment. This is especially true for students from varied cultures, students learning English as a second language, and less capable readers and writers.

Arranging the Classroom

The classroom arrangement should foster a community of learners. The physical arrangement and materials provided in the classroom play an important role in setting the stage for listening, talking, reading, and writing. In the past, textbooks were the primary instructional material, and students sat in desks arranged in rows facing the teacher. Now a wide variety of instructional materials are available in addition to textbooks, including trade books, newspapers, and audiovisual materials. Students' desks are arranged in small groups, and classrooms are visually stimulating, with signs, posters, charts, and other teacher-made and student-made displays related to the literature focus units and across-the-curriculum themes.

These are components of a literature-based reading classroom:

- desks arranged in groups to facilitate cooperative learning
- a classroom library stocked with many different kinds of reading materials
- posted messages about the current day
- displays of student work and projects
- a chair designated as the **author's chair**
- displayed signs, labels for items, and quotations
- posted directions for activities or use of equipment
- materials for recording language, including pencils, pens, paper, journals, books, computers, video cameras, and playback systems
- special places for reading and writing activities
- reference materials related to literature focus units and across-the-curriculum themes
- a listening center and other multimedia materials and equipment
- a puppet stage or area for storytelling and performing plays
- charts on which students record information (e.g., sign-in charts for attendance or writing group charts)
- world-related print (e.g., newspapers, maps, calendars)
- reading and writing materials in primary students' play centers (adapted from Hall, 1987)

These components of a literature-based reading classroom are elaborated on in Figure 2–6. Mrs. Bradshaw's multi-age classroom, described in the vignette at the beginning of this chapter, embodies many of these components. Her students' desks were arranged in groups, and literacy supplies were available for students to use as they participated in book clubs.

No single physical arrangement best represents a literature-based reading classroom, but the configuration of any classroom can be modified to include many of

FIGURE 2–6   Characteristics of Literature-Based Reading Classrooms

1. **Classroom Organization**
   - Desks are arranged in groups.
   - The arrangement facilitates group interaction.
   - Other parts of the classroom are organized into centers such as the library center, writing center, and theme center.

2. **Classroom Library Center**
   - There are at least four times as many books as there are students in the classroom.
   - Stories, informational books, and poetry are included.
   - Multicultural books and other reading materials are included.
   - Information about authors and illustrators is displayed.
   - Some of the books were written by students.
   - Books related to literature focus units and theme studies are highlighted.
   - Students monitor the center.

3. **Message Center**
   - Schedules and announcements about the current day are posted.
   - Some of the announcements are student-initiated.
   - There are mailboxes and/or a message board for students to use.
   - Students are encouraged to write notes to classmates.

4. **Display of Student Work and Projects**
   - All students have work displayed in the classroom.
   - Student work reflects a variety of curricular areas.
   - Students' projects and other student-made displays are exhibited in the class-room.
   - There is an area where students can display their own work.
   - Other student work is stored in portfolios.

5. **Author's Chair**
   - One chair in the classroom has been designated as the author's chair for students to use when sharing their writing.
   - The author's chair is labeled.

6. **Signs, Labels, and Quotations**
   - Equipment and other classroom items are labeled.
   - Words, phrases, and sentences are posted in the classroom.
   - Some signs, labels, and quotes are written by students.

the desirable characteristics. Student desks or tables should be grouped to encourage students to talk, share, and work cooperatively. Separate areas are needed for reading and writing, a classroom library, a listening center, centers for materials related to content-area theme studies, and dramatic activities. Kindergarten classrooms also need play centers. Some variations obviously occur at various grade levels. Older students, for example, use reference centers with materials related to the literature focus units and themes they are studying. The three diagrams in

FIGURE 2–6   *continued*

---

7. Directions

- Directions are provided in the classroom so that students can work independently.
- Some of the directions are written by students.

8. Materials for Writing

- Pencils, pens, paper, journals, books, computers, and other materials are available for recording language.
- Students have access to these materials.

9. Places for Reading and Writing

- There are special places in the classroom for reading and writing activities.
- These areas are quiet and separated from other areas.

10. Reference Materials

- Word walls list important words related to literature focus units and theme studies.
- Lists, clusters, pictures, charts, books, models, and other reference materials are available for content-area study.
- Artifacts and other items related to theme studies are labeled and displayed.
- Students use these materials as they work on projects related to theme studies.

11. Audiovisual Materials

- A listening center is available for students to use.
- Audiovisual materials—such as CD-ROM, filmstrips, videotapes, and films—related to literature focus units and theme studies are available.
- The equipment needed to use these audiovisual materials is available in the classroom.

12. Dramatic Center

- A puppet stage is set up in the classroom.
- Art materials are available for making puppets and other props.
- An area in the classroom is accessible for performing plays and telling stories.
- Props are available in the classroom.
- Primary-grade classrooms have dramatic play centers, including reading and writing materials.

Figure 2–7 suggest ways to arrange the classroom to foster a community of learners.

Three centers in literature-based reading classrooms are library centers, listening centers, and writing centers. Library centers are stocked with hundreds of trade books that are attractively displayed and available for students to peruse. These books might be from the teacher's own collection or borrowed from the school or public library. Many of the books should relate to units of study, and these should be changed peri-

KINDERGARTEN CLASSROOM

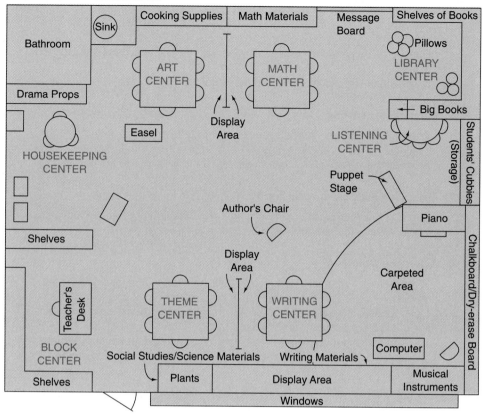

FIGURE 2–7   Three Classroom Diagrams

odically. Other books for students to read independently are also included in the library center. After studying library centers in classrooms, Leslie Morrow (1989) made the following recommendations:

■ The library center is inviting and affords privacy.

■ The library center has a physical definition with shelves, carpets, benches, sofas, or other partitions.

■ Five or six students fit comfortably in the center.

■ Two kinds of bookshelves are needed. Most of the collection is shelved with the spines facing outward, but some books are set so that the front covers are displayed.

■ Books are shelved by category and color-coded by type.

■ Books written by one author or related to a theme being studied are displayed prominently, and the displays are changed regularly.

■ The floor is covered with a rug, and the area is furnished with pillows, beanbag chairs, or comfortable furniture.

■ The center is stocked with at least four times as many books as there are students in the classroom.

THIRD-GRADE CLASSROOM

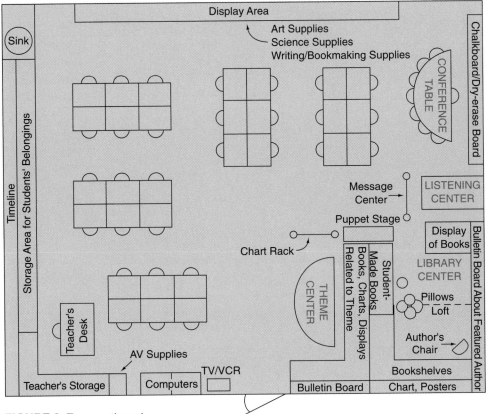

FIGURE 2–7 *continued*

- A variety of types of reading materials, including books, newspapers, magazines, posters, and charts, are available.
- Attractive posters that encourage reading, especially if they relate to books in the library center, are available.

These recommendations were based on research in primary-grade classrooms, but they are equally appropriate for older students.

Listening centers equipped with tape players and headphones are another essential part of language-rich classrooms. Students listen to cassette tapes of stories and sometimes follow along in accompanying books. Many commercially prepared tape recordings of children's books are available, and teachers can tape-record their own reading of books so that students can reread books and listen again and again to their favorite stories. Too often teachers think of listening centers as equipment for primary-grade classrooms and do not realize their potential usefulness with older students.

Supplies of writing and art materials for students to use as they write books and respond to books they read are stored in writing centers. These materials include:

- a variety of pens, pencils, crayons, markers, and other writing and drawing instruments
- lined and unlined paper of varied sizes and colors

SIXTH-GRADE CLASSROOM

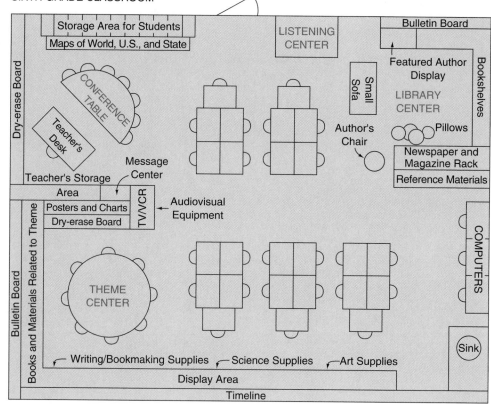

FIGURE 2–7   *continued*

- materials for making and binding books
- computers and printers
- a camera and film for taking illustration photos and photos of students for their "All About the Author" pages
- scrap art materials for illustrations

In primary-grade classrooms there is usually a table in the center where students gather to write and share their writing. In middle- and upper-grade classrooms, however, writing materials are stored on shelves or in cabinets, and students usually write at their own desks. To revise their writing, they meet with the teacher at a conference table or with small groups of classmates wherever there is space in the classroom.

Organizing the Instructional Program

Two approaches for literature-based reading instruction are literature focus units and reading and writing workshop. In literature focus units, students read books together and respond to them as a class or in small groups. Because students are reading together, they share their interpretations about the story and become a community of readers. Sometimes the unit focuses on a picture book such as *Rosie's Walk* (Hutchins, 1968) or *Cloudy With a Chance of Meatballs* (Barrett, 1978), or a chapter book such as *Bunnicula: A Rabbit-Tale of Mystery* (Howe & Howe, 1979). Other literature focus units feature a genre such as folktales or a study on an author or illustrator. Literature focus units have four components:

1. *Reading books.*   Students read books together as a class or in small groups. Students may read independently, read together with a partner, or read along as the teacher (or another fluent reader) reads the book aloud.

2. *Responding.*   Students respond to the book to record their initial impressions and develop their interpretations. Students write in reading logs and participate in grand conversations.

3. *Teaching minilessons.*   Teachers present **minilessons** on procedures, strategies, and skills and connect the lessons to books students are reading or compositions they are writing (Atwell, 1987). These lessons are brief explanations, discussions, and demonstrations and are usually completed in 15 or 20 minutes. Worksheets are not used in minilessons; instead, students apply the lesson to their own reading and writing activities. Minilessons can be conducted with the whole class, with small groups of students who have indicated that they need to learn more about a particular topic, and with individual students. Teachers can also plan minilessons on a regular basis to introduce or review topics.

4. *Creating projects.*   Students create projects to extend their reading. These projects can involve art, drama, reading, writing, music, research, and other types of responses (Gardner, 1983; Leland & Harste, 1994). Students usually choose the projects they create based on their interests and the opportunities the book

During a science fiction unit, sixth graders alternate reading chapters of a book with viewing chapters of an innovative video program.

presents to them. For example, after reading *Jumanji* (Van Allsburg, 1981), students might write sequels, design their own board games, or draw Venn diagrams comparing the book and the film. After reading *Sylvester and the Magic Pebble* (Steig, 1969), they might share their rock collections (or other things they collect) or read other books written by William Steig.

Two types of workshops are reading workshop and writing workshop. Reading workshop fosters real reading of self-selected stories, poems, and informational books, and writing workshop fosters real writing for genuine purposes and authentic audiences. Teachers often use both workshops, or if their schedule does not allow, they may alternate the two.

In reading workshop, students read books that they choose themselves, respond to books through writing in reading logs, and share the books with classmates (Atwell, 1987; Hornsby, Sukarna, & Parry, 1986). Reading workshop has five components:

1. *Reading.*   Students read books and other written materials independently.
2. *Responding.*   Students keep lists of books they have read and write their initial responses to their reading in reading logs.
3. *Sharing.*   The class gathers together as a community of learners to share books they have finished reading.
4. *Teaching minilessons.*   Teachers present brief lessons on reading workshop procedures and reading strategies and skills.
5. *Reading aloud to students.*   Teachers read books aloud to students, and students talk about the books in grand conversations. Primary-grade teachers often read picture books aloud, and middle- and upper-grade teachers read chapter books, completing one or two chapters each day.

Writing workshop is a new way of implementing the writing process (Atwell, 1987; Calkins, 1994; Graves, 1994; Parry & Hornsby, 1985). Students usually write on topics that they choose themselves, and they assume ownership of their learning. Students may write a sequel to a favorite book or retell a story from a different viewpoint. Primary-grade students often write innovations, in which they use the pattern of a book they have read to structure a book they are writing. Writing workshop is an hour to hour-and-a-half period scheduled each day. It has three components:

1. *Teaching minilessons.*   Teachers provide brief lessons on writing workshop procedures and writing strategies and skills.
2. *Writing.*   Students work independently on writing projects. They move through all five stages of the writing process—prewriting, drafting, revising, editing, and publishing—at their own pace. Many times students compile their final copies to make books during writing workshop, but sometimes they attach their writing to artwork, make posters, write letters that will be mailed, or perform scripts as skits or puppet shows.
3. *Sharing.*   Students gather together to share their new publications and make other related announcements. A student who has just finished writing a puppet show script and making puppets may ask for volunteers to help perform the puppet show, which could be held several days later during sharing time. Younger stu-

During writing workshop, students often draft, revise, and edit their compositions using computers in the classroom.

dents often sit in a circle or gather together on a rug for sharing time, and the students sit in a special author's chair to read their compositions.

Sometimes teachers organize their daily schedule to include both literature focus units and reading and writing workshop in their literacy block. When teachers don't have that much time available, Lewin (1992) recommends alternating teacher-led literature focus units with student-selected reading and writing workshop. Both teacher-led and student-selected instructional programs provide literacy opportunities that students need, and neither type of program can provide both types of opportunities. The logical solution is to use a combination of approaches.

Students also use reading and writing as they learn about social studies and science in theme studies. Across-the-curriculum themes are a new type of interdisciplinary unit that integrates language arts with social studies, science, and other curricular areas (Altwerger & Flores, 1994; Gamberg, Kwak, Hutchings, Altheim, & Edwards, 1988). Students use reading and writing as they investigate, solve problems, and learn during themes. Three types of literacy activities used during themes are:

1. *Keeping learning logs.*   Students keep **learning logs** to write entries about new concepts they are learning, record new and interesting words, make charts and diagrams, and write reflections about their learning.

2. *Reading books.*   Students read informational books and magazines as well as other types of books related to the theme.

3. *Creating projects.*   Students create projects to extend their learning and demonstrate their new knowledge. Projects include oral reports, poems, charts, dioramas, books, and skits.

What about teaching?

We could say that everything a teacher does during literature focus units and reading and writing workshop is teaching, and in a sense it is. If, however, we define teaching as providing information, literature-based reading teachers do two kinds of teaching. One kind is called direct instruction. In this kind of teaching, teachers provide systematic, planned lessons in which they explicitly present information, provide an opportunity for supervised practice, and then have students apply what they have learned through authentic reading and writing activities (Slaughter, 1988). Teachers often use direct instruction during minilessons in which they teach students about reading and writing procedures, skills, and strategies. Direct instruction has been associated with drill-and-practice activities, but it doesn't have to be. This kind of teaching is necessary to provide information and opportunities for students to apply what they are learning with guidance from the teacher (Spiegel, 1992). Some examples of direct instruction lessons are:

- presenting a biographical sketch of Chris Van Allsburg during a unit featuring the author and his fantasy stories
- highlighting important vocabulary from *Sarah, Plain and Tall* (MacLachlan, 1983) on the classroom **word wall**
- choosing a word from an across-the-curriculum theme (e.g., *evaporation*) and using the letters to build words (e.g., *pear, pave, port*) and review spelling rules
- explaining pourquoi (or "why") tales before reading *Iktomi and the Boulder* (Goble, 1988)
- demonstrating how to proofread a piece of writing to identify spelling, punctuation, and capitalization errors

The second kind of teaching is indirect teaching (Slaughter, 1988). Teachers use indirect teaching to take advantage of teachable moments as they respond to students' questions or when students demonstrate the need to know something. These lessons take place during whole-class activities, during conferences with students, and while working with small groups. Teachers also do indirect teaching as they model reading when reading aloud to the class and as they model writing when students are writing a **collaborative book.** Other examples include:

- demonstrating how to use an index when a student says she can't find anything about scorpions in the informational book *Desert Life* (Taylor, 1992)
- explaining how to use quotation marks while editing the student's piece of writing
- explaining what a prologue and an epilogue are during a conference with a student who is reading *Tuck Everlasting* (Babbitt, 1975)
- reviewing the spelling rule that *y* at the end of a word is usually changed to *i* before adding a suffix when a student asks how to spell *cries*
- showing a student how to write an innovation for *Dogs Don't Wear Sneakers* (Numeroff, 1993)

Although direct instruction is planned, teachers seize teachable moments for indirect instruction, as Mrs. Bradshaw did in the vignette at the beginning of this chapter. Both kinds of teaching are valuable and should be included in literature-based reading programs. Sometimes teachers ask how they should balance the two types of teaching. It is important to remember that most of the instructional time—perhaps as much as 70 to 80%—is devoted to real reading and writing (Goodman, Watson, & Burke, 1987). Of the remaining time—20 to 30%—probably one half is spent on unplanned, indirect instruction and the other half on planned, direct instruction. Because teachable moments may not present themselves for some important literacy strategies and skills, both direct and indirect instruction are needed (Baumann, 1991).

Teachers can turn to the Internet for more information and suggestions about teaching literature-based reading. As the Technology Link below suggests, teachers can collect lessons plans, share ideas for teaching skills and strategies, and dialogue with other teachers about teaching reading and writing on-line. The Internet provides an up-to-date listing of resources that can be very useful in teaching reading.

Technology Link
The NET Effect

There are many opportunities for teachers to share lesson plans and literature-based reading activities on the Internet, and to use the resources of the Internet in their classrooms. Almost all of the Internet access services (America Online, Prodigy, Compuserve) have an "Education" window on their general menu page. For example, on America Online, double-clicking on EDUCATION gets you access to specific education magazines, research groups, and bulletin boards. The "Teachers Information Network" screen is set up with icons representing each of the categories listed below.

■ "Professional Organizations," with information about convention dates and times

■ "Resource Pavilion," which provides original resources about educational topics, including adult literacy and gifted and talented students

■ "Electronic Schoolhouse," which provides bulletin boards to display and discuss lesson plans; on-line classroom links so that students reading the same book or studying the same theme can share their learning; and on-line chats with children's authors and educators

■ "Scholastic Network," with educational television channels and programming schedules, and information about new Scholastic programs such as new books and multimedia programs in the Magic School Bus series

■ "Computing Forums," with programs including a poetry anthology for students' poems, special writing projects for students, information about electronic books, and bulletin boards where teachers can post and collect messages

■ "Education Libraries," which displays libraries of lesson plans posted by teachers or professional organizations, and professional resources on literacy and a variety of other topics

Teachers can post and collect lesson plans and unit plans, engage in dialogues in "chat rooms," and learn how to integrate technology through using television programs and the print materials that the education channels provide for classroom use. Other resources are video and multimedia "stores" and libraries where materials may be obtained at little or no cost. Access to the Internet also allows teachers to obtain the latest research through ERIC-on-line.

In the classroom, students can use the Internet to read and write for authentic purposes. They "chat" with students in other classrooms during "classroom links," share their writing in electronic anthologies, participate in on-line chats with children's authors, locate resources related to theme studies, learn about electronic books and other media, and participate in special reading and writing programs announced through the Internet.

PARENT INVOLVEMENT

Effective teachers involve parents in the literacy program and extend their literacy programs from the classroom into the home. They communicate the importance of parent involvement to parents, view parents as teaching partners, and understand that even parents with limited education or those who do not speak English are valuable resources. They recognize that families from various cultures use literacy in different ways, but that parents from all sociocultural groups value literacy and want their children to succeed in school (Shockley, 1993).

Why involve parents?

Parents are the most powerful influence on children's literacy development, and they have a responsibility to be involved. What's more, when parents are involved in their children's literacy development, students become better readers and writers. Three ways that parents can become involved are as teaching partners in the classroom, as resource persons, and as teachers at home (Tinajero & Nagel, 1995).

Teachers are also learning that working with parents of preschoolers and kindergartners can help prevent children's reading problems later on (France & Hager, 1995). Through parent programs, low-income and minority parents can learn how to create a home environment that fosters literacy and how to read aloud to their young children. Parents with limited literacy skills benefit in other ways, too. They develop their own reading and writing abilities through family literacy programs.

Providing Literacy Information to Parents

Since the introduction of literature-based reading instruction, children are learning to read in new ways, and these new methods are often unfamiliar to parents. Not surprisingly, these changes have made many parents anxious about how their children are learning to read and write. Parent information programs are crucial in helping parents to understand why students may use trade books rather than textbooks, why children explore meanings of stories they have read through grand conversations, how skills and strategies are taught in minilessons, how writing supports children's reading development, and what invented spelling is. Teachers provide literacy information to parents in a variety of ways:

- back-to-school nights
- newsletters
- conferences with parents
- workshops on strategies for working with young readers and writers
- homework telephone hot lines
- telephone calls and notes with good news

In parent workshops and other information-sharing sessions, teachers use videotapes, demonstrations, and guest speakers to provide information about literacy development and the programs in their classrooms. Teachers share some of the books children are reading, especially books representing the cultures of the children in the classroom. Parents can write small books during a writing workshop session, use the

FIGURE 2–8   What Parents Can Learn in Literacy Information Programs

Components of literature-based reading programs
The importance of parents as literacy models for their children
How to read books to children
How to do shared reading
Ways to encourage children to read at home
How to observe in children's classrooms
How to conference with teacher
What to include in home literacy centers
How to record language experience stories with children
How to choose books appropriate for children's needs and interests
Ways to provide literacy learning opportunities through play
How to use the school library
How to select magazines for children
How computers can support children's literacy development
Ways to draw children's attention to print
How to teach children the letters of the alphabet
How to help children develop phonemic awareness
How to do assisted reading
How to be a role model for reading and writing
How to encourage children's writing at home
How to help children spell words
Ways to proofread children's rough drafts
How to share their own literacy uses with their children
How to help with and monitor children's homework even if parents can't do the
     homework themselves
Ways parents can talk to children about the literacy papers they bring home
How the school expects parents to help at home
How siblings can participate in home literacy programs

Adapted from Edwards, 1995; and Shanahan, Mulhern, and Rodriguez-Brown, 1995.

computer for literacy activities, and learn how to examine the work their children bring home. Teachers also show parents how to work with their children at home. Figure 2–8 presents a list of topics for literacy information programs. Without sharing these types of information, parents often feel isolated from the school and are unsure of how to help their children at home.

Patricia Edwards (1995) developed a literacy program for low-income parents in Louisiana, and she reports that parents want to know how to work with their children. Parents told her that they didn't know reading books aloud to their young children was so important and wished they had known sooner how to support their children's literacy development. In her study, parents were grateful that someone explained and demonstrated to them exactly what teachers expect them to do at home.

Parent Volunteers

Schools need lots of adults to read with students and to conference with students about books they are reading and compositions they are writing. Parents, grandparents, older students, and other community volunteers can be extremely useful, too.

Volunteer experiences can be extremely beneficial for parents, also, as they learn about the school and the literacy program. Come and Fredericks (1995) report that parents need to be involved in planning the program, and parents are more likely to become involved if they believe the school has their needs and those of their children at heart. Rasinski and Fredericks (1990) recommend five steps for establishing a quality volunteer program:

1. *Recruitment.*   Teachers invite parents and others to volunteer to assist in the classroom. Sometimes telephone calls and home visits are necessary to let parents know they are truly welcome and needed.
2. *Training.*   Teachers need to train volunteers so that they know how to work with students, where things are located in the school, and how to assist you.
3. *Variety.*   Teachers need to offer parents a variety of ways to be involved in schools. Volunteers may feel more comfortable helping in one way than in another, or they may have a special talent to share.
4. *Recognition.*   For a volunteer program to be successful, the volunteers need to know they are appreciated. Often schools plan recognition receptions each spring to publicly thank the volunteers for their dedication and service.
5. *Evaluation.*   Teachers evaluate their volunteer programs and make changes based on the feedback they get from the volunteers and students.

In bilingual schools with students from many cultural backgrounds, parents play a key role in their children's education. Monolingual English-speaking teachers rely on parents to develop an environment that is linguistically and culturally relevant for the children. Minority parents also provide a feeling of security and belonging for culturally and linguistically diverse students. Some parents from other cultures feel inadequate to help in schools, either because they speak another language or because they have limited education themselves, so it is the teacher's responsibility to let parents know they are valued (Tinajero & Nagel, 1995).

Supporting Literacy at Home

Parents are children's first and best teachers, and there are many things parents can do to support their children's literacy development at home (Tinajero & Nagel, 1995). In addition to reading to their children and listening to their children read to them, parents can build children's self-esteem and spend quality time together. Ten principles for parents as they work with their children at home are:

1. Make time for reading every day by establishing a daily read-aloud time. Make it a priority.
2. Make reading activities interesting and relevant to your children.
3. Read real books, and don't complete worksheets or other decontextualized skill activities.
4. Be patient with your child and understand that it takes time to become a fluent reader.
5. Support and encourage your child.
6. Keep reading experiences informal and relaxed.

7. Encourage your child to ask questions and talk about the books he or she is reading.

8. Encourage your child to read for fun.

9. Be a model for your child and read books, newspapers, and magazines every day.

10. Involve your child in writing activities (Come & Fredericks, 1995; Rasinski & Fredericks, 1988).

Families use literacy in many different ways. Some read the Bible and other religious publications, and others read the newspaper or novels as entertainment. In some homes, the main reading experience is reading *TV Guide,* while in other homes families write letters and sign greeting cards. Some parents read to their children each evening, and in other homes parents are busy catching up on work from the office while children do homework in the evening. In other homes, children and parents communicate by computer through the Internet. In many homes, there are daily living routines, such as making shopping lists, paying bills, and leaving messages for family members. Figure 2–9 identifies some of the many ways parents can support children's literacy development.

Many teachers assume that children from families with low socioeconomic status have few if any literacy events in their homes, but other teachers argue that such children live in homes where people use print for many and varied functions, even if many of those purposes might be different than those of middle-class families. In an interesting study, researchers uncovered great variation in the number and types of

FIGURE 2–9   Ways Parents Support Children's Literacy Development

Visit children's classrooms and get acquainted with their teachers
Talk to children about school activities
Display children's schoolwork at home
Place books in children's bedrooms and in living rooms
Keep pens and paper available in the home
Get a library card and take children to the library on a regular basis to check out books
Model reading and writing for children
Read to or with children every day
Subscribe to newspapers and magazines and read them
Write in family journals
Write letters and cards to extended family members and friends
Share family histories and memories with children
Set an area of the home aside for children to do their homework
Supervise children as they do homework and work on school projects
Watch literacy-related television programs such as *Sesame Street* and *Reading Rainbow* with children
Point out environmental signs and labels to young children
Volunteer to help in children's classrooms
Demonstrate that you value reading and writing
Audiotape and videotape children reading
Have high expectations for children
Encourage children to have hobbies and outside interests
Give children books as gifts

uses of reading and writing in low-income families (Purcell-Gates, L'Allier, & Smith, 1995). Included in the study were white, African-American, Hispanic-American, and Asian-American low-income families, and all children spoke English as their primary language. The findings confirm that teachers cannot make generalizations and must look at each child as an individual from a unique family setting. It is not enough to use demographic characteristics such as family income level to make assumptions about a child's literacy environment.

Family Literacy

Schools are designing family literacy programs for minority parents, parents who are not fluent readers and writers, and parents who are learning English as a second language. These programs are intergenerational and designed to improve the literacy development of both children and their parents. Adults learn to improve their literacy skills as well as how to work with their children to foster their literacy development (Morrow, Tracey, & Maxwell, 1995). Family literacy programs have four components:

1. *Parent literacy education.*   In these programs, parents develop their own reading and writing competencies.
2. *Information about how young children become literate.*   Parents learn how they can support their young children as they emerge into reading and writing and how they can work with their elementary-grade children at home.
3. *Support groups for parents.*   Parents get acquainted with other parents and share ways of working with their children.
4. *Planned interactions between parents and children.*   Parents and their children participate together in reading and writing activities.

Now family literacy programs are based on the "wealth model," which stresses that all families have literacy patterns within their homes and that family literacy programs should build on these patterns rather than impose mainstream school-like activities on parents (Morrow et al., 1995). Cultural differences in reading and writing development and literacy use are now regarded as strengths, not weaknesses. The wealth model has replaced the older deficit model, which assumed that children from minority groups and low-income families lacked the preschool literacy activities necessary for success in school (Auerbach, 1989).

Organizations dedicated to family literacy include The National Center for Family Literacy (NCFL), Reading is Fundamental (RIF), and the Barbara Bush Foundation for Family Literacy. These organizations have been instrumental in promoting family literacy initiatives at the national level. The NCFL, which began in 1989, disseminates information about family literacy and works to implement family literacy programs across the country. The NCFL has trained staff for almost 1,000 family literacy programs and sponsors an annual National Family Literacy Conference. RIF was formed in 1966 to promote children's reading, and the organization originally provided assistance to local groups in obtaining and distributing low-cost books for children and sponsoring reading-related events. Since 1982 RIF has developed other programs to support parents as children's first teachers. First Lady Barbara Bush organized the Barbara Bush

Foundation in 1989 to promote family literacy. This foundation provides grants for family literacy programs and published a book describing 10 model family literacy programs in the United States (The Barbara Bush Foundation for Family Literacy, 1989). A list of family literacy agencies and associations is presented in Figure 2–10.

A wide variety of local programs have been developed. Some programs are collaborations among local agencies, while others are run by adult literacy groups. Businesses, too, in many communities are forming partnerships to promote family literacy. Also, schools in multicultural communities are creating literacy programs for parents who are not yet proficient in English so that they can support their children's literacy learning. Shanahan, Mulhern, and Rodriguez-Brown (1995) developed a literacy project in a Chicago Latino neighborhood. Through this program, parents learned to speak and read English and became actively involved in their children's education. Spanish was used for instruction because that was the parents' home language.

Schools also organize writing programs for parents. Susan Akroyd (1995), a principal of a multicultural school in northern Virginia, developed a 10-week program for her school. She advertised the program in the school's newsletter for parents, and approximately 15 parents from different cultures and languages ranging from Korean and Vietnamese to Urdu attended. Many parents spoke very little English, but they came together to write and to learn more about writing. They wrote about memories, their experiences immigrating to America, and their hopes and dreams for their children. They also created a family history book. Some parents wrote in English, while others wrote in their native languages. Akroyd brought in translators so that the par-

FIGURE 2–10   Family Literacy Agencies and Associations

The Barbara Bush Foundation for Family Literacy 1002 Wisconsin Avenue, NW Washington, DC 20007	National Center for Family Literacy 401 South 4th Avenue, Suite 610 Louisville, KY 40202
Children's Television Workshop One Lincoln Plaza New York, NY 10023	National PTA 700 N. Rush Street Chicago, IL 60611
Even Start Program Compensatory Education Programs 400 Maryland Avenue, SW Room 2043 Washington, DC 20202	Reading Is Fundamental, Inc. 5500 Maryland Avenue, SW Washington, DC 20024
Family English Literacy Programs Office of Bilingual Education and Minority Language Affairs 400 Maryland Avenue, SW Room 5620 Washington, DC 20202	UNICEF 3 United Nations Plaza New York, NY 10017 Clearinghouse on Adult Education U.S. Department of Education Division of Adult Education 400 Maryland Avenue, SW Washington, DC 20201
Head Start Bureau P.O. Box 1182 Washington, DC 20013	

Effective Practices	Ineffective Practices
1. Teachers help students become independent learners and lifelong readers and writers.	**1.** Teachers focus on teaching reading and writing skills.
2. Teachers embrace cultural pluralism and recognize that each culture enriches American society.	**2.** Teachers expect all students to act like mainstream or European-American students.
3. Teachers support and value the native languages of students who are learning English as a second language.	**3.** Teachers use only English in their classrooms.
4. Teachers provide more explicit instruction and reading practice for students not making expected progress in learning to read and write.	**4.** Teachers provide the same instructional program for all students.
5. Teachers motivate students using intrinsic motivation and open-ended activities.	**5.** Teachers use praise, grades, and extrinsic motivation.
6. Teachers create a community of learners in their classrooms.	**6.** Teachers establish themselves as leaders of their classrooms.
7. Teachers orchestrate the life of the classroom as they assume a variety of roles.	**7.** Teachers view themselves as teachers.
8. Teachers arrange the classroom to facilitate collaboration and foster learning.	**8.** Teachers arrange the classroom in rows to ensure that students work quietly.
9. Teachers use a combination of literature focus units and reading and writing workshop.	**9.** Teachers use a basal reader program exclusively.
10. Teachers use both direct and indirect instruction.	**10.** Teachers use either direct or indirect instruction.
11. Teachers view literacy as a three-way partnership among students, teachers, and parents.	**11.** Teachers don't involve parents as partners in the classroom literacy program.

ents' writing could be shared with the group. At each class meeting, parents wrote, shared their writing in small groups, and then shared selected compositions with the class. At the end of the program, Akroyd collected pieces from each parent and published an anthology of their writing. The parents' children also wrote letters to their parents, complimenting them on their participation in this program. This sort of program can work in diverse communities, even when parents read and write in different languages.

Review

Students, teachers, and parents work together to foster children's literacy development. Students reflect our culturally pluralistic society, and teachers need to consider the needs of all students as they plan for instruction. Teachers have many roles in a literature-based reading classroom. They establish the classroom climate, organize for instruction, and manage the operation of the classroom. Teachers also arrange the classroom to facilitate children's literacy learning. Parents can be involved in their children's literacy development in several ways, such as volunteering to help in children's classrooms and reading and writing with their children at home. Multifaceted family literacy programs can also help parents expand their reading and writing abilities and learn ways to support their children's literacy development. The figure on page 78 shows some of the ways that effective teachers work with students and parents.

References

Akroyd, S. (1995). Forming a parent reading-writing class: Connecting cultures, one pen at a time. *The Reading Teacher, 48,* 580–584.

Allen, V. A. (1991). Teaching bilingual and ESL children. In J. Flood, J. M. Jensen, D. Lapp, & J. R. Squire (Eds.), *Handbook of research on teaching the English language arts* (pp. 356–364). New York: Macmillan.

Altwerger, B., & Flores, B. (1994). Theme cycles: Creating communities of learners. *Primary Voices K–6, 2,* 2–6.

American Council on Education and the Education Commission of the States. (1988). *One-third of a nation: A report of the Commission on minority participation in education and American life.* Washington, DC: American Council on Education.

Atwell, N. (1987). *In the middle: Writing, reading, and learning with adolescents.* Portsmouth, NH: Heinemann.

Auerbach, E. R. (1989). Toward a social-contextual approach to family literacy. *Harvard Educational Review, 59,* 165–181.

Banks, J. A. (1988). *Multiethnic education: Theory and practice.* Boston: Allyn & Bacon.

Barbara Bush Foundation for Family Literacy. (1989). *First teachers.* Washington, DC: Author.

Baumann, J. F. (1987). Direct instruction reconsidered. *Journal of Reading, 31,* 712–718.

Brooks, C. K. (Ed.). (1985). *Tapping potential: English and language arts for the black learner.* Urbana, IL: National Council of Teachers of English.

Calkins, L. M. (1994). *The art of teaching writing* (Rev. ed.). Portsmouth, NH: Heinemann.

Cheng, L. R. (1987). *Assessing Asian language performance.* Rockville, MD: Aspen.

Come, B., & Fredericks, A. D. (1995). Family literacy in urban schools: Meeting the needs of at-risk children. *The Reading Teacher, 48,* 566–570.

Edwards, P. A. (1995). Empowering low-income mothers and fathers to share books with young children. *The Reading Teacher, 48,* 558–564.

Faltis, C. J. (1993). *Joinfostering: Adapting teaching strategies for the multilingual classroom.* New York: Merrill/Macmillan.

France, M. G., & Hager, J. M. (1993). Recruit, respect, respond: A model for working with low-income families and their preschoolers. *The Reading Teacher, 46,* 568–572.

Freeman, D. E., & Freeman, Y. S. (1993). Strategies for promoting the primary languages of all students. *The Reading Teacher, 46,* 552–558.

Gamberg, R., Kwak, W., Hutchings, M., Altheim, J., & Edwards, G. (1988). *Learning and loving it: Theme studies in the classroom.* Portsmouth, NH: Heinemann.

Gardner, H. (1983). *Frames of mind: The theory of multiple intelligences.* New York: Basic Books.

Goodman, Y. M., Watson, D. J., & Burke, C. L. (1987). *Reading miscue inventory: Alternative procedures.* Katonah, NY: Richard C. Owen.

Graves, D. H. (1994). *A fresh look at writing.* Portsmouth, NH: Heinemann.

Hakuta, K., & Garcia, E. (1989). Bilingualism and education. *American Psychologist, 44,* 374–379.

Hall, N. (1987). *The emergence of literacy.* Portsmouth, NH: Heinemann.

Heath, S. B. (1983). *Ways with words: Language, life, and work in communities and classrooms.* Cambridge: Cambridge University Press.

Hornsby, D., Sukarna, D., & Parry, J. (1986). *Read on: A conference approach to reading.* Portsmouth, NH: Heinemann.

Kameenui, E. J. (1993). Diverse learners and the tyranny of time: Don't fix the blame; fix the leaky roof. *The Reading Teacher, 46,* 376–383.

Law, B., & Eckes, M. (1990). *The more than just surviving handbook: ESL for every classroom teacher.* Winnipeg, Canada: Peguis.

Leland, C. H., & Harste, J. C. (1994). Multiple ways of knowing: Curriculum in a new key. *Language Arts, 71,* 337–345.

Lewin, L. (1992). Integrating reading and writing strategies using an alternating teacher-led/student-selected instructional pattern. *The Reading Teacher, 45,* 586– 591.

Morrow, L. M. (1989). Designing the classroom to promote literacy development. In D. S. Strickland & L. M. Morrow (Eds.), *Emergent literacy: Young children learn to read and write* (pp. 121–134). Newark, DE: International Reading Association.

Morrow, L. M., Tracey, D. H., & Maxwell, C. M. (1995). *A survey of family literacy in the United States.* Newark, DE: International Reading Association.

Parry, J., & Hornsby, D. (1985). *Write on: A conference approach to writing.* Portsmouth, NH: Heinemann.

Purcell-Gates, V., L'Allier, S., & Smith, D. (1995). Literacy as the Harts' and Larsons': Diversity among poor, inner city families. *The Reading Teacher, 48,* 572–579.

Rasinski, T. V., & Fredericks, A. D. (1988). Sharing literacy: Guiding principles and practices for parent involvement. *The Reading Teacher, 41,* 508–512.

Rhodes, L. K., & Dudley-Marling, C. (1988). *Readers and writers with a difference: A holistic approach to teaching learning disabled and remedial students.* Portsmouth, NH: Heinemann.

Robb, L. (1993). A cause for celebration: Reading and writing with at-risk students. *The New Advocate, 6,* 25–40.

Ruddell, R. B. (1995). Those influential literacy teachers: Meaning negotiators and motivation builders. *The Reading Teacher, 48,* 454–463.

Scarcella, R. (1990). *Teaching language minority students in the multicultural classroom.* Englewood Cliffs, NJ: Prentice Hall.

Sears, S., Carpenter, C., & Burstein, N. (1994). Meaningful reading instruction for learners with special needs. *The Reading Teacher, 47,* 632–637.

Shanahan, T., Mulhern, M., & Rodriguez-Brown, F. (1995). Project FLAME: Lessons learned from a family literacy program for linguistic minority families. *The Reading Teacher, 48,* 586–593.

Shockley, B. (1993). Extending the literate community: Reading and writing with families. *The New Advocate, 6,* 11–24.

Slaughter, H. (1988). Indirect and direct teaching in a whole language program. *The Reading Teacher, 41,* 30–34.

Smith, F. (1988). *Joining the literacy club.* Portsmouth, NH: Heinemann.

Spiegel, D. L. (1992). Blending whole language and systematic direct instruction. *The Reading Teacher, 46,* 38–44.

Stanovich, K. E. (1986). Matthew effects in reading: Some consequences of individual differences in the acquisition of literacy. *Reading Research Quarterly, 21,* 360–407.

Sumara, D., & Walker, L. (1991). The teacher's role in whole language. *Language Arts, 68,* 276–285.

Tinajero, J. V., & Nagel, G. (1995). "I never knew I was needed until you called!": Promoting parent involvement in schools. *The Reading Teacher, 48,* 614–617.

Turner, J., & Paris, S. G. (1995). How literacy tasks influences children's motivation for literacy. *The Reading Teacher, 48,* 662–673.

Wood, J. W. (1993). *Mainstreaming: A practical approach for teachers* (2nd ed.) New York: Merrill/Macmillan.

Yokota, J. (1993). Issues in selecting multicultural children's literature. *Language Arts, 70,* 156–167.

Children's Book References

Babbitt, N. (1975). *Tuck everlasting.* New York: Farrar, Straus & Giroux.

Barrett, J. (1978). *Cloudy with a chance of meatballs.* New York: Macmillan.

Bauer, M. D. (1986). *On my honor.* Boston: Houghton Mifflin.

Blume, J. (1971). *Freckle juice.* New York: Bradbury Press.

Goble, P. (1988). *Iktomi and the boulder.* New York: Orchard Books.

Howe, D., & Howe, J. (1979). *Bunnicula: A rabbit-tale of mystery.* New York: Atheneum.

Hutchins, P. (1968). *Rosie's walk.* New York: Macmillan.

MacLachlan, P. (1983). *Sarah, plain and tall.* New York: Harper & Row.

Naylor, P. R. (1991). *Shiloh.* New York: Atheneum.

Numeroff, L. (1993). *Dogs don't wear sneakers.* New York: Simon & Schuster.

Paterson, K. (1977). *Bridge to Terabithia.* New York: Harper & Row.

Rockwell, T. (1973). *How to eat fried worms.* New York: Franklin Watts.

Sendak, M. (1962). *Where the wild things are.* New York: Harper & Row.

Steig, W. (1969). *Sylvester and the magic pebble.* New York: Farrar, Straus & Giroux.

Taylor, B. (1992). *Desert life.* New York: Dorling Kindersley.

Van Allsburg, C. (1981). *Jumanji.* Boston: Houghton Mifflin.

PART II
How Do Readers and Writers Construct Meaning?

A small group of third graders in Mrs. Donnelly's class read Judi Barrett's *Cloudy with a Chance of Meatballs* in their basal readers. Mrs. Donnelly also has several copies of the trade book available.

A student adds words to the word wall. Words from the story and other weather-related words are included.

Mrs. Donnelly collects these books for a text set on weather. Stories, informational books, and poems are included.

Mrs. Donnelly does a book talk to introduce students to the books displayed on the table in the reading area.

Students use the writing process to write wacky weather reports which they will present to their classmates and parents. Mrs. Donnelly meets with Charlie to revise his weather project.

Students present their completed wacky weather reports to classmates and parents. One student video-tapes the weather reports to replay later.

Today we can expect Cinnamon rolls with a chance of peaches followe-d by several apples. Several days of maceronis and cheese followed by grapes. Still a possibility of ornges on Sat-erday. Chiken becoming heavy at times on Sunday, Clouds of bananas moving into Michigan

Mrs. Donnelly teaches a minilesson on absurdity and students brainstorm a list of other fantasies, such as *Jumanji* by Chris Van Allsburg, that include absurd elements.

Students make posters to recommend favorite books from the text set that the third graders have read independently.

CHAPTER 3
Breaking the Code

The first graders in Mrs. Hoddy's classroom are involved in an author study on Eric Carle. They are reading many of the books Carle has written and illustrated, including *The Very Hungry Caterpillar* (1969), *The Very Busy Spider* (1984), *The Very Quiet Cricket* (1990), and *The Very Lonely Firefly* (1995). A list of these and other the Eric Carle books is presented in Figure 3–1. Mrs. Hoddy has a class set of *The Very Hungry Caterpillar* and several copies of each of the other books on a special shelf in the classroom library for students to read and reread.

For each book, Mrs. Hoddy begins by reading the book aloud to the students, and then students talk about the book, sharing their impressions and reactions. They make comparisons among the Eric Carle books they've read, pointing out the repetitive patterns, the themes, and Carle's unique illustration techniques. Students have watched *Eric Carle: Picture Writer* (Carle, 1993), a videotape of the author-illustrator demonstrating his illustration techniques, and they are creating their own books with bright tissue paper collage illustrations using the same illustration techniques that Eric Carle does.

Students read and reread books in small groups, at the listening center, with buddies, and independently. They add important vocabulary words from each story to the **word wall** (see the Compendium for more information about this and all other highlighted terms in this chapter) and participate in word-identification activities. Mrs. Hoddy reviews the letter-writing form, and students write letters to Eric Carle, telling him which of his books they like the best and about the books they are making with tissue paper collage illustrations.

FIGURE 3–1   Books by Eric Carle

The very hungry caterpillar. (1969). New York: Philomel.

Do you want to be my friend? (1971). New York: Harper & Row.

Rooster's off to see the world. (1972). New York: Franklin Watts.

What's for lunch? (1982). New York: Philomel.

The mixed-up chameleon. (1984). New York: Harper & Row.

The very busy spider. (1984). New York: Philomel.

The grouchy ladybug. (1986). New York: Harper & Row.

Papa, please get the moon for me. (1986). Saxonville, MA: Picture Book Studio.

Have you seen my cat? (1987). Saxonville, MA: Picture Book Studio.

A house for hermit crab. (1987). Saxonville, MA: Picture Book Studio.

The tiny seed. (1987). Saxonville, MA: Picture Book Studio.

Eric Carle's animals, animals. (1989). New York: Philomel.

The very quiet cricket. (1990). New York: Philomel.

The very lonely firefly. (1995). New York: Philomel.

Mrs. Hoddy teaches **minilessons** on phonics regularly during the author unit on Eric Carle. She uses a whole-part-whole approach. She begins by sharing the book with students, giving them opportunities to read and respond to the book—the whole. Then she focuses on skills and teaches minilessons on phonics using words from the story—the part. Afterwards, students apply the skills they are learning through reading and writing activities—the whole again. During this unit, students will continue reading Carle's books and write their own books.

After reading *The Very Hungry Caterpillar,* Carle's story about a caterpillar that eats through a large quantity of food before spinning a chrysalis, Mrs. Hoddy uses this book to teach a series of minilessons on phonics. In one lesson with the whole class she reviews the days of the week and focuses on the *-ay* rime using the days of the week and the words *bay, may, say, pay, ray, way, day, lay, play,* and *stay.* She begins by pointing out the days of the week on the calendar and reviewing with students what foods the caterpillar in the story ate each day. She writes the days of the week on the chalkboard and asks students to pronounce the words and note that they all rhyme. Then she asks one child to come to the chalkboard and circle the rime *-ay.* Next, she writes *say, may, play,* and several other *-ay* words on the chalkboard for children to decode. Then she distributes a small magic slate to each child, and students all write their favorite day of the week at the top of their slates and circle *-ay.* Then students take turns suggesting rhyming words to write on their slates. Mrs. Hoddy walks around the classroom, checking that students are sounding out the beginning sound and adding the rime correctly. For the last two minutes of the minilesson, she reviews the *-ill* rime that she taught last week, and students write *bill, still, will, mill, kill, gill, hill,* and *pill* on their magic slates.

Mrs. Hoddy alternates teaching minilessons to the whole class with teaching minilessons to small groups of students. She introduces new concepts, skills, and generalizations to the whole class and then reinforces, reviews, and extends the lessons with small groups. These groups change often, and students are grouped together according to their need to learn a specific skill.

One group of five students, for example, is still developing phonemic awareness—the ability to orally segment spoken words. Mrs. Hoddy meets with this group to orally segment words from the story, including *egg, moon, leaf, sun, food, pie, cheese, cupcake,* and *night.* When Mrs. Hoddy meets with the group, she brings along a copy of *The Very Hungry Caterpillar* and says to the group, "Let's find some interesting words in this book to break into sounds. How about *egg?*" The children respond, "e-gg." Students break the words into sounds and say the sounds together as a group, and then children take turns segmenting the words individually.

Another group of ten students reviews these six beginning sounds—/b/, /f/, /h/, /l/, /p/, and /s/—using words from the story. Mrs. Hoddy sets out six plastic baskets with a beginning sound written on the front of each basket. Then she shows students these objects and pictures—a butterfly puppet, the number four cut out of cardboard, a photo of a house, a lollipop, a jar of pickles, and a drawing of the sun—and students place each object in front of the appropriate basket. Then Mrs. Hoddy reads these words, which she has written on word cards:

b: butterfly, better, beautiful, big
f: five, four, fat, food
h: house, hole, hungry, he
l: light, lay, little, leaf, lollipop, look

    p: pushed, pop, pickle, piece, pears
    s: Sunday, Saturday, sun, salami, sausage

Students identify the beginning sound and place the cards in the appropriate basket. Afterwards, students add pictures on the back of each word card. Then they think of other words beginning with each sound and draw pictures representing the words on cards. They write the word on the back of the card and add these cards to the appropriate baskets.

Mrs. Hoddy passes out copies of *The Very Hungry Caterpillar* to another group of students, who look through the book to find examples of CVCe words (one-syllable words with a long vowel sound and ending with an *e*). Students locate these words and write them on cards that they place in the pocket chart: *came, ate, cake, ice, cone, slice, pie, ache, hole.* They also locate several words (e.g., *one, more*) that are exceptions to the rule. Mrs. Hoddy explains that *one* is a sight word and that the *r* in *more* overpowers the *o* and changes the sound, just like the *r* in *car* (a familiar word) is stronger than the *a*. The students reread the words several times, and all but two of them are able to read the cards easily. Mrs. Hoddy excuses the rest of the group and continues to work with the remaining two children for several more minutes. She gives them magic slates and asks them to draw three lines and write an *e:* __ __ __ e. Then she dictates *came* for the two children to write. They carefully sound out the word and spell it correctly. Then Mrs. Hoddy repeats the process with *hole* and *cone.* She makes a note to give these students more practice later the next day with these CVCe words.

With another group of six students, Mrs. Hoddy uses a set of word cards with the words *caterpillar, little, morning, sun, ate, plum, Thursday, strawberries, chocolate, pickle, lollipop, cupcake, watermelon, stomachache, green, leaf, big, butterfly,* and *beautiful.* As she shows the cards, students read the words. Then she has them read the words a second time and break the words into syllables. Children clap as they say each syllable: *cat-er-pill-ar.* After students take turns saying each word, syllable by syllable, Mrs. Hoddy asks the group to sort the word cards into four piles: one-syllable words, two-syllable words, three-syllable words, and four-syllable words. The group works independently, and then Mrs. Hoddy returns in a few minutes to check their work.

Several days later, Mrs. Hoddy teaches another minilesson to the entire class. She divides the class into groups of three and passes out packs of letter cards that together spell *caterpillar.* First, students arrange letters to spell the words *cat, pat,* and *rat.* Then they spell *it, pit,* and *lit.* Next, *cap, lap, tap,* and *trap.* Then, *car, are, art, part,* and *cart.* Children volunteer some other words they can make: *eat, late, ape,* and *tape.* Finally, Mrs. Hoddy asks students to guess the big word that all the letters spell together. They know it is a word on the word wall. Quickly, Jonas guesses that the word is *caterpillar* and all the children arrange the letters to spell the word. The next day, Mrs. Hoddy will repeat this activity in small groups, and she will take notes about the words that students in each group can build.

There are many phonics skills that Mrs. Hoddy could have chosen to teach through *The Very Hungry Caterpillar.* She could focus on one consonant sound—the *v* in *very,* the *h* in *hungry,* the *c* in *caterpillar,* or the *b* in *beautiful butterfly,* for example. Or she could have used the words *green leaf* from the story to focus on two vowel patterns used to spell long *e.* In order to show students how phonics can help them when they read, Mrs. Hoddy uses words from the book they are reading for minilessons.

FIGURE 3–2   First-Grade Phonics Checklist

Phonemic Awareness

____ segmenting   ____ blending   ____ rhyming

Consonants

____ b	____ f	____ j	____ m	____ qu	____ t
____ c (k)	____ g	____ k	____ n	____ r	____ v
____ d	____ h	____ l	____ p	____ s	____ w

Blends	**Digraphs**	**Rimes**
____ bl	____ ch	____ at
____ dr	____ sh	____ ill
____ fl	____ th	____ op
____ st	____ wh	____ ate
____ tr		____ ike
		____ ay

Short Vowels	**Long Vowels**	**Rules**
____ a (fan)	____ a (came, pail)	____ CVC
____ e (web)	____ e (be, feet, eat)	____ CVCe
____ i (sit)	____ i (ice, bite)	____ *r*-controlled
____ o (not)	____ o (go, soap)	____ syllables
____ u (cup)	____ u (mule)	

Mrs. Hoddy knows which phonics concepts, rules, and skills her first graders need to learn, and she develops minilessons and other activities using words drawn from the books she is reading during literature focus units. Together with the other first-grade teachers at her school, Mrs. Hoddy has developed a checklist of skills that she is responsible for teaching. A copy of the checklist is shown in Figure 3–2. The skills on this checklist include phonemic awareness, consonants, consonant blends and digraphs, rimes, short and long vowels, and vowel rules. Mrs. Hoddy chooses topics for minilessons from this checklist, and she uses one copy of the checklist to keep track of the skills she has introduced, practiced, and reviewed. She also makes copies of the checklist for each student and uses the checklists to document which skills children have learned. She uses the information on these checklists in putting together small groups for minilessons and related activities.

*T*he alphabetic principle suggests a one-to-one correspondence between phonemes (or sounds) and graphemes (or letters), such that each letter consistently represents one sound. English, however, is not a purely phonetic language. The 26 letters represent approximately 44 phonemes, and three letters—*c, q,* and *x*—are superfluous because they do not represent unique phonemes. The letter *c,* for example, can represent either /k/ as in *cat* or /s/ as in *city,* and it can be joined with *h* for the digraph /ch/. To further complicate the situation, there are more than 500 spellings to represent the 44 phonemes. Consonants are more consistent and predictable than vowels. Long *e,* for instance, is spelled 14 different ways in common words, depending on where the sound is in the word and whether or not the word entered English from another language (Horn, 1957).

Researchers estimate that words are spelled phonetically approximately half the time (Hanna, Hanna, Hodges, & Rudorf, 1966), and the nonphonetic spelling of many words reflects morphological information. The word *sign,* for instance, is a shortened form of *signature,* and the spelling shows this relationship. Spelling the word phonetically (e.g., *sine*) might seem simpler, but the phonetic spelling lacks semantic information (Venezky, 1970).

Other reasons for this mismatch between phonemes, graphemes, and spellings can be found by examining events in the history of the English language (Tompkins & Yaden, 1986). The introduction of the printing press in England in 1476 helped to stabilize spelling. The word *said,* for example, continues to be spelled as it was pronounced in Shakespeare's time. Our pronunciation does not reflect the word's meaning as the past tense of *say* because pronunciations have continued to evolve in the last 500 years but few spellings have been "modernized." In addition, 75% of English words have been borrowed from other languages around the world, and many words—especially those acquired more recently—have retained their native spellings. For example, *souvenir* was borrowed from French in the middle 1700s and retains its French spelling. Its literal meaning is "to remember."

The English spelling system can't be explained by the alphabetic principle alone because it is not merely a reflection of phoneme-grapheme correspondences. Our spelling system includes morphological, semantic, and syntactic elements, and it has been influenced by historical events.

As children begin to learn to read and write, they must learn how to "break the code." The process of learning about sound-symbol correspondences is often called "phonics," but it is more complex than that. As you read this chapter, you will learn

One of the first things that young children learn about the alphabet is the first letter of their name.

about phonemic awareness, children's ability to segment speech into sounds, phonics information children need to learn, and how children apply phonics through invented spelling. Children use what they have learned about sound-symbol correspondences and spelling patterns for both reading and writing. Think about these questions as you continue reading:

■ What knowledge about phonology do children need before they "break the code"?

■ Which phonics concepts are most important for children to learn?

■ What are the characteristics of effective phonics instruction?

■ How does invented spelling help children to learn phonics?

■ How should spelling be taught?

PHONEMIC AWARENESS

Phonemic awareness is children's basic understanding that speech is composed of a series of individual sounds, and it provides the foundation for "breaking the code" (Yopp, 1992). When children can choose a duck as the animal that begins with /d/ from a collection of toy animals, identify *duck* and *luck* as rhyming words in a song, or blend the sounds /d/, /u/, and /k/ to pronounce *duck,* they are phonemically aware. (Note that the emphasis is on the sounds of spoken words, not reading letters or pronouncing letter names.) Developing phonemic awareness enables children to use sound-symbol correspondences to read and spell words. Phonemic awareness is not sounding out words for reading, nor is it using spelling patterns to write words; rather, it is the foundation for phonics.

Phonemes are the smallest units of speech, and they are written as graphemes, or letters of the alphabet. In this book, phonemes are marked using diagonal lines (e.g., /d/) and graphemes are italicized (e.g., *d*). Sometimes phonemes (e.g., /k/ in *duck*) are spelled with two graphemes *(ck)*.

Understanding that words are composed of smaller units—phonemes—is a significant achievement for young children because phonemes are abstract language units. Phonemes carry no meaning, and children think of words according to their meanings, not their linguistic characteristics (F. Griffith & Olson, 1992). When children think about *ducks,* for example, they think of feathered animals that swim in ponds, fly through the air, and make noises we describe as "quacks." They don't think of *duck* as a word with three phonemes or four graphemes, as a word beginning with /d/ and rhyming with *luck*. Phonemic awareness requires that children treat speech as an object and that they shift their attention away from the meaning of words to the linguistic features of speech. This focus on phonemes is even more complicated because phonemes are not discrete units in speech. Often they are blended or slurred together in speech. Think about the blended initial sound in *tree* and the ending sound in *eating.*

Types of Activities

Children develop phonemic awareness in two ways. They learn through a language-rich environment as they sing songs, play with words, chant rhymes, and listen to parents and teachers read wordplay books to them (F. Griffith & Olson, 1992). Yopp (1995) recommends that teachers read books with wordplay aloud and encourage students to talk about the way the author manipulated words. Teachers ask questions

■ *Activity*

Phonics is a very controversial topic today. Before you continue reading, quickwrite about what you believe about phonics, comments you've read in newspaper articles, and television commercials you have seen. As you continue reading, compare your beliefs and today's "pop" notions with the information in this chapter.

and make comments, such as "Did you notice how _____ and _____ rhyme?" and "This book is fun because of all the words beginning with the /m/ sound." Once students are very familiar with the book, they can create new verses or make other variations. Books such as *Jamberry* (Degen, 1983) and *The Baby Uggs Are Hatching* (Prelutsky, 1982) stimulate children to experiment with sounds, create nonsense words, and become enthusiastic about reading. When teachers read books with alliterative or assonant patterns, such as *Faint Frogs Feeling Feverish and Other Terrifically Tantalizing Tongue Twisters* (Obligado, 1983), children attend to the smaller units of language. A list of wordplay books for young children is shown in Figure 3–3.

Teachers also teach lessons to help students understand that their speech is composed of sounds (Ball & Blachman, 1991; Hohn & Ehri, 1983; Lundberg, Frost, & Petersen, 1988). The goal of phonemic awareness activities is to break down and manipulate spoken words. Students who have developed phonemic awareness can manipulate spoken language in these five ways:

- match words with sounds
- isolate a sound in a word
- blend individual sounds to form a word
- substitute sounds in a word
- segment a word into its constituent sounds (Yopp, 1992)

FIGURE 3–3   Wordplay Books to Enhance Children's Phonemic Awareness

Ahlberg, J., & Ahlberg, A. (1978). *Each peach pear plum.* New York: Scholastic.

Cameron, P. (1961). *"I can't," said the ant.* New York: Coward McCann.

Degan, B. (1983). *Jamberry.* New York: Harper & Row.

Deming, A. G. (1994). *Who is tapping at my window?* New York: Penguin.

Dr. Seuss. (1963). *Hop on pop.* New York: Random House. (See also other books by the author.)

Ehlert, L. (1989). *Eating the alphabet: Fruits and vegetables from A to Z.* San Diego: Harcourt Brace Jovanovich.

Galdone, P. (1968). *Henny Penny.* New York: Scholastic.

Hague, K. (1984). *Alphabears.* New York: Henry Holt.

Hoberman, M. A. (1982). *A house is a house for me.* New York: Penguin.

Hutchins, P. (1976). *Don't forget the bacon!* New York: Mulberry Books.

Kuskin, K. (1990). *Roar and more.* New York: Harper & Row.

Lewiston, W. (1992). *"Buzz," said the bee.* New York: Scholastic.

Martin, B., Jr., & Archambault, J. (1987). *Chicka chicka boom boom.* New York: Simon & Schuster.

Most, B. (1991). *A dinosaur named after me.* San Diego: Harcourt Brace Jovanovich.

Obligado, L. (1983). *Faint frogs feeling feverish and other terrifically tantalizing tongue twisters.* New York: Puffin.

Prelutsky, J. (1982). *The baby uggs are hatching.* New York: Mulberry.

Prelutsky, J. (1989). *Poems of A. Nonny Mouse.* New York: Knopf. (See also the second volume in the series.)

Raffi. (1987). *Down by the bay.* New York: Crown.

Sendak, M. (1990). *Alligators all around: An alphabet.* New York: Harper & Row.

Shaw, N. (1986). *Sheep in a jeep.* Boston: Houghton Mifflin. (See also other books in this series.)

Showers, P. (1991). *The listening walk.* New York: Harper & Row.

Slepian, J., & Seidler, A. (1967). *The hungry thing.* New York: Scholastic.

Tallon, R. (1979). *Zoophabets.* New York: Scholastic.

Winthrop, E. (1986). *Shoes.* New York: Harper & Row.

Zemach, M. (1976). *Hush, little baby.* New York: Dutton.

Teachers teach minilessons focusing on each of these tasks using familiar songs with improvised lyrics, riddles and guessing games, and wordplay books. These activities should be playful and gamelike, and they should be connected to literature focus units and theme studies whenever possible. Five types of activities are sound matching, sound isolation, sound blending, sound addition and substitution, and segmentation.

Sound Matching.   In sound matching, children choose one of several words beginning with a particular sound or say a word that begins with a particular sound (Yopp, 1992). For these games, teachers use familiar objects (e.g., feather, toothbrush, book) and toys (e.g., small plastic animals, toy trucks, artificial fruits and vegetables), as well as pictures of familiar objects.

Teachers can play a sound-matching guessing game (Lewkowicz, 1994). For this game, teachers collect two boxes and pairs of objects to place in the boxes (e.g., forks, mittens, erasers, combs, and books). One item from each pair is placed in each box. After the teacher shows students the objects in the boxes and they name them together, two children play the game. One child selects an object, holds it, and pronounces the initial (or medial or final) sound. The second child chooses the same object from the second box and holds it up. Children check to see it the two players are holding the same object.

Children also identify rhyming words as part of sound-matching activities. Students name a word that rhymes with a given word and identify rhyming words from familiar songs and stories. As children listen to parents and teachers read Dr. Seuss books such as *Hop on Pop* (1963) and other wordplay books, students refine their understanding of rhyme.

Sound Isolation.   Students are given a word and then asked to identify the sounds at the beginning, middle, or end of the word. Yopp (1992) created new verses to the tune of "Old MacDonald Had a Farm":

> What's the sound that starts these words:
> Chicken, chin and cheek?
> (wait for response)
> /ch/ is the sound that starts these words:
> Chicken, chin, and cheek.
> With a /ch/, /ch/ here, and a /ch/, /ch/ there,
> Here a /ch/, there a /ch/, everywhere a /ch/, /ch/.
> /ch/ is the sound that starts these words:
> Chicken, chin, and cheek. (p. 700)

Teachers change the question at the beginning of the verse to focus on medial and final sounds. For example:

> What's the sound in the middle of these words?
> Whale, game, and rain. (p. 700)

And for final sounds:

> What's the sound at the end of these words?
> Leaf, cough, and beef. (p. 700)

Teachers can also set out a tray of objects and ask students to choose the one object that doesn't belong because it doesn't begin with the sound. For example, from a tray with a toy pig, a puppet, a teddy bear, and a pen, the teddy bear doesn't belong.

Sound Blending. Children blend sounds together in order to combine them to form a word. For example, children blend the sounds /d/, /u/, and /k/ to form the word *duck*. Teachers can play the "What am I thinking of?" guessing game with children by identifying several characteristics of the item and then saying the name of the item, articulating each of the sounds separately (Yopp, 1992). Then children blend the sounds together and identify the word, using the phonological and semantic information that the teacher provided. For example:

> We're studying about the pond and I am thinking of an animal that lives in the pond when it is young. When it is an adult, it lived on land and it is called a /f/, /r/, /o/, /g/. What is it?

The children blend the sounds together to pronounce the word *frog*. In this example, the teacher connects the game with a thematic unit, thereby making the game more meaningful for students.

Sound Addition and Substitution. Students play with words and create nonsense words as they add or substitute sounds in words in songs they sing or in books that are read aloud to them. Teachers read wordplay books such as Hutchins' *Don't Forget the Bacon!* (1976), in which a boy leaves for the store with a mental list of four items to buy. As he walks, he repeats his list, substituting words each time. "A cake for tea" changes to "a cape for me" and then to "a rake for leaves." Children suggest other substitutions, such as "a pail for maple sugar trees."

Students can substitute sounds in refrains of songs (Yopp, 1992). For example, students can change the "Ee-igh, ee-igh, oh!" refrain in "Old MacDonald Had a Farm" to "Bee-bigh, bee-bigh, boh!" to focus on the initial /b/ sound. Teachers can choose one sound, such as /sh/, and have children substitute this sound for the beginning sound in their names and in words for items in the classroom. For example, *Jimmy* becomes *Shimmy,* José becomes *Shosé,* and *clock* becomes *shock.*

Segmentation. One of the more difficult phonemic awareness activities is segmentation, in which children isolate the sounds in a spoken word (Yopp, 1988). An introductory segmentation activity is to draw out the beginning sound in words. Children enjoy exaggerating the initial sound in their own names and other familiar words. For example, a pet guinea pig named Popsicle lives in Mrs. Hoddy's classroom, and the children exaggerate the beginning sound of her name so that it is pronounced as "P-P-P-Popsicle." Children can also pick up objects or pictures of objects and identify the initial sound. A child who picks up a toy tiger says, "This is a tiger and it starts with /t/."

From that beginning, children move to identifying all the sounds in a word. Using a toy tiger again, the child would say, "This is a tiger, /t/, /i/, /g/, /er/." Yopp (1992) suggests singing a song to the tune of "Twinkle, Twinkle, Little Star" in which children segment entire words. Here is one example:

Listen, listen
To my word
Then tell me all the sounds you heard: coat
(slowly)
/k/ is one sound
/o/ is two
/t/ is last in coat
It's true. (p. 702)

After several repetitions of the verse segmenting other words, the song ends this way:

Thanks for listening
To my words
And telling all the sounds you heard! (p. 702)

Teachers also use Elkonin boxes teach students to segment words. This activity comes from the work of Russian psychologist D. B. Elkonin (Clay, 1985). As shown in Figure 3–4, the teacher shows an object or picture of an object and draws a series of boxes, with one box for each sound in the name of the object or picture. Then the teacher or a child moves a marker into each box as the sound is pronounced. Children can move small markers onto cards on their desks, or the teacher can draw the boxes on the chalkboard and use tape or small magnets to hold the larger markers in place. Elkonin boxes can also be used for spelling activities. When a child is trying to spell a word, such as *duck,* the teacher can draw three boxes, do the segmentation activity, and then have the child write the letters representing each sound in the boxes. Spelling boxes for *duck* and other words with two, three, or four sounds are also shown in Figure 3–4.

In these activities, students are experimenting with oral language. They do not usually read or write letters and words during phonemic awareness activities, because the focus is on speech. However, once children begin reading and writing, these activities reinforce the segmentation and blending activities they have learned. The phonemic awareness activities stimulate children's interest in language and provide valuable experiences with books and words. Effective teachers recognize the importance of building this foundation before children begin reading and writing. Guidelines for phonemic awareness activities are reviewed in Figure 3–5.

Why is phonemic awareness important?

The relationship between phonemic awareness and learning to read is extremely important, and researchers have concluded that at least some level of phonemic awareness is a prerequisite for learning to read (Tunmer & Nesdale, 1985; Yopp, 1985). In fact, phonemic awareness seems to be both a prerequisite for and a consequence of learning to read (Liberman, Shankweiler, Fischer, & Carter, 1974; Perfitti, Beck, Bell, & Hughes, 1987; Stanovich, 1980). As they become phonemically aware, children recognize that speech can be segmented into smaller units, and this knowledge is very useful when children learn about sound-symbol correspondences and spelling patterns.

Researchers have concluded that children can be explicitly taught to segment and manipulate speech, and children who receive training in phonemic awareness do

FIGURE 3–4   How to Use Elkonin Boxes for Segmentation Activities

1. The teacher shows students an object or the picture of an object, such as a duck, a bed, a game, a bee, a cup, or a cat.

2. The teacher prepares a diagram with a series of boxes, corresponding to the number of sounds heard in the name of the object. For example, the teacher draws three boxes side by side to represent the three sounds heard in the word *duck.* The teacher can draw the boxes on the chalkboard or on small cards for each child to use. The teacher also prepares markers to place on the boxes.

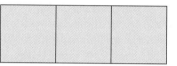

3. The teacher or students say the word slowly and move markers onto the boxes as each sound is pronounced.

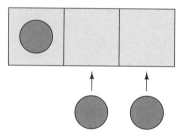

4. Elkonin boxes can also be used when spelling words. The teacher draws a series of boxes corresponding to the number of sounds heard in the word, and then the child and teacher pronounce the word, pointing to each box or sliding markers into each box. Then the child writes the letters representing each sound or spelling pattern in the boxes.

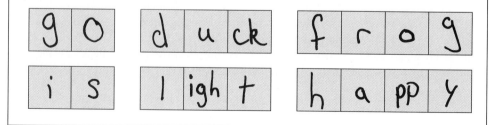

These vowel combinations often represent more than one sound and are used in only a few words:

> *au* as in *laugh* and *caught*
> *aw* as in *saw*
> *ew* as in *sew* and *few*
> *oi* as in *oil*
> *oo* as in *cook* and *moon*
> *ou* as in *about* and *through*
> *ow* as in *now*
> *oy* as in *toy*

Rimes and Rhymes.   One-syllable words and syllables in longer words can be divided into two parts, the onset and the rime. The onset is the consonant sound, if any, that precedes the vowel, and the rime is the vowel and any consonant sounds that follow it (Treiman, 1985). For example, in *show, sh* is the onset and *ow* is the rime, and in *ball, b* is the onset and *all* is the rime. For *at* and *up* there is no onset; the entire word is the rime. Research has shown that children make more errors decoding and spelling final consonants than initial consonants and that they make more errors on vowels than on consonants (Treiman, 1985). These problem areas correspond to rimes, and educators now speculate that onsets and rimes could provide the key to word identification.

Children can focus their attention on a rime, such as *ay*, and create rhyming words, including *bay, day, lay, may, ray, say,* and *way*, as Mrs. Hoddy did in the vignette at the beginning of this chapter. These words can be read and spelled by analogy because the vowel sounds are consistent in rimes. Wylie and Durrell (1970) identified 37 rimes that can be used to produce nearly 500 words that primary-grade students read and write. These rimes and some common words using them are presented in Figure 3–6.

Blending Into Words.   Readers "blend" or combine the sounds in order to decode words. Even though children may identify each sound in a word, one by one, they must be able to blend them together into a word. For example, in order to read the short-vowel word *best*, children identify /b/, /ĕ/, /s/, and /t/ and then combine them to form the word. For long-vowel words, children must identify the vowel pattern as well as the surrounding letters. In *pancake*, for example, children identify /p/, /ă/, /n/, /c/, /ā/, and /k/ and recognize that the *e* at the end of the word is silent and marks the preceding vowel as long. Shefelbine (1995) emphasizes the importance of blending and suggests that students who have difficulty decoding words usually know the sound-symbol correspondences but cannot blend the sounds together into recognizable words. The ability to blend sounds together into words is part of phonemic awareness, and students who have not had practice blending speech sounds into words are likely to have trouble blending sounds into words in order to identify unfamiliar written words.

Phonics Generalizations.   Because English does not have a one-to-one correspondence between sounds and letters, both linguists and educators have tried to create rules or generalizations to clarify English spelling patterns. One rule is that *q* is followed by *u* and pronounced /kw/, as in *queen, quick,* and *earthquake*. There are very few, if any, exceptions to this rule. Another generalization that has few exceptions re-

FIGURE 3–6   The 37 Rimes and Common Words Using Them

-ack	black, pack, quack, stack
-ail	mail, nail, sail, tail
-ain	brain, chain, plain, rain
-ake	cake, shake, take, wake
-ale	male, sale, tale, whale
-ame	came, flame, game, name
-an	can, man, pan, than
-ank	bank, drank, sank, thank
-ap	cap, clap, map, slap
-ash	cash, dash, flash, trash
-at	bat, cat, rat, that
-ate	gate, hate, late, plate
-aw	claw, draw, jaw, saw
-ay	day, play, say, way
-eat	beat, heat, meat, wheat
-ell	bell, sell, shell, well
-est	best, chest, nest, west
-ice	ice, mice, nice, rice
-ick	brick, pick, sick, thick
-ide	bride, hide, ride, side
-ight	bright, fight, light, might
-ill	fill, hill, kill, will
-in	chin, grin, pin, win
-ine	fine, line, mine, nine
-ing	king, sing, thing, wing
-ink	pink, sink, think, wink
-ip	drip, hip, lip, ship
-ir	fir, sir, stir
-ock	block, clock, knock, sock
-oke	choke, joke, poke, woke
-op	chop, drop, hop, shop
-ore	chore, more, shore, store
-or	for, or
-uck	duck, luck, suck, truck
-ug	bug, drug, hug, rug
-ump	bump, dump, hump, lump
-unk	bunk, dunk, junk, sunk

lates to *r*-controlled vowels: *r* influences the preceding vowel so that the vowel is neither long nor short. Examples are *car, market, birth,* and *four.* There are exceptions, however, and one example is *fire.*

Many generalizations aren't very useful because there are more exceptions to the rule than words that conform (Clymer, 1963). A good example is this rule for long vowels: When there are two vowels side by side, the long vowel sound of the first one is pronounced and the second is silent. Teachers sometimes call this the "when two vowels go walking, the first one does the talking" rule. Examples of words conforming to this rule are *meat, soap,* and *each.* There are many more exceptions, however, including *food, said, head, chief, bread, look, soup, does, too, again,* and *believe.*

Only a few phonics generalizations have a high degree of utility for readers. The generalizations that work most of the time are the ones that students should learn be-

FIGURE 3–7   The Most Useful Phonics Generalizations

Pattern	Description	Examples
1. Two sounds of *c*	The letter *c* can be pronounced as /k/ or /s/. When *c* is followed by *a, o,* or *u,* it is pronounced /k/—the hard *c* sound. When *c* is followed by *e, i,* or *y,* it is pronounced /s/—the soft *c* sound.	cat cough cut cent city cycle
2. Two sounds of *g*	The sound associated with the letter *g* depends on the letter following it. When *g* is followed by *a, o,* or *u,* it is pronounced as /g/—the hard *g* sound. When *g* is followed by *e, i,* or *y,* it is usually pronounced /j/—the soft *g* sound. Exceptions include *get* and *give.*	gate go guess gentle giant gypsy
3. CVC pattern	When a one-syllable word has only one vowel and the vowel comes between two consonants, it is usually short. One exception is *told.*	bat cup land
4. Final *e* or CVCe pattern	When there are two vowels in a one-syllable word and one of them is an *e* at the end of the word, the first vowel is long and the final *e* is silent. Two exceptions are *have* and *love.*	home safe cute
5. CV pattern	When a vowel follows a consonant in a one-syllable word, the vowel is long. Exceptions include *the, to,* and *do.*	go be
6. *R*-controlled vowels	Vowels that are followed by the letter *r* are overpowered and are neither short nor long. One exception is *fire.*	car for birthday
7. -*igh*	When *gh* follows *i,* the *i* is long and the *gh* is silent. One exception is *neighbor.*	high night
8. *Kn-* and *wr-*	In words beginning with *kn-* and *wr-,* the first letter is not pronounced.	knee write

Adapted from Clymer, 1963.

cause they are the most useful (Adams, 1990). Eight high-utility generalizations are listed in Figure 3–7. Even though these rules are fairly reliable, very few of them approach 100% utility. The *r*-controlled vowel rule mentioned above has been calculated to be useful in 78% of words in which the letter *r* follows the vowel (Adams, 1990). Other commonly taught, useful rules have even lower percentages of utility. The CVC pattern rule—which says that when a one-syllable word has only one vowel and the vowel comes between two consonants, it is usually short, as in *bat, land,* and *cup*—is estimated to work only 62% of the time. Exceptions include *told, fall, fork,* and *birth.* The CVCe pattern rule—which says that when there are two vowels in a one-syllable word and one vowel is an *e* at the end of the word, the first vowel is long and the final *e* is silent—is estimated to work in 63% of CVCe words. Examples of conforming words are *came, hole,* and *pipe,* and two very common exceptions are *have* and *love.*

Syllabication.   A syllable is a unit of pronunciation that includes a vowel sound. To determine the number of syllables in a word, students count the number of vowels they hear as the word is said aloud. They need to know about syllabication for both reading and writing. When reading they break long words into syllables in order to decode them, and when writing they break long words into syllables to spell them or divide them at the end of a line of writing.

These multisyllabic words were taken from *Cloudy With a Chance of Meatballs* (Barrett, 1978), and they illustrate how words are divided into syllables, as well as the CV, CVC, and CVCe spelling patterns within syllables:

Saturday	Sat-ur-day
incident	in-cid-ent
different	dif-fer-ent
potatoes	po-ta-toes
hamburger	ham-burg-er
prediction	pre-dic-tion
refrigerator	re-frig-er-a-tor
drizzle	driz-zle
absolute	ab-so-lute
department	de-part-ment
surrounding	sur-round-ing

Second graders clap the syllables as they pronounce a word.

The most useful syllabication rule is that when two consonants follow a vowel, the syllable is usually divided between the consonants. This rule works for many of the words listed above, but not all. In the word *surrounding,* for example, the rule works to divide the first and second syllables, but not to divide the second and third syllables. The suffix *-ing* is usually set off as a separate syllable. Pronouncing the word aloud is a good predictor of how to break the word into syllables. If a child who is decoding the word *surrounding* mistakenly breaks the word into these syllables—*sur-roun-ding*—it doesn't really matter as long as the child identifies the word.

Phonics Instruction

Phonics instruction is an important part of reading and writing instruction during the primary grades, but it is crucial that children are involved in real reading and writing activities as they learn phonics. Without this meaningful application of what they are learning, phonics instruction is often ineffective (Freppon & Dahl, 1991). Teachers use both direct and indirect methods for phonics instruction. They teach minilessons to introduce phonics concepts, skills, and generalizations in a systematic way, and they also take advantage of teachable moments to provide indirect instruction.

Minilessons. Teachers present short lessons on specific high-utility phonics concepts, skills, and generalizations as part of a systematic program. According to Shefelbine (1995), the program should be "systematic and thorough enough to enable most students to become independent and fluent readers, yet still efficient and streamlined" (p. 2). Phonics instruction is always tied to reading and writing.

The teacher presents a minilesson on /b/ as part of the literature focus unit on "The Three Bears."

Teachers emphasize that they are teaching phonics so that students can decode words fluently when reading and spell words conventionally when writing.

Teachers plan for the minilesson by identifying a phonics concept, skill, or generalization and choosing words from the story to introduce the lesson. Teachers clearly and explicitly present the phonics information and provide words to use in practicing the skill, as Mrs. Hoddy did in the vignette at the beginning of this chapter. During minilessons, teachers use the following activities to provide opportunities for students to read, write, and manipulate sounds, spelling patterns, and words:

- Locate other examples of the sound or pattern in words in a book.
- Sort objects and pictures by beginning sounds.
- Cut words and pictures from newspapers and magazines for phonics posters.
- Write words on magic slates or individual dry-erase boards.
- Make a poster or book of words fitting a pattern.
- Sort a group of word cards on the basis of spelling patterns.
- Take a group of magnetic letters or letter cards and arrange them to spell words.
- Read books with many phonetically regular words, such as Dr. Seuss books and Nancy Shaw's "sheep" series (e.g., *Sheep in a Jeep*, 1986).
- Write **alphabet books** and other books featuring phonetically regular words.
- Cut word cards apart into syllables.
- Make charts of words representing spelling patterns and other phonics generalizations, such as the two sounds of *g* and ways to spell long *o*.

While a regular program of minilessons is important, it is essential that they do not overshadow reading and writing as meaning-making processes. Figure 3–8 reviews the guidelines for phonics instruction.

Teachers have to be knowledgeable about phonics in order to teach it well. They need to be able to draw words from students' reading materials, understand the phonics principles operating in these words, and cite additional examples. They also need to know about exceptions so that they can explain why some words don't fit particular generalizations. Too often teachers want to purchase a packaged program, but I recommend that they plan their phonics program themselves, as Mrs. Hoddy did at the beginning of the chapter. She decided on the organization of her program using the checklist shown in Figure 3–2, and then she developed activities using words from the books her students were reading during literature focus units.

■ *Activity*

Choose a trade book and plan minilessons on five phonics concepts, skills, or generalizations that could be taught using the book. Identify words from the book that could be used for each minilesson and suggest ways students might apply what they are learning in reading and writing projects.

Teachable Moments.   Teachers often give impromptu phonics lessons as they engage children in authentic literacy activities using children's names, titles of books, and environmental print in the classroom. During these teachable moments, teachers answer students' questions about words, model how to use phonics knowledge to decode and spell words, and have students share the strategies they use for reading and writing (Mills, O'Keefe, & Stephens, 1992). For example, as she was introducing *The Very Hungry Caterpillar*, Mrs. Hoddy pointed out that *Very* begins with *v* and that not many words start with *v*. One child mentioned that *valentine* is another *v* word,

FIGURE 3–8   Guidelines for Phonics Instruction

---

1. High-Utility Phonics

Teachers teach the phonics concepts, skills, and generalizations that are most useful for decoding and spelling unfamiliar words. Some phonics rules, such as the CVVC long-vowel rule (e.g., *said, soap, head*), are not very useful.

2. Developmental Continuum

Teachers follow a developmental continuum for systematic phonics instruction, beginning with rhyming in kindergarten and ending with syllabication in third grade.

3. Whole-Part-Whole Instructional Sequence

Teachers plan phonics instruction that grows out of reading using a whole-part-whole sequence. Reading the literature is the whole, phonics instruction is the part, and applying the phonics in additional literacy activities is the second whole.

4. Minilessons

Teachers use minilessons to clearly and directly present information about phonics skills and generalizations and provide examples from books students are reading and other common words. They also provide opportunities for students to read and write words applying the concepts they are teaching.

5. Application of Phonics Skills

Students reinforce what they are learning about phonics skills and generalizations through spelling, word sorts, sound matching, word building, wordplay books such as Nancy Shaw's *Sheep in a Jeep* (1986), and other activities.

6. Teachable Moments

Teachers also take advantage of teachable moments when they can incorporate phonics information informally into reading and writing activities.

7. Phonemic Awareness

Teachers reinforce students' understanding of phonemic awareness as students segment and blend written words through phonics instruction and invented spelling.

8. Phonics Review

Upper-grade students review phonics generalizations and rules as part of the spelling program because some rules, such as changing the *y* at the end of a word to *i* before adding a suffix (e.g., *cherry* to *cherries*), are more useful for writing than for reading.

Adapted from Shefelbine, 1995; Stahl, 1992; and Trachtenburg, 1990.

and another said that her middle name is *Victoria*. Then a child who had been quietly looking at the cover of the book said, "I think *Very* is spelled wrong. The author made a mistake," and he pronounced the word *very*, emphasizing the final long *e* sound. "*Very* should have an *e* at the end, not a *y*," he concluded. This comment gave Mrs. Hoddy an opportunity to explain that long *e* at the end of a word is often spelled with a *y*.

Teachers also demonstrate how to apply phonics information as they read big books with the class and take children's dictation for **language experience approach (LEA)** charts. As they read and spell words, teachers break words apart into sounds and apply phonics rules and generalizations. For example, as Mrs. Hoddy talked about the life cycle of butterflies, the class created the chart shown in Figure 3–9. As she wrote, she talked about plural *-s* marker on *eggs* and *caterpillars* and the interesting *tw-* blend at the beginning of *twig*. Also, each time she wrote *butterfly* and *caterpillar,* she spelled the words syllable by syllable. Then as students reread the completed chart, she prompts them on the word *pupa* when they don't remember it, by sounding it out.

SPELLING

Learning to spell is also part of "breaking the code." As children learn about sound-symbol correspondences, they apply what they are learning through both reading and writing. Children's early invented spellings reflect what children know about phonics and spelling patterns, and as their knowledge grows, children's spelling increasingly approximates conventional spelling.

Students need to learn to spell words conventionally so that they can communicate effectively through writing. Learning phonics during the primary grades is part of spelling instruction, but students also need to learn other strategies and information about English orthography. In the past, weekly spelling tests were the main instructional strategy. Now, they are only one part of a comprehensive spelling program.

FIGURE 3–9   A Class Chart on Butterflies

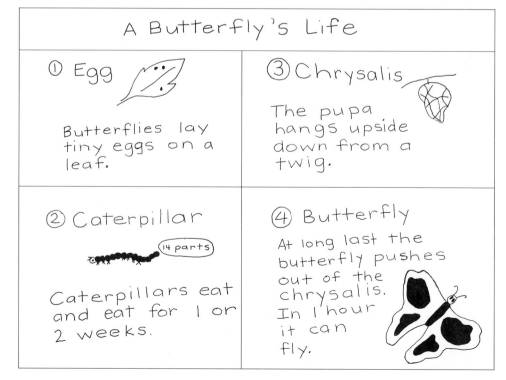

Stages of Invented Spelling

As young children begin to write, they create unique spellings, called invented spelling, based on their knowledge of sound-symbol correspondences and phonics generalizations. Other names for invented spelling are temporary spelling and kid spelling. Charles Read (1971, 1975, 1986) found that young children use their knowledge of phonology to invent spellings. The children in Read's studies used letter names to spell words, such as U *(you)* and R *(are)*, and they used consonant sounds rather consistently: GRL *(girl)*, TIGR *(tiger)*, and NIT *(night)*. They used several unusual but phonetically based spelling patterns to represent affricates. For example, they spelled *tr* with *chr* (e.g., CHRIBLES for *troubles*), *dr* with *jr* (e.g., JRAGIN for *dragon*), and substituted *d* for *t* (e.g., PREDE for *pretty*). Words with long vowels were spelled using letter names: MI *(my)*, LADE *(lady)*, and FEL *(feel)*. The children used several ingenious strategies to spell words with short vowels. The preschoolers selected letters to represent short vowels on the basis of place of articulation in the mouth. Short *i* was represented with *e*, as in FES *(fish)*, short *e* with *a*, as in LAFFT *(left)*, and short *o* with *i*, as in CLIK *(clock)*. These spellings may seem odd to adults, but they are based on phonetic relationships.

Based on observations of children's spellings, researchers have identified five stages that children move through on their way to becoming conventional spellers. At each stage they use different types of strategies. The stages are precommunicative spelling, semiphonetic spelling, phonetic spelling, transitional spelling, and conventional spelling (Gentry, 1978, 1981, 1982, 1987; Gentry & Gillet, 1993). The characteristics of the five stages of invented spelling are summarized in Figure 3–10.

Stage 1: Precommunicative Spelling.   Children string scribbles, letters, and letter-like forms together, but they do not associate the marks they make with any specific phonemes. Spelling at this stage represents a natural, early expression of the alphabet and other concepts about writing. Children may write from left to right, right to left, top to bottom, or randomly across the page. Some precommunicative spellers have a large repertoire of letter forms to use in writing, while others repeat a small number of letters over and over. They use both upper- and lowercase letters, but they show a distinct preference for uppercase letters. At this stage, children have not discovered how spelling works or that letters represent sounds in words. This stage is typical of preschoolers, ages three to five.

Stage 2: Semiphonetic Spelling.   At this stage, children begin to represent phonemes in words with letters, indicating that they have a rudimentary understanding of the alphabetic principle, that a link exists between letters and sounds. Spellings are quite abbreviated, and children use only one, two, or three letters to represent an entire word. Examples of Stage 2 spelling are DA *(day)*, KLZ *(closed)*, and SM *(swimming)*. Semiphonetic spellers use a letter-name strategy to determine which letters to use to spell a word. They pronounce words they want to spell slowly, listening for familiar letter names. Their spellings represent some sound features of words while ignoring other, equally important features. Spellers at this stage include five- and six-year-old children.

Stage 3: Phonetic Spelling.   Children's understanding of the alphabetic principle is further refined in this stage. They continue to use letter names to represent sounds, but they also use consonant and vowels sounds. Examples of Stage 3 spelling are LIV

FIGURE 3–10   Stages of Invented Spelling

Stage 1: Precommunicative Spelling

Child uses scribbles, letterlike forms, letters, and sometimes numbers to represent a message.

Child may write from left to right, right to left, top to bottom, or randomly on the page.

Child shows no understanding of phoneme-grapheme correspondences.

Child may repeat a few letters again and again or use most of the letters of the alphabet.

Child frequently mixes upper- and lowercase letters but shows a preference for uppercase letters.

Stage 2: Semiphonetic Spelling

Child becomes aware of the alphabetic principle that letters are used to represent sounds.

Child uses abbreviated one-, two-, or three-letter spelling to represent an entire word.

Child uses letter-name strategy to spell words.

Stage 3: Phonetic Spelling

Child represents all essential sound features of a word in spelling.

Child develops particular spellings for long and short vowels, plural and past-tense markers, and other aspects of spelling.

Child chooses letters on the basis of sound without regard for English letter sequences or other conventions.

Stage 4: Transitional Spelling

Child adheres to basic conventions of English orthography.

Child begins to use morphological and visual information in addition to phonetic information.

Child may include all appropriate letters in a word but reverse some of them.

Child uses alternate spellings for the same sound in different words, but only partially understands the conditions governing their use.

Child uses a high percentage of correctly spelled words.

Stage 5: Conventional Spelling

Child applies the basic rules of the English orthographic system.

Child extends knowledge of word structure including the spelling of affixes, contractions, compound words, and homonyms.

Child demonstrates growing accuracy in using silent consonants and doubling consonants before adding suffixes.

Child recognizes when a word doesn't "look right" and can consider alternate spellings for the same sound.

Child learns irregular spelling patterns.

Child learns consonant and vowel alternations and other morphological structures.

Child knows how to spell a large number of words conventionally.

Adapted from Gentry, 1982; Gentry & Gillet, 1993.

(live), DRAS *(dress)*, and PEKT *(peeked)*. As these examples show, children choose letters on the basis of sound alone, without considering acceptable English letter sequences (e.g., using *-t* rather than *-ed* as a past tense marker in *peeked*). These spellings do not resemble English words, but they can be deciphered. The major achievement of this stage is that, for the first time, children represent all essential sound features in the words. Phonetic spellers are typically about six years old.

Stage 4: Transitional Spelling.   Transitional spellers come close to the conventional spellings of English words. They spell many words correctly, but they continue to misspell words with irregular spellings. Examples of Stage 4 spelling are HUOSE *(house)*, TRUBAL *(trouble)*, EAGUL *(eagle)*, and AFTERNEWN *(afternoon)*. This stage is characterized by children's growing ability to represent the features of English orthography. Children include a vowel in every syllable and demonstrate knowledge of vowel patterns even though they make faulty decisions about which marker to use. For example, *toad* is often spelled TODE when children choose the wrong vowel marker, or TAOD when the two vowels are reversed. Also, transitional spellers use common letter patterns in their spelling, such as YOUNIGHTED for *united* and HIGHCKED for *hiked*. Transitional spelling resembles English orthography and can easily be read. As the examples show, children stop relying entirely on phonological information and begin to use visual clues and morphological information. Spellers in this stage are generally seven, eight, and nine years old.

Stage 5: Conventional Spelling.   As the name implies, children at this stage spell most words (90% or more) as they are spelled in the dictionary. They have mastered the basic principles of English spelling. Children typically reach Stage 5 by the age of eight or nine. During the next four or five years, they learn to control homonyms (e.g., *road–rode*), contractions, affixes (e.g., *run, running*), and alternative spellings (e.g., *city, sity*). They also learn to spell common irregularly spelled words (e.g., *school* and *they*). This is the stage when weekly spelling tests should begin, if they are used at all (Gentry & Gillet, 1993).

In a short period—four or five years—children move from precommunicative spelling to conventional spelling. This learning happens through reading and writing experiences and children's developing knowledge of phonics and words rather than through weekly spelling tests. Too often, children are advised to sound out spellings for unfamiliar words or to limit the words they use in their writing to words they are sure they already know how to spell, but these practices thwart children's spelling development. Sounding out spellings reinforces children's emphasis on the phoneme-grapheme correspondences rather than supporting students' experimentation with nonphonetic components of spelling as they move through the developmental sequence.

Researchers are continuing to study children's spelling development beyond age eight. Hitchcock (1989) studied children's spellings in grades two through six and classified the errors these older, conventional-stage spellers continue to make. More than half of their errors were classified as phonetic spellings, in which students spell words according to the way they sound or how they pronounce them (e.g., *wat* for *want, to* for *two, babes* for *babies*). That students continue to misspell words by spelling them phonetically is not surprising, because teachers and parents often encourage students to sound out the spelling when children ask how to spell an unknown word. Most of the other errors were transitional-stage spellings. Students misapplied rules about vowels, plurals, verb tenses, possessives, contractions, compound words, and affixes (e.g., *ca'nt* for *can't, alot* for *a lot, acter* for *actor,* and *huose* for *house*).

Other researchers have examined the spelling strategies of poor readers in fourth through sixth grade and found that these students are likely to use a sounding-out strategy (Anderson, 1985). Good readers, on the other hand, use a variety of spelling strategies, including visual information, knowledge about root words and affixes, and analogy to known words (Barron, 1980; Marsh, Friedman, Desberg, & Welsh, 1980). Frith (1980) concluded that older students who are good readers and spellers make spelling errors characteristic of the transitional stage, whereas students who are poor readers and spellers make spelling errors characteristic of the phonetic stage.

Teaching Spelling

Spelling instruction is more than weekly spelling tests. It is involving students in genuine reading and writing opportunities and teaching minilessons about phonics, spelling rules, and spelling strategies. Spelling instruction has seven components:

1. Daily writing opportunities.   Providing opportunities for students to write every day is prerequisite to any spelling program. Spelling is a writer's tool, and it is best learned through the experience of writing. Students who write daily and invent spellings for unfamiliar words move naturally toward conventional spelling. When they write, children predict spellings using their developing knowledge of sound-symbol correspondences and spelling patterns. Most of the informal writing that students do each day does not need to be graded, and spelling errors should not be marked. Learning to spell is a lot like learning to play the piano. These daily writing opportunities are the practice sessions, not the lesson with the teacher.

When students use the writing process to develop and polish their writing, emphasis on conventional spelling belongs in the editing stage. Through the process approach, children learn to recognize spelling for what it is—a courtesy to readers. As they write, revise, edit, and share their writing with genuine audiences, students understand the need to spell conventionally so that their audience can read their compositions.

2. Daily reading opportunities.   Reading also plays an enormous role in learning to spell. During reading, students store the visual shapes of words. The ability to recall how words look helps students decide when a spelling they are writing is correct. When students decide a word doesn't look right, they can rewrite the word several different ways until it does look right, ask the teacher or a classmate who knows the spelling, or check the spelling in a dictionary.

3. Word walls.   One way to highlight students' attention to words in books they are reading or social studies and science theme studies is through the use of word walls. Students and the teacher choose words to write on word walls, which are large sheets of paper hanging in the classroom. Then students refer to these word walls during word-study activities and also when they are writing. Seeing the words posted on word walls, **clusters,** and other charts in the classroom and using them in their writing helps students learn to spell the words.

Many teachers also hang word walls with high-frequency words. Researchers have identified the most commonly used words and recommend that elementary students learn to spell 100 of these words because of their usefulness. The most frequently used words represent more than 50% of all the words children and adults write (Horn, 1926)! Figure 3–11 lists the 100 most frequently used words. Some teachers alphabetize the 100 words and type them on small cards—personal word walls—that students keep at their desks.

4. Proofreading. Proofreading is a special kind of reading that students use to locate misspelled words and other mechanical errors in rough drafts. As students learn about the writing process, they are introduced to proofreading in the editing stage. More in-depth instruction about how to use proofreading to locate spelling errors and then correct these misspelled words is part of spelling instruction. Through a series of minilessons, students can proofread sample student papers and mark misspelled words. Then, working in pairs, students can correct the misspelled words.

Proofreading should be introduced in the primary grades. Young children and their teachers proofread **collaborative books** and dictated stories together, and students can be encouraged to read over their own compositions and make necessary corrections soon after they begin writing. This way students accept proofreading as a natural part of writing. Proofreading activities are more valuable for teaching spelling than are dictation activities, in which teachers dictate sentences for students to write and correctly capitalize and punctuate. Few people use dictation in their daily lives, but students use proofreading skills every time they polish a piece of writing.

5. Dictionary use. Students need to learn to locate the spelling of unfamiliar words in the dictionary. While it is relatively easy to find a "known" word in the dic-

FIGURE 3–11 The 100 Most Frequently Used Words

a	for	mother	there
about	from	my	they
after	get	no	things
all	got	not	think
am	had	now	this
an	have	of	time
and	he	on	to
are	her	one	too
around	him	or	two
as	his	our	up
at	home	out	us
back	house	over	very
be	how	people	was
because	I	put	we
but	if	said	well
by	in	saw	went
came	into	school	were
can	is	see	what
could	it	she	when
day	just	so	who
did	know	some	will
didn't	like	that	with
do	little	the	would
don't	man	them	you
down	me	then	your

tionary, it is hard to locate unfamiliar words, and students need to learn what to do when they do not know how to spell a word. One approach is to predict possible spellings for unknown words, then check the most probable spellings in a dictionary.

Students should be encouraged to check the spellings of words in a dictionary as well as to use dictionaries to check multiple meanings of a word or the etymology of the word. Too often students view consulting a dictionary as punishment. Teachers must work to change this view of dictionary use. One way to do this is to appoint some students in the classroom as dictionary checkers. These students have dictionaries to keep on their desks, and they are consulted whenever questions about spelling, word meaning, and word usage arise.

6. Spelling options.   In English, there are alternate spellings for many sounds because so many words have been borrowed from other languages and retain their native spellings. There are many more options for vowel sounds than for consonants. Even so, there are four spelling options for /f/ *(f, ff, ph, gh)*. Spelling options sometimes vary according to position in the word. For example, *ff* and *gh* are only used to represent /f/ at the end of a word, as in *cuff* and *laugh*. Common spelling options for phonemes are listed in Figure 3–12.

Teachers point out spelling options as they write words on word walls and when students ask about the spelling of a word. They also can use a series of minilessons to teach upper-grade students about these options. During each minilesson, students can focus on one phoneme, such as /f/ or /ar/, and as a class or small group they can develop a list of the various ways the sound is spelled in English, giving examples of each spelling. A sixth-grade chart on long *o* is presented in Figure 3–13.

7. Strategies for spelling unfamiliar words.   Students need to develop a repertoire of strategies in order to spell unfamiliar words. Some of these spelling strategies are:

■ inventing spellings for words based on students' phonological, semantic, and historical knowledge of words
■ proofreading to locate and correct spelling errors
■ locating words on word walls and other charts
■ predicting the spelling of a word by generating possible spellings and choosing the best alternative
■ applying affixes to root words
■ spelling unknown words by analogy to known words
■ locating the spelling of unfamiliar words in a dictionary or other resource book
■ writing a letter or two as a placeholder for a word they do not know how to spell when they are writing rough drafts and **quickwrites**
■ asking the teacher or another person how to spell a word

Instead of giving the traditional "sound it out" advice when students ask how to spell a word, teachers should suggest that students use a strategic "think it out" approach to spell unfamiliar words. This advice reminds students that spelling involves more than phonological information and suggests that students should think about spelling patterns, root words and affixes, and the shape of the word—what it looks like.

FIGURE 3–12 Common Spelling Options

Sound	Spellings	Examples	Sound	Spellings	Examples
long a	a-e	date	short oo	oo	book
	a	angel		u	put
	ai	aid		ou	could
	ay	day		o	woman
ch	ch	church	ou	ou	out
	t(u)	picture		ow	cow
	tch	watch	s	s	sick
	ti	question		ce	office
long e	ea	each		c	city
	ee	feel		ss	class
	e	evil		se	else
	e-e	these		x(ks)	box
	ea-e	breathe	sh	ti	attention
short e	e	end		sh	she
	ea	head		ci	ancient
f	f	feel		ssi	admission
	ff	sheriff	t	t	teacher
	ph	photograph		te	definite
j	ge	strange		ed	furnished
	g	general		tt	attend
	j	job	long u	u	union
	dge	bridge		u-e	use
k	c	call		ue	value
	k	keep		ew	few
	x	expect, luxury	short u	u	ugly
	ck	black		o	company
	qu	quite, bouquet		ou	country
l	l	last	y	u	union
	ll	allow		u-e	use
	le	automobile		y	yes
m	m	man		i	onion
	me	come		ue	value
	mm	comment		ew	few
n	n	no	z	s	present
	ne	done		se	applause
long o	o	go		ze	gauze
	o-e	note	syllabic *l*	le	able
	ow	own		al	animal
	oa	load		el	cancel
short o	o	office		il	civil
	a	all	syllabic *n*	en	written
	au	author		on	lesson
	aw	saw		an	important
oi	oi	oil		in	cousin
	oy	boy		contractions	didn't
long oo	u	cruel		ain	certain
	oo	noon	*r*-controlled	er	her
	u-e	rule		ur	church
	o-e	lose		ir	first
	ue	blue		or	world
	o	to		ear	heard
	ou	group		our	courage

117

FIGURE 3–13 Spelling Options Chart for Long *o*

		Location		
Spelling	**Word**	**Initial**	**Medial**	**Final**
o	oh, obedient	x		
	go, no, so			x
o-e	home, pole		x	
ow	own	x		
	known		x	
	blow, elbow, yellow			x
oa	oaf, oak, oat	x		
	boat, groan		x	
ew	sew			x
ol	yolk, folk		x	
oe	toe			x
ough	though			x
eau	beau			x
ou	bouquet		x	

Weekly Spelling Tests

Many teachers question the use of spelling tests to teach spelling, since research on invented spelling suggests that spelling is best learned through reading and writing (Gentry & Gillet, 1993; Wilde, 1992). In addition, teachers complain that lists of spelling words are unrelated to the words students are reading and writing and that the 30 minutes of valuable instructional time spent each day in completing spelling textbook activities is excessive. Weekly spelling tests, when they are used, should be individualized so that children learn to spell the words they need for their writing.

In the individualized approach to spelling instruction, students choose the words they will study, and many of the words they choose are words they use in their writing projects. Students study 5 to 10 specific words during the week using a study strategy. This approach places more responsibility on students for their own learning. Teachers develop a weekly word list of 20 to 50 words of varying difficulty from which students select words to study. Words for the master list are high-frequency words, words from the word wall related to literature focus units and theme studies, and words students needed for their writing projects during the previous week. Words from spelling textbooks can also be added to the list.

On Monday, the teacher administers a pretest using the master list of words, and students spell as many of the words as they can. Students correct their own pretests, and from the words that they misspell they create individual spelling lists. They make two copies of their study list, using the numbers on the master list to make it easier to take the final test on Friday. Students use one copy of the list for study activities, and the teacher keeps the second copy.

Students spend approximately 5 to 10 minutes studying the words on their study lists each day during the week. Instead of "busy-work" activities such as using their

HOW EFFECTIVE TEACHERS
Assist Students in "Breaking the Code"

Effective Practices	Ineffective Practices
1. Teachers develop students' phonemic awareness using songs, rhymes, and wordplay books.	1. Teachers focus only on teaching phonics using written words.
2. Teachers teach minilessons on segmenting and blending sounds in words using words drawn from literature focus units.	2. Teachers don't lay a foundation for phonics instruction by teaching students about phonemic awareness.
3. Teachers teach phonics using a whole-part-whole approach.	3. Teachers teach phonics in isolation without connecting phonics to real reading and writing.
4. Teachers teach the high-utility phonics concepts, skills, and generalizations.	4. Teachers don't consider the usefulness of the phonics generalizations they teach.
5. Teachers teach phonics through minilessons and "teachable moments."	5. Teachers depend on commercial phonics programs, including "Hooked on Phonics."
6. Teachers connect phonics instruction for decoding words to spelling words.	6. Teachers teach phonics using skill-and-practice activities and an abundance of worksheets and workbooks.
7. Teachers encourage students to apply what they know about phonics through invented spelling.	7. Teachers discourage students from using invented spelling.
8. Teachers analyze students' invented spelling as a measure of students' understanding of phonics.	8. Teachers consider students' spellings as right or wrong without analyzing the errors.
9. Teachers recognize that daily reading and writing experiences contribute to students' spelling development.	9. Teachers devalue the importance of reading and writing practice in students' spelling development.
10. Teachers teach minilessons on spelling using words from students' reading and writing. They may use spelling tests, but only as part of the spelling program.	10. Teachers teach spelling using spelling textbooks and weekly spelling tests.

spelling words in sentences or gluing yarn in the shape of the words, research shows it is more effective for students to use this study strategy:

1. Look at the word and say it to yourself.
2. Say each letter in the word to yourself.
3. Close your eyes and spell the word to yourself.
4. Write the word, and check that you spelled it correctly.
5. Write the word again and check that you spelled it correctly.

This strategy focuses on the whole word rather than breaking the word apart into sounds or syllables. Teachers explain how to use the strategy during a minilesson at the beginning of the school year and then post a copy of the strategy in the classroom. In addition to this study strategy, sometimes students trade word lists on Wednesday or Thursday or give each other a practice test.

A final test is administered on Friday. The teacher reads the master list, and students write only those words they have practiced during the week. To make it easier to administer the test, students first list the numbers of the words they have practiced from their study lists on their test papers. Any words that students misspell should be included on their lists the following week.

This individualized approach is recommended instead of a textbook approach. Typically, textbooks are arranged in week-long units, with lists of 10 to 20 words and practice activities that often require at least 30 minutes per day to complete. Research indicates that only 60 to 75 minutes per week should be spent on spelling instruction, as greater periods of time do not result in increased spelling ability (Johnson, Langford, & Quorn, 1981).

What is the controversy about spelling instruction?

The press and concerned parent groups periodically raise questions about invented spelling and the importance of weekly spelling tests. There is a misplaced public perception that today's children cannot spell. Researchers who are examining the types of errors students make have noted that the number of misspellings increases in grades one through four, as students write longer compositions, but that the percentage of errors decreases. The percentage continues to decline in the upper grades, although some students continue to make errors (Taylor & Kidder, 1988). The Educational Testing Service (Applebee, Langer, & Mullis, 1987) reported on the frequency of spelling errors in formal writing assessments. Nine-year-olds averaged 92% correct spelling, 13-year-olds spelled 97% of words correctly, and 17-year-olds scored 98%. These data suggest that by third or fourth grade most students are conventional spellers, making fewer than 10% errors.

Review

The three components involved in "breaking the code" are phonemic awareness, phonics, and spelling. Phonemic awareness is the ability to segment and blend spoken words, and it provides the foundation for phonics instruction. Phonics is the set of relationships between speech sounds and spelling patterns. During the primary grades, students learn phonics in order to decode words and invent spellings. In order to become fluent readers, students need to be able to decode unfamiliar words rapidly. As young children begin writing, they use invented spelling to apply what they know about English spelling patterns. Their spelling changes to reflect phonics skills and spelling patterns they are learning. The figure on page 119 reviews the recommended practices that effective reading teachers use in assisting students to "break the code."

References

Adams, M. J. (1990). *Beginning to read: Thinking and learning about print.* Cambridge, MA: MIT Press.

Anderson, K. F. (1985). The development of spelling ability and linguistic strategies. *The Reading Teacher, 39,* 140–147.

Applebee, A. N., Langer, J. A., & Mullis, I. V. S. (1987). *Grammar, punctuation, and spelling: Controlling the conventions of written English at ages 9, 13, and 17* (Report No. 15-W-03). Princeton, NJ: Educational Testing Service.

Ball, E., & Blachman, B. (1991). Does phoneme segmentation training in kindergarten make a difference in early word recognition and developmental spelling? *Reading Research Quarterly, 26,* 49–86.

Barron, R. W. (1980). Visual and phonological strategies in reading and spelling. In U. Frith (Ed.), *Cognitive processes in learning to spell.* London: Academic Press.

Carle, E. (1993). *Eric Carle: Picture writer* (videotape). New York: Philomel.

Clay, M. M. (1985). *The early detection of reading difficulties* (3rd ed.). Portsmouth, NH: Heinemann.

Clymer, T. (1963). The utility of phonic generalizations in the primary grades. *The Reading Teacher, 16,* 252–258.

Freppon, P. A., & Dahl, K. L. (1991). Learning about phonics in a whole language classroom. *Language Arts, 68,* 190–197.

Frith, U. (1980). Unexpected spelling problems. In U. Frith (Ed.), *Cognitive processes in learning to spell.* London: Academic Press.

Gentry, J. R. (1978). Early spelling strategies. *Elementary School Journal, 79,* 88–92.

Gentry, J. R. (1981). Learning to spell developmentally. *The Reading Teacher, 34,* 378–381.

Gentry, J. R. (1982). Developmental spelling: Assessment. *Diagnostique, 8,* 52–61.

Gentry, J. R. (1987). *Spel . . . is a four-letter word.* Portsmouth, NH: Heinemann.

Gentry, J. R., & Gillet, J. W. (1993). *Teaching kids to spell.* Portsmouth, NH: Heinemann.

Goodman, K. (1993). *Phonics phacts.* Portsmouth, NH: Heinemann.

Griffith, F., & Olson, M. (1992). Phonemic awareness helps beginning readers break the code. *The Reading Teacher, 45,* 516–523.

Griffith, P. L. (1991). Phonemic awareness helps first graders invent spellings and third graders remember correct spellings. *Journal of Reading Behavior, 23,* 215–232.

Hanna, P. R., Hanna, J. S., Hodges, R. E., & Rudorf, E. H. (1966). *Phoneme-grapheme correspondences as cues to spelling improvement.* Washington, DC: US Government Printing Office.

Hitchcock, M. E. (1989). *Elementary students' invented spellings at the correct stage of spelling development.* Unpublished doctoral dissertation, Norman, OK: University of Oklahoma.

Hohn, W., & Ehri, L. (1982). Do alphabet letters help prereaders acquire phonemic segmentation skill? *Journal of Educational Psychology, 75,* 752–762.

Horn, E. (1926). *A basic writing vocabulary.* Iowa City: University of Iowa Press.

Horn, E. (1957). Phonetics and spelling. *Elementary School Journal, 57,* 233–235, 246.

Johnson, T. D., Langford, K. G., & Quorn, K. C. (1981). Characteristics of an effective spelling program. *Language Arts, 58,* 581–588.

Juel, C., Griffith, P. L., & Gough, P. B. (1986). Acquisition of literacy: A longitudinal study of children in first and second grade. *Journal of Educational Psychology, 78,* 243–255.

Klesius, J. P., Griffith, P. L., & Zielonka, P. (1991). A whole language and traditional instruction comparison: Overall effectiveness and development of the alphabetic principle. *Reading Research and Instruction, 30,* 47–61.

Lewkowicz, N. K. (1994). The bag game: An activity to heighten phonemic awareness. *The Reading Teacher, 47,* 508–509.

Liberman, I., Shankweiler, D., Fischer, F., & Carter, B. (1974). Explicit syllable and phoneme segmentation in the young child. *Journal of Experimental Child Psychology, 18,* 201–212.

Lomax, R. G., & McGee, L. M. (1987). Young children's concepts about print and meaning: Toward a model of word reading acquisition. *Reading Research Quarterly, 22,* 237–256.

Lundberg, I., Frost, J., & Peterson, O. (1988). Effects of an extensive program for stimulating phonological awareness in preschool children. *Reading Research Quarterly, 23,* 263–284.

Marsh, G., Friedman, M., Desberg, P., & Welsh, V. (1981). The development of strategies in spelling. In U. Frith (Ed.), *Cognitive processes in learning to spell.* London: Academic Press.

McGee, L. M., & Richgels, D. J. (1989). "K is Kristen's": Learning the alphabet from a child's perspective. *The Reading Teacher, 43,* 216–225.

Mills, H., O'Keefe, T., & Stephens, D. (1992). *Looking closely: Exploring the role of phonics in one whole language classroom.* Urbana, IL: National Council of Teachers of English.

Perfitti, C., Beck, I., Bell, L., & Hughes, C. (1987). Phonemic knowledge and learning to read are reciprocal: A longitudinal study of first grade children. *Merrill-Palmer Quarterly, 33,* 283–319.

Read, C. (1971). Pre-school children's knowledge of English phonology. *Harvard Educational Review, 41,* 1–34.

Read, C. (1975). *Children's categorization of speech sounds in English* (NCTE Research Report No. 17). Urbana, IL: National Council of Teachers of English.

Read, C. (1986). *Children's creative spelling.* London: Routledge & Kegan Paul.

Shefelbine, J. (1995). *Learning and using phonics in beginning reading* (Literacy research paper; volume 10). New York: Scholastic.

Stahl, S. A. (1992). Saying the "p" word: Nine guidelines for exemplary phonics instruction. *The Reading Teacher, 45,* 618–625.

Stanovich, K. (1980). Toward an interactive-compensatory model of individual differences in the development of reading fluency. *Reading Research Quarterly, 16,* 37–71.

Taylor, K. K., & Kidder, E. B. (1988). The development of

spelling skills: From first grade through eighth grade. *Written Communication, 5,* 222–244.

Tompkins, G. E., & Yaden, D. B., Jr. (1986). *Answering students' questions about words.* Urbana, IL: ERIC Clearinghouse on Reading and Communication Skills and National Council of Teachers of English.

Trachtenburg, P. (1990). Using children's literature to enhance phonics instruction. *The Reading Teacher, 43,* 648–654.

Treiman, R. (1985). Onsets and rimes as units of spoken syllables: Evidence from children. *Journal of Experimental Child Psychology, 39,* 161–181.

Tunmer, W., & Nesdale, A. (1985). Phonemic segmentation skill and beginning reading. *Journal of Educational Psychology, 77,* 417–427.

Venezky, R. L. (1970). *The structure of English orthography.* The Hague: Mouton.

Wilde, S. (1992). *You kan red this! Spelling and punctuation for whole language classrooms, K–6.* Portsmouth, NH: Heinemann.

Wylie, R. E., & Durrell, D. D. (1970). Teaching vowels through phonograms. *Elementary English, 47,* 787–791.

Yopp, H. K. (1985). Phoneme segmentation ability: A prerequisite for phonics and sight word achievement in beginning reading? In J. Niles & R. Lalik (Eds.), *Issues in literacy: A research perspective* (pp. 330–336). Rochester, NY: National Reading Conference.

Yopp, H. K. (1988). The validity and reliability of phonemic awareness tests. *Reading Research Quarterly, 23,* 159–177.

Yopp, H. K. (1992). Developing phonemic awareness in young children. *The Reading Teacher, 45,* 696–703.

Yopp, H. K. (1995). Read-aloud books for developing phonemic awareness: An annotated bibliography. *The Reading Teacher, 48,* 538–542.

Children's Book References

Barrett, J. (1978). *Cloudy with a chance of meatballs.* New York: Atheneum.

Carle, E. (1969). *The very hungry caterpillar.* New York: Philomel.

Carle, E. (1984). *The very busy spider.* New York: Philomel.

Carle, E. (1990). *The very quiet cricket.* New York: Philomel.

Carle, E. (1995). *The very lonely firefly.* New York: Philomel.

Degen, B. (1983). *Jamberry.* New York: Harper & Row.

Dr. Seuss. (1963). *Hop on pop.* New York: Random House.

Hutchins, P. (1976). *Don't forget the bacon!* New York: Mulberry.

Obligado, L. (1983). *Faint frogs feeling feverish and other terrifically tantalizing tongue twisters.* New York: Puffin.

Prelutsky, J. (1982). *The baby uggs are hatching.* New York: Mulberry.

Sendak, M. (1963). *Where the wild things are.* New York: Harper & Row.

Shaw, N. (1986). *Sheep in a jeep.* Boston: Houghton Mifflin.

CHAPTER 4
Developing Strategic Readers and Writers

As part of a unit on weather, Mrs. Donnelly's third-grade class reads *Cloudy With a Chance of Meatballs* (Barrett, 1978), a fantasy picture book about the town of Chewandswallow, where food and drink fall from the sky like rain three times each day. After Mrs. Donnelly introduces the book as an "absurd" fantasy, most students read it independently, but a few choose to read it with the teacher. Students participate in a **grand conversation** and talk about their interpretations of the book (see the Compendium for a description of this and all other highlighted terms in this chapter). They also write in their **literature logs.** Later, students examine how the author combined fantasy and reality in the book through a **minilesson.** Students also create their own weather reports and write an **alphabet book** about weather. For more information about how Mrs. Donnelly's class read and responded to the book, see pages 82–85.

Josh, one of Mrs. Donnelly's students, agreed to talk to me about the book and what he does when he reads. The first question I asked was, "What did you think about before you started reading this book?"

"I just looked at the cover, and I knew right away that it would be a weird book. This picture of this man getting a meatball like rain falling on his plate made me think it would be funny—like it would make me laugh. Mrs. Donnelly told us a little about this book, and I know our theme is weather, so I thought about all the stuff I know about rain, snow, clouds, and stuff. But then I read this little writing at the bottom of the page—'If food dropped like rain from the sky, wouldn't it be marvelous! Or would it?'—and I was thinking that something bad was going to happen. Maybe their rain would stop."

"What were you thinking about as you read the book?"

"Well, I wondered why the writing was in yellow boxes on some pages and in pink and orange boxes on other pages. I thought that maybe that was important, but it wasn't. And I couldn't read this word—Chewandswallow—at first. I didn't know it was the name of the town, but I just skipped over it and went on reading. It didn't seem important, and then I saw it way back in the book and my eyes saw that it was three words and it was easy to read."

"Mrs. Donnelly told you that *Cloudy With a Chance of Meatballs* was a fantasy, didn't she?"

"That made me think that weird stuff would go on, and it did. I thought the weird stuff was going to start when Grandpa was making pancakes, but it didn't start until he told the story. That was sort of confusing, but I just kept reading and I figured it would make sense later on."

"After you finished reading, you wrote in your lit log, didn't you? Would you share it?"

"OK. This is my log: 'I would like to go to Chewandswallow. I want it to snow tacos and pizza and french fries and to rain Coke and hail chocolate chip cookies. I'd like all the free food, but I wouldn't like it when the weather got bad. Some of the weather was dangerous. I thought the book would have more information about weather but it didn't. It would have been more interesting if it did.'"

"That's very interesting. How do you decide what to write in your lit log?"

"Well, I write what is on my mind and the things I want to tell Mrs. Donnelly. I think about what I liked and I write that part and then I ask myself if there is anything that was bad for me and then I write that. I ask my brain what to write and it tells me and then I write it."

"When you're reading, do you imagine that you're right there in the story?"

"I guess so. Sometimes when I'm reading, I sort of become the character that is most like me and then I think I'm there. But I didn't really do that in this book. It was too weird. I couldn't think of being there because it's something that would probably never happen."

FIGURE 4–1   Josh's Page From the Class Alphabet Book on Weather

"Was there anything that you learned when your class talked about the book after you finished reading it?"

"The colors. I was just reading the book and I didn't see that the pages, you know, were all colors during Grandpa's story and the pictures were plain at the beginning and at the end. That's what Molly said and she was right."

Also, as part of the weather unit, Mrs. Donnelly's students wrote an alphabet book on weather. Students used the writing process to draft and refine their book. Each student wrote one page on a different letter, and Josh wrote about monsoons for the M page. His page is shown in Figure 4–1. He talked about the page he wrote and his writing.

"How did you decide to write about monsoons?"

"Mrs. Donnelly read us this book called *Jumanji* [Van Allsburg, 1981], and it was about a monsoon. I didn't know about them but I thought it was a kind of weather. I wanted to learn about it so I did. I would like to be in a monsoon someday if I went to places like India or Asia."

"What did you do when you were revising your page?"

"Well, monsoons are not easy to understand. Everybody knows about earthquakes and tornadoes because they happen in California, but monsoons are very unusual. Mrs. Donnelly told me that I had to make sure that everyone could understand my page. I read it to Mike and Perry and they said it was good but that I needed to make a chart about how a monsoon is made. So I did and my dad helped me do it. I made it like a math problem: hot land plus cold water equals a monsoon wind. I want it to be good so everyone will like it. Everybody liked it when I read it when we sat in a circle for a read-around. Then I made a fancy M on my page so it would be special."

*J*osh is an effective reader and writer. He makes predictions before beginning to read and organizes ideas before writing. Josh can talk about connecting what he is reading and writing to his own life and to books he has read. He also regulates or monitors what he does when he reads and writes. He has a sense of his audience when he writes. He tolerates confusion and ambiguity when he reads and writes, and he has confidence that he'll work through these problems. He applies a variety of skills automatically and uses problem-solving strategies in order to create meaning when he reads and writes.

We all have skills that we use automatically and self-regulated strategies for things that we do well, such as driving defensively, playing volleyball, training a new pet, or maintaining classroom discipline. We apply skills that we have learned unconsciously and choose among skills as we think strategically. The strategies we use in these activities are problem-solving mechanisms that involve complex thinking processes. When we are just learning how to drive a car, for example, we learn both skills and strategies. Some of the first skills we learn are how to start the engine, make left turns, and parallel park. With practice, these skills become automatic. Some of the first strategies that we learn are how to pass another car and stay a safe distance behind the cars ahead of us. At first we have only a small repertoire of strategies, and we don't always use them effectively. That's one reason why we take driving lessons from a driving instructor and have a learner's permit that requires a more experienced driver to ride along with us. These more experienced drivers teach us defensive driving strategies. We learn strategies for driving on interstate highways, on slippery roads, and at night. With practice and guidance, we become more successful drivers, able to anticipate driving problems and take defensive actions.

The same is true for literacy. Strategic readers and writers control their own reading and writing and apply skills and strategies as they need them. They set purposes before reading, revise their plans as they read, and deal with the difficulties that they encounter while reading and writing. Strategies allow students to monitor understanding and solve problems as they read. Students use strategies deliberately with some understanding of their usefulness or effectiveness. In order to become expert readers and writers, children must become strategic.

In this chapter, you will learn about strategic readers and writers and ways to teach students to use skills and strategies effectively. Use these questions to guide your reading:

- Which reading and writing strategies do elementary students use?
- Are there differences between how more capable and less capable readers and writers use strategies?
- How are strategies and skills different?
- How do students become strategic readers and writers?

■ *Activity*

Think about what you do when you read. What skills and strategies did you use as you read the beginning of this chapter? Make a list of the skills and strategies that you can identify. Next, spend 15 to 30 minutes reading a novel. What skills and strategies did you use? Make a second list. Then compare the two lists. Are there any differences? Why?

READING AND WRITING STRATEGIES

There is no single definition of a *strategy* or a single list of strategies on which all researchers can agree, but many of the things that Josh talked about in the vignette at the beginning of this chapter referred to strategies he was using. He talked about making predictions, monitoring his understanding, revising meaning, and making connections to personal experience and literature.

Good readers and writers are actively involved in creating meaning. They select and use appropriate strategies, monitor their understanding as they read, and refine their meaning as they write (Lewin, 1992; Paris & Jacobs, 1984; Schmitt, 1990). I will focus on 12 strategies that elementary students use when they read and write. These strategies are listed in Figure 4–2. These thinking or problem-solving strategies are used by both readers and writers.

1. Tapping prior knowledge. Students think about what they already know about the topic about which they will read or write. This knowledge includes information and vocabulary about topics such as dinosaurs, as well as information about authors and literary genres such as fantasies, alphabet books, and biographies. Students' knowledge is stored in schemata (or categories) and linked to other knowledge through a complex network of interrelationships. As students learn during the reading or writing task, they add the new information to their schemata.

2. Predicting. Students make predictions or thoughtful "guesses" about what will happen in the books they are reading. These guesses are based on what students already know about the topic and the literary genre, or on what they have read thus far. Students often make one prediction before beginning to read and several others at key points in the story or at the beginning of each chapter when reading chapter

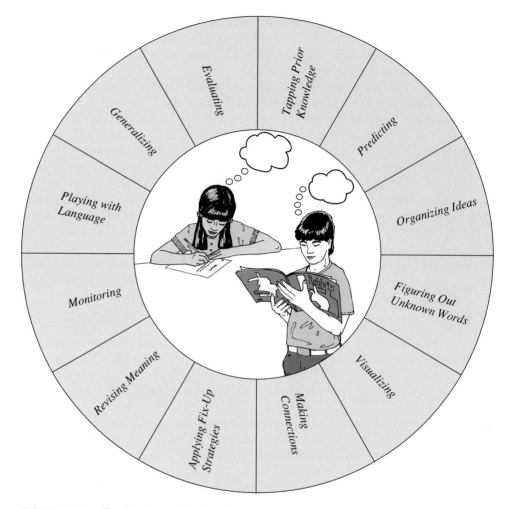

FIGURE 4–2   Twelve Strategies That Readers and Writers Use

books using the **Directed Reading-Thinking Activity** (DRTA) (Stauffer, 1975). As students read, their predictions are either confirmed or revised on the basis of what they have read. When they are preparing to read informational books or content-area textbooks, students often preview or look through the text in order to make predictions. They also ask questions for which they would like to find answers as they read or set purposes for reading.

When they are writing, students make plans and set purposes for the pieces they are writing. They make predictions about which ideas are important and which ones will interest their readers. They revise their plans as their writing moves in new or unexpected directions. Young children also make predictions about how long their writing will be when they count out the number of pages for their books.

3. Organizing ideas.   Students organize ideas and sequence story events as they read, and they organize their ideas for writing using **clusters** and other graphic organizers. The way students organize ideas varies depending on whether they are reading and writing stories, informational books, or poetry. Each type of text has unique organizational patterns. When students read and write stories, they often organize the events into the beginning, middle, and end. When they read and write informational books, they often use description, sequence, comparison, or cause-and-effect structures. When they read and write poetry, students use various poetic forms, including haiku, free verse, and acrostics.

4. Figuring out unknown words.   Students need to decide when to skip over a word and continue reading, when to use word-identification skills, and when to use context clues. Sometimes they check the dictionary or ask the teacher or a classmate. When students are writing, they often need to write words that they don't know how to spell. They can write several letters to serve as a placeholder. Later they will check the spelling by consulting a dictionary, a classmate, or the teacher. At other times, they sound out the word or "think it out." When thinking out the spelling, they have to consider root words, affixes, spelling patterns, and whether or not the word "looks right."

5. Visualizing.   Students create mental pictures of what they are reading or writing. They often place themselves in the images they create, becoming a character in the story they are reading, traveling to that setting, or facing the conflict situations that the characters themselves face. Teachers sometimes ask students to close their eyes to help visualize the story or to draw pictures of the scenes and characters they visualize. How well students use visualization often becomes clear when students view film versions of books they have read. Students who use the visualization strategy are often disappointed with the film version and the actors who perform as the characters, while students who don't visualize are often amazed by the film and prefer it to the book version.

When they are writing, students use description and sensory detail to make their writing more vivid and bring it to life for the people who will read their books. Sometimes teachers have students brainstorm lists of words related to each of the five senses and then incorporate some of the words in pieces they are writing. They also encourage students to use comparisons—metaphors and similes—to make their writing more vivid.

6. Making connections.   Students personalize what they are reading by relating what they are reading to their own lives. They recall similar experiences or compare the characters to people they know. They connect the book they are reading to other literature they have read. Readers often make connections among several books written by one author or between two versions of the same story. Similarly, when they are writing, students make connections between what they are writing and books they have read or experiences they have had.

The connections students make to books they have read previously are called "intertextuality" (de Beaugrande, 1980). Students also use intertextuality as they incorporate ideas and structures from the stories they have read into the stories they are writing. Five characteristics of intertextuality are:

■ *Individual and unique.* Students' literary experiences and the connections they make among them are different.
■ *Dependent on literary experiences.* Intertextuality is dependent on the types of books students have read, their purpose for and interest in reading, and the literary communities to which students belong.

Students apply reading strategies as they dramatize stories during literature focus units.

■ *Metacognitive awareness.* Most students are aware of intertextuality and consciously make connections among texts.

■ *Links to concept of story.* Students' connections among stories are linked to their knowledge about literature.

■ *Reading-writing connections.* Students make connections between stories they read and stories they write (Cairney, 1990, 1992).

The sum of students' experiences with literature—including the stories parents have read and told to young children, the books students have read or listened to the teacher read aloud, film versions they have viewed, their concepts of story and knowledge about authors and illustrators, and the books students have written—constitute their intertextual histories (Cairney, 1992). Cairney's research indicates that elementary students are aware of their past experiences with literature and use this knowledge as they read and write.

7. *Applying fix-up strategies.*   Sometimes when students are reading, they realize that something is not making sense or that they are not understanding what they are reading. Then they apply fix-up strategies. They may assume that things will make sense soon and continue reading, or they may reread, look at pictures, skip ahead, talk to a classmate about the book, or ask for help. Choosing an appropriate fix-up strategy is important so that students can continue reading productively.

When writing, students sometimes realize that their writing isn't working the way they want it to. Then they apply fix-up strategies. They might reread what they have written to get a jump start on their writing, do more prewriting to gather and organize ideas, read a book on the topic, talk about their ideas with a classmate, or ask a classmate or the teacher to read the piece and give some feedback. Sometimes they draw a picture.

8. Revising meaning.   Reading and writing are processes of making meaning, and as students read and write they are continually revising their understanding and the meaning they are creating. Students often reread for more information or because something doesn't make sense. They also study a book's illustrations, learn through the process of sharing, and get ideas from classmates during discussions. As they write in **reading logs,** students often gain new insights about a book.

Students meet in **writing groups** for classmates to read and react to their rough drafts so that writers can revise their writing and make it stronger. Writers revise on the basis of the feedback they get from classmates. As they revise, students add words and sentences, make substitutions and deletions, and move their text around to communicate more effectively. They also add titles and illustrations to clarify meaning.

9. Monitoring.   Students monitor their understanding as they read, though they may only be aware of this monitoring when comprehension breaks down. Students also monitor their writing to see how well they are communicating. When they are reading and writing, students ask themselves questions to monitor their understanding, and they use fix-up strategies when they realize that understanding has broken down.

10. Playing with language.   Students notice figurative and novel uses of language when they read, and they incorporate interesting language when they write. Some examples of playing with language are idioms, jokes, riddles, metaphors, similes, personification, sensory language, rhyme, alliteration, and invented words.

11. Generalizing.   Readers remember ideas and information and put them together to draw conclusions. Generalizing is important because big ideas are easier to remember than lots of details. Readers use these generalizations as they identify themes and articulate opinions. As students write, they often state their big ideas at the beginning of a paragraph and then support them with facts. They want their readers to be able to make generalizations. During revising, writers ask for feedback about how well their readers are drawing conclusions.

12. Evaluating.   Students make judgments about, reflect on, and value the books they are reading and writing. Readers think about what they have read, review the text, and evaluate their reading. They also value the books they read and what they do as readers. Writers do similar things. They ask themselves whether their own writing says what they want it to say—in other words, whether or not it is effective. They think about what they have experimented with in a particular piece of writing and reflect on the writing processes that they use. As a strategy, evaluation is not the teacher's judgment handed down to students, but rather students' own thinking about their goals and accomplishments.

Students don't use every one of these strategies every time they read or write, but effective readers and writers use most of them most of the time. Figure 4–3 shows how students in Mrs. Donnelly's classroom used these strategies in reading *Cloudy With a Chance of Meatballs* and in writing the class alphabet book about weather.

FIGURE 4–3   How Third Graders Use Reading and Writing Strategies

Strategy	How It Is Used When Reading *Cloudy With a Chance of Meatballs*	How It Is Used When Writing an Alphabet Book About Weather
Tapping Prior Knowledge	The teacher tells students that the book is a fantasy about weather, and students think about what they know about weather books and fantasy stories.	Students brainstorm weather words beginning with each letter of the alphabet. They choose the word for each page of the alphabet book.
Predicting	Students identify a purpose or reason for reading. They make "guesses" about what will happen next as they read, and then they read to confirm their predictions.	Students conference with the teacher, sharing their clusters before beginning to draft their page.
Organizing Ideas	Students think about the sequence of events in the story and chunk the events into three parts: beginning, middle, and end.	Students make a cluster to organize information about the word before beginning to write.
Figuring Out Unknown Words	Students skip some unfamiliar words and ask the teacher and classmates about other words. They also write unfamiliar words in their journals.	Students use invented spelling for unfamiliar words while drafting. Later, during editing, they check the spellings on the word wall, in a dictionary, or in an informational book.
Visualizing	Students visualize the events in the story or put themselves into the story and imagine the events happening to themselves.	Students think about the audience that will read their informational book. They imagine what their page in the finished book will look like.
Making Connections	Students think about how they would feel if the story happened in their community. They think about other books they have read in which impossible events occur.	Students think about what information might be interesting to readers. They think about informational books they have read that they can use as models for their books.

Why is it important that students become strategic readers and writers?

There are five reasons why it is so important that all students become strategic readers and writers. First, strategies allow readers and writers to generate, organize, and elaborate meaning more expertly than they can otherwise. Being strategic is an important characteristic of learning. Second, children learn all sorts of cognitive strategies during the elementary grades, and the acquisition of reading and writing strate-

FIGURE 4–3   *continued*

Strategy	How It Is Used When Reading *Cloudy With a Chance of Meatballs*	How It Is Used When Writing an Alphabet Book About Weather
Applying Fix-Up Strategies	Students are confused about the realistic event at the beginning of the story, but they decide to keep reading. They notice that the pictures at the beginning and end are black and white and the ones in the fantasy are in color. They reread to figure out why.	Students decide to add a comparison of lightning and thunder to make the section on thunderstorms clearer. They read more about fog to expand that part of the book.
Revising Meaning	Students turn back a page or two when something they read doesn't make sense. Students discuss the story after reading and elaborate their understanding as they talk and listen to classmates' comments.	Students stop drafting to reread what they have read and make revisions to communicate more effectively. Students meet in writing groups to share their drafts and get feedback to use in revising.
Monitoring	As they read, students ask themselves questions to be sure they understand what they are reading. The teacher asks students to notice characteristics of fantasy in the story, and students look for characteristics as they reread it.	As they draft, students check the accuracy and completeness of the information they are writing. They put themselves in the place of their readers and ask themselves if they would find the page interesting.
Playing With Language	Students notice that the town's name— Chewandswallow—is an invented word. They make up other invented words. *Lightning* becomes *flashandboom.*	Students decide to add a riddle to introduce each letter.
Generalizing	Students contrast the realism with the fantasy in the story. They identify several themes.	Students begin each page with a generalization, the most important fact, or a rule about the word. Then they add supporting or extending information.
Evaluating	In their journals or in conferences with the teacher, students give opinions about the story and say whether or not they liked it.	Students evaluate the effectiveness of each page and the accuracy of the information presented.

gies coincides with this cognitive development. As students learn to reflect on their learning, for example, they learn to reflect on themselves as readers and writers; and as they learn to monitor their learning, they learn to monitor their reading and writing. Many of the cognitive strategies that students learn have direct application to reading and writing. In this way, children's growing awarenesses about thinking, reading, and writing are mutually supportive.

Third, strategies are cognitive tools that students can use selectively and flexibly as they become independent readers and writers. In order for students to become independent readers and writers, they need these thinking tools. Fourth, reading and writing are tools for learning across the curriculum, and strategic reading and writing enhance learning in math, social studies, science, and other content areas. Children's competence in reading and writing affects all areas of the curriculum. Fifth, teachers can teach students how to apply reading and writing strategies (Paris, Wasik, & Turner, 1991). Just as driving instructors and more experienced drivers can teach novice drivers about defensive driving, teachers can demonstrate and explain strategic reading and writing and provide students with opportunities for guided practice.

Even though these strategies are called reading and writing strategies, they are the same strategies students use when they listen and talk (Brent & Anderson, 1993; Tompkins & Hoskisson, 1995). For example, when Mrs. Donnelly's students listen to her describe different cloud formations, they visualize the clouds in their minds and organize the information she is presenting. And when her students talk about their reflections of *Cloudy With a Chance of Meatballs,* they make connections to their own lives, revise meaning, and play with language.

Metacognitive Awareness

Students think about the strategies they use for reading and writing, and they apply and regulate their use of these strategies. This knowledge about their own thinking processes is called "metacognition" (Baker & Brown, 1984). During the elementary grades, students' metacognitive knowledge grows as they learn about the reading and writing processes and the strategies that readers and writers use. As students gain experience, their attention in reading moves from decoding to comprehension. In writing, their focus shifts from forming letters and spelling to communicating. As novice readers and writers, students apply strategies when teachers guide and direct them to, but as they become more proficient and more effective readers and writers, students regulate their use of strategies independently.

As teachers provide instruction about reading and writing strategies, students begin to notice what they do when they read and write—which strategies they use. When students work collaboratively, they notice the strategies that their classmates use, and they listen to classmates and the teacher talk about the strategies they use. They also interview visiting authors about how they write, and when community members come into the classroom to share favorite books, students ask them about their own reading processes. Despite instruction and activities such as these, some students reach high school with incomplete and mistaken knowledge about reading and writing strategies.

Comparing Capable and Less Capable Readers and Writers

Researchers have compared students who are capable readers and writers with other students who are less successful and have found some striking differences (Baker & Brown, 1984; Faigley, Cherry, Jolliffe, & Skinner, 1985; Paris et al., 1991). The researchers have found that capable readers

■ are fluent oral and silent readers
■ view reading as a process of creating meaning
■ decode rapidly

- have large vocabularies
- understand the organization of stories, plays, informational books, poems, and other texts
- use a variety of strategies
- monitor their understanding as they read

Similarly, capable writers

- vary how they write depending on the purpose for writing and the audience who will read the composition
- use the writing process flexibly
- focus on developing ideas and communicating effectively
- turn to classmates for feedback on how they are communicating
- monitor how well they are communicating in the piece of writing
- use formats and structures for stories, poems, letters, and other texts
- use a variety of strategies
- postpone attention to mechanical correctness until the end of the writing process

Teachers often notice that the more capable readers and writers in their own classes exemplify many of these characteristics.

Less successful readers exemplify fewer of these characteristics or behave differently when they are reading and writing. For example, more capable readers view reading as a process of creating meaning, while less capable readers focus on decoding. In writing, less capable writers make cosmetic changes when they revise, rather than changes to communicate meaning more effectively. A comparison of characteristics of capable and less capable readers and writers is presented in Figure 4–4. Young students who are learning to read and write often exemplify many of the characteristics of less capable readers and writers, but older students who are less successful readers and writers also exemplify these characteristics.

Perhaps the most remarkable difference between capable and less capable readers and writers is that those who are less successful are not strategic. They are naive. They seem reluctant to use unfamiliar strategies or those that require much effort. They do not seem to be motivated or to expect that they will be successful. Less capable readers and writers don't understand or use all stages of the reading and writing processes effectively. They do not monitor their reading and writing (Garner, 1987). Or, if they do use strategies, they remain dependent on primitive strategies. For example, as they read, less successful readers seldom look ahead or back into the text to clarify misunderstandings or make plans. Or, when they come to an unfamiliar word, they often stop reading, unsure of what to do. They may try to sound out an unfamiliar word, but if that is unsuccessful they give up. In contrast, capable readers know several strategies, and if one strategy isn't successful they try another one.

Less capable writers move through the writing process in a lockstep, linear approach. They use a limited number of strategies, most often a "knowledge-telling" strategy in which they list everything they know about a topic with little thought to choosing information to meet the needs of their readers or to organizing the information to put related information together (Faigley et al., 1985). In contrast, capable writers understand the recursive nature of the writing process and turn to classmates

▪ *Activity*

Observe a more capable student and a less capable student involved in reading and writing activities, and compare the strategies that the two students use. Which of the characteristics listed in Figure 4–4 does each student exhibit?

FIGURE 4-4 A Comparison of Capable and Less Capable Readers and Writers

Reader Characteristics	Writer Characteristics
1. Capable readers view reading as primarily a comprehending or meaning-making process, while less capable readers view reading as a decoding, not a comprehending, process.	1. Capable writers view writing as developing ideas, while less capable writers see writing as putting words on paper.
2. Capable readers adjust their reading speed or purpose according to the reading task, while less capable readers do not.	2. Capable writers are aware of audience, purpose, and form demands and adapt writing to meet these demands, but less capable writers do not.
3. Capable readers read fluently, while less capable readers read word by word and sometimes point at words as they read. Less capable readers do not read smoothly when reading orally, and they read slowly and move their lips as they actually say the words to themselves when reading silently.	3. Capable writers pause as they draft to think or reread what they have written, but less capable writers write without stopping to reread or think about their writing.
4. Capable readers relate what they are reading to their background knowledge, while less capable readers do not make this connection.	4. Capable writers are more concerned with ideas, while less capable writers are more concerned with mechanics than ideas and view correct spelling and punctuation as the hallmarks of a good writer.
5. Capable readers apply fix-up strategies effectively. Less capable readers are stumped when they come to unfamiliar words, or they skip over words and invent what they think is a reasonable text.	5. Capable writers vary the length of their writing depending on their purpose, but less capable writers assume that longer pieces of writing are better than short pieces.
6. Capable readers identify words more effectively than less capable readers do, whether the words are in context or in isolation.	6. Capable writers collaborate with classmates to write or revise their writing, but less capable writers do not collaborate as effectively.
7. Capable readers monitor their comprehension, but less capable readers don't. Neither do they realize or take action when they don't understand.	7. Capable writers assess their own writing, while less capable writers do not.
8. Capable readers have larger vocabularies than less capable readers do.	8. Capable writers make changes to communicate meaning more effectively when they revise, but less capable writers tend to make cosmetic changes.
9. Capable readers expect to be successful, while less capable readers have low expectations for success.	9. Capable writers use many strategies and vary them according to the assignment, but less capable writers use fewer strategies and don't monitor their use.

Adapted from Faigley, Cherry, Jolliffe, and Skinner, 1985; and Paris, Wasik, and Turner, 1991.

for feedback about how well they are communicating. They are more responsive to the needs of the audience that will read their papers, and they work to organize their paper in a cohesive manner.

This research on capable and less capable readers and writers has focused on differences in how students use strategies. It is noteworthy that all research comparing readers and writers focuses on how students use reading and writing strategies, not on differences in their use of skills.

Motivation for Strategic Reading and Writing

Motivation is intrinsic and internal—a driving force within us. Often students' motivation for becoming more capable readers and writers diminishes as they reach the upper grades. Penny Oldfather (1995) conducted a four-year study to examine the factors influencing students' motivation and found that when students had opportunities for authentic self-expression as part of literacy activities, they were more highly motivated. Students she interviewed reported that they were more highly motivated when they had ownership of the learning activities. Specific activities they mentioned included opportunities to

■ express their own ideas and opinions

■ choose topics for writing and books for reading

■ talk about books they are reading

■ share their writings with classmates

■ pursue "authentic" activities—not worksheets—using reading, writing, listening, and talking

Students who are strategic readers are more likely to become lifelong readers.

Some students are not strongly motivated to learn to read and write, and they adopt strategies for avoiding failure rather than strategies for making meaning. These strategies are defensive tactics (Dweck, 1986; Paris et al., 1991). Unmotivated readers give up or remain passive, uninvolved in reading (Johnston & Winograd, 1985). Some students feign interest or pretend to be involved even though they are not. Others don't think reading is important, and they choose to focus on other curricular areas—math or sports, for instance. Some students complain about feeling ill or that other students are bothering them. They place the blame on anything other than themselves.

There are other students who avoid reading and writing entirely. They just don't do it. Another group of students reads books that are too easy for them or writes short pieces so that they don't have to exert much effort. Even though these strategies are self-serving, students use them because they lead to short-term success. The long-term result, however, is devastating because these students fail to learn to read and write. Because it takes quite a bit of effort to read and write strategically, it is especially important that students experience personal ownership of the literacy activities going on in their classrooms and know how to manage their own reading and writing behaviors.

READING AND WRITING SKILLS

Skills are information-processing techniques that readers and writers use automatically and unconsciously as they construct meaning. Many skills focus at the word-level, but some require readers and writers to attend to larger chunks of text. For example, at the elementary level, readers use skills such as decoding unfamiliar words, noting details, and sequencing events; and writers employ skills such as forming contractions, using punctuation marks, and capitalizing people's names. Skills and strategies are not the same thing, since strategies are problem-solving tactics selected deliberately to achieve particular goals (Paris et al., 1991). The important difference between skills and strategies is how they are used.

Types of Skills

During the elementary grades, students learn to use five types of reading and writing skills:

1. *Meaning-making skills.*   These include summarizing, separating facts and opinions, comparing and contrasting, and recognizing literary genres and structures. Students use these skills in conjunction with reading and writing strategies as they comprehend what they are reading and compose what they are writing.

2. *Decoding and spelling skills.*   These include sounding out words, noticing word families, using root words and affixes to decode and spell words, and using abbreviations. Students use these skills as they decode words when reading and as they spell words when writing. They focus on spelling skills during the editing stage of the writing process.

3. *Language skills.*   These include identifying and inferring meanings of words, noticing idioms, dividing words into syllables, and choosing synonyms. Since reading and writing are language processes, students are continuously interacting with

language as they read and write, and they use these skills to analyze words they are reading and to choose more precise language when they are writing.

4. ***Study skills.*** These include skimming and scanning, taking notes, making clusters, and previewing a book before reading. Students use study skills during across-the-curriculum themes and when reading informational books, collecting information to use in writing reports, and studying for tests.

5. ***Reference skills.*** These include alphabetizing a list of words, using a dictionary, and reading and making graphs. Elementary students learn to use reference skills in order to read newspaper articles, locate information in dictionaries and other informational books, and use library references.

Examples of each of the five types of skills are presented in Figure 4–5. Students use these skills for various types of reading and writing tasks. For example, students use some of the skills when reading a newspaper, and they use other skills when writing a report. It is very unlikely that students use every skill listed in Figure 4–5 for any particular reading or writing task, but capable readers and writers are familiar with most of these skills and can use them automatically whenever they are needed.

Teachers often wonder when they should teach the skills listed in Figure 4–5. School districts often prepare curriculum guides that list the skills to be taught at each grade level, and they are usually listed on scope-and-sequence charts that accompany basal reader programs. On scope-and-sequence charts, textbook makers identify the grade level at which the skill should be introduced and the grade levels at which it is practiced. These resources provide guidelines, but teachers decide which skills to teach based on their children's level of literacy development and the reading and writing activities in which their students are involved. During literature focus units and reading and writing workshop, students use many skills, and teachers often go beyond the grade-level list of skills as students use reading and writing for a variety of purposes.

Mrs. Donnelly's students used reading skills as they read *Cloudy With a Chance of Meatballs* and used writing skills as they wrote their weather alphabet books. For example, when Mrs. Donnelly's students were checking a weather book for information about thunderstorms, they didn't start in the front of the book and hunt page by page through the book. Instead, they checked the index (or, if there wasn't an index, the table of contents) for the location of information about thunderstorms and then read that section. Using an index is a reference skill. When students wrote dialogue, they added quotation marks around the spoken words. They didn't make a conscious decision about whether or not to mark the dialogue; they automatically added the convention. Figure 4–6 provides other examples of the reading and writing skills that Mrs. Donnelly's students used.

Students often ask questions that lead to teachable moments, too. For example, during writing workshop, Shannon, one of Mrs. Donnelly's students, asked her teacher how to combine two sentences she was writing because they needed to be "close together." Mrs. Donnelly suggested using *and* to combine the sentences, but Shannon said that she tried that and the sentences weren't close enough together with that word. Then Mrs. Donnelly realized that Shannon was asking about semicolons without even knowing that such a punctuation mark even existed. She explained how to use a semicolon, Shannon added it to connect the two sentences, and then she continued writing.

FIGURE 4–5   Five Types of Skills That Readers and Writers Use

Meaning-Making Skills

Sequence
Summarize
Categorize
Classify
Separate facts and opinions
Note details
Identify cause and effect
Compare and contrast
Use context clues
Notice organizational patterns of poetry, plays, business and friendly letters, stories, essays, and reports
Recognize literary genres (traditional stories, fantasies, science fiction, realistic fiction, historical fiction, biography, autobiography, and poetry)

Decoding and Spelling Skills

Sound out words using knowledge of phonics
Notice word families
Look for picture cues
Ask a classmate or the teacher
Consult a dictionary or glossary
Apply spelling rules
Use root words and affixes
Capitalize proper nouns and adjectives
Use abbreviations

Study Skills

Skim
Scan
Preview
Follow directions
Make outlines and clusters
Take notes
Paraphrase

Language Skills

Notice compound words
Use contractions
Divide words into syllables
Use possessives
Notice propaganda
Use similes and metaphors
Notice idioms and slang
Choose synonyms
Recognize antonyms
Differentiate among homonyms
Appreciate rhyme and other poetic devices
Use punctuation marks (period, question mark, exclamation mark, quotation marks, comma, colon, semicolon, and hyphen)
Use simple, compound, and complex sentences
Combine sentences
Recognize parts of sentences
Avoid sentence fragments
Recognize parts of speech (nouns, pronouns, verbs, adjectives, adverbs, conjunctions, prepositions, and interjections)

Reference Skills

Sort in alphabetical order
Use a glossary or dictionary
Locate etymologies in the dictionary
Use the pronunciation guide in the dictionary
Locate synonyms in a thesaurus
Locate information in an encyclopedia, atlas, or almanac
Use a table of contents
Use an index
Use a card catalogue
Read and make graphs, tables, and diagrams
Read and make timelines
Read newspapers and magazines
Use bibliographic forms

Why distinguish between skills and strategies?

Skills are more commonly associated with reading and writing instruction than strategies are, and for many years teachers and parents equated teaching skills with teaching reading. They believed that the best way to help children learn to read was to teach them a set of discrete skills, using drill-and-practice worksheets and workbooks (Smith, 1965). But research during the last 20 years has shown that reading is a constructive process in which readers construct meaning by interacting with texts (Pearson, Roehler, Dole, & Duffy, 1990). Writing is also a constructive process, and writers construct meaning as they compose texts. Readers and writers use strategies

FIGURE 4–6   How Third Graders Use Reading and Writing Skills

Skills	How They Are Used When Reading *Cloudy With a Chance of Meatballs*	How They Are Used When Writing an Alphabet Book About Weather
Meaning-Making Skills	Students separate realism and fantasy in the story. They sequence story events. They compare real weather to the "food" weather.	Students add at least three details on each page. They reread classmates' pages to check the accuracy of information.
Decoding and Spelling Skills	Students use picture clues to read food words, including *frankfurter* and *syrup.* They sound out words like *prediction, Sanitation Department,* and *marvelous.*	During editing, students check the spelling of weather words in informational books. The teacher conferences with students about capitalization and punctuation marks.
Language Skills	Students notice weather-related words and phrases used in the story, such as "brief shower" and "gradual clearing."	Students use the " ___ is for _____ " form on each page of their books. They write in complete sentences.
Study Skills	Students scan the story looking for words for the word wall	Students skim sections of informational books as they gather information for the alphabet book. They take notes as they read. They make clusters as they prepare to write their pages.
Reference Skills	Students check the card catalogue for other books by the same author. They compare "The Chewandswallow Digest" with their local newspaper. They read weather reports and examine weather maps in their local newspaper.	Students use the index in books to locate information for the pages they are writing. They make charts and diagrams for their pages. They sort their pages into alphabetical order.

differently than skills: they use strategies to orchestrate higher-order thinking skills when reading and writing, whereas they use skills automatically and unconsciously when reading and writing.

While it continues to be important that students learn to use reading and writing skills automatically, of far greater importance is children's ability to use reading and writing strategies. When skills and strategies are lumped together, teachers tend to neglect reading and writing strategies because they are more familiar with skills.

TEACHING STRATEGIES AND SKILLS

Teachers use direct and indirect instruction to provide information that students need to know about strategies and skills when they need to know it (Kucer, 1991). Rather than teaching isolated skills with fragmented bits of language, stripped of meaning, teachers scaffold and support students' development of reading and writing skills and strategies through interaction with authentic and meaningful texts. As Kucer explains, "the ability to link classroom-based literacy lessons with real-world, authentic reading and writing experiences is critical if our instruction is to promote literacy development in the children we teach" (p. 532).

Through both direct and indirect instruction, students receive more detailed explanations and more precise descriptions of strategies, and then they learn when and how to use them during reading and writing (Duffy & Roehler, 1991; Duffy et al., 1987). It is essential that instruction enhance students' awareness of strategic reading and writing so that they can plan, evaluate, and regulate their own thinking.

Ineffective instruction has focused on isolated skills followed by lots of practice on worksheets. In contrast, effective instruction orients students to the task of constructing meaning from texts and provides a variety of tactics to use during the reading and writing processes. More than a decade ago, Anderson and his colleagues (1985) found that up to 70% of reading instructional time was spent on teaching fragmented skills. Now researchers recommend using a whole-part-whole approach to teach skills and strategies within the context of literature-based reading instruction.

In the whole-part-whole approach, skill and strategy instruction is the part in the middle (Flood & Lapp, 1994). First students read and respond to a piece of literature (the whole). Next they focus on skill and strategy instruction, using examples taken from the piece of literature (the part). Afterwards, students apply what they have learned in rereading or writing about the piece of literature (the whole).

Both direct and indirect instruction are used in literature-based reading classrooms (Spiegel, 1992). Teachers plan and teach minilessons on skills and strategies as part of literature focus units and during reading and writing workshop. These direct-instruction lessons are systematic and planned in conjunction with featured selections in literature focus units and based on students' needs during workshops. Students also learn some strategies and skills independently as they read and write, and they learn others indirectly as they observe and work collaboratively with parents, teachers, and classmates. In the classroom, teachers model reading naturally as they read a book aloud to the class or share a big book, and they model writing naturally as they write a class poem or take children's dictation of a story. Guidelines for skill and strategy instruction are presented in Figure 4–7.

Minilessons

Minilessons (Atwell, 1987) are brief direct-instruction lessons designed to help students learn literacy skills and become more strategic readers and writers. In these lessons, students and teacher are focused on a single goal; students are aware of why it is important to learn the skill or strategy, and they are explicitly taught how to use a particular skill or strategy through modeling, explanation, and practice. Then independent application takes place using authentic literacy materials. The steps in a minilesson are:

1. *Introduce the skill or strategy.* The teacher names the strategy or skill and explains why it is useful. The teacher also shares examples of how and when the skill or strategy is used.

2. *Demonstrate the skill or strategy.* The teacher explains the steps of the skill or strategy and models how to use it with authentic reading and writing activities.

FIGURE 4–7 Guidelines for Skill and Strategy Instruction

1. Minilessons

Teachers present minilessons when students demonstrate the need for instruction or are developmentally ready to learn a skill or strategy, rather than by adhering to a curriculum manual. Teachers who carefully observe and listen to their students recognize when students are ready for minilessons on particular skills and strategies.

2. Differentiation Between Skills and Strategies

Teachers understand that skills are automatic behaviors that readers and writers use, while strategies are problem-solving tactics, and they differentiate between skills and strategies as they teach minilessons and model how they use strategies. They are also careful to use the terms "skills" and "strategies" correctly when they talk to students.

3. Step-by-Step Explanations

Teachers describe the skill or strategy step by step so that it is sensible and meaningful to students. For strategies, they can use think-aloud or talk-aloud procedures to demonstrate how the strategy is used. Teachers also explain to students why they should learn the skill or strategy, how it will make reading and writing easier, and when to use it.

4. Modeling

Teachers model using strategies for students in the context of authentic reading and writing activities, rather than in isolation. Students are also encouraged to model using strategies for classmates.

5. Practice Opportunities

Students have opportunities to practice the skill or strategy in meaningful reading and writing activities. Teachers need to ensure that all students are successful using the skill or strategy so that they will be motivated to use it independently.

6. Across-the-Curriculum Applications

Teachers provide opportunities for students to use the skill or strategy in reading and writing activities related to social studies, science, and other content areas. The more opportunities students have to use the skill or strategy, the more likely they are to learn it.

7. Reflection

Teachers ask students to reflect on their use of the skill or strategy after they have had the opportunity to practice it and apply it in meaningful reading and writing activities.

8. Charts of Skills and Strategies

Teachers often hang lists of skills and strategies students are learning in the classroom and encourage students to refer to them when reading and writing. Separate charts should be used for skills and strategies so that students can remember which are which.

Adapted from Winograd and Hare, 1988; and Pressley and Harris, 1990.

Teachers provide opportunities for students to practice the strategy or skill they are learning during minilessons.

3. *Practice the skill or strategy.*   Students practice the skill or strategy that the teacher demonstrated, with the teacher's guidance and support. The teacher provides feedback to students about how well they are doing. Students make notes about the skill or strategy on a poster to be displayed in the classroom.

4. *Review the skill or strategy.*   Students reflect on what they have learned and how they can use this skill or strategy in reading and writing activities. Students look back and think about how they have used the skill or strategy. The teacher encourages students to talk about ways to improve and other times and places where they might use the skill or strategy.

5. *Apply the skill or strategy.*   Students use their newly learned skill or strategy in a new and authentic literacy activity. The teacher serves as a coach as students use the skill or strategy.

Through five-step minilessons, there is a transfer of responsibility from teacher to student (Bergman, 1992; Duffy & Roehler, 1987; Pearson & Gallagher, 1983). This minilesson procedure can be adapted to fit the skill or strategy being taught.

Figure 4–8 shows how Mrs. Donnelly used this five-step minilesson procedure to teach her third graders about literary opposites (Temple, 1992) during a literature focus unit on *Amos and Boris* (Steig, 1971), a story of true friendship between a whale and a mouse. In the story, a whale named Amos rescues a shipwrecked mouse named Boris, and later Boris saves Amos when he becomes beached. Literary opposites can be between settings, characters, events, and emotions in the story, and there is more than one pair of opposites in most stories. One of the opposites in the story is that the two animals, who are so different, become friends. Not only are they different in size, but one is a land animal and the other lives in the ocean.

FIGURE 4–8   Steps in Mrs. Donnelly's Minilesson on Literary Opposites

1. Introduce the Strategy

Mrs. Donnelly explains that one way of organizing events and characters in stories is to think of opposites. There are many different kinds of opposites in stories: kind and mean characters, day and night settings, and happy and sad events.

2. Demonstrate the Strategy

Mrs. Donnelly reviews Jan Brett's *Town Mouse, Country Mouse* (1994) and uses the think-aloud technique to point out these opposites:

town—country   mouse—owl
plain—fancy   dark—light
mouse—cat   quiet—noisy

She writes the list on the chalkboard and stands back to reflect on it. Then she circles "plain—fancy" and thinks aloud:

> Yes, I think these are all opposites, but I like plain and fancy best. It is the most important one. It sums up the essence of this story for me. I like it. I can think about all sorts of examples of plain and fancy: Plain and fancy clothes, plain and fancy food, and plain and fancy houses. All these differences. I want to think some more. Different—alike, alike—different. That's it! I think that even though there are all these differences, the author shows me that the two mouse families were alike. How are they alike? They both wanted what they didn't have, and they both had enemies, and they both wanted to go home at the end. Oh yes, they both made it home safely and a lot smarter, too.

3. Practice the Strategy

Mrs. Donnelly asks students to reread *Amos and Boris* (Steig, 1971)—a story her students read several days before as part of a unit on whales and other animals that live in the ocean—with partners and to look for opposites. After reading, Mrs. Donnelly's third graders list these opposites:

big—little   forgetting—remembering
land animal—sea animal   hope—hopeless
helping—being helped   in the sea—out of the sea
life—death   hello—good-bye

One student makes the intertextual tie between *Amos and Boris* and "The Lion and the Mouse," pointing out that both stories have the same theme. Then Mrs. Donnelly asks students to quickwrite and draw pictures about the opposites they think are most interesting. Students share their quickwrites with classmates.

4. Review the Strategy

Mrs. Donnelly asks students to reflect on literary opposites and to think about opposites in other stories they have read. Several students also make a chart on literary opposites to hang in the classroom.

5. Apply the Strategy

Mrs. Donnelly encourages students to think about opposites in the stories they are reading during reading workshop, and she asks students about the opposites as she conferences with them. She also asks students to talk about the opposites as they share the books they have read.

Indirect Instructional Techniques

Teachers often use informal, indirect instructional techniques to support students in their reading and writing (Staab, 1990). Three techniques that teachers use for indirect instruction about reading and writing skills and strategies are modeling, talk-alouds, and think-alouds. In each of these techniques, teachers share their knowledge as expert readers and writers, and students have opportunities to apply what they are learning in authentic reading and writing activities. Sometimes these techniques are used with the whole class, while at other times they are used with small groups of students. It is not enough to teach students how to use skills and strategies. Teachers must persuade students that they should continue to use the skills and strategies independently and to monitor their use. One of the differences mentioned earlier between capable and less capable readers and writers was their motivation to use strategies.

Modeling is an instructional technique that teachers use to demonstrate to students how to perform an unfamiliar reading or writing skill or strategy (Bergman, 1992). Teachers are expert readers and writers, and through modeling they show students—novice readers and writers—how to perform a strategy, skill, or other task so that students can build their own understanding of the activity. One of the advantages of heterogeneous classes and groups is that classmates also serve as models for each other.

Teachers informally model reading and writing strategies for students whenever teachers participate in literacy activities. Young children learn concepts about books as they watch teachers hold books, turn pages, and read from left to right and top to bottom, and middle-grade students learn about revising text as they work with the

Teachers model reading strategies and skills as they share big books with students.

teacher to revise the rough draft of a **collaborative report** that has been written on chart paper. As students work with teachers and observe them, they develop the understanding that readers and writers do some things automatically but at other times have to take risks, think out solutions to problems, and deal with ambiguities.

Teachers use talk-alouds to describe steps they use to apply a strategy or skill or complete a task (Baumann & Schmitt, 1986). Then teachers ask questions to guide students through the steps. In the vignette at the beginning of this chapter, Mrs. Donnelly used a talk-aloud as she introduced alphabet books to her third-grade class. She talked about how she looked at an alphabet book and what she noticed about the pattern of one letter per page with a picture and a sentence. She described the steps she used to examine an alphabet book, and then she passed out copies of various alphabet books for the students to examine. Here is an excerpt from Mrs. Donnelly's talk-aloud:

As I looked at *The Furry Alphabet Book* by Jerry Pallotta [1991], I was thinking about all the interesting information the author and illustrator included in this book about mammals. I read the "A" page, and I noticed that there is an illustration and a paragraph of text. The text has lots of information about a rare African animal called an aye-aye. The illustration was very useful, and I thought it would help me remember the information I was reading. I thought this mammal looked a lot like a bat and thought about it eating insects, just like bats do.

Then I read the "B" page, the "C" page, the "D" page, and the "E" page, and I noticed how much these pages were alike even though they were about different animals. They all had the upper- and lowercase letters written in a corner, a paragraph of text with lots of information, and a good illustration to show the animal and make the information easier to understand.

I always like to look to see what the author found for the hard letters, like "Q," "X," and "Z." I thought Jerry Pallotta was very smart to find animals for these letters. As I was looking for the "Q" page, I noticed that he put something special on the "P" page. He did a portrait of himself, I thought, and he added an extra fact: that people are mammals, too. For "Q," he chose quokka, a kind of small kangaroo from Australia. Then for "X," he used xukazi, the Zulu word for a female lamb, and for "Z," he described the zorilla, which is the smelliest skunk.

After the "Z" page, I found another special page about the naked mole rat, which the author said didn't deserve to be in this book because it didn't have any fur. I thought this was really cute, kind of like a secret between me and the author, so I decided to reread the book to look for more special pages, but I didn't find any more.

Then Mrs. Donnelly asked her students, to look through alphabet books, to notice the format of the pages and the interesting words chosen for the "hard" letters, and to look for any special pages. Using this talk-aloud, she articulated the procedure her students were to use to investigate alphabet books in preparation for writing their own class alphabet book about weather.

In this instructional technique, teachers share with students the thought processes they go through as they use a reading or writing skill or strategy (Davey, 1983; Wade, 1990). When teaching a writing strategy such as revision, teachers can say, "I'm going to show you how I revise a rough draft." Then they read the rough draft aloud and "think aloud," presenting a running commentary on their thoughts. Teachers continue to make revisions and reread to verify the revisions, again presenting a running commentary on their thoughts. For reading strategies, teachers can do similar think-alouds on tapping prior knowledge, monitoring, and making predictions (Bergman, 1992).

Talk-alouds and think-alouds are very similar techniques, and they are both useful. The difference is that for talk-alouds, teachers share what they have already done and articulate the steps students are to follow as they complete the task. In contrast, in a think-aloud, teachers perform the task in front of students, reflecting on their thoughts, explaining their reasoning, and showing their thinking as they perform a task.

Teachers also take advantage of teachable moments to share information about strategies and skills with students. They introduce, review, or extend a skill or strategy in these very brief lessons. As teachers listen to students read aloud or talk about the processes they use during reading, they often have an opportunity to teach a particular strategy or skill (Atwell, 1987). Similarly, as teachers conference with students about their writing or work with students to revise or edit their writing, teachers share information about writing skills and strategies with their students. Students also ask questions about skills and strategies or volunteer information about how they handled a reading or writing problem. Teachers who are careful observers and listen closely to their students don't miss these teachable moments.

Grouping for Instruction

Teachers use four grouping patterns for literacy instruction—whole class, small groups, partners, and individual—and they vary their use of the four types of groups according to the activity in which students are involved. These four grouping patterns are overviewed in Figure 4–9. Flood, Lapp, Flood, and Nagel (1992) and Berghoff and Egawa (1991) recommend that teachers vary the grouping patterns that they use and that when they use small groups, the groups are flexible and change often.

Teachers often use whole-class groups at the beginning of a literature focus unit, to introduce the featured selection and for **word walls,** and when students share during reading and writing workshop, to develop the classroom community and students' sense of belonging. When teachers read aloud to students or students create class projects such as a **story quilt,** a **read-around,** or a collaborative book, working together is a shared experience for students.

Students often work in small groups during literature focus units and reading and writing workshop. The makeup of the groups varies according to the activities in which students are involved. Sometimes the groups are formed according to interest, such as for book clubs, and at other times groups are formed according to students' need for skill and strategy instruction. The group makeup changes depending on what is being taught (Wiggins, 1994). Students usually sit in small groups in the classroom, and they work collaboratively in these groups as they do **word sorts** or make **story maps.** As they work collaboratively, students support each other and work as both teachers and learners. Students can often accomplish things working in groups that they could not do on their own.

Students often read and write with partners. They reread the featured selection with partners and work with partners as they proofread their compositions. Sometimes students work together on projects, such as making dioramas or scripting a puppet show. As they work together, students help each other and are more successful than they would be working independently. Sometimes teachers arrange for their students to be cross-age tutors or reading buddies with students in another class. These partnerships have both social and academic benefits.

FIGURE 4–9 Four Grouping Patterns

Advantages	Drawbacks	Possible Activities
Whole Class • Develops the classroom community and a sense of belonging • Provides a shared experience for students	• Large size of group • Fewer opportunities for individual students to interact • Often teacher-dominated	• Read aloud to students • Class collaborations • Grand conversations • Shared reading • Word walls • Story quilts
Small Group • Allows for flexible grouping and regrouping of students • Develops awareness of multiple perspectives • Encourages collaboration	• Grouping by ability may be detrimental to students' self-confidence and learning • Requires students to be able to work together	• Word sorts • Minilessons • Writing groups • Readers theatre • Book clubs • Story boards • K-W-L charts
Partners • Allows students to be successful • Provides opportunities for practice • Encourages collaboration • Provides support and assistance for classmates	• Students easily get "off task" • Requires students to be able to work together • Teachers feel a loss of control when students are involved in different activities	• Buddy reading • Proofreading • Cross-age tutors • Projects • Rereading books • Story maps and other charts • Choral reading
Individuals • Provides opportunity for sustained reading or writing • Develops reading fluency • Allows for personal choice • Reflects on events and learning	• Some students need support and assistance to be successful • Teachers feel a loss of control when students are involved in different activities	• Reading and writing workshop • Reading logs • Projects • Oral reports • Write books • Quickwrites • Portfolios

Adapted from Berghoff and Egawa, 1991; and Flood, Lapp, Flood, and Nagel, 1992.

Working individually is the fourth grouping pattern. Students read individually during reading workshop and write individually during writing workshop. The goal of literacy instruction is for students to become independent readers and writers, and when students read and write individually they are developing independence. Students also do **quickwrites** and **quickdraws** individually and create many projects individually.

Teachers often use small groups and whole-class groups for skill and strategy instruction. Whether teachers are using direct or indirect instructional techniques, they teach students who need the instruction, not the whole class. When teachers are introducing a new reading or writing skill or strategy, for example, it may be appropriate to present the lesson to the whole class. In contrast, teachers use small groups to review skills and provide extra follow-up practice. Teachers also use small groups to introduce new skills and strategies that only some students are interested in learning or ready to learn.

Reading instruction has traditionally been taught to students in small "ability groups." Students were permanently assigned to groups according to their level of reading achievement. Or, classes were regrouped with other classes on or across grade levels to form homogeneous classes. Homogeneous grouping is no longer recommended, because it creates serious academic and social problems, especially for students in the lowest group. Researchers report that homogeneous grouping does not result in increased student learning (Hiebert, 1983; Slavin, 1987). Teachers often treat students in the "low" group differently, even though they usually don't realize they are doing so. They focus more on correcting students' reading and writing errors, and their corrections are more simplistic and less meaning-oriented (Allington, 1980). Students in "low" groups spend less time on meaning-related activities and more time on decoding words. Also, Collins (1982) found that teachers change their focus with "high" and "low" reading groups. They focus on comprehension with higher groups and on decoding skills with lower groups, ask more thoughtful, higher-level questions with "high" groups, and involve readers in "high" groups in more discussion.

Why teach skills and strategies?

Some teachers argue about whether or not to teach strategies and skills—and, if they are taught, whether students should learn them inductively or whether teachers should teach explicitly. My position in this book is that teachers have the responsibility to teach students how to read and write, and part of that responsibility is teaching students the skills and strategies that capable readers and writers use. While it is true that students learn many things inductively through meaningful literacy experiences, instruction is important. Effective teachers do teach skills and strategies. The question is not whether or not to teach strategies and skills, but how, when, and why they are taught (Dudley-Marling & Dippo, 1991).

Researchers have compared classrooms in which teachers focused on teaching skills with other programs in which skills and strategies were taught inductively or using a whole-part-whole instructional sequence, and they concluded that the traditional skills programs were no more effective according to students' performance on standardized reading texts. Moreover, researchers suggest that traditional skills programs may be less effective when you take into account that students in the literature-based reading programs also think of themselves as readers and writers and have more knowledge about written language.

Freppon (1991) compared the reading achievement of first graders in traditional and literature-based reading classrooms and found that the literature group was more successful. Similarly, Reutzel and Hollingsworth (1991) compared students who were taught skills with students who spent an equal amount of time reading books, and they found that neither group did better on skill tests. This research suggests that students who do not already know skills and strategies can benefit from instruction, but the instruction must stress application to authentic reading and writing activities.

Carefully planned instruction, however, may be especially important for minority students. Lisa Delpit (1987) cautions that many students who grow up outside the dominant culture are disadvantaged when certain knowledge, strategies, and skills expected by teachers are not made explicit in their classrooms. Explicitness is crucial be-

Effective Practices

1. Teachers teach both skills and strategies.

2. Teachers teach twelve strategies: tap prior knowledge, predict, organize ideas, figure out unknown words, visualize, make connections, apply fix-up strategies, revise meaning, monitor, play with language, generalize, and evaluate.

3. Teachers teach five types of skills: meaning-making skills, decoding and spelling skills, language skills, study skills, and reference skills.

4. Teachers distinguish between skills and strategies.

5. Teachers use a whole-part-whole approach to skill and strategy instruction.

6. Teachers use both direct and indirect instruction techniques.

7. Teachers teach minilessons on skills and strategies to the whole class or to small groups, depending on students' needs.

8. Teachers model strategic reading and writing and use talk-aloud and think-aloud procedures.

9. Teachers take advantage of teachable moments to answer students' questions and clarify misconceptions.

10. Teachers use a variety of flexible grouping patterns, including whole class, small group, partners, and individuals.

Ineffective Practices

1. Teachers focus on teaching skills, not strategies.

2. Teachers teach very few strategies; sometimes they teach only prediction or ways to figure out unknown words.

3. Teachers teach many of these skills, but they view skill instruction as the most important part of reading instruction.

4. Teachers aren't aware of the importance of strategies and don't distinguish between skills and strategies.

5. Teachers teach skills in isolation, without making connections to literature.

6. Teachers use direct instruction and assign many worksheets.

7. Teachers group students into small "ability" groups for skill and strategy instruction.

8. Teachers do not model strategic reading and writing.

9. Teachers do not recognize teachable moments and focus on direct instruction.

10. Teachers either teach to the whole class or keep students in homogeneous small groups.

cause people from different cultures have different sets of understanding. When they teach children from other cultures, teachers often find it difficult to get their meaning across unless they are very explicit (Delpit, 1991). Delpit's writing has created a stir in the language arts community because she claims that literature-based reading has ignored the voices of African-American educators and that African-American children and other nonmainstream children frequently are not given access to the codes of power unless literacy instruction is explicit. Too often teachers assume that children make the connection between the strategies and skills they are teaching and the future use of those strategies and skills in reading and writing.

On the other hand, several studies suggest that both mainstream and nonmainstream students benefit from the same types of literature-based reading instruction. Lesley Morrow (1992) examined the impact of a literature-based reading program on minority students' reading achievement, and she found that both minority and mainstream children performed better in literature-based reading programs than in traditional classrooms on all measures of literacy development except on standardized tests, where there were no differences. Similarly, Karin Dahl and Penny Freppon (1995) found that minority students in literature-based reading classrooms do as well as students in skill-based classrooms, plus they develop a greater sense of the purposes of literacy and see themselves as readers and writers.

Review

Strategic readers and writers control their own reading and writing and apply skills and strategies as they need them. Twelve strategies were discussed in this chapter: tapping prior knowledge, predicting, organizing ideas, figuring out unknown words, visualizing, making connections, applying fix-up strategies, revising meaning, monitoring, playing with language, generalizing, and evaluating. Researchers have compared students who are capable readers and writers with other students who are less successful and found that those who are less successful are not strategic. Skills are information-processing techniques that readers and writers use automatically and unconsciously as they construct meaning. During the ele-

mentary grades, students learn to use five types of reading and writing skills: meaning-making skills, decoding and spelling skills, language skills, study skills, and reference skills.

Teachers use both direct and indirect skill and strategy instruction in literature-based reading classrooms. Teachers teach skills and strategies through minilessons; students learn some skills and strategies as they read and write, and they learn others as they work collaboratively with parents, teachers, and classmates. Ways that effective teachers assist their students in becoming strategic readers and writers are reviewed in the figure on page 153.

References

Allington, R. L. (1980). Teacher interruption behaviors during primary-grade oral reading. *Journal of Educational Psychology, 72,* 371–377.

Anderson, R. C., Hiebert, E. H., Scott, J. A., & Wilkinson, I. A. G. (1985). *Becoming a nation of readers: The report of the Commission on Reading.* Washington, DC: The National Institute of Education.

Atwell, N. (1987). *In the middle: Reading, writing, and thinking with adolescents.* Portsmouth, NH: Heinemann.

Baker, L., & Brown, A. L. (1984). Metacognitive skills and reading. In P. D. Pearson, M. Kamil, R. Barr, & P. Mosenthal (Eds.), *Handbook of reading research* (Vol. 1, pp. 353–394). New York: Longman.

Baumann, J. F., & Schmitt, M. C. (1986). The what, why, how, and when of comprehension instruction. *The Reading Teacher, 39,* 640–647.

Berghoff, B., & Egawa, K. (1991). No more "rocks": Grouping to give students control of their learning. *The Reading Teacher, 44,* 536–541.

Bergman, J. L. (1992). SAIL—A way to success and independence for low-achieving readers. *The Reading Teacher, 45,* 598–602.

Brent, R., & Anderson, P. (1993). Developing children's classroom listening strategies. *The Reading Teacher, 47,* 122–126.

Cairney, T. (1990). Intertextuality: Infectious echoes from the past. *The Reading Teacher, 43,* 478–484.

Cairney, T. (1992). Fostering and building students' intertextual histories. *Language Arts, 69,* 502–507.

Collins, J. (1982). Discourse style, classroom interaction and differential treatment. *Journal of Reading Behavior, 14,* 361–376.

Dahl, K. L., & Freppon, P. A. (1995). A comparison of

inner-city children's interpretations of reading and writing instruction in the early grades in skills-based and whole language classrooms. *Reading Research Quarterly, 30,* 50–74.

Davey, B. (1983). Think-aloud—Modelling the cognitive processes of reading comprehension. *Journal of Reading, 27,* 44–47.

de Beaugrande, R. (1980). *Text, discourse and process.* Norwood, NJ: Ablex.

Delpit, L. (1987). The silenced dialogue: Power and pedagogy in educating other people's children. *Harvard Educational Review, 58,* 280–298.

Delpit, L. (1991). A conversation with Lisa Delpit. *Language Arts, 68,* 541–547.

Dudley-Marling, C., & Dippo, D. (1991). The language of whole language. *Language Arts, 68,* 548–554.

Duffy, G. G., & Roehler, L. R. (1987). Improving reading instruction through the use of responsible elaboration. *The Reading Teacher, 20,* 514–520.

Duffy, G. G., & Roehler, L. R. (1991). Teachers' instructional actions. In R. Barr, M. Kamil, P. Mosenthal, & P. Pearson (Eds.), *Handbook of reading research* (Vol. 2, pp. 861 884). White Plains, NY: Longman.

Duffy, G. G., Roehler, L. R., Sivan, E., Rackliffe, G., Book, C., Meloth, M. S., Vavrus, L. G., Wesselman, R., Putnam, J., & Bassiri, D. (1987). Effects of explaining the reasoning associated with using reading strategies. *Reading Research Quarterly, 22,* 347–368.

Dweck, C. S. (1986). Motivational processes affecting learning. *American Psychologist, 41,* 1040–1048.

Faigley, L., Cherry, R. D., Jolliffe, D. A., & Skinner, A. M. (1985). *Assessing writers' knowledge and processes of composing.* Norwood, NJ: Ablex.

Flood, J., & Lapp, K. (1994). Developing literary appreciation and literacy skills: A blueprint for success. *The Reading Teacher, 48,* 76–79.

Flood, J., Lapp, D., Flood, S., & Nagel, G. (1992). Am I allowed to group? Using flexible patterns for effective instruction. *The Reading Teacher, 45,* 608–616.

Freppon, P. A. (1991). Children's concepts of the nature and purpose of reading in different instructional settings. *Journal of Reading Behavior, 23,* 139–163.

Garner, R. (1987). *Metacognition and reading comprehension.* Norwood, NJ: Ablex.

Hiebert, E. (1983). An examination of ability grouping for reading instruction. *Reading Research Quarterly, 18,* 231–255.

Johnston, P., & Winograd, P. (1985). Passive failure in reading. *Journal of Reading Behavior, 17,* 279–301.

Kucer, S. B. (1991). Authenticity as the basis for instruction. *Language Arts, 68,* 532–540.

Lewin, L. (1992). Integrating reading and writing strategies using an alternating teacher-led, student-selected instructional pattern. *The Reading Teacher, 45,* 586–591.

Morrow, L. M. (1992). The impact of a literature-based program on literacy achievement, use of literature, and attitudes of children from minority backgrounds. *Reading Research Quarterly, 27,* 251–275.

Oldfather, P. (1995). Commentary: What's needed to maintain and extend motivation for literacy in the middle grades. *Journal of Reading, 38,* 420–422.

Paris, S. G., & Jacobs, J. E. (1984). The benefits of informed instruction for children's reading awareness and comprehension skills. *Child Development, 55,* 2083–2093.

Paris, S. G., Wasik, B. A., & Turner, J. C. (1991). The development of strategic readers. In R. Barr, M. L. Kamil, P. B. Mosenthal, & P. D. Pearson (Eds.), *Handbook of reading research* (Vol. 2, pp. 609 640). New York: Longman.

Pearson, P. D., & Gallagher, M. C. (1983). The instruction of reading comprehension. *Contemporary Educational Psychology, 8,* 317–344.

Pearson, P. D., Roehler, L. R., Dole, J. A., & Duffy, G. G. (1990). *Developing expertise in reading comprehension: What should be taught? How should it be taught?* (Technical Report No. 512). Champaign, IL: University of Illinois, Center for the Study of Reading.

Pressley, M., & Harris, K. R. (1990). What we really know about strategy instruction. *Educational Leadership, 48,* 31–34.

Reutzel, D. R., & Hollingsworth, P. M. (1991). Reading comprehension skills: Testing the skills distinctiveness hypothesis. *Reading Research and Instruction, 30,* 32–46.

Schmitt, M. C. (1990). A questionnaire to measure children's awareness of strategic reading processes. *The Reading Teacher, 43,* 454–461.

Slavin, R. E. (1987). Ability grouping and student achievement in elementary schools: A best-evidence synthesis. *Review of Educational Research, 57,* 293–336.

Smith, N. B. (1965). *American reading instruction.* Newark, DE: International Reading Association.

Spiegel, D. L. (1992). Blending whole language and systematic direct instruction. *The Reading Teacher, 46,* 38–46.

Staab, C. F. (1990). Teacher mediation in one whole literacy classroom. *The Reading Teacher, 43,* 548–552.

Stauffer, R. G. (1975). *Directing the reading-thinking process.* New York: Harper & Row.

Taylor, B. M., Frye, B. J., Gaetz, T. M. (1990). Reducing the number of reading skill activities in the elementary classroom. *The Journal of Reading Behavior, 22,* 167–180.

Temple, C. (1992). Lots of plots: Patterns, meanings, and children's literature. In C. Temple & P. Collings (Eds.), *Stories and readers: New perspectives on literature in the elementary classroom* (pp. 3–13). Norwood, MA: Christopher-Gordon.

Tompkins, G. E., & Hoskisson, K. (1995). *Language arts: Content and teaching strategies* (3rd ed.). Englewood Cliffs, NJ: Merrill/Prentice Hall.

Wade, S. E. (1990). Using think alouds to assess comprehension. *The Reading Teacher, 43,* 442–453.

Wiggins, R. A. (1994). Large group lesson/small group follow-up: Flexible grouping in a basal reading program. *The Reading Teacher, 47,* 450–460.

Winograd, P., & Hare, V. C. (1988). Direct instruction of reading comprehension strategies: The nature of teacher explanation. In C. Weinstein, E. Goetz, & P. Alexander (Eds.), *Learning and study strategies: Issues in assessment, instruction, and evaluation* (pp. 121–139). San Diego, CA: Academic Press.

Children's Book References

Barrett, J. (1978). *Cloudy with a chance of meatballs.* New York: Macmillan.

Pallotta, J. (1991). *The furry alphabet book.* Watertown, MA: Charlesbridge Publishing.

Steig, W. (1971). *Amos and Boris.* New York: Farrar, Straus & Giroux.

Van Allsburg, C. (1981). *Jumanji.* Boston: Houghton Mifflin.

CHAPTER 5
Identifying and Understanding Words

Before Mrs. Dillon's second graders read Kevin Henkes's *Chrysanthemum* (1991), a picture book story about a mouse named Chrysanthemum who doesn't like her name, Mrs. Dillon brings a **book box** (see the Compendium for more information about this and all other highlighted terms in this chapter) full of artificial flowers to the classroom. She talks about how she loves flowers, especially these flowers. She takes each flower out of the box as she names it: rose, gladiola, daisy, chrysanthemum, pansy, delphinium, iris, and daffodil. Children mention names of flowers they like or that grow in their gardens. Mrs. Dillon writes *Chrysanthemum* on the chalkboard, and the students are amazed by the size of the word. Dean notices the word *the* in the middle of the word. Mrs. Dillon tells the class that it is the name of one of the flowers she showed them and also the title of the book they are going to read. Mrs. Dillon's students pride themselves on being word detectives. Several of them guess the flower name right away!

Mrs. Dillon uses shared reading to introduce the book to her students. She reads the book aloud as students follow in their own copies of the book. Afterwards, students identify these interesting and important words and phrases for the **word wall**— a large sheet of butcher paper hanging on the wall:

*Chrysanthemum	icing on her birthday cake
happiest day	sunniest dress
*absolutely perfect	Mrs. Chud
parents	*wilted
bathroom mirror	absolutely dreadful
entire alphabet	half the alphabet
miserably	Welcome home!
Oh, pish!	*precious
*priceless	*fascinating
winsome	*Parcheesi
macaroni and cheese	ketchup
extremely pleasant	*most comfortable
*jealous	*envious
begrudging	discontented
jaundiced	trifle better
*identity	chocolate cake
buttercream frosting	sprouted leaves and petals
Victoria	scrawny stem
worst nightmare	*miserably
*most prized possessions	good-luck charms
route to school	speechless
indescribable wonder	nice impression
class musicale	dainty Fairy Queen

Butterfly Princess	Pixie messenger
*daisy	*wildly funny
what's so humorous?	Mrs. Twinkle
*Delphinium	*blushed
beamed	bloomed
longingly	*Marigold
*Carnation	*Lily of the Valley
epilogue	huge success

There are many words in this list that students don't recognize by sight, such as *icing, sunniest,* and *absolutely,* even though they know the meanings of the words. They are able to figure out how to pronounce other words, such as *wilted,* using sound-symbol correspondences, but they don't know the meaning of the word. In the story, Chrysanthemum "wilted" when someone hurt her feelings. "Does the word mean she cried?" Lizzie asks. Lizzie makes a good guess using the context clues in the story, but she isn't correct, so Mrs. Dillon dramatizes the word to clarify the meaning. They talk about how clever the author was to choose this word because flowers wilt, too. Other words, such as *scrawny, Parcheesi, epilogue, jaundiced,* and *envious,* are new to them. Students don't know how to identify them or what they mean.

Mrs. Dillon won't try to teach all of these words. The ones she chooses to focus on (these words are marked with an asterisk in the list above) are ones that she thinks are important to the story and also common enough that her students will read them in other books. She chooses some fun words, too. *Parcheesi* is one of the fun words. She brings in a Parcheesi game and teaches the children how to play.

Mrs. Dillon uses a variety of activities to help students identify the words and learn their meanings. She teaches a **minilesson** on the /kri/ sound at the beginning of *Chrysanthemum,* and her students list other words with the same beginning sound, such as *Christmas, Christian, chrysalis, Christy,* and *Christopher.* The students talk about how both *i* and *y* are used as vowels in these words, and Christy shares that sometimes people spell her name *Kristi, Kristy,* or *Christie.* Students ask about these variations, and Mrs. Dillon explains that there's often more than one way to spell a sound because English is a "smart" language. (The *chri* and *chry* spelling options for /kri/ come from Greek, but Mrs. Dillon's second graders aren't ready to learn this yet. What's important to explain to them is that there are spelling options in English.) Other word activities include:

■ Teach a minilesson on syllables. *Victoria, Chrysanthemum,* and *Delphinium* all have four syllables.

■ Read other books on flowers, such as *The Rose in My Garden* (Lobel, 1984), *The Flower Alphabet Book* (Pallotta, 1988), *The Reason for a Flower* (Heller, 1983), and *Alison's Zinnia* (Lobel, 1990).

■ Teach a minilesson on capitalizing names. Students learn that *chrysanthemum* is a flower, but *Chrysanthemum* is a name.

■ Have students make word posters illustrating a word from the word wall and using that word in a sentence.

■ Talk with students about self-concept—how Chrysanthemum's classmates hurt her self-esteem and how Mrs. Twinkle made her feel better.

■ Make a Venn diagram comparing the characters Chrysanthemum and Victoria. The Venn diagram that Mrs. Dillon's class created is shown in Figure 5–1.

At the end of the unit, one of Mrs. Dillon's students, Lizzie, talks about the words in *Chrysanthemum*.

"I thought this book was going to be hard. *Chrysanthemum* is a big word and big words are hard sometimes. But this is a good book."

I asked whether she can read all the words in the book, and she is hesitant as she answers.

"Well, not all of them. I know *Chrysanthemum, absolutely perfect, wilted, Mrs. Chud, sunniest dress, Delphinium, Mrs. Twinkle, good-luck charms, Parcheesi, . . .*" (she continues reading from the word wall).

"Can you pick out some words from the word wall that describe Chrysanthemum?"

FIGURE 5–1   A Venn Diagram Comparing Two Characters

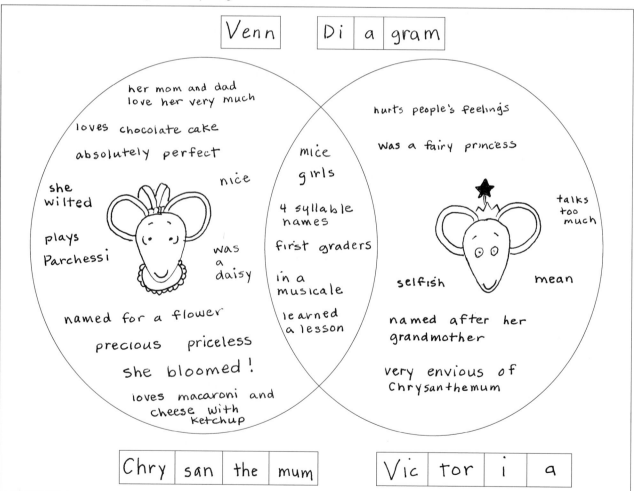

"Yes I can. Chrysanthemum is *wilted* [and she dramatizes the word as Mrs. Dillon had done]. And Chrysanthemum is *miserable* because Victoria and Rita and the other kids hurt her feelings, and she is named after a *flower,* and at the end she *bloomed* because she likes her name now because Mrs. Twinkle named her baby Chrysanthemum. This book is love. It's good, you know."

"How do you know these words?"

"I just do. We read and we talk about books every day. And we write lots of books. My teacher, Mrs. Dillon, says we are 'word detectives.' That means we know lots of words."

My last question was, "What do you do when you are reading and you come to a word you don't know?"

"Well, I try to sound it out but sometimes you can't. Then I try to think hard. I see if the pictures can tell me or I ask Jennifer or somebody else who's a good reader. If there's nobody to help me, I just keep reading. Sometimes the word gets in the way, but sometimes it's not important."

Mrs. Dillon incorporates word study throughout reading. She introduces a few key words before students read a book, but most of the word study comes after reading, when students are more interested in learning about the words in the book they have read. Creating and posting a word wall in the classroom is the most important thing Mrs. Dillon does. Her students choose the words and often write them on the word wall themselves. These words become their words. They refer to the list as they read and write and talk about the book.

Readers need to be able to quickly identify or decode words and know their meanings in order to read fluently. For young children, not recognizing high-frequency words such as *the, what,* and *of* makes reading difficult, and for older students, lacking background knowledge about a concept and being unfamiliar with related concept-words makes reading difficult. For example, students reading an informational book about rain forests can run into difficulty without a well-developed concept about this tropical landform and vocabulary such as *canopy, understory, ocelots, macaws, ferns,* and *kapok tree.* When students come to unfamiliar words as they read, they must focus a great deal of their mental energy on decoding the word, and this focus on decoding detracts from students' emphasis on making meaning.

Not all unfamiliar words are equally hard or easy to learn; the degree of difficulty depends on what the student already knows about the word. Graves (1985) identifies four possible situations for unfamiliar words:

1. *Sight word.* Students recognize the word, know what it means when they hear someone say it, and can use it orally, but they don't recognize its written form.

2. *New word.* Students have a concept related to the word, but they are not familiar with the word, either orally or in written form.

3. *New concept.* Students have little or no background knowledge about the concept underlying the word, and they don't recognize the word itself.

4. *New meaning.* Students know the word, but they are unfamiliar with the way the word is used and its meaning in this situation.

■ **ACTIVITY**

At the beginning of this chapter, Mrs. Dillon's students added words to the word wall that fit into each of these four categories. Give some examples of each type.

The most difficult category of words for students to learn is the one involving new concepts, because they must first learn the concepts and then attach word labels. Students benefit from direct instruction on these concepts and the words to explain them.

Our focus in this chapter is on words and how students learn to identify unfamiliar words as they read and how they learn the meanings of words. As you continue reading, think about these questions:

- What is the difference between identifying and understanding words?
- How do students learn to decode words?
- How do students become fluent readers?
- Why is fluent reading important?
- How do students learn the meanings of words?

WORD IDENTIFICATION

The two main ways that students identify words are by word recognition—recognizing many, many words automatically by sight and by decoding or analyzing unfamiliar words using cues in the text. Students use primarily graphophonic cues, but they also rely on syntactic and semantic cues, and sometimes an illustration provides a useful clue. Two other strategies that students use when they come to an unfamiliar word are to skip it and read on or to ask someone. Identifying words is not the same as reading, because readers sometimes recognize words without understanding them. At other times, students identify words but cannot comprehend the ideas presented among the sentences.

Sight Vocabulary

Students need to develop a large stock of words that they recognize and understand instantly and automatically, because it is impossible for them to analyze and decode every word that they encounter when reading or which they want to spell when writing. These recognizable words are called sight vocabulary. Through repeated reading experiences, students develop automaticity with most words they read and write (LaBerge & Samuels, 1976). Researchers report that the vital element in word recognition is learning each word's unique letter sequence (Eldredge, 1995). This knowledge about the sequence of letters is useful as students learn to spell. At the same time that students are becoming fluent readers, they are also learning to spell the words they write most often. Hitchcock (1989) found that by third grade most students spell 90% of the words they use correctly.

High-frequency words—those that readers and writers use again and again—are an important part of sight vocabulary. There have been numerous attempts to identify specific lists of these words and calculate their frequency in reading materials. Eldredge (1995, p. 93) identified these 36 most common words:

the	and	to	a	I	said
you	in	it	of	he	was
is	on	that	she	for	can
they	his	all	what	we	will
not	little	with	my	do	but
are	at	up	her	have	out

These 36 words accounted for 39% of the words in the first-grade basal programs and children's literature books that Eldredge analyzed. Some of these words, such as *it* and *can,* can be decoded, but others, such as *are* and *have,* are more easily learned as sight words. The 100 most frequently used words account for more than 55% of the words children read and write, and the 300 most frequently used words account for 72% (Eldredge, 1995). Figure 5–2 presents a list of 300 high-frequency words.

Why are high-frequency words important?   High-frequency words are so common in reading materials that it is essential that children learn to identify them, and many of these words are difficult to learn because they cannot be easily decoded. Try sounding out *the, what,* and *are* and you will see why they are called "sight" words. Because they can't be decoded easily, it is crucial that children learn to recognize these words instantly and automatically. A further complication is that many of these words are function words in sentences and don't carry much meaning. Children find it much easier to learn to recognize *whale* than *what,* because the word *whale* conjures up the image of the aquatic animal, while *what* is abstract. However, *what* is used much more frequently, and children need to learn to recognize it.

Children who recognize many high-frequency words are able to read more fluently than students who do not, and fluent readers are better able to understand what they are reading. Once children can read many of these words, they gain confidence in themselves as readers and begin reading books independently. Similarly, students who can spell these words are more successful writers.

Ways to Emphasize High-Frequency Words.   Effective teachers are aware of high-frequency words and understand their usefulness for beginning readers and writers. They emphasize these words during minilessons, plan reading and writing activities to

Children become fluent readers as they learn to recognize high-frequency words automatically.

FIGURE 5–2 A List of 300 High-Frequency Words

a	children	great	looking	ran	through
about	city	green	made	read	time
after	come	grow	make	red	to
again	could	had	man	ride	toad
all	couldn't	hand	many	right	together
along	cried	happy	may	road	told
always	dad	has	maybe	room	too
am	dark	hat	me	run	took
an	day	have	mom	said	top
and	did	he	more	sat	tree
animals	didn't	head	morning	saw	truck
another	do	hear	mother	say	try
any	does	heard	mouse	school	two
are	dog	help	Mr.	sea	under
around	don't	hen	Mrs.	see	until
as	door	her	much	she	up
asked	down	here	must	show	us
at	each	hill	my	sister	very
ate	eat	him	name	sky	wait
away	end	his	need	sleep	walk
baby	even	home	never	small	walked
back	ever	house	new	so	want
bad	every	how	next	some	wanted
ball	everyone	I	nice	something	was
be	eyes	I'll	night	soon	water
bear	far	I'm	no	started	way
because	fast	if	not	stay	we
bed	father	in	nothing	still	well
been	find	inside	now	stop	went
before	fine	into	of	stories	were
began	first	is	off	story	what
behind	fish	it	oh	sun	when
best	fly	it's	old	take	where
better	for	its	on	tell	while
big	found	jump	once	than	who
bird	fox	jumped	one	that	why
birds	friend	just	only	that's	will
blue	friends	keep	or	the	wind
book	frog	king	other	their	witch
books	from	know	our	them	with
box	fun	last	out	then	wizard
boy	garden	left	over	there	woman
brown	gave	let	people	these	words
but	get	let's	picture	they	work
by	girl	like	pig	thing	would
called	give	little	place	things	write
came	go	live	play	think	yes
can	going	long	pulled	this	you
can't	good	look	put	thought	you're
cat	got	looked	rabbit	three	your

reinforce some of these words, and take note when students read and write them without assistance. Five ways to call children's attention to sight words and provide practice activities are:

1. Word chart.   Post the 36 or 300 most common words alphabetically on a chart in the classroom or make individual bookmarks for students with the words listed (Cunningham, 1995). Teachers can begin the school year with the 36 highest-frequency words listed and add other words periodically during the year.

2. Reading and rereading books.   Have students read and reread trade books that have a high percentage of high-frequency words, such as *Pinkerton, Behave!* (Kellogg, 1979), *Whose Mouse Are You?* (Kraus, 1970), *There's a Nightmare in My Closet* (Mayer, 1968), and other easy-to-read books (Eeds, 1985).

3. Minilessons.   Teach brief, three-minute minilessons to emphasize the most frequently used words—especially those words that cannot be decoded easily—using a recite and spell-out strategy in which students read and spell several words (Shefelbine, 1995). Teachers take these words from big books and charts in the classroom that children have read. The teacher points to a word, pronounces the word, spells the word, and then asks the class to pronounce and spell it. Sometimes children clap as they spell out each letter:

Teacher: This word is "the," t-h-e. What is this word?
Students: "The," t-h-e.

Teachers often have students read and spell the same word two or three times and then repeat the process with several other words during each minilesson.

4. Dictionaries.   Help students make dictionaries with the 36 or 300 most frequently used words and put the words beginning with each letter on a separate page. Students keep the dictionaries at their desks and use them when writing. Encourage students to spell these words correctly, but allow them to use invented spelling for less common words.

5. Patterned writing.   Have students write books by completing a sentence stem on each page. Topics for these books should be related to literature children are reading or to theme studies. For example, when students are studying animals, they can write riddle books and repeat the pattern "What is it?" at the end of each riddle. One first grader wrote this riddle:

Page 1:   *It is a bird.*
Page 2:   *It can't fly but it can swim.*
Page 3:   *It is black and white.*
Page 4:   *It eats fish.*
Page 5:   *What is it?*
Page 6:   *A penguin.*

Of the words that the child wrote, two-thirds are among the 36 most common words listed above. Other sentence stems include:

I said . . .
I am . . .
I can . . .
I see . . .

Decoding Skills and Strategies

Beginning readers encounter many words that they don't recognize immediately, and more fluent readers also come upon words they don't recognize once in a while. To identify these words, students use word-identification skills and strategies and cues in the text. They use phonological information as well as semantic, syntactic, and pragmatic information. Phonological information is what most people call phonics, and for most words students can use phonics to sound out at least part of the word. Then students use semantic information to make logical guesses about the unfamiliar word. The word they are trying to identify must make sense in the context of the sentence or paragraph. Children call up their background information about the topic to help them make a logical guess. They also deduce the word using analogies to known words. For example, if the unknown word is *tureen,* students might notice that it ends like the familiar word *green.* Students also use syntactic information about sentence structure. If the unfamiliar word is a noun, students usually guess words that are also nouns. They also consider root words, prefixes, and suffixes. Efficient decoders use several strategies and related skills to identify words; they don't depend on just one strategy (Clay, 1985, 1991). Five word-identification strategies are summarized in Figure 5–3.

In order to become fluent readers, students need to be word detectives, just like Mrs. Dillon's students are. In this sentence, many of Mrs. Dillon's second graders could identify the word *icing:* "The mouse loved to eat chocolate cake and icing." They used a combination of phonological information and semantic clues. They might solve the problem this way: This word begins with *i* and ends with *-ing* and you eat it with chocolate cake. In contrast, the word *daisy* in this sentence is much more difficult to identify: "She played a daisy." Even though students might sound out part of the word *daisy,* the context offers them less help in identifying the word—unless there is an illustration showing the mouse dressed up in a flower costume and performing on a stage.

As students' sight vocabularies grow, they have less need to use these strategies, but all readers need them occasionally. The same is true for spelling. As students learn to spell more words, they need to figure out the spellings of fewer words, but everyone uses spelling skills and strategies or checks to see how a word is spelled in the dictionary occasionally.

Using Phonics. Students use what they know about sound-symbol correspondences, phonic generalizations, and spelling patterns to decode words. Even when students cannot sound out the entire word, they often decode the beginning sound or other phonetically regular parts of the word. (For more information on phonics, see Chapter 3, "Breaking the Code.")

Using Analogies. Students learn to decode many words by comparing them to words they already know. This procedure is known as decoding by analogy (Cunningham, 1975–1976; Gaskins, Gaskins, & Gaskins, 1991). For example, when read-

FIGURE 5–3   Five Word-Identification Strategies

Strategy	Description
Phonics	Students use their knowledge of sound-symbol correspondences and spelling patterns to decode words when reading and to spell words when writing. Examples: *fat, time, go, duck, fly.*
Analogies	Students use their knowledge of rhyming words to deduce the pronunciation or spelling of an unfamiliar word. Examples: *creep* from *sheep, think* from *pink, include* from *dude.*
Context Clues —	Students use semantic and syntactic information to predict unfamiliar words. They also use information from illustrations and their background knowledge of the topic. Example: "She bought beautiful flowers at the florist." Students predict the word *florist* from the gist of the sentence as well as an illustration of a florist working in a flower shop.
Morphemic Analysis	Students apply their knowledge of root words and affixes (prefixes at the beginning of the word and suffixes at the end) to identify an unfamiliar word. They "peel off" any prefixes or suffixes and identify the root word first. Then they add the affixes. Examples: *trans-port, astro-naut, bi-cycle, centi-pede, pseudo-nym, tele-scope.*
Syllabic Analysis	Students break multisyllabic words into syllables and then use phonics and analogies to decode the word, syllable by syllable. Examples: *cul-prit, tem-por-ary, vic-tor-y, neg-a-tive, sea-weed, bio-de-grad-able.*

ers come to an unfamiliar word such as *lend*, they might think of *send* and figure the word out by analogy; for *mound*, they might think of *found*. For the two-syllable word *margin*, students might think of *car* and *win* and figure the word out by analogy. Students use analogy to figure out the spelling of unfamiliar words as well. Students might use *cat* to help them spell *that*, for example. This strategy accounts for students' common misspelling of *they* as *thay*, because *they* is rhymed with *day, say*, and *may*.

Teachers give minilessons on how to decode by analogy whenever the words being studied are appropriate. For example, Mrs. Dillon asked her students to think of words that begin like *Chrysanthemum*. Teachers can also ask students to share examples of how they use analogies to figure out unknown words when reading independently.

Using Context Clues.   When words are read within the context of a sentence or paragraph, they are much easier to figure out than when they are read in isolation. The surrounding words and sentences provide context clues. Two kinds of context clues are the semantic and syntactic information in the sentence and paragraph surrounding the unfamiliar word. Semantic clues provide information about the meaning of the word, and syntactic clues provide information about the part of speech and how the unfamiliar word is used in a sentence. Other clues can come from illustrations or from the title of the book.

Teachers model how to use context clues to figure out the meaning of unfamiliar words when they read aloud to students. Before reading, teachers select several words with varying amounts of contextual amplification. Then as they read aloud, they stop at one word, question the word's meaning, and then think aloud as they figure it out. They think about their background knowledge and verbalize their choices, confusions, and decisions about the word.

Less capable readers often depend too heavily on context clues to figure out unfamiliar words, while more capable readers use all of the word-identification strategies and related skills (Stanovich, 1980). Using context clues is an effective strategy for beginning readers who are reading highly repetitive and predictable books such as Bill Martin, Jr.'s, *Brown Bear, Brown Bear, What Do You See?* (1983), but this technique does not work as well for less predictable books. Also, children who depend on context clues are not developing their understanding of the other word-identification skills and strategies, especially phonics.

Researchers have documented that children progress through three stages of early reading development (Juel, 1991). First is the selective-cue stage, when readers pay more attention to context clues and primarily read predictable books. Next is the spelling-sound stage, when students apply what they are learning about sound-symbol correspondences to decode unfamiliar words. The last stage is the automatic stage, when students are fluent readers. At this stage, students quickly recognize most words that they are reading and use all five word-identification skills and strategies to figure out unfamiliar words.

Using Morphemic Analysis.   Students examine the root word and affixes of longer unfamiliar words in order to identify the words. A root word is a morpheme, the basic part of a word to which affixes are added. Many words are developed from a single root word, For example, the Latin word *portare* (to carry) is the source of at least nine words: *deport, export, import, port, portable, porter, report, support,* and *transportation.* Latin is a common source of English root words, and Greek and English are two other sources.

Some root words are whole words, and others are parts of words. Some root words have become free morphemes and can be used as separate words, but others cannot. For instance, the word *act* comes from the Latin word *actus,* meaning *doing.* English uses part of the word and treats it as a root word that can be used independently, or in combination with affixes, as in *actor, activate, react,* and *enact.* In the words *alias, alien, alienate,* and *inalienable,* the root word *ali* comes from the Latin word *alius,* meaning *other;* it is not an independent root word in English. A list of root words appears in Figure 5–4.

Affixes are bound morphemes that are added to words and root words. Prefixes are added to the beginning of words, as in *reread,* and suffixes are added to the end of words, as in *singing* and *player.* Like root words, affixes come from Latin, Greek, and English. Affixes often change a word's meaning, such as adding *un-* to *happy* to form *unhappy.* Sometimes they change the part of speech, too. For example, when *-ion* is added to *attract* to form *attraction,* the verb *attract* becomes a noun.

When a word's affix is "peeled off," the remaining word is usually a real word. For example, when the prefix *pre-* is removed from *preview,* the word *view* can stand alone, and when the suffix *-able* is removed from *readable,* the word *read* can stand alone. Some words include letter sequences that might be affixes, but because the remaining word cannot stand alone, they are not affixes. For example, the *in-* at the beginning of *include* is not a prefix because *clude* is not a word. Similarly, the *-ic* at the

FIGURE 5–4   Root Words

ann/enn (year): anniversary, annual, biennial, centennial, perennial
ast (star): aster, asterisk, astrology, astronaut, astronomy
auto (self): autobiography, automatic, automobile
bio (life): biography, biology, autobiography, biodegradable
cent (hundred): cent, centennial, centigrade, centipede, century
circ (around): circle, circular, circus, circumspect
corp (body): corporal, corporation, corps
cycl (wheel): bicycle, cycle, cyclist, cyclone, tricycle
dict (speak): contradict, dictate, dictator, predict, verdict
geo (earth): geography, geology, geometry
graph (write): biography, graphic, paragraph, phonograph, stenographer
gram (letter): diagram, grammar, monogram, telegram
grat (pleasing, thankful): congratulate, grateful, gratitude
jus/jud/jur (law, right): injury, judge, justice
man (hand): manacle, manual, manufacture, manuscript
mand (order): command, demand, mandate, remand
mar (sea): aquamarine, marine, maritime, submarine
meter (measure): barometer, centimeter, diameter, speedometer, thermometer
min (small): miniature, minimize, minor, minute
mort (death): immortal, mortal, mortality, mortician, postmortem
ped/pod (foot): pedal, pedestrian, podiatry, tripod
phon (sound): earphone, microphone, phonics, phonograph, saxophone, symphony
photo (light): photograph, photographer, photosensitive, photosynthesis
quer/ques/quis (seek): query, question, inquisitive
rupt (break): abrupt, bankrupt, interrupt, rupture
scope (see): horoscope, kaleidoscope, microscope, periscope, telescope
struct (build): construction, indestructible, instruct
tele (far): telecast, telegram, telegraph, telephone, telescope, telethon, television
terr (land): terrace, terrain, terrarium, territory
tract (pull, drag): attraction, subtract, tractor
vict/vinc (conquer): convince, convict, evict, victor, victory
vis (see): television, visa, vision, visual
viv/vit (live): survive, vitamin, vivid
volv (roll): involve, revolutionary, revolver

end of *magic* is not a suffix because *mag* cannot stand alone as a word. Sometimes, however, the root word cannot stand alone. One example is *legible*. The *-ible* is a suffix, and *leg* is the root word even though it cannot stand alone.

A list of prefixes and suffixes is presented in Figure 5–5. White, Sowell, and Yanagihara (1989) researched affixes and identified those that are most commonly used in English words, and these affixes are marked with an asterisk in Figure 5–5. White and his colleagues recommend that the commonly used affixes be taught to middle- and upper-grade students because of their usefulness. Some of the most commonly used prefixes can be confusing because they have more than one meaning. The prefix *un-*, for example, can mean *not* (e.g., *unclear*) or it can reverse the meaning of a word (e.g., *tie–untie*).

Using Syllabic Analysis. Multisyllabic words, such as *biodegradable*, *admonition*, and *unforgettable*, are particularly difficult for many students to read. Students need

FIGURE 5–5   Affixes

Prefixes	Suffixes
a/an- (not): atheist, anaerobic	**-able/-ible** (worthy of, can be): lovable, audible
amphi- (both): amphibian	***-al/-ial** (action, process): arrival, denial
anti- (against): antiseptic	**-ance/-ence** (state or quality): annoyance, absence
bi- (two, twice): bifocal, biannual	**-ant** (one who): servant
contra- (against): contradict	**-ard** (one who is): coward
de- (away): detract	**-ary/-ory** (person, place): secretary, laboratory
di- (two): dioxide	
*dis- (not): disapprove	**-dom** (state or quality): freedom
*dis- (reversal): disinfect	**-ed** (past tense): played
ex- (out): export	**-ee** (one who is): trustee
hemi- (half): hemisphere	***-er/-or/-ar** (one who): teacher, actor, liar
*il-/im-/in-/ir- (not): illegible, impolite, inexpensive, irrational	**-er/-or** (action): robber
*in- (in, into): indoor	**-ern** (direction): northern
inter- (between): intermission	**-et/-ette** (small): booklet, dinette
kilo/milli- (one thousand): kilometer, milligram	**-ful** (full of): hopeful
micro- (small): microfilm	**-hood** (state of quality): childhood
*mis- (wrong): mistake	**-ic** (characterized by): angelic
mono- (one): monarch	**-icle/-ucle** (small): particle, molecule
multi- (many): multimillionaire	**-ify** (to make): simplify
omni- (all): omnivorous	**-ing** (participle): eating, building
*over- (too much): overflow	**-ish** (like): reddish
poly- (many): polygon	**-ism** (doctrine of): communism
post- (after): postwar	**-less** (without): hopeless
pre-/pro- (before): precede, prologue	**-ling** (young): duckling
quad-/quart- (four): quadruple, quarter	**-logy** (the study of): zoology
re- (again): repay	***-ly** (in the manner of): slowly
*re-/retro- (back): replace, retroactive	**-ment** (state or quality): enjoyment
*sub- (under): submarine	***-ness** (state or quality): kindness
super- (above): supermarket	**-s/-es** (plural): cats, boxes
trans- (across): transport	**-ship** (state, or art or skill): friendship, seamanship
tri- (three): triangle	***-sion/-tion** (state or quality): tension, attraction
*un- (not): unhappy	**-ster** (one who): gangster
*un- (reversal): untie	**-ure** (state or quality): failure
	-ward (direction): homeward
	*-y (full of): sleepy

*indicates the most commonly used affixes (White, Sowell, & Yanagihara, 1989)

to learn that longer words are composed of two or more syllables and that in order to decode multisyllabic words, students break the words down into syllables, the same way Mrs. Dillon did when she wrote *Chry-san-the-mum* on the chalkboard. Once the word is broken down, students can figure out the syllables using phonological cues and by analogy. Words that seem impossible to read become manageable when students break them apart.

Teaching Students to Identify Words

Three ways that students develop sight vocabularies and learn decoding skills to be able to identify words quickly and easily are wide reading, extensive writing opportunities, and minilessons on decoding strategies and skills. All three of these ways are important in helping students become more fluent readers.

Wide Reading.   Students need many varied reading experiences to develop a large sight vocabulary and to practice decoding strategies and skills. When teachers introduce books during literature focus units, they often use shared reading and then provide several opportunities for students to read and reread books. **Choral reading** of poems and **readers theatre** activities are also useful because students have opportunities to develop fluency. Students also need opportunities every day to read self-selected books independently.

Extensive Writing.   Students also learn sight words and develop spelling strategies through daily writing opportunities. Students reinforce their learning of sight words as they use words from the word wall to write reflections about the books they are reading and as they adapt those books for their own writing activities. After reading *Chrysanthemum,* for example, many of Mrs. Dillon's students wrote their own books. Carrie wrote a number book about flowers, and Missy wrote "How to Be a Good Friend." Pages from their books are shown in Figure 5–6. As these two examples show, students used several words from the class word wall. You may also notice that several words are misspelled in these two examples. Despite Mrs. Dillon's best efforts to help students edit their books, a few words continue to be misspelled. However, Carrie spelled 8 of 9 words correctly (89%) on the page from her number book, and Missy spelled 18 of 21 words correctly (86%) on the page from her "Friend" book.

Minilessons.   Word-level learning must be part of authentic literacy activities (Hiebert, 1991), and teaching minilessons about sight words and decoding is a useful way to help students focus on words. Minilessons grow out of meaningful literature experiences or theme studies, and teachers choose words for minilessons from books students are reading, as Mrs. Dillon did, or at least begin with several words from the book and then provide additional examples.

Delpit (1987) and Reyes (1991) have argued that learning words implicitly through reading and writing experiences assumes that students have existing literacy and language proficiencies and that the same sort of instruction works equally well for everyone. They point out that not all students have a rich background of literacy experiences before coming to school. Some students, especially those from nonmainstream cultural and linguistic groups, may not have been read to as preschoolers. They may not have recited nursery rhymes to develop phonemic awareness, or experimented with writing by writing letters to grandparents. Perhaps even more importantly, they are not familiar with the routines of school—sitting quietly and listening while the teacher reads, working cooperatively on group projects, answering questions and talking about books, and imitating the teacher's literacy behaviors. Delpit and Reyes conclude that explicit instruction is crucial for nonmainstream students who do not have the same literacy background as middle-class students.

Fluent readers develop a large repertoire of sight words and use phonological, semantic, and syntactic cues to decode unfamiliar words. Less capable readers, in contrast, cannot read as many sight words and do not use as many cues for decoding

FIGURE 5–6   A Page From Two Students' Books Written After Reading *Chrysanthemum*

words. Researchers have concluded again and again that students who do not become fluent readers depend on explicit instruction to learn how to identify words (Calfee & Drum, 1986; Gaskins et al., 1991; Johnson & Baumann, 1984).

Reading Recovery, a one-to-one tutorial for low-achieving first graders, involves children in repeated reading activities, writing experiences, and instruction in words until they reach the average level of their classmates (Clay, 1985, 1991). Others have adapted Reading Recovery procedures for teachers to use in classroom settings. These studies have combined multiple opportunities to read and reread literature with writing experiences and lessons about words. Based on this work, here is an instructional procedure for minilessons on word identification:

1. *Use shared reading.*   Teachers read a book with students using shared reading. A big book can be used with primary-grade students, while older students can use a class set of books. The teacher reads aloud while students follow along in individual copies of the book.

2. *Focus on a target word or words.*   Teachers choose one or more words from the class word wall for study. After highlighting the target word, teachers and students identify and list words with the same phonogram, or spelling pattern. Students write the words on individual magic slates or chalkboards. Students can also add the words to personal word banks and word booklets.

3. *Use target words in reading and writing activities.*   Students notice the words in books they read and report back to the class when they notice the word. Students also use the words when writing in response to reading and in various related activities. Students use the words on word posters and in books they write, as Mrs. Dillon's second graders did.

Teachers also present lessons to focus on sight words (Bridge, Winograd, & Haley, 1983). While practice in the context of **repeated readings** of predictable books is enough for some children, it is not enough for others. Some children do not notice individual words, and teachers need to call their attention to high-frequency words. Teachers can use the same three-step instructional procedure for minilessons on sight words.

Many fourth-grade teachers notice that their students seem to stand still or lose ground in their reading development. It has been assumed that the increased demands for reading informational books with unfamiliar vocabulary caused this phenomenon. Now researchers are suggesting that lack of instruction in word-identification strategies might be the cause of the "fourth-grade slump" (Chall, Jacobs, & Baldwin, 1990). Perhaps more minilessons on words will help eliminate this difficulty.

The guidelines for teaching word identification are summarized in Figure 5–7. In the vignette at the beginning of this chapter, Mrs. Dillon modeled many of these guidelines.

Developing Fluency

Reading fluency is the ability to read words accurately, rapidly, and automatically. Students who read fluently are better able to understand what they read because they can identify words easily (LaBerge & Samuels, 1976; Perfitti, 1985; Stanovich, 1986). Students who are not fluent readers often read hesitantly and with great effort. Less competent readers spend too much mental energy in identifying words, leaving little energy to focus on comprehension. Readers do not have an unlimited amount of mental energy to use when they read, and they cannot focus on both word identification and comprehension at the same time. So, as students become fluent readers, they use less energy for word identification and focus more energy on comprehending what they read.

FIGURE 5–7 Guidelines for Teaching Students to Identify Words

1. Part of Meaningful Reading Experiences

Teachers present word-identification lessons as part of literature focus units. A whole-part-whole approach for teaching word identification as well as other skills and strategies is recommended.

2. High-Frequency Words

Teachers choose both high-frequency words and other interesting words from the reading selections for minilessons and other word-study activities. It is especially important that students learn high-frequency words in order to become fluent readers.

3. Careful Selection of Words

Teachers consider the students, the text to be read, and the purpose for reading when deciding which words to focus on for word-study activities.

4. Key Words

Introduce only a few key words before beginning to read, and teach other words during and after reading. Key words are meaningful words in the reading selection, such as characters' names, or words related to a key concept.

5. Shared Reading

Teachers often use shared reading to introduce trade books and selections in basal reader textbooks. As teachers read they model word-identification strategies for students.

6. Word Walls and Word Banks

Students and teachers highlight important and interesting words from the reading selection on word walls and make word banks of high-frequency words for students to refer to when reading and spelling.

7. Word-Identification Strategies

Teachers present minilessons on the five word-identification strategies and related skills: phonics, analogies, context cues, morphemic analysis, and syllabic analysis.

8. Reading Workshop

Students need daily opportunities to read self-selected books during reading workshop, and as they read and reread books appropriate to their reading levels they apply word-identification strategies and related skills. Easy-to-read books written at the first-, second-, and third-grade levels are recommended for beginning readers.

9. Reading-Writing Connection

Integrated reading and writing instruction gives students many opportunities to write high-frequency words and other words related to reading selections in writing activities. Students write in reading logs, make story maps, and write innovations, or new versions of stories they are reading.

10. Fluency

The goal of word-identification lessons is to help students become fluent readers. Fluent readers can identify most words automatically and use word-identification strategies to figure out unfamiliar words.

Easy-to-Read Books.   Students need many opportunities to practice reading in order to develop fluency, and easy-to-read books are useful in developing reading fluency. Many easy-reader books written at the first- and second-grade reading levels are available, such as *Amelia Bedelia* (Parish, 1963), *"Buzz," Said the Bee* (Lewison, 1992), and *Hungry, Hungry Sharks* (Cole, 1986). These books provide many opportunities for students to apply word-identification skills and strategies and develop reading fluency. A list of easy-to-read books is presented in Figure 5–8. Some easy-to-read books are high-quality children's literature, such as Arnold Lobel's *Frog and Toad Are Friends* (1970), which was a Caldecott Honor Book, but many others are more "pop" literature—fun to read but rather ordinary. These books are often more effective than some high-quality literature selections in helping children develop fluency because the vocabulary is more controlled and students can be more successful. For young children and less capable readers, many high-quality literature selections are books for teachers to read aloud. A complete reading program includes both high-quality literature and books that children can read independently.

Ways to Promote Reading Fluency.   Teachers provide daily opportunities for children to practice reading and rereading familiar stories and other books. Some activities, such as choral reading, may be done together as a class or in small groups, while reading workshop is individualized and students read self-selected books. Students need both group reading experiences and independent practice to develop reading fluency. Often during the class or small-group activities, students read more challenging texts that they might not choose to read independently. They also notice how the teacher and classmates chunk words together into phrases and sentences. As they read orally as a group during choral reading, for example, students learn to pace their reading and add expression. During reading workshop, on the other hand, students often

As students reread books, they increase reading speed and develop reading fluency.

FIGURE 5–8   Easy-to-Read Books

Stories

Allard, H. (1979). *Bumps in the night.* New York: Bantam.

Benchley, N. (1979). *Running owl the hunter.* New York: Harper & Row.

Blume, J. (1971). *Freckle juice.* New York: Dell.

Blume, J. (1981). *The one in the middle is the green kangaroo.* New York: Dell.

Bonsall, C. (1980). *The case of the double cross.* New York: HarperCollins.

Brown, M. (1984). *There's no place like home.* New York: Parents Magazine Press.

Delton, J. (1992). *Lights, action, land-ho!* New York: Dell. (And other books in the series)

Giff, P. R. (1984). *The beast in Ms. Rooney's room.* New York: Dell. (And other books in the series)

Lewison, W. C. (1992). *"Buzz," said the bee.* New York: Scholastic.

Lobel, A. (1970). *Frog and Toad are friends.* New York: Harper & Row. (And other books in the Frog and Toad series)

Lobel, A. (1972). *Mouse tales.* New York: Harper & Row.

Marshall, E. (1983). *Fox on wheels.* New York: Puffin.

Marzollo, J., & Marzollo, C. (1987). *Jed and the space bandits.* New York: Dial.

Milios, R. (1988). *Bears, bears, everywhere.* Chicago: Childrens Press.

Parish, P. (1963). *Amelia Bedelia.* New York: Harper & Row. (And other books in the series)

Rylant, C. (1987). *Henry and Mudge: The first book.* New York: Aladdin.

Schwartz, A. (1982). *There is a carrot in my ear and other noodle tales.* New York: Harper & Row.

Schwartz, A. (1984). *In a dark, dark room.* New York: Scholastic.

Sharmat, M. W. (1974). *Nate the great goes undercover.* New York: Dell. (And other books in the Nate the Great series)

Yolen, J. (1980). *Commander Toad in space.* New York: Coward-McCann. (And other books in the Commander Toad series)

Ziefert, H. (1983). *Small potatoes club.* New York: Dell. (And other books in the series)

Poetry

Hopkins, L. B. (1984). *Surprises.* New York: Harper & Row.

Hopkins, L. B. (1985). *More surprises.* New York: Harper & Row.

Biographies

Adler, D. A. (1989). *A picture book of Abraham Lincoln.* New York: Holiday House. (And other biographies by the author)

Krensky, S. (1991). *Christopher Columbus.* New York: Random House.

History

Benchley, N. (1969). *Sam the minuteman.* New York: Harper & Row.

Benchley, N. (1977). *George the drummer boy.* New York: Harper & Row.

Brenner, B. (1978). *Wagon wheels.* New York: Harper & Row.

Byars, B. (1985). *The Golly sisters go west.* New York: Harper & Row.

Coerr, E. (1986). *The Josefina story quilt.* New York: Harper & Row.

Coerr, E. (1988). *Chang's paper pony.* New York: Harper & Row.

Greeson, J. (1991). *An American army of two.* Minneapolis: Carolrhoda.

Monjo, F. N. (1970). *The drinking gourd.* New York: Harper & Row.

Roop, P., & Roop, C. (1985). *Keep the lights burning, Abbie.* Minneapolis: Carolrhoda.

Roop, P., & Roop, C. (1986). *Buttons for General Washington.* Minneapolis: Carolrhoda.

Sandin, J. (1981). *The long way to a new land.* New York: Harper & Row.

Schultz, W. A. (1991). *Wil and Ory.* Minneapolis: Carolrhoda.

Wetterer, M. K. (1990). *Kate Shelley and the midnight express.* Minneapolis: Carolrhoda.

Science

Brown, M. (1984). *There's no place like home.* New York: Parents Magazine Press.

Cole J. (1986). *Hungry, hungry sharks.* New York: Random House.

Fowler, A. (1990). *It could still be a bird.* Chicago: Childrens Press. (And other books in the series)

Fowler, A. (1990). *It's a good thing there are insects.* Chicago: Childrens Press.

Milton, J. (1992). *Wild, wild wolves.* New York: Random House.

Parish, P. (1974). *Dinosaur time.* New York: Harper & Row.

Smith, M. (1991). *A snake mistake.* New York: HarperCollins.

Ziefert, H. (1991). *Bob and Shirley: A tale of two lobsters.* New York: HarperCollins.

read less challenging—"more comfortable"—books, and they read silently or by mumbling to themselves. Five instructional procedures to promote reading fluency are:

1. Repeated readings.   One strategy is repeated readings (Samuels, 1979), in which students reread a book several times, trying to improve their reading rate and decrease the number of miscues or errors they make. Yaden (1988) found that through

Technology Link
Screen Reading: Using Captioned Television Programs to Develop Reading Fluency

Reading captioned television programs provides students with opportunities for reading practice that is entertaining and self-correcting. On captioned television programs, sentences corresponding to the words spoken on the video are printed on the screen, much like the subtitles on foreign films. The captions can be seen on television sets that are equipped with special electronic TeleCaption decoders. These decoders can be purchased for less than $200 and can easily be attached to a television. All new televisions have the built-in circuitry to decode and display closed-captioned programming.

Captions were first developed for hearing-impaired viewers but now have a valuable instructional purpose: screen reading (Koskinen, Wilson, Gambrell, & Neuman, 1993). Koskinen and her colleagues found that less fluent readers and bilingual students become more motivated readers when they use captioned television and video, and they proposed that the simultaneous multisensory processing enhances learning.

Teachers can use captioned television programs when they are broadcast, or they can videotape the programs to use later. One of the best uses is to videotape a program and use it as a pre-reading activity to build background knowledge and introduce vocabulary. Teachers might show a video related to the text students will read, or they might show the video version of the book students will read. Many fine videos, including the Reading Rainbow programs featuring award-winning children's literature, are available. Children with reading difficulties can also practice rereading captioned videos, and they can view the videos as independent reading activities.

Guidelines for Using Captioned Television Programs

1. Choose programs related to literature and content-area instruction as a before-reading activity.

2. Introduce the program and provide key vocabulary words.

3. Plan related activities to use after viewing the program.

4. Allow students learning English as a second language and students with reading difficulties to view the program several times.

5. Create a text set of books and other reading materials to use with the program

6. Provide opportunities for students to review the program and read related texts.

7. Create a video library.

Some captioned videos such as Reading Rainbow programs can be purchased from video stores and from educational publishers. Captioned programs can be videotaped from television, but copyright laws restrict the length of time they can be saved and the number of times the tapes can be used.

For more information about captioned television programs and videos, contact The National Captioning Institute, 5203 Leesburg Pike, Falls Church, VA 22041; telephone 1-800-533-WORD.

repeated readings, students deepened their understanding of the books they reread. Screen reading is another way to provide reading practice. Check the Technology Link on page 179 for more information about how to use this innovative technology.

2. Choral reading.   Students and the teacher take turns reading in choral reading. This approach is especially useful for stories and other texts that students cannot yet read independently because students can read in small groups. One variation is unison reading, in which the teacher and students read a text together (Reutzel & Cooter, 1996). The teacher is the leader and reads loudly enough to be heard above the group. Another variation is echo reading, in which the teacher reads a paragraph or page of text and then students read the same material again. Echo reading is very useful for picture books with only a sentence or two of text on each page. These approaches are especially useful for helping students who are learning English as a second language to develop appropriate phrasing and intonation.

3. Readers theatre.   A readers theatre performance is a dramatic reading of a script by a group of students. Students assume roles and rehearse reading the script. During the rehearsals, students practice reading a particular character's lines in the script and interpret the story without using much action. They communicate the mood and theme by using their voices, gestures, and facial expressions. Then students give a performance of the script for a group of classmates or another audience.

4. Listening center.   Teachers set up a tape recording of a story or other book at the listening center, and students follow along in individual copies of the book as it is read aloud. Teachers can make their own tapes, and commercially prepared tapes are also available. Students need to understand the importance of reading along with the tape in order to develop fluency. One benefit of using cassette tapes is that students can listen to the tape again and again as they practice reading the book.

5. Reading workshop.   Students choose books and read independently for 15, 30, or 45 minutes or more each day during reading workshop. Students have opportunities to reread familiar texts as well as to read new texts. Reading workshop provides opportunities for extended reading practice.

VOCABULARY DEVELOPMENT

Students' vocabularies grow at an astonishing rate—about 3,000 words a year, or roughly 7 to 10 new words every day (Nagy & Herman, 1985). By the time students finish high school, their vocabularies reach 40,000 words. In order to learn words at such an astonishing rate, it seems obvious that students learn words both in school and outside of school. Television has a significant impact on children's vocabularies, too. Teachers often assume that students learn words primarily through the lessons they teach, but students actually learn the meanings of many more words through independent reading and writing projects than through instruction.

Capable readers have larger vocabularies and a wider repertoire of strategies for figuring out the meanings of unfamiliar words than less capable readers do (McKeown, 1985). Reading widely is one of the best ways students develop their vocabularies, and that is one reason why capable readers have larger vocabularies. They simply do more reading.

Vocabulary instruction also has a place in literature-based reading classrooms. Minilessons and other word-study activities focus on words from the trade books and textbooks that students are reading. The most successful activities are meaningful to students, involve the manipulation of the words from their reading, and teach students how to figure out the meaning of unfamiliar words (Blachowicz & Lee, 1991). In traditional classrooms, the most common vocabulary activities involved listing new words on the chalkboard and directing students to write the words and copy the definitions from a dictionary or use the words in sentences. These activities are not effective and are no longer recommended.

Word Walls

Words for study are chosen from books students are reading during literature focus units or from theme studies. Teachers post word walls, made from large sheets of butcher paper, in the classroom, as Mrs. Dillon did in the vignette at the beginning of this chapter. Students and the teacher write interesting, confusing, and important words on the word wall. Usually students choose the words to write on the word wall and may even do the writing themselves. Teachers add important words that students have not chosen. Words are added to the word wall as they come up in books students are reading or during a theme study, not in advance. Students use the word wall to locate a word they want to use during a **grand conversation** or to check the spelling of a word they are writing, and teachers use the words listed on the word wall for word-study activities.

Choosing Words for Study. Teachers choose the most important words from books to teach. Important words include words that are essential to understanding the text, words that may confuse students, and words students will use as they read other books. As teachers choose words for word walls and other vocabulary activities, they

Teachers use words from the word wall for minilessons and other vocabulary activities.

consider their students, the book being read, and the instructional context. For example, during a theme on bears, first graders listened to their teacher read these books:

The Three Bears (Galdone, 1972)

Somebody and the Three Blairs (Tolhurst, 1990)

Brown Bear, Brown Bear, What Do You See? (Martin, 1983)

Polar Bear, Polar Bear, What Do You Hear? (Martin, 1991)

Alaska's Three Bears (Cartwright, 1990)

and they added these words to their word wall:

shaggy	fur	dangerous
meat-eating	polar bear	grizzly bear
claws	hind legs	hibernate
cubs	tame	brown bear
den	black bear	sharp teeth

It is important to point out that these words are vocabulary words—content-related words—not high-frequency sight words such as *who* and *their* that students learn through repetition.

During a study of Martin Luther King, Jr., seventh graders listed these words on their word wall:

discrimination	slavery	integration
segregation	protest	sit-in
Nobel Peace Prize	Jim Crow laws	civil rights
boycott	Negro	prejudice
nonviolence	activist	assassinated
martyr	Rosa Parks	Ku Klux Klan
separate but equal	NAACP	James Earl Ray

Even though all of these words and perhaps more will be added to the word wall, not all of these words will be directly taught to students. As they plan, teachers create lists of words that will probably be written on word walls during the lesson. They try to identify which words will be the sight words for their students and which words will represent new concepts. From this list, teachers choose the key words—the ones that are critical to understanding the book or the theme—and these are the words that teachers plan to highlight or include in minilessons. They also choose any words that must be introduced before reading.

Identifying some word wall words as key words does not mean that the other words are unimportant. Students have many opportunities to use all the word wall words as they write and talk about what they are reading and studying. Teachers also plan word-study activities using many of the word wall words.

Activities for Exploring Words.   Word-study activities provide opportunities for students to explore the meaning of words listed on word walls, other words related to books they are reading, and words they are learning during social studies and science units. Through these activities, students learn the meanings of words and make associations among words. None of these activities require students to simply write words and their definitions or to use the words in sentences or a contrived story.

1. Word posters.   Students choose a word from the word wall and write it on a small poster. Then they draw and color a picture to illustrate the word. They may also want to use the word in a sentence on the poster. This is one way that students can visualize the meaning of a word.

2. Word maps.   Word maps are another way to visualize a word's meaning (Duffelmeyer & Banwart, 1992–1993; Schwartz & Raphael, 1985). Students choose a word from the word wall to write in the center circle. Then they draw rays from the center and write important information about the word to make connections between the word and what they are reading or studying. Three kinds of information are included in a word map: a category for the word, examples, and characteristics or associations. Figure 5–9 shows two word maps. First graders made the first cluster, on *fox,* after reading *Rosie's Walk* (Hutchins, 1968). For the examples section, the first graders identified four stories about foxes that they had read. A fifth grader who was reading *Bunnicula: A Rabbit-Tale of Mystery* (Howe & Howe, 1979) made the second word map, on *glistened,* a word from the first chapter.

3. Dramatizing words.   Students each choose a word from the word wall and dramatize it for classmates to guess. Sometimes an action is a more effective way to explain a word than a verbal definition. That's what Mrs. Dillon found when she dramatized the word *wilted* for her second graders. Drama is an especially effective activity for students who are learning English as a second language.

4. Word sorts.   Students sort a collection of words taken from the word wall into two or more categories in a **word sort.** Usually students choose the categories they will use for the sort, but sometimes the teacher chooses them. For example, words from a story might be sorted by character, or words from a theme on machines might be sorted according to type of machine. The words can be written on cards, and then students sort a pack of word cards into piles. Or, students can cut apart a list of words, sort them into categories, and then paste the grouped words together.

5. Word chains.   Students choose a word from the word wall and then identify three or four words to sequence before or after the word to make a chain. For example, the word *tadpole* can be chained this way: *egg, tadpole, frog;* and the word *aggravate* can be chained like this: *irritate, bother, aggravate, annoy.* Students can draw and write their chains on a sheet of paper, or they can make a construction paper chain and write the words on each link.

6. Semantic feature analysis.   Students select a group of related words, such as different kinds of birds, and then make a chart to classify them according to distinguishing characteristics (Heimlich & Pittelman, 1986). A semantic feature analysis on birds is presented in Figure 5–10. Students complete the semantic feature analysis by placing a check mark by the characteristics that each bird has and a circle by those the bird lacks.

FIGURE 5–9   Two Word Maps

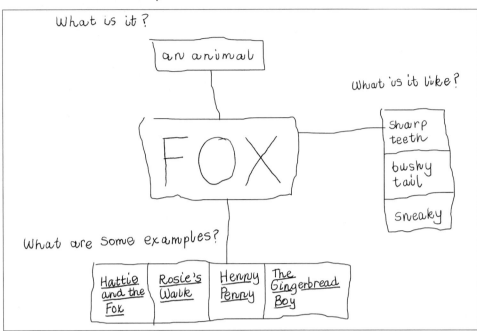

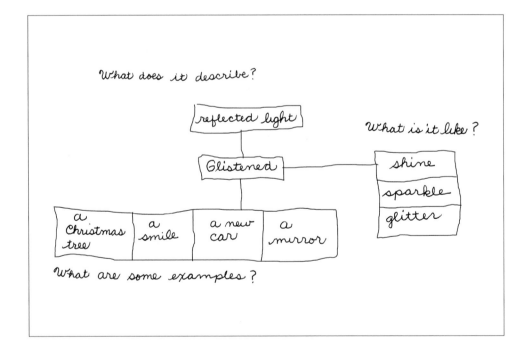

Word Meanings

As students experiment with words and concepts, their knowledge of words and meanings grows. Young children assume that every word has only one meaning, and words that sound alike, like *son* and *sun*, are confusing. Through continuing experiences with language, students become more sophisticated about words and their literal and figurative meanings. During the elementary grades, students learn about

	hatches from eggs	has feathers	has wings	can fly	can swim	migrates	is a bird of prey	is extinct
bluejay	✓	✓	✓	✓	○	○	○	○
owl	✓	✓	✓	✓	○	○	✓	○
roadrunner								
eagle								
pelican								
hummingbird								
quail								
ostrich								
dodo								
robin								
penguin								
chicken								
duck								
seagull								
peacock								
flamingo								

Code: ✓ = yes

○ = no

? = don't know

FIGURE 5–10   A Semantic Feature Analysis

words and word parts, words that mean the same as and the opposite of other words, words that sound alike, words with multiple meanings, the figurative language of idioms, and how words have been borrowed from languages around the world. They also learn about how words are created and can have fun playing with words (Tompkins, 1994; Tompkins & Yaden, 1986).

Understanding Multiple Meanings of Words.   Many words have more than one meaning. The word *bank,* for example, may have the following meanings: a piled-up mass of snow or clouds, the slope of land beside a lake or river, the slope of a road on a turn, the lateral tilting of an airplane in a turn, to cover a fire with ashes for slow burning, a business establishment that receives and lends money, a container in which money is saved, a supply for use in emergencies (e.g., a blood bank), a place for storage (e.g., a computer's memory bank), to count on, similar things arranged in a row (e.g., a bank of elevators), or to arrange things in a row. You may be surprised that there are at least a dozen meanings for the common word *bank.* How does this happen? The meanings of *bank* come from three sources. The first five meanings come from a Viking word, and they are related because they all deal with something slanted or making a slanted motion. The next five meanings come from the Italian word *banca,* a money changer's table. All these meanings deal with financial banking except for the tenth meaning, to count on, which requires a bit more thought. We use the saying "to bank on" figuratively to mean "to depend on," but it began more literally from the actual counting of money on a table. The last two meanings come from the French word *banc,* meaning bench. Words acquired multiple meanings as society became more complex and finer shades of meaning were necessary; for example, the meanings of *bank* as an emergency supply and a storage place are fairly new. As with many words with multiple meanings, it is just a linguistic accident that three original words from three languages with related meanings came to be spelled the same way.

Words assume new meanings when an affix is added or when they are compounded (combined with another word). Consider the word *fire* and the variety of words and phrases that incorporate *fire: fire hydrant, firebomb, fireproof, fireplace, firearm, fire drill, under fire, set the world on fire, fire away,* and *open fire.* Students can compile a list of words or make a booklet illustrating a set of words.

Recognizing Figurative Meanings.   Many words have both literal and figurative meanings. Literal meanings are the explicit, dictionary meanings, and figurative meanings are metaphorical or use figures of speech. For example, to describe winter as the coldest season of the year is literal, but to say that winter has icy breath is figurative. Two types of figurative language are idioms and metaphors.

Idioms are groups of words, such as "in hot water," that have a special meaning. Idioms can be confusing to students because they must be interpreted figuratively rather than literally. "In hot water" is an old expression meaning to be in trouble. Cox (1980) explains that hundreds of years ago there were no police officers and people had to protect themselves from robbers. When a robber tried to break into a house, the homeowner might pour boiling water from a second-floor window onto the head of the robber, who would then be "in hot water." There are hundreds of idioms in English, and we use them every day to create word pictures that make language more colorful. Some examples are "out in left field," "a skeleton in the closet," "stick your neck out," "a chip off the old block," and "don't cry over spilled milk."

Four excellent books of idioms for students are *Put Your Foot in Your Mouth and Other Silly Sayings* (Cox, 1980), *From the Horse's Mouth* (Nevin & Nevin, 1977), *Punching the Clock: Funny Action Idioms* (Terban, 1990), and *In a Pickle and Other Funny Idioms* (Terban, 1983). Because idioms are figurative sayings, many children—and especially those who are learning English as a second language—have difficulty learning them. It is crucial that children move beyond the literal meanings and become flexible in using language. One way for students to learn flexibility is to create idiom posters, as illustrated in Figure 5–11.

Metaphors and similes compare something to something else. A simile is a comparison signaled by the use of *like* or *as*. "The crowd was as rowdy as a bunch of marauding monkeys" and "In the moonlight the dead tree looked like a skeleton" are two examples. In contrast, a metaphor compares two things by implying that one is something else, without using *like* or *as*. "The children were frisky puppies playing in the yard" is an example. Metaphors are a stronger comparisons, as these examples show:

> She's as cool as a cucumber.
> She's a cool cucumber.

> In the moonlight, the dead tree looked like a skeleton.
> In the moonlight, the dead tree was a skeleton.

Differentiating between the terms *simile* and *metaphor* is less important than understanding the meaning of comparisons in books students read and having students use comparisons to make their writing more vivid. For example, two older students compared anger to a thunderstorm. Using a simile, one student wrote, "Anger is like a thunderstorm, screaming with thunder-feelings and lightning-words." And, as a

FIGURE 5–11   An Idiom Poster

metaphor, the other wrote, "Anger is a volcano, erupting with poisonous words and hot-lava actions."

Students begin by learning traditional comparisons such as "happy as a clam" and "high as a kite," and then they learn to notice and invent fresh, unexpected comparisons. To introduce traditional comparisons to primary-grade students, teachers use Audrey Wood's *Quick as a Cricket* (1982). Middle- and upper-grade students can locate in books and invent new comparisons for stale comparisons such as "butterflies in your stomach." In *Anastasia Krupnik,* for example, Lois Lowry (1979) substituted "ginger ale in her knees" for "butterflies in her stomach" to describe how nervous Anastasia was when she had to stand up to read her poem.

Using "Nym" Words.   There are three types of "nym" words—synonyms, antonyms, and homonyms. Synonyms are words that have the same or nearly the same meaning as other words. English has so many synonyms because so many words have been borrowed from other languages. Synonyms are useful because they provide options, allowing writers to be more precise. Think of all the different synonyms for the word *cold: cool, chilly, frigid, icy, frosty,* and *freezing.* Each word has a different shade of meaning: *cool* means moderately cold; *chilly* is uncomfortably cold; *frigid* is intensely cold; *icy* means very cold; *frosty* means covered with frost; and *freezing* is so cold that water changes into ice. Our language would be limited if we only had the word *cold.*

Antonyms are words that express the opposite meaning. Antonyms for *loud* include *soft, subdued, quiet, silent, inaudible, sedate, somber, dull,* and *colorless.* These words express shades of meaning just as synonyms do, and some opposites are more appropriate for one meaning of *loud* than for another. When *loud* means *gaudy,* for instance, opposites are *somber, dull,* or *colorless.*

Homonyms, words that have sound and spelling similarities, are divided into three categories: homophones, homographs, and homographic homophones. Homophones are words that sound alike but are spelled differently, such as *right* and *write, son* and *sun,* and *stationary* and *stationery.* Most homonyms are linguistic accidents, but *stationary* and *stationery* share an interesting history. *Stationery,* meaning paper and books, developed from *stationary.* In medieval England, merchants traveled from town to town selling their wares. The merchant who sold paper goods was the first to set up shop in one town. His shop was stationary because it did not move, and he came to be called the stationer. The spelling difference between the two words signifies the semantic difference.

Homographs are words that are spelled the same but pronounced differently. Examples of homographs are *bow, close, lead, minute, record, read,* and *wind. Bow* is a homograph that has four unrelated meanings. The verb form means "to bend in respect," and the noun form may mean "a gathering of ribbon," "a weapon for propelling an arrow," or the "forward end of a ship."

Homographic homophones are words that are spelled and pronounced alike, such as *bark, bat, bill, box, fair, fly, hide, jet, mine, pen, ring, row, spell, toast,* and *yard.* Some are related words, but most are linguistic accidents. The various meanings were never meant to be spelled the same. The different meanings of *toast,* for example, came from the same Latin source word, *torrere* (to parch, bake). The derivation of the noun *toast* as heated and browned slices of bread is obvious; however, the relationship between the source word and *toast* as a verb, drinking to someone's honor or health, is not immediately apparent. The connection is that toasted, spiced bread flavored the drinks used in making toasts. There are many books of homonyms for children, including Gwynne's *The King Who Rained* (1970), *A Chocolate Moose for Dinner*

(1976), *The Sixteen Hand Horse* (1980), and *A Little Pigeon Toad* (1988); Maestro's *What's a Frank Frank? Tasty Homograph Riddles* (1984); *Homographic Homophones* (Hanson, 1973); and *Eight Ate: A Feast of Homonym Riddles* (Terban, 1982).

Teaching Students How to Unlock Word Meanings

The goal of vocabulary instruction is for students to learn how to learn new words, but traditional approaches, such as assigning students to look up the definitions of a list of words in a dictionary, often fail to produce in-depth understanding (Nagy, 1988). Carr and Wixon (1986) provide four guidelines for effective instruction:

■ Instruction should help students relate new words to their background knowledge.

■ Instruction should help students develop ownership-level word knowledge.

■ Instruction should provide for students' active involvement in learning new words.

■ Instruction should develop students' strategies for learning new words independently.

Students use four strategies to learn the meanings of words as they read or listen to information presented orally. These strategies are similar to the ones students use to decode words. The four strategies are:

1. *Phonics.* Students use their knowledge of phoneme-grapheme relationships to pronounce an unknown word, and they often recognize the word's meaning when they hear it pronounced.

2. *Morphological analysis.* Students peel the affixes off the word and then use their knowledge of root words, prefixes, and suffixes to figure out the meaning of the word.

3. *Context clues.* Students use the surrounding information in the sentence to predict the meaning of the unknown word. Context clues take a variety of forms. Sometimes the word is defined in the sentence or later in the paragraph, while at other times synonyms or antonyms are used or examples give students an idea of the meaning of the word.

4. *Reference books.* Students locate the unknown word in a dictionary or thesaurus and read the definition or synonyms and antonyms to determine the meaning.

Students have opportunities to develop these strategies as they tap into prior knowledge, read widely and write often, participate in minilessons, and learn to use the dictionary and other reference books. Guidelines for vocabulary instruction are reviewed in Figure 5–12.

Tapping Into Prior Knowledge. Students recognize words they know slightly, and remember words they are learning more easily, when they tap into what they already know about a topic. Teachers help students think about what they know about a topic by collecting books into text sets and teaching social studies and science as units or theme studies. Words that are conceptually related are easier to remember. Students also tap into prior knowledge when they brainstorm lists, make **K-W-L charts,** draw **story maps** and **clusters,** record information on **data charts,** and use other graphic organizers.

FIGURE 5–12   Guidelines for Vocabulary Instruction

1. Words to Study

Teachers and students choose words for vocabulary instruction from literature focus units and across-the-curriculum theme studies. Word study grows out of what students are reading and learning about in the classroom.

2. Prior Knowledge

Teachers encourage students to activate their prior knowledge about the topic before reading. When students connect what they already know about a topic with what they are reading, learning new words is easier.

3. Word Walls

Students and teachers select important and interesting words to display on word walls during literature focus units and across-the-curriculum theme studies. Teachers highlight a few key terms before reading, and then students and teachers choose other words to add during and after reading.

4. Choosing Words to Teach

Teachers choose the most important words from reading selections to add to word walls and for word-study activities. These words are essential to understanding the text and useful enough that students will read them again in other books. These words are not high-frequency sight words such as *what* or *because,* but content-rich words.

5. The Four Language Arts

Teachers connect vocabulary study with all four language arts—listening, talking, reading, and writing. As students listen to classmates use the word wall words and use them themselves as they talk, read, and write, they learn how to use the words and what their meanings are.

6. Vocabulary Activities

Teachers plan word-study activities so that students can explore words after reading. Activities include word posters, word maps, dramatizing words, word sorts, word chains, and semantic feature analysis.

7. Minilessons

Teachers present minilessons on these strategies for unlocking word meanings: phonics, morphological analysis, context clues, and using reference books. Other minilessons focus on word-meanings, including multiple meanings, figurative meanings, and the "nym" words.

8. Wide Reading

Students learn only a small percentage of the 3,000 or more words they learn each year through teacher-directed lessons and activities. Wide reading is far more important in developing students' vocabularies.

9. Dictionaries and Reference Books

Students use dictionaries or other reference books to check the meaning of words or to learn more information about words. Teachers don't ask students to copy definitions of words or to write words in sentences or contrived stories.

In the vignette at the beginning of this chapter, Mrs. Dillon encouraged students to tap into their knowledge and experiences with flowers as they shared the vase of flowers she brought to class before introducing *Chrysanthemum*. And, because they had already accessed their schemata on flowers, Mrs. Dillon's second graders were better able to remember the names of the flowers mentioned in the story. An added benefit was that students were motivated to read the story to find out what the connection was between flowers and mice.

Wide Reading.   Researchers report that wide reading is an important contributor to general vocabulary development (Baumann & Kameenui, 1991; Beck & McKeown, 1991). In fact, encouraging students to read is probably the most important way teachers promote vocabulary growth (Nagy, 1988). As they read, students are actively engaged in meaningful, language-rich tasks and have many opportunities to develop problem-solving strategies for unlocking the meanings of words. Through repeated encounters with a word as they read text sets, students collect clues to the word's meaning and gather a variety of associations. They deepen their level of knowledge about words through reading, moving to a deeper, richer, and more flexible word knowledge. Wide reading also helps readers develop and retain meaningful personal contexts for words.

An interesting new approach is to use captioned television to promote vocabulary growth (Koskinen, Wilson, Gambrell, & Neuman, 1993). As students view captioned television programs and the videos made from these programs, they see the text printed on the screen as they hear the words spoken. This multisensory approach is especially powerful for students learning English as a second language and for poor readers. For more information about captioned videos, see the Technology Link on page 179.

Extensive Writing.   Writing is also important, because after students meet words in reading, they interact with the words a second time by writing them in **reading logs** or in projects. Repeated exposure to words is crucial because students need to see and use the word many times before it becomes a part of their "ownership dictionaries"— words they understand and use competently. Whenever students are writing responses to books or completing writing projects as part of literature focus units and theme studies, they are reinforcing their understanding of word meanings.

Students can also write definitions to reinforce their understanding of word meanings. The teacher provides a frame for the definition, such as:

Word is _____ . It is _____ , _____ , and _____ .
It is never _____ or _____ . *Word* is a _____ .

Mrs. Dillon's class wrote the following definition for *chrysanthemum* (the flower, not the mouse in the story) using this sentence frame:

> Chrysanthemum is a flower. It grows outside in the fall and you can buy it at Vons Supermarket anytime. It is sort of a smelly plant. It can be yellow or orange or white or purple. It is never pink or blue. Chrysanthemum is a flower with hundreds of little petals.

The students began composing their definition by brainstorming all the things they knew about chrysanthemums, and Mrs. Dillon wrote their brainstormed list on a chart. Then they chose information from their list to compose the definition.

Students learn words as they write reading log entries and participate in collaborative writing projects during literature focus units.

Here's a definition the class wrote for *epilogue:*

The epilogue is the part at the end of the book. It is short and it tells you how everything turns out. It is never at the beginning of a book. Only a few books like Chrysanthemum *have an epilogue at the end.*

Minilessons.   Teachers present minilessons to focus on key words and teach strategies for unlocking word meanings. These lessons should focus on words that students are reading and writing and involve students in meaningful activities. Students make tentative predictions about the meaning of unfamiliar words as they read, using a combination of context clues, structural analysis, and their own prior knowledge (Blachowicz, 1993). Later, teachers often ask students to return to important words after reading to check their understanding of the word. Teachers can use the following procedure to help students deepen their understanding of an unfamiliar word (Blachowicz & Zabroske, 1990):

1. *Highlight the sentence with the new word.*   The teacher rereads the sentence with the new word from the text that has already been read and then asks students to make a prediction about the word's meaning. They might offer a definition or suggest attributes, examples, and associations, and they also explain the rationalization for their hypotheses.

2. ***Provide information about the word.***   The teacher provides more information about the word or mentions other contexts in which the word is used. Then the teacher asks students to think about their predictions and confirm or refine them.

3. ***Ask questions.***   The teacher asks a question or two involving the meaning of the word or asks students to suggest a definition. If necessary, the teacher offers a definition.

4. ***Use the word meaningfully.***   The teacher encourages students to use the word in meaningful reading, writing, and talk activities.

This strategy works best for words that students have a background of knowledge about and for words that are concrete. It is not suitable for words that represent unfamiliar concepts.

For example, in the first chapter of *Bunnicula: A Rabbit-Tale of Mystery* (Howe & Howe, 1979), the word *mongrel* is presented in this sentence: "Now, most people might call me a mongrel, but I have some pretty fancy bloodlines running through these veins and Russian wolfhound happens to be one of them" (pp. 8–9). After reading the first chapter, the teacher might focus on the character of the dog named Harold and reread this sentence and ask students what the word *mongrel* means. The sentence provides some useful information about breeds that students can use to make a prediction about the meaning of the word. Students guess that a mongrel is a kind of dog or a breed of dog. Next the teacher might show a picture of her pet and say, "My dog is a mongrel, too. He's part collie and part German shepherd." The teacher's sentence helps to clarify the meaning of mongrel, and students notice the phrase "one of them" at the end of the sentence about Harold. They revise their predictions now that they understand that a mongrel is a mixed-breed dog. Several students talk about their pets and tell whether or not their dogs are mongrels. The discussion about Harold continues, and the information that he is a mixed-breed dog adds to the portrait of Harold created in the first chapter.

For other minilessons on key words and strategies for unlocking word meanings, teachers can use the following instructional procedure, which embodies Carr and Wixon's (1986) characteristics of effective vocabulary instruction and is based on the procedure for minilessons outlined in Chapter 4:

1. ***Introduce the word or strategy.***   Teachers introduce the key word (or words) and explain its meaning, tying the word to students' background knowledge and the context in which the word is used. Or they introduce the strategy and explain how it is used in reading or writing.

2. ***Add more explanation or information.***   Teachers and students use the word in context or practice the strategy. For word study, they identify the root word, talk about the etymology of the word, and consider related words or easily confused words, if appropriate.

3. ***Provide practice.***   Teachers involve students in activities to bring together all the information—semantic, structural, and contextual—presented earlier.

4. ***Review.***   Teachers and students review the word and the strategies used in identifying the word and learning its meaning. Students can add the word to vocabulary notebooks or make a poster to review the information they have learned. For

Effective Practices

1. Teachers teach high-frequency words because they are the most useful for students.

2. Teachers and students make dictionaries of high-frequency words and other sight words.

3. Teachers teach five decoding strategies and related skills—phonics, analogies, context clues, morphemic analysis, and syllabic analysis.

4. Teachers teach students to "peel" affixes from root words to identify the word and unlock the meaning of the word.

5. Students develop fluency by reading easy-to-read books and other books at their reading levels.

6. Students read stories and informational books daily because they learn many new words through reading.

7. Teachers and students post interesting content-related words on word walls after reading.

8. Teachers choose the most useful words from the word wall for vocabulary activities.

9. Teachers involve students in meaningful word-study activities, such as word maps, dramatizing words, and word sorts.

10. Teachers give minilessons on multiple meanings of words, figurative meanings, and "nym" words using examples from trade books.

Ineffective Practices

1. Teachers don't emphasize high-frequency words over less common words.

2. Teachers don't differentiate between sight words and words that can be decoded easily.

3. Teachers encourage students to depend on only one or two decoding strategies—usually phonics.

4. Teachers use worksheets to teach root words and affixes without explaining how to decode longer words when reading.

5. Teachers don't recognize the importance of having students become fluent readers.

6. Teachers provide few opportunities for students to read books.

7. Teachers introduce all vocabulary before reading.

8. Teachers expect students to study all vocabulary words.

9. Teachers have students copy definitions from the dictionary or use lists of words in sentences or stories.

10. Teachers don't connect lessons on words to literature students are reading.

strategies to unlock word meanings, students can review the steps in using the strategy and the contexts in which the strategy is useful.

5. *Apply.* Teachers provide opportunities for students to use the word in meaningful ways. They need to read the word; write the word; use the word in discussions, debates, and oral reports; and use the word in class, small-group, and individual projects. For strategies, teachers provide similar opportunities for students to apply the strategy and then reflect on how they have used it.

Using the Dictionary and Other References. Dictionaries, thesauruses, and other reference books should be available in the classroom for students to use. When students want to check meanings of unfamiliar words or learn how to pronounce and spell words, they should use a dictionary. A variety of dictionaries are available for primary-, middle-, and upper-grade students. Students use thesauruses to locate synonyms and related words, and they sometimes use rhyming dictionaries to locate rhyming words when writing poetry or making jingles. They use atlases, almanacs, and encyclopedias to locate facts and other kinds of information.

In order to use a dictionary or other reference book, students need to use alphabetical order to locate an item. It is helpful when students know how to use guide words located at the top of each dictionary page or how to use an index to locate information in reference books. Teachers can teach minilessons about how to use dictionaries and other reference books.

■ **Activity**

Choose a trade book or selection from a basal reading textbook and design vocabulary instruction using it. Identify a list of words for a word wall, plan several word-study activities, and develop several minilessons related to the words and strategies for unlocking the meanings of words.

Review

Students learn both to identify words in order to develop reading fluency and to understand the meanings of words as they add approximately 3,000 words to their vocabularies every year. They learn some of the words through instruction that teachers provide, but they learn far more words through reading, writing, watching television, and other activities outside of school. Teachers have an important role in teaching students how to use strategies for identifying words and unlocking their meanings so that they can figure out unfamiliar words independently. Words should always be studied as part of meaningful reading and writing activities or content-area study. The figure on page 194 presents a list of recommended practices that effective teachers use in teaching word identification and vocabulary.

References

Baumann, J. F., & Kameenui, E. J. (1991). Research on vocabulary instruction: Ode to Voltaire. In J. Flood, J. M. Jensen, D. Lapp, & J. R. Squire (Eds.), *Handbook on teaching the English language arts* (pp. 604–632). New York: Macmillan.

Beck, I., & McKeown, M. (1991). Conditions of vocabulary acquisition. In R. Barr, M. Kamil, P. Mosenthal, & P. D. Pearson (Eds.), *Handbook of reading research* (Vol. 2, pp. 789–814). White Plains, NY: Longman.

Blachowicz, C. L. Z. (1993). C(2)QU: Modeling context use in the classroom. *The Reading Teacher, 47,* 268–269.

Blachowicz, C. L. Z., & Lee, J. J. (1991). Vocabulary development in the whole literacy classroom. *The Reading Teacher, 45,* 188–195.

Blachowicz, C. L. Z., & Zabroske, B. (1990). Context instruction: A metacognitive approach for at-risk readers. *Journal of Reading, 33,* 504–508.

Bridge, C. A., Winograd, P. N., & Haley, D. (1983). Using predictable materials vs. preprimers to teach beginning sight words. *The Reading Teacher, 36,* 884–891.

Calfee, R., & Drum, P. (1986). Research on teaching reading. In M. W. Wittrock (Ed.), *Handbook of research on teaching* (3rd ed.) (pp. 804–849). New York: Macmillan.

Carr, E., & Wixon, K. K. (1986). Guidelines for evaluating vocabulary instruction. *Journal of Reading, 29,* 588–595.

Chall, J. S., Jacobs, V. A., & Baldwin, L. E. (1990). *The reading crisis: Why poor children fall behind.* Cambridge, MA: Harvard University Press.

Clay, M. M. (1985). *The early detection of reading difficulties* (2nd ed.). Portsmouth, NH: Heinemann.

Clay, M. M. (1991). *Becoming literate: The construction of inner control.* Portsmouth, NH: Heinemann.

Cunningham, P. M. (1975–1976). Investigating a synthesized theory of mediated word identification. *Reading Research Quarterly, 11,* 127–143.

Cunningham, P. M. (1995). *Phonics they use: Words for reading and writing* (2nd ed.). New York: Harper-Collins.

Delpit, L. (1987). The silenced dialogue: Power and pedagogy in educating other people's children. *Harvard Educational Review, 58,* 280–298.

Duffelmeyer, F. A., & Banwart, B. H. (1992–1993). Word maps for adjectives and verbs. *The Reading Teacher, 46,* 351–353.

Eeds, M. (1985). Bookwords: Using a beginning word list of high-frequency words from children's literature K–3. *The Reading Teacher, 38,* 418–423.

Eldredge, J. L. (1995). *Teaching decoding in holistic classrooms.* Englewood Cliffs, NJ: Prentice Hall.

Gaskins, R. W., Gaskins, J. W., & Gaskins, I. W. (1991). A decoding program for poor readers—and the rest of the class, too! *Language Arts, 68,* 213–225.

Graves, M. (1985). *A word is a word . . . or is it?* Portsmouth, NH: Heinemann.

Heimlich, J. E., & Pittelman, S. D. (1986). *Semantic mapping: Classroom applications.* Newark, DE: International Reading Association.

Hiebert, E. H. (1991). The development of word-level strategies in authentic literacy tasks. *Language Arts, 68,* 234–240.

Hitchcock, M. E. (1989). *Elementary students' invented spellings at the correct stage of spelling development.* Unpublished doctoral dissertation, Norman, University of Oklahoma.

Johnson, D. D., & Baumann, J. F. (1984). Word identification. In P. D. Pearson (Ed.), *Handbook of reading research* (pp. 583–608). New York: Longman.

Juel, C. (1991). Beginning reading. In R. Barr, M. Kamil, P. Mosenthal, & P. D. Pearson (Eds.), *Handbook of reading research* (Vol. 2, pp. 759–788). New York: Longman.

Koskinen, P. S., Wilson, R. M., Gambrell, L. B., & Neuman, S. B. (1993). Captioned video and vocabulary learning: An innovative practice in literacy instruction. *The Reading Teacher, 47,* 36–43.

LaBerge, D., & Samuels, S. J. (1976). Toward a theory of automatic information processing in reading. In H. Singer & R. Ruddell (Eds.), *Theoretical models and processes of reading* (pp. 548–579). Newark, DE: International Reading Association.

McKeown, M. G. (1985). The acquisition of word meaning from context by children of high and low ability. *Reading Research Quarterly, 20,* 482–496.

Nagy, W. E. (1988). *Teaching vocabulary to improve reading comprehension.* Urbana, IL: ERIC Clearinghouse on Reading and Communication Skills and the National Council of Teachers of English and the International Reading Association.

Nagy, W. E., & Herman, P. (1985). Incidental vs. instructional approaches to increasing reading vocabulary. *Educational Perspectives, 23,* 16–21.

Perfitti, C. A. (1985). *Reading ability.* New York: Oxford University Press.

Reutzel, D. R., & Cooter, R. B., Jr. (1996). *Teaching children to read: From basals to books* (2nd ed.). Englewood Cliffs, NJ: Merrill/Prentice Hall.

Reyes, M. de la Luz. (1991). A process approach to literacy using dialogue journals and literature logs with second language learners. *Research in the Teaching of English, 25,* 291–313.

Samuels, S. J. (1979). The method of repeated readings. *The Reading Teacher, 32,* 403–408.

Schwartz, R., & Raphael, T. (1985). Concept of definition: A key to improving students' vocabulary. *The Reading Teacher, 39,* 198–205.

Shefelbine, J. (1995). *The role of phonics in a balanced literacy program.* Staff development program at Madera Unified School District, Madera, CA.

Stanovich, K. (1980). Toward an interactive-compensatory model of individual differences in the development of reading fluency. *Reading Research Quarterly, 16,* 37–71.

Stanovich, K. E. (1986). Matthew effects in reading: Some consequences of individual differences in the acquisition of literacy. *Reading Research Quarterly, 21,* 360–406.

Tompkins, G. E. (1994). *Teaching writing: Balancing process and product* (2nd ed.). Englewood Cliffs, NJ: Merrill/Prentice Hall.

Tompkins, G. E., & Yaden, D. B., Jr. (1986). *Answering students' questions about words.* Urbana, IL: ERIC Clearinghouse on Reading and Communication Skills and the National Council of Teachers of English.

White, T. G., Sowell, J., & Yanagihara, A. (1989). Teaching elementary students to use word-part clues. *The Reading Teacher, 42,* 302–308.

Yaden, D. B., Jr. (1988). Understanding stories through repeated read-alouds: How many does it take? *The Reading Teacher, 41,* 556–560.

Children's Book References

Cartwright, S. (1990). *Alaska's three bears.* Homer, AK: Paws IV Publishing Company.

Cole, J. (1986). *Hungry, hungry sharks.* New York: Random House.

Cox, J. A. (1980). *Put your foot in your mouth and other silly sayings.* New York: Random House.

Galdone, P. (1972). *The three bears.* New York: Clarion Books.

Gwynne, F. (1970). *The king who rained.* New York: Windmill Books.

Gwynne, F. (1976). *A chocolate moose for dinner.* New York: Windmill Books.

Gwynne, F. (1980). *The sixteen hand horse.* New York: Prentice Hall.

Gwynne, F. (1988). *A little pigeon toad.* New York: Simon & Schuster.

Hanson, J. (1973). *Homographic homophones.* Minneapolis, MN: Lerner.

Heller, R. (1983). *The reason for a flower.* New York: Grosset & Dunlap.

Henkes, K. (1991). *Chrysanthemum*. New York: Greenwillow.

Howe, D., & Howe, J. (1979). *Bunnicula: A rabbit-tale of mystery*. New York: Atheneum.

Hutchins, P. (1968). *Rosie's walk*. New York: Macmillan.

Kellogg, S. (1979). *Pinkerton, behave!* New York: Dial.

Kraus, R. (1970). *Whose mouse are you?* New York: Macmillan.

Lewison, W. C. (1992). *"Buzz," said the bee*. New York: Scholastic.

Lobel, A. (1970). *Frog and toad are friends*. New York: Harper & Row.

Lobel, A. (1984). *The rose in my garden*. New York: Morrow.

Lobel, A. (1990). *Alison's zinnia*. New York: Greenwillow.

Lowry, L. (1979). *Anastasia Krupnik*. Boston: Houghton Mifflin.

Maestro, G. (1984). *What's a frank Frank? Tasty homograph riddles*. New York: Clarion Books.

Martin, B., Jr. (1983). *Brown bear, brown bear, what do you see?* New York: Holt, Rinehart & Winston.

Martin, B., Jr. (1991). *Polar bear, polar bear, what do you hear?* New York: Henry Holt.

Mayer, M. (1968). *There's a nightmare in my closet*. New York: Dial.

Nevin, A., & Nevin, D. (1977). *From the horse's mouth*. Englewood Cliffs, NJ: Prentice Hall.

Pallotta, J. (1988). *The flower alphabet book*. Watertown, MA: Charlesbridge.

Parish, P. (1963). *Amelia Bedelia*. New York: Harper & Row.

Terban, M. (1982). *Eight ate: A feast of homonym riddles*. New York: Clarion Books.

Terban, M. (1983). *In a pickle and other funny idioms*. New York: Clarion Books.

Terban, M. (1990). *Punching the clock: Funny action idioms*. New York: Clarion Books.

Tolhurst, M. (1990). *Somebody and the three Blairs*. New York: Orchard Books.

Wood, A. (1982). *Quick as a cricket*. London: Child's Play.

CHAPTER 6
The Structure of Text

The first graders in Mrs. Simmons's class are studying insects. They began by talking about insects and making a **K-W-L chart** (Ogle, 1986) (see the Compendium for more information about this and all other highlighted terms in this chapter), listing what they already know about insects in the "K: What We Know" column and things they want to learn in the "W: What We Want to Learn" column. At the end of the unit, students will finish the chart by listing what they have learned in the "L: What We Have Learned" column. The first graders name some of the insects they already know and ask if spiders are insects. Mrs. Simmons makes a mental note to teach a lesson comparing insects and spiders later in the unit.

The first graders read Eric Carle's insect stories: *The Very Hungry Caterpillar* (1969), a story that illustrates the life cycle of a butterfly; *The Very Quiet Cricket* (1990), a multisensory story about a cricket who is very quiet until he meets another cricket; and *The Grouchy Ladybug* (1986), a story about a ladybug who is looking for a fight and challenges every animal she meets. Mrs. Simmons encourages her students to read aesthetically and enjoy the reading experience. Later, as they reread the stories, Mrs. Simmons asks them to look for scientific information about insects, and she adds this information to the K-W-L chart.

Alberto talks about the scientific information he and his classmates found in *The Grouchy Ladybug:* "We learned that ladybugs like to eat things called aphids and we learned that ladybugs can fly. But we don't think that ladybugs are really grouchy or friendly like in the story. Something else is that they don't really try to fight with big animals like whales and rhinos."

Another day, Mrs. Simmons brings the materials to make an ant farm to the classroom. She reads *If You Were an Ant* (Calder, 1989), an informational book told through the eyes of an ant, and she asks students to try to remember the important information about ants so that they can make a chart after reading. This is their chart of 10 important facts about ants:

1. *Ants live together in colonies.*
2. *Worker ants make the nest and gather food.*
3. *The queen is the biggest ant and she lays eggs.*
4. *Ants are insects.*
5. *Ants have six legs.*
6. *Ants have combs on their front legs to comb their legs and antennae.*
7. *Ants eat caterpillars, flies, and beetles.*
8. *Ants can lift things that are 10 times heavier than they are.*
9. *Ants protect themselves by biting and stinging.*
10. *Enemies are anteaters, frogs, birds, and other ants.*

After compiling this information, Mrs. Simmons and her students follow the directions at the end of the book for making an ant farm as they make their own.

Mrs. Simmons gives students a purpose for reading or listening to each book read aloud. She asks her students to remember information for the class charts they plan to develop. Together they develop charts describing parts of an insect's body,

FIGURE 6–1   Two Pages From a First Grader's Insect Book

comparing insects and people, sequencing the stages in the life cycle of an insect, and listing ways insects help people.

Before reading *It's a Good Thing There Are Insects* (Fowler, 1990), an easy-to-read informational book, Mrs. Simmons asks her students whether insects are helpful or hurtful. Several students comment that insects like bees can hurt people and that most people don't like insects. She tells them that after reading she will ask them to decide if insects are helpful or not. She passes out copies of the book—one for each pair of students—and invites them to look through the book and identify many of the insects in the photo illustrations with their reading buddies. Then the class reads the book using shared reading. Students read along as Mrs. Simmons reads aloud. She often purchases enough copies of a book for half of her class and has the students read with buddies. In this way she can stretch her instructional materials budget and provide opportunities for buddy reading.

After reading, students have a **grand conversation** to talk about the book. Based on the information presented in the book, the class reaches the conclusion that insects are very helpful. From their discussion, the first graders compile this chart:

Ways Insects Help Us

1. *We get silk from silkworms.*

2. *We get honey from bees.*

3. Bees pollinate flowers.

4. Some insects are pretty to look at.

5. Ladybugs eat bad insects.

Alicia talks about this chart and how the first graders make charts: "Mrs. Simmons asked us if insects are good or bad, and we learned that they are good. We made this chart with five ways they are good. We learned about these five ways from a book that Mrs. Simmons read to us. We remembered the important stuff so we can make this chart."

Later, students use what they have learned about insects to write their own insect books. As they prepare to write, the first graders reread some of the insect books in the classroom library and the charts that the class has developed. Juan writes a book contrasting people and insects titled "I Am Not a Bug!" Two pages from his book are shown in Figure 6–1. He reflects on how he created his book: "I was just thinking about how I am not a bug and how bugs are different from people. Then I thought I could say 'I am not a bug' on every page. I looked at the chart and thought of these ways I am different. Then I just wrote my book. The best part is when I read it in the author's chair. I yelled the part 'But I am not!' and everybody laughed. That means I am a good writer."

Mrs. Simmons's students also read poems about insects from *The Random House Book of Poetry for Children* (Prelutsky, 1983) that she copied onto charts. Students read the poems using **choral reading.** One of their favorites is "Wasps" (p. 74), a very short rhyming verse. Students decide to write their own poems following the rhyming pattern of "Wasps," and here are two of their pattern poems:

Ants	*Beetles*
Ants like vanilla ice cream.	*Beetles like hot dogs.*
Peanut butter sandwiches.	*Potato chips.*
Tea.	*Tea.*
Chocolate cake.	*Watermelon.*
Apple juice.	*Chocolate chip cookies.*
Me.	*Me.*

Evelyn talks about the "Ants" poem she wrote and her classmates' poems: "We wanted to make our poems like 'Wasps' so we kept *tea* and *me* because they rhyme. Then we thought about other insects and we brainstormed foods that are sweet and insects would really like. I picked my favorite foods for my poem. I think ants would like them, too."

To end the unit, Mrs. Simmons asks her students to finish the K-W-L chart. In the third column, "L: What We Have Learned," students list some of the information they have learned, including:

Insects have six legs.
The life cycle of a butterfly is: egg, caterpillar, chrysalis, and adult.
Insects usually die before their first birthday.
It is good luck to find a ladybug.
Insects hatch from eggs.
Mosquitoes and fleas are pests.
Bees give us honey.

Insects have exoskeletons.
Insects and spiders are different.
Insects' noses are on their antennae.
Insects have three body parts.
Some insects can fly, but some cannot.
There are a million different insects on Earth.

*E*lementary students read all three types of literature—stories, informational books, and poems—just as the students in Mrs. Simmons's classroom do. These "real" books are called trade books. Most students also use reading textbooks (sometimes called basal readers) and social studies, science, math, and other content-area textbooks. Reading textbooks also contain stories, informational articles, and poetry. In recent years there has been a great deal of controversy about whether trade books or textbooks should be used to teach reading. Lapp, Flood, and Farnan (1992) believe that textbooks and trade books are compatible and that students should read both types.

In contrast, Goodman (1988) recommended using trade books because he found that more than half of the stories, informational articles, and poems were abbreviated in textbooks. Texts have been abbreviated by avoiding less frequently used words, shortening the sentences, and controlling the vocabulary. When these changes are made, the style and voice of the original is lost. Goodman called this the "basalization" of children's literature. Since he made this charge, textbook publishers have worked to increase the number of authentic texts in their books, but many times the stories and other pieces in basal readers are either adapted or especially written for the textbook. Newer textbooks contain complete stories, poems, and informational articles. The position in this book is that children need a wide range of reading materials, including the best literature available as well as books students can read independently. Beginning teachers often rely on basal readers and move toward incorporating trade books in their reading programs as they gain confidence in their teaching abilities, or in response to the expectations of administrators and parents.

Stories, informational books, and poems have unique structures or organizational patterns. Stories are organized differently from poems and informational books. For example, *The Very Hungry Caterpillar* (Carle, 1969) is a repetitive story that chronicles the life cycle of a butterfly, while *The Icky Bug Counting Book* (Pallotta, 1992) is an informational book highlighting 26 different species of insects, one on each page. Sometimes teachers call all literature that students read and write "stories," but stories are unique. They have specific structural elements, including characters and plot. Teachers need to introduce the three types of literature and use the labels for each type correctly.

The stories students write reflect the stories they have read. De Ford (1981) and Eckhoff (1983) found that when primary-grade students read the selections in basal reading textbooks, the stories they write reflect the short, choppy linguistic style of the readers, but when students read stories published as picture books and chapter books, their writing reflects the more sophisticated language structures and literary style of these books. Dressel (1990) also found that the quality of fifth graders' writing was dependent on the quality of the stories they read and listened to read aloud, regardless of students' reading levels. Similarly, when students learn about the structure of informational books and content-area textbooks, both their reading comprehension and their nonfiction writing improve (Flood, Lapp, & Farnan, 1986; McGee & Richgels, 1985; Piccolo, 1987).

In this chapter, you will learn about the structure of stories, informational books, and poems. As you read, think about these questions:

- How are stories organized?
- How are informational books organized?
- How are poems structured?
- How does the structure of text affect children's reading and writing?

■ *Activity*

Collect a text set of five or six stories, informational books, and poems on a science topic, such as whales, deserts, rain forests, insects, or frogs, to examine as you read this chapter.

ELEMENTS OF STORY STRUCTURE

Stories give meaning to the human experience, and they are a powerful way of knowing and learning. When preschool children listen to family members tell stories and read them aloud, they develop an understanding or concept about stories by the time they come to school. Students use and refine this knowledge as they read and write stories during the elementary grades. Many educators, including Jerome Bruner (1986), recommend using stories as a way into literacy.

Stories are available in picture book and chapter book formats. Picture books have brief texts, usually spread over 32 pages, in which text and illustrations combine to tell a story. The text is minimal, and the illustrations supplement the sparse text. The illustrations in many picture books are striking. Many picture books, such as *Rosie's Walk* (Hutchins, 1968), are for primary-grade students, but others, such as *Jumanji* (Van Allsburg, 1981), were written with middle-grade students in mind. Fairy tales have also been retold as picture books. Trina Schart Hyman's *The Sleeping*

Students learn about the structure of stories as they dramatize a familiar story.

Beauty (1977) is an especially beautiful picture book. Another type of picture book is wordless picture books, such as *Tuesday* (Wiesner, 1991) and *Good Dog, Carl* (Day, 1985), in which the story is told entirely through the illustrations.

Chapter books are longer stories written in a chapter format. Most are written for older students, but Patricia Reilly Giff's series of stories about the kids at the Polk Street School, including *The Beast in Ms. Rooney's Room* (1984) and *Fish Face* (1984), are for students reading at the second-grade level. Chapter books for middle-grade students include *Charlotte's Web* (White, 1952) and *Bunnicula: A Rabbit-Tale of Mystery* (Howe & Howe, 1979). Complex stories such as *The Giver* (Lowry, 1993) are more suitable for upper-grade students. Chapter books have few illustrations, if any, and the illustrations do not play an integral role in the book.

Stories have unique structural elements that distinguish them from other forms of literature. Five story elements are plot, characters, setting, point of view, and theme. These elements work together to structure a story, and authors manipulate them to make their stories hold readers' attention.

Plot

Plot is the sequence of events involving characters in conflict situations. A story's plot is based on the goals of one or more characters and the processes they go through to attain these goals (Lukens, 1995). The main characters want to achieve a goal, and other characters are introduced to oppose the main characters or prevent them from being successful. The story events are set in motion by characters as they attempt to overcome conflict, reach their goals, and solve their problems.

The most basic aspect of plot is the division of the main events of a story into three parts: beginning, middle, and end. In *The Tale of Peter Rabbit* (Potter, 1902), for instance, the three story parts are easy to pick out. As the story begins, Mrs. Rabbit sends her children out to play after warning them not to go into Mr. McGregor's garden. In the middle, Peter goes to Mr. McGregor's garden and is almost caught. Then Peter finds his way out of the garden and gets home safely—the end of the story. Students can make a **story map** of the beginning-middle-end of a story using words and pictures, as the story map for *The Tale of Peter Rabbit* in Figure 6–2 shows.

Specific types of information are included in each of the three story parts. In the beginning, the characters are introduced, the setting is described, and a problem is presented. Together, the characters, setting, and events develop the plot and sustain the theme through the story. In the middle, the plot unfolds, with each event preparing readers for what will follow. Conflict heightens as the characters face roadblocks that keep them from solving their problems. How the characters tackle these problems adds suspense to keep readers interested. In the end, all is reconciled, and readers learn whether or not the characters' struggles are successful.

Conflict is the tension or opposition between forces in the plot, and it is what interests readers enough to continue reading the story. Conflict usually occurs

- between a character and nature
- between a character and society
- between characters
- within a character (Lukens, 1995)

FIGURE 6–2   A Beginning-Middle-End Story Map for *The Tale of Peter Rabbit*

Conflict between a character and nature occurs in stories in which severe weather plays an important role, as in *Julie of the Wolves* (George, 1972), and in stories set in isolated geographic locations, such as *Island of the Blue Dolphins* (O'Dell, 1960), in which the Indian girl Karana struggles to survive alone on a Pacific island.

In some stories, a character's activities and beliefs differ from those of other members of the society, and the differences cause conflict between that character and the local society. One example of this type of conflict is *The Witch of Blackbird Pond* (Speare, 1958), in which Kit Tyler is accused of being a witch because she continues activities in a New England Puritan community that were acceptable in the Caribbean community where she grew up but are not acceptable in her new home. Conflict between characters is common in children's literature. In *Tales of a Fourth Grade Nothing* (Blume, 1972), for instance, the never-ending conflict between Peter and his little brother Fudge is what makes the story interesting. The fourth type of conflict is conflict within a character. In *Ira Sleeps Over* (Waber, 1972), six-year-old Ira must decide whether to take his teddy bear with him when he goes next door to spend the night with a friend. Figure 6–3 lists stories representing the four conflict situations.

The plot is developed through conflict that is introduced at the beginning of a story, expanded in the middle, and finally resolved at the end. Plot development involves four components:

1. A problem.   A problem that introduces conflict is presented at the beginning of the story.

FIGURE 6–3   Stories That Illustrate the Four Types of Conflict

Conflict Between a Character and Nature

George J. C. (1972). *Julie of the wolves.* New York: Harper & Row. (M–U)

O'Dell, S. (1960). *Island of the blue dolphins.* Boston: Houghton Mifflin. (M–U)

Paulsen, G. (1987). *Hatchet.* New York: Bradbury Press. (M–U)

Polacco, P. (1990). *Thundercake.* New York: Philomel. (P–M)

Sperry, A. (1968). *Call it courage.* New York: Macmillan. (U)

Steig, W. (1987). *Brave Irene.* New York: Farrar, Straus & Giroux. (M)

Conflict Between a Character and Society

Brett, J. (1994). *Town mouse, country mouse.* New York: Putnam. (P–M)

Bunting, E. (1994). *Smoky night.* San Diego: Harcourt Brace. (P–M)

Lowry, L. (1989). *Number the stars.* New York: Atheneum. (M–U)

Lowry, L. (1993). *The giver.* Boston: Houghton Mifflin. (U)

Nixon, J. L. (1987). *A family apart.* New York: Bantam. (M–U)

O'Brien, R. C. (1971). *Mrs. Frisby and the rats of NIMH.* New York: Atheneum. (M)

Speare, E. G. (1958). *The witch of Blackbird Pond.* Boston: Houghton Mifflin. (M–U)

Uchida, Y. (1971). *Journey to Topaz.* Berkeley, CA: Creative Arts. (U)

Conflict Between Characters

Blume, J. (1972). *Tales of a fourth grade nothing.* New York: Dutton. (M)

Bunting, E. (1994). *A day's work.* New York: Clarion. (P–M)

Cohen, B. (1983). *Molly's pilgrim.* New York: Lothrop, Lee & Shepard. (M)

Cushman, K. (1994). *Catherine called Birdy.* New York: HarperCollins. (U)

Hoban, R. (1970). *A bargain for Frances.* New York: Scholastic. (P)

Lester, H. (1988). *Tacky the penguin.* Boston: Houghton Mifflin. (P)

Say, A. (1995). *Stranger in the mirror.* Boston: Houghton Mifflin. (M–U)

Steig, W. (1982). *Doctor De Soto.* New York: Farrar, Straus & Giroux. (M)

Zelinsky, P. O. (1986). *Rumpelstiltskin.* New York: Dutton. (P–M)

Conflict Within a Character

Bauer, M. D. (1986). *On my honor.* Boston: Houghton Mifflin. (M–U)

Byars, B. (1970). *The summer of the swans.* New York: Viking. (M)

Carle, E. (1995). *The very lonely firefly.* New York: Philomel. (P)

Fritz, J. (1958). *The cabin faced west.* New York: Coward-McCann. (M)

Henkes, K. (1991). *Chrysanthemum.* New York: Greenwillow. (P)

Naylor, P. R. (1991). *Shiloh.* New York: Atheneum. (M–U)

Pinkney, A. D. (1995). *Hold fast to dreams.* New York: Morrow. (U)

Taylor, T. (1969). *The cay.* New York: Doubleday. (U)

Waber, B. (1972). *Ira sleeps over.* Boston: Houghton Mifflin. (P)

P = primary grades (K–2): M = middle grades (3–5); U = upper grades (6–8)

2. *Roadblocks.* Characters face roadblocks in attempting to solve the problem in the middle of the story.

3. *The high point.* The high point in the action occurs when the problem is about to be solved. This high point separates the middle and end of the story.

4. *The solution.* The problem is solved and the roadblocks are overcome at the end of the story.

The problem is introduced at the beginning of the story, and the main character is faced with trying to solve it. The problem determines the conflict. The problem in *The Ugly Duckling* (Mayer, 1987) is that the big, gray duckling does not fit in with the other ducklings, and conflict develops between the ugly duckling and the other ducks. This is an example of conflict between characters.

After the problem has been introduced, authors use conflict to throw roadblocks in the way of an easy solution. As characters remove one roadblock, the author devises another to further thwart the characters. Postponing the solution by introducing roadblocks is the core of plot development. Stories may contain any number of roadblocks, but many children's stories contain three, four, or five.

The first conflict in *The Ugly Duckling* comes in the yard when the ducks and the woman who feeds the ducks make fun of the duckling. The conflict is so great that he goes out into the world. Next, conflict comes from the wild ducks and other animals who scorn him, too. Third, the duckling spends a miserable, cold winter in the marsh.

The high point of the action occurs when the solution of the problem hangs in the balance. Tension is high, and readers continue reading to learn whether the main characters solve the problem. With *The Ugly Duckling*, readers are relieved that the duckling has survived the winter, but tension continues because he is still an outcast. Then the swan flies to a pond and sees three beautiful swans. He flies near to them even though he expects to be scorned.

As the story ends, the problem is solved and the goal is achieved. When the swan joins the other swans at the pond, they welcome him. The swan sees his reflection in the water and realizes that he is no longer an ugly duckling. Children come to feed the swans and praise the new swan's beauty. The new swan is happy at last!

Students can chart the plot of a story using a plot profile to track the tension or excitement in a story (Johnson & Louis, 1987). Figure 6–4 presents a plot profile for

FIGURE 6–4   A Plot Profile for *Stone Fox*

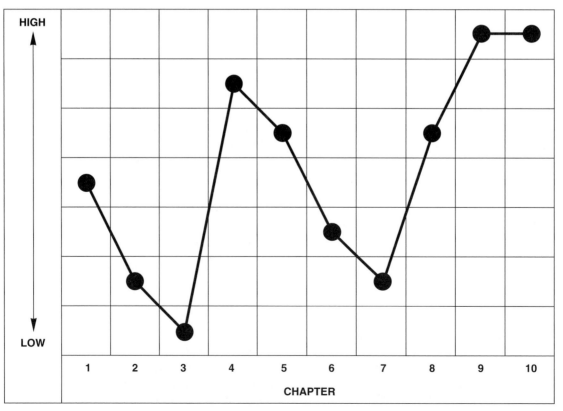

Stone Fox (Gardiner, 1980), a story about a boy who wins a dogsled race to save his grandfather's farm. A class of fourth graders met in small groups to talk about each chapter, and after these discussions the whole class came together to decide how to mark the chart. At the end of the story, students analyzed the chart and rationalized the tension dips in Chapters 3 and 7. They decided that the story would be too stressful without these dips.

Characters

Characters are the people or personified animals who are involved in the story. Characters are often the most important structural element because the story is centered around a character or group of characters. Usually, one or two fully rounded characters and several supporting characters are involved in a story. Fully developed main characters have many character traits, both good and bad. That is to say, they have all the characteristics of real people. Inferring a character's traits is an important part of reading. Through character traits we get to know a character well and the character seems to come alive. A list of stories with fully developed main characters is presented in Figure 6–5.

Characters are developed in four ways: appearance, action, dialogue, and monologue. Some description of the characters' physical appearance is usually included when they are introduced. Readers learn about characters by the description of their facial features, body shapes, habits of dress, mannerisms, and gestures. On the first page of *Tacky the Penguin* (Lester, 1988), the illustration of Tacky wearing a bright floral shirt and a purple-and-white tie suggests to readers that Tacky is an "odd bird"! Lester confirms this impression as she describes how Tacky behaves.

The second way—and often the best way—to learn about characters is through their actions. In Van Allsburg's *The Stranger* (1986), readers deduce that the stranger is Jack Frost because of what he does: He watches geese flying south for the winter, blows a cold wind, labors long hours without becoming tired, has an unusual rapport with wild animals, and is unfamiliar with modern conveniences.

Dialogue is the third way characters are developed. What characters say is important, but so is how they speak. The register of the characters' language is determined by the social situation. A character might speak less formally with friends than with respected elders or characters in positions of authority. The geographic location of the story and the characters' socioeconomic status also determine how characters speak. In *Roll of Thunder, Hear My Cry* (Taylor, 1976), for example, Cassie and her family speak Black English, a dialect.

Authors also provide insight into characters by revealing their thoughts, or internal monologue. In *Sylvester and the Magic Pebble* (Steig, 1969), thoughts and wishes are central to the story. Sylvester, a donkey, foolishly wishes to become a rock, and he spends a miserable winter that way. Steig shares the donkey's thinking with us. He thinks about his parents, who are frantic with worry, and we learn how Sylvester feels in the spring when his parents picnic on the rock he has become.

Setting

In some stories the setting is barely sketched, and these are called backdrop settings. The setting in many folktales, for example, is relatively unimportant, and the convention "Once upon a time . . ." may be used to set the stage. In other stories, the setting is elaborated and integral to the story's effectiveness. These settings are called integral settings (Lukens, 1995). A list of stories with integral settings is shown in

FIGURE 6–5   Stories With Fully Developed Main Characters

Character	Story
Queenie	Burch, R. (1966). *Queenie Peavy.* New York: Viking. (U)
Ramona	Cleary, B. (1981). *Ramona Quimby, age 8.* New York: Morrow. (M)
Leigh	Cleary, B. (1983). *Dear Mr. Henshaw.* New York: Morrow. (M)
Birdy	Cushman, K. (1994). *Catherine called Birdy.* New York: HarperCollins. (U)
Johnny	Forbes, E. (1974). *Johnny Tremain.* Boston: Houghton Mifflin. (U)
Little Willy	Gardiner, J. R. (1980). *Stone Fox.* New York: Harper & Row. (M–U)
Sam	George, J. C. (1959). *My side of the mountain.* New York: Dutton. (U)
Patty	Greene. B. (1973). *Summer of my German soldier.* New York: Dial. (U)
Beth	Greene, B. (1974). *Philip Hall likes me. I reckon maybe.* New York: Dial. (U)
Chrysanthemum	Henkes, K. (1991). *Chrysanthemum.* New York: Greenwillow. (P)
Tacky	Lester, H. (1988). *Tacky the penguin.* Boston: Houghton Mifflin. (P–M)
Frog, Toad	Lobel, A. (1970). *Frog and Toad are friends.* New York: Harper & Row. (P)
Jonas	Lowry, L. (1993). *The giver.* Boston: Houghton Mifflin. (U)
Sarah	MacLachlan, P. (1985). *Sarah, plain and tall.* New York: Harper & Row. (M)
Marty	Naylor, P. R. (1991). *Shiloh.* New York: Atheneum. (M–U)
Karana	O'Dell, S. (1960). *Island of the blue dolphins.* Boston: Houghton Mifflin. (M–U)
Gilly	Paterson, K. (1978). *The great Gilly Hopkins.* New York: Crowell. (M–U)
Peter	Potter, B. (1902). *The tale of Peter Rabbit.* New York: Warne. (P)
Billy	Say, A. (1990). *El Chino.* Boston: Houghton Mifflin. (M)
Matt	Speare, E. (1983). *The sign of the beaver.* Boston: Houghton Mifflin. (M–U)
Mafatu	Sperry, A. (1968). *Call it courage.* New York: Macmillan. (U)
Irene	Steig, W. (1986). *Brave Irene.* New York: Farrar, Straus & Giroux. (P–M)
Cassie	Taylor, M. (1976). *Roll of thunder, hear my cry.* New York: Dial. (U)
Moon Shadow	Yep, L. (1975). *Dragonwings.* New York: Harper & Row. (U)

Figure 6–6. The setting in these stories is specific, and authors take care to ensure the authenticity of the historical period or geographic location in which the story is set.

Four dimensions of setting are location, weather, time period, and time. Location is an important dimension in many stories. The Boston Commons in *Make Way for Ducklings* (McCloskey, 1969) and the Alaskan North Slope in *Julie of the Wolves*

FIGURE 6–6   Stories With Integral Settings

Babbitt, N. (1975). *Tuck everlasting.* New York: Farrar, Straus & Giroux. (M–U)

Bunting, E. (1994). *Smoky night.* San Diego: Harcourt Brace. (P–M)

Cauley, L. B. (1984). *The city mouse and the country mouse.* New York: Putnam. (P–M)

Choi, S. N. (1991). *Year of impossible goodbyes.* Boston: Houghton Mifflin. (U)

Cushman, K. (1994). *Catherine called Birdy.* New York: HarperCollins. (U)

Fleischman, S. (1963). *By the great horn spoon!* Boston: Little, Brown. (M–U)

Friedman, I. R. (1984). *How my parents learned to eat.* Boston: Houghton Mifflin. (P–M)

Gates, D. (1968). *Blue willow.* New York: Viking. (M–U)

George, J. C. (1972). *Julie of the wolves.* New York: Harper & Row. (M–U)

Harvey, B. (1988). *Cassie's journey: Going west in the 1860s.* New York: Holiday House. (M)

Johnston, T. (1994). *Amber on the mountain.* New York: Dial. (P–M)

Konigsburg, E. L. (1983). *From the mixed-up files of Mrs. Basil E. Frankweiler.* New York: Atheneum. (M)

L'Engle, M. (1962). *A wrinkle in time.* New York: Farrar, Straus & Giroux. (U)

Lester, H. (1989). *Tacky the penguin.* Boston: Houghton Mifflin. (P–M)

Lowry, L. (1989). *Number the stars.* Boston: Houghton Mifflin. (M–U)

Lowry, L. (1993). *The giver.* Boston: Houghton Mifflin. (U)

McCloskey, R. (1969). *Make way for ducklings.* New York: Viking. (P)

Myers, W. D. (1988). *Scorpions.* New York: Harper & Row. (U)

Ness, E. (1966). *Sam, Bangs, and moonshine.* New York: Holt, Rinehart & Winston. (P)

Paterson, K. (1977). *Bridge to Terabithia.* New York: Crowell. (M–U)

Paulsen, G. (1990). *Woodsong.* New York: Bradbury Press. (M–U)

Polacco, P. (1988). *The keeping quilt.* New York: Simon & Schuster. (M)

Polacco, P. (1988). *Rechenka's eggs.* New York: Philomel. (P–M)

Ringgold, R. (1991). *Tar beach.* New York: Crown. (P–M)

Roop, P., & Roop, C. (1985). *Keep the lights burning, Abbie.* Minneapolis: Carolrhoda. (P–M)

Say, A. (1990). *El Chino.* Boston: Houghton Mifflin. (M)

Speare, E. G. (1958). *The witch of Blackbird Pond.* Boston: Houghton Mifflin. (M–U)

Speare, E. G. (1983). *The sign of the beaver.* Boston: Houghton Mifflin. (M–U)

Uchida, Y. (1993). *The bracelet.* New York: Philomel. (P–M)

Wilder, L. I. (1971). *The long winter.* New York: Harper & Row. (M)

Yep, L. (1975). *Dragonwings.* New York: Harper & Row. (U)

(George, 1972) are integral to those stories' effectiveness. The settings are artfully described and add something unique to the story. In contrast, many stories take place in predictable settings that do not contribute to the story's effectiveness.

Weather is a second dimension of setting and, like location, is crucial in some stories. A rainstorm is essential to the plot development in *Bridge to Terabithia* (Paterson, 1977), but in other books weather is not mentioned because it does not affect the outcome of the story. Many stories take place on warm, sunny days.

The third dimension of setting is the time period, an important element in stories set in the past or future. If *The Witch of Blackbird Pond* (Speare, 1958) and *Number the Stars* (Lowry, 1989) were set in different eras, for example, they would lose much of their impact. Today, few people would believe that Kit Tyler is a witch or that Jewish people are the focus of government persecution. In stories that take place in the future, such as *A Wrinkle in Time* (L'Engle, 1962), things are possible that are not possible today.

The fourth dimension, time, includes both time of day and the passage of time. Most stories ignore time of day, except for scary stories that take place after dark. In stories such as *The Ghost-eye Tree* (Martin & Archambault, 1985), a story of two children who must walk past a scary tree at night to get a pail of milk, time is a more important dimension than in stories that take place during the day, because night makes things more scary.

Many short stories span a brief period of time—often less than a day, and sometimes less than an hour. In *Jumanji* (Van Allsburg, 1981), Peter and Judy's bizarre adventure, during which their house is overtaken by exotic jungle creatures, lasts only several hours. Other stories, such as *The Ugly Duckling* (Mayer, 1987), span a long enough period for the main character to grow to maturity.

Students can draw maps to show the setting of a story. These maps might show the path a character traveled or the passage of time in a story. Figure 6–7 shows a map for *Number the Stars* (Lowry, 1989). In this chapter book set in Denmark during World War II, a Christian girl and her family help a Jewish family flee to safety in Sweden. The map shows the families' homes in Copenhagen, their trip to a fishing village, and the ship they hid away on to escape to Sweden.

FIGURE 6–7   A Story Map for *Number the Stars*

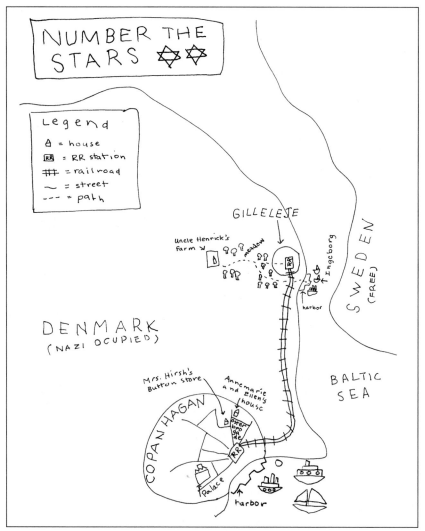

Point of View

Stories are written from a particular viewpoint, and this focus determines to a great extent readers' understanding of the characters and the events of the story. The four points of view are first-person viewpoint, omniscient viewpoint, limited omniscient viewpoint, and objective viewpoint (Lukens, 1995). A list of stories written from each point of view is presented in Figure 6–8.

The first-person viewpoint is used to tell a story through the eyes of one character using the first-person pronoun "I." In this point of view, the reader experiences the story as the narrator tells it. The narrator, usually the main character, speaks as an eyewitness and a participant in the events. For example, in *Alexander and the Terrible, Horrible, No Good, Very Bad Day* (Viorst, 1977), Alexander tells about a day everything seemed to go wrong for him. One limitation is that the narrator must remain an eyewitness.

In the omniscient viewpoint, the author is godlike, seeing and knowing all. The author tells readers about the thought processes of each character without worrying about how the information is obtained. *Doctor De Soto* (Steig, 1982), a story about a mouse dentist who outwits a fox with a toothache, is told from the omniscient view-

FIGURE 6–8   Stories That Illustrate the Four Points of View

First-Person Viewpoint

Bunting, E. (1994). *Smoky night.* San Diego: Harcourt Brace. (P–M)

Cushman, K. (1994). *Catherine called Birdy.* New York: HarperCollins. (U)

Greene, B. (1974). *Philip Hall likes me. I reckon maybe.* New York: Dial. (M–U)

Howard, E. F. (1991). *Aunt Flossie's hats (and crab cakes later).* New York: Clarion. (P)

Howe, D., & Howe, J. (1979). *Bunnicula: A rabbit-tale of mystery.* New York: Atheneum. (M)

MacLachlan, P. (1985). *Sarah, plain and tall.* New York: Harper & Row. (M)

Rylant, C. (1992). *Missing May.* New York: Orchard Books. (U)

Viorst, J. (1977). *Alexander and the terrible, horrible, no good, very bad day.* New York: Atheneum. (P)

Omniscient Viewpoint

Babbitt, N. (1975). *Tuck everlasting.* New York: Farrar, Straus & Giroux. (M–U)

Grahame, K. (1961). *The wind in the willows.* New York: Scribner, (M)

Lewis, C. S. (1981). *The lion, the witch and the wardrobe.* New York: Macmillan. (M–U)

Myers, W. D. (1988). *Scorpions.* New York: Harper & Row. (U)

Steig, W. (1982). *Doctor De Soto.* New York: Farrar, Straus & Giroux. (P)

Limited Omniscient Viewpoint

Burch, R. (1966). *Queenie Peavy.* New York: Dell. (U)

Cleary, B. (1981). *Ramona Quimby, age 8.* New York: Morrow. (M)

Gardiner, J. R. (1980). *Stone Fox.* New York: Harper & Row. (M)

Lionni, L. (1969). *Alexander and the wind-up mouse.* New York: Pantheon (P)

Lowry, L. (1989). *Number the stars.* Boston: Houghton Mifflin. (M–U)

Lowry, L. (1993). *The giver.* Boston: Houghton Mifflin. (U)

Objective Viewpoint

Brown, M. (1954). *Cinderella.* New York: Scribner. (P)

Cauley, L. B. (1988). *The pancake boy.* New York: Putnam. (P)

Lester, H. (1988). *Tacky the penguin.* Boston: Houghton Mifflin. (P–M)

Lobel, A. (1972). *Frog and Toad together.* New York: Harper & Row. (P)

Wells, R. (1973). *Benjamin and Tulip.* New York: Dial. (P)

Zemach, M. (1983). *The little red hen.* New York: Farrar, Straus & Giroux. (P)

point. Steig lets readers know that the fox wants to eat the dentist as soon as his toothache is cured and that the mouse dentist is aware of the fox's thoughts and plans a clever trick.

The limited omniscient viewpoint is used so that readers know the thoughts of one character. The story is told in third person, and the author concentrates on the thoughts, feelings, and experiences of the main character or another important character. Lowry used the limited omniscient viewpoint in *Number the Stars* (1989), and Annemarie, the Christian girl, is the character Lowry concentrates on, revealing her thoughts about the lies she tells to the Nazi soldiers.

In the objective viewpoint, readers are eyewitnesses to the story and confined to the immediate scene. They learn only what is visible and audible and are not aware of what any characters think. Most fairy tales, such as *The Little Red Hen* (Zemach, 1983), are told from the objective viewpoint. The focus is on recounting events, not on developing the personalities of the characters.

Most teachers postpone introducing the four viewpoints until the upper grades, but younger children can experiment with point of view to understand how the author's viewpoint affects a story. One way to demonstrate point of view is to contrast *The Three Little Pigs* (Galdone, 1970), the traditional version of the story told from an objective viewpoint, with *The True Story of the Three Little Pigs!* (Scieszka, 1989), a self-serving narrative told by Mr. A. Wolf from a first-person viewpoint. In this satirical retelling, the wolf tries to explain away his bad image. Even first graders are struck by how different the two versions are and how the narrator filters the information.

Theme

Theme is the underlying meaning of a story and embodies general truths about human nature (Lehr, 1991; Lukens, 1995). It usually deals with the characters' emotions and values. Themes can be stated either explicitly or implicitly. Explicit themes are stated openly and clearly in the story, while implicit themes must be inferred from the story. Themes are developed as the characters attempt to overcome the obstacles that prevent them from reaching their goals. They are often stated explicitly at the end of fables, but in most stories the theme emerges through the thoughts, speech, and actions of the characters as they seek to resolve their conflicts. In *A Chair for My Mother* (Williams, 1982), a young girl demonstrates the importance of sacrificing personal wants for her family's welfare as she and her mother collect money to buy a new chair.

Stories usually have more one theme, and their themes usually cannot be articulated with a single word. *Charlotte's Web* (White, 1952) has several "friendship" themes, one explicitly stated and others inferred from the text. Friendship is a multidimensional theme—qualities of a good friend, unlikely friends, and sacrificing for a friend, for instance. Teachers can probe students' thinking as they work to construct a theme and move beyond one-word labels (Au, 1992).

Why do teachers need to know about story elements?

Most teachers are familiar with story terms such as *character, plot,* and *setting,* but teachers need to understand how authors combine the story elements to craft stories as they read stories aloud and plan for reading instruction. Teachers cannot assume that teacher's manuals or other guides will be available for every story they read with their students. Teachers must be prepared to think about the structure of stories they will use in their classrooms.

Students make a story quilt with memorable quotes after reading stories and informational books about the Underground Railroad.

For example, after reading *Sarah, Plain and Tall* (MacLachlan, 1985), teachers might choose Caleb as their favorite character and think about how the story would be different if Sarah, not Anna, were telling the story. They might wonder if the author meant to send a message of promise of future happiness for the family by setting the story in the springtime. They also might speculate that the storm was the turning point in the story or wonder about the role of colors in the story. This kind of thoughtful reflection allows teachers to know the story better, prepare themselves to guide their students through the story, and plan activities to help students explore the story's meaning.

While teachers do not ask students to identify conflict situations or points of view in stories, they may organize students' dramatization of a story into beginning-middle-end or direct students' attention to how a particular conflict situation or viewpoint has influenced a story. Teachers often teach **minilessons** about story elements to provide students with background information that they can apply when reading and writing stories. Primary-grade students can organize their retellings of favorite fairy tales and picture books into beginning-middle-end parts, and they can write innovations for familiar stories like *Brown Bear, Brown Bear, What Do You See?* (Martin, 1983). Middle-grade students use their knowledge of setting and plot as they write sequels after reading *Jumanji* (Van Allsburg, 1981). Teachers must know about story structure in order to plan these types of writing projects. Similarly, when teachers want to react to stories students are writing, having this knowledge about stories is helpful for providing useful information about story elements for students to apply in the stories they are writing.

■ *Activity*

Compare the story elements in *Rosie's Walk, Cloudy With a Chance of Meatballs,* and *Bunnicula: A Rabbit-Tale of Mystery* or three other stories. How are these books alike, and how are they different?

EXPOSITORY TEXT STRUCTURES

Stories have been the primary genre for reading and writing instruction in the elementary grades because it has been assumed that constructing stories in the mind is a fundamental way of learning (Wells, 1986). Recent research, however, suggests that children may prefer to read informational books and are able to understand them as well as they do stories (Pappas, 1991, 1993). Certainly, children are interested in learning about their world—about baleen whales, how a road is built, threats to the environment of Antarctica, or Helen Keller's courage—and informational books provide this knowledge. Even young children read informational books, as Mrs. Simmons's first graders did in the vignette.

Students often assume an efferent stance as they read informational books to locate facts, but students do not always use efferent reading (Rosenblatt, 1978). Many times they pick up an informational book to check a fact and then continue reading—aesthetically—because they are fascinated by what they are reading. They get carried away in the book, just as they do when reading stories. At other times, students read books about topics they are interested in, and they read aesthetically, engaging in the lived-through experience of reading and connecting what they are reading to their own lives and prior reading experiences.

Russell Freedman, who won the 1988 Newbery Award for *Lincoln: A Photobiography* (1987), talks about the purpose of informational books and explains that it is not enough for an informational book to provide information: "[An informational book] must create a vivid and believable world that the reader will enter willingly and leave only with reluctance. . . . It should be just as compelling as a good story" (1992, p. 3). High-quality informational books like Freedman's encourage students to read aesthetically because they engage readers and tap their curiosity.

There is a new wave of engaging and artistic informational books being published today, and these books show increased respect for children. Peter Roop (1992) explains that for years informational books were the "ugly duckling" of children's literature, but now they have grown into a beautiful swan. Four qualities of informational books are accuracy, organization, design, and style (Vardell, 1991). First and foremost, the facts must be current and complete. They must be well researched, and, when appropriate, varying points of view should be presented. Stereotypes are to be avoided, and details in both the text and the illustrations must be authentic. Second, information should be presented clearly and logically, using organizational patterns to increase the book's readability. Third, the book's design should be eye-catching and enhance its usability. Illustrations should complement the text, and explanations should accompany each illustration. Last, the style should be lively and stimulating so as to engage readers' curiosity and wonder.

Informational books are available today on topics ranging from biological sciences, physical sciences, and social sciences to arts and biographies. *Cactus Hotel* (Guiberson, 1991) is a fine informational book that shows the desert ecosystem. The author discusses the life cycle of a giant saguaro cactus and describes its role as a home for desert creatures. Other books, such as *Whales* (Simon, 1989), illustrated with striking full-page color photos, and *Antarctica* (Cowcher, 1990), illustrated with dramatic double-page paintings, are socially responsible and emphasize the threats people present to animals and the earth.

Other books present historical and geographic concepts. *New Providence: A Changing Cityscape* (von Tscharner & Fleming, 1987), for instance, traces the evolution of a small fictional city, and *Surrounded by Sea: Life on a New England Fishing Is-*

land (Gibbons, 1991) describes the social life and customs of island residents through the four seasons. These books provide an enriching reading experience for elementary students.

Some informational books focus on letters and numbers. While many alphabet and counting books with pictures of familiar objects are designed for young children, others provide a wealth of information on various topics. In his alphabet book *Illuminations* (1989), Jonathan Hunt presents detailed information about medieval life, and in *The Underwater Alphabet Book* (1991), Jerry Pallotta provides information about 26 types of fish and other sea creatures. Muriel and Tom Feelings present information about Africa in *Moja Means One: Swahili Counting Book* (1971), and Ann Herbert Scott presents information about cowboys in *One Good Horse: A Cowpuncher's Counting Book* (1990). In some of these books, new terms are introduced and illustrated, and in others, the term is explained in a sentence or a paragraph. Other informational books focus on mathematical concepts (Whitin & Wilde, 1992). Tana Hoban's *26 Letters and 99 Cents* (1987) presents concepts about money, *What Comes in 2's, 3's and 4's?* (Aker, 1990) introduces multiplication, and *If You Made a Million* (Schwartz, 1989) focuses on big numbers.

Biographies are also informational books, and the biographies being written today are more realistic than in the past, presenting well-known personalities warts and all. Jean Fritz's portraits of Revolutionary War figures, such as *Will You Sign Here,*

Students apply what they are learning about the structure of informational books as they write their own weather books.

John Hancock? (1976), are among the best-known, but she has also written comprehensive biographies, including *The Great Little Madison* (1989). Fritz and other authors often include notes in the back of books to explain how the details were researched and to provide additional information. Only a few autobiographies are available to students, but more are being published each year. Autobiographies about authors and illustrators, such as Cynthia Rylant's *Best Wishes* (1992), are also popular.

Other books present information within a story context. Authors are devising innovative strategies for combining information with a story. Margy Burns Knight's *Who Belongs Here? An American Story* (1993), a two-part book, is a good example. One part is the story of Nary, a young Cambodian refugee who escapes to the United States after his parents are killed by the Khmer Rouge. This story is told in a picture book format, with the story text accompanying each picture. The second part of the book is information about refugees, immigration laws, and cultural diversity in America. The text for this second part is printed in a different typeface and appears below the story text on each page. Additional information about America as a nation of immigrants is presented at the back of the book. The two parts work together to create a very powerful book.

Some combination informational/story books are imaginative fantasies. The Magic School Bus series is perhaps the best-known. In *The Magic School Bus Inside the Earth* (Cole, 1987), for example, Ms. Frizzle and her class study the earth and take a field trip on the magic school bus to the inner core of the earth and out again through a volcano. The page layout is innovative, with charts and reports containing factual information presented at the outside edges of most pages.

Informational books are organized in particular ways called expository text structures. Five of the most common organizational patterns are description, sequence, comparison, cause and effect, and problem and solution (Meyer & Freedle, 1984; Niles, 1974). Figure 6–9 describes these patterns and presents sample passages and cue words that signal use of each pattern. When readers are aware of these patterns, they understand what they are reading better, and when writers use these structures to organize their writing, it is more easily understood by readers. Sometimes the pattern is signaled clearly by means of titles, topic sentences, and cue words, and sometimes it is not.

Description

In this organizational pattern, a topic is described by listing characteristics, features, and examples. Phrases such as *for example* and *characteristics are* cue this structure. Examples of books using description include *Spiders* (Gibbons, 1992) and *Mercury* (Simon, 1993), in which the authors describe may facets of their topic. When students delineate any topic, such as the Mississippi River, eagles, or Alaska, they use description.

Sequence

In this pattern, items or events are listed or explained in numerical or chronological order. Cue words for sequence include *first, second, third, next, then,* and *finally.* Caroline Arnold describes the steps in creating a museum display in *Dinosaurs All Around: An Artist's View of the Prehistoric World* (1993), and David Macaulay describes how a castle is built in *Castle* (1977). Students use the sequence pattern to write directions for completing a math problem or for the stages in an animal's life cycle. The events in a biography are often written in the sequence pattern.

FIGURE 6–9 The Five Expository Text Structures

Pattern	Description	Cue Words	Graphic Organizer	Sample Passage
Description	The author describes a topic by listing characteristics, features, and examples.	*for example* *characteristics are*		The Olympic symbol consists of five interlocking rings. The rings represent the five continents—Africa, Asia, Europe, North America, and South America—from which athletes come to compete in the games. The rings are colored black, blue, green, red, and yellow. At least one of these colors is found in the flag of every country sending athletes to compete in the Olympic games.
Sequence	The author lists items or events in numerical or chronological order.	*first, second, third* *next* *then* *finally*	1. _____ 2. _____ 3. _____ 4. _____ 5. _____	The Olympic games began as athletic festivals to honor the Greek gods. The most important festival was held in the valley of Olympia to honor Zeus, the king of the gods. It was this festival that became the Olympic games in 776 B.C. These games were ended in A.D. 394 by the Roman Emperor who ruled Greece. No Olympic games were held for more than 1,500 years. Then the modern Olympics began in 1896. Almost 300 male athletes competed in the first modern Olympics. In the games held in 1900, female athletes were allowed to compete. The games have continued every four years since 1896 except during World War II, and they will most likely continue for many years to come.
Comparison	The author explains how two or more things are alike and/or how they are different.	*different* *in contrast* *alike* *same as* *on the other hand*		The modern Olympics is very unlike the ancient Olympic games. Individual events are different. While there were no swimming races in the ancient games, for example, there were chariot races. There were no female contestants and all athletes competed in the nude. Of course, the ancient and modern Olympics are also alike in many ways. Some events, such as the javelin and discus throws, are the same. Some people say that cheating, professionalism, and nationalism in the modern games are a disgrace to the Olympic tradition. But according to the ancient Greek writers, there were many cases of cheating, nationalism, and professionalism in their Olympics, too.

219

FIGURE 6-9 *continued*

Pattern	Description	Cue Words	Graphic Organizer	Sample Passage
Cause and Effect	The author lists one or more causes and the resulting effect or effects.	*reasons why* *if . . . then* *as a result* *therefore* *because*	Cause → Effect #1, Effect #2, Effect #3	There are several reasons why so many people attend the Olympic games or watch them on television. One reason is tradition. The name *Olympics* and the torch and flame remind people of the ancient games. People can escape the ordinariness of daily life by attending or watching the Olympics. They like to identify with someone else's individual sacrifice and accomplishment. National pride is another reason, and an athlete's or a team's hard earned victory becomes a nation's victory. There are national medal counts and people keep track of how many medals their country's athletes have won.
Problem and Solution	The author states a problems and lists one or more solutions for the problem. A variation of this pattern is the question-and-answer format in which the author poses a question and then answers it.	*problem is* *dilemma is* *puzzle is* *solved* *question . . . answer*	Problem → Solution	One problem with the modern Olympics is that it has become very big and expensive to operate. The city or country that hosts the games often loses a lot of money. A stadium, pools, and playing fields must be built for the athletic events and housing is needed for the athletes who come from around the world. And all of these facilities are used for only 2 weeks! In 1984, Los Angeles solved these problems by charging a fee for companies who wanted to be official sponsors of the games. Companies like McDonald's paid a lot of money to be part of the Olympics. Many buildings that were already built in the Los Angeles area were also used. The Coliseum where the 1932 games were held was used again and many colleges and universities in the area became playing and living sites.

Comparison

In the comparison structure, two or more things are compared. *Different, in contrast, alike,* and *on the other hand* are cue words and phrases that signal this structure. In *Horns, Antlers, Fangs, and Tusks* (Rauzon, 1993), for example, the author compares animals with distinctive types of headgear. When students compare and contrast book and movie versions of a story, reptiles and amphibians, or life in ancient Greece with life in ancient Egypt, they use this organizational pattern.

Cause and Effect

The writer explains one or more causes and the resulting effect or effects. *Reasons why, if . . . then, as a result, therefore,* and *because* are words and phrases that cue this structure. Explanations of why dinosaurs became extinct, the effects of pollution on the environment, or the causes of the Civil War are written using the cause and effect pattern. *How Do Apples Grow?* (Maestro, 1992) and *What Happens to a Hamburger?* (Showers, 1985) are two books that exemplify this structure.

Problem and Solution

In this expository structure, the writer states a problem and offers one or more solutions. In *Man and Mustang* (Ancona, 1992), for example, the author describes the problem of wild mustangs and explains how they are rescued. A variation is the question-and-answer format, in which the writer poses a question and then answers it. One question-and-answer book is . . . *If You Traveled West in a Covered Wagon* (Levine, 1986). Cue words and phrases include *the problem is, the puzzle is, solve,* and *question . . . answer.* Students use this structure when they write about why money was invented, why endangered animals should be saved, or why dams are needed to ensure a permanent water supply. They often use the problem-solution pattern in writing advertisements and other persuasive writing as well.

Figure 6–10 lists other books that illustrate each of the five expository text structures.

Why do teachers need to know about expository text structures?

When teachers use informational books and content-area textbooks, they should consider how the books are organized as they prepare for instruction. Often teachers do what Mrs. Simmons did in the vignette at the beginning of this chapter: They give students a purpose for reading and use a graphic organizer to record information after reading.

Researchers have confirmed that when students use the five expository text structures to organize their reading and writing, they are more effective readers and writers. Most of the research on expository text structures has focused on older students' use of these patterns in reading; however, elementary students also use the patterns and cue words in their writing (Langer, 1986; Raphael, Englert, & Kirschner, 1989; Tompkins, 1994).

Students also use the five expository text structures when they write informational books, essays, and other nonfiction forms. A class of second graders examined the five expository text structures and learned that authors use cue words as a secret code to signal the structures. Then the students read informational books that used

FIGURE 6–10 Informational Books Representing the Expository Test Structures

Description

Balestrino, P. (1971). *The skeleton inside you.* New York: Crowell. (P)

Branley, F. M. (1986). *What the moon is like.* New York: Harper & Row. (M)

Fowler, A. (1990). *It could still be a bird.* Chicago: Childrens Press. (P–M)

Hansen, R., & Bell, R. A. (1985). *My first book of space.* New York: Simon & Schuster. (M)

Horvatic, A. (1989). *Simple machines.* New York: Dutton. (M)

Morris, A. (1989). *Hats, hats, hats.* New York: Mulberry Books. (P)

Patent, D. H. (1992). *Feathers.* New York: Cobblehill. (M–U)

Simon, S. (1992). *Wolves.* New York: HarperCollins. (M–U)

Sequence

Aliki. (1992). *Milk from cow to carton.* New York: HarperCollins. (P–M)

Cole, J. (1991). *My puppy is born.* New York: Morrow. (P–M)

Gibbons, G. (1993). *Pirates.* Boston: Little, Brown. (P–M)

Jaspersohn, W. (1988). *Ice cream.* New York: Macmillan. (M–U)

Lasky, K. (1983). *Sugaring time.* New York: Macmillan. (M–U)

Provensen, A. (1990). *The buck stops here.* New York: HarperCollins. (M–U)

Wheatley, N. (1992). *My place.* New York: Kane/Miller. (M–U)

Comparison

Gibbons, G. (1984). *Fire! Fire!* New York: Harper & Row. (P–M)

Lasker, J. (1976). *Merry ever after: The story of two medieval weddings.* New York: Viking. (M–U)

Markle, S. (1993). *Outside and inside trees.* New York: Bradbury Press. (M)

Munro, R. (1987). *The inside-outside book of Washington, D.C.* New York: Dutton. (M–U)

Rauzon, M. J. (1993). *Horns, antlers, fangs, and tusks.* New York: Lothrop, Lee & Shepard. (P–M)

Spier, P. (1987). *We the people.* New York: Doubleday. (M–U)

Cause and Effect

Branley, F. M. (1985). *Flash, crash, rumble, and roll.* New York: Harper & Row. (P–M)

Branley, F. M. (1985). *Volcanoes.* New York: Harper & Row. (P–M)

Branley, F. M. (1986). *What makes day and night?* New York: Harper & Row. (P–M)

Heller, R. (1983). *The reason for a flower.* New York: Grosset & Dunlap. (M)

Selsam, M. E. (1981). *Where do they go? Insects in winter.* New York: Scholastic. (P–M)

Showers, P. (1985). *What happens to a hamburger?* New York: Harper & Row. (P–M)

Problem and Solution

Cole, J. (1983). *Cars and how they go.* New York: Harper & Row. (P–M)

Heller, R. (1986). *How to hide a whippoorwill and other birds.* New York: Grosset & Dunlap. (P–M)

Lauber, P. (1990). *How we learned the earth is round.* New York: Crowell. (P–M)

Levine, E. (1988). *If you traveled on the underground railroad.* New York: Scholastic. (M–U)

Showers, P. (1980). *No measles, no mumps for me.* New York: Crowell. (P–M)

Simon, S. (1984). *The dinosaur is the biggest animal that ever lived and other wrong ideas you thought were true.* New York: Harper & Row. (M)

Combination

Aliki (1981). *Digging up dinosaurs.* New York: Harper & Row. (M)

Carrick, C. (1993). *Whaling days.* New York: Clarion (P–M)

Guiberson, B. Z. (1991). *Cactus hotel.* New York: Henry Holt. (P–M)

Hoyt-Goldsmith, D. (1992). *Hoang Anh: A Vietnamese-American boy.* New York: Holiday House. (M)

Simon, S. (1985). *Meet the computer.* New York: Harper & Row. (M–U)

Venutra, P., & Ceserani, G. P. (1985). *In search of Tutankhamun.* Morristown, NJ: Silver Burdett. (U)

FIGURE 6–11 Second Graders' Graphic Organizers and Paragraphs Illustrating the Five Expository Text Structures

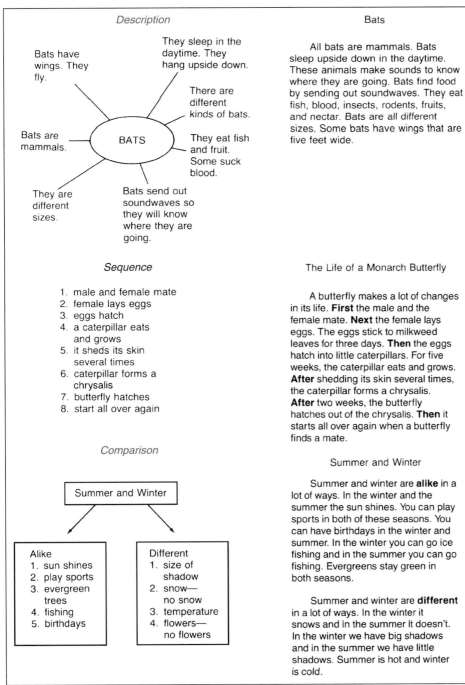

Description

Bats have wings. They fly.

They sleep in the daytime. They hang upside down.

There are different kinds of bats.

Bats are mammals.

BATS

They eat fish and fruit. Some suck blood.

They are different sizes.

Bats send out soundwaves so they will know where they are going.

Bats

All bats are mammals. Bats sleep upside down in the daytime. These animals make sounds to know where they are going. Bats find food by sending out soundwaves. They eat fish, blood, insects, rodents, fruits, and nectar. Bats are all different sizes. Some bats have wings that are five feet wide.

Sequence

1. male and female mate
2. female lays eggs
3. eggs hatch
4. a caterpillar eats and grows
5. it sheds its skin several times
6. caterpillar forms a chrysalis
7. butterfly hatches
8. start all over again

The Life of a Monarch Butterfly

A butterfly makes a lot of changes in its life. **First** the male and the female mate. **Next** the female lays eggs. The eggs stick to milkweed leaves for three days. **Then** the eggs hatch into little caterpillars. For five weeks, the caterpillar eats and grows. **After** shedding its skin several times, the caterpillar forms a chrysalis. **After** two weeks, the butterfly hatches out of the chrysalis. **Then** it starts all over again when a butterfly finds a mate.

Comparison

Summer and Winter

Alike
1. sun shines
2. play sports
3. evergreen trees
4. fishing
5. birthdays

Different
1. size of shadow
2. snow—no snow
3. temperature
4. flowers—no flowers

Summer and Winter

Summer and winter are **alike** in a lot of ways. In the winter and the summer the sun shines. You can play sports in both of these seasons. You can have birthdays in the winter and summer. In the winter you can go ice fishing and in the summer you can go fishing. Evergreens stay green in both seasons.

Summer and winter are **different** in a lot of ways. In the winter it snows and In the summer it doesn't. In the winter we have big shadows and in the summer we have little shadows. Summer is hot and winter is cold.

FIGURE 6–11   *continued*

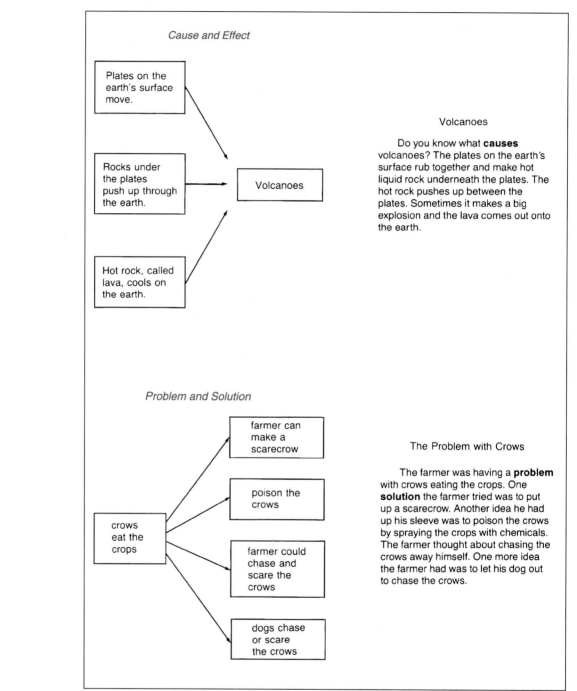

Cause and Effect

Plates on the earth's surface move.

Rocks under the plates push up through the earth.

Volcanoes

Hot rock, called lava, cools on the earth.

Volcanoes

Do you know what **causes** volcanoes? The plates on the earth's surface rub together and make hot liquid rock underneath the plates. The hot rock pushes up between the plates. Sometimes it makes a big explosion and the lava comes out onto the earth.

Problem and Solution

farmer can make a scarecrow

poison the crows

crows eat the crops

farmer could chase and scare the crows

dogs chase or scare the crows

The Problem with Crows

The farmer was having a **problem** with crows eating the crops. One **solution** the farmer tried was to put up a scarecrow. Another idea he had up his sleeve was to poison the crows by spraying the crops with chemicals. The farmer thought about chasing the crows away himself. One more idea the farmer had was to let his dog out to chase the crows.

each of the expository text structures, developed graphic organizers to record the information in the books, and wrote paragraphs on the same topics to exemplify each of the five organizational patterns. The graphic organizers and paragraphs are presented in Figure 6–11, and the secret code (or cue) words in each paragraph appear in boldface type. These paragraphs show that even primary-grade students can learn about expository text structures and use them to organize their writing.

POETIC FORMS

Poetry "brings sound and sense together in words and lines," according to Donald Graves, "ordering them on the page in such a way that both the writer and reader get a different view of life" (1992, p. 3). Poetry surrounds us; children chant jump-rope rhymes on the playground and dance in response to songs and their lyrics. Larrick (1991) believes that we enjoy poetry because of the physical involvement that the words evoke. Also, people play with words as they invent rhymes and ditties, create new words, and craft powerful comparisons.

Today more poets are writing for children, and more books of poems for children are being published than ever before. No longer is poetry confined to rhyming verse about daffodils, clouds, and love. Recently published poems about dinosaurs, Halloween, chocolate, baseball, and insects are very popular. Children choose to read poetry and share favorite poems with classmates. They read and respond to poems containing beautiful language and written on topics that are meaningful to them.

Three types of poetry books are published for children. A number of picture book versions of single poems in which each line or stanza is illustrated on a page are available, such as *Paul Revere's Ride* (Longfellow, 1990). Other books are specialized collections of poems, either written by a single poet or related to a single theme, such as dinosaurs. Comprehensive anthologies are the third type of poetry books for children, and they feature 50 to 500 or more poems arranged by category. One of the best anthologies is *The Random House Book of Poetry for Children* (Prelutsky, 1983). A list of poetry books that includes examples of each of the three types is presented in Figure 6–12.

Poems for children assume many different forms, including rhymed verse, narrative poems, haiku, and free verse. Additional forms are useful for elementary students who write poems.

Rhymed Verse

The most common type of poetry is rhymed verse, as in *Hailstones and Halibut Bones* (O'Neill, 1989), *My Parents Think I'm Sleeping* (Prelutsky, 1985), and *Sierra* (Siebert, 1991). Poets use various rhyme schemes, and the effect of the rhyming words is a poem that is pleasurable to read and to listen to when it is read aloud. Children should savor the rhyming words but not be expected to pick out the rhyme scheme.

Rhyme is the sticking point for many would-be poets. In searching for a rhyming word, children often create inane verse; for example:

> I see a funny little goat
> Wearing a blue sailor's coat
> Sitting in an old motorboat.

Certainly children should not be forbidden to write rhyming poetry, but rhyme should never be imposed as a criterion for acceptable poetry. Children may use rhyme when it fits naturally into their writing. When children write poetry, they are searching for their own voices, and they need freedom to do that. Freed from the pressure to create rhyming poetry and from other constraints, children create sensitive word pictures, vivid images, and unique comparisons.

One type of rhymed verse—limericks—can be used effectively with older students. A limerick is a short verse form popularized by Edward Lear that incorporates

FIGURE 6–12   Collections of Poetry Written for Children

Picture Book Versions of Single Poems

Carroll, L. (1977). (Ill. by J. B. Zalben). *Lewis Carroll's Jabberwocky.* New York: Warne. (M–U)

Frost, R. (1988). (Ill. by E. Young). *Birches.* New York: Henry Holt. (U)

Lear, E. (1986). (Ill. by L. B. Cauley) *The owl and the pussycat.* New York: Putnam. (P–M)

Longfellow, H. W. (1990). (Ill. by T. Rand). *Paul Revere's ride.* New York: Dutton. (M–U)

Mahy, M. (1987). *17 kings and 42 elephants.* New York: Dial. (M)

Moore, C. (1980). *The night before Christmas.* New York: Holiday House. (P–M)

Noyes, A. (1981). (Ill. by C. Keeping). *The highwayman.* Oxford, England: Oxford University Press. (U)

Sandburg, C. (1993). *Arithmetic.* New York: Harcourt Brace. (P–M)

Thayer, E. L. (1988). (Ill. by P. Polacco). *Casey at the bat: A ballad of the republic, sung in the year 1888.* New York: Putnam. (M–U)

Westcott, N. B. (1988). *The lady with the alligator purse.* Boston: Little, Brown. (P–M)

Specialized Collections

Carle, E. (1989). *Animals, animals.* New York: Philomel. (P–M)

Dickinson, E. (1978). *I'm nobody! Who are you? Poems of Emily Dickinson for children.* Owing Mills, MD: Stemmer House. (M–U)

Fleischman, P. (1985). *I am phoenix: Poems for two voices.* New York: Harper & Row. (M–U)

Fleischman, P. (1988). *Joyful noise: Poems for two voices.* New York: Harper & Row. (M–U)

Froman, R. (1974). *Seeing things: A book of poems.* New York: Crowell. (M)

Frost, R. (1982). *A swinger of birches: Poems of Robert Frost for young people.* Owing Mills, MD: Stemmer House. (U)

Greenfield, E. (1988). *Under the Sunday tree.* New York: Harper & Row. (M)

Hopkins, L. B. (1984). *Surprises* (An I Can Read Book). New York: Harper & Row. (P)

Hopkins, L. B. (1987). *Click, rumble, roar: Poems about machines.* New York: Crowell. (M)

Janeczko, P. B. (Sel.). (1993). *Looking for your name: A collection of contemporary poems.* New York: Orchard Books. (U)

Jones, H. (Ed.). (1993). *The trees stand shining: Poetry of the North American Indians.* New York: Dial. (M–U)

Kuskin, K. (1980). *Dogs and dragons, trees and dreams.* New York: Harper & Row. (P–M)

Lewis, R. (1965). *In a spring garden.* New York: Dial. (haiku) (M–U)

Livingston, M. C. (1985). *Celebrations.* New York: Holiday House. (M)

Lobel, A. (1983). *The book of pigericks.* New York: Harper & Row. (limericks) (P–M)

Livingston, M. C. (1986). *Earth songs.* New York: Hoiday House. (See also *Sea songs* and *Space songs.*) (M–U)

McCord, D. (1974). *One at a time.* Boston: Little, Brown. (M–U)

Pomerantz, C. (1982). *If I had a paka: Poems in 11 languages.* New York: Greenwillow. (M–U)

Prelutsky, J. (1981). *It's Christmas.* New York: Scholastic. (Collections for other holidays, too.) (P–M)

Prelutsky, J. (1984). *The new kid on the block.* New York: Greenwillow. (P–M)

Prelutsky, J. (1989). *Poems of A. Nonny Mouse.* New York: Knopf. (P–M)

Prelutsky, J. (1990). *Something big has been here.* New York: Greenwillow. (P–M)

Prelutsky, J. (1993). *A. Nonny Mouse writes again!* New York: Knopf. (M–U)

Siebert, D. (1984). *Truck song.* New York: Harper & Row. (P–M)

Siebert, D. (1989). *Heartland.* New York: Crowell. (M–U)

Silverstein, S. (1974). *Where the sidewalk ends.* New York: Harper & Row. (P–M–U)

Yolen, J. (1990). *Bird watch: A book of poetry.* New York: Philomel. (M–U)

Comprehensive Anthologies

de Paola, T. (Compiler). (1988). *Tomie de Paola's book of poems.* New York: Putnam. (P–M)

de Regniers, B. S., Moore, E., White, M. M., & Carr, J. (Compilers). (1988). *Sing a song of popcorn: Every child's book of poems.* New York: Scholastic. (P–M–U)

Dunning, S., Leuders, E., & Smith, H. (Compilers). (1967). *Reflections on a gift of watermelon pickle, and other modern verse.* New York: Lothrop, Lee & Shepard. (U)

Kennedy, X. J. (Compiler). (1985). *The forgetful wishing well: Poems for young people.* New York: McElderry Books. (U)

Kennedy, X. J., & Kennedy, D. M. (Compilers). (1982). *Knock at a star: A child's introduction to poetry.* Boston: Little, Brown. (P–M–U)

Prelutsky, J. (Compiler). (1983). *The Random House book of poetry for children.* New York: Random House. (P–M–U)

both rhyme and rhythm. The poem consists of five lines; the first, second, and fifth lines rhyme, while the third and fourth lines rhyme with each other and are shorter than the other three. The rhyme scheme is a-a-b-b-a. The last line often contains a funny or surprise ending, as in this limerick written by an eighth grader.

> *There once was a frog named Pete*
> *Who did nothing but sit and eat.*
> *He examined each fly*
> *With so careful an eye*
> *And then said, "You're dead meat."*

Poet X. J. Kennedy (1982) suggests introducing students to limericks by reading aloud some of Lear's verses so that students can appreciate the rhythm of the verse. Two collections of Lear's limericks for elementary students are *There Was an Old Man: A Gallery of Nonsense Rhymes* (Lear, 1994) and *How Pleasant to Know Mr. Lear!* (Livingston, 1982). Younger children especially enjoy *AnimaLimericks* (Driver, 1994), which feature animals instead of people. Writing limericks can be a challenging assignment for many upper-grade students, but middle-grade students can write limericks, too, especially if they write a class collaboration poem. Arnold Lobel has also written a book of unique pig limericks, *Pigericks* (1983). After reading Lobel's pigericks, students will want to write "fishericks."

Narrative Poems

Poems that tell a story are narrative poems. Perhaps our best-known narrative poem is Clement Moore's classic, "The Night Before Christmas." Other narrative poems include Longfellow's *Paul Revere's Ride* (1990), illustrated by Ted Rand; Alfred Noyes's *The Highwayman* (1983), illustrated by Charles Mikolaycak; and Jeanette Winter's *Follow the Drinking Gourd* (1988), which is about the Underground Railroad.

Haiku and Related Forms

Haiku is a Japanese poetic form that contains just 17 syllables arranged in three lines of 5, 7, and 5 syllables. Haiku poems deal with nature and present a single clear image. Haiku is a concise form, much like a telegram. Because of its brevity, it has been considered an appropriate form of poetry for children to read and write. A fourth grader wrote this haiku about a spider web she saw one morning.

> *Spider web shining*
> *Tangled on the grass with dew*
> *Waiting quietly.*

Books of haiku to share with students include *Shadow Play: Night Haiku* (Harter, 1994), *Haiku: The Mood of the Earth* (Atwood, 1971), and *In a Spring Garden* (Lewis, 1965). The photographs and artwork in these picture books may give students ideas for illustrating their haiku poems.

A poetic form similar to haiku is the cinquain, a five-line poem containing 22 syllables in a 2-4-6-8-2 syllable pattern. Cinquains often describe something, but they may also tell a story. Have students ask themselves what their subject looks like, smells like, sounds like, and tastes like, and record their ideas using a five-senses **cluster.** The formula is as follows.

Line 1: a one-word subject with two syllables ✓
Line 2: four syllables describing the subject ✓
Line 3: six syllables showing action ✓
Line 4: eight syllables expressing a feeling or observation about the subject ✓
Line 5: two syllables describing or renaming the subject

Students in a fourth-grade class wrote cinquains as part of a theme study on westward movement. One student wrote this cinquain about the transcontinental railroad:

Railroads
One crazy guy's
Transcontinental dream . . .
With a golden spike it came true.
Iron horse

Another student wrote about the gold rush:

Gold rush
Forty-niners
were sure to strike it rich.
Homesickness, pork and beans, so tired.
Panning

Another related form is the diamante (Tiedt, 1970), a seven-line contrast poem written in the shape of a diamond. This poetic form helps students apply their knowledge of opposites and parts of speech. The formula is:

Line 1: one noun as the subject
Line 2: two adjectives describing the subject
Line 3: three participles (ending in *-ing*) telling about the subject
Line 4: four nouns (the first two related to the subject and the last two related to the opposite)
Line 5: three participles telling about the opposite
Line 6: two adjectives describing the opposite
Line 7: one noun that is the opposite of the subject

A third-grade class wrote this diamante poem about the stages of life:

Baby
wrinkled tiny
crying wetting sleeping
rattles diapers money house
caring working loving
smart helpful
Adult

Students read books of poetry written by Jack Prelutsky during an author study.

Notice that the students created a contrast between *baby,* the subject represented by the noun in the first line, and *adult,* the opposite in the last line. This contrast gives students the opportunity to play with words and apply their understanding of opposites. The third word, *money,* in the fourth line begins the transition from *baby* to its opposite, *adult.*

Free Verse

Free verse is unrhymed poetry, and rhythm is less important in free verse than in other types of poetry. Word choice and visual images take on greater importance in free verse. *Nathaniel Talking* (Greenfield, 1988) and *Neighborhood Odes* (Soto, 1992) are two collections of free verse. In *Nathaniel Talking,* Eloise Greenfield writes from the viewpoint of a young African-American child who has lost his mother but not his spirit. Most of the poems are free verse, but one is a rap and several others rhyme. Greenfield uses few capital letters or punctuation marks. In *Neighborhood Odes,* Gary Soto writes about his childhood as a Mexican-American child living in Fresno, California. Soto adds a few Spanish words to his poems to sharpen the pictures the poems paint of life in his neighborhood.

In free verse, children choose words to describe something and put them together to express a thought or tell a story, without concern for rhyme or other arrangements. The number of words per line and use of punctuation vary. In the following poem, an eighth grader poignantly describes "Loneliness" using only 15 well-chosen words.

> *A lifetime*
> *Of broken dreams*
> *And promises*

Lost love
Hurt
My heart
Cries
In silence

Students can use several methods for writing free verse. They can select words and phrases from brainstormed lists and clusters to create the poem, or they can write a paragraph and then "unwrite" it to create the poem by deleting unnecessary words. They arrange the remaining words to look like a poem.

During a literature focus unit on MacLachlan's *Sarah, Plain and Tall* (1985), a third-grade class wrote this free-form poem after discussing the two kinds of dunes in the story:

Dunes

Dunes of sand
on the beach.
Sarah walks on them
and watches the ocean.

Dunes of hay
beside the barn.
Papa makes them for Sarah
because she misses Maine.

A unique type of free verse is poems for two voices. These poems are written in two columns, side by side, and the columns are read together by two readers. The two best-known books of poems for two voices are Paul Fleischman's *I Am Phoenix* (1985), which is about birds, and the Newbery Award–winning *Joyful Noise* (1988), which is about insects.

A third-grade class wrote this poem for two voices about whales as part of their across-the-curriculum theme on the ocean:

Whales

Whales	*Whales*
dive deep	*dive deep*
into the ocean	
	then surface for air
breathing	
	through blowholes
always	*always*
swimming	*looking for food*
looking for food	*swimming*
whales	*whales*
mammals	
	look like fish
but they aren't	*but they aren't*
two groups	*two groups*
baleen whales	
	toothed whales

the humpback whale

    a baleen whale

fast swimmer   fast swimmer

little beluga whale

    a toothed whale

all white

    very unusual

the blue whale

    a baleen whale

the biggest

    of all

big blue   big blue

narwhal

    a toothed whale

that looks like

    a unicorn

killer whale

    a toothed whale

black and white   white and black

dangerous attacker   dangerous attacker

whales   whales

Another type of free verse is found poems. Students create found poems by culling words from other sources, such as newspaper articles, stories, and informational books. Found poems give students the opportunity to manipulate words and sentence structures they don't write themselves. A small group of third graders composed the following found poem, "This Is My Day," after reading *Sarah Morton's Day: A Day in the Life of a Pilgrim Girl* (Waters, 1989):

Good day.
I must get up and be about my chores.
The fire is mine to tend.
I lay the table.
I muck the garden.
I pound the spices.
I draw vinegar to polish the brass.
I practice my lessons.
I feed the fire again.
I milk the goats.
I eat dinner.
I say the verses I am learning.
My father is pleased with my learning.
I fetch the water for tomorrow.
I bid my parents good night.
I say my prayers.
Fare thee well.
God be with thee.

To compose the found poem, the students collected their favorite words and sentences from the book and organized them sequentially to describe the pilgrim girl's day.

Other Poetic Forms

Students use a variety of other forms when they write poems, even through few adults use these forms. These forms provide a scaffold or skeleton for students' poems. After collecting words, images, and comparisons, students craft their poems, choosing words and arranging them to create a message. Meaning is always most important, and form follows the search for meaning. Poet Kenneth Koch (1970), working with students in the elementary grades, developed some simple formulas that make it easy for nearly every child to become a successful poet. These formulas call for students to begin every line the same way or to insert a particular kind of word in every line. The formulas use repetition, a stylistic device that is more effective for young poets than rhyme. Some forms may seem more like sentences than poems, but the dividing line between poetry and prose is a blurry one, and these poetry experiences help children move toward poetic expression.

1. "I wish . . ." poems.   Children begin each line of their poems with the words "I wish" and complete the line with a wish (Koch, 1970). In this second-grade class collaboration poem, children simply listed their wishes:

> *Our Wishes*
>
> *I wish I had all the money in the world.*
> *I wish I was a star fallen down from Mars.*
> *I wish I were a butterfly.*
> *I wish I were a teddy bear.*
> *I wish I had a cat.*
> *I wish I were a pink rose.*
> *I wish it wouldn't rain today.*
> *I wish I didn't have to wash a dish.*
> *I wish I had a flying carpet.*
> *I wish I could go to Disney World.*
> *I wish school was out.*
> *I wish I could go outside and play.*

After this experience, students choose one of their wishes and expand on the idea in another poem. Brandi expanded her wish this way:

> *I wish I were a teddy bear*
> *Who sat on a beautiful bed*
> *Who got a hug every night*
> *By a little girl or boy*
> *Maybe tonight I'll get my wish*
> *And wake up on a little girl's bed*
> *And then I'll be as happy as can be.*

2. Color poems.   Students begin each line of their poems with a color. They can repeat the same color in each line or choose a different color (Koch, 1970). In this example, a class of seventh graders writes about yellow:

> *Yellow is shiny galoshes*
> *splashing through mud puddles.*
> *Yellow is a street lamp*

beaming through a dark, black night.
Yellow is the egg yolk
bubbling in a frying pan.
Yellow is the lemon cake
that makes you pucker your lips.
Yellow is the sunset
and the warm summer breeze.
Yellow is the tingling in your mouth
after a lemon drop melts.

Students can also write more complex poems by expanding each idea into a stanza, as this poem about black illustrates.

Black

Black is a deep hole
sitting in the ground
waiting for animals
that live inside.

Black is a beautiful horse
standing on a high hill
with the wind
swirling its mane.

Black is a winter night sky
without stars
to keep it
company.

Black is a panther
creeping around a jungle
searching for
its prey.

As part of a unit on *Where the Wild Things Are* (Sendak, 1963), first graders made "wild thing" costumes out of large paper grocery bags and then wrote color poems about the wild things they created. This is one boy's poem:

My Wild Thing

Purple hair
it's like spaghetti.
Black eyes
they stare inside you.
Yellow teeth
they're sharp and long.
Green scales
he's just like a fish.
Red feet
and he's got fifty toes.
Orange face
he's my wild thing.

Hailstones and Halibut Bones (O'Neill, 1989) is another source of color poems; however, O'Neill uses rhyme as a poetic device, and it is important to emphasize that students' poems need not rhyme.

3. Acrostic poems.   Students write acrostic poems by taking a word and writing it vertically. They write a word or phrase beginning with each letter to complete the poem. As part of literature focus units, students can write about a book title or a character's name. This acrostic poem about *Jumanji* (Van Allsburg, 1981) was written by a fourth grader:

> **J**ungle adventure game and
> f**U**n for a while.
> **M**onkeys ransacking kitchens
> **A**nd boa constrictors slithering past.
> **N**o way out until the game is done—
> **J**ust reach the city of Jumanji.
> **I** don't want to play!

4. Five-senses poems.   Students write about a topic using each of the five senses. Sense poems are usually five lines long, with one line for each sense, as this poem written by a sixth grader demonstrates:

> *Being Heartbroken*
>
> *Sounds like thunder and lightning*
> *Looks like a carrot going through a blender*
> *Tastes like sour milk*
> *Feels like a splinter in your finger*
> *Smells like a dead fish*
> *It must be horrible!*

It is often helpful to have students develop a five-senses cluster and collect ideas for each sense. Students select from the cluster the most vivid or strongest idea for each sense to use in a line of the poem.

5. "If I were . . ." poems.   Children write about how they would feel and what they would do if they were something else—a dinosaur, a hamburger, sunshine (Koch, 1970). They begin each poem with "If I were" and tell what it would be like to be that thing. In this example, seven-year-old Robbie writes about what he would do if he were a dinosaur:

> *If I were a Tyrannosaurus Rex*
> *I would terrorize other dinosaurs*
> *And eat them up for supper.*

In composing "If I were . . ." poems, students use personification, explore ideas and feelings, and consider the world from a different vantage point.

6. Preposition poems.   Students begin each line of a preposition poem with a preposition, and a delightful poetic rewording of lines often results from the attempt. Seventh grader Mike wrote this preposition poem about a movie super-hero:

> *Superman*
>
> *Within the city*
> *In a phone booth*
> *Into his clothes*
> *Like a bird*
> *In the sky*
> *Through the walls*
> *Until the crime*
> *Among us*
> *is defeated!*

It is helpful for children to brainstorm a list of prepositions to refer to when they write preposition poems. Students may find that they need to ignore the formula for a line or two to give the content of their poems top priority, or they may mistakenly begin a line with an infinitive (e.g., "to say") rather than a preposition. These forms provide a structure or skeleton for students' writing that should be adapted as necessary.

Why do teachers need to know about poetic forms?

When students in the elementary grades read and recite poetry, the emphasis is on introducing them to poetry so that they have a pleasurable experience. Students need to have fun as they do choral readings of poems, pick out favorite lines, and respond to poems. Teachers need to be aware of poetic forms so that they can point out the form when it is appropriate or provide information about a poetic form when students ask. For example, sometimes when students read free verse they say it isn't poetry because it doesn't rhyme. At this time, it's appropriate to point out that poetry doesn't have to rhyme and that this poem is a poem—that this type of poetry is called free verse. Teachers might also explain that in free verse, creating an image or projecting a voice is more important than the rhyme scheme. It is not appropriate for students to analyze the rhyme scheme or search out the meaning of the poem. Instead, children should focus on what the poem means to them. Teachers introduce poetic forms when students are writing poetry. When students use poetic formulas such as color poems, acrostics, and haiku they are often more successful than when they attempt to create rhyming verse, because the formulas provide a framework for students' writing.

Review

Three broad types of literature are stories, informational books, and poetry, and they are included in basal readers and published as trade books. Each type of text has a unique structure or organization. Story elements include plot, characters, setting, point of view, and theme. Informational books are organized into expository text structures, of which the five most common patterns are description, sequence, comparison, cause and effect, and problem and solution. The most common poetic forms for children are rhymed verse, narrative poems, haiku, and free verse. Teachers need to be aware of the structure of text so that they can help students become more successful readers and writers. Guidelines for effectively teaching students about the structure of text are summarized in the figure on page 236.

HOW EFFECTIVE TEACHERS
Teach the Structure of Text

Effective Practices

1. Teachers point out differences among stories, informational books, and poems.

2. Teachers help students set aesthetic or efferent purposes for reading.

3. Teachers include all three types of literature—stories, informational books, and poems—in text sets.

4. Teachers choose high-quality literature because they understand that students' writing reflects what they are reading.

5. Teachers teach minilessons about story elements, expository text structures, and poetic forms.

6. Students examine story elements in stories they are reading as part of literature focus units.

7. Students examine expository text structure in informational books they are reading as part of theme studies.

8. Students make charts to emphasize the structure of texts while taking notes.

9. Students examine the patterns authors use to write poems and then write poems using the same patterns.

10. Students use their knowledge of text structure when writing stories, informational books, and poems.

Ineffective Practices

1. Teachers call all texts "stories" and don't differentiate among the three types of literature.

2. Teachers don't teach students to set purposes for reading.

3. Teachers don't consider whether all three types of literature are included in text sets for students to read.

4. Teachers don't consider the impact of the quality of literature on students' reading and writing development.

5. Teachers focus on other aspects of reading instruction and rarely teach about text structure.

6. Students don't understand that authors use plot, setting, and other elements as they develop stories.

7. Students don't examine the structure of the text in materials they read.

8. Students complete worksheets instead of making structural charts and diagrams.

9. Students don't examine the organization of poems and rarely write any poems.

10. Teachers focus on other aspects of writing and do not ask students to organize their writing according to text structure.

References

Au, K. H. (1992). Constructing the theme of a story. *Language Arts, 69,* 106–111.

Bruner, J. (1986). *Actual minds, possible worlds.* Cambridge, MA: Harvard University Press.

De Ford, D. (1981). Literacy: Reading, writing, and other essentials. *Language Arts, 58,* 652–658.

Dressel, J. H. (1990). The effects of listening to and discussing different qualities of children's literature on the narrative writing of fifth graders. *Research in the Teaching of English, 24,* 397–414.

Eckhoff, B. (1983). How reading affects children's writing. *Language Arts, 60,* 607–616.

Flood, J., Lapp, D., & Farnan, N. (1986). A reading-writing procedure that teaches expository paragraph structure. *The Reading Teacher, 39,* 556–562.

Freedman, R. (1992). Fact or fiction? In E. B. Freeman & D. G. Person (Eds.), *Using nonfiction tradebooks in the elementary classroom: From ants to zeppelins* (pp. 2–10). Urbana, IL: National Council of Teachers of English.

Goodman, K. S. (1988). Look what they've done to Judy Blume!: The "basalization" of children's literature. *The New Advocate, 1,* 29–41.

Graves, D. H. (1992). *Explore poetry.* Portsmouth, NH: Heinemann.

Johnson, T. D., & Louis, D. R. (1987). *Literacy through literature.* Portsmouth, NH: Heinemann.

Koch, K. (1970). *Wishes, lies, and dreams.* New York: Vintage.

Langer, J. A. (1986). *Children reading and writing: Structures and strategies.* Norwood, NJ: Ablex.

Lapp, D., Flood, J., & Farnan, N. (1992). Basal readers and literature: A tight fit or a mismatch? In K. D. Wood & A. Moss (Eds.), *Exploring literature in the classroom: Contents and methods* (pp. 35–57). Norwood, MA: Christopher Gordon.

Larrick, N. (1991). *Let's do a poem! Introducing poetry to children.* New York: Delacorte.

Lehr, S. S. (1991). *The child's developing sense of theme: Responses to literature.* New York: Teachers College Press.

Lukens, R. J. (1995). *A critical handbook of children's literature* (5th ed.). Glenview, IL: Scott, Foresman.

McGee, L. M., & Richgels, D. J. (1985). Teaching expository text structures to elementary students. *The Reading Teacher, 38,* 739–745.

Meyer, B. J., & Freedle, R. O. (1984). Effects of discourse type on recall. *American Educational Research Journal, 21,* 121–143.

Niles, O. S. (1974). Organization perceived. In H. L. Herber (Ed.), *Perspectives in reading: Developing study skills in secondary schools.* Newark, DE: International Reading Association.

Ogle, D. M. (1986). K-W-L: A teaching model that develops active reading of expository text. *The Reading Teacher, 39,* 564–570.

Pappas, C. (1991). Fostering full access to literacy by including information books. *Language Arts, 68,* 449–462.

Pappas, C. (1993). Is narrative "primary"? Some insights from kindergartners' pretend readings of stories and information books. *Journal of Reading Behavior, 25,* 97–129.

Piccolo, J. A. (1987). Expository text structures: Teaching and learning strategies. *The Reading Teacher, 40,* 838–847.

Raphael, T. E., Englert, C. S., & Kirschner, B. W. (1989). Acquisition of expository writing skills. In J. M. Mason (Ed.), *Reading and writing connections* (pp. 261–290). Boston: Allyn & Bacon.

Roop, P. (1992). Nonfiction books in the primary classroom: Soaring with the swans. In E. B. Freeman & D. G. Person (Eds.), *Using nonfiction tradebooks in the elementary classroom: From ants to zeppelins* (pp. 106–112). Urbana, IL: National Council of Teachers of English.

Rosenblatt, L. (1978). *The reader, the text, the poem: The transactional theory of the literary work.* Carbondale: Southern Illinois University Press.

Tiedt, I. (1970). Exploring poetry patterns. *Elementary English, 45,* 1082–1084.

Tompkins, G. E. (1994). *Teaching writing: Balancing process and product* (2nd ed.). New York: Merrill/Macmillan.

Vardell, S. (1991). A new "picture of the world": The NCTE Orbis Pictus Award for outstanding nonfiction for children. *Language Arts, 68,* 474–479.

Wells, G. (1986). *The meaning makers: Children learning language and using language to learn.* Portsmouth, NH: Heinemann.

Whitin, D. J., & Wilde, S. (1992). *Read any good math lately? Children's books for mathematical learning, K–6.* Portsmouth, NH: Heinemann.

Children's Book References

Aker, S. (1990). *What comes in 2's, 3's, and 4's?* New York: Simon & Schuster.

Ancona, G. (1992). *Man and mustang.* New York: Macmillan.

Arnold, C. (1993). *Dinosaurs all around: An artist's view of the prehistoric world.* New York: Clarion.

Atwood, S. (1971). *Haiku: The mood of the earth.* New York: Scribner.

Blume, J. (1972). *Tales of a fourth grade nothing.* New York: Dutton.

Calder, S. J. (1989). *If you were an ant.* Englewood Cliffs, NJ: Silver Books/Silver Burdett.

Carle, E. (1969). *The very hungry caterpillar.* New York: Philomel.

Carle, E. (1986). *The grouchy ladybug.* New York: Harper & Row.

Carle, E. (1990). *The very quiet cricket.* New York: Philomel.

Cole, J. (1987). *The magic school bus inside the earth.* New York: Scholastic.

Cowcher, H. (1990). *Antarctica.* New York: Farrar, Straus & Giroux.

Day, A. (1985). *Good dog, Carl.* New York: Green Tiger Press.

Driver, R. (1994). *AnimaLimericks.* New York: Half Moon Books.

Feelings, M., & Feelings, T. (1971). *Moja means one: Swahili counting book.* New York: Dial.

Fleischman, P. (1985). *I am phoenix: Poems for two voices.* New York: Harper & Row.

Fleischman, P. (1988). *Joyful noise: Poems for two voices.* New York: Harper & Row.

Fowler, A. (1990). *It's a good thing there are insects.* Chicago: Childrens Press.

Freedman, R. (1987). *Lincoln: A photobiography.* New York: Clarion.

Fritz, J. (1976). *Will you sign here, John Hancock?* New York: Coward-McCann.

Fritz, J. (1989). *The great little Madison.* New York: Putnam.

Galdone, P. (1970). *The three little pigs.* New York: Seabury.

Gardiner, J. R. (1980). *Stone Fox.* New York: Harper & Row.

George, J. C. (1972). *Julie of the wolves.* New York: Harper & Row.

Gibbons, G. (1991). *Surrounded by sea: Life on a New England fishing island.* Boston: Little, Brown.

Gibbons, G. (1992). *Spiders.* New York: Holiday House.

Giff, P. R. (1984). *The beast in Ms. Rooney's room.* New York: Bantam.

Giff, P. R. (1984). *Fish face.* New York: Bantam.

Greenfield, E. (1988). *Nathaniel talking.* New York: Black Butterfly Children's Books.

Guiberson, B. Z. (1991). *Cactus hotel.* New York: Henry Holt.

Harter, P. (1994). *Shadow play: Night haiku.* New York: Simon & Schuster.

Hoban, T. (1987). *26 letters and 99 cents.* New York: Greenwillow.

Howe, D., & Howe, J. (1979). *Bunnicula: A rabbit-tale of mystery.* New York: Atheneum.

Hunt, J. (1989). *Illuminations.* New York: Bradbury.

Hutchins, P. (1968). *Rosie's walk.* New York: Macmillan.

Hyman, T. S. (1977). *The sleeping beauty.* New York: Holiday House.

Kennedy, X. J. (1982). *Knock at a star: A child's introduction to poetry.* Boston: Little, Brown.

Knight, M. B. (1993). *Who belongs here? An American story.* Gardiner, ME: Tulbury House.

Lear, E. (1994). *There was an old man: A gallery of nonsense rhymes.* New York: Morrow.

L'Engle, M. (1962). *A wrinkle in time.* New York: Farrar, Straus & Giroux.

Lester, H. (1988). *Tacky the penguin.* Boston: Houghton Mifflin.

Levine, E. (1986). *. . . If you traveled west in a covered wagon.* New York: Scholastic.

Lewis, R. (1965). *In a spring garden.* New York: Dial.

Livingston, M. C. (Ed.). (1982). *How pleasant to know Mr. Lear!* New York: Holiday House.

Lobel, A. (1983). *Pigericks: A book of pig limericks.* New York: Harper & Row.

Longfellow, H. W. (1990). *Paul Revere's ride.* New York: Dutton.

Lowry, L. (1989). *Number the stars.* Boston: Houghton Mifflin.

Lowry, L. (1993). *The giver.* Boston: Houghton Mifflin.

Macaulay, D. (1977). *Castle.* Boston: Houghton Mifflin.

MacLachlan, P. (1985). *Sarah, plain and tall.* New York: Harper & Row.

Maestro, B. (1992). *How do apples grow?* New York: Harper Collins.

Martin, B., Jr. (1983). *Brown bear, brown bear, what do you see?* New York: Holt, Rinehart & Winston.

Martin, B., Jr., & Archambault, J. (1985). *The ghost-eye tree.* New York: Holt, Rinehart & Winston.

Mayer, M. (1987). *The ugly duckling.* New York: Macmillan.

McCloskey, R. (1969). *Make way for ducklings.* New York: Viking.

Noyes, A. (1983). *The highwayman.* New York: Lothrop, Lee & Shepard.

O'Dell, S. (1960). *Island of the blue dolphins.* Boston: Houghton Mifflin.

O'Neill, M. (1989). *Hailstones and halibut bones.* New York: Doubleday.

Pallotta, J. (1991). *The underwater alphabet book.* Watertown, MA: Charlesbridge.

Pallotta, J. (1992). *The icky bug counting book.* Watertown, MA: Charlesbridge.

Paterson, K. (1977). *Bridge to Terabithia.* New York: Crowell.

Potter, B. (1902). *The tale of Peter Rabbit.* New York: Warne.

Prelutsky, J. (1983). *The Random House book of poetry for children.* New York: Random House.

Prelutsky, J. (1985). *My parents think I'm sleeping.* New York: Greenwillow.

Rauzon, M. J. (1993). *Horns, antlers, fangs, and tusks.* New York: Lothrop, Lee & Shepard.

Rylant, C. (1992). *Best wishes.* Katonwah, NY: Richard C. Owen.

Schwartz, D. (1989). *If you made a million.* New York: Lothrop, Lee & Shepard.

Scieszka, J. (1989). *The true story of the three little pigs!* New York: Viking.

Scott, A. H. (1990). *One good horse: A cowpuncher's counting book.* New York: Greenwillow.

Sendak, M. (1963). *Where the wild things are.* New York: Harper & Row.

Showers, P. (1985). *What happens to a hamburger?* New York: Harper & Row.

Siebert, D. (1991). *Sierra.* New York: HarperCollins.

Simon, S. (1989). *Whales.* New York: Crowell.

Simon, S. (1993). *Mercury.* New York: Morrow.

Soto, G. (1992). *Neighborhood odes.* San Diego: Harcourt Brace Jovanovich.

Speare, E. G. (1958). *The witch of blackbird pond.* Boston: Houghton Mifflin.

Steig, W. (1969). *Sylvester and the magic pebble.* New York: Simon & Schuster.

Steig, W. (1982). *Doctor De Soto*. New York: Farrar, Straus & Giroux.

Taylor, M. D. (1976). *Roll of thunder, hear my cry*. New York: Dial.

Van Allsburg, C. (1981). *Jumanji*. Boston: Houghton Mifflin.

Van Allsburg, C. (1986). *The stranger*. Boston: Houghton Mifflin.

Viorst, J. (1977). *Alexander and the terrible, horrible, no good, very bad day*. New York: Atheneum.

von Tscharner, R., & Fleming, R. L. (1987). *New Providence: A changing cityscape*. San Diego: Harcourt Brace Jovanovich.

Waber, B. (1972). *Ira sleeps over*. Boston: Houghton Mifflin.

Waters, K. (1989). *Sarah Morton's day: A day in the life of a pilgrim girl*. New York: Scholastic.

White, E. B. (1952). *Charlotte's web*. New York: Harper & Row.

Wiesner, D. (1991). *Tuesday*. New York: Clarion.

Williams, V. B. (1982). *A chair for my mother*. New York: Mulberry.

Winter, J. (1988). *Follow the drinking gourd*. New York: Knopf.

Zemach, M. (1983). *The little red hen*. New York: Farrar, Straus & Giroux.

PART III

How Do Teachers Organize for Literacy Instruction?

Mrs. Peterson shares objects from a book box—white vegetables, a bunny, and a children's version of *Dracula*—as she introduces *Bunnicula: A Rabbit-Tale of Mystery*.

TEXT SET

Featured Selection

Howe, D., & Howe, J. (1979). *Bunnicula: A rabbit-tale of mystery.* New York: Atheneum.

Related Books

Howe, J. (1982). *Howliday Inn.* New York: Atheneum.
Howe, J. (1984). *The celery stalks at midnight.* New York: Atheneum.
Howe, J. (1987) *Nighty-nightmare.* New York: Atheneum.
Howe, J. (1989). *Harold and Chester in Scared silly: A Halloween treat.* New York: Morrow.
Howe, J. (1990). *Hot fudge.* New York: Morrow.
Howe, J. (1992). *Return to Howliday Inn.* New York: Atheneum.

About the Author

Howe, J. (1994). *Playing with words.* Katonah, NY: Richard C. Owen.

Mrs. Peterson joins a small group of sixth graders to talk about the fifth chapter and make predictions about what will happen next.

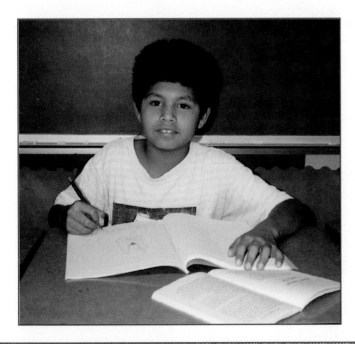

Students write responses in reading logs after they read each chapter. They focus on making connections to their own lives.

Mrs. Peterson shares information about author James Howe and reads aloud his autobiography *Playing With Words.*

Students learn one way new words are created through a minilesson on portmanteau words.

Bunny + Dracula = Bunnicula

Students extend their learning as they develop projects. This student shares vampire jokes and riddles with classmates

These girls share their "Count Dracula's Vampire Facts" poster with the class.

CHAPTER 7

The Reading and Writing Processes

The seventh graders in Mrs. Lentz's class are reading the Newbery Award–winning book *The Giver* (Lowry, 1993). In this futuristic story, 12-year-old Jonas is selected to become the next Keeper of the Memories, and he discovers the terrible truth of his community. Mrs. Lentz has a class set of paperbacks of the book, and her students use the reading process as they read and explore the book.

To introduce the book to her students, she asks them to get into small groups and brainstorm lists of all the things they would change about life if they could. They write the lists on butcher paper. Their lists include: getting $200 for allowance every week, no more homework, no AIDS, no crime, no gangs, no parents, no taking out the garbage, and being allowed to drive a car at age 10. The groups hang their lists on the chalkboard and share their lists. Then Mrs. Lentz puts check marks by many of the items, seeming to agree with the points. Next she explains that the class is going to read a story about life in the future. She explains that *The Giver* takes place in a planned utopian, or "perfect," society with the qualities that she checked on students' brainstormed lists.

She passes out copies of the book and uses shared reading as she reads the first chapter aloud and students follow along in their books. Then the class talks about the first chapter, and they ask a lot of questions. They want to know: Why were there so many rules? Doesn't anyone drive a car? What does "released" mean? Why are children called a "Seven" or a "Four"? What does it mean that people are "given" spouses—don't they fall in love and get married? Why does Jonas have to tell his feelings? Why can't he keep them to himself? Classmates share their ideas and are eager to continue reading. Mrs. Lentz's reading aloud of the first chapter and the questions that the students raise cause everyone in the class to become interested in the story, even several students who often try to remain uninvolved in class activities. The power of this story grabs them all.

The class sets up a schedule for reading and discussion. Every three days they will come together to talk about the chapters they have read, and over two weeks the class will read and talk about the story. They will also write in **reading logs** (see the Compendium for more information about this and all other highlighted terms in this chapter) after reading the first chapter and then five more times as they are reading. In their reading logs, students write reactions to the story. Maria wrote this journal entry after she finished reading the book:

> *Jonas had to do it. He had to save Gabriel's life because the next day Jonas's father was going to release (kill) him. He had it all planned out. That was important. He was very brave to leave his parents and his home. But I guess they weren't his parents really and his home wasn't all that good. I don't know if I could have done it but he did the right thing. He had to get out. He saved himself and he saved little Gabe. I'm glad he took Gabriel. That community was supposed to be safe but it really was dangerous. It was weird to not have colors. I guess that things that at first seem to be good are really bad.*

Ron explored some of themes of the story:

> *Starving. He has memories of food. He's still hungry. But he's free. Food is safe. Freedom is surprises. Never saw a bird before. Same-same-same. Be-*

fore he was starved for colors, memories and choice. Choice. To do what you want. To be who you can be. He won't starve.

Alicia thought about a lesson her mother taught her as she wrote:

As Jonas fled from the community he lost his memories so that they would go back to the people there. Would they learn from them? Would they remember them? Or would life go on just the same? I think you have to do it yourself if you are going to learn. That's what my mom says. Somebody else can't do it for you. But Jonas did it. He got out with Gabe.

Tomas wrote about the Christmas connection at the end of the story:

Jonas and Gabe came to the town at Christmas. Why did Lois Lowry do that? Gabe is like the baby Jesus, I think. It is like a rebirth—being born again. Jonas and his old community didn't go to church. Maybe they didn't believe in God. Now Jonas will be a Christian and the people in the church will welcome them. Gabe won't be released. I think Gabe is like Jesus because people tried to release Jesus.

During their discussions, which Mrs. Lentz calls "conversations," students talk about many of the same points they raise in their journal entries. The story fascinates her students—at first they think about how simple and safe life would be, but then they think about all the things they take for granted that they would have to give up to live in Jonas's ordered society. They talk about bravery and making choices, and applaud Jonas's decision to flee with Gabriel. They also speculate about Jonas's and Gabe's new lives in Elsewhere. Will they be happy? Will they ever go back to check on their old community? Will other people escape to Elsewhere?

The students collect "important" words from the story for their **word wall.** After reading Chapters 4, 5, and 6, students add these words to the word wall:

leisurely pace	bikeports	regulated
invariably	gravitating	rehabilitation
serene	chastised	rule infraction
the wanting	stirrings	reprieve
relinquish	chastisement	assignment

Sometimes students choose unfamiliar or long words, but they also choose words like *assignment* that are important to the story. Students refer to the list for words and their spellings for the various activities they are involved in. Later during the unit, Mrs. Lentz teaches a minilesson about root words using some of these words.

Mrs. Lentz teaches a series of **minilessons** about reading strategies and skills as students read the story. The day after students read about colors in the story, she teaches a minilesson on the visualization strategy. She begins by rereading excerpts from Chapters 7 and 8 about Jonas being selected to be the next Receiver and asks students to try to draw a picture of the scene in their minds. Mrs. Lentz asks students to focus on the sights, sounds, smells, and feelings, and she talks about the importance of bringing a story to life in their minds as they read. Then students draw pictures of their visualizations and share them in small groups.

To review spelling patterns and phonics rules, Mrs. Lentz divides the class into six groups and gives each group a different set of letter cards that can be sorted to spell a word from the word wall: *stirrings, release, memories, receiver, fascinated,* or *ceremony.* She asks the students in each group to sort the letter cards to spell as many different words as they can. Letters from *ceremony,* for example, can be used to spell *me, my, on, no, more, core, cone, come,* and *money.* Then they arrange all of the letters to spell the word wall word.

Another minilesson is about literary opposites. She explains that authors often introduce conflict and develop themes using contrasts or opposites. She asks students to think of opposites in *The Giver.* One example that she suggests is *safe* and *free.* Other opposites that the students suggest include:

alive—released	color—black and white
choice—no choice	conform—do your own thing
rules—anarchy	stirrings—the pill
families—family units	memories—no memories

Mrs. Lentz asks students to think about how the opposites relate to the development of the story and how Lois Lowry made the opposites explicit in *The Giver.* Students

FIGURE 7–1   One Square for a Story Quilt on *The Giver*

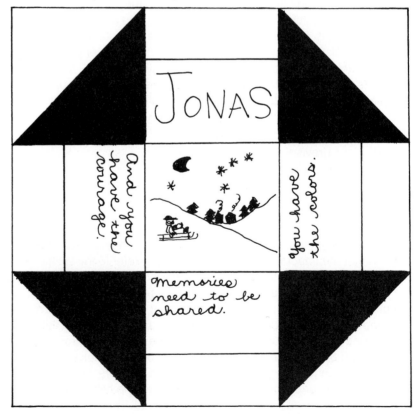

talk about how the community seemed safe at the beginning of the story, but chapter by chapter Lowry uncovered the shortcomings of the community. They also talk about themes of the story reflected in these opposites. Mrs. Lentz ends the minilesson by asking students to look for opposites in other stories they read.

After they finish reading the book, students have a **read-around** in which they select and read aloud favorite passages to the class. Then students make a **story quilt.** Each student prepares a quilt piece made of construction paper and writes a favorite quote on the square. One quilt square is shown in Figure 7–1. The students decide to use white, gray, and black for most of the quilt square to represent the sameness of Jonas's community, and they add color in the center to represent Else-where.

Students also choose projects that they will work on individually or in small groups to extend their reading of *The Giver.* One student makes a **book box** with objects related to the story, and two other students read *Hailstones and Halibut Bones* (O'Neill, 1989) and then write their own collection of color poetry. One student makes an **open-mind portrait** of Jonas to show his thoughts the night he decided to escape with Gabe. Some students read other books with similar themes or other books by Lois Lowry, and they share their books with the class during a **book talk.** Other students write about memories of their own lives. They use the writing process to draft, refine, and publish their writing. They share their published pieces at a class meeting at the end of the unit.

The reading process that Mrs. Lentz uses represents a significant shift in thinking about what people do as they read. Mrs. Lentz understands that readers create meaning as they negotiate the texts they are reading, and that they use their life and literature experiences and knowledge of written language as they read. She knows that it is quite common for two people to read the same story and come away with different interpretations, and that their understanding of the story will depend on things that have happened in their own lives. Meaning does not exist on the pages of the book readers are reading; instead, meaning is created through the interaction between readers and what they are reading.

The reading process involves a series of stages during which readers construct interpretations as they read and respond to the text. The term *text* includes all reading materials—stories, maps, newspapers, cereal boxes, textbooks, and so on; it is not limited to basal reader textbooks. The writing process is a similar recursive process involving a variety of activities as students gather and organize ideas, draft their compositions, revise and edit the drafts, and, finally, publish their writings.

Reading and writing have been thought of as the flip sides of a coin—as opposites; readers decoded or deciphered written language, and writers encoded or produced written language. Then researchers began to note similarities between reading and writing and talked of both of them as processes. Now reading and writing are viewed as parallel processes of meaning construction, and readers and writers use similar strategies for making meaning with text.

Fluent readers create meaning as they read.

In this chapter you will read about the reading and writing processes and how teachers use these process in designing literacy instruction. As you continue reading, think about these questions:

■ What are the stages in the reading process?
■ What are the stages in the writing process?
■ How are the two processes alike?
■ How do teachers use these two processes in teaching reading and writing?

THE READING PROCESS

Reading is a process in which readers create meaning or develop an interpretation. During reading, the meaning does not go from the page to readers. Instead, it is a complex negotiation between the text and readers that is shaped by many factors: readers' knowledge about the topic; their purpose for reading; the language community readers belong to; how closely that language matches the language used in the text; readers' culturally based expectations about reading; and readers' expectations about reading based on their previous experiences (Weaver, 1988). The reading process involves five stages: preparing to read, reading, responding, exploring, and extending. These stages are overviewed in Figure 7–2.

Stage 1: Preparing

The reading process does not begin as readers open a book and read the first sentence. The first stage is preparing to read. In the vignette, Mrs. Lentz developed her students' background knowledge and stimulated their interest in *The Giver* as they brainstormed lists and talked about how wonderful life would be in a "perfect" world. As readers prepare to read, they make connections, set purposes, and plan for reading.

FIGURE 7–2 Key Features of the Reading Process

Stage 1: Preparing to Read

- Students set purposes.
- Students connect to prior personal experiences.
- Students connect to prior literary experiences.
- Students connect to theme studies or special interests.
- Students make predictions.
- Students preview the text.
- Students consult the index to locate information.

Stage 2: Reading

- Students make predictions.
- Students apply skills and strategies.
- Students read independently; with a partner; using shared reading or guided reading; or listen to the text read aloud.
- Students read the illustrations, charts, and diagrams.
- Students read the entire text from beginning to end.
- Students read one or more sections of text to learn specific information.
- Students take notes.

Stage 3: Responding

- Students write in a reading log.
- Students participate in a grand conversation.

Stage 4: Exploring

- Students reread and think more deeply about the text.
- Students make connections with personal experiences.
- Students make connections with other literary experiences.
- Students examine the author's craft.
- Students identify memorable quotes.
- Students learn new vocabulary words.
- Students participate in minilessons on reading procedures, concepts, strategies, and skills.

Stage 5: Extending

- Students construct projects.
- Students use information in theme cycles.
- Students connect with related books.
- Students reflect on their interpretation.
- Students value the reading experience.

Making Connections. Readers activate their prior (background) knowledge or schemata about the book or other text they plan to read. They make connections to personal experiences, to literary experiences, or to theme studies in the classroom. The topic of the book, the title, the author, the genre, an illustration, a comment someone makes about the text, or something else may trigger this activation, but for readers to make meaning with the text, schemata must be activated. For instance, readers who love horses and are very knowledgeable about them often choose horse books like *Misty of Chincoteague* (Henry, 1963) to read. Those who like books written by Beverly Cleary or Dr. Seuss choose books by their favorite authors.

Sometimes teachers collect objects related to the book and create a book box to use in introducing the book to the class. As you saw on pages 240–243, Mrs. Peterson collected objects related to *Bunnicula: A Rabbit-Tale of Mystery* (Howe & Howe, 1979). She painted fabric vegetables white and added two little "fang" holes in each one and placed them in the box. She also added a small black-and-white stuffed bunny and a book about vampires. As she introduced the book, she showed students the objects, talked about each one, and asked students to speculate on how they might be related to the story.

Setting Purposes.   The two overarching purposes for reading are pleasure and information. When students read for pleasure or enjoyment, they read aesthetically, to be carried into the world of the text; when they read to locate information or for directions about how to do something, they read efferently (Rosenblatt, 1978). Often readers use elements of both purposes as they read, but usually one purpose is more primary to the reading experience than the other. For example, when students pick up *The Sweetest Fig* (1993) or *Bad Day at Riverbend* (1995), two of the newest Chris Van Allsburg picture book fantasies, their primary purpose is enjoyment. They want to experience the story, but at the same time, they search for the white dog, a trademark that Van Allsburg includes in all of his books, and they compare this book with others of his they have read. As they search for the white dog or make comparisons, they add efferent purposes to their primarily aesthetic reading experience.

Purpose-setting is usually directed by the teacher during literature focus units, but in reading workshop students set their own purposes because everyone is reading different self-selected books. For teacher-directed purpose-setting, teachers explain how students are expected to read and what they will do after reading. The goal of teacher-directed purpose-setting is to help students learn how to set personally relevant purposes when they are reading independently (Blanton, Wood, & Moorman, 1990). Students should always have a purpose for reading, whether they are reading aesthetically or efferently, whether reading a text for the first time or the tenth. Readers are more successful when they have a single purpose for reading the entire selection. A single purpose is more effective than multiple purposes, and sustaining a single purpose is more effective than presenting students with a series of purposes as they read.

When readers have purposes for reading, their comprehension of the selection they are reading is enhanced in three ways, whether teachers provide the purpose or students set their own purpose (Blanton et al., 1990). First of all, the purpose guides the reading process that students use. Having a purpose provides motivation and direction for reading, as well as a mechanism that students use for monitoring their reading. As they monitor their reading, students ask themselves whether or not they are fulfilling their purpose.

Second, setting a purpose activates a plan for readers to use while reading. Purpose-setting causes students to draw on background knowledge, consider strategies they might use as they read, and think about the structure of the text they are reading. Third, students are better able to sort out important from unimportant information as they read when they have a purpose for reading. Teachers direct students' attention to relevant concepts as they set purposes for reading and show them how to connect the concepts they are reading about to their prior knowledge about a topic.

Students read differently depending on the purpose for reading, a[nd] [the instruc]tional procedures that teachers use also vary according to the purpo[se]. When students are reading stories, teachers might use the **Directed Re[ad]ing Activity** (DRTA) to help students predict and then read to confirm [their] predictions, or have students create **story maps** to focus their attention [on char]acters, or another element of story structure. When students are rea[ding informa]tional books and content-area textbooks, teachers might use an **antici[pation guide]** to activate prior knowledge, or **cubing** to explore a concept from d[ifferent view]points.

In contrast to teacher-directed purpose-setting, students set their [own purposes] for reading during reading workshop and at other times when they cho[ose the] books to read. Often they choose materials that are intrinsically interest[ing or that] describe something they want to learn more about. As students gain [experience in] reading, identify favorite authors and illustrators, and learn about genre, they have other criteria to use in choosing books and setting purposes for reading. When teachers conference with students during reading workshop, they often ask students about their purposes for reading and why they choose particular books to read.

Planning for Reading. Students often preview the reading selection as they prepare to read. They look through the selection and check its length, the reading difficulty of the selection, and the illustrations in order to judge the general suitability of the selection for them as readers. Previewing serves an important function as students connect their prior knowledge, identify their purpose for reading, and take their first look at the selection. Teachers set the guidelines for the reading experience. Teachers explain how the book will be read—independently, in small groups, or as a class—and set the schedule for reading. Setting the schedule is especially important when students are reading a chapter book. Often teachers and students work together to create a two-, three-, or four-week schedule for reading and responding and then write the schedule on a calendar to which students can refer.

Students make other types of plans depending on the type of selection they will read. Students who are preparing to read stories make predictions about the story. Their predictions often focus on the characters and events in the story. Students often use the title of the selection and the illustration on the cover of the book or on the first page as a basis for their predictions. If they have read other books by the same author or other selections in the same genre, students also use this information in making their predictions. Sometimes students share their predictions orally as they talk about the selection, while at other times they write and draw their predictions as the first entry in their reading logs.

When students are preparing to read informational books, they preview the selection by flipping through the pages and noting section headings, illustrations, diagrams, and other charts. Sometimes they examine the table of contents to see how the book is organized, or consult the index to locate specific information they want to read. They may also notice unfamiliar terminology and other words they can check in the glossary, ask a classmate or the teacher about, or look up in a dictionary. Teachers also use anticipation guides, **prereading plans** (PRePs), and the survey step of the **SQ3R** study procedure as they introduce informational books and content-area textbooks.

Students often make notes in **learning logs** as they explore informational books and content-area textbooks. They do **quickwrites** and **quickdraws** to activate prior knowledge and explore the concepts to be presented in the selection, write important terminology, and draw **clusters, data charts,** and other diagrams they will complete as they read. As they move through the remaining stages in the reading process, students add other information to their learning logs.

Stage 2: Reading

In this stage, students read the book or other selection. They use their knowledge of word identification, sight words, strategies, skills, and vocabulary while they read. Fluent readers are better able to understand what they are reading because they identify most words automatically and use decoding skills when necessary. They also apply their knowledge of the structure of text as they create meaning. They continue reading as long as what they are reading fits the meaning they are constructing. When something doesn't make sense, readers slow down, back up, and reread until they are making meaning again.

Students may read the entire text or only read sections. When students are reading aesthetically, they usually read the entire text, but when they are reading efferently, they may be searching for specific information and read only until they locate that information. Also, students may decide to put a book down if it does not capture their interest, if it is too difficult to read, or if it does not have the information they are searching for. It is unrealistic to assume that students will always read entire texts or finish reading every book they begin.

Outside of school, readers usually read silently and independently. Sometimes, however, people listen as someone else reads. Young children often sit in a parent's lap and look at the illustrations as the parent reads a picture book aloud. Adults also listen to books read aloud on cassette tapes. In the classroom, teachers and students use five types of reading: shared reading, guided reading, independent reading, buddy reading, and reading aloud to students.

Shared Reading.   Teachers use shared reading during literature focus units to introduce a book or other reading selection to students before the students read the selection with partners or individually. In this type of reading, students follow along as the teacher reads the selection aloud. Kindergarten teachers and other primary-grade teachers often use big books—enlarged versions of the selection—for shared reading (Holdaway, 1979). Students sit so that they can see the book, and they either listen to the teacher read aloud or join in and read along with the teacher. The teacher or a student points to each line of text as it is read to draw students' attention to the words and to highlight important concepts about the direction of print on a page and about letters, words, and sentences.

Teachers also use shared reading when students have individual copies of the reading selection. Students follow along in their copies as the teacher or another fluent reader reads aloud. This "first" reading is preparation for students so that they become familiar enough with the story line and the vocabulary that they can read the text independently later during the literature focus unit.

When students are reading chapter books, shared reading is used as the main reading approach during the unit when students can't read the selection independently. The teacher and other fluent readers take turns reading aloud as students follow along in their copies of the selection. To ensure that all the students are following along in their copies of the book, teachers sometimes ask all students or a group of students to read aloud very softly or "mumble" along as they read aloud. Sometimes teachers read the first chapter or two of a chapter book together as a class using shared reading, and then students use other types of reading as they read the rest of the book. Only students for whom the book is too difficult continue to use shared reading and read along with the teacher.

There are several variations of shared reading. One is **choral reading,** when students divide into groups to read poems aloud. Another type is **readers theatre,** in which students read play scripts aloud. A third type of shared reading is the listening center. Students often listen to a book read aloud as they follow along in the book. Listening centers are a good way to provide additional reading practice to help students become fluent readers.

Guided Reading.   Students and the teacher read and talk their way through the reading of a text together in guided reading. This type of reading is teacher-directed and usually done in small groups. Teachers invite students to make predictions before reading or ask questions to guide students' reading, and students read short sections of the selection. Students can read the selection orally or silently, but if the selection is appropriate for their reading levels, it is usually read silently. Then students stop reading at a predetermined point in the selection and talk about their reading. Then the cycle of asking questions, reading, and discussing is repeated several times as students and the teacher read the selection. One example of guided reading is the Directed Reading-Thinking Activity (DRTA) (Stauffer, 1975).

Guided reading is often used in literature focus units. Teachers read the featured selection in small groups, and they have opportunities to demonstrate reading strategies, clarify misconceptions as students read, point out key vocabulary words, and take advantage of many teachable moments. The small-group arrangement also gives

In guided reading, small groups of students read and discuss the story with the teacher.

teachers the opportunity to observe individual students as they read, monitor their comprehension, and informally assess their reading progress. However, the ask-read-discuss cycle can become intrusive and interfere with students' understanding of the selection if teachers repeat it too often.

Independent Reading.   When students read independently, they read silently by themselves, for their own purposes, and at their own pace (Hornsby, Sukarna, & Parry, 1986). In order for students to read independently, the reading selections must be at their reading level. Students read the featured selection independently during literature focus units, but this is often after they have already read the selection once or twice with assistance from the teacher. They also read related books from the text set independently as part of these units.

During reading workshop, students almost always read independently. They choose the books they want to read, and they need to learn how to choose books that are written at an appropriate level of difficulty. Even young children in kindergarten can do a variation of independent reading when they look at books, creating their own text to accompany the illustrations.

Independent reading is an important part of the literature-based reading program because it is the most authentic type of reading. This type of reading is what most people do when they read, and this is the way students develop a love of reading and come to think of themselves as readers. The reading selection, however, must be either at an appropriate level of difficulty or very familiar so that students can read it independently. Otherwise, teachers use one of the other four types of reading to support students and make it possible for them to participate in the reading experience.

Buddy Reading.   In buddy reading, students read or reread a selection with a classmate. Sometimes students read with buddies because it is an enjoyable social activity, and sometimes they read together to help each other. Often students can read selections together that neither student could read individually. Buddy reading is a good alternative to independent reading because students can choose books they want to read and then read at their own pace. By working together they are often able to figure out unfamiliar words and talk out comprehension problems.

During literature focus units, students often reread the featured selection with buddies after the teacher has presented it using shared reading. Students read and reread books from the text set this way, too. Buddy reading is used less often during reading workshop, but students might decide once in a while to read a book together, especially if it is a book they both want to read and neither could read independently.

As teachers introduce buddy reading, they show students how to read with buddies and how to support each other as they read. Unless the teacher has explained the approach and taught students how to work collaboratively, buddy reading often deteriorates into the stronger of the two buddies reading aloud to the other student, and that is not the intention of this type of reading. Students take turns reading aloud to each other or read in unison. They often stop and help each other identify an unfamiliar word or take a minute or two at the end of each page to talk about what they have read. Buddy reading is a valuable way of providing the practice that beginning readers need to become fluent readers, and it is also an effective way to work with students with special learning needs and students who are learning English.

Reading Aloud to Students.   In kindergarten through eighth grade, teachers read aloud to students for a variety of purposes each day. During literature focus units, teachers read aloud featured selections that are appropriate for students' interest level but too difficult for students to read themselves. They also read aloud the featured selection if they have only one copy of the book available. Sometimes it is also appropriate to read the featured selection aloud before distributing copies of the selection for students to read with buddies or independently. When they read aloud during literature focus units, teachers model what good readers do and how good readers use reading strategies. Reading aloud also provides an opportunity for teachers to think aloud about their use of reading strategies.

During reading workshop, teachers also read aloud stories and other books to introduce students to literature they might not choose to read on their own. The reading aloud component of reading workshop provides students with a shared social experience and an opportunity to talk about literature and reading. In addition, teachers also read aloud books related to science, social studies, and other across-the-curriculum themes.

Reading aloud to students is not the same as "round-robin" reading, a practice that is no longer recommended in which students take turns reading paragraphs aloud as the rest of the class listens. Round-robin reading has been used for reading chapter books aloud, but it is more commonly used for reading chapters in content-area textbooks, even though there are more effective ways to teach content-area information and read textbooks. For more information on using content-area textbooks, see Chapter 11, "Reading and Writing Across the Curriculum."

Round-robin reading is no longer recommended, for several reasons (True, 1979). First, if students are going to read aloud, they should read fluently. When less capable readers read, their reading is often difficult to listen to and embarrassing to them personally. Less capable readers need reading practice, but performing in front of the entire class is not the most productive way for them to practice. They can read with buddies and in small groups during guided reading. Second, if the selection is appropriate for students to read aloud, they should be reading independently. Whenever the reading level of the text is appropriate for students, they should be reading independently. During round-robin reading, students often only follow along just before it is their turn to read. Third, round-robin reading is often tedious and boring, and students lose interest in reading.

The advantages and drawbacks for each type of reading are outlined in Figure 7–3. In the vignette at the beginning of this chapter, Mrs. Lentz used a combination of these approaches. She used shared reading as she read the first chapter aloud, with students following in their own copies of *The Giver*. Later, students read together in small groups, with a buddy, or independently. As teachers plan their instructional programs, they include reading aloud to students, teacher-led student reading, and independent reading each day.

Stage 3: Responding

During the third stage, readers respond to their reading and continue to negotiate the meaning. Two ways that students make tentative and exploratory comments immediately after reading are by writing in reading logs and participating in grand conversations.

Writing in Reading Logs. Students write and draw their thoughts and feelings about what they have read in reading logs. Rosenblatt (1978) explains that as students write about what they have read, they unravel their thinking and, at the same

FIGURE 7–3   Types of Reading

Type	Advantages	Drawbacks
Shared Reading Teacher reads aloud while students follow along using individual copies of book, a class chart, or a big book.	• Access to books students could not read themselves. • Teacher models fluent reading. • Opportunities to model reading strategies. • Students practice fluent reading. • Develops a community of readers.	• Multiple copies, a class chart, or a big book needed. • Text may not be appropriate for all students. • Students may not be interested in the text.
Guided Reading Teachers use the prediction cycle to guide students as they read a text.	• Practice the prediction cycle. • Teacher provides direction and scaffolding. • Opportunities to model reading strategies. • Use with unfamiliar texts.	• Multiple copies of text needed. • Teacher controls the reading experience. • Some students may not be interested in the text.
Independent Reading Students read a text independently and often choose the text themselves.	• Develops responsibility and ownership. • Self-selection of texts. • Experience is more authentic.	• Students may need assistance to read the text. • Little teacher involvement and control.
Buddy Reading Two students read or reread a text together.	• Collaboration between students. • Students assist each other. • Use to reread familiar texts. • Develops reading fluency. • Students talk and share interpretations.	• Limited teacher involvement. • Less teacher control.
Reading Aloud to Students Teacher or other fluent reader reads aloud to students.	• Access to books students could not read themselves. • Teacher models fluent reading. • Opportunities to model reading strategies. • Develops a community of readers. • Use when only one copy of text is available.	• No opportunity for students themselves to read. • Text may not be appropriate for all students. • Students may not be interested in the text. • Does not require students to take turns reading.

time, elaborate on and clarify their responses. When students read informational books, they sometimes write in reading logs, as they do after reading stories and poems, but at other times they make notes of important information or draw charts and diagrams to use in theme studies.

Students usually make reading logs by stapling together 10 to 12 sheets of paper at the beginning of a literature focus unit or reading workshop. At the beginning of a theme study, students make learning logs to write in during the unit. They decorate the covers, keeping with the theme of the unit, and write entries related to their reading and make notes related to what they are learning in minilessons. Teachers monitor students' entries during the unit, often reading and responding to students' entries. Because these journals are learning tools, teachers rarely correct students' spellings. They focus their responses on the students' ideas, but they expect students to spell the title of the book and the names of characters accurately. At the end of the unit, teachers review students' work and often grade the journals based on whether students completed all the entries and on the quality of the ideas in their entries.

Participating in Grand Conversations.   Students also talk about the text with classmates in **grand conversations** or other literature discussions. Peterson and Eeds (1990) explain that in this type of discussion students share their personal responses and tell what they liked about the text. After sharing personal reactions, they shift the focus to "puzzle over what the author has written and . . . share what it is they find revealed" (p. 61). Often students make connections between the text and their own lives or between the text and other literature they have read. If they are reading a chapter book, they also make predictions about what they think will happen in the next chapter.

Teachers often participate in grand conversations, but they act as interested participants, not leaders. The talk is primarily among the students, but teachers ask questions regarding things they are genuinely interested in learning more about and share information in response to questions that students ask. In the past, many discussions have been "gentle inquisitions" during which students recited answers to factual questions teachers asked about books that students were reading (Eeds & Wells, 1989). Teachers asked these questions in order to determine whether or not students read and understood an assignment. While teachers can still judge whether or not students have read the assignment, the focus in grand conversations is on clarifying and deepening students' understanding of the selection they have read.

Grand conversations can be held with the whole class or in small groups. Young children usually meet together as a class, while older students often prefer to talk with classmates in small groups. When students meet together as a class, there is a shared feeling of community, and the teacher can be part of the group. When students meet in small groups, students have more opportunities to participate in the discussion and share their interpretations, but fewer viewpoints are expressed in each group and teachers must move around, spending only a few minutes with each group. Some teachers compromise and have students begin their discussions in small groups and then come together as a class and have each group share what their group discussed.

Stage 4: Exploring

During this stage, students go back into the text to explore it more analytically. They reread the selection, examine the author's craft, and focus on words from the selection. Teachers also present minilessons on procedures, concepts, strategies, and skills.

Rereading the Selection.   Through **repeated readings,** students reread the selection and think again about what they have read. Each time they reread a selection, students benefit in specific ways (Yaden, 1988). They deepen their interpretations and make further connections between the selection and their own lives or between the selection and other literature they have read. Students often reread a selection several times. If the teacher used shared reading to read the selection with students in the reading stage, students might reread it with a buddy once or twice, read it with their parents, and, after these experiences, read it independently.

Examining the Author's Craft.   Teachers plan exploring activities to focus students' attention on the structure of text and the literary language that authors use. Students notice opposites in the story, use **story boards** to sequence the events in the story, and make story maps to highlight the plot, characters, and other elements of story structure. Another way students learn about the structure of stories is by writing books based on the selection they have read. Students write sequels, telling what happens to the characters after the story ends. Stories such as *Jumanji* (Van Allsburg, 1981) suggest another episode at the end of the story and invite students to create a sequel. Students also write innovations, or new versions, for the selection. In these innovations, students follow the same sentence pattern but use their own ideas. First graders often write innovations for Bill Martin, Jr.'s, *Brown Bear, Brown Bear, What Did You See?* (1983) and *Polar Bear, Polar Bear, What Did You Hear?* (1992), and older students write innovations for *Alexander and the Terrible, Horrible, No Good, Very Bad Day* (Viorst, 1977).

Teachers share information about the author of the featured selection and introduce other books by the same author. Sometimes teachers help students make comparisons among several books written by a particular author. They also provide information about the illustrator and the illustration techniques used in the book. To focus on literary language, students often reread favorite excerpts in read-arounds and write memorable quotes on story quilts that they create.

Focusing on Words.   Teachers and students add "important" words to word walls after reading and post these word walls in the classroom. Students refer to the word walls when they write, using these words for a variety of activities during the exploring stage. Students make word clusters and posters to highlight particular words. They also make word chains, sort words, create a semantic feature analysis to analyze related words, and play word games.

Teachers choose words from word walls to use in minilessons, too. Words can be used to teach phonics skills, such as beginning sounds, rhyming words, vowel patterns, *r*-controlled vowels, and syllabication. Other concepts, such as root words and affixes, compound words, contractions, and metaphors, can also be taught using examples from word walls. Sometimes teachers decide to teach a minilesson on a particular concept, such as words with the *-ly* suffix, because five or six words representing the concept are listed on the word wall.

Teaching Minilessons.   Teachers present minilessons on reading procedures, concepts, strategies, and skills during the exploring stage. (For a review of the steps in a minilesson, check the entry on minilessons in the Compendium.) In a minilesson, teachers introduce the topic and make connections between the topic and examples in the featured selection students have read. In this way, students are better able to connect the information teachers are presenting with their own reading process. In the vignette, Mrs. Lentz presented minilessons on the visualization strategy and on root words and affixes using examples from *The Giver.*

FIGURE 7–4   Type of Projects

Art Projects

1. Experiment with the illustration techniques (e.g., collage, watercolor, line drawing) used in a favorite book. Examine other books illustrated with the same technique.
2. Make a diagram or model using information from a book.
3. Create a collage to represent the theme of a book.
4. Design a book jacket for a book, laminate it, and place it on the book.
5. Decorate a coffee can or a potato chip can using scenes from a book. Fill the can with quotes from characters in the story. Other students can guess the identity of the characters. Or fill the can with quotes from a poem with words missing. Other students guess the missing words.
6. Construct a shoebox or other miniature scene of an episode for a favorite book (or use a larger box to construct a diorama).
7. Make illustrations for each important event in a book.
8. Make a map or relief map of a book's setting or something related to the book.
9. Construct the setting of the book in the block center, or use other construction toys such as Lego's or Lincoln Logs.
10. Construct a mobile illustrating a book.
11. Make a roll-movie of a book by drawing a series of pictures on a long strip of paper. Attach ends to rollers and place in a cardboard box cut like a television set.
12. Make a comic strip to illustrate the sequence of events in a book.
13. Make a clay or soap model of a character.
14. Prepare bookmarks for a book and distribute them to classmates.
15. Prepare flannel board pictures to use in retelling the story.
16. Use or prepare illustrations of characters for pocket props to use in retelling the story.
17. Use or prepare illustrations of the events in the story for clothesline props to use in retelling the story.
18. Experiment with art techniques related to the mood of a poem.
19. Make a mural of the book.
20. Make a book box and decorate it with scenes from a book. Collect objects, poems, and illustrations that represent characters, events, or images from the book to add to the box.
21. Make an open-mind portrait to probe the thoughts of one character.

Writing Projects

22. Write a review of a favorite book for a class review file.
23. Write a letter about a book to a classmate, friend, or pen pal.
24. Dictate or write another episode or sequel for a book.
25. Create a newspaper with news stories and advertisements based on characters and episodes from a book.
26. Make a five-senses cluster about the book.
27. Write a letter to a favorite character (or participate in a class collaboration letter).
28. Write a simulated letter from one book character to another.
29. Copy five "quotable quotes" from a book and list them on a poster.
30. Make a scrapbook about the book. Label all items in the scrapbook and write a short description of the most interesting ones.
31. Write a poem related to the book. Some types of poems to choose from are acrostic, concrete poem, color poem, "I wish" poem, "If I were" poem, haiku, or limerick.

FIGURE 7–4 *continued*

32. Write a lifeline related to the book, the era, the character, or the author.
33. Write a business letter to a company or organization requesting information on a topic related to the book.
34. Keep a simulated journal from the perspective of one character from the book.
35. Write a dictionary defining specialized vocabulary in a book.
36. Write the story from another point of view (e.g., write the story of *The Little Red Hen* from the perspective of the lazy characters).
37. Make a class collaboration book. Each child dictates or writes one page.
38. Write a letter to a famous person from a character in a book.
39. Make a ladder to accomplishment listing the steps taken to achieve some goal.

Reading Projects

40. Read another book by the same author.
41. Read another book by the same illustrator.
42. Read another book on the same theme.
43. Read another book in the same genre.
44. Read another book about the same character.
45. Read and compare another version of the same story.
46. Listen to and compare a tape, filmstrip, film, or video version of the same story.
47. Tape-record a book or an excerpt from it to place in the listening center.
48. Read a poem that complements the book aloud to the class. Place a copy of the poem in the book.
49. Tape-record a book using background music and sound effects.

Drama and Talk Projects

50. Give a readers theatre presentation of a book.
51. Improvise the events in a book.
52. Write a script and present a play about a book.
53. Make puppets and use them in retelling a book.
54. Dress as a character from the book and answer questions from classmates about the character.
55. Have a grand conversation with a small group or the whole class about a book.
56. Write and present a rap about the book.
57. Videotape a commercial for a book.
58. Interview someone in the community who is knowledgeable about a topic related to the book.

Literary Analysis Projects

59. Make a chart to compare the story with another version or with the film version of the story.
60. Make a character cluster.
61. Make a character sociogram.
62. Make a plot diagram of the book.
63. Make a plot profile of the book.

Research Projects

64. Research the author of the book and compile information in a chart or summary. Place the chart or summary in the book.
65. Research a topic related to the book. Present the information in a report.

Stage 5: Extending

During the extending stage, readers deepen their interpretations, reflect on their understanding, and value the reading experience. Building on the initial and exploratory responses they made immediately after reading, students create projects. These projects can involve reading, writing, talk and drama, art, or research and may take many forms, including murals, readers theatre scripts, and **individual books and reports,** as well as reading other books by the same author. Usually students choose which projects they will do rather than having the entire class do the same project. Sometimes, however, the class decides to work together on a project. In Mrs. Lentz's class, for example, some students wrote color poems, while others read books and wrote about memories. A list of projects is presented in Figure 7–4. The purpose of these activities is for students to expand the ideas they read about, create a personal interpretation, and value the reading experience.

■ *Activity*

Reread the vignette at the beginning of this chapter and identify the activities that Mrs. Lentz used during each stage of the reading process.

THE WRITING PROCESS

The focus in the writing process is on what students think and do as they write. The five stages are prewriting, drafting, revising, editing, and sharing, and the key features of each stage are shown in Figure 7–5. The labeling and numbering of the stages does not mean that the writing process is a linear series of neatly packaged categories. Research has shown that the process involves recurring cycles, and labeling is only an aid to identifying and discussing writing activities. In the classroom, the stages merge and recur as students write.

Stage 1: Prewriting

Prewriting is the getting-ready-to-write stage. The traditional notion that writers have a topic completely thought out and ready to flow onto the page is ridiculous. If writers wait for ideas to fully develop, they may wait forever. Instead, writers begin tentatively—talking, reading, writing—to see what they know and what direction they want to go in. Prewriting has probably been the most neglected stage in the writing process; however, it is as crucial to writers as a warm-up is to athletes. Murray (1982) believes that at least 70% of writing time should be spent in prewriting. During the prewriting stage, students choose a topic, consider function, form, and audience, and generate and organize ideas for writing.

Choosing a Topic.   Choosing a topic for writing can be a stumbling block for students who have become dependent on teachers to supply topics. For years, teachers have supplied topics by suggesting gimmicky story starters and relieving students of the "burden" of topic selection. Often, these "creative" topics stymied students, who were forced to write on topics they knew little about or were not interested in. Graves (1976) calls this "writing welfare." Instead, students need to choose their own writing topics.

Some students complain that they do not know what to write about, but teachers can help them brainstorm a list of three, four, or five topics and then identify the one topic they are most interested in and know the most about. Students who feel they cannot generate any writing topics are often surprised that they have so many options available. Then, through prewriting activities, students talk, draw, read, and even write to develop information about their topics.

FIGURE 7–5   Key Features of the Writing Process

Stage 1: Prewriting

- Students write on topics based on their own experiences.
- Students engage in rehearsal activities before writing.
- Students identify the audience to whom they will write.
- Students identify the function of the writing activity.
- Students choose an appropriate form for their compositions based on audience and function.

Stage 2: Drafting

- Students write a rough draft.
- Students emphasize content rather than mechanics.

Stage 3: Revising

- Students reread their own writing.
- Students share their writing in writing groups.
- Students participate constructively in discussions about classmates' writing.
- Students make changes in their compositions to reflect the reactions and comments of both teacher and classmates.
- Between the first and final drafts, students make substantive rather than only minor changes.

Stage 4: Editing

- Students proofread their own compositions.
- Students help proofread classmates' compositions.
- Students increasingly identify and correct their own mechanical errors.
- Students meet with the teacher for a final editing.

Stage 5: Publishing

- Students publish their writing in an appropriate form.
- Students share their finished writing with an appropriate audience.

Asking students to choose their own topics for writing does not mean that teachers never give writing assignments; teachers do provide general guidelines. They may specify the writing form, and at other times they may establish the function, but students should choose their own content.

Considering Purpose.   As students prepare to write, they need to think about the purpose of their writing. Are they writing to entertain? To inform? To persuade? Setting the purpose for writing is just as important as setting the purpose for reading, because purpose influences decisions students make about audience and form.

Considering Audience.   Students may write primarily for themselves, to express and clarify their own ideas and feelings, or they may write for others. Possible audiences include classmates, younger children, parents, foster grandparents, children's authors, and pen pals. Other audiences are more distant and less well known. For example, students write letters to businesses to request information, articles for the local newspaper, or stories and poems for publication in literary magazines.

Children's writing is influenced by their sense of audience. Britton and his colleagues (1975) define audience awareness as "the manner in which the writer expresses a relationship with the reader in respect to the writer's understanding" (pp. 65–66). Students adapt their writing to fit their audience just as they vary their speech to meet the needs of the people who are listening to them.

Considering Form.   One of the most important considerations is the form the writing will take: A story? A letter? A poem? A journal entry? A writing activity could be handled in any one of these ways. As part of a science theme study on hermit crabs, for instance, students could write a story about a hermit crab, draw a picture and label body parts, explain how hermit crabs obtain shells to live in, or keep a log of observations about the pet hermit crabs in the classroom. There is an almost endless variety of forms that children's writing may take. A list of these forms is presented in Figure 7–6. Students need to experiment with a wide variety of writing forms and explore the potential of these functions and formats.

FIGURE 7–6   Writing Forms

advertisements	diagrams	persuasive letters
"All About the Author"	dictionaries	poems
alphabet books	directions	postcards
announcements	editorials	posters
anthologies	essays	proverbs
apologies	evaluations	puzzles
applications	explanations	questionnaires
autobiographies	fables	questions
awards	fairy tales	quickwrites
ballots	folktales	quizzes
bibliographies	freewrites	recipes
biographies	greeting cards	research reports
book jackets	hink-pinks	reviews
book reports	instructions	riddles
books	interviews	schedules
brochures	invitations	scripts
bumper stickers	jokes	sentences
campaign speeches	journals	signs
captions	labels	slogans
cartoons	lab reports	stories
catalogues	learning logs	study guides
certificates	letters to the editor	tall tales
character sketches	lists	telegrams
charts	lyrics	telephone directories
clusters	maps	thank-you notes
comics	menus	thesauruses
comparisons	mysteries	thumbnail sketches
complaints	myths	tongue twisters
computer programs	newspapers	valentines
coupons	notes	Venn diagrams
crossword puzzles	obituaries	word-finds
definitions	oral histories	wordless picture books
descriptions	paragraphs	words
dialogue	personal narratives	

Through reading and writing, students develop a strong sense of these forms and how they are structured. Langer (1985) found that by third grade, students responded in distinctly different ways to story- and report-writing assignments; they organized the writing differently and included varied kinds of information and elaboration. Similarly, Hidi and Hildyard (1983) found that elementary students could differentiate between stories and persuasive essays. Because children are clarifying the distinctions between various writing forms during the elementary grades, it is important that teachers use the correct terminology and not label all children's writing "stories."

Decisions about function, audience, and form influence each other. For example, if the function is to entertain, an appropriate form might be a story, poem, or script—and these three forms look very different on a piece of paper. Whereas a story is written in the traditional block format, scripts and poems have unique page arrangements. Scripts are written with the character's name and a colon, and the dialogue is set off. Action and dialogue, rather than description, carry the story line in a script. In contrast, poems have unique formatting considerations, and words are used judiciously. Each word and phrase is chosen to convey a maximum amount of information.

Gathering and Organizing Ideas.   Students engage in activities to gather and organize ideas for writing. Graves (1983) calls what writers do to prepare for writing "rehearsal" activities. Rehearsal activities take many forms, including:

1. *Drawing.*   Drawing is the way young children gather and organize ideas for writing. Primary-grade teachers often notice that students draw before they write and, thinking that they are eating dessert before the meat and vegetables, insist that they write first. But many young children cannot write first because they don't know what to write until they see what they draw (Dyson, 1982, 1986).

2. *Clustering.*   Students make clusters (weblike diagrams) in which they write the topic in a center circle and then draw rays from the circle for each main idea. Then they add details and other information on rays drawn from each main idea. Through clustering, students organize their ideas for writing. Clustering is a better prewriting strategy than outlining because it is nonlinear.

3. *Talking.*   Students talk with their classmates to share ideas about possible writing topics, try out ways to express an idea, and ask questions.

4. *Reading.*   Students gather ideas for writing and investigate the structure of various written forms through reading. They may retell a favorite story in writing, write new adventures for favorite story characters, or experiment with repetition, onomatopoeia, or another poetic device used in a poem they have read. Informational books also provide raw material for writing. For example, if students are studying polar bears, they read to gather information about the animal—its habitat and predators, for example—that they may use in writing a report.

5. *Role-playing.*   Children discover and shape ideas they will use in their writing through role-playing. During theme cycles and after reading stories, students can reenact events to bring an experience to life. Teachers should choose a particular critical moment for students to reenact. For example, after reading *Sarah, Plain and Tall* (MacLachlan, 1985), children might reenact the day Sarah took the wagon to town. This is a critical moment: Does Sarah like them and their prairie home well enough to stay?

6. *Quickwriting.* Students can expand a quickwrite (or journal entry) that they wrote during a literature focus unit or a theme cycle into a polished composition.

Stage 2: Drafting

Students write and refine their compositions through a series of drafts. During the drafting stage, they focus on getting their ideas down on paper. Because writers don't begin writing with their compositions already composed in their minds, students begin with tentative ideas developed through prewriting activities. The drafting stage is the time to pour out ideas, with little concern about spelling, punctuation, and other mechanical errors.

Students skip every other line when they write their rough drafts to leave space for revisions. They use arrows to move sections of text, cross-outs to delete sections, and scissors and tape to cut apart and rearrange text, just as adult writers do. They write only on one side of a sheet of paper so it can be cut it apart or rearranged. As word processors become more available in elementary classrooms, revising, with all its moving, adding, and deleting of text, will be much easier. However, for students who handwrite their compositions, the wide spacing is crucial. Teachers might make small *x*'s on every other line of students' papers as a reminder to skip lines as they draft their compositions.

Students label their drafts by writing *Rough Draft* in ink at the top or by using a ROUGH DRAFT stamp. This label indicates to the writer, other students, parents, and administrators that the composition is a draft in which the emphasis is on content, not mechanics. It also explains why the teacher has not graded the paper or marked mechanical errors.

Instead of writing drafts by hand, students can write using computers to compose rough drafts, polish their writing, and print out final copies. There are many benefits of using computers for word processing. Students are often more motivated to write, and they tend to write longer pieces. Their writing looks neater, and they can use spellcheck programs to identify and correct misspelled words. Even young children can word-process their compositions using FirstWriter, Bank Street Prewriter, Magic Slate, and other programs designed for beginning writers. To learn more about word-processing programs for elementary students, check the Technology Link on page 268.

During drafting, students may need to modify their earlier decisions about function, audience, and, especially, the form their writing will take. For example, a composition that began as a story may be transformed into a report, letter, or poem. The new format allows the student to communicate more effectively. The process of modifying earlier decisions continues into the revising stage.

As students write rough drafts, it is important not to emphasize correct spelling and neatness. In fact, pointing out mechanical errors during the drafting stage sends students a false message that mechanical correctness is more important than content (Sommers, 1982). Later, during editing, students can clean up mechanical errors and put their composition into a neat, final form.

Stage 3: Revising

During the revising stage, writers refine ideas in their compositions. Students often break the writing process cycle as soon as they complete a rough draft, believing that once they have jotted down their ideas, the writing task is complete. Experienced writers, however, know they must turn to others for reactions and revise on the basis

Technology Link
Word-Processing Programs

Word-processing programs support students who are learning to use the process approach to writing (Cochran-Smith, Kahn, & Paris, 1988; DeGroff, 1990). Students revise and edit their rough drafts more easily when they use word processors, and they print out neat and "clean" final copies without the drudgery of recopying their compositions. Many word-processing and publishing programs are available for elementary students, including:

Title	Publisher
Appleworks (U)*	South-Western 5101 Madison Road Cincinnati, OH 45227
Bank Street Prewriter (P)	Scholastic 555 Broadway New York, NY 10012
Bank Street Writer (M–U)	Scholastic 555 Broadway New York, NY 10012
Children's Writing and Publishing Center (P–M)	The Learning Company 6493 Kaiser Drive Freemont, CA 94555
Easy Book (M–U)	Tom Snyder Productions 80 Coolidge Hill Road Watertown, MA 02172
FirstWriter (P–M)	Houghton Mifflin One Beacon Street Boston, MA 02108
Hyperscreen (M–U)	Scholastic 555 Broadway New York, NY 10012
MacWrite (M–U)	Claris 5201 Patrick Henry Drive Santa Clara, CA 95052
Magic Slate (P–M)	Sunburst Communications 39 Washington Street Pleasantville, NY 10570
Print Shop Deluxe (P–M–U)	Broderbund Software P.O. Box 6125 Novato, CA 94948
Process Writer (M–U)	Scholastic 555 Broadway New York, NY 10012
Quill (M–U)	D. C. Heath 125 Spring Street Lexington, MA 02173
Writing Center (P–M)	The Learning Company 6493 Kaiser Drive Freemont, CA 94555
Writing Workshop (M–U)	Milliken 1100 Research Blvd. P.O. Box 21579 St. Louis, MO 63132

Students learn to use the word-processing program using tutorial lessons that accompany most programs. Students work through the lessons in small groups. It's a good idea to make the first writing project a class collaboration so students can review word-processing procedures. The next several writing projects should be short so that students can concentrate on working through the word-processing procedures. Often one or two students will assume an important new status as "computer expert" because of special interest or expertise. These experts help other students with word-processing tasks and using the printer.

———————

*P = primary grades (K–2); M = middle grades (3–5); U = upper grades (6–8).

of these comments. Revision is not just polishing; it is meeting the needs of readers by adding, substituting, deleting, and rearranging material. The word *revision* means "seeing again," and in this stage writers see their compositions again with the help of classmates and the teacher. The revising stage includes three activities: rereading the rough draft, sharing the rough draft in a writing group, and revising on the basis of feedback.

Rereading the Rough Draft.   After finishing the rough draft, writers need to distance themselves from the draft for a day or two, then reread the draft from a fresh perspective, as a reader might. As they reread, students make changes—adding, substituting, deleting, and moving—and place question marks by sections that need work. It is these trouble spots that students ask for help with in their writing groups.

Sharing in Writing Groups.   Students meet in **writing groups** to share their compositions with classmates. They respond to the writer's rough draft and suggest possible revisions. Writing groups provide a scaffold in which teachers and classmates talk about plans and strategies for writing and revising (Applebee & Langer, 1983; Calkins, 1983).

Writing groups can form spontaneously when several students have completed drafts and are ready to share their compositions, or they can be formal groupings with identified leaders. In some classrooms writing groups form when four or five students finish writing their rough drafts. Students gather around a conference table or in a corner of the classroom and take turns reading their rough drafts aloud. Classmates in the group listen and respond, offering compliments and suggestions for revision. Sometimes the teacher joins the writing group, but if the teacher is involved in something else, students work independently.

In other classrooms, the writing groups are assigned. Students get together when all students in the group have completed their rough drafts and are ready to share their writing. Sometimes the teacher participates in these groups, providing feedback along with the students. Or, the writing groups can function independently. For these assigned groups, each cluster is made up of four or five students, and a list of groups and their members is posted in the classroom. The teacher puts a star by one student's name, and that student serves as a group leader. The leader changes every quarter.

Making Revisions.   Students make four types of changes to their rough drafts: additions, substitutions, deletions, and moves (Faigley & Witte, 1981). As they revise, students might add words, substitute sentences, delete paragraphs, and move phrases. Students often use a blue or red pen to cross out, draw arrows, and write in the space left between the double-spaced lines of their rough drafts so that revisions will show clearly. That way teachers can examine the types of revisions students make by examining their revised rough drafts. Revisions are another gauge of students' growth as writers.

Stage 4: Editing

Editing is putting the piece of writing into its final form. Until this stage, the focus has been primarily on the content of students' writing. Once the focus changes to mechanics, students polish their writing by correcting spelling and other mechanical errors. The goal here is to make the writing "optimally readable" (Smith, 1982). Writers who write for readers understand that if their compositions are not readable, they have written in vain because their ideas will never be read.

Mechanics are the commonly accepted conventions of written Standard English. They include capitalization, punctuation, spelling, sentence structure, usage, and formatting considerations specific to poems, scripts, letters, and other writing forms. The use of these commonly accepted conventions is a courtesy to those who will read the composition.

During editing, students proofread with partners to identify and correct errors.

Students learn mechanical skills best during through hands-on editing of their own compositions, not through workbook exercises. When they edit a composition that will be shared with a genuine audience, students are more interested in using mechanical skills correctly so they can communicate effectively. In a study of two third-grade classes, Calkins (1980) found that the students who learned punctuation marks as a part of editing could define or explain more marks than the students in the other class, who were taught punctuation skills in a traditional manner, with instruction and practice exercises on each punctuation mark. In other words, the results of this research, as well as other studies (Bissex, 1980; Elley, Barham, Lamb, & Wyllie, 1976; Graves, 1983), suggest that teaching mechanical skills as part of the writing process is more effective than practice exercises.

Students move through three activities in the editing stage: getting distance from the composition, proofreading to locate errors, and correcting errors.

Getting Distance.   Students are more efficient editors if they set the composition aside for a few days before beginning to edit. After working so closely with a piece of writing during drafting and revising, they are too familiar with it to be able to locate many mechanical errors. With the distance gained by waiting a few days, children are better able to approach editing with a fresh perspective and gather the enthusiasm necessary to finish the writing process by making the paper optimally readable.

Proofreading.   Students proofread their compositions to locate and mark possible errors. Proofreading is a unique type of reading in which students read slowly, word by word, hunting for errors rather than reading quickly for meaning (King, 1985). Concentrating on mechanics is difficult because of our natural inclination to read for meaning. Even experienced proofreaders often find themselves reading for meaning and thus overlooking errors that do not inhibit meaning. It is important, therefore, to take time to explain proofreading and demonstrate how it differs from regular reading.

To demonstrate proofreading, teachers take a piece of student writing and copy it on the chalkboard or display it on an overhead projector. The teacher reads it several times, each time hunting for a particular type of error. During each reading, the teacher reads the composition slowly, softly pronouncing each word and touching the word with a pencil or pen to focus attention on it. The teacher marks possible errors as they are located.

Errors are marked or corrected with special proofreaders' marks. Students enjoy using these marks, the same ones that adult authors and editors use. Proofreaders' marks that elementary students can learn to use in editing their writing are presented in Figure 7–7.

Editing checklists help students focus on particular types of errors. Teachers can develop checklists with two to six items appropriate for the grade level. A first-grade checklist, for example, might include only two items—perhaps one about capital letters at the beginning of sentences and a second about periods at the end of sentences. In contrast, a middle-grade checklist might include items such as using commas in a series, paragraph indention, capitalizing proper nouns and adjectives, and spelling homonyms correctly. Teachers can revise the checklist during the school year to focus attention on skills that have recently been taught.

FIGURE 7–7   Proofreaders' Marks

Delete	ℓ	Most whales are ~~big and~~ huge creatures.
Insert	∧	**called** A baby whale is ∧ a calf.
Indent paragraph	¶	¶Whales look a lot like fish, but the two are quite different.
Capitalize	≡	In the United s̲t̲a̲t̲e̲s̲ it is illegal to hunt whales.
Change to lower case	/	Why do beached W̸hales die?
Add period	⊙	Baleen whales do not have any teeth⊙
Add comma	⌃	Some baleen whales are blue whales ⌃ gray whales and humpback whales.
Add apostrophe	⌄	People are the whale⌄s only enemy.

A sample third-grade editing checklist is presented in Figure 7–8. The writer and a classmate work together as partners to edit their compositions. First, students proofread their own compositions, searching for errors in each category on the checklist, and, after proofreading, check off each item. After completing the checklist, students sign their names and trade checklists and compositions. Now they become editors and complete each other's checklist. Having writer and editor sign the checklist helps them to take the activity seriously.

Correcting Errors. After students proofread their compositions and locate as many errors as they can, they correct the errors individually or with an editor's assistance. Some errors are easy to correct, some require use of a dictionary, and others involve instruction from the teacher. It is unrealistic to expect students to locate and correct every mechanical error in their compositions. Not even published books are always error-free! Once in a while, students may change a correct spelling or punctuation mark and make it incorrect, but they correct far more errors than they create.

Editing can end after students and their editors correct as many mechanical errors as possible, or after students meet with the teacher in a conference for a final editing. When mechanical correctness is crucial, this conference is important. Teachers proofread the composition with the student, and they identify and make the remaining corrections together, or the teacher makes check marks in the margin to note errors for the student to correct independently.

Stage 5: Publishing

In this stage, students bring their compositions to life by publishing them or by sharing them orally with an appropriate audience. When they share their writing with real

FIGURE 7–8   A Third-Grade Editing Checklist

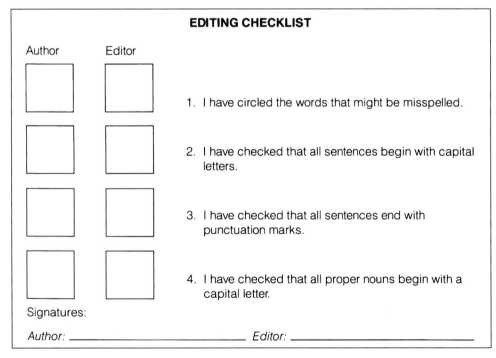

EDITING CHECKLIST

Author   Editor

1. I have circled the words that might be misspelled.

2. I have checked that all sentences begin with capital letters.

3. I have checked that all sentences end with punctuation marks.

4. I have checked that all proper nouns begin with a capital letter.

Signatures:

Author: _____   *Editor:* _____

audiences of classmates, other students, parents, and the community, students come to think of themselves as authors.

Making Books.   One of the most popular ways for children to publish their writing is by making books. Simple booklets can be made by folding a sheet of paper into quarters, like a greeting card. Students write the title on the front and use the three remaining sides for their composition. They can also construct booklets by stapling sheets of writing paper together and adding covers made out of construction paper. Sheets of wallpaper cut from old sample books also make sturdy covers. These stapled booklets can be cut into various shapes, too. Students can make more sophisticated books by covering cardboard covers with contact paper, wallpaper samples, or cloth. Pages are sewn or stapled together, and the first and last pages (endpapers) are glued to the cardboard covers to hold the book together. Directions for making one type of hardcover book are shown in Figure 7–9.

In addition, students can add an "All About the Author" page with a photograph at the end of their books, just as information about adult authors is often included on the jackets of published books. A fifth grader's "All About the Author" page from a collection of poetry he wrote is presented in Figure 7–10. Notice that the student wrote about himself in the third person, as in adult biographical sketches.

Sharing Writing.   Students read their writing to classmates or share it with larger audiences through hardcover books placed in the class or school library, plays performed for classmates, or letters sent to authors, businesses, and other correspondents. Other ways to share children's writing are:

Submit the piece to writing contests
Display the writing as a mobile
Contribute to a class anthology
Contribute to the local newspaper
Make a shape book
Record the writing on a cassette tape
Submit it to a literary magazine
Read it at a school assembly
Share it at a read-aloud party
Share it with parents and siblings
Display poetry on a "poet-tree"
Send it to a pen pal
Display it on a bulletin board
Make a big book
Design a poster about the writing
Read it to foster grandparents
Share it as a puppet show
Display it at a public event
Read it to children in other classes

Through this sharing, students communicate with genuine audiences who respond to their writing in meaningful ways. Sharing writing is a social activity that helps children develop sensitivity to audiences and confidence in themselves as authors. Dyson (1985) advises that teachers consider the social interpretations of sharing— the students' behavior, the teacher's behavior, and the interaction between students

FIGURE 7–9 Directions for Making Hardcover Books

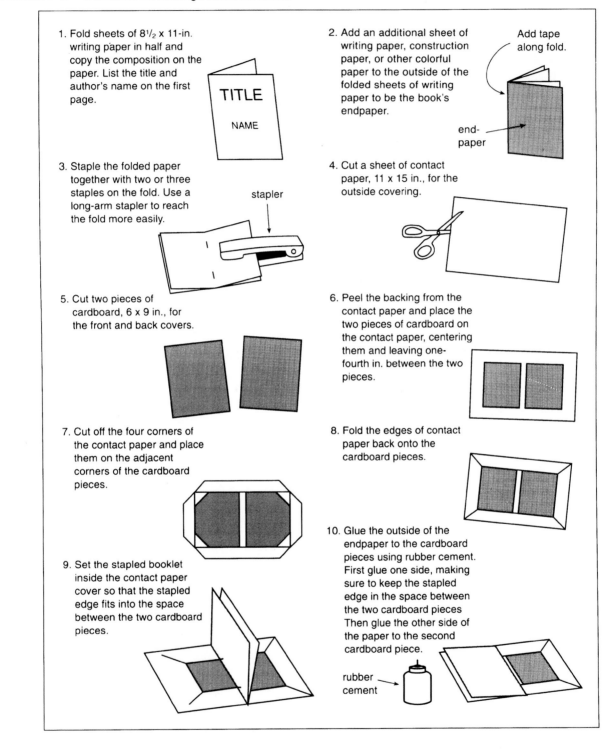

1. Fold sheets of 8½ x 11-in. writing paper in half and copy the composition on the paper. List the title and author's name on the first page.

TITLE

NAME

2. Add an additional sheet of writing paper, construction paper, or other colorful paper to the outside of the folded sheets of writing paper to be the book's endpaper.

Add tape along fold.

end-paper

3. Staple the folded paper together with two or three staples on the fold. Use a long-arm stapler to reach the fold more easily.

stapler

4. Cut a sheet of contact paper, 11 x 15 in., for the outside covering.

5. Cut two pieces of cardboard, 6 x 9 in., for the front and back covers.

6. Peel the backing from the contact paper and place the two pieces of cardboard on the contact paper, centering them and leaving one-fourth in. between the two pieces.

7. Cut off the four corners of the contact paper and place them on the adjacent corners of the cardboard pieces.

8. Fold the edges of contact paper back onto the cardboard pieces.

9. Set the stapled booklet inside the contact paper cover so that the stapled edge fits into the space between the two cardboard pieces.

10. Glue the outside of the endpaper to the cardboard pieces using rubber cement. First glue one side, making sure to keep the stapled edge in the space between the two cardboard pieces Then glue the other side of the paper to the second cardboard piece.

rubber cement

FIGURE 7–10   A Fifth Grader's "All About the Author" Page

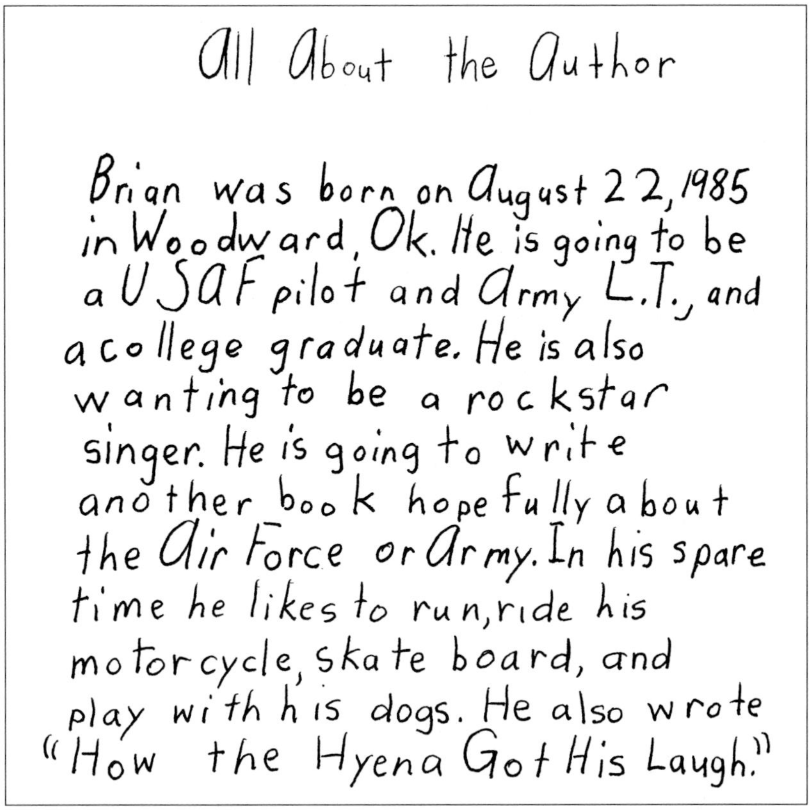

All About the Author

Brian was born on August 22, 1985 in Woodward, Ok. He is going to be a USAF pilot and Army L.T., and a college graduate. He is also wanting to be a rockstar singer. He is going to write another book hopefully about the Air Force or Army. In his spare time he likes to run, ride his motorcycle, skate board, and play with his dogs. He also wrote "How the Hyena Got His Laugh."

and teacher—within the classroom context. Individual students interpret sharing differently. Beyond just providing the opportunity for students to share writing, teachers need to teach students how to respond to their classmates. Teachers themselves serve as a model for responding to students' writing without dominating the sharing.

Why Are Reading and Writing Similar Processes?

In both reading and writing the goal is to construct meaning, and the reading and writing processes have comparable activities at each stage (Butler & Turbill, 1984). Figure 7–11 shows the similarities between reading and writing activities at each stage. Notice the activities listed for the third stages, responding and revising, for example. Fitzgerald (1989) analyzed these two activities and concluded that they draw on similar processes of author-reader-text interaction. Similar analyses can be made for reading and writing activities in each of the other stages, as well.

Tierney (1983) explains that reading and writing are multidimensional and involve concurrent, complex transactions between writers, between writers as readers, between readers, and between readers as writers. Writers participate in several types of reading activities. They read other authors' works for ideas and to learn about the structure of stories, but they also read and reread their own work—to problem-solve,

FIGURE 7–11 A Comparison of the Reading and Writing Processes

	What Readers Do	What Writers Do
Stage 1	*Preparing to Read* Readers use knowledge about • the topic • reading • literature • language systems Readers' expectations are cued by • previous reading/writing experiences • format of the text • purpose for reading • audience for reading Readers make predictions.	*Prewriting* Writers use knowledge about • the topic • writing • literature • language systems Writers' expectations are cued by • previous reading/writing experiences • format of the text • purpose for writing • audience for writing Writers gather and organize ideas.
Stage 2	*Reading* Readers • use word identification strategies • use meaning-making strategies • monitor reading • create meaning	*Drafting* Writers • use transcription strategies • use meaning-making strategies • monitor writing • create meaning
Stage 3	*Responding* Readers • respond to the text • interpret meaning • clarify misunderstandings • expand ideas	*Revising* Writers • respond to the text • interpret meaning • clarify misunderstandings • expand ideas
Stage 4	*Exploring the Text* Readers • examine the impact of words and literary language • explore structural elements • compare the text to others	*Editing* Writers • identify and correct mechanical errors • review paragraph and sentence structure
Stage 5	*Extending the Interpretation* Readers • go beyond the text to extend their interpretations • share projects with classmates • reflect on the reading process • make connections to life and literature • value the piece of literature • feel success • want to read again	*Publishing* Writers • produce the finished copy of their compositions • share their compositions with genuine audiences • reflect on the writing process • value the composition • feel success • want to write again

Adapted from Butler and Turbill, 1984.

discover, monitor, and clarify. The quality of these reading experiences seems closely tied to success in writing. "Readers as writers" is a newer idea, but readers are involved in many of the same activities that writers use. They generate ideas, organize, monitor, problem-solve, and revise. Smith (1983) believes that reading influences writing skills because readers unconsciously "read like writers":

> To read like a writer we engage with the author in what the author is writing. We can anticipate what the author will say, so that the author is in effect writing on our behalf, not showing how something is done but doing it with us. . . . Bit by bit, one thing at a time, but enormous numbers of things over the passage of time, the learner learns through reading like a writer to write like a writer. (pp. 563–564)

Also, both reading and writing are recursive, cycling back through various parts of the process, and, just as writers compose text, readers compose their meaning.

Teachers can help students appreciate the similarities between reading and writing in many ways. Tierney (1983) explains: "What we need are reading teachers who act as if their students were developing writers and writing teachers who act as if their students were readers" (p. 151). These are some ways to point out the relationships between reading and writing:

■ Help writers assume alternative points of view as potential readers.

■ Help readers consider the writer's purpose and viewpoint.

■ Point out that reading is much like composing, so that students will view reading as a process, much like the writing process.

■ Talk with students about the reading and writing processes.

■ Talk with students about reading and writing strategies.

Students conference with the teacher as they draft, revise, and edit their writing.

Readers and writers use a number of strategies for constructing meaning as they interact with print. As readers, we use a variety of problem-solving strategies to make decisions about an author's meaning and to construct meaning for ourselves. As writers we also use problem-solving strategies to decide what our readers need as we construct meaning for them and for ourselves. Comparing reading to writing, Tierney and Pearson (1983) described reading as a composing process because readers compose and refine meaning through reading, much like writers compose and refine meaning through writing.

Langer (1985) followed this line of thinking in identifying four strategies that both readers and writers use to interact with text. The first strategy is generating ideas: both readers and writers generate ideas as they get started, as they become aware of important ideas and experiences, and as they begin to plan and organize the information. Formulating meaning is the second strategy—the essence of both reading and writing. Readers and writers formulate meaning by developing the message, considering the audience, drawing on personal experience, choosing language, linking concepts, summarizing, and paraphrasing. Assessing is the third strategy. In both reading and writing, students review, react, and monitor their understanding of the message and the text itself. The fourth strategy is revising, wherein both readers and writers reconsider and restructure the message, recognize when meaning has broken down, and take appropriate action to change the text to improve understanding.

There are practical benefits of connecting reading and writing. Reading contributes to students' writing development, and writing contributes to students' reading development. Shanahan (1988) has outlined seven instructional principles for relating reading and writing so that students develop a clear conception of literacy. The principles are:

1. Involve students in reading and writing experiences every day.
2. Introduce reading and writing processes in kindergarten.
3. Expect students' reading and writing to reflect their stage of literacy development.
4. Make the reading-writing connection explicit to students.
5. Emphasize both the processes and the products of reading and writing.
6. Emphasize the functions for which students use reading and writing.
7. Teach reading and writing through authentic literacy experiences.

These principles are integrated into the two instructional approaches—literature focus units and reading and writing workshop—presented in this textbook and discussed in the next two chapters.

Review

Teachers incorporate the five stages of the reading process—preparing, reading, responding, exploring, and extending—in planning for instruction. Teachers include shared reading, guided reading, independent reading, buddy reading, and reading aloud to students in their instructional programs. Teachers also use the five stages of the writing process—prewriting, drafting, revising, editing, and publishing—in teaching students how to write and refine their compositions. The goal of both reading and writing is to construct meaning, and the two processes involve similar activities at each stage. Researchers recommend that teachers connect reading and writing because they are mutually supportive processes. The figure on page 279 presents guidelines for effectively teaching the reading and writing processes to students.

HOW EFFECTIVE TEACHERS...
Teach the Reading and Writing Processes

Effective Practices	Ineffective Practices
1. Teachers use the five-stage reading process to plan an integrated, balanced instructional program.	1. Teachers segment instruction, with separate reading and skills programs.
2. Teachers and students set purposes for reading.	2. Teachers and students don't set purposes for reading, or set inappropriate purposes.
3. Teachers incorporate different types of reading: shared reading, guided reading, independent reading, buddy reading, and reading aloud to students.	3. Teachers use only one type of reading.
4. Students respond to their reading as they participate in grand conversations and write in reading logs.	4. Teachers ask questions to assess children's understanding of the reading selection.
5. Students reread the selection, examine the author's craft, and focus on words during the exploring stage.	5. Teachers assign students worksheets to practice vocabulary words and check comprehension skills.
6. Teachers teach skills and strategies during the exploring stage.	6. Teachers don't coordinate skills instruction with literature.
7. Teachers provide opportunities for students to complete self-selected projects.	7. Teachers assign more practice activities and worksheets.
8. Teachers view reading and writing as processes of creating meaning.	8. Teachers see reading and writing as instructional activities.
9. Teachers teach students how to use each of the five stages in the writing process.	9. Teachers assign single-draft writing activities.
10. Teachers involve students in genuine and meaningful reading and writing activities.	10. Teachers assign worksheets and other practice activities.

References

Applebee, A. N., & Langer, J. A. (1983). Instructional scaffolding: Reading and writing and natural language activities. *Language Arts, 60,* 168–175.

Bissex, G. L. (1980). *Gyns at wrk: A child learns to write and read.* Cambridge, MA: Harvard University Press.

Blanton, W. E., Wood, K. D., & Moorman, G. B. (1990). The role of purpose in reading instruction. *The Reading Teacher, 43,* 486–493.

Britton, J., Burgess, T., Martin, N., McLeod, A., & Rosen, H. (1975). *The development of writing abilities (11–18).* London: Schools Council Publications.

Butler, A., & Turbill, J. (1984). *Towards a reading-writing classroom.* Portsmouth, NH: Heinemann.

Calkins, L. M. (1980). When children want to punctuate: Basic skills belong in context. *Language Arts, 57,* 567–573.

Calkins, L. M. (1983). *Lessons from a child: On the teaching and learning of writing.* Portsmouth, NH: Heinemann.

Cochran-Smith, M., Kahn, J., & Paris, C. L. (1988). When word processors come into the classroom. In J. L. Hoot & S. B. Silvern (Eds.), *Writing with computers in the early grades* (pp. 43–74). New York: Teachers College Press.

DeGroff, L. (1990). Is there a place for computers in whole language classrooms? *The Reading Teacher, 43,* 568–572.

Dyson, A. H. (1982). The emergence of visible language: Interrelationships between drawing and early writing. *Visible Language, 6,* 360–381.

Dyson, A. H. (1985). Second graders sharing writing: The multiple social realities of a literacy event. *Written Communication, 2,* 189–215.

Dyson, A. H. (1986). The imaginary worlds of childhood: A multimedia presentation. *Language Arts, 63,* 799–808.

Eeds, M., & Wells, D. (1989). Grand conversations: An exploration of meaning construction in literature study groups. *Research in the Teaching of English, 23,* 4–29.

Elley, W. B., Barham, I. H., Lamb, H., & Wyllie, M. (1976). The role of grammar in a secondary school English curriculum. *Research in the Teaching of English, 10,* 5–21.

Faigley, L., & Witte, S. (1981). Analyzing revision. *College Composition and Communication, 32,* 400–410.

Fitzgerald, J. (1989). Enhancing two related thought processes: Revision in writing and critical thinking. *The Reading Teacher, 43,* 42–48.

Graves, D. H. (1976). Let's get rid of the welfare mess in the teaching of writing. *Language Arts, 53,* 645–651.

Graves, D. H. (1983). *Writing: Teachers and children at work.* Exeter, NH: Heinemann.

Hidi, S., & Hildyard, A. (1983). The comparison of oral and written productions in two discourse modes. *Discourse Processes, 6,* 91–105.

Holdaway, D. (1979). *The foundations of literacy.* Portsmouth, NH: Heinemann.

Hornsby, D., Sukarna, D., & Parry, J. (1986). *Read on: A conference approach to reading.* Portsmouth, NH: Heinemann.

King, M. (1985). Proofreading is not reading. *Teaching English in the Two-Year College, 12,* 108–112.

Langer, J. A. (1985). Children's sense of genre. *Written Communication, 2,* 157–187.

Murray, D. H. (1982). *Learning by teaching.* Montclair, NJ: Boynton/Cook.

Peterson, R., & Eeds, M. (1990). *Grand conversations: Literature groups in action.* New York: Scholastic.

Rosenblatt, L. (1978). *The reader, the text, the poem: The transactional theory of the literary work.* Carbondale: Southern Illinois University Press.

Shanahan, T. (1988). The reading-writing relationship: Seven instructional principles. *The Reading Teacher, 41,* 636–647.

Smith, F. (1982). *Writing and the writer.* New York: Holt, Rinehart and Winston.

Smith, F. (1983). *Essays into literacy.* Portsmouth, NH: Heinemann.

Sommers, N. (1982). Responding to student writing. *College Composition and Communication, 33,* 148–156.

Stauffer, R. G. (1975). *Directing the reading-thinking process.* New York: Harper & Row.

Tierney, R. J. (1983). Writer-reader transactions: Defining the dimensions of negotiation. In P. L. Stock (Ed.), *Forum: Essays on theory and practice in the teaching of writing* (pp. 147–151). Upper Montclair, NJ: Boynton/Cook.

Tierney, R. J., & Pearson, P. D. (1983). Toward a composing model of reading. *Language Arts, 60,* 568–580.

True, J. (1979). Round robin reading is for the birds. *Language Arts, 56,* 918–921.

Weaver, C. (1988). *Reading process and practice: From socio-psycholinguistics to whole language.* Portsmouth, NH: Heinemann.

Yaden, D. B., Jr. (1988). Understanding stories through repeated read-alouds: How many does it take? *The Reading Teacher, 41,* 556–560.

Children's Book References

Henry, M. (1963). *Misty of Chincoteague.* Chicago: Rand McNally.

Howe, D., & Howe, J. (1979). *Bunnicula: A rabbit-tale of mystery.* New York: Atheneum.

Lowry, L. (1993). *The giver.* Boston: Houghton Mifflin.

MacLachlan, P. (1985). *Sarah, plain and tall.* New York: Harper & Row.

Martin, B., Jr. (1983). *Brown bear, brown bear, what do you see?* New York: Holt, Rinehart & Winston.

Martin, B., Jr. (1992). *Polar bear, polar bear, what do you hear?* New York: Holt, Rinehart & Winston.

O'Neill, M. (1989). *Hailstones and halibut bones.* New York: Doubleday.

Van Allsburg, C. (1981). *Jumanji.* Boston: Houghton Mifflin.

Van Allsburg, C. (1993). *The sweetest fig.* Boston: Houghton Mifflin.

Van Allsburg, C. (1995). *Bad day at Riverbend.* Boston: Houghton Mifflin.

Viorst, J. (1977). *Alexander and the terrible, horrible, no good, very bad day.* New York: Atheneum.

CHAPTER 8
Literature Focus Units

"Who knows the story of 'The Three Little Pigs'?" Mrs. Dillon asks her second-grade class as she holds up a double-sided doll with the faces of two of the pigs on one side and the face of the third pig and a wolf on the other side. The students talk about pigs who build houses of straw, brick, and "something else that isn't very good." They remember the nasty wolf who blows down the houses not made of bricks. Mrs. Dillon tells the students that "The Three Little Pigs" is a folktale and that most folktales have threes in them. "Sometimes there are three characters," she says, "there might be three events, a character might have three objects, or a character does something three times." Then she asks her students to listen for threes as she reads aloud James Marshall's *The Three Little Pigs* (1989).

After she is finished reading, students move into a circle to participate in a **grand conversation** (see the Compendium for more information about this and all other highlighted terms in this chapter) about the book. Maria begins: "That wolf deserved to die. I'm glad the third pig cooked him up and ate him up." Angela says, "The first little pig and the second little pig were pretty dumb. Their houses weren't very strong." Several children agree that the third little pig was the smart one. Jim remembers that the second building material was sticks, and several children identify threes in the story: three pigs, three houses, three visits by the wolf, three tricks planned by the wolf and foiled by the third little pig.

Then Mrs. Dillon passes out paperback copies of *The Three Little Pigs* and invites the students to reread the story with partners. Afterwards, students suggest words for the class **word wall.** Their completed list includes these words:

old sow	seek their fortune	straw
house	mind your own business	wolf
lean	my chinny chin chin	annoyed
huff and puff	gobbled up	sticks
blew-blue	capital idea	bricks
sturdy	nice and solid	still hungry
loitering around	blue in the face	dazzling smile
displeasure	scrumptious turnips	splendid
shimmied	empty butter churn	frightened
mean	iron pot	

Mrs. Dillon's second graders spend two weeks reading and comparing versions of the familiar folktale "The Three Little Pigs." She has 15 paperback copies (half of a class set) of James Marshall's *The Three Little Pigs,* as well as one or two copies of eight other versions of the folktale. She also has many other stories and informational books about pigs that students can read independently. These books are listed in Figure 8–1. Mrs. Dillon has arranged the books on one shelf of the classroom library, and she introduces the books to her students during a **book talk.**

During the first week of the two-week unit, Mrs. Dillon's students read the story several times—they read the story independently to themselves, the class reads the book together as a **readers theatre,** and each child reads a favorite excerpt to Mrs.

FIGURE 8–1   Trade Books Used in Mrs. Dillon's Literature Focus Unit

Versions of "The Three Little Pigs"

Bishop, G. (1989). *The three little pigs.* New York: Scholastic.

Galdone, P. (1970). *The three little pigs.* New York: Seabury.

Hooks, W. H. (1989). *The three little pigs and the fox.* New York: Macmillan.

Lowell, S. (1992). *The three little javelinas.* Flagstaff, AZ: Northland.

Marshall, J. (1989). *The three little pigs.* New York: Dial.

Scieszka, J. (1989). *The true story of the three little pigs.* New York: Viking.

Trivizas, E. (1993). *The three little wolves and the big bad pig.* New York: McElderry Books.

Zemach, M. (1988). *The three little pigs.* New York: Farrar, Straus & Giroux.

Other Stories and Informational Books About Pigs

Axelrod, A. (1994). *Pigs will be pigs.* New York: Four Winds.

Carlson, N. (1988). *I like me!* New York: Viking.

Dubanevich, A. (1983). *Pigs in hiding.* New York: Scholastic.

Galdone, P. (1981). *The amazing pig.* New York: Clarion.

Geisert, A. (1992). *Pigs from 1 to 10.* Boston: Houghton Mifflin.

Geisert, A. (1993). *Oink oink.* Boston: Houghton Mifflin.

Grossman, P. (1989). *Tommy at the grocery store.* New York: Harper & Row.

Heller, N. (1994). *Woody.* New York: Greenwillow.

Hutchins, P. (1994). *Little pink pig.* New York: Greenwillow.

Johnson, A. (1993). *Julius.* New York: Orchard.

Kasza, K. (1988). *The pigs' picnic.* New York: Scribner.

Keller, H. (1994). *Geraldine's baby brother.* New York: Greenwillow.

Kimmel, E. (1992). *The old woman and her pig.* New York: Holiday.

King-Smith, D. (1993). *All pigs are beautiful.* New York: Candlewick.

Ling, B. (1993). *Pig.* London: Dorling Kindersley.

Lobel, A. (1969). *Small pig.* New York: Harper & Row.

McPhail, D. (1993). *Pigs aplenty, pigs galore!* New York: Dutton.

Rayner, M. (1977). *Garth pig and the ice cream lady.* New York: Atheneum.

Rayner, M. (1993). *Garth pig steals the show.* New York: Dutton.

Rayner, M. (1994). *10 pink piglets: Garth pig's wall song.* New York: Dutton.

Steig, W. (1994). *Zeke Pippin.* New York: Harper-Collins.

Van Leeuwen, H. (1979). *Tales of Oliver pig.* New York: Dial.

Wilhelm, H. (1988). *Oh, what a mess.* New York: Crown.

Dillon. They reread the story for other purposes, too. They sequence the events using **story boards** and choose a favorite quote to use in making a **story quilt.** Mrs. Dillon teaches a **minilesson** on quotation marks, and then students make a booklet with dialogue among the characters in the story.

Mrs. Dillon teaches a series of minilessons on the /k/ sound at the end of short-vowel words such as *brick* or *stick* and at the end of long-vowel words such as *make* or *steak*. She chooses this minilesson because the words *brick* and *stick* are used in this story. During the minilesson, students hunt for words ending with /k/, and Mrs. Dillon writes them on the chalkboard. Then the students sort the words into two columns: words spelled with *ck* and words spelled with *k*. Together the students deduce that most short-vowel words are spelled *ck* (exceptions include *pink* and *thank*), while long-vowel words are spelled *k*. In a follow-up lesson, students practice spelling *ck* and *k* words using erasable magic slates.

Students continue to add important words to the word wall. One day students divide into four groups: first little pig, second little pig, third little pig, and big bad wolf. Each group makes a vocabulary mobile. Students draw and color a picture of the character and then add at least five words and phrases from the word wall related to that character on word cards hanging below their picture. The second little pig mobile, for example, included these words and phrases: "sticks," "build a house," "not by the hair of my chinny chin chin," "ha ha ha," and "gobbled up."

Mrs. Dillon reads a different version of "The Three Little Pigs" each day, and students compare the versions. They add information to a comparison chart they are compiling, as shown in Figure 8–2. While several of the versions are very similar, others are unique. In Hooks's Appalachian version (1989), the third little pig, Hamlet, is a girl, and she saves her brothers. In this version Hamlet builds the only house using rocks. In Lowell's Southwestern version (1992), the pigs are javelinas and are pursued by a coyote, not a wolf. This story also ends happily as all three javelina brothers live together in a strong adobe house.

During the second week, students read a variety of pig books independently and work on projects that extend their interpretation of "The Three Little Pigs" stories. Some of the projects they choose are:

- making puppets of pigs and wolf
- creating a **choral reading** from the story
- writing several poems
- drawing a **story map**
- making a Venn diagram comparing pigs and wolves
- dramatizing the story
- writing and mailing a letter to the author
- making houses out of straw, sticks, and bricks
- writing a retelling of the story
- writing an "All About . . ." book about pigs

Students work on projects individually or in pairs or small groups, and then they share their projects during the last two days of the unit.

Mrs. Dillon teaches a series of minilessons this week on using *y* at the end of words. She begins the lesson by writing *by the hair of my chinny chin chin* on the chalkboard and underlines the words *by, my,* and *chinny.* Students read the words and note that *y* in the first two words is pronounced as a long *i,* but in the third word it's pronounced as a long *e.* Then she asks students to think of five other words ending in *y.* She writes students' words on a chart and then divides them into two groups according to the sound the *y* represents:

try	sunny
by	baby
sky	hairy
my	Jimmy
why	bunny

Then Mrs. Dillon spends several days on follow-up minilessons on using *y* at the end of words. Students also practice sorting the words (see **word sorts**) and writing and spelling the words using magic slates.

Students have samples of straw, sticks, and bricks—the three house-building materials mentioned in the story—in the classroom, and Mrs. Dillon spends time during the second week talking with students about houses, the advantages and draw-

FIGURE 8–2   A Chart Comparing Versions of "The Three Little Pigs"

Book	Who Are the Three Main Characters?	Who Is the Bad Character?	What Kinds of Houses?	What Happens to the Three Characters?	What Happens to the Bad Character?
The Three Little Pigs James Marshall	3 boy pigs	wolf	1. straw 2. sticks 3. bricks	#1 eaten #2 eaten #3 lives happily ever after	He is cooked and eaten.
The Three Little Pigs Gavin Bishop	3 boy pigs	cool fox	1. straw 2. sticks 3. bricks	#1 eaten #2 eaten #3 lives happily	He is cooked and eaten.
The Three Little Pigs Paul Galdone	3 boy pigs	wolf	1. straw 2. sticks 3. bricks	#1 eaten #2 eaten #3 lives happily	He is cooked and eaten.
The Three Little Javelinas Susan Lowell	2 boy javelinas 1 girl javelina	coyote	1. tumbleweeds 2. cactus 3. adobe	#1 escapes #2 escapes #3 lives safely with her brothers	He is burned up and becomes smoke.
The Three Little Pigs and the Fox William Hooks	3 pigs: Rooter—boy Oinky—boy Hamlet—girl	fox	Only Hamlet builds a rock house.	#1 caught by fox #2 caught by fox #3 catches fox and saves her brothers	He is stuffed in a churn and floats down the river.
The Three Little Wolves and the Big Bad Pig Eugene Trivizas	3 boy wolves: #1 black #2 gray #3 white	big, bad pig	1. brick 2. concrete 3. armor-plated 4. flowers	#1 escaped #2 escaped #3 escaped to live together	He becomes a good pig and lives with the wolves.
The Three Little Pigs Margot Zemach	3 boy pigs	wolf	1. straw 2. sticks 3. bricks	#1 eaten #2 eaten #3 lives happily	He is cooked and eaten.
The True Story of the Three Little Pigs Jon Scieszka	The wolf is the good character. He was framed.	the 3 pigs	1. straw 2. sticks 3. bricks	#1 eaten #2 eaten #3 lives happily	The "good" wolf goes to jail.

FIGURE 8-3 Mrs. Dillon's Two-Week Lesson Plan for "The Three Little Pigs"

	MONDAY	TUESDAY	WEDNESDAY	THURSDAY	FRIDAY
WEEK 1	Introduce "The Three Little Pigs" and 3's in fairy tales	Sequence the story boards	ML: *ck* and *k* spelling at the end of words	Do word sorts in small groups	Spell words using magic slates
	Read aloud James Marshall's *The Three Little Pigs*	ML: Comparing versions of stories	Make vocabulary mobiles in 4 groups	Reread story using readers theatre	Make story quilt
	Have a grand conversation about the book / Begin word wall	Begin comparison chart	ML: Dialogue and how to use " "	Make dialogue books with quotes from each character	Also finish dialogue book
	Reread the book with partners / Introduce text set	Read Bishop's version and add information to the chart	Read Galdone's version and add to chart	Read Lowell's version and add to chart	Read Hooks's version and add to chart
WEEK 2	Independent reading of pig books				
	Work on projects				
	ML: *y* at the end of words	ML: Focus on 1-syllable words	ML: Focus on 2-syllable words	Share projects	Share projects
	Read Trivizas's version and add to chart	Read Zemach's version and add to chart	Read Scieszka's version and finish chart	Vote on favorite version and compile graph	Write letters to Mrs. Dillon. Collect materials and assignment checklists.

backs of building materials, how houses are constructed in the United States, and the types of houses people live in around the world. She shares *Houses and Homes* (Morris, 1992) and *This Is My House* (Dorros, 1992), two related books, with students, and they learn that today people continue to live in houses made of straw, sticks, and bricks around the world.

Mrs. Dillon continues to read different versions of "The Three Little Pigs" to the class this week, and they complete the chart shown in Figure 8–2. After reading all of the versions, students vote on their favorite version and create a graph to show the results. Not surprisingly, Scieszka's *The True Story of the Three Little Pigs!* (1989), a story told from the wolf's viewpoint, is the class's favorite. The style of this spirited version and its surrealistic illustrations make it popular with students.

Mrs. Dillon's language arts period lasts approximately two hours each morning, and for this period she plans a variety of activities that are appropriate to the students' attention span and literacy abilities. The lesson plan shown in Figure 8–3 shows how Mrs. Dillon taught this two-week literature focus unit on "The Three Little Pigs" stories.

*L*iterature focus units are the most common way teachers organize for literacy instruction. Teachers choose a trade book or basal reader selection and build a literature focus unit around the featured selection or selections, as Mrs. Dillon did in the vignette. Her featured book was James Marshall's version of *The Three Little Pigs* (1989), and she developed a two-week unit around that book. Literature focus units include these components:

■ a related text set of reading materials
■ multiple opportunities to read and reread the featured book as well as the text set
■ ways to create meaning and respond to the featured book
■ vocabulary activities
■ minilessons on strategies, skills, and procedures
■ projects to extend students' understanding of the book

Literature focus units include activities incorporating all five stages of the reading process. Teachers involve students in preparing-to-read activities as they build background experiences and activate students' prior knowledge. Next, students read the featured book and respond to it in grand conversations and entries in **reading logs.** Students participate in exploring activities as they learn vocabulary and participate in minilessons. Last, students extend their interpretations as they create projects and share them with their classmates at the end of the unit. Through these activities, students read together, share their interpretations, and become a community of readers.

In this chapter, you will learn ways to select books for literature focus units and the steps to follow in developing a literature focus unit. As you read, think about these questions:

■ Which books should students read during literature focus units?
■ How can teachers make literature accessible to every student?

■ How can basal reader selections be used?

■ What components should be included in a literature focus unit?

■ What kinds of units can teachers develop?

CHOOSING LITERATURE FOR UNITS

Choosing the literature that students read is one of teachers' most important responsibilities. When teachers choose high-interest pieces of literature written at an appropriate reading level, their students are more likely to become readers. When students are expected to read pieces that they can't relate to, that don't interest them, or that are too difficult or too easy, they don't become readers. The two main sources of literature are trade books and textbooks. In many reading textbook series, students are not required to read story-by-story from front to back anymore. Teachers can choose the most appropriate pieces for their students from basal readers and select trade books, magazines, and other reading materials to create text sets.

In the vignette, Mrs. Dillon was familiar with the wide range of books available for children today. Because she was knowledgeable about literature, she was able to make wise choices and connect language arts and literature. She chose one version of "The Three Little Pigs" as her main selection. Beginning with multiple copies of that book, she added other versions of the folktale and other books about pigs to create a text set.

Teachers need to consider the types of books they choose and the impact of their choices on their students. Researchers who have examined the books that teachers select for classroom use have found that their choices suggest an unconscious gender or racial bias because few books that are chosen feature the experiences of females or of ethnic minorities, and even fewer were written by people from these groups (Jipson & Paley, 1991; Shannon, 1986; Traxel, 1983). These researchers call this pattern the "selective tradition," and they believe that books reflect and convey sociocultural values, beliefs, and attitudes to readers. It is important that teachers be aware of the ideas conveyed by their selection patterns and become more reflective about the books they choose for classroom use.

The Best of the Best

Teachers who want to use literature as the basis for their reading programs must be knowledgeable about children's literature. The first step in becoming knowledgeable about children's literature is to read many of the stories, informational books, and poems available for children today. Many of the stories in basal readers today are also available as trade books or are excerpted from chapter books. Teachers need to locate the complete versions of basal reader selections to share with their students. Children's librarians and the salespeople in children's bookstores are very helpful and willing to suggest books for teachers.

As they read and make selections for classroom use, teachers should keep in mind guidelines for selecting literature. The most important guideline is that teachers should choose books that they like themselves. Teachers are rarely, if ever, successful in teaching books they don't like. The message that they don't like the book comes across loud and clear, even when teachers try to hide their feelings. Other guidelines for choosing stories, informational books, and poems and books of poetry are pre-

These students made cubes after reading E. B. White's *Charlotte's Web,* one of the "best of the best" books.

sented in Figure 8–4. The trade books and basal reader selections that teachers use as featured selections for literature focus units should embody these qualities.

Each year a number of books written for children are recognized for excellence and receive awards. The two best-known awards are the Caldecott Medal for excellence in illustration and the Newbery Medal for excellence in writing. Lists of the previous winners of the Caldecott and Newbery Medal and Honor Books are given in Appendix A. Teachers should be familiar with many of these outstanding books and consider selecting one of more of them to use in their classrooms as featured selections in literature focus units and as part of text sets.

Multicultural Literature

Multicultural literature is "literature that represents any distinct cultural group through accurate portrayal and rich detail" (Yokota, 1993, p. 157); it has generally been described as stories and books by and about people of color. Stories such as Faith Ringgold's *Tar Beach* (1991), about how an African-American child spends a hot summer evening on the roof of her New York City apartment house, and Gary Soto's *Too Many Tamales* (1993), about a Mexican-American child who loses her mother's diamond ring in a batch of tamales she is making, provide glimpses of contemporary life in two cultural groups. Other books tell the history of various cultural and ethnic groups. *Journey to Topaz* (Uchida, 1971), for instance, tells how Japanese Americans were interned in desolate camps during World War II, and *Anthony Burns: The Defeat and Triumph of a Fugitive Slave* (Hamilton, 1988) describes how slaves risked their lives to be free.

FIGURE 8–4 Guidelines for Selecting Books

Stories

- Is the book a good story?
- Is the plot original and believable?
- Are the characters real and believable?
- Do the characters grow and change in the story?
- Does the author avoid stereotyping?
- Does the story move beyond the setting and have universal implications?
- Is the theme worthwhile?
- Are the style of writing and use of language appropriate?
- Does the book exemplify the characteristics of a genre?
- How does the book compare with others on the same subject or in the same genre?

Informational Books

- Does the book stimulate children's curiosity and wonder?
- Is the information accurate, complete, and up to date?
- Does the author use facts to support generalizations?
- Is the information presented without anthropomorphism (assigning human characteristics and feelings to animals, plants, or objects)?
- Are there any racial, cultural, or sexual stereotypes?
- Is the organization clear and logical?
- Is vocabulary related to the subject introduced in the text?
- Do illustrations (including photographs and charts) complement and clarify the text?
- Does the author use a lively and stimulating writing style?
- Are reference aids, such as a table of contents, a glossary, and an index, included?

Poems and Books of Poetry

- Is the poem lively, with exciting meters and rhythms?
- Does the poem emphasize the sounds of language and encourage wordplay?
- Does the poem encourage children to see or hear the world in a new way?
- Does the poem allow children to feel emotions?
- Does the poem create an image that appeals to a child's imagination?
- Is the poem good enough for children to want to hear it again and again?
- Is the cover of the book appealing to children?
- Do poems in the book meet the criteria listed above?
- Are the poems arranged on the page so as to not overwhelm children?
- Do the illustrations clarify and extend the image the poem creates, or do they merely distract the reader?

Adapted from Huck, Hepler, and Hickman, 1987; Norton, 1995; Sutherland and Arbuthnot, 1986; and Vardell, 1991.

For this discussion of multicultural literature, the literature about American cultural groups has been divided into five main groups: African Americans, Asian Americans, Hispanic Americans, Native Americans, and other American groups. These umbrella labels can be deceiving, however, as there are substantial differences among the cultures within a label. For example, there are no composite Native Americans; instead, Eskimos and the more than 100 Indian tribes in North America are grouped together under the Native American umbrella label. Books written for children about each of these cultures are presented in Figure 8–5. For an annotated listing of more than 300 multicultural books, see *Kaleidoscope: A Multicultural Booklist for Grades K–8* (Bishop, 1994).

1. African Americans.   More books are available today about African Americans than about other cultural groups. Some books, such as *Follow the Drinking Gourd* (Winter, 1988), about the Underground Railroad, and *Roll of Thunder, Hear My Cry* (Taylor, 1976), about discrimination in the South during the 1930s, document events in the history of African Americans, and other books focus on contemporary events, such as *Ben's Trumpet* (Isadora, 1979), about a boy who wants to become a jazz musician.

2. Asian Americans.   Books about Asian Americans in Figure 8–5 deal with specific Asian-American groups, not in generalities. The characters in the books go beyond common stereotypes and correct historical errors and omissions. Many of the books have been written by Asian Americans and are about their own assimilation experiences or remembrances as children in the United States. For example, *Angel Child, Dragon Child* (Surat, 1983) is the story of a Vietnamese-American child who adjusts to life in the United States.

3. Hispanic Americans.   Few Hispanic-American writers are writing literature for children, and fewer books about Hispanic Americans are available than for other cultural groups, despite the fact that Hispanic Americans are one of the largest cultural groups in the United States. Two authors who are making a significant contribution are Nicholasa Mohr, who writes about life in the Puerto Rican–American community in New York, and Gary Soto, who writes about life in the Mexican-American community in California. Both writers bring firsthand knowledge of life in a barrio (a Spanish-speaking neighborhood in the United States) to make their writing authentic (Soto, 1992; Zarnowski, 1991). Books by these two authors are included in Figure 8–5.

4. Native Americans.   Many books are available about Native Americans, but few have been written by Native American authors. Most books about Native Americans are retellings of traditional folktales, myths, and legends, such as *The Legend of the Indian Paintbrush* (de Paola, 1988) and *Iktomi and the Boulder* (Goble, 1988). A number of biographies about Indian chiefs are also available, and other books describe Indian rituals and ceremonies, such as *Totem Pole* (Hoyt-Goldsmith, 1990), in which a contemporary Indian boy describes how his father carves a totem pole.

5. Other American groups.   Other distinct regional and religious groups in the United States include Jewish, Amish, Cajun, and Appalachian cultures. As the majority culture, European Americans are sometimes ignored in discussions of cultural groups, but to ignore them denies the distinct cultures of many Americans (Yokota, 1993). Within the European-American umbrella category are a variety of groups,

FIGURE 8–5 Multicultural Books

Primary Grades

Aliki. (1976). *Corn is maize: The gift of the Indians.* New York: Crowell. (Native American)

Armstrong, J. (1993). *Cleversticks.* New York: Crown. (Asian American)

Cazet, D. (1993). *Born in the gravy.* New York: Orchard. (Hispanic)

Crews, D. (1991). *Bigmama's.* New York: Greenwillow. (African American)

de Paola, T. (1983). *The legend of the bluebonnet.* New York: Putnam. (Native American)

Dooley, N. (1991). *Everybody cooks rice.* Minneapolis: Carolrhoda. (all)

Dorros, A. (1991). *Abuela.* New York: Dutton. (Hispanic)

Garza, C. L. (1990). *Family pictures.* San Francisco: Children's Book Press. (Hispanic)

Greenfield, E. (1991). *Night on Neighborhood Street.* New York: Dial. (African American)

Hoffman, M. (1991). *Amazing Grace.* New York: Dial. (African American)

Martin, B., & Archambault, J. (1987). *Knots on a counting rope.* New York: Holt, Rinehart & Winston. (Native American)

Ringgold, F. (1991). *Tar beach.* New York: Crown. (African American)

Soto, G. (1993). *Too many tamales.* New York: Putnam. (Hispanic)

Stolz, M. (1988). *Storm in the night.* New York: HarperCollins. (African American)

Towle, W. (1993). *The real McCoy: The life of an African-American inventor.* New York: Scholastic. (African American)

Waters, K. (1990). *Lion dancer: Ernie Wan's Chinese New Year.* New York: Scholastic. (Asian American)

Middle Grades

Ancona, G. (1993). *Powwow.* Orlando: Harcourt Brace. (Native American)

Anzaldua, G. (1993). *Friends from the other side/Amigos del otro lado.* San Francisco: Children's Book Press. (Hispanic)

Golenbock, P. (1990). *Teammates.* San Diego: Harcourt Brace Jovanovich. (African American)

Hamilton, V. (1985). *The people could fly: American Black folktales.* New York: Knopf. (African American)

Hewett, J. (1990). *Hector lives in the United States now: The story of a Mexican-American child.* New York: Lippincott. (Hispanic)

Hopkinson, D. (1993). *Sweet Clara and the freedom quilt.* New York: Knopf. (African American)

Jones, H. (1993). *The trees standing shining: Poetry of the North American Indians.* New York: Dial. (Native American)

Keegan, M. (1991). *Pueblo boy: Growing up in two worlds.* New York: Cobblehill. (Native American)

Lord, B. B. (1984). *In the year of the boar and Jackie Robinson.* New York: HarperCollins. (Asian American)

Mathis, S. B. (1975). *The hundred penny box.* New York: Viking. (African American)

Mochizuki, K. (1993). *Baseball saved us.* New York: Lee & Low Books. (Asian American)

Mohr, N. (1979). *Felita.* New York: Dial. (Hispanic)

Soto, G. (1992). *The skirt.* New York: Delacorte. (Hispanic)

Speare, E. G. (1983). *The sign of the beaver.* Boston: Houghton Mifflin. (Native American)

Whelan, G. (1992). *Goodbye, Vietnam.* New York: Knopf. (Asian American)

Winter, J. (1988). *Follow the drinking gourd.* New York: Knopf. (African American)

Yarbrough, C. (1979). *Cornrows.* New York: Coward McCann. (African American)

Upper Grades

Armstrong, W. H. (1969). *Sounder.* New York: Harper & Row. (African American)

Cisneros, S. (1983). *The house on Mango Street.* New York: Vintage Books. (Hispanic)

George, J. C. (1972). *Julie of the wolves.* New York: Harper & Row. (Native American)

George, J. C. (1989). *Shark beneath the reef.* New York: HarperCollins. (Hispanic)

Gilson, J. (1985). *Hello, my name is scrambled eggs.* New York: Morrow. (Asian American)

Hamilton, V. (1974). *M. C. Higgins, the great.* New York: Macmillan. (African American)

Levne, E. (1993). *Freedom's children.* New York: Putnam. (African American)

Mazer, A. (Ed.). (1993). *America street: A multicultural anthology of stories.* New York: Persea Books. (all)

Meltzer, M. (1982). *The Hispanic Americans.* New York: Crowell. (Hispanic)

Mohr, N. (1988). *In Nueva York.* Houston: Arte Publico. (Hispanic)

Myers, W. D. (1988). *Scorpions.* New York: HarperCollins. (African American)

Slote, A. (1991). *Finding Buck McHenry.* New York: HarperCollins. (African American)

Soto, G. (1992). *Neighborhood odes.* Orlando: Harcourt Brace. (Hispanic)

Uchida, Y. (1971). *Journey to Topaz.* Berkeley, CA: Creative Arts. (Asian American)

Yep, L. (1975). *Dragonwings.* New York: HarperCollins. (Asian American)

including German Americans, Italian Americans, Swedish Americans, and Russian Americans. Some books describing other American regional and religious groups are also included in Figure 8–5.

Educators recommend selecting multicultural literature that is "culturally conscious" (Sims, 1982)—that is to say, literature that accurately reflects a group's culture, language, history, and values without perpetuating stereotypes. Such literature often deals with issues of prejudice, discrimination, and human dignity. According to Yokota (1993), these books should be rich in cultural details, use authentic dialogue, and present cultural issues in enough depth that readers can think and talk about them. Inclusion of cultural group members should be purposeful. They should be distinct individuals whose lives are rooted in the culture; they should never be included simply to fulfill a quota.

Multicultural literature must meet the criteria for good literature as well as for cultural consciousness. One example is *The Gold Cadillac* (Taylor, 1987), a story about the harsh realities of racial discrimination that an African-American family encounters they travel from Ohio to Mississippi in their new Cadillac during World War II. This well-written story is both historically and culturally accurate (Yokota, 1993).

Until recently, most books about Native Americans, Hispanic Americans, and other cultural groups have been written by European-American authors who, because of their own ethnicity, represent an "outside" viewpoint (Bishop, 1992). An inside perspective is more likely to give an authentic view of what members of the cultural group believe to be true about themselves, while an outside perspective describes how others see that group's beliefs and behaviors. The difference in perspective means there is a difference in what the authors say and how they say it, as well as a difference in their purpose for writing (Reimer, 1992). Some authors, however, do successfully write about another culture. Byrd Baylor and Paul Goble are notable examples. They have a sensitivity learned through research about and participation in another cultural group. Today more people within each cultural group are writing about their own cultures and providing more authentic "inside" viewpoints in multicultural literature.

Why use multicultural literature? There are many reasons to use multicultural literature in elementary classrooms, whether students represent diverse cultures or not. First of all, multicultural literature is good literature. Students enjoy reading stories, informational books, and poems, and through reading they learn more about what it means to be human and that people of all cultural groups are real people with similar emotions, needs, and dreams (Bishop, 1994). Allen Say's *El Chino* (1990), for example, tells about a Chinese American who achieves his dream of becoming a great athlete, and the book provides a model for children and adults of all ethnic groups.

Second, through multicultural books, students learn about the wealth of diversity in the United States and develop sensitivity to and appreciation for people of other cultural groups (Walker-Dalhouse, 1992). *Teammates* (Golenbock, 1990), for example, tells about the friendship of baseball greats Jackie Robinson and Pee Wee Reese, and it teaches a valuable lesson in tolerance and respect. Multicultural literature also challenges racial and ethnic stereotypes by providing an inside view of a culture.

Third, students broaden their knowledge of geography and learn different views of history through multicultural literature. They read about the countries that minority groups left as they immigrated to America, and often students gain nonmainstream perspectives about historical events. For example, Yoshiko Uchida tells of her experiences in Japanese-American internment camps in the United States during

World War II in *The Bracelet* (1993) and *Journey to Topaz* (1971). As they read and respond to multicultural books, students challenge traditional assumptions and gain a more balanced view of historical events and the contributions of people from cultural groups. They learn that traditional historical accounts have emphasized the contributions of European Americans, particularly those made by men.

Fourth, multicultural literature raises issues of social injustice—prejudice, racism, discrimination, segregation, colonization, anti-Semitism, and genocide. Two books that describe the discrimination and mistreatment of Chinese Americans during the 1800s, as well as their contributions to the settlement of the western United States, are *Chang's Paper Pony* (Coerr, 1988), a story set during the California gold rush, and *Ten Mile Day and the Building of the Transcontinental Railroad* (Fraser, 1993), a factual account of the race to complete the construction of the first railroad across North America.

Using multicultural literature has additional benefits for nonmainstream students. When students read books about their own cultural group, they develop pride in their cultural heritage and learn that their culture has made important contributions to the United States and the world (Harris, 1992a, 1992b). In addition, these students often become more interested in reading because they are able to better identify with the characters and with the events in those characters' lives.

Teachers' choices of books for instruction and for inclusion in the classroom library influence students in other ways, too. Students tend to choose familiar books and those that reflect their own cultures for reading workshop and other independent reading activities (Rudman, 1976). If teachers read aloud culturally conscious books, include them in literature focus units and theme studies, and display them in the classroom library, these books become familiar and are more likely to be picked up and read independently by students.

Ways to Incorporate Multicultural Books.   Some teachers periodically share books of multicultural literature with their students, some teachers include multicultural components in lessons they teach, and other teachers teach literature focus units to raise students' awareness of social issues. Rasinski and Padak (1990) have identified four approaches for teaching students about cultural diversity and integrating concepts about cultural pluralism into literature focus units and theme studies. These approaches are based on Banks's (1989) multicultural curriculum model and differ in the extent to which multicultural issues become a central part of the curriculum.

1. The contributions approach.   In this approach, special lessons are taught in connection with a holiday or other special occasions (Rasinski & Padak, 1990). The purpose of activities is to familiarize students with holidays, specific customs, or the contributions of important people, but these activities do not teach cultural values or challenge students to reexamine their beliefs. Single lessons might focus on reading *Seven Candles for Kwanzaa* (Pinkney, 1993), a story about Kwanzaa, an African-American holiday celebrated from December 26 to January 1, or *How My Parents Learned to Eat* (Friedman, 1984), a story about an American sailor who courts a young Japanese woman after World War II. In the latter book, the young woman learns to eat with a knife and fork to surprise the sailor, and the sailor learns to eat with chopsticks to surprise the woman. Or, teachers might read *A Picture Book of Martin Luther King, Jr.* (Adler, 1989), to celebrate the Civil Rights leader's birthday. This approach is an easy way to include a multicultural component in the curriculum, but students gain only a superficial understanding of cultural diversity.

2. *The additive approach.* In this approach, multicultural literature is added to existing literature focus units and across-the-curriculum themes (Rasinski & Padak, 1990). In a unit on folktales, for example, *Mufaro's Beautiful Daughters: An African Tale* (Steptoe, 1987), *Yeh-Shen: A Cinderella Story From China* (Louie, 1982), and *The Egyptian Cinderella* (Climo, 1989) are added as international versions of the Cinderella story. Or, an upper-grade teacher might choose *Year of Impossible Goodbyes* (Choi, 1991), the story of a Korean girl who immigrates to America after enduring the cruelties of the Japanese military force occupying her country at the end of World War II, for a literature focus unit. The teacher could choose this book because it is a powerful, well-written book, not because it is a "token" multicultural book. The additive approach is similar to the contributions approach because the curriculum is based in the European-American perspective. Cultural diversity is added to the curriculum but not woven through it.

3. *The transformation approach.* In this approach, literature focus units are modified to promote the study of historical events and contemporary issues from culturally diverse viewpoints (Rasinski & Padak, 1990). First graders, for instance, might read *A Chair for My Mother* (Williams, 1982), *Everybody Cooks Rice* (Dooley, 1991), and *Bigmama's* (Crews, 1991) as part of a unit on families and talk about the common features of families from diverse cultural groups. Or, during a study of World War II, upper-grade students might read *Journey to Topaz* (Uchida, 1971) to learn about Japanese Americans' viewpoint about the war and their unfair internment. These literature experiences and extension projects allow students to see the interconnectedness of the ethnic groups within American society and understand how diverse cultural groups have shaped American history.

4. *The social action approach.* In this approach, students study important social issues and take action to solve problems (Rasinski & Padak, 1990). Students read culturally conscious literature in order to gain an "inside" view on social issues. For example, students learning about immigration might begin by reading *How Many Days to America? A Thanksgiving Story* (Bunting, 1988) to learn about modern-day refugees who risk their lives coming to America. Afterwards they can talk about their own attitudes toward immigrant groups and research how and when their family came to America. Another book they might read is *Who Belongs Here? An American Story* (Knight, 1993). The question "Who belongs here?" might direct their study and lead them to find ways to encourage tolerance and assist with refugee programs in their community. In this approach, students read and do research, think deeply about social issues, and apply what they are learning in their own communities.

Students can also create multicultural books, both through the content of the books they write and through the types of books they construct. Students often write books as extension projects, and their books may reflect their cultures. Students write about how their families or ancestors immigrated to the United States as part of a unit on immigration, or they devise new versions of "The Gingerbread Man" story, substituting ethnic foods for gingerbread cookies. They also construct book forms representing many cultures. Gaylord (1994) suggests African scrolls, Native American hides, Aztec accordion books, American comic books, Southeast Asian palm leaf books, Japanese Haiku books, Viking rune stones, and European newsbooks. The materials students use to construct books also reflect various cultures. They can use paper with varied textures, cardboard, cloth, yarn and ribbon, beads, and other decorations.

Textbooks

Another source of literature is basal reading textbooks. In recent years, basal readers have been criticized for their controlled vocabulary, for their emphasis on isolated skills, and for stories that lack conflict or authentic situations. Stories in these textbooks have been excerpted from children's literature and rewritten, often substituting simpler or more decodable words for the author's original language (Goodman, Shannon, Freeman, & Murphy, 1988). The literature-based reading movement has called for the use of authentic texts—selections that have not been edited or abridged—and during the past few years, publishers of basal reading programs have redesigned their programs to make them more in line with the literature-based reading movement. Now many basal readers include authentic, unadapted literature in their series and support materials.

McCarthey and Hoffman (1995) compared newer first-grade-level literature-based basal readers with older editions and found that the newer editions were very different from the older ones. They examined five characteristics of basal readers and reported their findings:

1. **Word and sentence difficulty.**   The researchers reported that the total number of words was smaller in the new programs, but the newer basal readers contained more unique words. They concluded that the vocabulary was much less controlled and that there was significantly less repetition of words in the new programs.

2. **Literary characteristics.**   The researchers found that the new editions included different formats. Reading materials were packaged in a variety of ways—as big books, in trade books, and in anthologies. The new editions included a wider variety of genres with very few adaptations of children's literature.

3. **Literacy features.**   The researchers also evaluated the literary quality of the selections and found that the selections in the new basals had more complex plots, more highly developed characters, and more idiomatic and metaphorical language. They concluded that the newer basals were more engaging than the older ones, but the researchers' average rating of the newer basals was only a 3 on a scale of 1 to 5.

4. **Predictability.**   The researchers found that more than half of the selections in the new basal readers had predictable features, including repeated patterns, rhyme, and rhythm. In contrast, less than 20% of the stories in the older editions had predictable features.

5. **Decodability.**   The researchers examined the word-level decoding demands placed on the reader and concluded that the new basal readers placed much higher decoding demands on readers than the older ones did.

McCarthey and Hoffman concluded that skills are still prevalent in newer reading textbooks, but they are slightly more integrated. They noted that assessment tools broadened from a testing-only mentality to include portfolios and other innovative assessment strategies. They also found that the tone of the teacher's manual was less prescriptive and advocated that teachers become decision makers.

One big advantage of basal readers is their availability. These textbooks provide teachers with multiple copies of reading materials to use for literature focus units,

■ *Activity*

Visit a classroom where reading is taught using basal readers and another classroom where reading is taught with trade books. Compare the instructional programs using the characteristics discussed in this section.

and the reading difficulty level is usually appropriate for the students' grade placement. Teachers should consider the selections in basal readers when planning literature focus units, and it is important to point out that teachers can use selections from reading textbooks without doing all of the accompanying workbook and related activities.

Determining the Difficulty Level of Books

When teachers want to estimate the difficulty level of a particular trade book or textbook, they can use a readability formula. Readability levels can serve as rough gauges of text difficulty, and they are reported as grade-level scores. If a book has a readability score of fifth grade, then teachers can assume that many average fifth-grade readers will be able to read the book. Sometimes readability scores are marked RL and a grade level, such as RL 5, on the back covers of paperback trade books.

There are limitations associated with readability formulas. The scores that readability formulas provide are estimates, not absolute scores of reading difficulty, because only two of the many factors that affect readability are measured by readability formulas. These estimates are usually determined using vocabulary difficulty and sentence complexity, measured by word and sentence length. These two variables are most often used to predict the difficulty of a text. Readability formulas don't take into account the experience and knowledge that readers bring to the reading experience. Nor do they take into account readers' cognitive and linguistic backgrounds or their motivation or purpose for reading. It is also important to note that different formulas sometimes yield different results.

One fairly quick and simple readability formula is the Fry Readability Graph, developed by Edward Fry (1968). Figure 8–6 presents the Fry Readability Graph and lists the steps in using the formula to predict the grade-level score for the material, ranging from first grade through college level. Teachers should always consider using a readability formula as an aid in evaluating textbook and trade book selections for classroom use, but they cannot assume that materials that are rated as appropriate for a particular grade level will be appropriate for all students at that grade level. Teachers need to recognize the effectiveness of readability formulas as a tool but remember that these formulas have limitations.

Many reading selections that might seem very different actually score at the same level. For example, *Sarah, Plain and Tall* (MacLachlan, 1985), *Tales of a Fourth Grade Nothing* (Blume, 1972), *Bunnicula: A Rabbit-Tale of Mystery* (Howe & Howe, 1979), and *The Hundred Penny Box* (Mathis, 1975) all score at the third-grade level according to Fry's Readability Graph, even though some of the books are longer, have fewer illustrations, are written on very different topics, and are printed in different-sized type.

Making Books Accessible

Sometimes the books that teachers choose for literature focus units are difficult for the less capable readers to read. Teachers sometimes wonder if they should choose a less difficult book for the weaker readers, but all students deserve the opportunity to experience the same high-quality literature as well as opportunities to read reading-level-appropriate books independently. Teachers can use a variety of techniques to make difficult books more accessible and even enticing to students who are not fluent readers. The most common way that teachers make books accessible is by reading

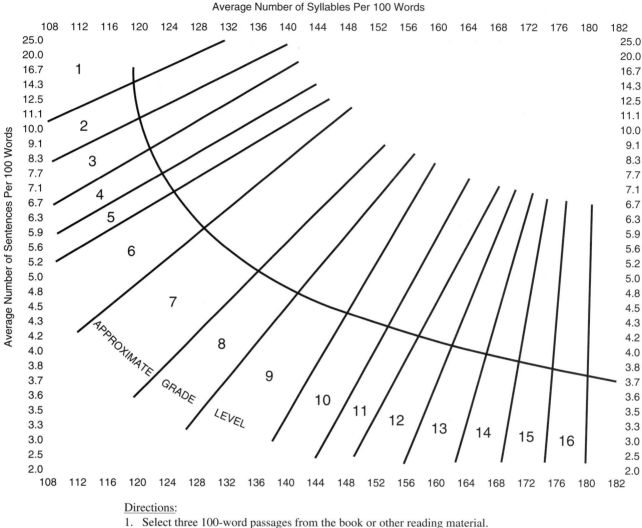

FIGURE 8–6   The Fry Readability Graph
Note. From "A Readability Formula That Saves Time," by E. Fry, 1968, *Journal of Reading, 11,* p. 587.

Directions:
1. Select three 100-word passages from the book or other reading material.
2. Count the number of syllables in each 100-word passage and average them.
3. Count the number of sentences in each 100-word passage and average them.
4. Plot the average numbers on the graph to determine the grade-level reading difficulty of the material. A few scores will fall outside the lined area, and these scores are not valid.

them aloud. In a literature focus unit featuring a picture book, teachers often read the book aloud before students read the book themselves, and in units featuring a chapter book, teachers read the book aloud as students follow along in their own copies. When teachers read aloud for students, they are providing a scaffold to support fledgling readers. Teachers also use preparing activities and provide tape-recorded versions of the books. A list of seven ways to make difficult books more accessible for students is presented in Figure 8–7.

FIGURE 8–7   Seven Ways to Make Books More Accessible

1. Build Background

Students who have an adequate background of knowledge and experiences will be better prepared to read a book. Try these activities to build background:

• Read another book (or show a film) on the same topic.
• As a class, brainstorm a list of words or make a semantic map on the topic.
• Use a field trip as the first activity, not the culminating activity.
• As a group, talk or quickwrite about a similar experience in students' own lives.
• Dramatize the book for students.
• Share small objects related to the book.

2. Read Aloud

While some students can read a book independently, others need to have you read aloud as they follow along. Round-robin reading is a mistake because many students do not read fluently and it becomes a painful experience both for the student who is struggling to read and for others who are listening.

3. Use Echo Reading

When reading a picture book with only a sentence on each page, students "echo" read by repeating the text after you read it. Students who are reading chapter books mumble along as you read. They're more likely to look at the words and practice the phrasing that fluent readers use. Even though mumbling creates an undercurrent of noise in the classroom, it's worthwhile because students are actually involved in reading.

4. Reread the Book

When readers reread a book they notice subtle meanings and catch more of the author's powerful language. Younger students reread favorite picture books, and older students reread chapter books that were read aloud to them months or even years earlier.

5. Use Listening Center

Students can listen to the book read aloud again and again at the listening center. Tape-record the book as you read it aloud, and don't worry about reading miscues and extraneous noises. It is important for students to reread the book again without having to purchase a professionally read tape.

6. Use Buddy Reading

Buddy reading is a popular technique in which students read with a classmate. As students read together, they practice reading, assist each other with unfamiliar words, and model reading strategies.

7. Delay Independent Reading

Too often students are asked to do the most difficult assignment—reading the book independently—first. Instead, read the book aloud, do related activities, and then ask students to read the book independently. By reversing the order, students will build background to use when reading independently.

Adapted from Tompkins, 1992.

One way to make books more accessible is for students to read along as they listen to a tape of the book.

Fielding and Roller (1992) emphasize the importance of both making difficult books accessible for less capable readers and making easier books acceptable for these readers. All students need daily opportunities to actually read and be immersed in the experience of making meaning from the symbols on the pages and their world of experiences. Research has shown that primary-grade students spend as little as 7 or 8 minutes a day reading, and middle-grade students read only 15 minutes a day in traditional classrooms (Anderson, Hiebert, Scott, & Wilkinson, 1985). Teachers need to ensure that their students spend much more time each day reading and rereading books.

When teachers collect a text set of books to accompany the featured selection, both fiction and nonfiction books at a varying levels of difficulty are needed. Less able readers need access to easier books to read independently. Unfortunately, some students see a stigma to "easy" books—those books that are shorter, have more pictures, are printed in large type, or which teachers read to students a year or two earlier. Teachers can do a lot to legitimize picture books and other easy-to-read books. They can read picture books to the class and value them. They can point out to students that most of the pleasure reading that adults do is easy (Fielding & Roller, 1992). Teachers also need to challenge some students' preconceptions that easy books are boring by sharing some of the fine picture books designed for middle- and upper-grade students. They can also read an exciting excerpt from an easy-to-read book during a book talk introducing books in a text set.

FRAMEWORK FOR A LITERATURE FOCUS UNIT

Teachers plan literature focus units featuring popular and award-winning stories for children and adolescents. Some literature focus units feature a single book, either a picture book or a chapter book, while others feature a text set of books for a genre unit or an author study unit. Figure 8–8 presents a list of trade books, genres, and authors recommended for literature focus units for kindergarten through eighth grade. During these units, students move through the five stages of the reading process as they read and respond to stories and learn more about reading and writing.

Steps in Developing a Unit

Teachers develop a literature focus unit through a six-step series of activities, beginning with choosing the literature for the unit and setting goals, then identifying and scheduling activities, and finally deciding how to assess students' learning. Whether teachers are using trade books or textbook selections, they develop a unit using these steps to meet the needs of their students. An overview of the six steps in developing a literature focus unit is presented in Figure 8–9. Effective teachers do not simply follow directions in basal reader teacher's manuals and literature focus unit planning guides that are available for purchase in school supply stories. Teachers need to make the plans themselves because they are the ones most knowledgeable about their students, the literature books they have available, the time available for the unit, the skills and strategies they want to teach, and the activities they want to develop.

Usually literature focus units featuring a picture book are completed in one week, and units featuring a chapter book are completed in two, three, or four weeks. Genre and author units may last two, three, or four weeks. Rarely, if ever, do literature focus units continue for more than a month. When teachers drag out a unit for six weeks or longer they risk killing students' interest in that particular book or, worse yet, their love of literature or reading.

Step 1: Select the Literature.   Teachers begin by selecting the reading material for the literature focus unit. The featured selection may be a story in a picture book format, a chapter book, or a story selected from a basal reading textbook. The reading materials should be high-quality literature. Sometimes teachers select several related stories—books representing the same genre, books written by the same author (for an author study), or books illustrated by same artist (for an illustrator study). Teachers collect multiple copies of the book or books for the literature focus unit. When teachers use trade books, they have to collect class sets of the books for the unit. In some school districts, class sets of selected books are purchased and loaned to teachers. However, in other school districts, teachers have to request that administrators purchase multiple copies of books or buy them themselves through book clubs. When teachers use picture books, students can share books so only half as many books as students are needed.

Once the book (or books) is selected, teachers collect additional related books for the text set. Books for the text set include:

■ other versions of the same story
■ other books written by the same author
■ other books illustrated by the same artist
■ books with the same theme
■ books with similar settings
■ books in the same genre
■ informational books on a related topic
■ books of poetry on a related topic

FIGURE 8–8   Topics for Literature Focus Units

Books	Genres	Authors and Illustrators
Primary Grades (K–2)		
Blume, J. (1971). *Freckle juice.* New York: Bradbury Press.	Number books	Jan Brett
Brett, J. (1989). *The mitten.* New York: Putnam.	Folk tales	Eric Carle
Carle, E. (1970). *The very hungry caterpillar.* New York: Viking.	Pattern stories	Donald Crews
Dorros, A. (1991). *Abuela.* New York: Dutton.	Alphabet books	Tomie de Paola
Galdone, P. (1972). *The three bears.* New York: Clarion.	Fairy tales	Dr. Suess
Henkes, K. (1991). *Chrysanthemum.* New York: Greenwillow.	Biographies	Lois Ehlert
Hutchins, P. (1968). *Rosie's walk.* New York: Macmillan.		Mem Fox
Lionni, L. (1969). *Alexander and the wind-up mouse.* New York: Knopf.		Tana Hoban
Martin, B. Jr. (1983). *Brown bear, brown bear, what do you see?* New York: Holt, Rinehart & Winston.		Steven Kellogg
Most, B. (1978). *If the dinosaurs came back.* San Diego: Harcourt Brace.		James Marshall
Noble, T. H. (1980). *The day Jimmy's boa ate the wash.* New York: Dial.		Bill Martin and John Archambault
Numeroff, L. (1985). *If you give a mouse a cookie.* New York: Harper & Row.		Patricia and Frederick McKissack
Rylant, C. (1985). *The relatives came.* New York: Bradbury Press.		Bernard Most
Lester, H. (1988). *Tacky the penguin.* Boston: Houghton Mifflin.		Bernard Waber
Westcott, N. B. (1980). *I know an old lady who swallowed a fly.* Boston: Little, Brown.		Audrey and Don Wood
Middle Grades (3–5)		
Barrett, J. (1978). *Cloudy with a chance of meatballs.* New York: Macmillan.	Biography	Byrd Baylor
Blume, J. (1972). *Tales of a fourth grade nothing.* New York: Dutton.	Fables	Beverly Cleary
Cleary, B. (1981). *Ramona Quimby, age 8.* New York: Morrow.	Native American myths	Jean Fritz
Coerr, E. (1977). *Sadako and the thousand paper cranes.* New York: Putnam.	Poetry	Paul Goble
Cohen, B. (1983). *Molly's pilgrim.* New York: Morrow.	Tall tales	Eloise Greenfield
Cole, J. (1992). *The magic school bus on the ocean floor.* New York: Scholastic.	Wordplay books	Patricia MacLachlan
Gardiner, J. R. (1980). *Stone Fox.* New York: Harper & Row.		Ann Martin
King-Smith, D. (1988). *Martin's mice.* New York: Crown.		Patricia Polacco
		Jack Prelutsky
		Cynthia Rylant
		William Steig
		R. L. Stine
		Marvin Terban
		Chris Van Allsburg
		Jane Yolen

FIGURE 8–8   *continued*

Books	Genres	Authors and Illustrators
Middle Grades (continued)		
Lowry, L. (1989). *Number the stars.* Boston: Houghton Mifflin.		
MacLachlan, P. (1985). *Sarah, plain and tall.* New York: Harper & Row.		
Mathis, S. B. (1975). *The hundred penny box.* New York: Viking.		
Naylor, P. R. (1991). *Shiloh.* New York: Macmillan.		
Paterson, K. (1977). *Bridge to Terabithia.* New York: Crowell.		
Speare, E. G. (1983). *The sign of the beaver.* Boston: Houghton Mifflin.		
White, E. B. (1952). *Charlotte's web.* New York: Harper & Row.		
Upper Grades (6–8)		
Avi. (1991). *Nothing but the truth.* New York: Orchard.	Science fiction	Lloyd Alexander
Babbitt, N. (1975). *Tuck everlasting.* New York: Farrar, Straus & Giroux.	Myths	Avi
Fox, L. (1984). *One-eyed cat.* New York: Bradbury Press.	Poetry	Paula Danziger
George, J. C. (1972). *Julie of the wolves.* New York: Harper & Row.		Russell Freedman
Hamilton, V. (1967). *Zeely.* New York: Macmillan.		Virginia Hamilton
Hinton, S. E. (1967). *The outsiders.* New York: Viking.		David Macaulay
Howe, D., & Howe, J. (1979). *Bunnicula: A rabbit-tale of mystery.* New York: Atheneum.		Walter Dean Myers
Uchida, Y. (1971). *Journey to Topaz.* Berkeley, CA: Creative Arts.		Scott O'Dell
L'Engle, M. (1962). *A wrinkle in time.* New York: Farrar, Straus & Giroux.		Katherine Paterson
Lewis, C. S. (1950). *The lion, the witch and the wardrobe.* New York: Macmillan.		Gary Paulsen
Lowry, L. (1993). *The giver.* Boston: Houghton Mifflin.		Richard Peck
Paulsen, G. (1987). *The hatchet.* New York: Viking.		Jerry Spinelli
Peck, R. (1972). *A day no pigs would die.* New York: Knopf.		Yoshiko Uchida
Taylor, M. (1976). *Roll of thunder, hear my cry.* New York: Dial.		Laurence Yep
Voigt, C. (1982). *Dicey's song.* New York: Atheneum.		Paul Zindel

FIGURE 8–9   Steps in Developing a Literature Focus Unit

Step 1: Select the Literature

- Identify the featured selection for the unit.
- Collect multiple copies of the featured selection for students to read individually, with partners, or in small groups.
- Collect related books for the text set, including stories, informational books, and poems.
- Identify supplemental materials, including puppets, information about the author and illustrator, and multimedia resources.

Step 2: Set Goals

- Identify four or five broad goals or learning outcomes for the unit.
- Choose skills and strategies to teach.
- Expect to refine these goals as the unit is developed.

Step 3: Develop a Unit Plan

- Read or reread the featured selection.
- Think about the focus for the unit and the goals or learning outcomes.
- Plan activities for each of the five stages of the reading process.

Step 4: Coordinate Grouping Patterns With Activities

- Decide how to incorporate whole-class, small-group, partner, and individual activities.
- Double-check that all four types of grouping are used during the unit.

Step 5: Create a Time Schedule

- Include activities representing all five stages of the reading process in the schedule for the literature focus unit.
- Incorporate minilessons to teach reading and writing procedures, concepts, skills, and strategies.
- Write weekly lesson plans.

Step 6: Manage Record Keeping

- Use unit folders in which students keep all assignments.
- Develop assignment checklists for students to use to keep track of their work during the unit.
- Monitor students' learning using observations, anecdotal notes, conferences, and work samples.

Teachers collect one or two copies of 10, 20, 30, or more books for the text set and add these to the classroom library during the focus unit. Text set books are set on a special shelf or in a crate in the library center. At the beginning of the unit, teachers do a book talk to introduce the books in the text set, and then students read them during independent reading time.

Teachers also identify and collect supplemental materials related to the featured selection, including puppets, stuffed animals, and toys; charts and diagrams; **book**

boxes of materials to use in introducing in the book; and information about the author and illustrator. For many picture books, big book versions are also available, and these versions can be used in introducing the featured selection. Teachers also locate multimedia resources, including films and videotapes of the featured selection, compact disks and other multimedia materials to provide background knowledge on the topic, and videotapes, films, and filmstrips about the author and illustrator. For information on materials about authors and illustrators, see Appendix B.

Step 2: Set Goals.   Teachers set goals or learning outcomes for the literature focus unit. They make choices about what they want their students to learn during the unit, what skills and strategies they plan to teach, and what types of activities they want students to learn how to do. Teachers identify four or five broad goals for the unit and then refine these goals as they develop the unit.

Step 3: Develop a Unit Plan.   Teachers read or reread the selected book or books and then think about the focus they will use for the unit. Sometimes teachers focus on an element of story structure, the historical setting, wordplay, the author or genre, or a concept or topic related to the book, such as weather or life in the desert. In the vignette at the beginning of this chapter, Mrs. Dillon selected Marshall's *The Three Little Pigs* and read it with her students to introduce a genre unit.

   After determining the focus, teachers think about which activities they will use at each of the five stages of the reading process. For each stage, teachers ask themselves these questions:

1. *Preparing to Read*
   - What background knowledge do students need before reading?
   - What key concepts and vocabulary should I teach before reading?
   - How will I introduce the story and stimulate students' interest for reading?

2. *Reading*
   - How will students read this story?
   - What reading strategies will I model or ask students to use?
   - How can I make the story more accessible for less able readers?

3. *Responding*
   - Will students write in reading logs? How often?
   - Will students participate in grand conversations? How often?

4. *Exploring*
   - What words might be added to the word wall?
   - What vocabulary activities might be used?
   - Will students reread the story?
   - What skill and strategy minilessons might be taught?
   - What word-study or wordplay activities might be used?
   - How will books from the text set be used?
   - What writing, drama, and other reading activities might be used?
   - What can I share about the author, illustrator, or genre?

Students learn about scarecrows during a literature focus unit on *Barn Dance!* by Bill Martin, Jr., and John Archambault.

5. Extending

- What projects might students choose to pursue?
- How will books from the text set be used?
- How will students share projects?

Teachers often jot notes on a chart divided into sections for each stage. Then they use the ideas they have brainstormed as they plan the unit. Usually, not all of the brainstormed activities will be used in the literature focus unit, but teachers select the most important ones according to their focus and the available time. Teachers do not omit any of the stages, however, in an attempt to make more time available for activities during any one stage.

Step 4: Coordinate Grouping Patterns With Activities.   Teachers think about how to incorporate whole-class, small-group, partner, and individual activities into their unit plans. It is important that students have opportunities to read and write independently as well as to work with small groups and to come together as a class. If the featured selection that students are reading will be read together as a class, then students need opportunities to reread it with a buddy or independently or to read related books independently. These grouping patterns should be alternated during various activities in the unit. Teachers often go back to their planning sheet and highlight activities with colored markers according to grouping patterns.

Step 5: Create a Time Schedule.   Teachers create a time schedule that enables students to have sufficient time to move through the five stages of the reading process and to complete the activities planned for the literature focus unit. Literature-based reading programs require large blocks of time—at least two hours in length—in which students read, listen, talk, and write about the literature they are reading.

Teachers also plan for minilessons to teach reading and writing procedures, concepts, skills, and strategies identified in their goals and those needed for students to complete the activities that teachers plan. Of course, teachers also present impromptu minilessons when students ask questions or need to know how to use a procedure, skill, or strategy, but many minilessons are planned. Sometimes teachers have a set time for minilessons in their weekly schedule, and sometimes teachers arrange their schedules so that they teach minilessons just before they introduce related activities or assignments.

Using this block of time, teachers write weekly lesson plans, as Mrs. Dillon did in Figure 8–3. Mrs. Dillon used a two-hour time block broken into four 30-minute sections. She listed the activities representing each of the five stages of the reading process during the two-week unit. The stages are not clearly separated and they do overlap, but preparing, reading, responding, exploring, and extending activities are included in the lesson plan.

Step 6: Manage Record Keeping.   Teachers often distribute unit folders for students to use. They keep all work, reading logs, reading materials, and related materials in the folder. Then at the end of the unit, students turn in their completed folders for teachers to evaluate. Keeping all the materials together makes the unit easier for both students and teachers to manage.

Teachers also plan ways to document students' learning and assign grades. One type of record keeping is an assignment checklist. This sheet is developed with students and distributed at the beginning of the literature focus unit. Students keep track of their work during the unit and sometimes negotiate to change the sheet as the unit evolves. Students keep the lists in unit folders, and they mark off each item as it is completed. At the end of the unit, students turn in their completed assignment checklist and other completed work. A copy of an assignment checklist for Mrs. Dillon's literature unit on "The Three Little Pigs" is presented in Figure 8–10. While this list does not include every activity students were involved in, it does list the activities and other assignments Mrs. Dillon holds the students accountable for. Students complete the checklist on the left side of the sheet and add titles of books and other requested information.

Teachers also monitor students' learning as they observe students reading, writing, and working in small groups. Students and teachers also meet together in brief conferences during literature focus units to talk about the featured selection and other books in the text set students are reading, projects students do during the extending stage of the reading process, and other assignments. Often these conferences are brief, but they give teachers insight into students' learning. Teachers make anecdotal notes of their observations and conferences, and they also examine students' work samples to monitor learning.

Units Featuring a Picture Book

In literature focus units featuring picture books, younger children read predictable picture books or books with very little text, such as *Rosie's Walk* (Hutchins, 1968), and older students read more sophisticated picture books with more text, such as *Ju-*

■ *Activity*
Analyze Mrs. Dillon's lesson plan in Figure 8–3 and identify activities representing each of the five stages of the reading process.

FIGURE 8–10   An Assignment Checklist for Mrs. Dillon's Focus Unit

Three Little Pigs Unit

Name _____

____ 1. Read *The Three Little Pigs.*

_____

_____

____ 2. Read to Mrs. Dillon.

____ 3. Make a vocabulary mobile.

____ 4. Make a quotes book.

____ 5. Make a square for the quilt.

____ 6. Read four pig books.

_____

_____

_____

_____

____ 7. Do a project.

What is your project? _____

____ 8. Write a letter to Mrs. Dillon.

____ 9. Write in your journal.

☐ draw pigs

☐ draw wolves

☐ write about the three pigs

☐ write about the wolf

manji (Van Allsburg, 1981). Teachers use the same five-step approach for developing units featuring a picture book for younger and older students. Second graders, for example, might spend a week reading *Tacky the Penguin* (Lester, 1988), a popular story about an oddball penguin who saves all the penguins from some hunters. During the unit, students read the story several times, share their responses to the story, participate in a variety of exploring activities, and do projects to extend their interpretations. A week-long plan for teaching a unit on *Tacky the Penguin* is presented in Figure 8–11.

Several types of exploring activities are included in this plan. One type focuses on vocabulary. On Monday, students list words from the story on a word wall, the next day they reread the words and sort them according to the character they refer to, and on Thursday the teacher teaches a minilesson about peeling off the *-ly* suffix to learn the "main" word (root word). It's not typical to teach a lesson on derivational suffixes in second grade, but second graders notice that many of the words on the word wall have *-ly* at the end of them and often ask about the suffix.

Another activity examines character. The teacher gives a minilesson on characters on Tuesday. Then students make a character **cluster** about Tacky and draw open minds to show what Tacky is thinking. To make an **open-mind portrait,** students

FIGURE 8–11 A Week-Long Lesson Plan for *Tacky the Penguin*

	MONDAY	TUESDAY	WEDNESDAY	THURSDAY	FRIDAY
8:45	Talk about penguins Begin KWL chart Begin word wall	Have students share reading log entries in small groups Reread word wall	Have students make open-mind portraits of Tacky →	Reread *Tacky* in small groups while other students work on projects	Finish projects →
9:15	Read *Tacky the Penguin* using guided reading Have grand conversation. Ask: Is Tacky an "odd" bird?	Reread story with reading buddies	Discuss possible projects		Sequence story boards with students who are done with their projects
9:45	BREAK				
10:00	Add words to word wall Have students write in reading logs	Sort words: 1. Tacky words 2. Other penguin words 3. Hunter words	Begin work on projects	ML: Suffix *-ly.* Show students how to peel off suffix →	Share projects →
10:30	Introduce text set Read aloud *Three Cheers for Tacky*	ML: Character development Make a character cluster for Tacky	Add to KWL chart Read *A Penguin Year* aloud	Read aloud two other books by Helen Lester: *Me First* *A Porcupine Named Fluffy*	
11:00	Reading Workshop			←	Add favorite story quotes and interesting penguin facts to penguin bulletin board to make a story quilt

311

draw a portrait of the penguin, cut around the head so that it will flip open, and draw or write what Tacky is thinking on another sheet of paper that has been attached behind the paper with the portrait.

Units Featuring a Chapter Book

Teachers develop literature focus units using chapter books, such as *Bunnicula: A Rabbit-Tale of Mystery* (Howe & Howe, 1979), *Sarah, Plain and Tall* (MacLachlan, 1985), *The Sign of the Beaver* (Speare, 1983), and *Number the Stars* (Lowry, 1989). The biggest difference between picture books and chapter books is their length, and when teachers plan literature focus units featuring a chapter book, they need to decide how to schedule the reading of the book. Will students read one or two chapters each day? How often will they respond in **literature logs** or grand conversations? It is important that teachers reread the book to note the length of chapters and identify key points in the book where students will want time to respond to and explore the ideas presented in the book.

Figure 8–12 presents a four-week lesson plan for Lois Lowry's *Number the Stars*, a story of friendship and courage set in Nazi-occupied Denmark during World War II. The daily routine during the first two weeks is:

1. **Reading.**   Students and the teacher read two chapters using shared reading.
2. **Responding to the reading.**   Students participate in a grand conversation about the chapters they have read, write in reading logs, and add important words from the chapters to the class word wall.

Students read and respond to three versions of "The Mitten" folktale during a genre unit.

FIGURE 8–12   A Four-Week Lesson Plan for *Number the Stars*

	MONDAY	TUESDAY	WEDNESDAY	THURSDAY	FRIDAY
WEEK 1	Build background on World War II; The Resistance movement; ML: Reading maps of Nazi-occupied Europe; Read aloud *The Lily Cupboard*	Introduce NTS; Begin word wall; Read Ch. 1 & 2; Grand conversation; Lit log; Add to word wall; Book talk on text set	Read Ch. 3 & 4; Grand conversation; Lit log; Word wall; ML: Connecting with a character; Read text set books	Read Ch. 5; Grand conversation; Lit log; Word wall; ML: Visualizing Nazis in apartment (use drama)	Read Ch. 6 & 7; Grand conversation; Lit log; Word wall; ML: Information about the author and why she wrote the book
WEEK 2	Read Ch. 8 & 9; Grand conversation; Lit log; Word wall; ML: Compare home front and war front; Read text set books	Read Ch. 10 & 11; Grand conversation; Lit log; Word wall; ML: Visualizing the wake (use drama) →	Read Ch. 12 & 13; Grand conversation; Lit log; Word wall; ML: Compare characters—make Venn diagram →	Read Ch. 14 & 15; Grand conversation; Lit log; Word wall; ML: Make word maps of key words →	Finish book; Grand conversation; Lit log; Word wall; ML: Theme of book →
WEEK 3	Plan class interview project; Choose individual projects; Independent reading/projects →	Activities: 1. Story map 2. Word sort 3. Plot profile 4. Story quilt →	→	→	→
WEEK 4	Revise interviews; Independent reading/projects →	→	Edit interviews; Share projects →	Make final copies →	Compile interview book →

3. Minilesson.   The teacher teaches a minilesson on a reading strategy or presents information about World War II or the author.

4. More reading.   Students read related books from the text set independently.

The schedule for the last two weeks is different. During the third week, students choose a class project (interviewing people who were alive during World War II) and individual projects. They work in teams on two of four activities related to the book and continue to read other books about the war. During the final week, students finish the class interview project and share their completed individual projects.

Units Focusing on a Genre

Genre units provide an opportunity for students to learn about a particular genre or category of literature, such as folktales or science fiction. Students read stories illustrating the genre and then participate in a variety of activities to deepen their interpretations and knowledge about the genre. In these units, students participate in these activities:

- reading several stories illustrating a genre
- learning the characteristics of the genre
- reading other stories illustrating the genre
- responding to and exploring the genre stories
- writing or rewriting stories exemplifying the genre

Genre studies about traditional literature, including fables, folktales, legends, and myths, are very appropriate for elementary students. A list of recommended genre units was also included in Figure 8–8.

During a genre study of folktales, for example, third-grade students read folktales such as *The Little Red Hen* (Zemach, 1983), *The Mitten* (Brett, 1989), and *Little Red Riding Hood* (Hyman, 1983), and the teacher explains that these stories are folktales and that folktales are relatively short stories that originated as part of the oral tradition. They make a list of these characteristics of folktales:

- The story is often introduced with the words "Once upon a time."
- The setting is usually generalized and could be located anywhere.
- The plot structure is simple and straightforward.
- The problem usually revolves around a journey from home to perform some tasks, a journey that involves a confrontation with a monster, the miraculous change from a harsh home to a secure home, or a confrontation between a wise character and a foolish character.
- Characters are portrayed in one dimension, either good or bad, stupid or clever, industrious or lazy.
- The ending is happy, and everyone "lives happily ever after."

Then students spend several days reading and responding to other folktales from a special display set up in the classroom. The teacher brings the class together, and they share the folktales they have read and find examples of the characteristics in the

HOW EFFECTIVE TEACHERS
Develop Literature Focus Units

Effective Practices	Ineffective Practices
1. Teachers choose high-quality literature—either trade books or textbooks—for literature focus units.	**1.** Teachers teach stories and other pieces without considering their literary value or interest to students.
2. Teachers introduce students to Caldecott and Newbery award books.	**2.** Teachers don't include award-winning books in their reading program.
3. Teachers select multicultural books for featured selections and for text sets.	**3.** Teachers use few multicultural books.
4. Teachers determine the difficulty level of books they use for literature focus units.	**4.** Teachers do not know how to determine the difficulty level of books.
5. Teachers find ways to make difficult books accessible for students.	**5.** Teachers allow students to "sink or swim" when reading books.
6. Teachers also provide daily opportunities for students to choose and read books at their own reading levels from text sets.	**6.** Teachers use very few related books or don't collect books for text sets.
7. Teachers carefully develop literature focus units using the six-step approach described in this chapter.	**7.** Teachers follow teachers' manuals or commercial unit plans for teaching literature focus units.
8. Teachers spend approximately one week on a picture book unit and no longer than a month on other types of units.	**8.** Teachers spend more than one week on a picture book unit and more than a month on other types of units.
9. Teachers consider using four types of literature focus units: picture book units, chapter book units, genre units, and author or illustrator units.	**9.** Teachers use only one type of literature focus unit.
10. Teachers incorporate activities from all five stages of the reading process in literature focus units.	**10.** Teachers emphasize only reading and exploring activities.

Just a Dream (1990), the story of how Walter learns to value the environment through a series of dreams

The Wretched Stone (1991), a story told as a ship captain's log of how the crew turned into monkeys after staring mindlessly at a glowing stone

The Widow's Broom (1992), the story of a magical broom and how the villagers feared the broom because it was different

The Sweetest Fig (1993), the story of Monsieur Bibot, a coldhearted dentist who gets what he deserves when his long-suffering dog eats a fig with magical powers

Bad Day at Riverbend (1995), the story of Riverbend, a colorless, sleepy western town, and what happens when it is covered with a greasy slime of color

Next, teachers decide which books to focus on and read together as a class, which books students will read in small groups, and which books students will read independently. They also choose activities based on the books and plan minilesson topics. Then they develop a lesson plan according to the time and resources they have available for the unit.

A plan for a three-week author unit is presented in Figure 8–14. In this plan, the teacher spends the first two days on *Jumanji* and the next day on *The Polar Express*. Then students spend four days in book clubs. Students divide into small groups, and each day they read one of Van Allsburg's books. Students rotate through groups so that in four days they read four books. Next, students read *The Z Was Zapped* and write a class alliterative **alphabet book.** For the next two days, students read and respond to *The Wretched Stone* and *Bad Day at Riverbend* as a class, and the teacher teaches minilessons on theme using these two books as examples. During the third week, students write descriptions and stories for the illustrations in *The Mysteries of Harris Burdick* and write letters to Chris Van Allsburg. They also read and reread Van Allsburg's books independently and with buddies. To end the unit, students vote on their favorite Van Allsburg book, make a story quilt with a white dog in the center of each square, and have a **read-around** in which they read their favorite quotes from various books aloud.

Review

Students need opportunities to read and respond to quality literature. Books that have received the Caldecott Award or the Newbery Award are often chosen for literature focus units. Multicultural literature should also be used as an integral part of literature focus units. Literature from basal readers can be used for literature focus units as long as it is fine literature. Teachers develop literature focus units to highlight quality literature. Four types of literature focus units are picture book units, chapter book units, genre units, and author units. Six steps are used to develop a unit: selecting the literature, setting goals, developing the unit plan, coordinating grouping patterns with activities, creating a time schedule, and managing record keeping. Effective teaching practices for using literature focus units are reviewed in the figure on page 319.

References

Anderson, R. C., Hiebert, E. H., Scott, J. A., & Wilkinson, I. A. G. (1985). *Becoming a nation of readers: The report of the Commission on Reading.* Washington, DC: National Institute on Education.

Banks, J. A. (1989). Integrating the curriculum with ethnic content: Approaches and guidelines. In J. A. Banks & C. A. McGee Banks (Eds.), *Multicultural education: Issues and perspectives* (pp. 189–207). Boston: Allyn & Bacon.

Bishop, R. S. (1992). Multicultural literature for children: Making informed choices. In V. J. Harris (Ed.), *Teaching multicultural literature in grades K–8* (pp. 37–54). Norwood, MA: Christopher-Gordon.

Bishop, R. S. (Ed.). (1994). *Kaleidoscope: A multicultural booklist for grades K–8.* Urbana, IL: National Council of Teachers of English.

Cummings, P. (Ed.). (1992). *Talking with artists.* New York: Bradbury.

Fielding, L., & Roller, C. (1992). Making difficult books accessible and easy books acceptable. *The Reading Teacher, 45,* 678–685.

Fry, E. (1968). A readability formula that saves time. *Journal of Reading, 11,* 587.

Gaylord, S. K. (1994). *Multicultural books to make and share.* New York: Scholastic.

Goodman, K. S., Shannon, P., Freeman, V. S., & Murphy, S. (1988). *Report on basal readers.* Katonah, NY: Richard C. Owen.

Harris, V. J. (1992a). Multiethnic children's literature. In K. D. Wood & A. Moss (Eds.), *Exploring literature in the classroom: Content and methods* (pp. 169–201). Norwood, MA: Christopher-Gordon.

Harris, V. J. (Ed.). (1992b). *Teaching multicultural litera-ture in grades K–8*. Norwood, MA: Christopher-Gordon.

Huck, C. S., Hepler, S., & Hickman, J. (1987). *Children's literature in the elementary school* (4th ed.). New York: Holt, Rinehart & Winston.

Jipson, J., & Paley, N. (1991). The selective tradition in teachers' choice of children's literature: Does it exist in the elementary classroom? *English Education, 23,* 148–159.

McCarthey, S. J., & Hoffman, J. V. (1995). The new basals: How are they different? *The Reading Teacher, 49,* 72–75.

Norton, D. E. (1995). *Through the eyes of a child: An intro-duction to children's literature* (4th ed.). New York: Merrill/Prentice-Hall.

Rasinski, T. V., & Padak, N. D. (1990). Multicultural learning through children's literature. *Language Arts, 67,* 576–580.

Reimer, K. M. (1992). Multiethnic literature: Holding fast to dreams. *Language Arts, 69,* 14–21.

Roginsky, J. (1985, 1989). *Behind the covers: Interviews with authors and illustrators of books for children and young adults* (Vols. 1–2). Englewood, CO: Libraries Unlimited.

Rudman, M. (1976). *Children's literature: An issues ap-proach* (2nd ed.). New York: Longman.

Shannon, P. (1986). Hidden within the pages: A study of social perspective in young children's favorite books. *The Reading Teacher, 39,* 656–661.

Sims, R. B. (1982). *Shadow and substance*. Urbana, IL: National Council of Teachers of English.

Soto, G. (1992). Author for a day: Glitter and rainbows. *The Reading Teacher, 46,* 200–202.

Sutherland, Z., & Arbuthnot, M. H. (1986). *Children and books* (7th ed.). Glenview, IL: Scott Foresman.

Tompkins, G. E. (1992). The scaffolding principle: What to do when the book is too difficult. *The California Reader, 25,* 2–4.

Traxel, J. (1983). The American Revolution in children's fiction. *Research in the Teaching of English, 17,* 61–83.

Vardell, S. (1991). A new "picture of the world": The NCTE Orbis Pictus Award for outstanding nonfiction for children. *Language Arts, 68,* 474–479.

Walker-Dalhouse, D. (1992). Using African-American lit-erature to increase ethnic understanding. *The Reading Teacher, 45,* 416–422.

Yokota, J. (1993). Issues in selecting multicultural chil-dren's literature. *Language Arts, 70,* 156–167.

Zarnoski, M. (1991). An interview with author Nicholasa Mohr. *The Reading Teacher, 45,* 100–106.

Children's Book References

Adler, D. A. (1989). *A picture book of Martin Luther King, Jr.* New York: Holiday House.

Blume, J. (1972). *Tales of a fourth grade nothing*. New York: Dutton.

Brett, J. (1989). *The mitten*. New York: Putnam.

Bunting, E. (1988). *How many days to America? A Thanks-giving story*. New York: Clarion.

Choi, S. N. (1991). *Year of impossible goodbyes*. Boston: Houghton Mifflin.

Climo, S. (1989). *The Egyptian Cinderella*. New York: Crowell.

Coerr, E. (1988). *Chang's paper pony*. New York: Harper & Row.

Crews, D. (1991). *Bigmama's*. New York: Greenwillow.

de Paola, T. (1988). *The legend of the Indian paintbrush*. New York: Putnam.

Dooley, N. (1991). *Everybody cooks rice*. Minneapolis: Car-olrhoda.

Dorros, A. (1992). *This is my house*. New York: Scholastic.

Fraser, M. A. (1993). *Ten mile day and the building of the transcontinental railroad*. New York: Henry Holt.

Friedman, I. R. (1984). *How my parents learned to eat*. Boston: Houghton Mifflin.

Goble, P. (1988). *Iktomi and the boulder*. New York: Or-chard.

Golenbock, P. (1990). *Teammates*. San Diego: Harcourt Brace Jovanovich.

Hamilton, V. (1988). *Anthony Burns: The defeat and tri-umph of a fugitive slave*. New York: Knopf.

Hooks, W. H. (1989). *The three little pigs and the fox*. New York: Macmillan.

Howe, D., & Howe, J. (1979). *Bunnicula: A rabbit-tale of mystery*. New York: Atheneum.

Howe, J. (1994). *Playing with words*. Katonah, NY: Richard C. Owen.

Hoyt-Goldsmith, D. (1990). *Totem pole*. New York: Holi-day House.

Hutchins, P. (1968). *Rosie's walk*. New York: Macmillan.

Hyman, T. S. (1983). *Little Red Riding Hood*. New York: Holiday House.

Isadora, R. (1979). *Ben's trumpet*. New York: Morrow.

Knight, M. B. (1993). *Who belongs here? An American story*. Gardiner, ME: Tilbury House.

Lester, H. (1988). *Tacky the penguin*. Boston: Houghton Mifflin.

Louie, A. (1982). *Yeh-Shen: A Cinderella story from China*. New York: Philomel.

Lowell, S. (1992). *The three little javelinas*. Flagstaff, AZ: Northland.

Lowry, L. (1989). *Number the stars.* Boston: Houghton Mifflin.

MacLachlan, P. (1985). *Sarah, plain and tall.* New York: Harper & Row.

Marshall, J. (1989). *The three little pigs.* New York: Dial.

Mathis, S. B. (1975). *The hundred penny box.* New York: Viking.

Morris, A. (1992). *Houses and homes.* New York: Mulberry Books.

Pinkney, A. (1993). *Seven candles for Kwanzaa.* New York: Dial.

Polacco, P. (1994). *Firetalking.* Katonah, NY: Richard C. Owen.

Ringgold, F. (1991). *Tar beach.* New York: Crown.

Say, A. (1990). *El Chino.* Boston: Houghton Mifflin.

Scieszka, J. (1989). *The true story of the three little pigs!* New York: Viking.

Soto, G. (1993). *Too many tamales.* New York: Putnam.

Speare, E. G. (1983). *The sign of the beaver.* Boston: Houghton Mifflin.

Steptoe, J. (1987). *Mufaro's beautiful daughters: An African tale.* New York: Lothrop, Lee & Shepard.

Surat, M. M. (1983). *Angel child, dragon child.* Milwaukee: Raintree.

Taylor, M. D. (1976). *Roll of thunder, hear my cry.* New York: Dial.

Taylor, M. D. (1977). *The gold Cadillac.* New York: Dial.

Uchida, Y. (1971). *Journey to Topaz.* Berkeley, CA: Creative Arts.

Uchida, Y. (1993). *The bracelet.* New York: Philomel.

Van Allsburg, C. (1979). *The garden of Abdul Gasazi.* Boston: Houghton Mifflin.

Van Allsburg, C. (1981). *Jumanji.* Boston: Houghton Mifflin.

Van Allsburg, C. (1982). *Ben's dream.* Boston: Houghton Mifflin.

Van Allsburg, C. (1983). *The wreck of the Zephyr.* Boston: Houghton Mifflin.

Van Allsburg, C. (1984). *The mysteries of Harris Burdick.* Boston: Houghton Mifflin.

Van Allsburg, C. (1985). *The polar express.* Boston: Houghton Mifflin.

Van Allsburg, C. (1986). *The stranger.* Boston: Houghton Mifflin.

Van Allsburg, C. (1987). *The Z was zapped.* Boston: Houghton Mifflin.

Van Allsburg, C. (1988). *Two bad ants.* Boston: Houghton Mifflin.

Van Allsburg, C. (1990). *Just a dream.* Boston: Houghton Mifflin.

Van Allsburg, C. (1991). *The wretched stone.* Boston: Houghton Mifflin.

Van Allsburg, C. (1992). *The widow's broom.* Boston: Houghton Mifflin.

Van Allsburg, C. (1993). *The sweetest fig.* Boston: Houghton Mifflin.

Van Allsburg, C. (1995). *Bad day at Riverbend.* Boston: Houghton Mifflin.

Williams, V. B. (1982). *A chair for my mother.* New York: Mulberry.

Winter, J. (1988). *Follow the drinking gourd.* New York: Knopf.

Zemach, M. (1983). *The little red hen.* New York: Farrar, Straus & Giroux.

CHAPTER 9

Reading and Writing Workshop

The 29 students in Mrs. Donnelly's third-grade classroom spend 75 minutes after lunch each day in reading and writing workshop. Mrs. Donnelly alternates reading workshop and writing workshop month by month, and this month students are involved in reading workshop. During reading workshop, they read for the first 45 minutes. As they return from lunch, they pick up the books they are reading that are stored in their desks and begin reading. Most of the students are reading Beverly Cleary chapter books, including *Ramona and Her Father* (1977), *The Mouse and the Motorcycle* (1965), and *Two Dog Biscuits* (1961), and they continue to wear the sock puppets of Cleary characters that they made as part of their just concluded author study on Beverly Cleary. This is one of the students' favorite parts of the school day. They enter the classroom after lunch eager to read and begin reading immediately, with little or no direction from Mrs. Donnelly.

Those students who are ready for a new book browse in the classroom library and choose one. Mrs. Donnelly surveys the class as students begin reading, and stops briefly to help Noelle, who can't find her book and is beginning to clean out her desk. Then she walks to the library corner to check on four students who are browsing. Students are responsible for choosing their own books, and all but one make choices and return to their desks. She talks briefly with Marcus, who is still browsing.

Mrs. Donnelly goes to the conference table in one corner of the classroom, where she meets with students who have completed reading a book and have signed up to have a conference. She wants to conference with each child at least once a week. Sometimes she conferences individually with students, and at other times, like today, she meets with small groups. She consults the sign-up list and invites four children who have finished reading Beverly Cleary books to participate in a group conference. Students bring their books (and their puppets!) and come to the table.

Mrs. Donnelly asks students to go around the table, taking turns and telling a little about their books. Jenny shares that she has finished reading *Ramona and Her Mother* (Cleary, 1984), but she liked *Ramona and Her Father* (1975) and *Ramona Forever* (1979) better. "This Ramona book is sort of dumb. She makes a toothpaste cake in the sink to get more attention and all she gets is being in trouble. She has to use that toothpaste in the sink to brush her teeth every day until it is all used up."

Mrs. Donnelly asks students if they are using the "making connections to your own life" reading strategy she taught last week in a **minilesson** (see the Compendium for more information about this and all other highlighted terms in this chapter), and students talk about how they made connections as they read. Jenny talks about some of the ways her family is like Ramona's. To end the 15-minute discussion, Mrs. Donnelly asks students what they plan to read next. Most of the students in the group have already picked out their next book. Jenny says, "I don't think I am going to read any more Ramona books for a while. I'm sort of full of them. I think I'll read *The Magic Finger* [Dahl, 1966]. Lindy said it was good. She read it and it's real weird." Mrs. Donnelly smiles to herself, thinking about how the students have become a community of readers. Once someone in the class reads a book, it often travels around the class from student to student. Several students have begun reading Roald Dahl books, and Mrs. Donnelly decides to plan a minilesson later in the week about the British author.

As students talk, Mrs. Donnelly takes notes in her reading workshop notebook. She has a page for each student and notes the date, title, and author of the book and

FIGURE 9–1   Mrs. Donnelly's Reading Workshop Conference Notes

Jenny

2/25   *Swamp Angel* [Isaacs, 1994]. Continuing to read award books. Recognizes the Caldecott and Newbery seals on books. Asked her to pull these books from the class library and put on a special shelf and share with class. Asked what a tall tale was. Suggested that she read some of Steven Kellogg's tall tales.

3/1   *Pecos Bill* and *Paul Bunyan* [Kellogg, 1986, 1988]. Likes *Swamp Angel* better. Why? Female character and illustration techniques—paint on wood. Asks if tall tales are real. Says her parents know about Pecos Bill and Paul Bunyan but not Swamp Angel. Plans to write a tall tale at home.

3/9   *The Courage of Sarah Noble* [Dalgliesh, 1982]. Got this book from Angela. She loved it. Says she "lived this story and my heart was beating so hard." Wants to read another pioneer book that is scary. Recommended *The Cabin Faced West* [Fritz, 1958].

3/16   *Ramona Forever* [Cleary, 1979]. Excited about Beverly Cleary. Likes this one and *Ramona and Her Father* [1977] that we read together in class. Has already started *Ramona and Her Mother* [1984]. Asked about *The Cabin Faced West* and she said it was boring. Dropped it when we started reading Cleary books.

3/24   *Ramona and Her Mother.* Doesn't like this one as well as the other two Ramona books she's read. Thinks story is simplistic—"dumb." Talked about realistic fiction and compared it to historical fiction. Is applying connecting-to-your-own life strategy. Plans to read Dahl's *The Magic Finger* [1966] next—suggested by Lindy.

summarizes the conference. Mrs. Donnelly's notes about Jenny, who participated in the conference, are reproduced in Figure 9–1.

Mrs. Donnelly doesn't have her students write in **reading logs,** as many teachers do. She prefers that they spend all of the reading time doing just that—reading. They write in reading logs as part of literature focus units and theme studies. Students, do, however, keep a list of all the books they have read during the year.

When the reading time ends, Mrs. Donnelly gathers the class together for 15 minutes of sharing or a minilesson. On sharing days, students who have finished reading a book and have conferenced with her take turns sharing their books with the class. They give a **book talk,** in which they show the book and tell a little about it, and then they offer it to a classmate who wants to read it or put it back in the classroom library. Each student takes two or three minutes to share, and usually five or six students share each day.

On other days, Mrs. Donnelly takes these 15 minutes to teach a reading minilesson. She reviews how to use reading strategies and provides opportunities for students to share how they use the strategies as they read. She also teaches reading workshop procedures, including how to select books, how to apply word-identification skills when students encounter an unfamiliar word, and how to share a book in a book talk. She also introduces new books and authors. On this day she introduces two new chapter books, *Sideways Stories From Wayside School* (Sachar, 1978) and *Wayside School Is Falling Down* (Sachar, 1985). She talks a little about the stories and explains how the Wayside School is organized. She reads the brief, first chapter of each book aloud and then passes out the new books to two eager students.

Mrs. Donnelly spends the last 15 minutes reading a book aloud to the class. Sometimes she reads a picture book, while at other times she reads one or two chapters from a chapter book. Today she is beginning *Strider* (1991), Beverly Cleary's sequel to *Dear Mr. Henshaw* (1983), which she finished reading yesterday. Both books are about an unhappy boy named Leigh, who lives with his mother after his parents' divorce and who shows talent as a writer. From the illustration on the cover, students accurately predict that Leigh will adopt a dog, and they listen intently as Mrs. Donnelly reads aloud the first four chapters. Then students talk about the book in a **grand conversation.** They talk about their pets and agree that people who abandon dogs should be punished. They make predictions about how Leigh will change now that he has a dog, and they compare Leigh and his dog Strider to Henry and his dog Ribsy.

When Mrs. Donnelly does writing workshop, she uses a similar format. Students begin by writing for 45 minutes. They write on self-selected topics and usually prepare their writings as picture books or as chapter books with illustrations for each chapter. After students prepare the final copy of their books, they read them aloud to classmates during sharing. Then Mrs. Donnelly teaches a minilesson on writing strategies, writing workshop procedures, or other writing-related topics during the last 15 minutes.

During the school year, each of Mrs. Donnelly's students writes 20 or more books, and she keeps track of students' work in a writing workshop notebook similar to the reading workshop notebook that she keeps. During writing workshop, Mrs. Donnelly conferences with students as they revise and edit their writing, making notes about the topics students choose, the writing forms they use, their application of writing strategies, the types of revisions students make, students' questions and concerns, and possible minilesson topics.

Reading and writing workshop is a new approach to literacy instruction, in which students are involved in authentic reading and writing projects. They read and respond to self-selected books and write and publish books and other compositions, as the students did in Mrs. Donnelly's third-grade classroom. The workshop approach involves three key characteristics: time, choice, and response. First, in reading and writing workshop, students have large chunks of time and the opportunity to read and write. Instead of being add-ons for when students finish schoolwork, reading and writing become the core of the literacy curriculum.

Second, students have ownership of their learning through self-selection of books they read and their topics for writing. Instead of reading books selected by the teacher or reading the same book together as a class, students select the books they want to read, books that are suitable to their interests and reading levels. Usually students choose whatever book they want to read—a story, a book of poems, or an informational book—but sometimes teachers set parameters as Mrs. Donnelly did. During writing workshop students plan their writing projects. They choose topics related to hobbies, content-area themes, and other interests, and they also select the format for their writing. Often they choose to construct books.

The third characteristic is response. In reading workshop, students have opportunities to respond to books they are reading in reading logs they share with classmates and the teacher or during conversations with the teacher and classmates. Similarly, in writing workshop, students share rough drafts of books and other compositions they are writing with classmates, and they share their completed and published compositions with genuine audiences.

Reading workshop and writing workshop are two different types of workshops. Reading workshop fosters real reading of self-selected stories, poems, and informational books. Students read hundreds of books during reading workshop. At the first-grade level, students might read or reread three or four books each day, totaling close to a thousand books during the school year, and older students read fewer, longer books. Even so, Cora Lee Five, a fifth-grade teacher, reported that her students read between 25 and 144 books (Five, 1988).

Similarly, writing workshop fosters real writing (and the use of the writing process) for genuine purposes and authentic audiences. Each student writes and publishes as many as 50 to 100 short books in the primary grades and 20 to 25 longer books in the middle and upper grades. As they write, students come to see themselves as authors and become interested in learning about the authors of the books they read.

Teachers often use both workshops, or if their schedule does not allow, they may alternate the two, like Mrs. Donnelly does. Schedules for reading and writing workshop at the first-, third-, sixth-, and eighth-grade levels are presented in Figure 9–2.

Why Use Reading and Writing Workshop?

There are many reasons to recommend the workshop approach. In reading workshop, students select and read genuine literature that is interesting and written at their reading level. The literature has complex sentence patterns and presents challenging concepts and vocabulary. Through reading workshop students become more fluent readers and learn to deepen their appreciation of books and reading. As students read they are developing lifelong reading habits. They are introduced to different genres and choose favorite authors. Most importantly, they come to think of themselves as readers.

In writing workshop, students create their own compositions and come to see themselves as writers. They practice writing strategies and skills and learn to choose words carefully to articulate their ideas. Perhaps most importantly, they see firsthand the power of writing to entertain, inform, and persuade.

Samway, Whang, and their students (1991) reported that the two most important benefits of reading workshop are that students become a community of learners and that students view themselves as readers. As students read and respond to books, they understand themselves and their classmates better. They gain confidence in themselves as readers. In addition, their ability to choose reading materials becomes more sophisticated during the school year. Students are much more enthusiastic about reading workshop than traditional reading approaches. The authors offer advice to teachers about the necessary components of reading workshop: Students want to read complete books, not excerpts; they want to choose the books they read; and they need plenty of time to read and talk about books.

Many teachers fear that their students' standardized achievement test scores will decline if they implement a workshop approach in their classrooms, even though

FIGURE 9–2 Schedules for Reading and Writing Workshop

First Grade

9:00–9:10	The teacher rereads several familiar big books with students. Then the teacher introduces a new big book and reads it with the students.
9:10–9:30	Students read matching small books independently and reread other familiar books.
9:30–9:40	Students choose one of the books they have read or reread during independent reading to draw and write a quickwrite.
9:40–9:50	Students share the favorite book and quickwrite.
9:50–10:05	The teacher teaches a reading/writing minilesson.
10:05–10:30	Students write independently on self-selected topics and conference with the teacher.
10:30–10:40	Students share their published books with classmates.
10:40–10:45	The class uses choral reading to enjoy poems and charts hanging in the classroom.

Third Grade

10:30–11:00	Students read self-selected books and respond to the books in reading logs.
11:00–11:15	Students share books they have finished reading with classmates and do informal book talks about them. Students often pass the "good" books to classmates who want to read them next.
11:15–11:30	The teacher teaches a reading/writing minilesson.
11:30–11:55	The teacher reads aloud picture books or chapter books, one or two chapters each day. After reading, students talk about the book in a grand conversation.
	— Continued after lunch —
12:45–1:15	Students write books independently.
1:15–1:30	Students share their published books with classmates.

Sixth Grade

8:20–8:45	The teacher reads aloud a chapter book to students, and students talk about their reactions in a grand conversation.
8:45–9:30	Students write independently using the writing process. They also conference with the teacher.
9:30–9:40	The teacher teaches a reading/writing minilesson.
9:40–10:25	Students read self-selected books independently.
10:25–10:40	Students share published writings and give book talks about books they have read with with classmates.

Eighth Grade

During alternating months, students participate in reading workshop or writing workshop.

1:00–1:45	Students read or write independently.
1:45–2:05	The teacher presents a minilesson on a reading or writing procedure, concept, strategy, or skill.
2:05–2:15	Students share with their classmates books they have read or compositions they have published.

many teachers have reported either an increase in test scores or no change at all (Five, 1988, Swift, 1993). Kathleen Swift (1993) reported the results of a year-long study comparing two groups of her students. One group read basal reader stories, and the other participated in reading workshop. The reading workshop group showed significantly greater improvement, and Swift also reported that students participating in reading workshop showed more positive attitudes toward reading.

In this chapter, you will learn how to set up and manage reading and writing workshop in an elementary classroom. Think about these questions as you read:

■ What are the components of reading workshop?

■ What are the components of writing workshop?

■ How do teachers manage a workshop classroom?

■ How are workshops different from other instructional approaches?

READING WORKSHOP

Nancie Atwell (1987) introduced reading workshop as an alternative to traditional reading instruction. In reading workshop, students read books that they choose themselves and respond to books through writing in reading logs and conferences with teachers and classmates. This approach represents a change in what we believe about how children learn and how literature should be used in the classroom. While traditional reading programs emphasized dependence on a teacher's guide to

Students choose books they want to read during reading workshop from a well-stocked classroom library.

determine how and when particular strategies and skills should be taught, reading workshop is an individualized reading program. Atwell developed reading workshop with her middle-school students, but it has been adapted and used successfully at every grade level, first through eighth (Hornsby, Parry, & Sukarna, 1992; Hornsby, Sukarna, & Parry, 1986; McWhirter, 1990). There are several different versions of reading workshop, but they usually contain five components: reading, responding, sharing, teaching minilessons, and reading aloud to students.

Reading

Students spend 30 to 60 minutes independently reading books and other written materials. Frank Smith (1984) claims that to learn to read, children need to read every day, and several times each day for varied purposes. Teachers need to provide plenty of time in class, and not simply assume that students will practice at home what they are learning at school. In a report entitled *Becoming a Nation of Readers,* researchers reported that, in classrooms that don't have a reading workshop component, primary-grade students typically spend only 7 to 8 minutes each day reading independently, and middle-grade students spend only about 15 minutes each day reading independently (Anderson, Hiebert, Scott, & Wilkinson, 1985). Similarly, McWhirter (1990) surveyed her eighth graders and found that 97% reported that they do not read on their own for pleasure. Moreover, research suggests that higher achievement is associated with more time allocated to academic activities (Brophy & Good, 1986).

Students choose the books that they read during reading workshop. Often they depend on recommendations from classmates. They also read books on particular topics—horses, science fiction, dinosaurs—or by favorite authors, such as Judy Blume, Chris Van Allsburg, and Dr. Seuss. Ohlhausen and Jepsen (1992) developed a strategy for choosing books that they called the "Goldilocks Strategy." These teachers developed three categories of books—"Too Easy" books, "Too Hard" books, and "Just Right" books—using "The Three Bears" folktale as their model. The books in the "Too Easy" category were books students had read before or could read fluently. "Too Hard" books were unfamiliar and confusing, and books in the "Just Right" category were interesting and had just a few unfamiliar words. The books in each category vary according to the student's reading level. This approach works at any grade level. Figure 9–3 presents a chart about choosing books using the Goldilocks Strategy. This chart was developed by Mrs. Donnelly's students, the class that was spotlighted at the beginning of this chapter.

When students choose their own books, they take ownership of the reading. Students' reading fluency and enjoyment of reading are related to sustained encounters with interesting texts (Smith, 1984). Reading and responding to literature is the heart of reading workshop.

Teachers often read their own books and magazines or read a book of children's literature during reading workshop. Through their example, they are modeling and communicating the importance of reading. Teachers also conference with students about the books they are reading. As they conference, they talk briefly and quietly with students about their reading. Students may also read aloud favorite quotes or an interesting passage to the teacher.

Students read all sorts of books during reading workshop, including stories, informational books, biographies, and books of poetry. They also read magazines. Most of their reading materials are selected from the classroom library, but students also

FIGURE 9–3   A Third-Grade Chart Applying the Goldilocks Strategy

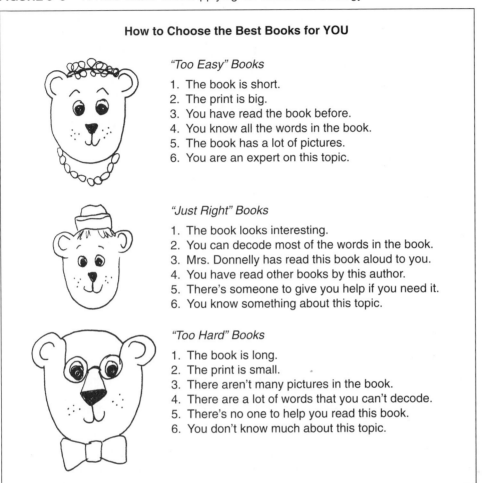

How to Choose the Best Books for YOU

"Too Easy" Books

1. The book is short.
2. The print is big.
3. You have read the book before.
4. You know all the words in the book.
5. The book has a lot of pictures.
6. You are an expert on this topic.

"Just Right" Books

1. The book looks interesting.
2. You can decode most of the words in the book.
3. Mrs. Donnelly has read this book aloud to you.
4. You have read other books by this author.
5. There's someone to give you help if you need it.
6. You know something about this topic.

"Too Hard" Books

1. The book is long.
2. The print is small.
3. There aren't many pictures in the book.
4. There are a lot of words that you can't decode.
5. There's no one to help you read this book.
6. You don't know much about this topic.

bring other books from home and borrow books from classmates, from the public library, and from the school library. Students read many award-winning books during reading workshop, but they also read series of popular books and technical books related to their hobbies and special interests. These books are not necessarily the same books that teachers use for literature focus units, but students often choose to reread books they have read earlier in the school year or the previous year in literature studies.

Teachers need to have literally hundreds of books in their class libraries, including books written at a range of reading levels, in order to have enough books so that every student can read during reading workshop. Primary teachers often worry about finding books that their emerging readers can handle independently. Wordless picture books in which the story is told entirely through pictures, **alphabet books,** number books, pattern and predictable books, and books the teacher has read aloud several times are often the most accessible for kindergartners and first graders. Primary-grade children often read and reread easy-to-read books such as those in the Scholastic Bookshelf series and the Wright Group's Story Box kits. Figure 9–4 lists many trade books that might be placed in classroom libraries and used for reading workshop in

FIGURE 9–4   Books for Reading Workshop Collections

Kindergarten

Ahlberg, J., & Ahlberg, A. (1978). *Each peach, pear, plum.* New York: Scholastic.

Baker, K. (1990). *Who is the beast?* Orlando, FL: Harcourt Brace.

Barton, B. (1990). *Bones, bones, dinosaur bones.* New York: HarperCollins.

Burningham, J. (1994). *The friend.* Cambridge, MA: Candlewick.

Carlson, N. (1988). *I like me!* New York: Viking.

Crews, D. (1982). *Carousel.* New York: Greenwillow.

Cristini, E. (1984). *The pond.* New York: Picture Book Studio.

Dr. Seuss. (1963). *Hop on pop.* New York: Random House. (And other books by this author.)

Dubanevich, A. (1983). *Pigs in hiding.* New York: Scholastic.

Ehlert, L. (1990). *Fish eyes: A book you can count on.* Orlando, FL: Harcourt Brace.

Martin, B., Jr. (1983). *Brown bear, brown bear, what do you see?* New York: Holt.

McPhail, D. (1988). *David McPhail's animals A to Z.* New York: Scholastic Hardcover.

Morris, A. (1989). *Hats, hats, hats.* New York: Mulberry Books.

Rockwell, A. (1986). *Fire engines.* New York: Dutton.

Tafuri, N. (1986). *Who's counting?* New York: Mulberry Books.

Turkle, B. (1976). *Deep in the forest.* New York: Dutton.

Westcott, N. B. (1980). *The lady with the alligator purse.* New York: Lippincott.

Wood, A. (1982). *Quick as a cricket.* London: Child's Play.

First Grade

Carle, E. (1994). *Today is Monday.* New York: Philomel. (And other books by this author.)

de Paola, T. (1978). *Pancakes for breakfast.* New York: Harcourt Brace Jovanovich.

Dr. Seuss. (1988). *Green eggs and ham.* New York: Random House. (And other books by Dr. Seuss.)

Ehlert, L. (1989). *Eating the alphabet: Fruits and vegetables from A to Z.* Orlando: Harcourt Brace.

Galdone, P. (1968). *Henny penny.* New York: Clarion.

Guarino, D. (1989). *Is your mama a llama?* New York: Scholastic.

Hoberman, M. A. (1978). *A house is a house for me.* New York: Penguin.

Mayer, M. (1968). *There's a nightmare in my closet.* New York: Dial. (And other books by this author.)

Morris, A. (1989). *Bread, bread, bread.* New York: Scholastic.

Most, B. (1978). *If the dinosaurs came back.* Orlando: Harcourt Brace.

Numeroff, L. J. (1985). *If you give a mouse a cookie.* New York: Harper & Row.

Raffi. (1988). *Wheels on the bus.* New York: Crown.

Rosen, M. (1989). *We're going on a bear hunt.* New York: McElderry.

Sendak, M. (1962). *Where the wild things are.* New York: Harper & Row.

Shaw, N. (1986). *Sheep in a jeep.* Boston: Houghton Mifflin. (And other books in the series.)

Walsh, E. S. (1989). *Mouse paint.* Orlando: Harcourt Brace.

Wood, A. (1984). *The napping house.* Orlando: Harcourt Brace Jovanovich.

Ziefert, H. (1993). *Harry's bath.* New York: Bantam.

Second Grade

Blume, J. (1971). *Freckle juice.* New York: Dell.

Brett, J. (1989). *The mitten.* New York: Putnam.

Cazet, D. (1993). *Never spit on your shoes.* New York: Orchard.

Coerr, E. (1986). *The Josefina story quilt.* New York: Harper & Row.

Conrad, P. (1989). *The tub people.* New York: Harper & Row.

Fletcher, N. (1993). *Penguin.* London: Dorling Kindersley.

Fowler, A. (1990). *It could still be a tree.* Chicago: Childrens Book Press.

Gibbons, G. (1993). *Pirates: Robbers of the high seas.* Boston: Little, Brown.

Giff, P. R. (1984). *The beast in Ms. Rooney's room.* New York: Bantam. (And other books in the series.)

Heller, R. (1981). *Chickens aren't the only ones.* New York: Grosset & Dunlap. (And other books by this author.)

Kasza, K, (1987). *The wolf's chicken stew.* New York: Putnam.

Kellogg, S. (1979). *Pinkerton, behave!* New York: Dial.

Kroll, S. (1993). *Andrew wants a dog.* New York: Hyperion.

Lester, H. (1988). *Tacky the penguin.* Boston: Houghton Mifflin.

Noble, T. H. (1980). *The day Jimmy's boa ate the wash.* New York: Dial.

Numeroff, L. (1993). *Dogs don't wear sneakers.* New York: Simon & Schuster.

Sachar, L. (1992). *Monkey soup.* New York: Knopf.

Zemach, M. (1983). *The little red hen.* New York: Farrar, Straus & Giroux.

FIGURE 9–4 *continued*

Third Grade

Brenner, B. (1978). *Wagon wheels.* New York: Harper & Row.

Cherry, L. (1993). *The great Kapok tree.* Orlando: Harcourt Brace Jovanovich.

Cleary, B. (1981). *Ramona Quimby, age 8.* New York: Morrow. (And other books in the series.)

Cohen, B. (1983). *Molly's pilgrim.* New York: Bantam.

Cole, J. (1992). *The magic school bus on the ocean floor.* New York: Scholastic.

Dahl, R. (1966). *The magic finger.* New York: Puffin.

Danziger, P. (1994). *Amber Brown is not a crayon.* New York: Putnam.

Hulme, J. N. (1991). *Sea squares.* New York: Hyperion.

Maestro, B. (1993). *The story of money.* New York: Mulberry Books.

Martin, B., Jr. & Archambault, J. (1986). *White Dynamite and Curley Kidd.* New York: Henry Holt.

Prelutsky, J. (1985). *My parents think I'm sleeping.* New York: Greenwillow.

Sachar, L. (1978). *Sideways stories from Wayside School.* New York: Avon Books.

Shannon, G. (1994). *Still more stories to solve: Fourteen folktales from around the world.* New York: Greenwillow.

Spier, P. (1980). *People.* New York: Doubleday.

Viorst, J. (1972). *Alexander and the terrible, horrible, no good, very bad day.* New York: Atheneum.

Wells, R. E. (1993). *Is a blue whale the biggest thing there is?* Morton Grove, IL: Whitman.

Yolen, J. (1980). *Commander Toad in space.* New York: Coward-McCann. (And other books in the series.)

Fourth Grade

Blume, J. (1972). *Tales of a fourth grade nothing.* New York: Dutton. (And the sequel.)

Dahl, R. (1992). *Esio trot.* New York: Viking.

Fritz, J. (1976). *What's the big idea, Ben Franklin?* New York: Coward-McCann.

Gardiner, J. R. (1980). *Stone Fox.* New York: Crowell.

Goble, P. (1988). *Her seven brothers.* New York: Bradbury. (And other books by this author.)

Haskins, J. (1989). *Count your way through Mexico.* Minneapolis: Carolrhoda.

Levine, E. (1986). *. . . If you traveled west in a covered wagon.* New York: Scholastic.

MacLachlan, P. (1985). *Sarah, plain and tall.* New York: Harper & Row.

Monjo, F. N. (1970). *The drinking gourd.* New York: Harper & Row.

Prelutsky, J. (1982). *The baby uggs are hatching.* New York: Greenwillow.

Rockwell, T. (1973). *How to eat fried worms.* New York: Franklin Watts.

Scieszka, J. (1989). *The true story of the three little pigs.* New York: Viking.

Smith, R. K. (1972). *Chocolate fever.* New York: Coward.

Spinelli, J. (1993). *Fourth grade rats.* New York Scholastic.

Thaler, M. (1985). *Cream of creature from the school cafeteria.* New York: Avon.

Van Allsburg, C. (1981). *Jumanji.* Boston: Houghton Mifflin.

Waters, K. (1991). *The story of the White House.* New York: Scholastic.

Fifth Grade

Anno, M. (1983). *Anno's USA.* New York: Philomel.

Avi. (1984). *The fighting ground.* New York: Harper & Row.

Cleary, B. (1983). *Dear Mr. Henshaw.* New York: Morrow.

Coerr, E. (197). *Sadako and the thousand paper cranes.* New York: Putnam.

Cole, J. (1989). *Anna Banana: 101 jump-rope rhymes.* New York: Morrow.

Dahl, R. (1964). *Charlie and the chocolate factory.* New York: Knopf.

Hurwitz, J. (1994). *School spirit.* New York: Morrow.

King-Smith, D. (1988). *Martin's mice.* New York: Crown.

Kline, S. (1990). *Horrible Harry in room 2B.* New York: Viking.

McAfee, A. (1987). *Kirsty knows best.* New York: Knopf.

McGovern, A. (1992). *. . . . If you lived in colonial times.* New York: Scholastic.

Packard, E. (1979). *The mystery of chimney rock (Choose your own adventure).* New York: Bantam.

Pinkwater, D. M. (1977). *Fat men from space.* New York: Dell.

Schwartz, D. M. (1985). *How much is a million?* New York: Scholastic.

Taylor, M. D. (1990). *Mississippi bridge.* New York: Dial.

Van Allsburg, C. (1985). *The polar express.* Boston: Hougton Mifflin. (And other books by this author.)

Wiesner, D. (1991). *Tuesday.* New York: Clarion.

Wilder, L. I. (1953). *Little house in the big woods.* New York: Harper & Row. (And other books in the series.)

Sixth Grade

Byars, B. (1968). *The midnight fox.* New York: Viking.

Filipovic, Z. (1993). *Zlata's diary: A child's life in Sarajevo.* New York: Viking.

FIGURE 9–4 *continued*

Fleischman, S. (1990). *The midnight horse.* New York: Greenwillow.

Gilson, J. (1985). *Thirteen ways to sink a sub.* New York: Lothrop, Lee & Shepard.

Hart, G. (1990). *Ancient Egypt.* New York: Knopf.

Howe, D., & Howe, J. (1979). *Bunnicula: A rabbit-tale of mystery.* New York: Atheneum. (And other books in the series.)

Kehret, P. (1993). *Terror at the zoo.* New York: Cobble-hill.

L'Engle, M. (1962). *A wrinkle in time.* New York: Farrar, Straus & Giroux.

Lewis, C. S. (1950). *The lion, the witch and the wardrobe.* New York: Macmillan.

Lowry, L. (1989). *Number the stars.* Boston: Houghton Mifflin. (And other books by this author.)

Macaulay, D. (1975). *Pyramid.* Boston: Houghton Mifflin.

Mazer, A. (Ed.). (1993). *America street: A multicultural anthology of stories.* New York: Persea.

Naylor, P. R. (1991). *Shiloh.* New York: Atheneum.

Paterson, K. (1977). *Bridge to Terabithia.* New York: Harper & Row.

Patterson, F. (1985). *Koko's kitten.* New York: Scholastic.

Ride, S., & O'Shaughnessy, T. (1994). *The third planet: Exploring the earth from space.* New York: Crown.

Silverstein, S. (1974). *Where the sidewalk ends.* New York: Harper & Row.

Slote, A. (1991). *Finding Buck McHenry.* New York: HarperCollins.

Soto, G. (1990). *Baseball in April and other stories.* Orlando: Harcourt Brace.

Seventh Grade

Aaseng, N. (1992). *Navajo code talkers.* New York: Walker.

Avi. (1991). *Nothing but the truth.* New York: Orchard.

Caras, R. (1987). *Roger Caras' treasury of great cat stories.* New York: Dutton.

Conrad, P. (1985). *Prairie songs.* New York: HarperCollins.

Cushman, K. (1994). *Catherine called Birdy.* New York: Dutton.

Danzinger, P. (1979). *Can you sue your parents for malpractice?* New York: Delacorte.

Fox, P. (1984). *One-eyed cat.* New York: Bradbury.

Hinton, S. E. (1967). *The outsiders.* New York: Viking.

Jukes, M. (1988). *Getting even.* New York: Knopf.

Krementz, J. (1989). *How it feels to fight for your life.* Boston: Little, Brown.

McKinley, R. (1984). *The hero and the crown.* New York: Greenwillow. (And other books by this author.)

O'Dell, S. (1960). *Island of the blue dolphins.* Boston: Houghton Mifflin.

Paulson, G. (1987). *Hatchet.* New York: Delacorte. (And other books by this author.)

Rawls, W. (1961). *Where the red fern grows.* New York: Doubleday.

Service, P. F. (1988). *Stinker from space.* New York: Fawcett.

Siebert, D. (1991). *Sierra.* New York: Harper & Row.

Wallace, B. (1992). *Buffalo gal.* New York: Holiday House.

Eighth Grade

Adams, R. (1974). *Watership down.* New York: Macmillan.

Brooks, B. (1984). *The moves make the man.* New York: HarperCollins.

Duncan, L. (1981). *Stranger with my face.* Boston: Little, Brown.

Freedman, R. (1987). *Lincoln: A photobiography.* New York: Clarion.

Gallo, D. R. (Ed.). (1993). *Join in: Multiethnic short stories.* New York: Delacorte.

George, J. C. (1989). *Shark beneath the reef.* New York: Harper & Row.

Hermes, P. (1991). *Mama, let's dance.* Boston: Little, Brown.

Janeczko, P. (Ed.). (1991). *Preposterous: Poems of youth.* New York: Orchard.

Macaulay, D. (1988). *The way things work: From levers to lasers, cars to computers—A visual guide to the world of machines.* Boston: Houghton Mifflin.

Moore, K. (1994). *. . . If you lived at the time of the Civil War.* New York: Scholastic.

Murphy, C. R. (1992). *To the summit.* New York: Lodestar.

Myers, W.D. (1990). *The mouse rap.* New York: HarperCollins

Naylor, P. R. (1992). *All but Alice.* New York: Atheneum

Paterson, K. (1980). *Jacob have I loved.* New York: HarperCollins.

Peck, R. N. (1972). *A day no pigs would die.* New York: Knopf.

Reaver, C. (1994). *A little bit dead.* New York: Delacorte.

Sleator, W. (1986). *Interstellar pig.* New York: Dutton.

Sperry, A. (1968). *Call it courage.* New York: Collier.

Zindel, P. (1968). *The pigman.* New York: HarperCollins.

kindergarten through eighth grade. Of course, many of the books listed are suitable for other grade levels, too.

Teachers need to introduce students—especially reluctant readers—to the books in the classroom library so that they can more effectively choose books to read during reading workshop. The best way to preview books is using a very brief book talk to interest students in the book. In a book talk, teachers tell students a little about the book, show the cover, and perhaps read the first paragraph or two (Prill, 1994–1995). Teachers also give book talks to introduce text sets of books, and students give book talks as they share books they have read with the class during the sharing part of reading workshop.

Responding

Students usually keep journals or reading logs in which they write their initial responses to the books they are reading. Sometimes students dialogue with the teacher about the book they are reading. A journal allows for ongoing written conversation between the teacher and individual students (Atwell, 1987; Staton, 1988). Responses often demonstrate students' reading strategies and offer insights into their thinking about literature. Seeing how students think about their reading helps teachers guide their learning.

Teachers play an important role in helping students expand and enrich their responses to literature (Hancock, 1993). They help students move beyond writing summaries and toward reflecting and making connections between literature and their own lives (Barone, 1990, Kelly, 1990). Excerpts from students' reading log entries about *Bunnicula: A Rabbit-Tale of Mystery* (Howe & Howe, 1979) are presented in Figure 9–5. These excerpts reflect the depth of students' responses to the book.

Teachers can collect students' journals periodically to monitor their reflections, and Wollman-Bonilla (1989) recommends writing back and forth with students, with the idea that students write more if the teacher responds. Also, teachers can model and support students' responses in their responses. However, because responding to students' journals is very time-consuming, teachers should keep their responses brief and not respond to every entry.

Teachers and researchers have examined students' responses and noticed patterns in their responses. Hancock (1992, 1993) identified these eight categories:

1. *Monitoring understanding.*   Students get to know the characters and explain how the story is making sense to them. These responses usually occur at the beginning of a book.

2. *Making inferences.*   Students share their insights into the feelings and motives of a character. They often begin their comment with "I think."

3. *Making, validating, or invalidating predictions.*   Students speculate about what will happen later in the story and also confirm or deny predictions they made previously.

4. *Expressing wonder or confusion.*   Students reflect on the way the story is developing. They ask "I wonder why" questions and write about confusions.

5. *Character interaction.*   Students show that they are personally involved with a character, sometimes writing "If I were _____ , I would." They express empathy and share related experiences from their own lives. Also, they may give advice to the character.

FIGURE 9–5   Excerpts from Students' Responses to *Bunnicula*

I think the Monroes will find out what Chester and Harold are doing.

Bunnicula must really be scared of Harold and Chester. I wouldn't trust Chester either. He's sneaky.

That was stupid! They were pounding a steak—MEAT—into the bunny's heart. That won't work!

I know how Chester and Harold feel. It's like when I got a new baby sister and everyone paid attention to her. I got ignored a lot.

I just can't stop reading. This book is so cool. And it's funny, too.

Can a bunny be a vampire? I don't think so. A bunny couldn't suck the blood out of a vegetable. They don't even have blood.

I think Chester is jealous of the baby rabbit.

Gross!!! The vegetables are all white and there are two little fang holes in each one.

I was right! I knew Harold and Chester would try to take care of Bunnicula. What I didn't know was that the Monroes would come home early.

Mrs. S., I want to write a letter to this author. I've got questions for him. Also, are there more Bunnicula books? I gotta keep reading.

I wonder why the vegetables are turning white. I know it's not Bunnicula but I don't know why.

If I were Bunnicula, I'd run away. He's just not safe in that house!

Those Monroes don't know what is happening in their own house. Are they blind?

My dog is a lot like Harold. He gets on my bed with me and he loves snacks, but you should never feed a dog chocolate.

I guess Bunnicula really is a vampire.

The Monroes got Bunnicula at a movie theater. They named him Bunnicula because they found him when a Dracula movie was on. Bunny + Dracula = Bunnicula.

This is a great book! I know stuff like this couldn't happen but it would be awesome if it could. It's just fantasy but it's like I believe it.

6. ***Character assessment.***   Students judge a character's actions and often use evaluative terms such as "nice" or "dumb."

7. ***Story involvement.***   Students reveal their involvement in the story as they express satisfaction with how the story is developing. They may comment on their desire to continue reading or use terms such as "disgusting," "weird," or "awesome" to react to sensory aspects of the story.

8. *Literary criticism.* Students offer "I liked/I didn't like" opinions and praise or condemn an author's style. Sometimes students compare the book with others they have read or compare the author with other authors with whom they are familiar.

The first four categories are personal meaning-making options in which students make inferences about characters, offer predictions, ask questions, or discuss confusions. The next three categories focus on character and plot development. Students are more involved with the story, and they offer reactions to the characters and events of the story. The last category is literary evaluation, in which students evaluate books and reflect on their own literary tastes.

These categories can extend the possibilities of response by introducing teachers and students to a wide variety of response options. Hancock (1992, 1993) recommends that teachers begin by assessing the kinds of responses students are currently making. They can read students' journals, categorize entries, and make an assessment. Often students use only a few types of responses, not the wide range that is available. Teachers can teach minilessons and model types of responses that students aren't using, and they can ask questions in journals to prompt students to think in new ways about the story they are reading.

Some students write minimal or very limited responses in journals. It is important that students read books they find personally interesting and that they feel free to share their thoughts, feelings, and questions with a trusted audience—usually the teacher. Sometimes writing entries on computer and using a modem to share the entries with students in another class or with other interested readers increases students' interest in writing more elaborate responses, as the Technology Link on page 340 shows.

Responding in reading logs replaces doing workbook pages or worksheets. Teachers traditionally use worksheets as a management tool or because they think their use will increase students' reading levels. In *Becoming a Nation of Readers* (Anderson et al., 1985), the authors reported that children spend up to 70% of reading instructional time engaged in completing worksheets and workbook pages, even though these provide only perfunctory levels of reading practice in traditional classrooms.

During reading and responding time, there is little or no talking. Students are engrossed in reading and writing independently. Rarely do students interrupt classmates, go to the rest room, or get drinks of water, except in case of emergency. They do not use reading workshop time to do homework or other schoolwork.

Sharing

For the last 15 minutes of reading workshop, the class gathers together to discuss books they have finished reading. Students talk about the book and why they liked it. Sometimes they read a brief excerpt aloud or formally pass the book to a classmate who wants to read it. Sharing is important because it helps students form a community to value and celebrate each other's accomplishments (Hansen, 1987).

Teaching Minilessons

The teacher spends 10 to 20 minutes teaching minilessons, brief lessons on reading workshop procedures and reading strategies and skills. Topics for minilessons are usually drawn from students' observed needs, comments students make during

■ *Activity*

Analyze the excerpts from students' responses to *Bunnicula* that were shown in Figure 9–5 using Hancock's eight categories. What conclusions can you draw about the types of responses these students made?

Technology Link
Electronic Dialoguing About Reading, Literature, and Books

Students can share responses about books they are reading using modems and computers. Students write responses to books they are reading independently and send them to students in another classroom, older students, or preservice teachers at a university. Moore (1991) described a program set up between Eastern Michigan University and a fifth-grade class in the Ypsilanti School District in which teachers in a graduate course dialogued with students in the class. Students wrote about books they were reading, and the teachers responded. The teachers encouraged students to expand their entries, make personal connections, and reflect on their reading. One fifth grader, Chih Ping, wrote these responses about Judy Blume's *Superfudge* (1980):

> 11/7
> I am enjoying *Superfudge.* My favorite character is Fudge. I like him because he is so funny.

> 11/21
> I think Peter's new house is real good because in

Pine Grove the apartments aren't as good. I have moved before. I just moved here and lived here like about two years. This is my second year at Chapelle. It also seemed hard for me at school. After I met Robert (one of my best friends) it became easy at school. He plays in band and I play in orchestra. I am good at playing in orchestra. I play a violin. Sometimes the teacher tells me to teach the violinist how to play a song (Violinist = people who want to play violin) while she taught other people how to play the guitar and a person how to play the viola. (p. 283)

These two entries show how this student's responses and interpretations became more elaborate through dialoguing over the computer.

———————————

For more information about electronic dialoguing, see Moore, M. A. (1991). Electronic dialoguing: An avenue to literacy. *The Reading Teacher, 45,* 280–286.

conferences, and procedures that students need to know how to do for reading workshop. Figure 9–6 lists possible minilesson topics.

Reading workshop minilessons are sometimes taught to the whole class, while at other times they are taught to small groups. At the beginning of the school year, Mrs. Donnelly teaches minilessons to the whole class on choosing books to read during reading workshop, and later in the year she teaches minilessons on noticing literary language and creating images in your mind as you read. She also teaches minilessons on particular authors when she introduces their stories to the whole class. In addition, she teaches minilessons on literary genre—contemporary realism, science fiction, historical fiction, folktales—when she sets out collections of books representing each genre in the classroom library. When she noticed that several students seemed unfamiliar with making predictions, she worked with that group, and when several other students questioned her about the flashback at the beginning of *The Day Jimmy's Boa Ate the Wash* (Noble, 1980), she taught a minilesson on this literary device.

Reading Aloud to Students

Teachers often read picture books and chapter books aloud to the class as part of reading workshop. They choose high-quality literature that students might not be able to read themselves, award-winning books that they feel every student should be exposed to, or books that relate to a social studies or science theme. After reading, students par-

FIGURE 9–6   Minilesson Topics for Reading and Writing Workshop

Procedures	Concepts	Strategies/Skills
Reading Workshop		
Choose a book	Aesthetic reading	Identify unfamiliar words
Abandon a book	Efferent reading	Visualize
Listen to book read aloud	Interpretation	Predict and confirm
Read independently	Story genre	Engage with text
Decode unfamiliar words	Story elements	Identify with characters
Respond in reading logs	Intertextuality	Elaborate on the plot
Use double-entry journals	Sequels	Notice opposites
Give a book talk	Author information	Monitor understanding
Conference		Connect to one's own life
		Connect to previously read stories
		Value the story
		Evaluate the story
Writing Workshop		
Choose a topic	The writing process	Gather ideas
Cluster ideas	Audience	Organize ideas
Make a table of contents	Purposes for writing	Draft
Participate in writing groups	Writing forms	Revise
Proofread	Proofreaders' marks	Use metaphors and similes
Use the dictionary	Authors	Use imagery
Conference with the teacher	Illustration techniques	Sentence combining
Write an "All About the Author" page	Wordplay	Edit
Make hardcover books		Identify and correct spelling errors
Share published writing		Use capital letters correctly
Use author's chair		Use punctuation marks correctly
Use rubrics		Use dialogue
		Value the composition

[handwritten annotation:] Minilesson

ticipate in a grand conversation to talk about the book and share the reading experience. This activity is important because students listen to a story read aloud and respond to the story together as a community of learners, not as individuals.

Variations of Reading Workshop

Teachers adapt reading workshop in a variety of ways. Sometimes students choose and read books from a special themed text set as part of a social studies or science theme study such as the ocean or ancient Egypt. For example, when Mrs. Donnelly's students study the desert, they spend a week reading only desert-related books during reading workshop. Mrs. Donnelly sets out a collection of more than 50 desert books from which students choose. Teachers also collect books for literature-related text sets. Students might read books from a collection written by one author, such as Lois

Ehlert, Eve Bunting, Chris Van Allsburg, or Gary Paulsen. Or they might read books representing one genre, such as folktales or science fiction.

Another variation is book clubs (Raphael & McMahon, 1994)—also called literature study groups (Peterson & Eeds, 1990)—in which students divide into small groups to read one of five or six related books. For example, first graders might choose and read Dr. Seuss stories in small groups; second graders might read different versions of a fairy tale, such as "The Three Little Pigs"; fourth graders might read informational books in the Magic School Bus series (e.g., *The Magic School Bus in the Time of the Dinosaurs* [Cole, 1994]); and sixth graders might read survival stories. A list of suggested text sets for book clubs is presented in Figure 9–7.

For book clubs, teachers design text sets with five, six, or seven related titles and collect six copies of each book. Then the teacher gives a book talk about each book, and students sign up for the book they want to read. One way to do this is to set each book on the chalk tray and have students sign their names on the chalkboard above the book they want to read. Or, teachers can set the books on a table and place a sign-up sheet beside each book. Students need time to preview the books, and then they select the book they want to read. Once in a while, students don't get to read their first-choice book, but they can always read it later during reading workshop.

The books in the text set often vary in length and difficulty, but students are not placed in groups according to reading level. Students choose the books they want to read, and as they preview the books they consider how good a "fit" the book is, but that is not their only consideration. They often choose to read the book they find most interesting or the book their best friend has chosen. Students can usually manage whatever book they choose because of support and assistance from their group or

During reading workshop, teachers conference with students about the stories and other books they are reading.

FIGURE 9–7   Text Sets for Book Clubs

Primary Grades

Dr. Seuss Stories

Dr. Seuss. (1960). *Green eggs and ham.* New York: Random House.

Dr. Seuss. (1960). *One fish, two fish, red fish, blue fish.* New York: Random House.

Dr. Seuss. (1963). *Hop on pop.* New York: Random House.

Dr. Seuss. (1967). *The cat in the hat.* New York: Random House.

Dr. Seuss. (1968). *The foot book.* New York: Random House.

Frog and Toad Books

Clarke, B. (1990). *Amazing frogs and toads.* New York: Knopf.

Lobel, A. (1970). *Frog and Toad are friends.* New York: Harper & Row.

Mayer, M., & Mayer, M. (1975). *One frog too many.* New York: Dial.

Pallotta, J. (1990). *The frog alphabet book.* Watertown, MA: Charlesbridge.

Yolen, J. (1980). *Commander Toad in space.* New York: Coward-McCann.

Versions of "The Three Little Pigs"

Bishop, G. (1989). *The three little pigs.* New York: Scholastic Hardcover.

Lowell, S. (1992). *The three little javelinas.* Flagstaff, AZ: Northland.

Marshall, J. (1989). *The three little pigs.* New York: Dial.

Scieszka, J. (1989). *The true story of the three little pigs.* New York: Viking.

Trivizas, E. (1993). *The three little wolves and the big bad pig.* New York: McElderry Books.

Middle Grades

Magic School Bus Books

Cole, J. (1987). *The magic school bus inside the earth.* New York: Scholastic.

Cole, J. (1989). *The magic school bus inside the human body.* New York: Scholastic.

Cole, J. (1990). *The magic school bus lost in the solar system.* New York: Scholastic.

Cole, J. (1992). *The magic school bus on the ocean floor.* New York: Scholastic.

Cole, J. (1994). *The magic school bus in the time of the dinosaurs.* New York: Scholastic.

Tall Tales

Kellogg, S. (1984). *Paul Bunyan.* New York: Morrow.

Kellogg, S. (1986). *Pecos Bill.* New York: Morrow.

Kellogg, S. (1992). *Mike Fink.* New York: Morrow.

Lester, J. (1994). *John Henry.* New York: Dial.

Isaacs, A. (1994). *Swamp angel.* New York: Dutton.

Bevery Cleary Books

Cleary, B. (1954). *Henry and Ribsy.* New York: Morrow.

Cleary, B. (1965). *The mouse and the motorcycle.* New York: Morrow.

Cleary, B. (1975). *Ramona and her father.* New York: Morrow.

Cleary, B. (1981). *Ramona Quimby, age 8.* New York: Morrow.

Cleary, B. (1983). *Dear Mr. Henshaw.* New York: Morrow.

Upper Grades

Arthurian Legends

Andronik, C. M. (1989). *Quest for a king: Searching for the real King Arthur.* New York: Atheneum.

Pyle, H. (1984). *The story of King Arthur and his knights.* New York: Scribner.

Riordan, J. (1982). *Tales of King Arthur.* New York: Macmillan.

Sutcliff, R. (1980). *The light beyond the forest: The quest for the Holy Grail.* New York: Dutton.

Tennyson, A. L. (1986). *The lady of Shalott.* Oxford, England: Oxford University Press.

Survival Stories

George, J. C. (1972). *Julie of the wolves.* New York: Harper & Row.

Hamilton, V. (1971). *The planet of Junior Brown.* New York: Macmillan.

Lowry, L. (1993). *The giver.* Boston: Houghton Mifflin.

Paulsen, G. (1987). *Hatchet.* New York: Viking.

Sperry, A. (1940). *Call it courage.* New York: Macmillan.

Ancient Egypt

Bradshaw, G. (1991). *The dragon and the thief.* New York: Greenwillow.

Carter, D. S. (1987). *His majesty, Queen Hatshepsut.* New York: HarperCollins.

Dexter, C. (1992). *The gilded cat.* New York: Morrow.

McMullan, K. (1992). *Under the mummy's spell.* New York: Farrar, Straus & Giroux.

Snyder, Z. K. (1967). *The Egypt game.* New York: Atheneum.

through determination. Once in a while, teachers counsel students to choose another book or provide an additional copy of the book so the students can practice at home or with a tutor at school.

Students use reading workshop time to read the book. Teachers set a time schedule for students to follow as they read, respond to the book, and participate in grand conversations. As students read, the teacher moves around the classroom, meeting with each group. During group meetings, the teacher may read along with students, read their reading log entries, or participate in grand conversations. While the teacher is meeting with one group, the other groups read independently or participate in other activities, such as writing in reading logs.

Since everyone in the book club is reading the same book, students talk about the book in a grand conversation. Sometimes teachers participate in these conversations, and sometimes they don't. When the teachers are participants, they participate as fellow readers who share joys and difficulties, insights and speculations. They also help students develop literary insights by providing information, asking insightful ques-

FIGURE 9–8   Questions to Ask During Grand Conversations to Help Students Focus on Literary Qualities

---

1. Plot

* What are the conflicts in the story?
* How does the author develop the conflicts?
* What events lead to the high point in the story?
* What devices did the author use to develop the plot?

2. Character

* Which characters are fully developed and which are flat?
* How does the author tell us about the characters? By what they do? By how they look? By what they say? By what they think?
* How does the story show the development of the characters?
* If you were a character in the story, which character would you be? Why?

3. Setting

* How does the setting influence the story?
* Is the setting important to the story?
* How is time marked in the story?
* Does the author use flashbacks or foreshadowing?
* How much time passes in the story?

4. Point of View

* Is the story written from first person or third person?
* Are the characters' feelings and thoughts presented?
* How does the author describe the characters?

5. Theme

* What symbols does the author use?
* What universal truths does the story present?

Adapted from Eeds and Peterson, 1991; and Peterson and Eeds, 1990.

tions, and guiding students to make comments. Teachers might use some of the questions listed in Figure 9–8 to help students dig more deeply into books during grand conversations. Teachers ask questions judiciously to help students think more deeply about the stories. Eeds and Peterson (1991) advise teachers to listen carefully to what students say as they talk about a book and to introduce literary terminology such as conflict, foreshadowing, and theme when appropriate.

In addition to identifying the elements of story structure, teachers also help students make connections between the story and their own lives and between the story and other stories they have read. Students often notice literary language and read memorable passages aloud. For example, when Mrs. Donnelly was talking with a small group of third graders who had read Gloria Houston's *My Great-Aunt Arizona* (1992), one student made an insightful comment about the theme and then connected the story to another one the class had read. Kristy remarked, "I think this story is about Arizona's journey through life, and it is a lot like *Miss Rumphius* [Cooney, 1982]. That book was about Miss Rumphius's life's journey. Journeys— that's how they are alike." Mrs. Donnelly used Kristy's comment to ask another question about theme and to talk about intertextuality.

For years teachers have devoted 10, 20, or 30 minutes a day to silent reading in the classroom. Lyman Hunt (1970) called it Uninterrupted Sustained Silent Reading (USSR), the McCrackens (1972) called it Sustained Silent Reading, and teachers have created their own acronyms, such as DEAR (Drop Everything and Read) Time. Students read self-selected library books during these practice periods. The idea behind these programs is that students need lots of reading practice in addition to the regular reading instruction. These add-on programs were very innovative when they were developed because research showed that children had few opportunities to read for sustained periods in school and to transfer the skills and strategies they were learning to more genuine reading activities. However, it is important to note that these practice programs are not the same as reading workshop, because they lack instructional components.

WRITING WORKSHOP

Writing workshop is a new way to implement the writing process (Atwell, 1987; Calkins, 1994; Graves, 1983, 1994; Hornsby, Parry, & Sukarna, 1992). Students write on topics that they choose themselves, and they assume ownership of their writing and learning. At the same time, the teacher's role changes from being a provider of knowledge to serving as a facilitator and guide. The classroom becomes a community of writers who write and share their writing. There is a spirit of pride and acceptance in the classroom.

In a writing workshop classroom, students have writing folders in which they keep all papers related to the writing project they are working on. They also keep writing notebooks in which they jot down images, impressions, dialogue, and experiences that they can build upon for writing projects (Calkins, 1991). Students have access to different kinds of paper, some lined and some unlined, as well as writing instruments such as pencils and red and blue pens. They also have access to the classroom library. Many times students' writing grows out of favorite books they have read. They may write a sequel to a book or retell a story from a different viewpoint. Primary-grade students often use patterns from books they have read to structure a book they are writing.

Students sit at desks or tables arranged in small groups as they write. The teacher circulates around the classroom, conferencing briefly with students, and the classroom atmosphere is free enough that students converse quietly with classmates and move around the classroom to assist classmates or share ideas. There is space for students to meet together for **writing groups,** and often a sign-up sheet for writing groups is posted in the classroom. A table is available for the teacher to meet with individual students or small groups for conferences, writing groups, proofreading, and minilessons.

Writing workshop is a 60- to 90-minute period scheduled each day. During this time students are involved in three components: minilessons, writing, and sharing. Sometimes a fourth activity, reading aloud to students, is added to writing workshop when it is not used in conjunction with reading workshop.

Teaching Minilessons

During this 10- to 20-minute period, teachers provide brief lessons on writing workshop procedures and writing strategies and skills, such as organizing ideas, proofreading, and using quotation marks in marking dialogue. In the middle and upper grades, teachers often make a transparency of an anonymous student's piece of writing (often a student in another class or from a previous year) and then display it using an overhead projector. Students read the writing, and the teacher uses it to teach the lesson, which may focus on giving suggestions for revision, combining sentences, proofreading, or writing a stronger lead sentence. Teachers also use excerpts from books students are reading for minilessons to show students how published authors use writing skills and strategies. Refer back to Figure 9–6 for a list of minilessons for writing workshop. These minilessons are similar to those taught in reading workshop.

Teachers teach brief minilessons on writing procedures, skills, and strategies during writing workshop.

Teachers also share information about authors and how they write during minilessons. In order for students to think of themselves as writers, they need to know what writers do. Each year there are more autobiographies written by authors. James Howe, author of *Bunnicula: A Rabbit-Tale of Mystery* (Howe & Howe, 1979), has written an autobiography, *Playing With Words* (1994), in which he reflects on his desire since childhood to make people laugh and describes his writing routine and how he makes time to read and write every day. Some of the other books in the "Meet the Author" series are *Firetalking,* by Patricia Polacco (1994), *Hau Kola/Hello Friend,* by Paul Goble (1994), and *Surprising Myself,* by Jean Fritz (1992).

Filmstrip and video productions about authors and illustrators are also available. For example, in American School Publishers' Meet the Newbery Author Series, Arnold Lobel (1978) describes his writing process and calls his revising "unwriting." He shows how he uses a pen to cross out the unnecessary words so that his stories will fit within the 32-page picture book format. Videos are an excellent medium for authors and illustrators to demonstrate their craft. In a 27-minute video *Eric Carle: Picture Writer* (1993), Eric Carle demonstrates how he uses paint and collage to create the illustrations for his popular picture books. A list of books, journal articles, and audiovisual materials about authors and illustrators is presented in Appendix B.

Writing

Students spend 30 to 45 minutes or longer working independently on writing projects. Just as students in reading workshop choose and read books at their own pace, in writing workshop students work at their own pace on writing projects they have chosen themselves. Most students move through all five stages of the writing process—prewriting, drafting, revising, editing, and publishing—at their own pace, but young children often use an abbreviated process of prewriting, drafting, and publishing. Teachers often begin writing workshop by reviewing the five stages of the writing process, setting guidelines for writing workshop, and taking students through one writing activity together. A set of guidelines for writing workshop that one seventh-grade class developed is presented in Figure 9–9.

Teachers conference with students as they write. Many teachers prefer moving around the classroom to meet with students rather than having the students come to a table to meet with the teacher. Too often a line forms as students wait to meet with the teacher, and students lose precious writing time. Some teachers move around the classroom in a regular pattern, meeting with one-fifth of the students each day. In this way they can conference with every student during the week.

Other teachers spend the first 15 to 20 minutes of writing workshop stopping briefly to check on 10 or more students each day. Many use a zigzag pattern to get to all parts of the classroom each day. These teachers often kneel down beside each student, sit on the edge of the student's seat, or carry their own stool to each student's desk. During the one- or two-minute conference, teachers ask students what they are writing, listen to students read a paragraph or two, and then ask what they plan to do next. Then these teachers use the remaining time during writing workshop to more formally conference with students who are revising and editing their compositions. Students often sign up for these conferences. The teachers find strengths in students' writing, ask questions, and discover possibilities during these revising conferences. Some teachers like to read the pieces themselves, while others like to listen to students read their papers aloud. As they interact with students, teachers model the kinds of responses that students are learning to give to each other.

FIGURE 9–9   A Seventh–Grade Class's Guidelines for Writing Workshop

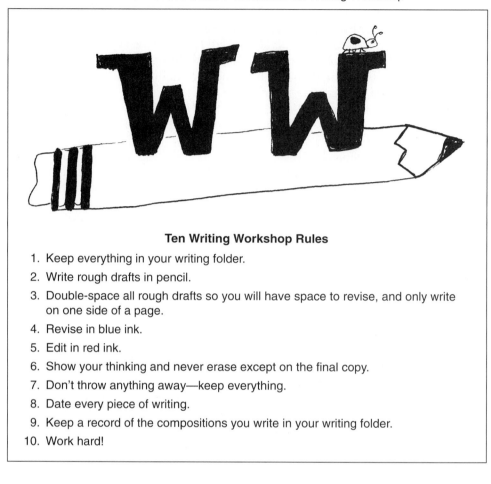

Ten Writing Workshop Rules

1. Keep everything in your writing folder.
2. Write rough drafts in pencil.
3. Double-space all rough drafts so you will have space to revise, and only write on one side of a page.
4. Revise in blue ink.
5. Edit in red ink.
6. Show your thinking and never erase except on the final copy.
7. Don't throw anything away—keep everything.
8. Date every piece of writing.
9. Keep a record of the compositions you write in your writing folder.
10. Work hard!

As students meet together to share their writing during revising and editing, they continue to develop their sense of community. They share their rough drafts with classmates in writing groups composed of four or five students. In some classrooms, teachers join the writing groups whenever they can, but students normally run the groups themselves. They take turns reading their rough drafts to each other and listen as their classmates offer compliments and suggestions for revision. In contrast, students usually work with one partner to edit their writing, and they often use red pens.

After proofreading their drafts with a classmate and then meeting with the teacher for final editing, students make the final copy of their writings. Students often want to put their writings on the computer so that their final copies will appear professional. Many times students compile their final copies to make books during writing workshop, but sometimes they attach their writing to artwork, make posters, write letters that will be mailed, or perform scripts as skits or puppet shows. Not every piece is necessarily published, however. Sometimes students decide not to continue with a piece of writing. They file the piece in their writing folders and start something new.

Even kindergartners, first graders, and second graders can work productively during writing workshop. They often write single-draft books and use their developing knowledge of phoneme-grapheme correspondence to spell words. One page from a kindergartner's turtle book is shown in Figure 9–10. The text reads, "Turtles hide in

FIGURE 9–10   A Page From a Kindergartner's Book About Turtles

their shells." After drawing a picture of a turtle and cutting it out for the cover of the book, William asked a parent volunteer to cut eight sheets of paper in the same shape and to help punch holes and bind the book together with yarn. William worked for several days to write and illustrate the book. He copied some of the correctly spelled words from a book on turtles that he found in the library center, and other words were spelled by a parent volunteer. Here is the complete text of the book, along with a translation:

Cover	*The Turtle Bok.*	The Turtle Book
	by William	by William
1	*Trt hv lz*	Turtles have shells.
2	*T id in their shells.*	Turtles hide in their shells.
3	*T r gre and br*	Turtles are green and brown.
4	*Turtls etlus and fiz*	Turtles eat lettuce and flies.
5	*Tls knsm*	Turtles can swim.
6	*T lv biapd*	Turtles live by a pond.
7	*Turtles r cbd reptiles.*	Turtles are cold-blooded reptiles.
8	*I luv trlsss.*	I love turtles.

Primary-grade students make literally hundreds of little books bound with yarn and staples as they experiment with writing. Like William, many students write books about favorite animals. They also make color books, number books, pattern books, and books about their families, and they retell familiar stories such as "Little Red Riding Hood" and "The Three Billy Goats Gruff."

Parent volunteers, aides, and cross-age tutors support students as they write, encouraging them to experiment with spellings and punctuation marks. They also demonstrate how to form letters, and listen as children reread their books. Because students' spellings are not conventional, it is important that students reread their books several times to parents and tutors so that they can remember them. As students gain experience with writing, parent volunteers and cross-age tutors begin conferencing with students and guiding them into revising and editing (Baker, 1994). These volunteers help students reflect on their writing by asking pertinent questions to help them clarify or refine their thinking.

Sharing

For the last 10 to 15 minutes of writing workshop, the class gathers together to share their new publications and make other related announcements. Younger students often sit in a circle or gather together on a rug for sharing time. If an **author's chair** is available, each student sits in the special chair to read his or her composition. After each reading, classmates clap and offer compliments. They may also make other comments and suggestions, but the focus is on celebrating completed writing projects, not on revising the composition to make it better. Classmates help celebrate after the child shares by clapping, and perhaps the best praise is having a classmate ask if he or she can read the newly published book.

■ *Activity*

Think about how Mrs. Donnelly might organize her 75-minute workshop period for writing workshop. Set up a schedule that includes all the writing workshop components.

Students share their newly published books with classmates.

Variations of Writing Workshop

Sometimes teachers set up writing workshop for a limited period of time when their students are working on a project and need lengthy periods of time for writing. For example, as third graders write weather reports after reading *Cloudy With a Chance of Meatballs* (Barrett, 1978), or as upper-grade students write simulated journals or reports about the Civil War, they participate in writing workshop for a week or two. During these project-oriented writing workshops, teachers sometimes teach minilessons on topics related to the assignment, but usually all of the writing workshop time is used for writing and then for sharing when students have completed their projects.

A second variation is poetry workshop, which incorporates components of both reading workshop and writing workshop (Tompkins & McGee, 1993). Students read and respond to poems during the reading workshop component and write poems during the writing workshop component. One possible schedule for a two-hour poetry workshop is:

15 minutes	The teacher leads a whole-class meeting to give a book talk on a new poetry book, talk about a poet, read several favorite poems using **choral reading,** or talk about a "difficult" or "confusing" poem.
30 minutes	Students read poems independently.
15 minutes	Students share favorite poems with classmates.
15 minutes	The teacher teaches a poetry minilesson, perhaps on a poetic form or on using sensory words, metaphors, or alliteration.
30 minutes	Students write poems using the writing process.
15 minutes	Students share their poems with classmates.

Duthie and Zimet (1992) describe a similar poetry workshop for first graders that combines reading and writing. Students read poems individually or with partners, and the teacher reads poems aloud to students. Writing workshop follows reading workshop, and students also write poems. They draft poems and share them with classmates from the author's chair. Teachers also teach minilessons related to reading and writing poetry. Their minilesson topics include rhyming versus nonrhyming poetry, invented words, poetry anthologies, arranging lines of poetry, sound words, alliteration, titles for poems, and shape poems. As a culminating project, students compile an anthology of original poems.

Teachers can use this combined reading-writing workshop format when studying any literary genre. Students can read and write biographies, tall tales, pourquoi tales, or collections of letters or journals.

MANAGING A WORKSHOP CLASSROOM

It takes time to establish a workshop approach in the classroom, especially if students are used to reading from basal readers. Students need to learn how to become responsible for their own learning. They need to develop new ways of working and learning, and they have to form a community of readers and writers in the classroom. For reading workshop, students need to know how to select books, how to read aesthetically, and other reading workshop procedures. For writing workshop, students need to know how to develop and refine a piece of writing, how to make books and booklets for their compositions, and other writing workshop procedures. Sometimes students complain that they don't know what to write about, but in time they learn how to brainstorm possible topics and to keep a list of topics in their writing workshop notebooks.

Teachers begin to establish the workshop environment in their classroom from the first day of the school year by providing choice and time for their students to read and write and by offering opportunities for response. Through their interactions with students, the respect they show to students, and the way they model reading and writing, teachers establish the classroom as a community of learners.

Teachers develop a schedule for reading and writing workshop with time allocated for each component, or alternating the two types of workshop, as shown in Figure 9–2. In their schedules, teachers allot as much time as possible for students to read and write. After developing the schedule, teachers post it in the classroom and talk with students about the activities and discuss their expectations with students. Teachers teach the workshop procedures and continue to model the procedures as students become comfortable with the routines. As students share what they are reading and writing at the end of workshop sessions, their enthusiasm grows and the workshop approaches are successful.

Students keep two folders—one for reading workshop and one for writing workshop. In the reading workshop folder, students keep a list of books they have read, notes from minilessons, reading logs, and other materials. In the writing workshop folder, they keep all rough drafts and other compositions, a list of all compositions, topics for future pieces, and notes from minilessons.

Writing Workshop Chart

Names	Dates 10/18	10/19	10/20	10/21	10/22	10/25	10/26	10/27
Antonio	4 5	5	5	6	7	8	8	8 9
Bella	2	2	2 3	2	2	4	5	6
Charles	8 9 1	3 1	1	2	2 3	4	5	6 7
Dina	6	6	6	7 8	8	9 1	1	2 3
Dustin	7 8	8	8	8	8	8	9 1	1
Eddie	2 3	2	2 4	5 6	8	9 1	1 2	2 3
Elizabeth	7	6	7	8	8	8	9	1 2
Elsa	2	3	4 5	5 6	6 7	8	8	9 1

Code:
1 = Prewrite   4 = Writing Group   7 = Conference
2 = Draft   5 = Revise   8 = Make Final Copy
3 = Conference   6 = Edit   9 = Publish

FIGURE 9–11   "State of the Class" Chart

Effective Practices

1. Students choose the books they want to read.

2. Teachers teach students how to select books using the Goldilocks Strategy.

3. Teachers recognize reading workshop as an instructional approach and provide plenty of time for students to read and respond to books.

4. Teachers use conferences and responses students write in reading logs to monitor their reading progress.

5. Teachers build students' enthusiasm for reading and books through book talks and sharing.

6. Teachers teach minilessons and have students apply what they have learned through reading and writing.

7. Teachers include both reading and writing workshop, or alternate them.

8. Students choose their own topics and forms for writing.

9. Students learn to use the writing process to develop and refine their compositions.

10. Students publish writing in books and booklets.

11. Students celebrate their completed writings and share them using an author's chair.

Ineffective Practices

1. Teachers assign books for students to read.

2. Teachers don't teach students how to select books because they assign books for students to read.

3. Teachers view reading workshop as supplementary to the reading program and provide limited time for it.

4. Teachers use book report forms to monitor students' progress.

5. Teachers deemphasize sharing.

6. Teachers use worksheets instead of minilessons to teach concepts and skills.

7. Teachers do only reading or writing workshop, and only use the approach once in a while.

8. Teachers assign topics and forms for writing.

9. Teachers collect single-draft compositions to edit and grade.

10. Students write compositions on sheets of paper like other school assignments.

11. Students don't share their completed compositions.

Many teachers use a classroom chart to monitor students' work on a daily basis. At the beginning of reading workshop, students (or the teacher) record what book they are reading or if they are writing in a reading log, waiting to conference with the teacher, or browsing in the classroom library. For writing workshop, students identify the writing project they are involved in or the stage of the writing process they are at. A sample writing workshop chart is shown in Figure 9–11. Teachers can also use the chart to award weekly "effort" grades, to have students indicate their need to conference with the teacher, or to have students announce that they are ready to share the book they have read or to publish their writing. Nancie Atwell (1987) calls this chart "the state of the class." Teachers can review students' progress and note which students need to meet with the teacher or receive additional attention. When students fill in the chart themselves, they develop responsibility for their actions and a stronger desire to accomplish tasks they set for themselves.

To monitor primary-grade students, teachers might use a pocket chart and have students place a card in their pocket, indicating whether they are choosing a new book, reading, or responding during reading workshop or at which stage of the writing process they are working during writing workshop.

Teachers should take time during reading and writing workshop to observe students as they interact and work together in small groups. Researchers who have observed in reading and writing workshop classrooms report that some students, even as young as first graders, are excluded from group activities because of gender, ethnicity, and socioeconomic status (Henkin, 1995; Lensmire, 1992). The socialization patterns in elementary classrooms seem to reflect society's. Henkin recommends that teachers be alert to the possibility that boys might only share books with other boys or that some students won't find anyone willing to be their editing partner. If teachers see instances of discrimination in their classrooms, they should confront it directly and work to foster a classroom environment where students treat each other equitably.

Review

The innovative workshop approach involves students in meaningful reading and writing experiences. Students read and respond to books in reading workshop, and they write and publish books in writing workshop. Effective teachers incorporate the three key characteristics of the workshop approach—time, choice, and response—in their workshops. The five components of reading workshop are reading, responding, sharing, teaching minilessons, and reading aloud to students. The components of writing workshop are similar: teaching minilessons, writing, and sharing. Sometimes teachers combine reading and writing workshop, alternate them, or use writing workshop as students complete projects related to literature focus units or across-the-curriculum theme studies. A list of effective practices for the workshop approach is presented in the figure on page 353.

References

Anderson, R. C., Hiebert, E. H., Scott, J. A., & Wilkinson, I. A. G. (1985). *Becoming a nation of readers.* Washington, DC: National Institute of Education.

Atwell, N. (1987). *In the middle: Reading and writing with adolescents.* Upper Montclair, NJ: Boynton/Cook.

Baker, E. C. (1994). Writing and reading in a first-grade writers' workshop: A parent's perspective. *The Reading Teacher, 47,* 372–377.

Barone, D. (1990). The written responses of young children: Beyond comprehension to story understanding. *The New Advocate, 3,* 49–56.

Brophy, J. E., & Good, T. L. (1986). Teacher behavior and student achievement. In M. C. Wittrock (Ed.), *Handbook of research on teaching* (3rd ed., pp. 328–375). New York: Macmillan.

Calkins, L. M. (1991). *Living between the lines.* Portsmouth, NH: Heinemann.

Calkins, L. M. (1994). *The art of teaching writing* (Rev. ed.). Portsmouth, NH: Heinemann.

Carle, E. (1993). *Eric Carle: Picture writer* (videotape). New York: Philomel.

Duthie, C., & Zimet, E. K. (1992). "Poetry is like directions for your imagination!" *The Reading Teacher, 46,* 14–24.

Eeds, M., & Peterson, R. (1991). Teacher as curator: Learning to talk about literature. *The Reading Teacher, 45,* 118–126.

Five, C. L. (1988). From workbook to workshop: Increasing children's involvement in the reading process. *The New Advocate, 1,* 103–113.

Graves, D. H. (1983). *Writing: Teachers and students at work*. Portsmouth, NH: Heinemann.

Graves, D. H. (1994). *A fresh look at writing*. Portsmouth, NH: Heinemann.

Hancock, M. R. (1992). Literature response journals: Insights beyond the printed page. *Language Arts, 69,* 36–42.

Hancock, M. R. (1993). Exploring and extending personal response through literature journals. *The Reading Teacher, 46,* 466–474.

Hansen, J. (1987). *When writers read*. Portsmouth, NH: Heinemann.

Henkin, R. (1995). Insiders and outsiders in first-grade writing workshops: Gender and equity issues. *Language Arts, 72,* 429–434.

Hornsby, D., Parry, J., & Sukarna, D. (1992). *Teach on: Teaching strategies for reading and writing workshops*. Portsmouth, NH: Heinemann.

Hornsby, D., Sukarna, D., & Parry, J. (1986). *Read on: A conference approach to reading*. Portsmouth, NH: Heinemann.

Hunt, L. C., Jr. (1970). The effect of self-selection, interest and motivation upon independent, instructional and frustration levels. *The Reading Teacher, 24,* 416.

Kelly, P. R. (1990). Guiding young students' response to literature. *The Reading Teacher, 43,* 464–470.

Lensmire, T. (1992). *When children write*. New York: Teachers College Press.

McCracken, R. A., & McCracken, M. J. (1972). *Reading is only the tiger's tail*. San Rafael, CA: Leswing Press.

McWhirter, A. M. (1990). Whole language in the middle school. *The Reading Teacher, 43,* 562–565.

Moore, M. A. (1991). Electronic dialoguing: An avenue to literacy. *The Reading Teacher, 45,* 280–286.

Ohlhausen, M. M., & Jepsen, M. (1992). Lessons from Goldilocks: "Somebody's been choosing my books but I can make my own choices now!" *The New Advocate, 5,* 31–46.

Peterson, R., & Eeds, M. (1990). *Grand conversations: Literature groups in action*. Toronto: Ontario: Scholastic-TAB.

Prill, P. (1994–1995). Helping children use the classroom library. *The Reading Teacher, 48,* 363–364.

Raphael, T. E., & McMahon, S. I. (1994). Book club: An alternative framework for reading instruction. *The Reading Teacher, 48,* 102–116.

Samway, K. D., Whang, G., Cade, C., Gamil, M., Lubandina, M. A., & Phommachanh, K. (1991). Reading the skeleton, the heart, and the brain of a book: Students' perspectives on literature study circles. *The Reading Teacher, 45,* 196–205.

Smith, F. (1984). *Reading without nonsense*. New York: Teachers College Press.

Staton, J. (1988). ERIC/RCS report: Dialogue journals. *Language Arts, 65,* 198–201.

Swift, K. (1993). Try reading workshop in your classroom. *The Reading Teacher, 46,* 366–371.

Tompkins, G. E., & McGee, L. M. (1993). *Teaching reading with literature: Case studies to action plans*. New York: Merrill/Macmillan.

Wollman-Bonilla, J. E. (1989). Reading to participate in literature. *The Reading Teacher, 43,* 112–120.

Children's Literature References

Barrett, J. (1978). *Cloudy with a chance of meatballs*. New York: Atheneum.

Blume, J. (1980). *Superfudge*. New York: Dutton.

Cleary, B. (1961). *Two dog biscuits*. New York: Morrow.

Cleary, B. (1965). *The mouse and the motorcycle*. New York: Morrow.

Cleary, B. (1977). *Ramona and her father*. New York: Morrow.

Cleary, B. (1979). *Ramona forever*. New York: Morrow.

Cleary, B. (1983). *Dear Mr. Henshaw*. New York: Morrow.

Cleary, B. (1984). *Ramona and her mother*. New York: Morrow.

Cleary, B. (1991). *Strider*. New York: Morrow.

Cole, J. (1994). *The magic school bus in the time of the dinosaurs*. New York: Scholastic.

Cooney, B. (1982). *Miss Rumphius*. New York: Viking.

Dahl, R. (1966). *The Magic finger*. New York: Puffin.

Dalgliesh, A. (1982). *The courage of Sarah Noble*. New York: Scribner.

Fritz, J. (1958). *The cabin faced west*. New York: Coward-McCann.

Fritz, J. (1992). *Surprising myself*. Katonah, NY: Richard C. Owen.

Goble, P. (1994). *Hau kola/Hello friend*. Katonah, NY: Richard C. Owen.

Houston, G. (1992). *My great-aunt Arizona*. New York: HarperCollins.

Howe, D., & Howe, J. (1979). *Bunnicula: A rabbit-tale of mystery*. New York: Atheneum.

Howe, J. (1994). *Playing with words*. Katonah, NY: Richard C. Owen.

Isaacs, A. (1994). *Swamp angel*. New York: Dutton.

Kellogg, S. (1986). *Pecos Bill*. New York: Morrow.

Kellogg, S. (1988). *Paul Bunyan*. New York: Morrow.

Meet the Newbery author: Arnold Lobel. (1978). Hightstown, NJ: American School Publishers.

Noble, T. H. (1980). *The day Jimmy's boa ate the wash.* New York: Dial.

Polacco, P. (1994). *Firetalking.* Katonah, NY: Richard C. Owen.

Sachar, L. (1978). *Sideways stories from Wayside School.* New York: Avon Books.

Sachar, L. (1985). *Wayside School is falling down.* New York: Avon Books.

Polar bears live in ice and snow.
Polar bears have good noses. They can smell a seal 20 miles away.
Polar bears eat meat—seals, walruses, and foxes.

Mrs. Mast laminates the chart, and students read and reread it each day. Soon children have memorized most of the sentences. After they reread the chart, children pick out and circle particular letters and words such as *Polar bears* with a pen for writing on laminated charts.

Mrs. Mast notices a note to Goldilocks on the classroom message board, and she takes the note and jots an answer in a childlike handwriting. Soon more children are writing notes to Goldilocks from the perspective of a bear. Most of the children realize that Mrs. Mast is pretending to be Goldilocks, and they are anxious for her to write notes back to them. One note reads:

GOOOOS	Goldilocks,
D U NO	Don't you know (that it is)
DDZTO GOTO	dangerous to go to
A BearH?	a bear's house?
BS.	Be safe.
FMBear	From Mother Bear

FIGURE 10–1   One Page From a Kindergarten Collaborative "Book of Threes"

Mrs. Mast writes back:

> Dear Mother Bear,
> I have learned a good lesson.
> I will never go into a bear's house again.
> Love, Goldilocks

The children have been writing notes and sending pictures back and forth to classmates for several months, but this is the first time they assume the role of a character in a book they are reading.

At the end of the unit, Mrs. Mast places one copy of each of "The Three Bears" books, the story boards for Galdone's version of the book, and three small teddy bears—one brown, one black, and one white—in a small "traveling" bag. Children will take turns taking the traveling bag home to share with their parents.

Mrs. Mast's language arts block is fast-paced, taking into account young children's short attention spans, their need for active involvement, and their desire to manipulate materials. Her schedule is:

8:30–8:45	*Morning Message* Mrs. Mast talks briefly with students about their news and compiles important news and daily activities in a paragraph-length message that she writes while the children observe. After writing, Mrs. Mast reads the message aloud twice and children join in to read familiar words.
8:45–9:15	*Shared Reading/Reading Aloud* Mrs. Mast reads aloud (or rereads) the focus book or related books. After reading, children participate in a grand conversation or other whole-class activity. She also reads and recites poems, sings songs, and does finger plays with students during this time.
9:15–9:35	*Focus Book Centers* Students work at one of five centers related to the focus book set up in the classroom, rotating so that each week students work at all five centers.
9:35–10:00	*Other Centers* Students choose from the literacy play center, blocks, water and sand tray, art project, puzzles, and other rotating activities.
10:00–10:25	*Recess and Snack*
10:25–10:55	*Other Focus Book Activities* Students work in groups or together as a class in other reading and writing activities or related drama and art activities. One day each week, fifth graders come to Mrs. Mast's class to read books to the kindergartners using **assisted reading.**

FIGURE 10–2 Mrs. Mast's Unit Plan for "The Three Bears"

	ACTIVITY	MONDAY	TUESDAY	WEDNESDAY	THURSDAY	FRIDAY
8:30–8:45	Morning Message	→				
8:45–9:15	Shared Reading/ Reading Aloud	Read Galdone's *The Three Bears* using a big book Grand conversation	Read Cauley's *Goldilocks and the Three Bears* Grand conversation	Read *Alaska's Three Bears* Grand conversation	Make charts on three kinds of bears: Grizzly bears Black bears Polar bears	Read *Deep in the Forest* Retell story Grand conversation
9:15–9:35	Focus Book Centers (rotate)	Listening	Literacy play	(parent volunteer) Reading	(aide) Writing	(Mrs. M.) Skills
9:35–10:00	Other Centers					→
10:00–10:25	Recess and Snack					→
10:25–10:55	Other Focus Book Activities	Begin word wall Sequence *The Three Bears* story boards Talk about threes in story	Read Brett's *Goldilocks and the Three Bears* Compare three versions	Talk about threes in folktales Make a class "Book of Three" Compile the book	Fifth-grade reading buddies read "bear" books	Dramatize *Deep in the Woods* Sequence story boards Graph favorite story
10:55–11:00	Songs, Poems, and Fingerplays					→

| 10:55–11:00 | *Songs, Poems, and Fingerplays* |
| | Mrs. Mast leads the class in songs, poems, fingerplays, and other oral language activities. Whenever possible, she relates the wordplay activities to the featured book. |

Mrs. Mast's lesson plan for the week-long focus unit on "The Three Bears" is shown in Figure 10–2.

---

*L*iteracy is a process that begins well before the elementary grades and continues into adulthood, if not throughout life. It used to be that five-year-old children came to kindergarten to be "readied" for reading and writing instruction, which would formally begin in first grade. The implication was that there was a point in children's development when it was time to begin teaching them to read and write. For those not ready, a variety of "readiness" activities would prepare them for reading and writing. Since the 1970s this view has been discredited by both teachers' and researchers' observations (Clay, 1989). The children themselves demonstrated that they could recognize signs and other environmental print, retell stories, scribble letters, invent printlike writing, and listen to stories read aloud to them. Some children even taught themselves to read.

This new perspective on how children become literate—that is, how they learn to read and write—is known as emergent literacy. New Zealand educator Marie Clay is credited with coining the term. Studies from 1966 on have shaped the current outlook (Clay, 1967; Durkin, 1966; Holdaway, 1979; Taylor, 1983; Teale, 1982; Teale & Sulzby, 1989). Now, researchers are looking at literacy learning from the child's point of view. The age range has been extended to include children as young as one or two who listen to stories being read aloud, notice labels and signs in their environment, and experiment with pencils. The concept of literacy has been broadened to include the cultural and social aspects of language learning, and children's experiences with and understandings about written language—both reading and writing—are included as part of emergent literacy.

Teale and Sulzby (1989) paint a portrait of young children as literacy learners with these characteristics:

■ Children begin to learn to read and write very early in life.

■ Young children learn the functions of literacy through observing and participating in real-life settings in which reading and writing are used.

■ Young children's reading and writing abilities develop concurrently and interrelatedly through experiences in reading and writing.

■ Young children learn through active involvement with literacy materials, by constructing their understanding of reading and writing.

In the vignette at the beginning of this chapter, Mrs. Mast's students exemplified many of these characteristics.

Teale and Sulzby describe young children as active learners who construct their own knowledge about reading and writing with the assistance of parents and other literate persons. These caregivers help by demonstrating literacy as they read and write, by supplying materials, and by structuring opportunities for children to be involved in reading and writing. The environment is positive, with children experiencing reading and writing in many facets of their everyday lives and observing others who are engaged in literacy activities.

As you read this chapter, think about these questions:

■ How do teachers foster children's interest in literacy?

■ How do teachers adapt literature focus units and reading workshop for emergent readers?

■ What other instructional approaches are used with young children?

■ How do teachers adapt the writing process for young children?

FOSTERING YOUNG CHILDREN'S INTEREST IN LITERACY

Children's introduction to written language begins before they come to school. Parents and other caregivers read to young children, and children observe adults reading. They learn to read signs and other environmental print in their community. Children experiment with writing and have their parents write for them. They also observe adults writing. When young children come to kindergarten, their knowledge about written language expands quickly as they participate in meaningful, functional, and genuine experiences with reading and writing.

Concepts About Written Language

Through experiences in their homes and communities, young children learn that print carries meaning and that reading and writing are used for a variety of purposes. They read menus in restaurants to know what foods are being served, write and receive letters to communicate with friends and relatives, and read and listen to stories for enjoyment. Children also learn about language purposes as they observe parents and teachers using written language for all these purposes.

Children's understanding about the purposes of reading and writing reflects how written language is used in their community. While reading and writing are part of daily life for almost every family, families use written language for different purposes in different communities (Heath, 1983). It is important to make clear that children have a wide range of literacy experiences in both middle-class and working-class families, even though those experiences might be different (Taylor, 1983; Taylor & Dorsey-Gaines, 1987). In some communities, written language is used mainly as a tool for practical purposes such as paying bills, while in other communities, reading and writing are also used for leisure-time activities. In still other communities, written language serves even wider functions, such as debating social and political issues.

Mrs. Mast and other primary-grade teachers can demonstrate the purposes of written language and provide opportunities for students to experiment with reading and writing in many ways:

- posting signs in the classroom
- making a list of classroom rules
- using reading and writing materials in literacy play centers
- writing notes to students in the class
- exchanging messages with classmates
- reading and writing stories
- making posters about favorite books
- labeling classroom items
- drawing and writing in journals
- writing morning messages
- recording questions and information on charts
- writing notes to parents
- reading and writing letters to pen pals
- reading and writing charts and maps

Through their early experiences with reading and writing, children learn that talk can be written down and read and see how text is arranged in books, letters, charts, and other reading materials. They acquire three types of concepts about print:

1. **Book-orientation concepts.** Students learn how to hold books and turn pages, and they learn that the text, not the illustrations, carries the message.
2. **Directional concepts.** Students learn that print is written and read from left to right and from top to bottom on a page, and they match voice to print, pointing

Young children learn concepts about written language as they exchange letters at the message center.

FIGURE 10–5 *continued*

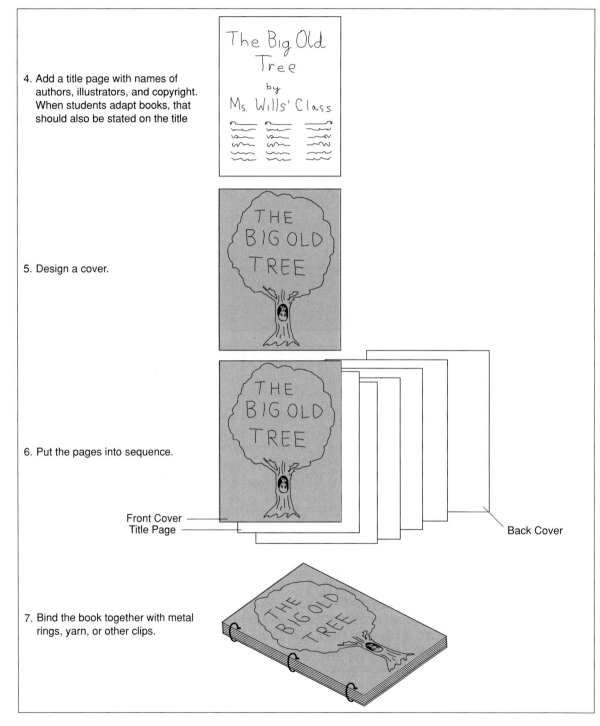

4. Add a title page with names of authors, illustrators, and copyright. When students adapt books, that should also be stated on the title

5. Design a cover.

6. Put the pages into sequence.

Front Cover
Title Page

Back Cover

7. Bind the book together with metal rings, yarn, or other clips.

pages. Teachers can use the book with young children just as they would use commercially produced big books and big books they made themselves.

Predictable Books.   The stories and other books that teachers use for shared reading with young children often have repeated words and sentences, rhyme, or other patterns. Books that use these patterns are known as predictable books. These books are a valuable tool for emergent readers because the repeated words and sentences, patterns, and sequences enable children to predict the next sentence or episode in the story or other book (Bridge, 1979; Heald-Taylor, 1987; Tompkins & Webeler, 1983). Four characteristics of predictable books are:

1. *Repetitive sentences.*   In some books, phrases and sentences are repeated over and over. Sometimes each episode or section of the text ends with the same words or a refrain, and in other books the same statement or question is repeated. In *The Little Red Hen* (Galdone, 1973), the animals repeat "Not I" when the Little Red Hen asks them to help her plant the seeds, harvest the wheat, and bake the bread; after their refusals to help, the hen says, "Then I will."

2. *Repetitive sentences in a cumulative sequence.*   In some books the phrases or sentences are repeated and expanded in each episode. In *The Gingerbread Boy* (Galdone, 1975), for instance, the Gingerbread Boy repeats and expands his boast as he meets each character on his run away from the Little Old Man and the Little Old Woman.

3. *Rhyme and rhythm.*   Rhyme and rhythm are important devices in some books. The sentences have a strong beat, and rhyme is used at the end of each line or in another poetic scheme. Also, some books have an internal rhyme within lines rather than at the end of rhymes. One example of a book in this category is Dr. Seuss's *Hop on Pop* (1963).

4. *Sequential patterns.*   Some books use a familiar sequence, such as months of the year, days of the week, numbers 1 to 10, or letters of the alphabet, to structure the text. For example, *The Very Hungry Caterpillar* (Carle, 1969) combines number and day-of-the-week sequences as the caterpillar eats through an amazing array of foods during the week.

A list of predictable books illustrating each of these patterns is presented in Figure 10–6.

Adapting Reading Workshop for Emergent Readers

Even emergent readers can participate in reading workshop. Like all students, young children need opportunities to look at books, reread favorite stories, and explore new texts. Young children read and reread many predictable books and read easy-to-read books with decodable words and familiar sight words, such as *Commander Toad in Space* (Yolen, 1980) and *The Josefina Story Quilt* (Coerr, 1986). As they read and reread books, children gain valuable experience with books, develop concepts about print, and practice decoding words. Providing daily opportunities for children to practice reading and rereading books that they have chosen themselves is an essential part of a balanced reading program.

Kindergartners and other children who are not yet reading can "look" at books, too. Teachers begin by demonstrating looking at both familiar and unfamiliar books.

FIGURE 10–6   Predictable Books

Repetitive Sentences

Asch, F. (1981). *Just like Daddy.* New York: Simon & Schuster.

Bennett, J. (1985). *Teeny tiny.* New York: Putnam.

Brown, R. (1981). *A dark, dark tale.* New York: Dial.

Carle, E. (1973). *Have you seen my cat?* New York: Philomel.

Carle, E. (1984). *The very busy spider.* New York: Philomel.

Carle, E. (1990). *The very quiet cricket.* New York: Philomel.

Gag, W. (1956). *Millions of cats.* New York: Coward-McCann.

Galdone, P. (1973). *The little red hen.* New York: Seabury.

Guarino, D. (1989). *Is your mama a llama?* New York: Scholastic.

Hill, E. (1980). *Where's Spot?* New York: Putnam.

Hutchins, P. (1972). *Good-night, owl!* New York: Macmillan.

Hutchins, P. (1986). *The doorbell rang.* New York: Morrow.

Martin, B., Jr. (1983). *Brown bear, brown bear, what do you see?* New York: Holt, Rinehart & Winston.

Martin, B., Jr. (1992). *Polar bear, polar bear, what do you hear?* New York: Holt, Rinehart & Winston.

Peek, M. (1981). *Roll over!* Boston: Houghton Mifflin.

Peek, M. (1985). *Mary wore her red dress.* New York: Clarion.

Rosen, M. (1989). *We're going on a bear hunt.* New York: Macmillan.

Weiss, N. (1987). *If you're happy and you know it.* New York: Greenwillow.

Weiss, N. (1989). *Where does the brown bear go?* New York: Viking.

Westcott, N. B. (1988). *The lady with the alligator purse.* Boston: Little, Brown.

Wickstrom, S. K. (1988). *Wheels on the bus.* New York: Crown.

Williams, S. (1989). *I went walking.* San Diego: Harcourt Brace Jovanovich.

Repetitive Sentences in a Cumulative Structure

Brett, J. (1989). *The mitten.* New York: Putnam.

Flack, M. (1932). *Ask Mr. Bear.* New York: Macmillan.

Fox, H. (1986). *Hattie and the fox.* New York: Bradbury.

Galdone, P. (1975). *The gingerbread boy.* New York: Seabury.

Kellogg, S. (1974). *There was an old woman.* New York: Parents.

Kraus, R. (1970). *Whose mouse are you?* New York: Macmillan.

Tolstoi, A. (1968). *The great big enormous turnip.* New York: Watts.

Westcott, N. B. (1980). *I know an old lady who swallowed a fly.* Boston: Little, Brown.

Zemach, H. (1969). *The judge.* New York: Farrar, Straus & Giroux.

Zemach, M. (1983). *The little red hen.* New York: Farrar, Straus & Giroux.

Rhyme and Rhythm

Brown, M. (1987). *Play rhymes.* New York: Dutton.

de Paola, T. (1985). *Hey diddle diddle and other Mother Goose rhymes.* New York: Putnam.

Messenger, J. (1986). *Twinkle, twinkle, little star.* New York: Macmillan.

Sendak, M. (1962). *Chicken soup with rice.* New York: Harper & Row.

Seuss, Dr. (1963). *Hop on Pop.* New York: Random House.

Seuss, Dr. (1988). *Green eggs and ham.* New York: Random House.

Sequential Patterns

Alain. (1964). *One, two, three, going to sea.* New York: Scholastic.

Carle, E. (1969). *The very hungry caterpillar.* Cleveland: Collins-World.

Carle, E. (1977). *The grouchy ladybug.* New York: Crowell.

Carle, E. (1987). *A house for a hermit crab.* Saxonville, MA: Picture Book Studio.

Domanska, J. (1985). *Busy Monday morning.* New York: Greenwillow.

Keats, E. J. (1973). *Over in the meadow.* New York: Scholastic.

Mack, S. (1974). *10 bears in my bed.* New York: Pantheon.

Numeroff, L. J. (1985). *If you give a mouse a cookie.* New York: HarperCollins.

Numeroff, L. J. (1991). *If you give a moose a muffin.* New York: HarperCollins.

Wood, A. (1984). *The napping house.* San Diego: Harcourt Brace Jovanovich.

For familiar texts, teachers demonstrate how to think about the book and, perhaps, how to remember the title, characters, or plot. Then teachers model how to turn the pages and think aloud about the story, re-creating it in their minds. For unfamiliar books, teachers show children how to carefully examine the illustrations and create a probable text for the books. Without this training, young children often flip through a book without looking at each page and developing an appreciation for the book.

Reading workshop is often used in conjunction with literature focus units, but some first- and second-grade teachers alternate the two. Once children are able to read and reread predictable texts and decode some words, they can use reading workshop. First and second graders can read independently for 20 to 30 minutes and participate in minilessons and sharing, as older students do.

Other Instructional Approaches

Two other instructional approaches that teachers use with young children are assisted reading and language experience. These approaches are more personal, based on children's own experiences and language, and they more closely approximate the literacy activities that go on at home. These two approaches are both useful for older nonreaders, too.

Assisted Reading.   **Assisted reading** extends the familiar routine of parents reading to their children (Hoskisson, 1975). In this approach, a child and a teacher, parent, or other fluent reader sit together to read a book. At first, the teacher does most of the reading, and gradually the child assumes more and more of the reading until the child is doing most of it, with the teacher supplying only a few unfamiliar words. Teachers, aides, and parent volunteers can use assisted reading one-on-one with children to introduce them to concepts about written language. The main drawback is that one-on-one reading is time-consuming. Even spending ten minutes a week with each child can take five hours per week—approximately one hour each day—with a class of 30 students.

One way to make assisted reading more feasible in classrooms is to use a class of upper-grade students in a cross-age reading buddies program with primary-grade children. Older students read books aloud to younger children, and they also read with the children using assisted reading. The effectiveness of cross-age tutoring is supported by research (Cohen, Kulik, & Kulik, 1982), and teachers report that students' reading fluency and attitudes toward school and learning improve (Labbo & Teale, 1990; Morrice & Simmons, 1991).

Teachers arranging a buddy-reading program decide when students will get together, how long each session will last, and what the schedule will be. Primary-grade teachers explain the program to their students and talk about activities the buddies will be doing together, and upper-grade teachers explain to their students how to work with young children. In particular, they should teach students how to read aloud and encourage children to make predictions, how to use assisted reading, how to select books to appeal to younger children, and how to help them respond to books. Then older students choose books to read aloud and practice reading them until they can read the books fluently.

At the first meeting, the students pair off, get acquainted, and read together. They also talk about the books they read and perhaps write in special reading logs. Buddies also may want to go to the library and choose the books they will read at the next session.

There are significant social benefits to cross-age tutoring programs, too. Children get acquainted with other children they might otherwise not meet and learn how to work with older or younger children. As they talk about books they have read, they share personal experiences and interpretations. They also talk about reading strategies, how to choose books, and their favorite authors or illustration styles. Sometimes reading buddies write notes back and forth, or the two classrooms plan holiday celebrations together. These activities strengthen the social connections between the children.

A second way to encourage more one-on-one reading is to involve parents in the program by using traveling bags of books. Teachers collect text sets of four or five books on various topics for children to take home and read with their parents (Reutzel & Fawson, 1990). For example, teachers might collect copies of *Hattie and the Fox* (Fox, 1986), *The Gingerbread Boy* (Galdone, 1975), *Flossie and the Fox* (McKissack, 1986), and *Rosie's Walk* (Hutchins, 1968) for a traveling bag of fox stories. Then children and their parents read one or more of the books using assisted reading and draw or write a response to the books they have read in the reading log that accompanies the books in the traveling bag. Children keep the bag at home for several days, often rereading the books each day with their parents, and then return it to school so that another child can borrow it. Text sets for ten traveling bags are listed in Figure 10–7. Many of these text sets include combinations of stories, informational books, and poems. Teachers can also add small toys, stuffed animals, audiotapes of one or more of the books, or other related objects to the bags.

Teachers often introduce traveling bags at a special parents' meeting or open-house get-together and explain to parents how to use assisted reading to read with their children. It is important that parents understand that their children may not be familiar with the books and that children are not expected to be able to read them independently. Teachers also talk about the responses children and parents write in the reading log and show sample entries from the previous year.

Language Experience Approach. The **language experience approach** (LEA) is based on children's language and experiences (Ashton-Warner, 1965; Stauffer, 1970). In this approach, children dictate words and sentences about their experiences, and the teacher writes down what the children say. The text they develop becomes the reading material. Because the language comes from the children themselves and the content is based on their experiences, they are usually able to read the text easily. Reading and writing are connected, as students are actively involved in reading what they have written.

Using this approach, students can create individual booklets. They draw pictures on each page or cut pictures from magazines to glue on each page, and then they dictate the text that the teacher writes beside the illustration on each page. Students can also make a class book, or they can each create one page to be added to a class book. For example, as part of the unit on "The Three Bears," Mrs. Mast's students wrote a collaborative book on bears. Students each chose a fact they knew about bears for their page. They drew an illustration and dictated the text for Mrs. Mast to record. An example of one page from the class book is shown in Figure 10–8. Mrs. Mast took the students' dictation rather than having the children write the book themselves because she wanted it to be written in conventional spelling so that students could read and reread the book.

Teachers also take children's dictation to write charts about what the class is learning about literature or in connection with social studies or science themes. Stu-

FIGURE 10–7   Text Sets for Traveling Bags

Books About Airplanes

Barton, R. (1982). *Airport*. New York: Harper & Row.
McPhail, D. (1987). *First flight*. Boston: Little, Brown.
Petersen, D. (1981). *Airplanes* (A new true book). Chicago: Childrens Press.
Ziegler, S. (1988). *A visit to the airport*. Chicago: Childrens Press.

Books About Dogs

Barracca, D., & Barracca, S. (1990). *The adventures of taxi dog*. New York: Dial.
Bridwell, N. (1963). *Clifford the big red dog*. New York: Greenwillow.
Cole, J. (1991). *My puppy is born*. New York: Morrow.
Reiser, L. (1992). *Any kind of dog*. New York: Greenwillow.

Books by Ezra Jack Keats

Keats, E. J. (1962). *The snowy day*. New York: Viking.
Keats, E. J. (1964). *Whistle for Willie*. New York: Viking.
Keats, E. J. (1967). *Peter's chair*. New York: Harper & Row.
Keats, E. J. (1969). *Goggles*. New York: Macmillan.
Keats, E. J. (1970). *Hi cat!* New York: Macmillan.

Books About Frogs and Toads

Lobel, A. (1970). *Frog and toad are friends*. New York: Harper & Row.
Mayer, M. (1974). *Frog goes to dinner*. New York: Dial.
Pallotta, J. (1990). *The frog alphabet book: And other awesome amphibians*. Watertown, MA: Charlesbridge.
Watts, B. (1991). *Frog*. New York: Lodestar.
Yolen, J. (1980). *Commander Toad in space*. New York: Coward-McCann.

Books About Mice

Cauley, L. B. (1984). *The town mouse and the country mouse*. New York: Putnam.
Henkes, K. (1991). *Chrysanthemum*. New York: Greenwillow.
Lionni, L. (1969). *Alexander and the wind-up mouse*. New York: Pantheon.
Lobel, A. (1977). *Mouse soup*. New York: Harper & Row.
Numeroff, L. J. (1985). *If you give a mouse a cookie*. New York: Harper & Row.

Books About Numbers

Aker, S. (1990). *What comes in 2's, 3's, & 4's?* New York: Simon & Schuster.
Bang, M. (1983). *Ten, nine, eight*. New York: Greenwillow.
Giganti, P., Jr. (1992). *Each orange had 8 slices: A counting book*. New York: Greenwillow.
Tafuri, N. (1986). *Who's counting?* New York: Greenwillow.

Books About Plants

Ehlert, L. (1991). *Red leaf, yellow leaf*. San Diego: Harcourt Brace Jovanovich.
Fowler, A. (1990). *It could still be a tree*. Chicago: Childrens Press.
Gibbons, G. (1984). *The seasons of Arnold's apple tree*. San Diego: Harcourt Brace Jovanovich.
King, E. (1990). *The pumpkin patch*. New York: Dutton.
Lobel, A. (1990). *Alison's zinnia*. New York: Greenwillow.

Books About Rain

Branley, F. M. (1985). *Flash, crash, rumble, and roll*. New York: Harper & Row.
Polacco, P. (1990). *Thunder cake*. New York: Philomel.
Shulevitz, U. (1969). *Rain rain rivers*. New York: Farrar, Straus & Giroux.
Spier, P. (1982). *Rain*. New York: Doubleday.

Books About the Three Bears

Cauley, L. B. (1981). *Goldilocks and the three bears*. New York: Putnam.
Galdone, P. (1972). *The three bears*. New York: Clarion Books.
Tolhurst, M. (1990). *Somebody and the three Blairs*. New York: Orchard Books.
Turkle, B. (1976). *Deep in the forest*. New York: Dutton.

Books About Trucks

Crews, D. (1980). *Truck*. New York: Greenwillow.
Owen, A. (1990). *Bumper to bumper*. New York: Knopf.
Rockwell, A. (1984). *Trucks*. New York: Dutton.
Rockwell, A. (1986). *Big wheels*. New York: Dutton.
Siebert, D. (1984). *Truck song*. New York: Harper & Row.

FIGURE 10–8   One Page From a Kindergarten Class Book About Bears

Polar bears live in ice and snow.

Jesse

dents in Mrs. Mast's kindergarten class, for example, dictated the facts they learned about grizzly, brown, and polar bears in the vignette at the beginning of this chapter. After watching a video about trees, kindergartners in another class dictated this message during a theme on the four seasons:

> *Trees change during the four seasons. New leaves and flowers grow on trees during the spring. In the summer, leaves are pretty green. Fruit is growing on apple trees and on peach trees. Nuts grow on some trees, too. In the autumn the fruit is ready to pick and eat. The leaves turn colors—yellow, orange, red, and brown—and then they fall to the ground. In the winter the trees rest and get ready for the next year.*

It is a great temptation to change the child's language to the teacher's own, in either word choice or grammar, but editing should be kept to a minimum so that children do not get the impression that their language is inferior or inadequate.

It is interesting that, as children become familiar with dictating to the teacher, they learn to pace their dictation to the teacher's writing speed. At first, children dictate as they think of ideas, but with experience they watch as the teacher writes and supply the text word by word.

The language experience approach is an effective way to help children emerge into reading. Even students who have not been successful with other types of reading activities can read what they have dictated. There is a drawback, however; teachers provide a "perfect" model when they take children's dictation—they write neatly and spell words correctly. After language experience activities, some young children are not eager to do their own writing. They prefer their teacher's "perfect" writing to their own childlike writing. To avoid this problem, young children should be doing their own writing in personal journals and responding to literature activities at the same time they are participating in language experience activities. This way, they will learn that sometimes they do their own writing and at other times the teacher takes their dictation.

YOUNG CHILDREN EMERGE INTO WRITING

Many young children become writers before entering kindergarten, and the rest are introduced to writing during their first year of school (Harste, Woodward, & Burke, 1984; Temple, Nathan, Burris, & Temple, 1988). Young children's writing development follows a pattern similar to children's reading development: emergent writing, beginning writing, and fluent writing. In the first stage, emergent writing, children make scribbles to represent writing. At first the scribbles may appear randomly on a page, but with experience children line up the letters or scribbles from left to right and from top to bottom. Children also begin to "read," or tell what their writing says. The next stage is beginning writing, and it marks children's growing awareness of the alphabetic principle. Children use invented spelling to represent words, and as they learn more about sound-symbol correspondences their writing approximates conventional spelling. The third stage is fluent writing, when children use conventional spelling and other conventions of written language, including capital letters and punctuation marks.

Opportunities for writing begin on the first day of kindergarten and continue on a daily basis through the primary grades, regardless of whether children have already learned to read or write letters and spell words. Children often begin using a combination of art and scribbles or letterlike forms to express themselves, and their writing moves toward conventional forms as they apply concepts they are learning about written language.

Young children participate in many of the same types of writing activities that older students do. They use letters or words to label pictures they have drawn, describe experiences in journals, write letters to family members, and make books to share information. In their writing, children use a combination of adult spelling and invented spelling, or they have an idiosyncratic approach of using letters and other marks to represent words.

Introducing Young Children to Writing

Children are introduced to writing as they watch their parents and teachers write and as they experiment with drawing and writing. Teachers help children emerge into writing as they show them how to use kid writing, teach minilessons about written language, and involve children in writing activities.

Teachers demonstrate to children through morning messages and language experience approach activities that people use written language to represent their thoughts. However, adult models can be very intimidating to young children who feel at a loss to produce adult writing that is neatly written and spelled conventionally. Teachers can contrast their writing—adult writing—with the "kid" writing that children can do. Kid writing takes many different forms. It can be scribbles or a collection of random marks on paper. Sometimes children are imitating adults' cursive writing as they scribble. Children can string together letters that have no phoneme-grapheme correspondences, or they can use one or two letters to represent entire words. Children with more experience with written language can invent spellings that represent more sound features of words, and they can apply spelling rules. A child's spellings of "Abbie is my good dog. I love her very much" over a year and a half are presented in Figure 10–9. The child moves from using scribbles to using single letters to represent words, then to invented spelling, and finally to conventional spelling. In the fourth example, the child is experimenting with using periods to mark spaces between words.

FIGURE 10–9   Stages of Development in a Child's "Kid" Writing

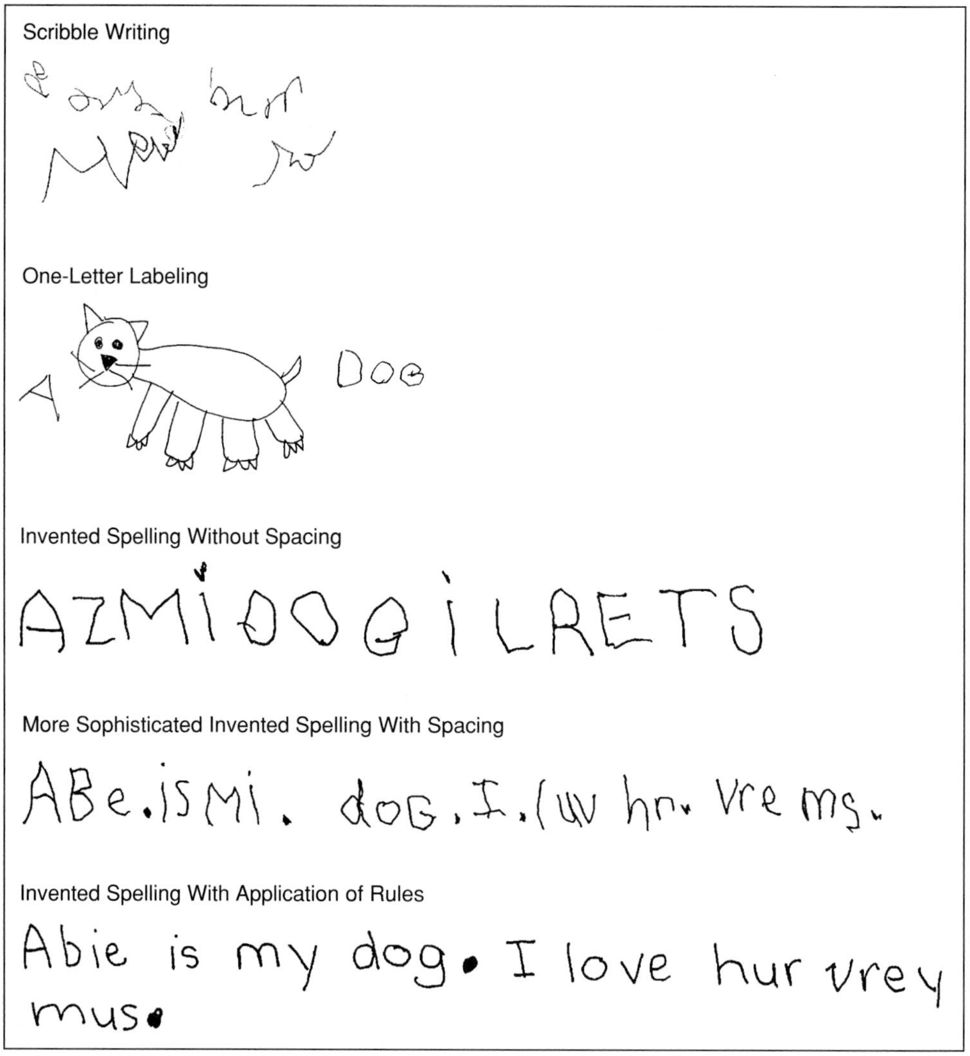

Kid writing is an important concept for young children because it gives them permission to experiment with written language when they draw and write. Too often children assume they should write and spell like adults do, and they cannot. Without this confidence, children do not want to write, or they ask teachers to spell every word or copy text out of books or from charts. Kid spelling teaches students several strategies for writing, and it gives them permission to invent spellings that reflect their knowledge of written language.

Young children's writing grows out of talk and drawing. As children begin to write, their writing is literally their talk written down, and they can usually express in writing the ideas they talk about. At the same time, children's letterlike marks develop from their drawing. With experience, children differentiate between drawing and writing. Some kindergarten teachers explain to children that they should use crayons when they draw and use pencils when they write. Teachers can also differentiate where on a page children write and draw. The writing might go at the top or bottom of a page, or children can use paper with space for drawing at the top and lines for writing at the bottom.

Adapting the Writing Process for Young Children

Teachers often simplify the writing process for young children by abbreviating the revising and editing stages of the writing process. At first children's revising is limited to reading the text to themselves or to the teacher to check that they have written all that they want to say. Revising becomes more formal as children learn about audience and decide they want to "add more" or "fix" their writing to make it appeal to their classmates. Some emergent writers ignore editing altogether—as soon as they have dashed off their drafts, they are ready to publish or share their writing. However, others change a spelling, fix a poorly written letter, or add a period to the end of the text as they read over their writings. When children begin writing, teachers accept children's writing as it is written and focus on the message. As children gain experience with writing, teachers encourage children to "fix" more and more of their errors. Guidelines for adapting the writing process for emergent writers are presented in Figure 10–10.

Writing Centers.   Writing centers can be set up in kindergarten classrooms so that children have a special place where they can go to write. The center should be located at a table with chairs, and a box of supplies, including pencils, crayons, a date stamp, different kinds of paper, journal notebooks, a stapler, blank books, notepaper, and envelopes, should be stored nearby. The alphabet, printed in upper- and lowercase letters, should be available on the table for children to refer to as they write. In addition,

Young children draw and write in journals and make books at the writing center.

FIGURE 10–10   Guidelines for Adapting the Writing Process for Emergent Writers

Prewriting

Prewriting is as important to young children as it is to other writers. Children write about topics they know well and have the vocabulary to express ideas about. Topics include personal experiences, classroom activities, stories students have listened to read aloud or have read independently, and theme cycle topics. Children use drawing to gather and organize ideas before writing. Children often talk about the topic or dramatize it before beginning to write.

Drafting

Young children usually write single-draft compositions. They add words to accompany drawings they have already made. The emphasis is on expressing ideas, not on handwriting skills or conventional spelling. Often children write in small booklets of paper, and they write equally well on lined or unlined paper.

Revising

Teachers play down this stage until children have learned the importance of revising to meet the needs of their readers. At first children reread their writings to see that they have included everything they wanted to say, and they make very few changes. As they gain experience, they begin to make changes to make their writing clearer and add more information to make their writing more complete.

Editing

Like revising, this stage is de-emphasized until children have learned conventional spellings for some words and have gained control over rules for capitalizing words and adding punctuation marks. To introduce editing, teachers help children make one or two corrections by erasing the error and writing the correction in pencil on the child's writing. Teachers do not circle errors on a child's paper with a red pen. As children become more fluent writers, teachers help them make more corrections.

Publishing

Children read their writings to their classmates and share their drawings. Through sharing, children develop a concept of audience and learn new ways of writing from their classmates. Kindergartners and first graders usually do not recopy their writings, but sometimes the teacher or an assistant types the final copy, changing the child's writing into conventional form. When adults recopy children's writing, however, they send a strong message that the children's writing is inadequate, unless there is a good reason for converting the kid writing to adult writing.

there should be a crate for children to file their work in. They can also share their completed writings by sending them to classmates or sharing them in the author's chair.

When children come to the writing center, they draw and write in journals, compile books, and write messages to classmates. Teachers should be available to encourage and assist children at the center. They can observe children as they invent spellings and can provide information about letters, words, and sentences as needed. If the teacher cannot be at the writing center, perhaps an aide, a parent volunteer, or an upper-grade student can assist.

The Author's Chair.   In primary-grade classrooms a special chair should be designated as the **author's chair** (Graves & Hansen, 1983). This chair might be a rocking chair, a lawnchair with a padded seat, a wooden stool, or a director's chair, and it should be labeled "Author's Chair." Children and the teacher sit in the chair to share books they have read and other books they have written, and this is the only time anyone sits in the chair.

When teachers sit in the chair to read books aloud to children, they name the author of the book and, if possible, tell a little something about the author. In this way, children gain an awareness of authors, the people who write books. Children also sit in the author's chair to share books and other compositions they have written. Sitting in the special author's chair helps children to gradually realize that they are authors. Graves and Hansen (1983) identify three stages in children's growing awareness of authors and of themselves as authors:

1. *Authors write books.*   After hearing many books read to them and reading books themselves, children develop the concept that authors are the people who write books.

2. *I am an author.*   Sharing the books they have written with classmates from the author's chair helps children view themselves as authors.

3. *If I wrote this published book now, I wouldn't write it this way.*   Children learn that they have options when they write, and this awareness grows after experimenting with various writing functions, forms, and audiences.

When children share their writings, one child sits in the author's chair and a group of children sit on the floor or in chairs in front of the author's chair. The child sitting in the author's chair reads the book or other piece of writing aloud and shows the accompanying illustrations. Then children who want to make a comment raise their hands, and the author chooses several children to ask questions, give compliments, and make comments. Then the author chooses another child to share and takes a seat in the audience.

Writing as Part of Literature Focus Units

Young children use writing during several steps of the reading process. As they read and respond to books, emergent readers use a combination of art and writing as they make entries in their reading logs. Figure 10–11 presents two reading log entries. The first shows a kindergartner's response to *If You Give a Mouse a Cookie* (Numeroff, 1985). The child's kid writing says, "I love chocolate chip cookies." The second entry was written by a first grader after reading *Are You My Mother?* (Eastman, 1965). The child wrote, "The bird said, 'Are you my mother, you big ole Snort?'" After students shared their log entries during a grand conversation, this student added, "The mommy said, 'Here is a worm. I am here. I'm here.'" You will notice that the part that the mother says is written as though it were coming out of the bird's mouth and going up into the air.

FIGURE 10–11   Two Emergent Writers' Reading Log Entries

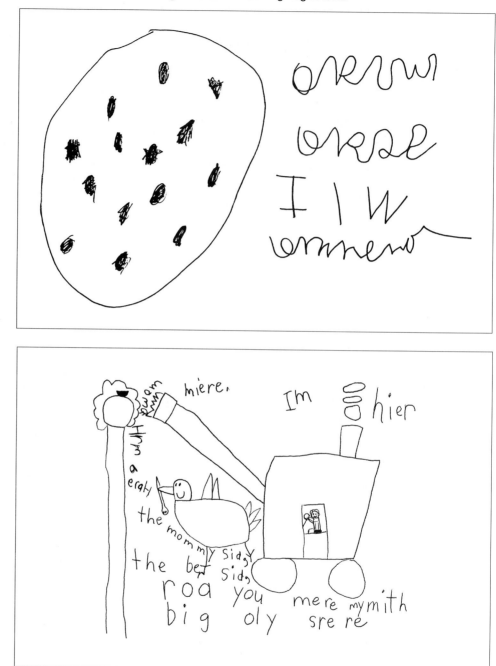

Young children also use writing as they develop projects after reading. They make books based on the books they have read. They can use the same patterns as in *Polar Bear, Polar Bear, What Do You Hear?* (Martin, 1991), *If You Give a Mouse a Cookie* (Numeroff, 1985), and *If the Dinosaurs Came Back* (Most, 1978), for example, to create innovations, or new versions of familiar stories. A first grader's four-page book about a mouse named Jerry, written after reading *If You Give a Mouse a Cookie*, is

FIGURE 10–12 A First Grader's Innovation for *If You Give a Mouse a Cookie*

shown in Figure 10–12. In these writing projects, children often use invented spelling, but they are encouraged to spell familiar words correctly. They also learn to use the books they are reading to check the spelling of characters' names and other words from the story.

Review

Emergent literacy is the new way of looking at how children begin to read and write. Children's emergent literacy provides a foundation for their later literacy learning. Teachers foster young children's interest in written language through morning messages, literacy play centers, sign-in sheets, and mailboxes for exchanging messages. Literature focus units and reading workshop are used in kindergarten and the primary grades for reading instruction. Assisted reading and language experience approach are ways to introduce young children to reading. As children emerge into writing they move from scribbling to using letters to represent their thoughts, and they refine their "kid" writing as they learn about phoneme-grapheme correspondences and spelling patterns. Effective teaching practices for working with emergent readers and writers are reviewed in the figure on page 392.

Effective Practices

1. Children begin developmentally appropriate reading and writing activities on the first day of kindergarten.

2. Teachers teach concepts about print through shared reading, language experience approach, and other instructional strategies.

3. Teachers provide opportunities for children to practice writing their names for genuine purposes, including sign-in sheets in kindergarten.

4. Teachers include literacy materials in play centers.

5. Teachers incorporate all five steps of the reading process in literature focus units.

6. Teachers use shared reading with big books.

7. Teachers provide opportunities for daily reading and writing experiences.

8. Teachers adapt the writing process and emphasize prewriting, drafting, and publishing stages.

9. Teachers introduce "kid" writing and encourage children to use invented spelling.

10. Teachers set up a writing center, mailboxes, and an author's chair in their classrooms.

11. Teachers use predictable books and encourage children to use the pattern in order to read independently.

Ineffective Practices

1. Teachers provide readiness activities to prepare children for reading and writing instruction.

2. Teachers rarely model reading and writing for children.

3. Teachers write children's names for them because they do not realize children can write them themselves.

4. Teachers do not include materials for functional reading and writing activities in play centers.

5. Teachers do not teach using literature focus units, or use only two or three steps in their instructional units.

6. Teachers only use small books.

7. Teachers emphasize play and provide few opportunities for reading and writing.

8. Teachers rarely have children do writing and do not introduce the writing process.

9. Teachers assume children can't write because they can't write like adults.

10. Teachers focus on teaching handwriting, not writing.

11. Teachers assume children can't read independently, so they don't show them how to use the patterns in predictable books.

References

Ashton-Warner, S. (1965). *Teacher.* New York: Simon & Schuster.

Bridge, C. A. (1979). Predictable materials for beginning readers. *Language Arts, 56,* 503–507.

Clay, M. M. (1967). The reading behaviour of five year old children. *New Zealand Journal of Educational Studies, 2,* 11–31.

Clay, M. M. (1972). *Reading: The patterning of complex behavior.* Portsmouth, NH: Heinemann.

Clay, M. M. (1975). *What did I write? Beginning writing behavior.* Portsmouth, NH: Heinemann.

Clay, M. M. (1979). *The early detection of reading difficulties.* Portsmouth, NH: Heinemann.

Clay, M. M. (1989). Foreword. In D. S. Strickland & L. M. Morrow (Eds.)., *Emerging literacy: Young children learn to read and write.* Newark, DE: International Reading Association.

Cohen, P., Kulik, J. A., & Kulik, C. (1982). Educational outcomes of tutoring: A meta-analysis of findings. *American Educational Research Journal, 19,* 237–248.

Downing, J. (1970). The development of linguistic concepts in children's thinking. *Research in the Teaching of English, 4,* 5–19.

Downing, J. (1971–1972). Children's developing concepts of spoken and written language. *Journal of Reading Behavior, 4,* 1–19.

Downing, J., & Oliver, P. (1973–1974). The child's conception of "a word." *Reading Research Quarterly, 9,* 568–582.

Durkin, D. (1966). *Children who read early.* New York: Teachers College Press.

Dyson, A. H. (1984). "N spells my grandmama": Fostering early thinking about print. *The Reading Teacher, 38,* 262–271.

Fisher, B. (1991). *Joyful learning: A whole language kindergarten.* Portsmouth, NH: Heinemann.

Graves, D. H., & Hansen, J. (1983). The author's chair. *Language Arts, 60,* 176–183.

Harste, J., Woodward, V., & Burke, C. (1984). *Language stories and literacy lessons.* Portsmouth, NH: Heinemann.

Heald-Taylor, G. (1987). How to use predictable books for K–2 language arts instruction. *The Reading Teacher, 40,* 656–661.

Heath, S. B. (1983). *Ways with words.* New York: Oxford University Press.

Holdaway, D. (1979). *The foundations of literacy.* Portsmouth, NH: Heinemann.

Hoskisson, K. (1975). The many facets of assisted reading. *Elementary English, 52,* 312–315.

Juel, C. (1991). Beginning reading. In R. Barr, M. L. Kamil, P. Mosenthal, & P. D. Pearson (Eds.), *Handbook of reading research* (Vol. 2, pp. 759–788). New York: Longman.

Kawakami-Arakaki, A., Oshiro, M., & Farran, S. (1989). Research to practice: Integrating reading and writing in a kindergarten curriculum. In J. Mason (Ed.), *Reading and writing connections* (pp. 199–218). Boston: Allyn & Bacon.

Labbo, L. D., & Teale, W. H. (1990). Cross-age reading: A strategy for helping poor readers. *The Reading Teacher, 43,* 362–369.

Morrice, C., & Simmons, M. (1991). Beyond reading buddies: A whole language cross-age program. *The Reading Teacher, 44,* 572–577.

Papandropoulou, I., & Sinclair, H. (1974). What is a word? Experimental study of children's ideas on grammar. *Human Development, 17,* 241–258.

Reutzel, D. R., & Fawson, P. C. (1990). Traveling tales: Connecting parents and children in writing. *The Reading Teacher, 44,* 222–227.

Schickedanz, J. A. (1990). *Adam's righting revolutions: One child's literacy development from infancy through grade one.* Portsmouth, NH: Heinemann.

Slaughter, J. P. (1983). Big books for little kids: Another fad or a new approach for teaching beginning reading? *The Reading Teacher, 36,* 758–762.

Stauffer, R. G. (1970). *The language experience approach to the teaching of reading.* New York: Harper & Row.

Sulzby, E. (1985). Kindergartners as readers and writers. In M. Farr (Ed.), *Advances in writing research. Vol. 1: Children's early writing development* (pp. 127–199). Norwood, NJ: Ablex.

Taylor, D. (1983). *Family literacy: Young children learning to read and write.* Exeter, NH: Heinemann.

Taylor, D., & Dorsey-Gaines, C. (1987). *Growing up literate: Learning from inner-city families.* Portsmouth, NH: Heinemann.

Teale, W. H. (1982). Toward a theory of how children learn to read and write. *Language Arts, 59,* 555–570.

Teale, W. H., & Sulzby, E. (1989). Emerging literacy: New perspectives. In D. S. Strickland & L. M. Morrow (Eds.), *Emerging literacy: Young children learn to read and write* (pp. 1–15). Newark, DE: International Reading Association.

Temple, C., Nathan, R., Burris, N., & Temple, F. (1988). *The beginnings of writing.* Boston: Allyn & Bacon.

Templeton, S. (1980). Young children invent words: Developing concepts of "word-ness." *The Reading Teacher, 33,* 454–459.

Tompkins, G. E., & Webeler, M. (1983). What will happen next? Using predictable books with young children. *The Reading Teacher, 36,* 498–502.

Trachtenburg, R., & Ferruggia, A. (1989). Big books from little voices: Reaching high risk beginning readers. *The Reading Teacher, 42,* 284–289.

Children's Book References

Brett, J. (1987). *Goldilocks and the three bears*. New York: Sandcastle.

Bridwell, N. (1963). *Clifford the big red dog*. New York: Four Winds Press.

Carle, E. (1969). *The very hungry caterpillar*. Cleveland: Collins-World.

Cauley, L. B. (1981). *Goldilocks and the three bears*. New York: Putnam.

Coerr, E. (1986). *The Josefina story quilt*. New York: Harper & Row.

Dr. Seuss. (1963). *Hop on pop*. New York: Random House.

Eastman, P. D. (1960). *Are you my mother?* New York: Random House.

Fowler, A. (1992). *It could still be water*. Chicago: Childrens Press.

Fox, M. (1986). *Hattie and the fox*. New York: Bradbury Press.

Galdone, P. (1972). *The three bears*. Boston: Houghton Mifflin.

Galdone, P. (1973). *The little red hen*. New York: Seabury.

Galdone, P. (1975). *The gingerbread boy*. New York: Seabury.

Gill, S. (1990). *Alaska's three bears*. Homer, AK: Paws IV.

Hutchins, P. (1968). *Rosie's walk*. New York: Macmillan.

Martin, B., Jr. (1991). *Polar bear, polar bear, what do you hear?* New York: Henry Holt.

Mayer, M. (1992). *Just Grandma and me*. Novato, CA: Broderbund.

McKissack, P. C. (1986). *Flossie and the fox*. New York: Dial.

Most, B. (1978). *If the dinosaurs came back*. San Diego: Harcourt Brace.

Numeroff, L. J. (1985). *If you give a mouse a cookie*. New York: Harper & Row.

Prelutsky, J. (1984). *The new kid on the block*. New York: Greenwillow.

Turkle, B. (1976). *Deep in the forest*. New York: Dutton.

Waber, B. (1972). *Ira sleeps over*. Boston: Houghton Mifflin.

Yolen, J. (1980). *Commander Toad in space*. New York: Coward McCann.

CHAPTER 11
Reading and Writing Across the Curriculum

do they live.
ks their eggs?
r enemies?
ir eggs hatch?
ey black and white?
y live in places that
cold?
me different colors?
re so many different

nt names?
they have fur instead
y fly?
penguin?
so fuzzy?
called penguins?

Mrs. Roberts's first and second graders begin their two-week unit on penguins by starting a **K-W-L chart** (Ogle, 1986) (see the Compendium for more information about this and all other highlighted terms in this chapter). Mrs. Roberts asks students what they already know about penguins and records their information in the "K: What We Know" column. Students mention that penguins live at the South Pole, that they eat fish, and that they can swim. Paula asks if penguins can fly, and Mrs. Roberts writes this question as the first entry in the "W: What We Want to Learn" column. As the discussion continues, more information and questions are added to the chart. The third column, "L: What We Learned," is still empty, but later in the unit Mrs. Roberts and her students will add entries for that column.

Students read stories and informational books about penguins during their language arts block and continue studying about penguins during science. During the first week of the two-week theme study, they read *Tacky the Penguin* (Lester, 1988) and examine the beginning, middle, and end of the story. They make posters diagramming the three parts. Students also make "circles" of a **story quilt** to celebrate the story. Students write their favorite quotes from the story around the outside of the circles, and in the middle of the circles they draw pictures of Tacky.

Mrs. Roberts has collected a text set of books about penguins for this theme study. Some books are stories, and others are informational books. She also locates several poems to display on large charts. She reads some of the books aloud, such as *Little Penguin's Tale* (Wood, 1989), students read some books during reading workshop, and others she saves for students to read during book clubs during the second week of the unit.

Mrs. Roberts's class has reading workshop for 30 minutes each day. In order to have books that all children can read, in addition to books in the text set, Mrs. Roberts develops predictable books and other patterned books so that all children can read at their own developmental level. She created one book based on *Brown Bear, Brown Bear, What Do You See?* (Martin, 1983). The book begins this way:

Page 1:   *Little penguin, little penguin, what do you see?*
Page 2:   *I see a leopard seal looking at me.*
Page 3:   *Leopard seal, leopard seal, what do you see?*
Page 4:   *I see two gulls looking at me.*
Page 5:   *Two gulls, two gulls, what do you see?*

Mrs. Roberts has also created a number book with pictures of penguins and related objects. It begins this way:

Page 1:   *One fish for a hungry penguin.*
Page 2:   *Two penguins standing by a nest.*
Page 3:   *Three seals hunting for a penguin.*

Another book is a "T is for Tacky" book. On each page, Mrs. Roberts has drawn a picture of something beginning with *T* (e.g., a telephone, a taxi, a tiger) along with a picture of Tacky and a talking balloon. In the talking balloon is the single word for the item beginning with *T*. On the page with the telephone, the sentence at the bottom of the page says, "T is for Tacky and telephone."

Each year when Mrs. Roberts teaches this unit, she works with a small group of emergent readers in her class to create another predictable book. This year the small group decides to make "What Can Penguins Do?" Students decide on these sentences:

Penguins can swim.
Penguins can dive
Penguins can eat fish.
Penguins can waddle.
Penguins can sit on nests.
Penguins can lay eggs.
Penguins can feed babies.
But, penguins cannot fly!

Together, Mrs. Roberts and the small group of students draw and color the pictures, add the sentences, and compile the book. Then they share it with the other students in the class.

During the second week of the unit, students form book clubs. Mrs. Roberts does a **book talk** about these four informational books, and students choose one of them to read:

■ *It Could Still Be a Bird* (Fowler, 1990), a book that describes the characteristics of birds, using the predictable pattern "It could still be a bird."
■ *Penguin* (Fletcher, 1993), a book that describes the first two and a half years of a penguin's life.
■ *Antarctica* (Cowcher, 1990), a vividly illustrated book about penguins and other animals living in Antarctica.
■ *A Penguin Year* (Bonners, 1981), a book showing what penguins do during each season.

Students read the book they have chosen and talk about the book in a **grand conversation** with Mrs. Roberts or the student teacher. Later during the week, students reread the book as scientists, hunting for information about penguins to share with classmates. Students take notes on chart paper and then share what they have learned.

At the beginning of the unit, Mrs. Roberts posts a **word wall,** and she and her students add "science" words to the word wall during the unit. At the end of the unit, these words have been added:

Emperor penguins	rookery	Leopard seals
Adelie penguins	stand upright	birds
hatch from eggs	Antarctica	feathers
waddle	crests	flippers
swimmers	webbed feet	waterproof coat
divers	chicks	crop in throat
krill	skua gulls	nursery

Students use the words from the word wall as they write and talk about penguins, the books they are reading, and science they are learning. Students draw pictures of Antarctica and label at least eight things in their pictures using words from the word wall.

One of Mrs. Roberts's favorite vocabulary activities is "What Words Don't Belong?" (also called exclusion brainstorming). She makes a list of words, including some that don't relate to penguins:

penguins	polar bears	fly	swim
arctic	sing	chicks	webbed feet
krill	fur	seals	birds
wear clothes	eggs	nursery	hot
fish	ice	trees	rock nests

Students work in small groups to circle the words that don't belong, such as *polar bears, fly, hot,* and *trees.* As they share their papers with the class, students explain why the words they circled don't belong.

Mrs. Roberts uses words from the word wall as she teaches **minilessons** on phonemic awareness (segmenting and blending sounds in words), building words that rhyme with *chick* and with *coat,* and comparing *e* sounds in *egg, nests, feet,* and *seal.* She also teaches minilessons on *r*-controlled vowels, using *bIRds, LeopARd seals, nURsERy,* and *AntARctica* for the more advanced readers in her class.

As their project for the unit on penguins, Mrs. Roberts's students write "All About Penguins" books. They use a modified version of the writing process as they write their books. To begin, students brainstorm facts that they have learned about penguins, such as:

Penguins are black and white birds.

Penguins are covered with feathers.

Penguins are good swimmers, but they can't fly.

Mother penguins lay eggs.

Father penguins hold the eggs on their feet to keep them warm.

Penguin chicks stay together in the rookery.

Penguins look funny when they waddle on land.

Penguins eat fish and krill.

Leopard seals are a dangerous enemy, but people may be an even worse enemy.

Mrs. Roberts writes these facts on sentence strips (long strips of paper that fit into pocket charts). Students read and reread these facts and think about the facts they want to include in their "All About . . ." books.

Next, students collect five or six sheets of white paper for the inside of their books. They draw a picture and write a fact on each page. Most students invent spellings as they write, but a few locate the sentence strips and dutifully copy the fact so that their book will be written in "adult" spelling. As students write and draw, Mrs. Roberts circulates around the classroom, helping students choose facts, correcting their misconceptions about life in Antarctica, showing them how to draw penguins and

FIGURE 11–1   Excerpts From Two Students' Books About Penguins

other animals, and encouraging them to invent spellings. The only word Mrs. Roberts insists that students spell correctly is *penguin,* and she places word cards with the word at each table. All students are encouraged to check their spellings with words on the word wall, but Mrs. Roberts is more insistent that the more fluent writers check their spelling.

Pages from two students' penguin books are shown in Figure 11–1. The page about laying eggs was written by a second grader, and it says, "Penguins lay eggs and keep them warm with their feet and their stomachs." The page about seals eating penguins was written by a first grader who is learning English as a second language. The page says, "The seal likes to eat penguins." This first grader is experimenting with word boundaries, and he adds a dot between words. As he says the sentence, "to eat" sounds like one word to him. He also makes two word cards beside his picture.

After students finish drawing and writing facts, they compile their pages and add black and orange covers—penguin colors. Before students make their covers, Mrs. Roberts teaches a brief minilesson on choosing titles and explains how to capitalize all the important words in a title. Most students title their books "The Penguin Book" or "All About Penguins," but several students experiment with other titles. One child chooses "Penguins in Antarctica," and another child selects "The Adventures of Penguins." Students also add their names as the authors.

Students use reading and writing throughout the school day and across the curriculum as they learn science, social studies, math, and other curriculum areas. Just as Mrs. Roberts's first and second graders learned about penguins as they read stories and informational books, students at all grade levels read informational books, stories, and poems as they learn about insects, World War II, rain forests, flight, and ancient civilizations. They use particular reading and writing procedures and activities, such as K-W-L charts, exclusion brainstorming, and **individual reports,** as tools for learning.

Literature is just as important in learning about the world as it is for learning how to read. Students learn about energy, pioneers, fractions, the Constitution—all areas of the curriculum—through trade books. There are also content-area textbooks in social studies, science, math, and other curricular areas. In fact, sometimes the phrase "content-area reading and writing" is used instead of "reading and writing across the curriculum" to point out that students read content-area textbooks as they learn about science, social studies, and math.

The overall goal of content-area instruction is to help students construct their own understanding of key concepts. Students are naturally curious about the world, and they learn as they investigate new ideas. Students learn labels for concepts and develop new ways of expressing ideas. Reading and writing are useful learning tools, and through talking, reading, and writing, students explore concepts and make connections between what they are learning and what they already know. Students also apply what they are learning to their own lives; in order for students to learn, they must make connections between the concepts they are learning and their own lives.

Teachers organize content-area study into theme studies (also called themes, thematic units, and theme cycles) and identify key concepts for students to investigate. Often theme studies connect social studies, science, and other curricular areas. Themes are time-consuming because student-constructed learning takes time. Teachers can't try to cover every topic; if they do, their students will probably learn very little. Teachers must make careful choices as they plan units, because only a relatively few topics can be presented in-depth during a school year. During theme studies, students need opportunities to question, discuss, explore, and apply what they are learning. It takes time for students to become deeply involved in learning so that they can apply what they are learning in their own lives. The only way students acquire a depth of knowledge is by focusing on the big ideas or key concepts. Even the first and second graders in Mrs. Roberts's class learned key concepts about penguins. They learned (1) about the ecosystem in Antarctica, (2) how penguins have adapted to their environment, (3) about the life cycle of a penguin, and (4) that people pose a threat to the environment of Antarctica.

Think about these questions as you read this chapter:

- How do students use informational books, stories, and poems to learn science, social studies, and math?
- How can teachers help students read and understand content-area textbooks?
- How do students use reading and writing as tools for learning?
- How do teachers develop theme studies?

READING IS A LEARNING TOOL

Informational books are the most common type of literature used in teaching students about social studies, science, and math concepts, and students are often encouraged to read these books efferently, that is, to locate and remember information. However, students use both aesthetic and efferent reading as they read all types of reading materials. In addition to informational books, students read maps, newspapers, magazines, letters, brochures, and charts.

Reading is a tool for making sense of everyday life (Winograd & Higgins, 1994–1995). Many times students read entire books about content-area topics, and they may read the books aesthetically—to be carried off to Antarctica or somewhere else in the world, back in time to ancient Egypt or another period in history, or, through a biography or autobiography, to walk in someone else's shoes and see the world from someone else's perspective—Theodore Roosevelt's or Helen Keller's, for example. At other times, students use either skimming or scanning to read rapidly through a book, especially an informational book. When students skim, they read rapidly to get a general idea of material that they will later reread more slowly and carefully. At other times, they scan or search through a book to locate specific information. As they use informational books in social studies and science, students learn how to skim and scan as well as when these two types of reading are appropriate.

Reading Informational Books

Children are curious, and they read informational books to know about the world around them. They learn about whales in *Going on a Whale Watch* (McMillan, 1992),

Children learn many concepts as they listen to teachers read aloud informational books.

colonial life in . . . *If You Lived in Colonial Times* (McGovern, 1964), the human body in *The Magic School Bus Inside the Human Body* (Cole, 1989), multiplication in *Anno's Mysterious Multiplying Jar* (Anno, 1983), and levers, inclined planes, and other simple machines and how they work in *Simple Machines* (Horvatic, 1989). In fact, high-quality informational books are available about almost any topic that interests children, and reading informational books is fun. According to Horowitz and Freeman (1995), high-quality trade books play a significant role in science and other across-the-curriculum theme studies. Doiron (1994) argues that nonfiction also has an aesthetic quality that makes it very attractive and motivating for young readers.

Informational books are different from stories, and they place different demands on readers. They differ from stories in three basic ways:

1. **Organizational patterns.** Informational books are organized using expository text structures (the five basic expository patterns are explained in Chapter 6, "The Structure of Text").

2. **Vocabulary.** Informational books include technical vocabulary related to concepts presented in the book.

3. **Special features.** Informational books include special features, including a table of contents, an index, a glossary, and charts, graphs, maps, and other diagrams.

When teachers introduce informational books to students, they explain these differences and show students how they can take advantage of the special features to enhance their comprehension. Teachers also take these differences into account as they read informational books with students as part of theme studies. Guidelines for using informational books are presented in Figure 11–2.

Teachers help students read expository text by teaching them about expository text structures. Teachers teach students to recognize the organizational patterns and how to adjust their purposes for reading to fit the structure. Students also need to know the cue words that authors use to signal structures and be able to recognize them.

The four informational books about penguins that Mrs. Roberts used in the vignette at the beginning of this chapter illustrate three expository text structures. *It Could Still Be a Bird* (Fowler, 1990) is organized using a description structure. The book points out these characteristics of birds:

1. All birds have feathers.
2. Birds have wings
3. Birds usually can fly.
4. Birds lay eggs.
5. Some birds can swim.
6. Birds can be big or little.
7. Birds can be many different colors.
8. Birds can live almost anywhere.

Both *Penguin* (Fletcher, 1993) and *A Penguin Year* (Bonners, 1981) employ a sequence structure. *Penguin* focuses on a penguin's development from hatching to age two and a half, and on the last page of the book a series of photographs reviews the sequence. *A Penguin Year* shows how penguins live from the dark winter through

FIGURE 11–2   Guidelines for Using Informational Books

1. Efferent Reading

Teachers explain to students that they should read or listen to informational books efferently when they want to remember information. They compare the efferent and aesthetic stances and point out the differences between the two.

2. Unique Components of Informational Books

Teachers point out to students the unique components of informational books: table of contents, index, glossary, highlighted vocabulary, charts, maps, and diagrams.

3. Setting Purposes

Teachers give students a specific purpose for reading or listening, and they understand that students will not remember everything they read or listen to.

4. Building Background

Teachers activate students' prior knowledge, build background for topics that are new to students, and introduce technical vocabulary before reading.

5. Arrangements for Reading

Teachers use a variety of arrangements for reading. They ask students to overview or preview the book before reading, divide into small groups to read a book, or reread the book for a specific reason.

6. Rereading

Teachers have students reread informational books for specific reasons—to locate specific information, verify a fact, or gather evidence for a position.

7. Questions

Teachers have students write questions before reading and then read to find answers to their questions. This activity motivates students for reading and sets a meaningful purpose for reading.

8. Real-Life Experiences

Teachers use concrete objects, videos, field trips, and dramatizations whenever possible to help build students' background knowledge and motivation for reading.

9. Graphic Organizers

Teachers use clusters and graphic organizers to help students identify main ideas and remember important information from their reading. Students can use graphic organizers teachers have created or can develop their own.

10. Text Sets

Teachers create text sets to connect informational books with stories and poems.

spring, summer, and fall. The author emphasizes that in the spring penguins return to the rookery where they were hatched in order to lay eggs, and she explains how penguin parents hatch and care for their chicks season by season.

In *Antarctica* (1990), Helen Cowcher uses a problem-solution structure to identify three of the penguins' enemies—leopard seals, skua gulls, and people—and to make a plea that people do not destroy the penguins' environment. Figure 11–3 shows a chart that Mrs. Roberts's students made to emphasize the information they learned about penguins' enemies. The students shared this information with other students during a book talk.

Teachers consider the structure of text as they decide how to introduce an informational book, what type of graphic organizer or diagram to make to help emphasize the key points, and what points to emphasize in discussions. When teachers provide this type of structure, students are better able to focus on key concepts in each book rather than trying to remember a number of unrelated or unorganized facts.

Integrating Stories and Poetry

Children's literature brings content-area studies to life (C. S. Nelson, 1994; Smith & Johnson, 1994). Stories provide a window through which students view yesterday's world and today's. Facts and across-the-curriculum concepts are imbedded in fiction (Doiron, 1994). The settings of many stories provide historical and geographic information, and the conflict situations the characters face provide a glimpse into cultural, economic, and political issues. For example, students learn about penguins in *Tacky the Penguin* (Lester, 1988), step into Nazi-occupied Denmark in *Number the Stars* (Lowry, 1989), understand the discrimination that immigrants face in *Molly's Pilgrim*

FIGURE 11–3   A Problem-Solving Chart

(Cohen, 1983), relive the dangerous days of pre–Revolutionary War Boston in *Johnny Tremain* (Forbes, 1970), and think about the consequences of pollution in *Ben's Dream* (Van Allsburg, 1990). Whether students are reading stories as part of literature focus units or as part of across-the-curriculum theme studies, they read aesthetically, for the lived-through literary experience. Even though students aren't reading efferently to pick out information, they are learning information and developing concepts as they read aesthetically. As they develop their understanding of a story, students often ask questions about historical settings, political situations, and unfamiliar cultural traditions during grand conversations. Stories are an important way of learning social studies, science, and math.

Drama is an effective way to evoke an aesthetic response to literature and deepen students' understanding of stories (Fennessey, 1995). As students role-play events, especially events from biographies and stories of historical fiction, they step into the lives of the characters, understand the characters' motivations, empathize with characters, and appreciate the cultural dynamics in the time period. Teachers integrate drama easily into reading and responding to literature because it is impromptu and no planning or supplies are needed.

Poetry is also used as part of across-the-curriculum learning. Many books of poetry written for children can be used in teaching social studies and science. Figure 11–4 presents a list of some of these poetry books. For example, *Desert Voices* (Baylor, 1981), a collection of poems written in the first person from the viewpoint of desert animals, and *Mojave* (Siebert, 1988), a book-length poem written from the viewpoint of the desert and illustrated with striking full-page illustrations, can be used in a unit on the desert.

Using Content-Area Textbooks

Content-area texts are no longer viewed as the only source for learning, but they continue to be useful tools for learning across the curriculum and are available in most classrooms. Tierney and Pearson (1992) recommend that teachers shift from teaching *from* textbooks to teaching *with* textbooks and that they strive to incorporate other types of reading materials and activities into theme studies.

Content-area textbooks are often difficult for students to read—more difficult, in fact, than many informational books. One reason textbooks are difficult is that they briefly mention many topics without developing any of them in-depth. A second reason is that content-area textbooks are read differently than stories. Teachers need to show students how to approach content-area textbooks by teaching students how to use specific expository text reading strategies and procedures to make comprehension easier. Figure 11–5 presents a list of guidelines for using content-area textbooks.

There are specific procedures for students to use before, during, and after reading to make content-area textbooks more readable and to remember what they have read. Before reading, students can use one of these strategies to activate prior knowledge, set purposes for reading, or build background knowledge:

1. *Preview.* In this procedure, students note main headings in the chapter and then skim or rapidly read the chapter to get a general idea about the topics covered in the reading assignment.

2. *Prereading plan (PReP).* In a **prereading plan,** teachers introduce a key concept discussed in the reading assignment and ask students to brainstorm words and

FIGURE 11–4 Books of Poetry That Can Be Used in Theme Studies

Adoff, A. (1979). *Eats poems.* New York: Lothrop. (P–M)

Amon, A. (Sel.). (1981). *The earth is sore: Native Americans on nature.* New York: Atheneum. (M–U)

Baylor, B. (1981). *Desert voices.* New York: Scribner. (P–M)

Benet, R., & Benet, S. V. (1961). *A book of Americans.* New York: Holt. (M–U)

Carle, E. (Sel.). (1989). *Eric Carle's animals, animals.* New York: Philomel. (P–M)

Esbensen, B. J. (1984). *Cold stars and fireflies: Poems of the four seasons.* New York: Crowell. (U)

Fisher, A. (1983). *Rabbits, rabbits.* New York: Harper & Row. (P)

Fisher, A. (1988). *The house of a mouse.* New York: Harper & Row. (Poems about mice) (P–M)

Fleischman, P. (1985). *I am phoenix: Poems for two voices.* New York: Harper & Row. (Poems about birds) (M–U)

Fleischman, P. (1988). *Joyful noise: Poems for two voices.* New York: Harper & Row. (Poems about insects) (M–U)

Goldstein, B. S. (Sel.). (1989). *Bear in mind: A book of bear poems.* New York: Puffin. (P–M)

Goldstein, B. S. (Sel.). (1992). *What's on the menu?* New York: Viking. (Poems about food) (P–M)

Harvey, A. (Sel.). (1992). *Shades of green.* New York: Greenwillow. (Poems about ecology) (U)

Hopkins, L. (Sel.). (1985). *Munching: Poems about eating.* Boston: Little, Brown. (M–U)

Hopkins, L. B. (Sel.). (1976). *Good morning to you, valentine.* New York: Harcourt Brace Jovanovich. (See other collections of holiday poems by the same selector.) (P–M)

Hopkins, L. B. (Sel.). (1983). *A song in stone: City poems.* New York: Crowell. (M)

Hopkins, L. B. (Sel.). (1983). *The sky is full of song.* New York: Harper & Row. (Poems about the seasons). (P–M)

Hopkins, L. B. (Sel.). (1987). *Dinosaurs.* San Diego: Harcourt Brace Jovanovich. (M–U)

Hopkins, L. B. (Sel.). (1987). *Click, rumble, roar: Poems about machines.* New York: Crowell. (M)

Hopkins, L. B. (Sel.). (1991). *On the farm.* Boston: Little, Brown. (P–M)

Hopkins, L. B. (Sel.). (1992). *To the zoo: Animal poems.* Boston: Little, Brown. (P–M)

Janeczko, P. B. (Sel.). (1984). *Strings: A gathering of family poems.* New York: Bradbury Press. (U)

Larrick, N. (Sel.). (1988). *Cats are cats.* New York: Philomel. (M–U)

Larrick, N. (Sel.). (1990). *Mice are nice.* New York: Philomel. (M)

Livingston, M. C. (1982). *Circle of seasons.* New York: Holiday House. (M–U)

Livingston, M. C. (1985). *Celebrations.* New York: Holiday House. (Poems about holidays) (P–M)

Livingston, M. C. (Sel.). (1986). *Earth songs.* New York: Holiday House. (M–U)

Livingston, M. C. (Sel.). (1987). *Cat poems.* New York: Holiday House. (P–M–U)

Livingston, M. C. (Sel.). (1987). *New year's poems.* New York: Holiday House. (See other collections of holiday poems by the same selector.) (P–M–U)

Livingston, M. C. (Sel.). (1988). *Space songs.* New York: Holiday House. (M–U)

Livingston, M. C. (Sel.). (1990). *If the owl calls again: A collection of owl poems.* New Year: McElderry Books. (U)

Livingston, M. C. (Sel.). (1990). *Dog poems.* New York: Holiday House. (M–U)

Livingston, M. C. (Sel.). (1992). *If you ever meet a whale.* New York: Holiday House. (P–M)

Morrison, L. (1985). *The break dance kids: Poems of sport, motion, and locomotion.* New York: Lothrop, Lee & Shepard. (U)

Prelutsky, J. (1984). *It's snowing! It's snowing!* New York: Greenwillow. (P–M)

Prelutsky, J. (1977). *It's Halloween.* New York: Greenwillow. (See other books of holiday poems by the same author.) (P–M)

Prelutsky, J. (1983). *Zoo doings: Animal poems.* New York: Greenwillow. (P–M)

Prelutsky, J. (1988). *Tyrannosaurus was a beast: Dinosaur poems.* New York: Greenwillow. (P–M)

Provensen, A. (1990). *The buck stops here: Presidents of the United States.* New York: HarperCollins. (M–U)

Russo, S. (Sel.). (1984). *The ice cream ocean and other delectable poems of the sea.* New York: Lothrop, Lee & Shepard. (P–M)

Siebert, D. (1988). *Mojave.* New York: Harper & Row. (M–U)

Siebert, D. (1991). *Sierra.* New York: HarperCollins. (M–U)

Sneve, V. D. H. (1989). *Dancing teepees: Poems of American Indian youth.* New York: Holiday House. (M–U)

Turner, A. (1986). *Street talk.* Boston: Houghton Mifflin. (Poems about city life) (M–U)

Yolen, J. (1990). *Bird watch: A book of poetry.* New York: Philomel. (M–U)

Yolen, J. (1990). *Dinosaur dances.* New York: Putnam. (M)

P = primary grades (K–2); M = middle grades (3–5); U = upper grades (6–8).

FIGURE 11–5   Guidelines for Using Content-Area Textbooks

1. Comprehension Aids

Teachers show students how to use the comprehension aids in content-area textbooks, including chapter overviews, headings that outline the chapter, helpful graphics such as maps, charts, tables, graphs, diagrams, photos, and drawings, technical words defined in the text, end-of-chapter summaries, and review questions.

2. Questions for Reading

Before reading each section of a chapter, students turn the section heading into a question and read to find the answer to the question. As they read students take notes about the section, and then they answer the question they created after reading.

3. Expository Text Structures

Teachers assist students in identifying the expository text structures used in the reading assignment, especially cause-and-effect or problem-and-solution patterns, before reading.

4. Key Terms

Teachers introduce only the key terms as part of an introductory presentation or discussion before students read the textbook assignment. Other vocabulary is presented during reading, if needed, and after reading the teacher and students develop a word wall with the important words.

5. Big Ideas

Students focus on the big ideas or key concepts instead of trying to remember all the facts or other information.

6. Reading Strategies

Students use reading strategies such as PReP, clusters, and anticipation guides to help them comprehend what they are reading.

7. Headings

Teachers encourage students to use headings to select and organize relevant information. The headings can be used to create a cluster, and students add details as they read.

8. Self-Questions

Teachers encourage students to be active readers, to ask themselves questions as they read, and to monitor their reading.

9. Listen-Read-Discuss Format

Teachers use a listen-read-discuss format. To begin, the teacher presents the key concepts orally, and then students read and discuss the chapter. Or, the students read the chapter as a review activity rather than as the introductory activity.

10. Text Set

Teachers supplement content-area textbook assignments with a text set of informational books, stories, poems, and other reading materials.

ideas related to the concept (Langer, 1981). Afterwards students quickwrite or quickdraw to reflect on the concept.

3. *Anticipation guides.*   In **anticipation guides,** teachers present a set of statements on the topic to be read. Students agree or disagree with each statement and then read the assignment to see if they were right (Head & Readence, 1986).

4. *Exclusion brainstorming.*   In this procedure, teachers distribute a list of words, most of which are related to the key concepts presented in the reading assignment. Teachers ask students to circle the words that are related to a key concept and then read the assignment to see if they circled the right words (Johns, VanLeirsburg, & Davis, 1994).

Teachers teach students to use the following strategies during reading to help them identify main ideas and details and organize what they are reading:

1. *Cluster.*   Teachers distribute a **cluster** or other graphic organizer with main ideas marked. Students complete the graphic organizer by adding details as they read.

2. *Note-taking.*   Students develop an outline by writing the main headings and then take notes after reading each section.

Students can use other strategies after reading to review what they have read or to locate specific information:

1. *Scanning.*   Students reread quickly to locate specific information.

2. *Quickwrites.*   Students **quickwrite** or **quickdraw** about the key concepts or important information presented in the reading assignment (Tompkins, 1994).

■ *Activity*

Choose a topic presented in a social studies or science textbook and collect a text set of informational books, stories, poems, or other reading materials on the topic. Then compare these two ways of teaching the concept. Which is more likely to appeal to students? Which presents the concept in a more comprehensible way? What are the advantages and disadvantages of each?

Students in the upper grades also need to learn how to use the **SQ3R study strategy,** a five-step technique in which students survey, question, read, recite, and review as they study a content-area reading assignment. The SQ3R study strategy incorporates before-, during-, and after-reading components. This study strategy was devised in the 1930s and has been researched and thoroughly documented as a very effective technique when used properly (Anderson & Armbruster, 1984; Caverly & Orlando, 1991).

Teachers introduce the SQ3R study strategy and provide opportunities for students to practice each step. At first, students can work together as a class as they use the strategy with a text the teacher is reading to students. Then students can work with partners and in small groups before using the strategy individually. Teachers need to emphasize that if students simply begin reading the first page of the assignment without doing the first two steps, they won't be able to remember as much of what they read. When students are in a hurry and skip some of the steps, the strategy will not be as successful.

Using Books to Teach Math Concepts

The most common type of mathematics book is a counting book, such as Eric Carle's *1, 2, 3 to the Zoo* (1968), but a variety of children's books that present more complex mathematical concepts have been published in the past few years. In books such as *The Grouchy Ladybug* (Carle, 1986), *Fraction Action* (Leedy, 1994), *Anno's Magic Seeds* (Anno, 1992), and *How Much Is a Million?* (Schwartz, 1985), mathematics is fun and is portrayed in a meaningful context (Whitin & Wilde, 1992). Children's books also demonstrate that mathematics develops out of human experience, integrating math across the curriculum, into literature, social studies, and science.

Students read and respond to books incorporating math concepts, and they listen to teachers read these books aloud. Sometimes the books are read as part of a theme study, while at other times they are chosen to teach a mathematical concept. A list of books that incorporate mathematical concepts about counting, addition and subtraction, multiplication and division, fractions, geometry, and measurement are presented in Figure 11–6.

FIGURE 11–6   Books About Mathematical Concepts

Akers, S. (1990). *What comes in 2's, 3's, and 4's?* New York: Simon & Schuster. (P–M)

Anno, M. (1983). *Anno's mysterious multiplying jar.* New York: Philomel. (M)

Anno, M. (1986). *All in a day.* New York: Philomel. (M)

Anno, M. (1992). *Anno's magic seeds.* New York: Philomel. (P–M)

Ashabranner, M., & Ashabranner, B. (1989). *Counting America: The study of the United States Census.* New York: Putnam. (M–U)

Bang, M. (1983). *Ten, nine, eight.* New York: Greenwillow. (P)

Carle, E. (1968). *1, 2, 3 to the zoo.* New York: Philomel. (P)

Carle, E. (1969). *The very hungry caterpillar.* New York: Putnam. (P)

Carle, E. (1977). *The grouchy ladybug.* New York: Crowell. (P)

Coerr, E. (1977). *Sadako and the thousand paper cranes.* New York: Putnam. (M)

Ehlert, L. (1989). *Color zoo.* New York: Lippincott. (P)

Ehlert, L. (1990). *Fish eyes: A book you can count on.* San Diego: Harcourt Brace Jovanovich. (P)

Falwell, C. (1993). *Feast for 10.* New York: Clarion. (P)

Feelings, M. (1971). *Moja means one: A Swahili counting book.* New York: Dial. (M)

Fisher, L. E. (1987). *Calendar art: Thirteen days, weeks, months, and years from around the world.* New York: Four Winds. (M–U)

Gibbons, G. (1979). *Clocks and how they go.* New York: Crowell. (M–U)

Giganti, P., Jr. (1988). *How many snails? A counting book.* New York: Mulberry. (P–M)

Giganti, P., Jr. (1992). *Each orange had 8 slices.* New York: Greenwillow. (P–M)

Haskins, J. (1987). *Count your way through Japan.* Minneapolis: Carolrhoda. (See other books in the series.) (M)

Hoban, T. (1973). *Over, under and through, and other spatial concepts.* New York: Macmillan. (P–M)

Hoban, T. (1974). *Circles, triangles, and squares.* New York: Macmillan. (P)

Hoban, T. (1981). *More than one.* New York: Greenwillow. (P)

Hopper, M. (1985). *Seven eggs.* New York: Harper & Row. (P)

Hulme, J. N. (1991). *Sea squares.* New York: Hyperion. (P–M)

Hutchins, P. (1982). *1 hunter.* New York: Mulberry. (P)

Hutchins, P. (1986). *The doorbell rang.* New York: Greenwillow. (P)

Leedy, L. (1994). *Fraction action.* New York: Holiday House. (M)

Macaulay, D. (1975). *Pyramid.* Boston: Houghton Mifflin. (U)

Macaulay, D. (1980). *Unbuilding.* Boston: Houghton Mifflin. (U)

McGrath, B. B. (1994). *The M&M's counting book.* Watertown, MA: Charlesbridge. (P–M)

McMillan, B. (1989). *Super super superwords.* New York: Lothrop, Lee & Shepard. (P–M)

Merriam, E. (1993). *12 ways to get to 11.* New York: Dell. (P)

Myller, R. (1990). *How big is a foot?* New York: Dell. (M)

Peek, M. (1981). *Roll over!* New York: Clarion. (P)

Schwartz, D. (1985). *How much is a million?* New York: Lothrop, Lee & Shepard. (P–M)

Schwartz, D. (1989). *If you made a million.* New York: Lothrop, Lee & Shepard. (P–M)

Scott, A. H. (1990). *One good horse: A cowpuncher's counting book.* New York: Greenwillow. (P–M)

Tafuri, N. (1986). *Who's counting?* New York: Greenwillow. (P)

Tombert, A. (1990). *Grandfather Tang's story.* New York: Crown. (M–U)

Walsh, E. S. (1991). *Mouse count.* Orlando: Harcourt Brace. (P)

Williams, V. B. (1982). *A chair for my mother.* New York: Mulberry. (P)

Wood, A. (1984). *The napping house.* San Diego: Harcourt Brace Jovanovich. (P)

FIGURE 11–7   Two Pages From a Second Grader's Science Log

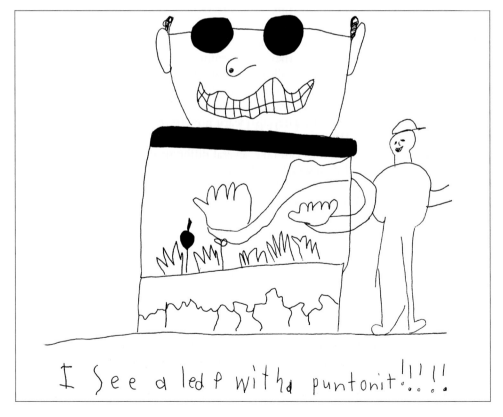

ing words related to the theme, create timelines, and draw diagrams, charts, and maps. For example, as part of a study of the Civil War, eighth graders might include the following in their learning logs:

- informal quickwrites about the causes of the war and other topics related to the war
- a list of words related to the theme
- a chart of major battles in the war
- a Venn diagram comparing the Northern and Southern viewpoints
- a timeline showing events related to the war
- a map of the United States at the time of the war, with battle locations marked
- notes after viewing several films about the Civil War era
- a list of favorite quotes from Lincoln's "Gettysburg Address"
- a response to a chapter book such as *Charley Skedaddle* (Beatty, 1987), *Brady* (Fritz, 1987), or *Across Five Aprils* (Hunt, 1987)

Through these learning log activities, student explore concepts they are learning and record information they want to remember about the Civil War.

Simulated Journals

In simulated journals, students assume the role of another person and write from that person's viewpoint. They can assume the role of a historical figure when they read biographies or as part of social studies units. As they read stories, students can assume the role of a character in the story. In this way, students gain insight into other people's lives and into historical events. When students write from the viewpoint of a famous person, they begin by making a "lifeline," a timeline of the person's life. Then they pick key dates in the person's life and write entries about those dates. A look at a series of diary entries written by a fifth grader who has assumed the role of Benjamin Franklin shows how the student chose the important dates for each entry and wove in factual information:

December 10, 1719
Dear Diary,
My brother James is so mad at me. He just figured out that I'm the one who wrote the articles for his newspaper and signed them Mistress Silence Dogood. He says I can't do any more of them. I don't understand why. My articles are funny. Everyone reads them. I bet he won't sell as many newspapers anymore. Now I have to just do the printing.

February 15, 1735
Dear Diary,
I have printed my third "Poor Richard's Almanack." It is the most popular book in America and now I am famous. Everyone reads it. I pretend that somebody named Richard Saunders writes it, but it's really me. I also put my wise sayings in it. My favorite wise saying is "Early to bed, early to rise, makes a man healthy, wealthy, and wise."

FIGURE 11–8   Two Clusters on Birds

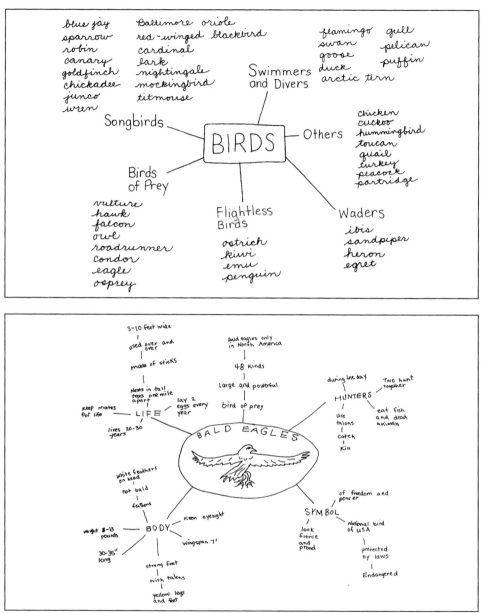

The name of this procedure comes from the fact that, just as cubes have six sides, cubing includes six dimensions. As students think about the topic from all six dimensions, they consider varied viewpoints and think more deeply about the topic. Middle- and upper-grade students can divide into six groups to cube the Civil War, deserts, or another topic they are studying. Students in each group draw a picture and write a quickwrite to reflect their thinking, and then they share their work with classmates and compile the papers to make a large cube. Students can also make individual cubes.

Reports

Students in the elementary grades write many different types of reports. The three most common types are "All About . . ." books, **collaborative reports,** and **individual reports.** Too often students are not exposed to report writing until they are faced with writing a term paper in high school, and then they are overwhelmed with learning how to take notes on note cards, how to organize and write the paper, and how to compile a bibliography. There is no reason to postpone report writing until students reach high school. Early, successful experiences with informative writing teach students about content-area topics as well as how to write reports (Krogness, 1987; Queenan, 1986; Tompkins, 1994).

The first reports that young children write are "All About . . ." books, in which they provide information about familiar topics, including "Signs of Fall" and "Sea Creatures" (Bonin, 1988; Sowers, 1985). Young children write an entire booklet on a single topic. Usually one piece of information and an illustration appear on each page. Mrs. Roberts's first and second graders wrote "All About Penguins" books in the vignette at the beginning of this chapter.

For collaborative reports, the whole class or small groups of students work together to write sections of the report, which are then compiled. Students benefit from writing a collaborative report before writing individual reports because they learn how to write a report, with the group as a scaffold or support system, before tackling

Students can publish reports as posters with text, maps, charts, and illustrations.

FIGURE 11–9   A Page From a Class Book About Martin Luther King, Jr.

Martin Luther King, Jr. won the Nobel Peace Prize. He receive da Medal and $54,600.00.

individual reports. Also, working in groups lets them share the laborious parts of the work.

Students often each write one page for a collaborative report. Alphabet books are one kind of collaborative report. Teachers and students can also develop collaborative reports on almost any science or social studies topic. For example, as part of a unit on Martin Luther King, Jr., a first-grade class wrote a collaborative biography of the great Civil Rights leader. The teacher began by drawing a lifeline, and the students added 16 important events from King's life. Then students chose the events to draw and write about. Some students worked individually, while others worked with a partner. After students completed their pages, they were compiled and bound into a book. One page from the class book is shown in Figure 11–9.

Students also write individual reports as projects during theme studies. Toby Fulwiler (1985) recommends that students do "authentic" research, in which they explore topics that interest them or hunt for answers to questions that puzzle them. When students become immersed in content-area study, questions arise that they want to explore. During a study of life in ancient Egypt, a class of sixth graders generated a long list of questions they wanted to research. Each student chose three or four questions to research, and then they wrote reports with the answers they found.

An excerpt from one sixth grader's report on ancient Egypt is presented in Figure 11–10. This chapter focuses on one of the questions the student researched: How was King Tut's tomb discovered? Other chapters in this student's book examine the Egyptian gods and goddesses, the annual floodings of the Nile River, and a comparison of the living conditions of the rich and poor.

FIGURE 11–10   An Excerpt From a Sixth Grader's Report on Ancient Egypt

---

Chapter II

The Discovery of Tut's Tomb

In 1916 Howard Carter and his employer Lord Canarvan went digging in the sand of the Sahara Desert to find the tomb of the Young Pharoah, King Tutankhamun. They dug and dug for almost six years. In fact, it was probably over six years. That's how they discovered the tomb of King Tut.

Who was King Tut? Why wasn't he buried in the Valley of the Kings? Where was he buried? Keep reading to find the answers to these mysteries.

Going back thousands of years ago there was a young pharoah, King Tutankhamun (King Tut for short). He was eight when he married, nine when crowned as a boy king, and 18 or 19 when he died. He was married to Queen Nefertiti's daughter.

King Tut wasn't buried in the Valley of the Kings because he wanted to be buried where no man had been buried before. He knew that robbers had been known to steal the gold and jewelry from the other pyramids. He didn't want to be one of the kings who had been robbed. Where was King Tut buried? By our knowledge his tomb was found in northern Egypt and west of the Nile River.

It was 1922, November 26, when the shovel of Howard Carter hit something as hard as a rock. All of Howard Carter's employees and workers gathered around and began digging. They were all digging together, using their picks, axes, shovels, and possibly wheelbarrows. The workers and everyone finally reached the sixteenth step. There was sixteen steps leading down to a door made of heavy metal. It appeared to be metal, but no one knows for sure. It could have been stone, steel, or brick. Who knows?

Well, anyway, they drilled a peephole as small as a quarter. It was pitch dark when everyone took a peek. Howard Carter sent someone up to get their flashlights that they had brought along if needed. Now they finally got a sight of what was really in the tomb. Almost in every direction that they looked they saw glittering, shiny objects. After a moment of gazing around, they immediately drilled a hole big enough for each and everyone to crawl through. Howard sent a few workers across the desert to get some photographers. The workmen told them to wait until they got back. Howard Carter, Lord Canarvan, other employees, and workmen all sat down to wait. They waited a while and then finally they decided to crawl on in.

There were chariots made of gold that had fallen into many broken pieces. Hierglyphics were found on many walls. King Tut's chalice (which also had hieroglyphics) was in the tomb, a child-size throne, roast duck (King Tut's favorite food), a good dagger, and a bust of Nefertiti. This was because King Tut was the son-in-law of Queen Nefertiti. They finally found the body of the boy king, King Tut. Tut's pine scented aftershave was in there also. Many games were found in there, for example: draught, sennet, and a game somewhat like parchesi. There were 5,000 objects and almost all were made of gold because there was very little silver. It took ten years to sort out and record all of the 5,000 objects. These objects have traveled around the world, and still are to this day.

THEME STUDIES

Theme studies are interdisciplinary units that integrate reading and writing with social studies, science, math, and other curricular areas (Altwerger & Flores, 1994; Gamberg, Kwak, Hutchings, Altheim, & Edwards, 1988). Sometimes they focus on one curricular area, such as a theme study on insects or the Revolutionary War; at other times they extend across most or all of the school day, and students are involved in planning the direction for the theme. Topics for these extended theme studies are broad and encompass many possible directions for exploration, such as houses and homes, or people who have changed the world.

Students are involved in planning the theme studies and identifying some of the questions they want to explore and the activities that interest them. Students are involved in authentic and meaningful learning activities, not reading chapters in content-area textbooks in order to answer the questions at the end of the chapter. Textbooks might be used as a resource, but only as one of many available resources. Students explore topics that interest them and research answers to questions they have posed and are genuinely interested in answering. Students share their learning at the end of the theme study and are assessed on what they have learned as well as the processes they used in learning and working in the classroom.

How to Develop a Theme Study

To begin planning a theme study, teachers choose the general topic and then identify three or four key concepts that they want to develop through the theme. The goal of a theme study is not to teach a collection of facts but to help students grapple with several big understandings (Tunnell & Ammon, 1993). Next, teachers identify the resources that they have available for the theme and develop their teaching plan. Ten important considerations in developing a theme study are:

1. Collect a text set of stories, informational books, and poems. Teachers collect stories, poems, informational books, magazines, newspaper articles, and reference books for the text set related to the theme. The text set is placed in the special area for materials related to the theme in the classroom library. Teachers plan to read aloud some books to students (or tape-record them for the listening center), some will be

A text set is a collection of stories, informational books, and poems related to a theme.

read independently, and others students will read together as shared or guided reading. These materials can also be used for minilessons—to teach students, for example, about reading strategies and expository text structure. Other books can be used as models or patterns for writing projects. Teachers also write the poems on charts to share with students or arrange a bulletin board display of the poems.

2. Set up a listening center.   Teachers select tapes to accompany stories or informational books or create their own tapes so that absent students can catch up on a book being read aloud day by day, or the tapes can be used to provide additional reading experiences for students who listen to a tape when they read or reread a story or informational book.

3. Coordinate content-area textbook readings.   Teachers can teach theme studies without textbooks; however, when information is available in a literature or content-area textbook, it can be used. Upper-grade students, in particular, read and discuss concepts presented in textbooks or use them as a reference for further study.

4. Locate multimedia materials.   Teachers plan the films, videotapes, filmstrips, charts, timelines, maps, models, posters, and other displays to be used in connection with the theme study. Some materials are used to develop children's background knowledge about the theme, and other materials are used in teaching the key concepts. They can be displayed in the classroom, and students can make other materials during the theme.

5. Identify potential words for the word wall.   Teachers preview books in the text set and identify potential words for the word wall. This list is useful in planning vocabulary activities, but teachers do not simply use their word lists for the classroom word wall. Students and the teacher develop the classroom word wall as they read and discuss the key concepts and other information related to the theme.

6. Plan how students will use learning logs.   Teachers plan for students to keep learning logs in which students can take notes, write questions, make observations, clarify their thinking, and write reactions to what they read during theme studies (Tompkins, 1994). They also write quickwrites and makes clusters to explore what they are learning.

7. Identify literacy skills and strategies to teach during the theme.   Teachers plan minilessons to teach literacy skills and strategies, such as expository text structures, how to use an index, skimming and scanning, how to write an alphabet book, and interviewing techniques. Minilessons are taught using a whole-part-whole approach so that students can apply what they are learning in reading and writing activities.

8. Plan talk and drama activities related to the theme.   Students use talk and drama to learn during the theme study and to demonstrate their learning (Erickson, 1988; P. A. Nelson, 1988; San Jose, 1988). These are possible activities:

Give oral reports.

Interview someone with special expertise on the theme.

Participate in a debate related to the theme.

Role-play a historical event.

Assume the role of a historical figure.

Participate in a **readers theatre** presentation of a story or poem.

Tell or retell a story, biography, or event.

Use a puppet show to tell a story, biography, or event.

Write and perform a skit or play.

9. Brainstorm possible projects students may create to extend their learning.
Teachers think about projects students may choose to develop to extend and personalize their learning during theme studies. This advance planning makes it possible for teachers to collect needed supplies and to have suggestions ready to offer to students who need assistance in choosing a project. Students work on the project independently or in small groups and then share the project with the class at the end of the theme. Projects involve reading, writing, talk, art, music, or drama. Some suggestions are:

Read a biography related to the theme study.

Create a poster to illustrate a key concept.

Write and mail a letter to get information related to the theme.

Write a story related to the theme.

Perform a readers theatre production, puppet show, or other dramatization related to the theme.

Write a poem, song, or rap related to the theme.

Write an "All About . . ." book or report about one of the key concepts.

Create a commercial or advertisement related to the theme.

Create a tabletop display or diorama about the theme.

10. Plan for the assessment of the theme.   Teachers consider how they will assess students' learning as they make plans for activities and assignments. In this way, teachers can explain to students how they will be assessed at the beginning of the theme study and check to see that their assessment will emphasize students' learning of the key concepts and important ideas.

Teachers consider the resources they have available, brainstorm possible activities, and then develop clusters to guide their planning. The goal in developing plans for a theme study is to consider a wide variety of resources that integrate listening, talking, reading, and writing with the content of the theme (Pappas, Kiefer, & Levstik, 1990).

Why aren't content-area textbooks enough?

Sometimes content-area textbooks are used as the entire instructional program in social studies or science, and that's not a good idea. Textbooks typically only survey topics; other instructional materials are needed to provide the depth and understanding. Students need to read, write, and discuss topics. It is most effective to use the reading process and then extend students' learning with projects. Developing theme studies and using content-area textbooks as one resource is a much better idea than using content-area textbooks as the only reading material.

W
desert
Death V
Sahara
Mojave
kangaro
barrel c:
dunes
Gobi De
Bedouin
oasis
scorpion
coral sn;

Maps a
• Read
• Draw
• Draw
  anim
• Make
  chart

Aut
• S
• R
• V

FIGURE

A Primary-Grade Theme: Houses and Homes

In this three-week theme, students learn that people and animals live in different sorts of houses depending where they live and what their needs are. They also learn about how houses are built in the United States and the types of building materials that are used. Through field trips to a site where a house is being built in town, students learn the steps in building a house. Two books are available as big books, and a variety of stories, informational books, and poems are available as small books. Students read and respond to Ann Morris's *Houses and Homes* (1992) during the first week of the theme, to *A House Is a House for Me* (Hoberman, 1978) during the second week, and to Eric Carle's *A House for Hermit Crab* (1987) during the third week. Students interview builders, carpenters, plumbers, and other people who build houses and manipulate some of the tools and building supplies. They learn the names for tools and building supplies as well as the names for various types of houses that people and animals live in. Students work in small groups to create projects, including making books and making a cluster of the types of houses different animals live in. A planning cluster for a theme on houses and homes is presented in Figure 11–11.

A Middle-Grade Theme: Desert Life

Students investigate the plants, animals, and people that live in the desert during this three-week theme. They learn about desert ecosystems, how deserts form, and how they change. They keep learning logs in which they take notes and write reactions to books they are reading. Students divide into book clubs during the first week to read one of six books about the desert. During the second week of the unit, students participate in an author study of Byrd Baylor, a woman who lives in the desert and writes about desert life, and they read many of her books. During the third week, students participate in a reading workshop and read other desert books and reread favorite books. To extend their learning, students participate in projects, including writing desert riddles, making a chart of a desert ecosystem, and making a desert mural. Together as a class, students can write a desert alphabet book or a collaborative report about deserts. A planning cluster for a theme on desert life is presented in Figure 11–12.

An Upper-Grade Theme: Ancient Egypt

Students learn about this great ancient civilization during a month-long theme study. Key concepts include the influence of the Nile River on Egyptian life, the contributions of this civilization to twentieth-century America, a comparison of ancient to modern Egypt, and the techniques Egyptologists use to locate tombs of the ancient rulers and to decipher Egyptian hieroglyphics. Students will read books in book clubs and choose other books from the text set to read during reading workshop. Students and the teacher will add vocabulary to the word wall, and students will use the words in a variety of activities.

Teachers will teach minilessons on writing simulated journals, map-reading skills, Egyptian gods, mummification, and writing poems for two voices. Students will also work in writing workshop as they write reports, biographies, or collections of poetry related to the theme study. As a culminating activity, students will create individual projects and share them on Egypt day, when students assume the roles of ancient Egyptians, dress as ancient people did, and eat foods of the period. Figure 11–13 presents a planning cluster for an upper-grade unit on ancient Egypt.

■ *Activity*

Develop a planning cluster for Mrs. Roberts's theme on penguins described in the vignette at the beginning of this chapter. Or, develop a planning cluster for a theme study you are preparing to teach.

Word Wall

Egypt	embalming
pharoahs	Africa
Nile River	lotus
Ramses the Great	obelisk
Tutankhamun	papyrus
Nefertiti	scribes
Hatshepsut	hieroglyphs
natron	Imhotep
mummification	Champollion
canopic jars	Amun-Ra
pyramids	dynasty
Valley of the Kings	Luxor
senet	Memphis
irrigation	Rosetta stone
Old Kingdom	vizier
Middle Kingdom	Egyptologist
New Kingdom	

Cubing

Make a cube exploring the ancient Egyptian civilization.

K-W-L Chart

- Introduce K-W-L chart at the beginning of the unit.
- Identify research questions for collaborative or individual reports.
- Use to conclude the unit.

Learning Logs

Keep a learning log with quickwrites, notes, maps, charts, and diagrams.

Maps and Diagrams

- Make a timeline of ancient Egypt.
- Create a Venn diagram comparing ancient and modern Egypt.
- Read maps of ancient and modern Egypt.
- Draw maps of Egypt.

Projects

- Keep a simulated journal as an ancient Egyptian.
- Make a timeline of the ancient civilization.
- Make a poster about a god or goddess.
- Present an oral report about how to mummify someone.
- Make a salt map of Egypt and mark ancient landmarks.
- Write a collection of poems about ancient Egypt.
- Make paper.
- Present an "interview" of several ancient Egyptians.
- Write a book about the ways the Egyptian civilization has influenced ours.
- Research the Rosetta stone.
- Read two books about ancient Egypt.
- Make a chart comparing ancient and modern Egypt.

Literacy Skills and Strategies

- Use anticipation guides.
- Use the SQ3R study strategy.
- Read expository text using efferent stance.
- Make a timeline.
- Analyze root words and affixes.
- Use syllabication to identify words.

Word-Study Activities

- Make word maps.
- Do a word sort.
- Create a semantic feature analysis.
- Make a word chain.
- Write an alphabet book on Egypt.

ANCIENT EGYPT

Books

Aliki. (1979). *Mummies made in Egypt*. New York: HarperCollins.

Bendick, J. (1989). *Egyptian tombs*. New York: Franklin Watts.

Carter, D. S. (1987). *His majesty, Queen Hatshepsut*. New York: HarperCollins.

Climo, S. (1989). *The Egyptian Cinderella*. New York: HarperCollins.

Giblin, J. C. (1990). *The riddle of the Rosetta stone*. New York: HarperCollins.

Harris, G. (1992). *Gods and pharoahs from Egyptian mythology*. New York: Peter Bedrick.

Katan, N. J., & Mintz, B. (1981). *Hieroglyphs: The writing of ancient Egypt*. New York: McElderry.

Lattimore, D. N. (1992). *The winged cat: A tale of ancient Egypt*. New York: HarperCollins.

Macaulay, D. (1975). *Pyramid*. Boston: Houghton Mifflin.

McGraw, E. J. (1961). *The golden goblet*. New York: Puffin.

McMullen, K. (1992). *Under the mummy's spell*. New York: Farrar, Straus & Giroux.

Perl, L. (1987). *Mummies, tombs, and treasure: secrets of ancient Egypt*. New York: Clarion.

Price, L. (1990). *Aida*. San Diego: Harcourt Brace.

Raphael, E., & Bolognese, D. (1989). *Drawing history: Ancient Egypt*. New York: Franklin Watts.

Reeves, C. N. (1992). *Into the mummy's tomb*. New York: Scholastic.

Stanley, D., & Vennema, P. (1994). *Cleopatra*. New York: Morrow.

Stolz, M. (1978). *Cat in the mirror*. New York: Dell.

Stolz, M. (1988). *Zekmet the stone carver: A tale of ancient Egypt*. San Diego: Harcourt Brace.

Ventura, P. & Ceserani, G. P. (1985). *In search of Tutankhamun*. Morristown, NJ: Silver Burdett.

Woodruff, E. (1994). *The magnificent mummy maker*. New York: Scholastic.

FIGURE 11–13 A Planning Cluster for an Upper-Grade Theme on Ancient Egypt

expected to read at least two books. Students document their reading by writing reactions in literature logs, and they conference once a week with Mrs. Peterson.

During writing workshop, students use the writing process to write stories, poems, essays, how-to manuals, and other types of writing. Most students use a computer to print out their final copies and then bind them into books. Students are expected to complete two books during the four-week unit. The weekly assignment sheet that Mrs. Peterson's students use during reading and writing workshop is shown in Figure 12–1.

Mrs. Peterson collects other types of assessment information about her students on a regular basis during this quarter. She does the following activities:

■ listens to students read aloud excerpts of books they are reading and takes **running records** to check their fluency

■ reviews students' literature logs to check for comprehension

■ listens to comments students make during grand conversations to check for comprehension

■ checks their understanding of story elements as they develop charts during book clubs

■ analyzes spelling errors in students' literature logs and on students' rough drafts during editing conferences in writing workshop

■ observes students and makes anecdotal notes each week to monitor their work habits and learning

Mrs. Peterson keeps a literacy folder for each student in which she places the assessment information she collects as well as notes from each conference. She brings these folders to the conferences at the end of the third quarter and will add the notes she makes during this conference to the folders.

During the last week of the quarter, Mrs. Peterson conferences with each student. She spends approximately 15 minutes talking with each student about his or her work and making plans for the next quarter. She uses a conference sheet to take notes about these conferences, and both she and the student sign this sheet. A copy of the conference sheet is shown in Figure 12–2. At the conference, Mrs. Peterson accomplishes these things:

■ reviews the student's work during the three units and the grades the student received

■ examines the items the student has chosen to add to his or her portfolio and asks the student to explain why these items were chosen

■ presents some of the assessment information she has collected about the student

■ determines the student's reading and writing grades for the report card

■ sets goals with the student for the next quarter

■ completes the conference sheet

After the conference, students finish writing reflections to attach to the new portfolio items and then add them to their portfolios. Students will take the rest of the unit folders home with their report cards. They will also take a copy of the conference sheet with their goals for the next quarter.

FIGURE 12–1   Record Sheet Used by Mrs. Peterson's Sixth Graders

Weekly Assignment Sheet

Name _____   Week _____

READING WORKSHOP

1. What books did you read?

2. Did you write in your reading log?

3. Did you conference with Mrs. Peterson?

4. What did you do during Reading Workshop?

M	T	W	Th	F

WRITING WORKSHOP

1. What did you write?

2. Did you use the writing process?

   • prewriting   • drafting   • revising   • editing   • publishing

3. Did you conference with Mrs. Peterson?

4. What did you do during Writing Workshop?

M	T	W	Th	F

FIGURE 12–2   Mrs. Peterson's Assessment Form

End-of-Quarter Conference Sheet

Name _____   Date _____

Unit 1

Unit 2

Unit 3

_____

Items Chosen for Portfolio

_____

Accomplishments

_____

Concerns and Issues

_____

Goals for the Next Quarter

_____

Grades   [ ] Reading   [ ] Writing   [ ] Work Habits

_____   _____
Student   Teacher

Today Mrs. Peterson conferences with Ted. They go over his three unit folders and set goals for the next quarter. Ted explains that he really didn't like *Tuck Everlasting* and didn't work as hard as he usually does. He says that the unit grade he received—B—reflects the grade he would give the book. Ted asks if he can choose five items from the other two units because he really doesn't have anything in this unit folder that he wants to put into his portfolio, and Mrs. Peterson agrees.

Ted participated in the book club reading *Bunnicula: A Rabbit-Tale of Mystery* (Howe & Howe, 1979), and he says that this is one of his favorite books. Through his reading log and participation in grand conversations, Ted demonstrated his comprehension of the story and knowledge of story structure. Mrs. Peterson recalls that Ted asked her about humor and whether or not it was an element of story structure. He says that he now thinks humor is the glue that holds the story together because it is a combination of characters, plot, setting, and point of view. He tells Mrs. Peterson that he has concluded that he likes stories like *Bunnicula* that are told in the first person best.

Ted shows Mrs. Peterson his literature log, written from Harold the dog's viewpoint, and a chart he has made about the humor in the book that he wants to place in his portfolio. Mrs. Peterson agrees. Ted's grade for this book club unit is an A on his assignment sheet, and Ted agrees that he deserved it.

During reading workshop, Ted has continued reading *Bunnicula* sequels. He has read *Howliday Inn* (Howe, 1981), *The Celery Stalks at Midnight* (Howe, 1983), *Nighty-Nightmare* (Howe, 1987), and *Return to Howliday Inn* (Howe, 1992). He made an audiotape of his reading of excerpts from each of the books, and this is one of the items he wants to put in his portfolio. He is especially proud of the voices he uses for each character. Mrs. Peterson praises Ted for his enthusiasm and the number of books he has read in reading workshop. His grade for reading workshop will be an A. She also asks if the Bunnicula books are challenging him, or if they are easy for him. He admits that they are "sort of easy" and agrees to choose some more challenging books during the next quarter.

During writing workshop, Ted has written and mailed a letter to author James Howe. He wants to put a copy of the letter in his portfolio, along with the response he is eagerly awaiting. He became interested in vampires through the *Bunnicula* books and has researched them. Now he is finishing a book he's calling "What's True and What's Not About Vampires," and he wants to place it in his portfolio, too. He is preparing his final copy on the computer so that it will be neat.

Mrs. Peterson talks with Ted about his writing process. He talks about how he draws a series of small boxes representing each page on a sheet of paper during prewriting to plan his book. He tries to plan out the entire book in his head, and then he writes the book straight through, paying little attention to revising. He met with Mrs. Peterson several days earlier to edit his book, and although there were several places where he might have made some revisions, he didn't want to. Mrs. Peterson expresses her concern that he isn't giving adequate attention to revising and that this is affecting the quality of his writing. His grade for writing workshop will be a B.

During the last several minutes of the conference, Ted sets goals for the next quarter. For reading, he wants to read ten books and agrees to choose more challenging books. For writing, he reluctantly agrees to take time to revise his work, and, because Ted enjoys word processing, Mrs. Peterson suggests that he do both his rough drafts and final copies on the computer. Ted also volunteers that he would like to try his hand at writing a play during writing workshop in the next quarter. He had attended a play with his family and learned about scripts. Now he wants to write one. He thinks perhaps that he will feature Bunnicula, Harold, and Chester in the play.

The conference ends, Ted returns to his desk, and Mrs. Peterson calls another student to the conference table.

A ssessing students' literacy development is a difficult task. Although it may seem fairly easy to develop and administer a criterion-referenced test, tests measure reading and writing skills rather than students' abilities to use literacy in authentic ways. Tests in which students match characters and events or write the meanings of words do not measure comprehension very well, and a test on punctuation marks, for example, does not indicate students' ability to use punctuation marks correctly in their own writing. Instead, tests typically evaluate students' ability to add punctuation marks to a set of sentences created by someone else, or to proofread and spot punctuation errors in someone else's writing.

Traditional assessment reflects outdated views of how students learn to read and write, and they are incomplete assessments of students' literacy abilities. Tests and other traditional assessment procedures focus on only a few aspects of what readers do as they read, and of what writers do as they write. Traditional reading assessment fails to use authentic reading tasks or to help teachers find ways to help students succeed.

Assessment should resemble real reading and real writing (Valencia, Hiebert, & Afflerbach, 1994). A better approach is authentic assessment, in which teachers examine both the processes that students use as they read and write and the artifacts or products that readers and writers produce, such as projects and reading logs. Students, too, participate in reflecting and self-assessing their learning. Authentic assessment has five purposes:

- to document mileposts in students' development as readers and writers
- to identify students' strengths in order to plan for instruction
- to document students' reading and writing activities
- to determine grades
- to help teachers learn more about how children become strategic readers and writers

Assessment is more than testing—it is an integral part of teaching and learning (K. S. Goodman, Goodman, & Hood, 1989). The purpose of classroom assessment is to inform and influence instruction. Through authentic assessment, teachers learn about their students, about themselves as teachers, and about the impact of the instructional program. Similarly, when students reflect on their learning and use self-assessment, they learn about themselves as learners and also about their learning. Figure 12–3 presents guidelines for authentic assessment and describes how students can use authentic assessment tools in their classrooms.

FIGURE 12–3 Guidelines for Authentic Assessment

1. Appropriate Assessment Tools

Teachers identify their purpose for assessment and choose an appropriate assessment tool. To gauge students' reading fluency, for example, teachers can do a running record, and to judge whether or not students are comprehending, they can examine students' reading logs and listen to their comments during a grand conversation.

2. Variety of Assessment Tools

Teachers learn how to use and then regularly use a variety of assessment tools that reflect current theories about how children learn and become literate, including running records, anecdotal notes, and reading logs.

3. Integration of Instruction and Assessment

Teachers use the results of assessment to inform their teaching. They observe and conference with students as they teach and supervise students during reading and writing activities. When students do not understand what teachers are trying to teach, teachers need to try other instructional procedures.

4. Positive Focus

Teachers focus on what students can do, not what they can't do. Too often teachers want to diagnose students' problems and then remediate or "fix" these problems, but teachers should focus on how to facilitate students' development as readers and writers.

5. Both Processes and Products

Teachers examine both the processes and the products of reading and writing. Teachers notice the strategies that students use as well as assess the products they produce through reading and writing.

6. Multiple Contexts

Teachers assess students' literacy development in a variety of contexts, including literature focus units, reading and writing workshop, and theme studies. Multiple contexts are important because students often do better in one type of activity than another.

7. Individual Students

In addition to whole-class assessments, teachers make time to observe, conference with, and do other assessment procedures with individual students in order to develop clear understandings of the student's development as a reader or writer.

8. Self-Assessment

Students' reflection and self-assessment of their progress in reading and writing should be an integral part of assessment.

In this chapter you will learn how to assess students' learning in literature-based reading classrooms. As you read, think about these questions:

■ How do teachers monitor students' progress?
■ What procedures can teachers use to assess students' development in reading and writing?
■ How do students use portfolios?
■ How do teachers assign grades?

LITERACY ASSESSMENT TOOLS

Teachers use a variety of literacy assessment tools and procedures to monitor, document, and examine students' reading and writing development. These tools examine students' ability to identify words, read fluently, comprehend what they are reading, use the writing process, and invent spellings. These tools are informal and created by teachers. They are usually used with individual students, and even though it takes time to administer individual assessments, the information the teacher gains is useful and valuable. Giving a paper-and-pencil test to the entire class rarely provides much useful information. Teachers learn much more about their students as they listen to individual students read, watch individual students write, and talk with individual students about their reading and writing.

Monitoring Students' Progress

Teachers monitor students' learning continuously in literature-based reading classrooms, and they use the results of their monitoring to inform their teaching (Baskwill & Whitman, 1988; K. S. Goodman et al., 1989). As they monitor students' learning, teachers learn about their students, about themselves as teachers, and about the impact of the instructional program. Five ways to monitor students' progress are:

1. Observing students as they read and write. Literature-based reading teachers are "kid watchers," a term Yetta Goodman (1978) coined and defined as "direct and informal observation of students" (p. 37). To be an effective kid watcher, teachers must understand how children learn to read and write. Some observation times should be planned when the teacher focuses on particular students and makes anecdotal notes about the students' involvement in literacy events. The focus is on what students do as they read or write, not on whether or not they are behaving properly or working quietly. Of course, little learning can occur in disruptive situations, but during these observations the focus is on literacy, not behavior.

2. Taking anecdotal notes of literacy events. Teachers write brief notes as they observe students, and the most useful notes describe specific events, report rather than evaluate, and relate the events to other information about the student (Rhodes & Nathenson-Mejia, 1992). Teachers make notes about students' reading and writing activities, the questions students ask, and the strategies and skills they use fluently or indicate confusion about. These records document students' growth and pinpoint

Teachers monitor students' learning as they work with small groups of students.

problem areas for future minilessons or conferences. Mrs. Peterson's anecdotal notes about sixth-grade students in the book club reading *Bunnicula: A Rabbit-Tale of Mystery* (Howe & Howe, 1979) appear in Figure 12–4.

3. Conferencing with students.   Teachers talk with students to monitor their progress in reading and writing activities as well as to set goals and help students solve problems. Figure 12–5 presents a list of seven types of conferences that teachers have with students. Often these conferences are brief and impromptu, held at students' desks as the teacher moves around the classroom, while at other times the conferences are planned and students meet with the teacher at a designated conference table, as Mrs. Peterson did with her sixth graders in the vignette at the beginning of this chapter.

4. Documenting students' learning with checklists.   Teachers use checklists as they observe literacy events, track students' progress during literature focus units or reading and writing workshop, and document students' use of literacy skills, strategies, and procedures. Teachers also develop checklists for students to use to keep track of assignments during literature focus units or to use as they edit their writing.

5. Collecting students' work samples.   Teachers have students collect their work in folders to document learning during literature focus units and reading and writing workshop. Work samples might include reading logs, audiotapes of a students' reading, photos of projects, videotapes of puppet shows and oral presentations, and books students have written. Students often choose some of these work samples to place in their portfolios.

FIGURE 12–4 Mrs. Peterson's Anecdotal Notes About a Book Club

March 2

Met with the *Bunnicula* book club as they started reading the book. They have their reading, writing, and discussion schedule set. Sari questioned how a dog could write the book. We reread the Editor's Note. She asked if Harold really wrote the book. She's the only one confused in the group. Is she always so literal? Mario pointed out that you have to know that Harold supposedly wrote the book to understand the first-person viewpoint of the book. Talked to Sari about fantasy. Told her she'll be laughing out loud as she reads this book. She doubts it.

March 3

Returned to *Bunnicula* book club for first grand conversation, especially to check on Sari. Annie, Mario, Ted, Rod, Laurie, and Belinda talked about their pets and imagine them taking over their homes. Sari is not getting into the book. She doesn't have any pets and can't imagine the pets doing these things. I asked if she wanted to change groups. Perhaps a realistic book would be better. She says no. Is that because Ted is in the group?

March 5

The group is reading Chapters 4 and 5 today. Laurie asks questions about white vegetables and vampires. Rod goes to get an encyclopedia to find out about vampires. Mario asks about DDT. Everyone—even Sari—involved in reading.

March 8

During a grand conversation, students compare the characters Harold and Chester. The group plans to make a Venn diagram comparing the characters for the sharing on Friday. Students decide that character is the most important element, but Ted argues that humor is the most important element in the story. Other students say humor isn't an element. I asked what humor is a reaction to—characters or plot? I checked journals and all are up to date.

March 10

The group has finished reading the book. I share sequels from the class library. Sari grabs one to read. She's glad she stayed with the book. Ted wants to write his own sequel in writing workshop. Mario plans to write a letter to James Howe.

March 12

Ted and Sari talk about *Bunnicula* and share related books. Rod and Mario share the Venn diagram of characters. Annie reads her favorite part, and Laurie shows her collection of rabbits. Belinda hangs back. I wonder if she has been involved. I need to talk to her.

FIGURE 12–5   Seven Types of Conferences

---

1. On-the-Spot Conferences

Teachers visit briefly with students at their desks to monitor some aspect of the students' work or to check on progress. These conferences are brief; the teacher may spend less than a minute at each student's desk.

2. Prereading or Prewriting Conferences

The teacher and student make plans for reading or writing at the conference. At a prereading conference, they may talk about information related to the book, difficult concepts or vocabulary words related to the reading, or the reading log the student will keep. At a prewriting conference, they may discuss possible writing topics or how to narrow a broad topic.

3. Revising Conferences

A small group of students and the teacher meet to get specific suggestions about revising their compositions. These conferences offer student writers an audience to provide feedback on how well they have communicated.

4. Book Discussion Conferences

Students and the teacher meet to discuss the book they have read. They may share reading log entries, discuss plot or characters, compare the story to others they have read, or make plans to extend their reading.

5. Editing Conferences

The teacher reviews students' proofread compositions and helps them correct spelling, punctuation, capitalization, and other mechanical errors.

6. Minilesson Conferences

The teacher meets with students to explain a procedure, strategy, or skill (e.g., writing a table of contents, using the visualization strategy when reading, capitalizing proper nouns).

7. Assessment Conferences

The teacher meets with students after they have completed an assignment or project to talk about their growth as readers or writers. Students reflect on their competencies and set goals.

Examining Students' Oral Reading

Teachers observe individual students as they read aloud and also take **running records** of students' reading to assess their reading fluency (Clay, 1985). With a running record, teachers calculate the percentage of words the student reads correctly and then analyze the miscues or errors. Teachers make a check mark on a sheet of paper as the child reads each word correctly. Teachers use other marks to indicate words that the student substitutes, repeats, pronounces incorrectly, or doesn't know. While teachers can make the running record on a blank sheet of paper, it is much easier to duplicate a copy of the page or pages the student will read and take the running

Teachers take running records as they listen to students read books aloud.

record next to or on top of the actual text. Making a copy of the text is especially important for middle- and upper-grade students who read more complex texts and read them more quickly than younger students do.

After identifying the words that the student read incorrectly, teachers calculate the percentage of words the student read correctly. Teachers use the percentage of words read correctly to determine whether or not the book or other reading material is too easy, too difficult, or appropriate for the student at this time. If the student reads 95% or more of the words correctly, the book is easy or at the independent reading level for that child. If the student reads 90–94% of the words correctly, the book is at the student's instructional level. If the student reads fewer than 90% of the words correctly, the book is too difficult for the student to read. It is at the student's frustration level.

Running records are easy for teachers to take, although teachers need some practice before they are comfortable with the procedure. Figure 12–6 presents a running record done with a sixth grader in Mrs. Peterson's classroom. This student was reading the beginning of Chapter 1 of *Bunnicula: A Rabbit-Tale of Mystery* (Howe & Howe, 1979) when the reading record was taken.

Teachers can categorize and analyze the student's errors to identify patterns of error, as shown at the bottom of Figure 12–6. Then teachers use this information as they plan minilessons and other word-study activities. Another way to analyze students' errors is called miscue analysis (K. S. Goodman, 1976). "Miscue" is another word for "error," and it suggests that students used the wrong cueing system to figure out the word. For example, if a student reads "Dad" for "Father," the error is meaning-related because the student over-relied on the semantic system. If a student reads "Feather" for "Father," the error is more likely graphophonic (or phonological), because the student over-relied on the beginning sound in the word and didn't evaluate whether or

FIGURE 12–6 Running Record and Analysis

Text	Running Record
I shall never forget the first time I laid these	✓ *will/shall* ✓ ✓ ✓ ✓ ✓ ✓
now tired old eyes on our visitor. I had been	— *tie-red/now tired* ✓ ✓ ✓ ✓ ✓ ✓ ✓
left home by the family with the admonition	✓ ✓ ✓ ✓ ✓ ✓ *T/admonition*
to take care of the house until they returned.	✓ ✓ ✓ ✓ ✓ ✓ ✓ ✓
That's something they always say to me when	✓ ✓ ✓ ✓ ✓ ✓ ✓
they go out: "Take care of the house, Harold.	✓ ✓ ✓ ✓ ✓ ✓ ✓ ✓
You're the watchdog." I think it's their	✓ ✓ *wa-wash-watchdog/watchdog* ✓ ✓ ✓
way of making up for not taking me with	✓ ✓ ✓ ✓ ✓ ✓ ✓ ✓
them. As if I wanted to go anyway. You can't	✓ ✓ ✓ ✓ ✓ ✓ ✓ ✓ ✓
lie down at the movies and still see the screen.	*lay/lie* ✓ ✓ ✓ ✓ ✓ ✓ ✓ ✓
And people think you're being impolite if you	— /*And* ✓ ✓ ✓ ✓ *impo-impo-T/impolite* ✓ ✓
fall asleep and start to snore, or scratch	✓ ✓ ✓ ✓ ✓ ✓ *scrap/scratch*
yourself in public. No thank you, I'd rather	✓ ✓ ✓ ✓ ✓ ✓
be stretched out on my favorite rug	✓ *streaked/stretched* ✓ ✓ ✓ ✓
in front of a nice, whistling radiator.	✓ ✓ ✓ ✓ ✓ *radio/radiator*

Analysis

Total words 128
Errors 11
Accuracy rate 92% (instructional level)

This student read the text with interest, enthusiasm, and good expression. After reading, the student was able to talk about what he had read and to make predictions about Harold's role in the story. The errors are:

Substitution	will/shall
	lay/lie
	scrap/scratch
	streaked/stretched
	radio/radiator
Omission	now
	and
Mispronounced	tie-red/tired
Teacher told	admonition
	impolite
Prolonged decoding	watchdog

Most of the errors were multisyllabic words, which the student was unable to break apart. A series of minilessons on breaking apart multisyllabic words to decode them is recommended for this student. The first two substitution errors did not affect meaning, and the two omission errors did not affect meaning either.

Reprinted with the permission of Atheneum Books for Young Readers, an imprint of Simon and Schuster Children's Publishing Division. From *Bunnicula: A Rabbit-Tale of Mystery* by Deborah Howe and James Howe. Text copyright © 1979 James Howe.

not the word made sense semantically. The Dad/Father and Feather/Father miscues are both syntactically correct because a noun was substituted for a noun. Sometimes, however, students substitute words that don't make sense syntactically. For example, if a student reads "tomorrow" for "through" in the sentence "Father walked through the door," the error doesn't make sense either semantically or syntactically, even though both words begin with *t*.

Teachers can categorize students' miscues or errors according to the semantic, graphophonic, and syntactic cueing systems in order to examine what word-identification strategies students are using. As they categorize the miscues, teachers should ask themselves:

- Does the reader self-correct the miscue?
- Does the miscue change the meaning of the sentence?
- Is the miscue phonologically similar to the word in the text?
- Is the miscue acceptable within the syntax (or structure) of the sentence?

The errors that interfere with meaning and the errors that are syntactically unacceptable are the most serious because the student doesn't realize that reading should make sense. Errors can be classified and charted, as shown in Figure 12–7. These errors were taken from the sixth grader's running record presented in Figure 12–6. Only words that students mispronounce or substitute can be analyzed. Repetitions and omissions are not calculated.

■ *Activity*

Take a running record of several students reading passages of at least 100 words. Calculate the students' accuracy levels and analyze their errors.

Determining Students' Reading Levels

Teachers use a commercial test called an informal reading inventory (IRI) to determine students' reading levels. The reading levels are grade-level scores—second-grade level or sixth-grade level, for example. The IRI is an individually administered reading test and is typically composed of graded word lists, graded passages from stories and informational books, and comprehension questions. This inventory can also be used to assess students' reading strengths and weaknesses.

The graded word lists consist of 10 to 20 words at each grade level, from first grade through eighth or ninth. Students read the lists of words until they reach a point when the words become too difficult for them. This indicates an approximate level for students to begin reading the graded reading passages. In addition, teachers can note the decoding skills that students use to identify words presented in isolation.

The graded reading passages are series of narrative and expository passages, ranging in difficulty. Students read these passages orally or silently and then answer a series of comprehension questions. The questions are designed to focus on main ideas, inferences, and vocabulary. Teachers use scoring sheets to record students' performance, and they analyze the results to see how readers use strategies in context, how they identify unknown words, and how they comprehend what they read.

Students' scores on the IRI can be used to calculate their independent, instructional, and frustration reading levels. At the independent level, students can read the text comfortably and without assistance. Students read books at this level for pleasure and during reading workshop. At the instructional level, students can read textbooks and trade books successfully with teacher guidance. Books selected for literature focus

FIGURE 12–7   Miscue Analysis of Student's Errors From Running Record

Student _____   Date _____

Text _____

WORDS			SEMANTICS	PHONOLOGY	SYNTAX
Text	Student	Self-corrected?	Similar meaning?	Graphophonic similarity?	Syntactically acceptable?
shall	will		✓		✓
tired	tie-red			✓	
lie	lay		✓	✓	✓
scratch	scrap			✓	
stretched	streaked			✓	✓
radiator	radio			✓	✓

Analysis:

This student seems to rely on graphophonic similarities—particularly beginning sounds—more than semantic similarities. The student did not self-correct any words.

units and book clubs should be at students' instructional levels. At the frustration level, the reading materials are too difficult for students to read, so students often don't understand what they are reading. As the name implies, students become very frustrated when they attempt to read trade books and textbooks at this level. When books featured in literature focus units are too difficult for some students to read, teachers need to make provisions for these students. Teachers can use shared reading, buddy reading, or reading aloud to students.

IRIs can also be used to identify students' listening capacity levels. Teachers read aloud passages written at or above students' frustration levels and ask students the comprehension questions. If students can answer the questions, they understand the passage. Teachers then know that students will be able to understand books being read aloud during literature focus units and that students have the potential to improve their reading to this level.

A variety of commercially published IRIs are available. Some of the better-known IRIs are:

Analytical Reading Inventory (Woods & Moe, 1995)
Classroom Reading Inventory (Silvaroli, 1994)
The Flynt/Cooter Reading Inventory for the Classroom (Flynt & Cooter, 1995)

Other IRIs accompany basal reading series, and teachers can construct their own using textbooks or trade books written at each reading level.

Assessing Students' Comprehension

Since the goal of reading is comprehension, it is especially important that teachers assess whether or not students understand what they are reading, However, because comprehension is an invisible process, teachers must find ways to examine what students say and write about their reading to see how well they comprehend. The traditional way to check on students' comprehension is to ask questions, but there are more authentic ways to assess comprehension. Three ways are the cloze procedure, story retellings, and reading logs. Other ways include noting students' comments during grand conversations, talking with students about the story they are reading in conferences, and noticing how students apply what they have learned in books in the projects they develop.

The **cloze procedure** is an informal tool for assessing students' comprehension. The word *cloze* comes from the word *closure*. Teachers create the reading material by selecting an excerpt of 100 to 300 words from a story, informational book, or textbook that students have read. Then they delete every fifth word in the passage and replace each deleted word with a blank. Then students read the passage and write the missing words in the blanks. Students use their knowledge of the topic, of narrative or expository texts, of word order in English, and of the meaning of words within sentences to successfully guess the missing words in the passage. Only the exact word is considered the correct answer.

Teachers often vary the cloze procedure and delete specific content words rather than every fifth word. Character names and words related to key events in the story might be omitted. For passages from informational books, teachers often delete key terms. If students are to be graded on how well they complete this assignment, teachers can calculate a percentage or set a grading scale so that zero or one error is an A, two, three, or four errors are a B, and so on.

The following cloze procedure was devised by a fourth-grade teacher to assess students' understanding during a unit on astronomy. The three paragraphs were taken from a class book, and each was written by a different student:

> The _____ planets travel around the _____ . The _____ is a
> planet that travels around the sun once a year. The planets between the sun
> and the Earth are called the _____ planets and the others are the _____
> planets. The planets are Mercury, _____ , Earth, Mars, Jupiter, _____ ,
> Uranus, _____ , and Pluto. The sun, the planets, and their _____ make
> up the _____ system.

Stars are giant shining balls of hot _____ . The _____ are dark, and we can only _____ them because they reflect the _____ of the sun. Planets and stars look almost the same at night, but planets do not _____ . Stars stay in the same place in the _____ , but planets _____ around.

Jupiter is the _____ planet in the solar system. It is the _____ planet from the _____ . Jupiter is covered with thick _____ so we can't see it from Earth. Astronomers can see a giant _____ spot on the clouds. Maybe it is sort of like a hurricane. Believe it or not, Jupiter has both _____ and _____ . It is very _____ on Jupiter, but there could be life there.

A second way to find out if students understand a story they have read is through story retelling (Gambrell, Pfeiffer, & Wilson, 1985; Morrow, 1985). This procedure is especially useful with emergent readers. The teacher asks students to retell the story in their own words. Sometimes the teacher turns the pages through a picture book or uses **story boards** to prompt the child. The teacher can also have students retell everything they remember about the story. Afterwards the teacher asks questions or prompts, "What else can you remember?" A story retelling sheet is presented in Figure 12–8. The teacher makes notes about the student's unaided retelling in the column on the left side, asks the prompts written in the middle column as needed, and adds the student's prompted responses in the right column.

FIGURE 12–8   A Story Retelling Sheet

Story Retelling Sheet

Name _____   Date _____
Story _____

Student's familiarity with the story:

●——●——●——●——●
one reading   many readings

Part	Student's Unaided Retelling	Prompts	Student's Aided Retelling
Beginning		What happened at the beginning? Where did the story take place? Who were the characters? What was the main problem?	
Middle		What happened in the middle? What happened next? What did—do?	
End		How was the problem solved? What happened at the end? What was the author's message?	

A third way teachers assess students' comprehension is by reviewing their reading logs. Wollman-Bonilla (1991) identified four kinds of assessment information teachers can cull from reading logs:

1. *Comprehension.* Students' entries reveal their understanding of story events and characters.
2. *Reading processes.* Students write their about predictions, how they monitor their reading, and what they do when they are confused or the reading isn't going well.
3. *Literary knowledge.* Students write about genre, literary language and favorite quotes, authors and how they manipulate story elements, and illustrators and their illustrations.
4. *Engagement with reading.* Students relate how they empathize with characters, connections they make between the stories and their own lives, and connections with other literature they have read.

As teachers review reading logs, they can note these four kinds of comments in students' entries. If students don't make these types of comments, teachers can ask questions to further probe their understandings.

Documenting Students' Growth as Writers

As students' writing develops, it gets more complex in a variety of ways. One of the most obvious changes is that it gets longer. Longer doesn't mean better, but as students write longer pieces, their writing often shows other signs of growth, too. Four ways that elementary students' writing develops are:

1. *Ideas.* Students' writing is creative, and they develop the main ideas and provide supporting details. Their writing is tailored to both purpose and audience.
2. *Organization.* Writers present ideas in a logical sequence and provide transitions between ideas. The composition is divided into paragraphs. For stories, students organize their writing into beginning, middle, and end, and for informational pieces, topic sentences clarify the organization.
3. *Language.* Students use words effectively, including figurative language. They choose language that is appropriate for purpose and audience. Students use Standard English word forms and sentence constructions. They also vary the types of sentences they write.
4. *Mechanics.* Students use correct spelling, punctuation, and capitalization. The composition is formatted appropriately for the writing form (e.g., letters, poems, plays, or stories), and the final copy is neat (Tompkins, 1994).

Teachers develop rubrics, or scoring guides, to assess students' growth as writers (Farr & Tone, 1994). Rubrics make the analysis of writing simpler and the assessment process more reliable and consistent. Rubrics may have three, four, five, or six levels, with descriptors related to ideas, organization, language, and mechanics at each level. Some rubrics are general and appropriate for almost any writing assignment, while others are designed for a specific writing assignment. Figure 12–9 presents two rubrics. One is a general five-level rubric for middle-grade students, and the other is a four-level rubric for assessing sixth graders' reports on ancient Egypt. In contrast to

FIGURE 12–9   Two Rubrics for Assessing Students' Writing

Middle-Grade Writing Rubric
5   EXCEPTIONAL ACHIEVEMENT
• Creative and original • Clear organization • Precise word choice and figurative language • Sophisticated sentences • Essentially free of mechanical errors
4   EXCELLENT ACHIEVEMENT
• Some creativity, but more predictable than an exceptional paper • Definite organization • Good word choice but not figurative language • Varied sentences • Only a few mechanical errors
3   ADEQUATE ACHIEVEMENT
• Predictable paper • Some organization • Adequate word choice • Little variety of sentences and some run-on sentences • Some mechanical errors
2   LIMITED ACHIEVEMENT
• Brief and superficial • Lacks organization • Imprecise language • Incomplete and run-on sentences • Many mechanical errors
1   MINIMAL ACHIEVEMENT
• No ideas communicated • No organization • Inadequate word choice • Sentence fragments • Overwhelming mechanical errors

the general rubric, the report rubric includes specific components that students were to include in their reports.

Both teachers and students can assess writing with rubrics. They read the composition and highlight words in the rubric that best describe the composition. The score is determined by examining the highlighted words and determining which level has the most highlighted words.

FIGURE 12–9 *continued*

Rubric for Assessing Reports on Ancient Egypt	

4 EXCELLENT REPORT
_____ Three or more chapters with titles
_____ Main idea clearly developed in each chapter
_____ Three or more illustrations
_____ Effective use of Egypt-related words in text and illustrations
_____ Very interesting to read
_____ Very few mechanical errors
_____ Table of contents

3 GOOD REPORT
_____ Three chapters with titles
_____ Main idea somewhat developed in each chapter
_____ Three illustrations
_____ Some Egypt-related words used
_____ Interesting to read
_____ A few mechanical errors
_____ Table of contents

2 AVERAGE REPORT
_____ Three chapters
_____ Main idea identified in each chapter
_____ One or two illustrations
_____ A few Egypt-related words used
_____ Some mechanical errors
_____ Sort of interesting to read
_____ Table of contents

1 POOR REPORT
_____ One or two chapters
_____ Information in each chapter rambles
_____ No illustrations
_____ Very few Egypt-related words used
_____ Many mechanical errors
_____ Hard to read and understand
_____ No table of contents

Analyzing Students' Invented Spellings

Teachers analyze children's invented spellings by examining their writing and classifying the words not spelled conventionally according to the five stages of spelling development (discussed in Chapter 3, "Breaking the Code"). This analysis provides information about the child's level of spelling development and the kinds of errors the child makes. Knowing the stage of a student's spelling development suggests the appropriate type of instruction. A composition written by Marc, a first grader, is presented in Figure 12–10. He reverses *b* and *s,* and these two reversals

FIGURE 12–10 An Analysis of an Emergent Writer's Invented Spelling

To bay a perezun at home kob
uz anb seb that a bome wuz in
or skuwl anb mab uz go at zib
anb makbe uz wat a haf uf
a awr anb it mab uz wazt or
time on l oren ee ing.

THE eNb

Precommunicative	Semiphonetic	Phonetic	Transitional	Conventional
	kod	sed	peresun	today
		wus	bome	a
		or	skuwl	at
		mad	makde	home
		at sid	uf	us
		wat	loreneeing	and
		haf		that
		awr		a
		mad		in
		wast		and
		or		us
				go
				and
				us
				a
				a
				and
				it
				us
				time
				on
				the
				end
Total 0	1	11	6	23
Percent 0	2	27	15	56

make his writing more difficult to decipher. Here is a translation of Marc's composition:

Today a person at home called us and said that a bomb was in our school and made us go outside and made us wait a half of an hour and it made us waste our time on learning. The end.

Marc was writing about a traumatic event, and it was appropriate to use invented spelling in his composition. Primary-grade students should write using invented spelling, and conventional spelling should be required only if the composition will "go public." Prematurely differentiating between "kid" and "adult" spelling interferes with children's natural spelling development and makes them dependent on adults to supply the "adult" spelling.

Teachers categorize children's invented spellings using a chart like the one at the bottom of Figure 12–10. They list each invented spelling in one of the categories, ignoring proper nouns, capitalization errors, and poorly formed or reversed letters. They calculate the number of invented spellings in each category. If the student spells 90% or more words correctly, the student is classified as a conventional speller. Otherwise, the student is classified as spelling at the stage where most of the invented spellings fall.

Perhaps the most interesting thing about Marc's writing is that he spelled 56% of the words correctly. Only one word, *kod (called),* is categorized as semiphonetic, and it is classified this way because the spelling is extremely abbreviated, with only the first and last sounds represented. The 11 words categorized as phonetic are words in which it appears that his spelling represents only the sounds heard; unpronounced letters, such as the final *e* in *made* and the *i* in *wait,* are not represented. Marc pronounces *our* as though it were a homophone for *or,* so *or* is a reasonable phonetic spelling. Homophone errors are phonological because the child focuses on sound, not on meaning.

The words categorized as transitional exemplify a spelling strategy other than sound. In *bome (bomb),* for example, Marc applied the rule he recently learned about final *e,* even though it isn't appropriate in this word. In time he will learn to spell the word with an unpronounced *b* and know that this *b* is needed because *bomb* is a newer, shortened form of *bombard,* in which the *b* in the middle of the word is pronounced. The *b* remains in *bomb* because of the etymology of the word. The word *makde* is especially interesting. Marc pronounced the word "maked," and the *de* is a reversal of letters, a common characteristic of transitional spelling. Transitional spellers often spell *girl* as *gril* and *friend* as *freind.* That *made,* not *maked,* is the past tense of *make* is a grammatical error and unimportant in determining the stage of spelling development. *Loreneeing (learning)* is categorized as transitional because Marc added long-vowel markers (an *e* after *lor* and *ee* after *n*). Because the spelling is based on his pronunciation of *learning,* the long-vowel markers and the conventional spelling of the suffix *-ing* signal a transitional spelling. Categorizing spelling errors in a child's composition and computing the percentage of errors in each category is a useful tool for diagnosing the level of spelling development and deciding whether or not to begin formal spelling instruction.

From the spelling in Marc's composition, he might be classified as a phonetic speller who is moving toward the transitional stage. Marc's paper was written in January of his first-grade year, and he is making expected progress in spelling. During the next few months, he will begin to notice that his spelling doesn't look right (e.g., *sed* for *said*) and will note visual features of words. He will apply the vowel rules he is learning more effectively, particularly the final *e (mad* will become *made, sid* will become *side,* and *wast* will become *waste).*

Marc is not ready for weekly spelling tests, in which he would memorize correct spellings of words, because he has not yet internalized the visual and morphological spelling strategies of the transitional stage. Also, Marc will probably self-correct the *b* and *s* reversals through daily writing experiences, as long as he is not placed under great pressure to form the letters correctly.

IMPLEMENTING PORTFOLIOS IN THE CLASSROOM

Portfolios are systematic and meaningful collections of artifacts documenting students' literacy development over a period of time (Graves & Sunstein, 1992; Porter & Cleland, 1995; Tierney, Carter, & Desai, 1991). These collections are dynamic and reflect students' day-to-day reading and writing activities as well as across-the-curriculum activities. Students' work samples provide "windows" on the strategies that students use as readers and writers. Students not only select pieces to be placed in their portfolios but learn to establish criteria for their selections. Because of students' involvement in selecting pieces for their portfolios and reflecting on them, portfolio assessment respects students and their abilities. Portfolios help students, teachers, and parents see patterns of growth from one literacy milestone to another in ways that are not possible with other types of assessment.

Why are portfolio programs worthwhile?

There are many reasons why portfolio programs complement a literature-based reading programs. The most important one is that students become more involved in the assessment of their work and more reflective about the quality of their reading and writing. Other benefits include:

- Students feel ownership of their work.
- Students become more responsible about their work.
- Students set goals and are motivated to work toward accomplishing them.
- Students reflect on their accomplishments.
- Students make connections between learning and assessing.
- Students' self-esteem is enhanced.
- Students recognize the connection between process and product.
- Portfolios eliminate the need to grade all student work.
- Portfolios are used in student and parent conferences.
- Portfolios complement the information provided in report cards.

Rolling Valley Elementary School in Springfield, Virginia, implemented a portfolio program schoolwide several years ago. The students overwhelmingly reported that by using portfolios they were better able to show their parents what they were learning and also better able to set goals for themselves (Clemmons, Laase, Cooper, Areglado, & Dill, 1993). The teachers also reported that by using portfolios they

Students choose items for their portfolios that reflect their growth as readers and writers.

were able to assess their students more thoroughly and that their students were better able to see their own progress.

Collecting Work in Portfolios

Portfolios are folders, large envelopes, or boxes that hold students' work. Teachers often have students label and decorate large folders and then store them in plastic crates or large cardboard boxes. Students date and label items as they place them in their portfolios, and they often attach notes to the items to explain the context for the activity and why they selected this particular item. Students' portfolios should be stored in the classroom in a place where they are readily accessible to students. Students like to review their portfolios periodically and add new pieces to them.

Students usually choose the items to place in their portfolios within the guidelines provided by the teacher. Some students submit the original piece of work; others want to keep the original, so they place a copy in the portfolio instead. In addition to the reading and writing samples that can go directly into portfolios, students also record oral language and drama samples on audiotapes and videotapes to place in their portfolios. (To learn more about videotape portfolios, check the Technology Link on page 459.) Large-size art and writing projects can be photographed, and the photographs placed in the portfolio. The following types of student work might be placed in a portfolio:

"All About . . ." books

alphabet books

autobiographies

biographies

books

choral readings (on audiotape)

clusters

drawings, diagrams, and charts

learning log entries

letters to pen pals, businesses, authors (copies, because the originals have been sent)

lists of books read

newspaper articles

oral reading (on audiotape or videotape)

oral reports (on audiotape or videotape)

poems

projects

puppets (on photographs)

puppet shows (on videotape)

quickwrites

readers theatre presentations (on audiotape or videotape)

reading log entries

reports

simulated journal entries

stories

This variety of work samples takes into account all four language arts. Samples from literature focus units, reading and writing workshop, and across-the-curriculum theme studies should be included.

One piece of writing from a third grader's portfolio is shown in Figure 12–11. This sample is a simulated letter written to Peter Rabbit from Mr. McGregor as a project during a literature focus unit on *The Tale of Peter Rabbit* (Potter, 1902). The student's teacher taught a minilesson on persuasive writing, and this student applied what he had learned in his letter. He placed it in his portfolio because it looked good and because his classmates had really liked it when he had shared it with them. His prewriting, the rough draft, and a scoring rubric were tacked to the final copy shown in the figure. The scoring rubric is also shown.

The student and teacher scored the letter together using the rubric and rated it a 4 out of a possible 5 points. First, the child used the friendly letter format, so a check mark was placed on that line. Second, in the letter he had applied what he learned about persuasion. He suggested a deal to Peter and made a threat about what will

Technology Link
Videotape Portfolios

Teachers can document students' learning using a camcorder in ways that reading logs, lists of books students' have read, and conference notes cannot. The saying that "a picture is worth a thousand words" really is true! Students each bring a blank VCR tape at the beginning of the school year for their video portfolios. A sheet of paper is attached to each tape case to note dates and topics of the tapings. This sheet becomes the table of contents for the videotape.

When a camcorder is first introduced, students are distracted and "mug" for the camera, but after a few days they get used to it. Using a camcorder frequently is the best way to acclimate students. The teacher and student videographers film students as they are involved in a variety of literacy activities:

■ Record individual students reading aloud at the beginning of the year and at the end of each grading period.

■ Film students during reading and writing workshop.

■ Document student-teacher conferences.

■ Film oral performances, including puppet shows, readers theatre presentations, book talks, and reports.

■ Include group activities such as grand conversations and read-arounds.

■ Document students' work on projects, especially projects such as dioramas, book boxes, and murals, that can't be saved in traditional portfolio folders.

Keeping a camcorder in the classroom with batteries charged allows students and the teacher to capture ongoing classroom activities.

Creating video portfolios is too heavy a burden if teachers do all of the videotaping. Students—even second and third graders—can learn how to use the camcorder. Teachers identify guidelines for videotaping and establish routines for regular taping. They also experiment to determine how to get the best sound quality for individual and group activities, how long to film episodes, and how to transition between episodes. Aides and parents volunteers can be enlisted to assist, too.

Video portfolios often have jerky starts and abrupt stops, and sometimes the audio is difficult to hear, but nevertheless they are a meaningful record of students' literacy development and reading and writing activities spanning a school year. Even though video portfolios are rarely polished productions, they are valuable documentation for students, teachers, and parents.

happen if the rabbit comes back into the garden. A check mark was also placed on the second line. Next, he used character names and other information from the story in the persuasive argument, so the third item was checked, too. Fourth, the student and teacher looked at the spelling and other conventions. The teacher pointed out five misspelled words (*stesling-stealing, vegetbles-vegetables, rember-remember, vegtables-vegetables*, and *sind-signed*) and checked to see if they had been corrected on the rough draft during editing. All but one had, but the student had failed to use the corrected spellings in his final draft. After some consideration, the student and his teacher decided not to add a check mark on this item, even though the errors were minor and did not interfere with reading the letter. The student recognized that he needed to be more careful when he made his final copy. The paper was neat, and the last item was checked. In addition, the teacher commended this student for his lively writing style and the way he highlighted important words in his letter.

Dear Peter,

      I wish you would stop stesling my vegetables! I'll tell you what, I'll make a deal. I'll leave some vegetbles out once a week. **OK?** But if you go in my garden one more time with out permission then I will put you in my **Pie!** OH and....ammm.... thanks for the clothes. And rember all you have to do is **tell Me** that you want some vegtables.

SiNd BY Mr. McgregoR

Rubric for Scoring Peter Rabbit Letters

- ✓ Uses the friendly letter format
- ✓ Is persuasive
- ✓ Uses information from the story
- ____ Uses mostly correct spelling and other mechanics
- ✓ Paper is neat

Other comments:

Very persuasive! I like the way you highlighted the important words.
I hear Mr. McGregor's voice clearly in your letter.

Scoring guide:

4 or 5 ✓	= A
3 ✓	= B
2 ✓	= C
1 ✓	= D

Many teachers collect students' work in folders, and they assume portfolios are basically the same as work folders; however, the two types of collections differ in several important ways. Perhaps the most important difference is that portfolios are student-oriented, while work folders are usually teachers' collections. Students choose which samples will be placed in portfolios, while teachers often place all completed assignments in work folders (Clemmons et al., 1993). Next, portfolios focus on students' strengths, not their weaknesses. Because students choose items for portfolios, they choose samples that best represent their literacy development. Another difference is that portfolios involve reflection (D'Aoust, 1992). Through reflection, students pause and become aware of their strengths as readers and writers. They also use their work samples to identify the literacy procedures, concepts, skills, and strategies they already know and ones they need to focus on.

Involving Students in Self-Assessment

A portfolio is not just a collection of work samples; instead, it is a vehicle for engaging students in self-evaluation and goal-setting (Clemmons et al., 1993). Students can learn to reflect on and assess their own reading and writing activities and their development as readers and writers (Stires, 1991). Teachers begin by asking students to think about their reading and writing in terms of contrasts. For reading, students identify the books they have read that they liked most and least, and ask themselves what these choices suggest about themselves as readers. They also identify what they do well in reading and what they need to improve about their reading. In writing, students make similar contrasts. They identify the compositions they thought were

Students conference with the teacher about items they select for their portfolios.

their best and others that were not so good, and think about what they do well when they write and what they need to improve. By making these comparisons, students begin to reflect on their literacy development.

Teachers use minilessons and conferences to talk with students about the characteristics of good readers and writers. In particular, they discuss:

- what fluent reading is
- what reading skills and strategies students use
- how students demonstrate their comprehension
- how students value books they have read
- what makes a good project to extend reading
- what makes an effective piece of writing
- what writing skills and strategies students use
- how to use writing rubrics
- how the effective use of mechanical skills is a courtesy to readers

As students learn about what it means to be effective readers and writers, they acquire the tools they need to reflect on and evaluate their own reading and writing. They learn how to think about themselves as readers and writers and acquire the vocabulary to use in their reflections, such as "goal," "strategy," and "rubric."

Students write notes on items they choose to put into their portfolios. In these self-assessments, students explain their reasons for the selection and identify strengths and accomplishments in their work. In some classrooms students write their reflections and other comments on index cards, while in other classrooms students design special comment sheets that they attach to the items in their portfolios. Two students' self-assessments are shown in Figure 12–12. In the first one, "Portfolio Notes," a fifth grader assesses his simulated journal, written from the viewpoint of Benjamin Franklin. In the second, a first grader writes about having read five books written and illustrated by Eric Carle, and this note is attached to her reading workshop book list for the week.

Clemmons et al. (1993) recommend collecting baseline reading and writing samples at the beginning of the school year and then conducting portfolio review conferences with students at the end of each grading period. At these conferences, the teacher and student talk about the items placed in the portfolio and the self-assessments the student has written. Together they also set goals for the next grading period. Students talk about what they want to improve or what they want to accomplish during the next grading period, and these points become their goals.

Self-assessment can also be used for an assessment at the end of the school year. Coughlan (1988) asked his seventh-grade students to "show me what you have learned about writing this year" and "explain how you have grown as a written language user, comparing what you knew in September to what you know now" (p. 375). These upper-grade students used a process approach to develop and refine their compositions, and they submitted all drafts with their final copies. Coughlan examined both the content of students' compositions and the strategies they used in thinking through the assignment and writing their responses. He found this "test" to be a very worthwhile project because it "forced the students to look within themselves . . . to realize just how much they had learned" (p. 378). Moreover, students' compositions verified that they had learned about writing and that they could articulate that learning.

FIGURE 12–12 Two Students' Self-Assessments of Items Placed in Their Porfolios

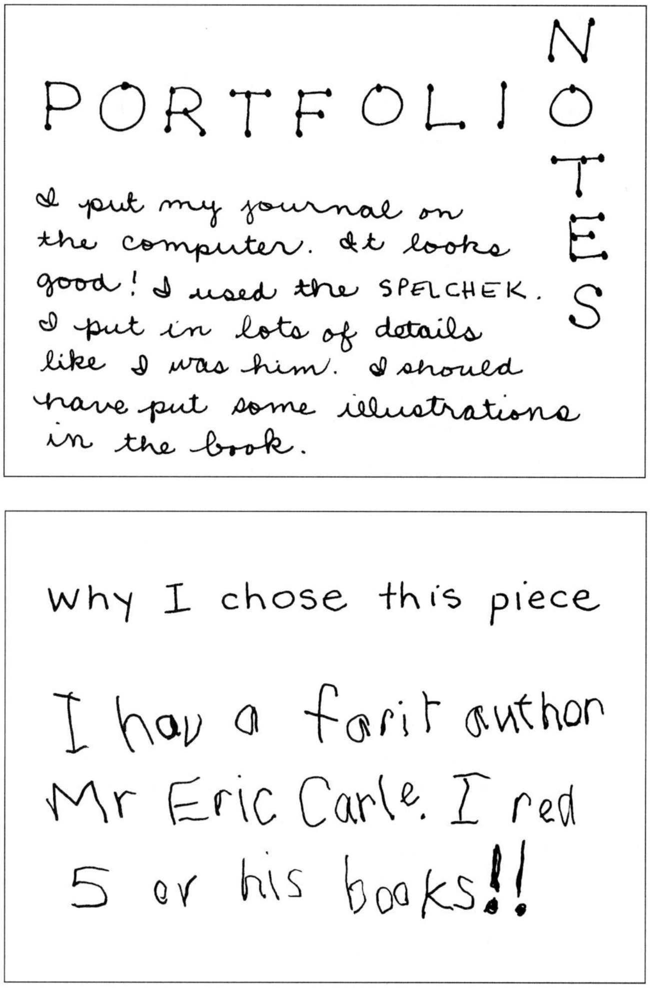

PORTFOLIO NOTES

I put my journal on the computer. It looks good! I used the SPELCHEK. I put in lots of details like I was him. I should have put some illustrations in the book.

Why I chose this piece

I hav a farit author Mr Eric Carle. I red 5 or his books!!

Showcasing Students' Portfolios

At the end of the school year, many teachers organize "Portfolio Share Days" to celebrate students' accomplishments and to provide an opportunity for students to share their portfolios with classmates and the wider community (Porter & Cleland, 1995). Often family members, local business people, school administrators, local politicians, college students, and others are invited to attend. Students and community members form small groups, and students share their portfolios, pointing out their accomplishments and strengths. This activity is especially useful in involving community members in the school and showing them the types of literacy activities in which students are involved as well as how students are becoming effective readers and writers.

These sharing days also help students accept responsibility for their own learning—especially those students who have not been as motivated as their classmates. When less-motivated students listen to their classmates talk about their work and how they have grown as readers and writers, these students often decide to work harder the next year.

■ *Activity*

Examine a student's portfolio and talk with the student about the literacy activities in which he or she has been involved and what the samples document about the student as a reader and writer. Encourage the student to talk about strengths and future goals.

ASSIGNING GRADES

Assigning grades is one of the most difficult responsibilities placed on teachers. "Grading is a fact of life," according to Donald Graves (1983, p. 93), but he adds that teachers should use grades to encourage students, not to hinder their achievement. The authentic assessment procedures described in this chapter encourage students because they document what students can do as they read and write. They focus on students' strengths, not their weaknesses. Reviewing and translating this documentation into grades is the difficult part.

Literature Focus Unit Assignment Sheets

One way for students to keep track of assignments during literature focus units is to use assignment sheets. Teachers create the assignment sheet as they plan the unit and then use the sheet to grade students' work. A sample assignment sheet for a fifth-grade unit on *The Sign of the Beaver* (Speare, 1983) is shown in Figure 12–13. Students receive a copy of the assignment sheet at the beginning of the unit and keep it in their unit folder. Then, as they complete the assignments, they check them off, and it is easy for the teacher to make periodic checks to monitor students' progress. At the end of the unit, the teacher collects the unit folders and grades the work.

FIGURE 12–13　　An Assignment Sheet for a Literature Focus Unit

Checklist for *The Sign of the Beaver*

Name _____　　Date _____

Student's Check		Teacher's Check
_____	1. Read *The Sign of the Beaver.*	_____
_____	2. Make a map of Matt's journey in 1768. (10)	_____
_____	3. Keep a simulated journal as Matt or Attean. (20)	_____
_____	4. Do a word sort by characters. (5)	_____
_____	5. Listen to Elizabeth George Speare's taped interview and do a quickwrite about her. (5)	_____
_____	6. Do an open-mind portrait about one of the characters. (10)	_____
_____	7. Make a Venn diagram to compare/contrast Matt or Attean with yourself. (10)	_____
_____	8. Contribute to a model of the Indian village or the clearing.	_____
_____	9. Write a sequel or do another project. (20) My project is _____	_____
_____	10. Read other books from the text set. (10)	_____
	_____ _____ _____	
_____	11. Write a self-assessment about your work, behavior, and effort in this unit. (10)	_____

TOTAL POINTS _____

Assignments can be graded as "done" or "not done," or they can graded for quality. Teachers of middle- and upper-grade students often assign points to each activity on the assignment sheet so that the total point value for the unit is 100 points. Activities that involve more time and effort earn more points. The maximum number of points possible for each assignment is listed in parentheses in Figure 12–13.

Reading and Writing Workshop Assignment Sheets

Students and the teacher set guidelines for what students are to accomplish during reading and writing workshop and how students will be graded, as Mrs. Peterson did in the vignette at the beginning of this chapter. Then teachers design assignment sheets for reading and writing workshop, and students use the assignment sheets to keep track of the books they are reading and their writing projects. At the end of the workshop, teachers collect students' reading and writing workshop folders, conference with students, and assign grades.

Grading Across-the-Curriculum Theme Studies

Teachers design assignment sheets for theme studies that are similar to those for literature focus units. Teachers can also design tests that allow students to show teachers what they have learned about a key concept. Teachers review the key concepts in a theme study with students and then have students choose one of the concepts to write and draw about on the test. Students divide a piece of a paper into two parts. On one part they draw pictures, diagrams, maps, or charts to describe the concept, and they label the drawings with key words and phrases. On the other part of the paper, they write about the concept. Then teachers grade the test according to the number of components related to the key concept students included in their drawings or writings.

A third grader's test on the skeletal system is presented in Figure 12–14. Students could choose to draw and write about one of three major systems in the human body: the skeletal, circulatory, or digestive system. In their tests, students were to draw at

FIGURE 12–14 A Third Grader's "Show-Me" Test

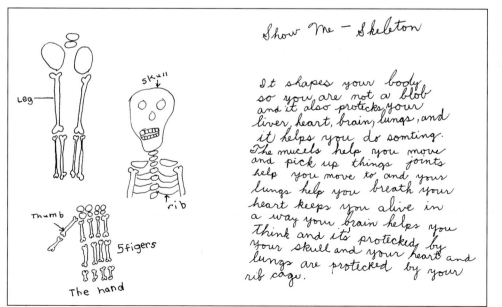

Effective Practices

1. Teachers use authentic assessment tools to assess students' literacy development.

2. Teachers monitor students' learning using observation and anecdotal notes, conferences, checklists, and collections of students' work samples.

3. Teachers take running records to assess students' reading fluency.

4. Teachers use informal reading inventories to determine students' reading levels.

5. Teachers use cloze procedure, story retellings, and reading logs to assess students' comprehension.

6. Teachers document students' growth, and students assess their own growth as writers using rubrics.

7. Teachers analyze young children's invented spellings for signs of growth.

8. Students choose work samples to document their literacy development for portfolios.

9. Students self-assess their work samples and set goals for future learning.

10. Teachers use assignment sheets for literature focus units, reading and writing workshop, and theme studies.

Ineffective Practices

1. Teachers use tests to assess students' literacy development.

2. Teachers collect and grade students' assignments.

3. Teachers listen to students read aloud, but they don't analyze students' errors.

4. Teachers have all students read the same grade-level textbook.

5. Teachers ask students to answer a series of questions orally or in writing to assess their comprehension.

6. Teachers grade students' writing according to how well ideas are developed and according to mechanical correctness.

7. Teachers either accept all invented spellings or correct all spellings.

8. Teachers file students' work samples in folders.

9. Teachers assess students' work.

10. Teachers score students' daily work and tests to determine grades.

least three pieces of information and write three important things about the system. This student drew three pictures of the skeleton system, illustrating different kinds of bones, and he wrote about two functions of the skeleton—to give the body shape and to protect organs. He also points out that the bones, joints, and muscles work together to help a person move. Two other things that the class studied about the skeletal system that this child did not mention are that bone marrow helps keep blood healthy and that there are 206 bones in the body. In the middle of the written part, the child included unrelated information about the functions of the heart, lungs, and brain. Out of a possible score of 6, the child received a 5. There are a few misspelled words and missing punctuation marks in the test, but they do not affect the grade since they do not interfere with the information presented.

Review

Assessment is more than testing; it is an essential part of teaching and learning. In authentic assessment, teachers examine both the processes of reading and writing and the artifacts that students produce. Teachers use a variety of literacy assessment tools, including procedures to monitor students' progress, determine students' reading levels, assess students' comprehension, document students' growth as writers, and analyze students' spelling development. Teachers help students collect their work samples in portfolios and document their literacy development. Teachers use assignment sheets to monitor students' work during literature focus units, reading and writing workshop, and theme studies, and to assign grades. Effective practices for assessing students' literacy learning are reviewed in the figure on page 466.

References

Baskwill, J., & Whitman, P. (1988). *Evaluation: Whole language, whole child.* New York: Scholastic.

Clay, M. M. (1985). *The early detection of reading difficulties* (3rd ed.). Portsmouth, NH: Heinemann.

Clemmons, J., Laase, L., Cooper, D., Areglado, N., & Dill, M. (1993). *Portfolios in the classroom: A teacher's sourcebook.* New York: Scholastic.

Coughlan, M. (1988). Let the students show us what they know. *Language Arts, 65,* 375–378.

D'Aoust, C. (1992). Portfolios: Process for students and teachers. In K. B. Yancy (Ed.), *Portfolios in the writing classroom* (pp. 39–48). Urbana, IL: National Council of Teachers of English.

Farr, R., & Tone, B. (1994). *Portfolio and performance assessment.* Orlando: Harcourt and Brace.

Flynt, E. S., & Cooter, R. B., Jr. (1995). *The Flynt/Cooter reading inventory for the classroom* (2nd ed.). Scottsdale, AZ: Gorsuch Scarisbrick Publishers.

Gambrell, L. B., Pfeiffer, W., & Wilson, R. (1985). The effects of retelling upon reading comprehension and recall of text information. *Journal of Educational Research, 78,* 216–220.

Goodman, K. S. (1976). Behind the eye: What happens in reading. In H. Singer & R. B. Ruddell (Eds.), *Theoretical models and processes of reading* (2nd ed., pp. 470–496). Newark, DE: International Reading Association.

Goodman, K. S., Goodman, Y. M., & Hood, W. J. (1989). *The whole language evaluation book.* Portsmouth, NH: Heinemann.

Goodman, Y. M. (1978). Kid watching: An alternative to testing. *National Elementary Principals Journal, 57,* 41–45.

Graves, D. H. (1983). *Writing: Teachers and students at work.* Portsmouth, NH: Heinemann.

Graves, D. H., & Sunstein, B. S. (Eds.). (1992). *Portfolio portraits.* Portsmouth, NH: Heinemann.

Morrow, L. M. (1985). Retelling stories: A strategy for improving children's comprehension, concept of story structure, and oral language complexity. *Elementary School Journal, 85,* 647–661.

Porter, C., & Cleland, J. (1995). *The portfolio as a learning strategy.* Portsmouth, NH: Heinemann.

Rhodes, L. K., & Nathenson-Mejia, S. (1992). Anecdotal records: A powerful tool for ongoing literacy assessment. *The Reading Teacher, 45,* 502–511.

Silvaroli, N. J. (1994). *Classroom reading inventory* (7th ed.). Madison, WI: Brown & Benchmark.

Stires, S. (1991). Thinking through the process: Self-evaluation in writing. In B. M. Power & R. Hubbard (Eds.), *The Heinemann reader: Literacy in process* (pp. 295–310). Portsmouth, NH: Heinemann.

Tierney, R., Carter, M., & Desai, L. (1991). *Portfolio assessment in the reading-writing classroom.* Norwood, MA: Christopher-Gordon.

Tompkins, G. E. (1994). *Teaching writing: Balancing process and product* (2nd ed.). New York: Merrill/Macmillan.

Valencia, S. W., Hiebert, E. H., Afflerbach, P. P. (1994). *Authentic reading assessment: Practices and possibilities.* Newark, DE: International Reading Association.

Wollman-Bonilla, J. (1991). *Response journals.* New York: Scholastic.

Woods, M. L., & Moe, A. J. (1995). *Analytical reading inventory* (5th ed.). Englewood Cliffs, NJ: Merrill/Prentice-Hall.

Children's Book References

Babbitt, N. (1975). *Tuck everlasting.* New York: Farrar, Straus & Giroux.

Byars, B. (1968). *The midnight fox.* New York: Viking.

George, J. C. (1972). *Julie of the wolves.* New York: Harper & Row.

Howe, J. (1981). *Howliday Inn.* Boston: Atheneum.

Howe, J. (1983). *The celery stalks at midnight.* Boston: Atheneum.

Howe, J. (1987). *Nighty-nightmare.* Boston: Atheneum.

Howe, J. (1992). *Return to Howliday Inn.* Boston: Atheneum.

Howe, D., & Howe, J. (1979). *Bunnicula: A rabbit-tale of mystery.* Boston: Atheneum.

Lewis, C. S. (1950). *The lion, the witch and the wardrobe.* New York: Macmillan.

Naylor, P. R. (1991). *Shiloh.* New York: Atheneum.

Paulsen, G. (1987). *Hatchet.* New York: Viking.

Potter, B. (1902). *The tale of Peter Rabbit.* New York: Warne.

Speare, E. G. (1983). *The sign of the beaver.* Boston: Houghton Mifflin.

PART IV
Compendium of Instructional Procedures

ALPHABET BOOKS

Students construct alphabet books much like the alphabet trade books published for children (Tompkins, 1994). These student-made books are useful reading materials for beginning readers, and students often make alphabet books as part of literature focus units and across-the-curriculum themes. Students can make alphabet books collaboratively as a class or in a small group. Interested students can make individual alphabet books, but with 26 pages to complete, it is an arduous task. The steps in constructing an alphabet book with a group of students are:

1. Have students examine alphabet trade books published for children, such as *Eating the Alphabet: Fruits and Vegetables From A to Z* (Ehlert, 1989) or *Illuminations* (Hunt, 1989), or student-made alphabet books made by other classes.
2. Write the letters of the alphabet in a column on a long sheet of butcher paper.
3. Have students brainstorm words related to the literature focus unit or across-the-curriculum theme study beginning with each letter of the alphabet, and then write these words on the sheet of butcher paper. Students often consult the **word wall** and books in the text set as they try to think of related words.
4. Have students each choose a letter for their page.
5. Design the format of the page as a class, deciding where the letter, the illustration, and the text will be placed.
6. Have students use the writing process to draft, revise, and edit their pages.
7. Have students make the final copies of their pages.
8. Have one student make the cover.
9. Compile the pages in alphabetical order and bind the book.

Alphabet books are often used as projects at the end of a unit of study, such as the oceans, the desert, World War II, and California missions. The *U* page from a fourth-grade class's alphabet book on the California missions is shown in Figure 1.

ANTICIPATION GUIDES

Anticipation guides (Head & Readence, 1986) are used before reading content-area textbooks and informational books. In an anticipation guide, the teacher prepares a list of statements about the topic for students to discuss before reading. Some of the statements should be true and accurate, and others incorrect or based on misconceptions. Students discuss each statement and agree or disagree with it. The purpose of this activity is to stimulate students' interest in the topic and to activate prior knowledge. An anticipation guide about Canada might include these statements:

Canada is the second-largest country in the world.

The official language of Canada is English.

Canada is very much like the United States.

Canada's economy is based on its wealth of natural resources.

Canada has always fought on the American side during wars.

Today most Canadians live within 200 miles of the American border.

FIGURE 1   The "U" Page From a Fourth-Grade Class Alphabet Book

The steps in developing an anticipation guide are:

1. Identify several major concepts related to the reading assignment or unit.

2. Consider your students' knowledge about the topic and any misconceptions they might have.

3. Develop a list of three or more statements that are general enough to stimulate discussion and can be used to clarify misconceptions. The list can be written on a chart or on paper so that students can have individual copies.

4. Introduce the anticipation guide and have students respond to the statements. They should think about the statements and decide whether they agree or disagree with each one.

5. Discuss each statement with the class and ask students to defend their positions.

6. Have students read the text and compare their responses to what the reading material states.

7. Discuss each statement again and have students cite information in the text that supports or discounts the statement. Also, ask students if they have changed their responses.

Students can also try their hand at writing anticipation guides. When students are reading informational books in book clubs, they can create an anticipation guide after reading and then share the guide with classmates when they present the book during a sharing time.

ASSISTED READING

Assisted reading is one approach to help young children emerge into reading. It extends the familiar routine of parents reading to their children (Hoskisson, 1975). In this approach, a child and a teacher (or other fluent reader) sit together to read a book. The child listens and looks at the illustrations in the book as the teacher reads aloud. Gradually the child assumes more and more of the reading until the child is doing most of the reading and the teacher fills in the difficult words. The three stages in assisted reading are:

1. Reading to children.   Teachers read to children and have them repeat each phrase or sentence. At first most children's attention will not be on the lines of print

Teachers use assisted reading as they read along with beginning readers.

as they repeat the words. They may be looking around the room or at the pictures in the book. To direct their attention to the lines of print, the teacher points to the words on each line as they are read. This allows children to see that lines of print are read from left to right, not randomly. Many different books are read and reread during this stage. Rereading is important because the visual images of the words must be seen and read many times to ensure their recognition in other books. Later, one repetition of a word may be sufficient for subsequent recognition of the word in context.

2. Shared reading.   When children begin to notice that some words occur repeatedly from book to book, they enter the second stage of assisted reading. In this stage, the teacher reads and children repeat or echo the words; however, the teacher does not read the words the children seem to recognize. The teacher omits those words, and children fill them in. The fluency, or flow, of the reading should not be interrupted. If fluency is not maintained during this stage, children will not grasp the meaning of the passage, because the syntactic and semantic cues that come from a smooth flow of language will not be evident to them.

3. Independent reading.   The transition to independent reading occurs when children begin to ask the teacher to let them read the words themselves. When children know enough words to do the initial reading themselves, they read and the teacher willingly supplies any unknown words. It is important to assist children so that the fluency of the reading is not disrupted. Children do the major portion of the reading, but they tire more easily because they are struggling to use all the information they have acquired about written language. Children at this stage need constant encouragement; they must not feel a sense of frustration, because moving to independent reading is a gradual process.

AUTHOR'S CHAIR

A special chair is designated as the author's chair. This chair might be a rocking chair, a lawn chair with a padded seat, a wooden stool, or a director's chair, and it should be labeled "Author's Chair." Children and the teacher sit in this chair to share books they have written and other books they have read, and this is the only time anyone sits in the chair. Teachers at all grade levels use author's chairs, but these special chairs are most important in primary classrooms, where students are developing a concept of authorship.

When teachers sit in the chair to read books aloud to students, they name the author of the book and tell a little something about the author. In this way, students gain an awareness of authors, the people who write books. Students also sit in the author's chair to share books and other compositions they have written. Sitting in the special author's chair helps young children, in particular, gradually realize that they are authors, too (Graves & Hansen, 1983).

When children share their writings, one child sits in the author's chair, and a group of children sit on the floor or in chairs in front of the author's chair. The child sitting in the author's chair reads the book or other piece of writing aloud and shows the accompanying illustrations. Then children who want to make a comment raise their hands, and the author chooses several children to ask questions, give compliments, and make comments. Then the author chooses another child to share and takes a seat in the audience.

Students sit in the author's chair to share their writing with classmates.

BOOK BOXES

Teachers and students collect three or more objects or pictures related to a story, informational book, or poem and put them in a box along with the book or other reading material. For example, a book box for *Sarah, Plain and Tall* (MacLachlan, 1983) might include seashells, a train ticket, a yellow bonnet, colored pencils, a map of Sarah's trip from Maine to the prairie, and letters. Or, for *Eating the Alphabet: Fruits and Vegetables From A to Z* (Ehlert, 1989), teachers can collect plastic fruits and vegetables. The steps in preparing a book box are:

1. Read the book and notice important objects that are mentioned.
2. Find a box, basket, or plastic tub to hold the objects, and decorate the box with the name of the book, pictures, and words.
3. Place three or more objects and pictures in the box. When students are making book boxes, they may place an inventory sheet in the box with all the items listed and an explanation of why the items were selected.
4. Share the completed box with students. When teachers make book boxes, they use them to introduce the book and provide background information before reading. In contrast, students often make book boxes as a project during the extending stage of the reading process.

Book boxes are especially useful for students learning English as a second language and for nonverbal students who have small vocabularies and difficulty developing sentences to express ideas.

Book talks are brief teasers that teachers give to interest students in particular books. Teachers use book talks to introduce students to books in the classroom library, books for a book club, or a text set of books for a theme or by a particular author. Students also give book talks to share books they have read during reading workshop or during a theme study. The steps are:

BOOK TALKS

1. Select one or more books to share. When more than one book is shared, the books are usually related in some way—on the same theme, written by the same author, or on a related topic.
2. Plan a brief one- or two-minute presentation for each book. The presentation should include the title and author of the book, the genre or topic, a brief summary, why the teacher liked it, and why students might be interested in it. The teacher may also read a short excerpt and show an illustration.
3. Display the books on a chalk tray or shelf and present the planned book talk.

The same steps are used when students give the book talk. If students have also prepared a project related to the book, they also share it during the book talk.

One way for students to read poems is by using choral reading. In choral reading, students take turns reading a poem together. Students may read the poem aloud together as a class or in small groups. Or, individual students read particular lines or stanzas. Four possible arrangements for choral reading are:

CHORAL READING

1. *Echo reading.*   The leader reads each line, and the group repeats it.
2. *Leader and chorus reading.*   The leader reads the main part of the poem, and the group reads the refrain or chorus in unison.
3. *Small-group reading.*   The class divides into two or more groups, and each group reads one part of the poem.
4. *Cumulative reading.*   One student or one group reads the first line or stanza, and another student or group joins in as each line or stanza is read so that a cumulative effect is created.

The steps in choral reading are:

1. Select a poem to use for choral reading and copy it onto a chart or make multiple copies for students to read.
2. Work with students to decide how to arrange the poem for reading. Add marks to the chart or have students mark individual copies so that they can follow the arrangement.
3. Read the poem with students several times. Emphasize that students should pronounce words clearly and read with expression. Teachers may want to tape-record students' reading so that they can hear themselves.

Choral reading makes students active participants in the poetry experience, and it helps them learn to appreciate the sounds, feelings, and magic of poetry. Many poems can be used for choral reading; try, for example, Shel Silverstein's "Boa Constrictor," Karla Kuskin's "Full of the Moon," Laura E. Richards's "Eletelephony," and Eve Merriam's "Catch a Little Rhyme."

CLOZE PROCEDURE

The cloze procedure is an informal diagnostic procedure that teachers use to gather information about readers' abilities to deal with the content and structure of texts they are reading. Teachers construct a cloze passage by taking an excerpt from a book—a story, an informational book, or a content-area textbook—that students have read and deleting every fifth word in the passage. The deleted words are replaced with blanks. Then students read the passage and add the missing words. Students use their knowledge of syntax (the order of words in English) and semantics (the meaning of words within sentences) to successfully predict the missing words in the text passage. Only the exact word is considered the correct answer.

The steps in the cloze procedure are:

1. Select a passage from a textbook or trade book. The selection may be either a story or an informational piece.

2. Retype the passage. The first sentence is typed exactly as it appears in the original text. Beginning with the second sentence, one of the first five words is deleted and replaced with a blank. Then every fifth word in the remainder of the passage is deleted and replaced with a blank.

3. Have students read the passage all the way through once silently and then reread the passage and predict or "guess" the word that goes in each blank. Students write the deleted words in the blanks.

4. Score the student's work, awarding one point each time the missing word is correctly identified. A percentage of correct answers is determined by dividing the number of points by the number of blanks.

5. Compare the percentage of correct word replacements with this scale:

61% or more correct:	independent level
41–60% correct:	instructional level
less than 40% correct:	frustration level

The cloze procedure has other uses also. When used to assess students' understanding of the text, specific words (e.g., character names, words related to the setting or key events in the story) can be deleted rather than every fifth word. Grading is done using a percentage, allowing one or two errors for an A, three, four, or five for a B, and so on.

The cloze procedure can also be used to judge whether or not an unfamiliar trade book or textbook is appropriate to use for classroom instruction. Teachers prepare a cloze passage and have all students or a random sample of students follow the procedure identified above. Then teachers score the passages and use a one-third to one-half formula to determine the text's appropriateness for their students. If students correctly predict more than 50% of the deleted words, the passage is easy reading. If students predict less than 30% of the missing words, the passage is too difficult for classroom instruction. The instructional range is 30–50% correct predictions (Reutzel & Cooter, 1996). The percentages are different from those in the scale because students are reading an unfamiliar passage instead of a familiar one.

CLUSTERS

Clusters are weblike diagrams with the topic written in a circle centered on a sheet of paper. Main ideas are written on rays drawn out from the circle, and branches with details and examples are added to complete each main idea (Rico, 1983). Students use clusters to organize information they are learning and to organize ideas before beginning to write a composition. The steps are:

1. Select a topic and write the word in the center of a circle drawn on a chart or sheet of paper.
2. Have students brainstorm as many words and phrases as they can that are related to the topic and then organize the words into categories. The teacher may prompt students for additional words or suggest categories.
3. Have students determine main ideas and details. The main ideas are written on rays drawn out from the circled topic, and details are written on rays drawn out from the main ideas.

Clusters are often called maps and webs, and they are similar to **story maps.** When the purpose of the diagram is writing, the diagrams are arbitrarily called clusters in this book, and when the purpose of the diagram is reading, the diagrams are called maps.

COLLABORA-TIVE BOOKS AND REPORTS

Students divide the work of writing an informational book or report when they work collaboratively. Students each contribute one page for a class book or work with partners or in small groups to research and write sections of the report. Then the students' work is compiled, and the book or report is complete (Tompkins, 1994). Students use a process approach as they research their topics and compose their sections of the report or book. The steps are:

1. Choose a topic for the informational book or report related to a literature focus unit or theme study. Almost any social studies or science topic that can be subdivided into four or more parts works well for collaborative reports and books.
2. Have students choose specific topics related to the general topic for their pages or sections. Students work in small groups, with partners, or individually to research and write their sections of the informational book or report.
3. Introduce the organization for each section of the book or report. If students are each contributing one page for a class informational book, they will draw a picture and add a fact or other piece of information. Students working on chapters for a longer report will need to design research questions. These questions emerge as students study a topic and brainstorm a list of questions on a chart posted in the classroom. If they are planning a report on the human body, for example, the small groups that are studying each organ may decide to research the same three questions: "What does the organ look like?" "What job does the organ do?" and "Where is the organ located in the human body?"

4. Rehearse the procedure and write one section of the report or book together as a class before students begin working on their section of the report.

5. Have students gather and organize information for their sections. Students writing pages for informational books often draw pictures as prewriting. Students working in small groups or with partners search for answers to the research questions. Students can use **clusters** or **data charts** to record the information they gather. A data chart for a report on the human body is shown in Figure 2. The research questions are the same for each data-collection instrument. On a cluster, students add information as details to each main idea ray; if they are working with data charts, they record information from the first source in the first row under the appropriate question, from the second source in the second row, and so on.

6. Draft the sections of the report. Students write rough drafts of their sections. When students are working in small groups, one student is the scribe and writes the draft while the other students dictate sentences, using information from a cluster or data chart. Next, they share their drafts with the class and make revisions on the basis of feedback they receive. Last, students proofread and correct mechanical errors.

FIGURE 2   A Data Chart for A Report on the Human Body

Human Body Report Data Chart				
Organ _____ Researchers				
Source of information	What does it look like?	Where is it located?	What job does it do?	Other important information

7. Compile the pages or sections. Students compile their completed pages or sections, and then the entire book or report is read aloud so students can catch inconsistencies or redundant passages.

8. Add front and back pages. For an informational book, students add a title page and covers. For reports, students also write a table of contents, an introduction, and a conclusion and add a bibliography at the end.

9. Publish the informational book or report. Students make a final copy with all the parts of the book or report in the correct sequence. For longer reports, it is much easier to print out the final copy if the sections have been drafted and revised on a computer. To make the book sturdier, teachers often laminate the covers (or all pages in the book) and bind everything together using yarn ties, brads, or metal rings.

10. Make copies of the book or report for students. Teachers often make copies of the informational book or report for each student, whereas the special bound copy is often placed in the class or school library.

CUBING

In cubing, students explore a topic from six dimensions or viewpoints (Neeld, 1986). The name comes from the fact that cubes have six sides and there are six dimensions in this instructional procedure. These six dimensions are:

- Describe the topic, including its colors, shapes, and sizes.
- Compare the topic to something else. Consider how it is similar to or different from this other thing.
- Associate the topic with something else and explain why the topic makes you think of this other thing.
- Analyze the topic and tell how it is made or what it is composed of.
- Apply the topic and tell how it can be used or what can be done with it.
- Argue for or against the topic. Take a stand and list reasons to support it.

Cubing involves the following steps:

1. Choose a topic.
2. Examine the topic from each of the six dimensions.
3. Move quickly, spending only five to ten minutes thinking about each dimension and writing a **quickwrite** or making a **quickdraw.**
4. Construct a cube using cardboard and attach the quickwrites or quickdraws. Cardboard boxes shaped like cubes can also be used.

Cubing is a useful procedure for across-the-curriculum themes, and middle- and upper-grade students can cube topics such as Antarctica, the U.S. Constitution, tigers or other endangered animals, the Underground Railroad, and the Nile River.

See **Collaborative Books and Reports.**

DATA CHARTS

DIRECTED READING-THINKING ACTIVITY

In the Directed Reading-Thinking Activity (DRTA), students are actively involved in reading stories or listening to stories read aloud because they make predictions and read or listen to confirm their predictions (Stauffer, 1975). DRTA is a useful approach for teaching students how to use the predicting strategy. It can be used for both picture books and chapter books. The steps in DRTA are:

1. Introduce the story before beginning to read. Teachers might discuss the topic or show objects and pictures related to the story in order to draw on prior knowledge or create new experiences.

2. Show students the cover of the book and ask them to make a prediction about the story using these questions:

   ■ What do you think a story with a title like this might be about?

   ■ What do you think might happen in this story?

   ■ Does this picture give you any ideas about what might happen in this story?

   If necessary, the teacher reads the first paragraph or two to provide more information for students to use in making their predictions. After a brief discussion in which all students commit themselves to one or another of the alternatives presented, the teacher asks these questions:

   ■ Which of these ideas do you think would be the likely one?

   ■ Why do you think that idea is a good one?

3. Have students read the beginning of the story or listen to the beginning of the story read aloud. Then the teacher asks students to confirm or reject their predictions by responding to questions such as:

   ■ What do you think now?

   ■ What do you think will happen next?

   ■ Would happen if . . . ?

   ■ Why do you think that idea is a good one?

   Students continue reading or the teacher continues reading aloud, stopping at several key points to repeat this step.

4. Have students reflect on their predictions. Students talk about the story, expressing their feelings and making connections to their own lives and experiences with literature. Then students reflect on the predictions they made as they read or listened to the story read aloud, and they provide reasons to support their predictions. Teachers ask these questions to help students think about their predictions:

   ■ What predictions did you make?

   ■ What in the story made you think of that prediction?

   ■ What in the story supports that idea?

The Directed Reading-Thinking Activity is only useful when students are reading or listening to an unfamiliar story so that they can be actively involved in the prediction-confirmation cycle.

A special type of **reading log** is a double-entry journal (Barone, 1990; Berthoff, 1981). Students divide their journal pages into two columns. In the left column students write quotes from the story or informational book they are reading, and in the right column they reflect on each quote. They may relate a quote to their own lives, react to it, write a question, or make some other comment. Excerpts from a fifth grader's double-entry journal about *The Lion, the Witch and the Wardrobe* (Lewis, 1950) are shown in Figure 3. The steps are:

1. Have students divide the pages in their reading logs into two columns, labeling the left column "In the Text" or "Quotes" and the right column "My Responses," "Comments," or "Reflections."

2. As students read, or immediately after reading, have students copy one or more important or interesting quotes in the left column of the reading logs.

3. Ask students to reread the quotes and make notes in the right column about their reasons for choosing the quote. Sometimes it is easier if students share the quotes

FIGURE 3　Excerpts From a Fifth Grader's Double-Entry Journal About *The Lion, the Witch and the Wardrobe*

In the Text	My Response
Chapter 1 I tell you this is the sort of house where no one is going to mind what we do.	I remember the time that I went to Beaumont, Texas to stay with my aunt. My aunt's house was very large. She had a piano and she let us play it. She told us what we could do whatever we wanted to.
Chapter 5 "How do you know?" he asked, "that your sister's story is not true?"	It reminds me of when I was little and I had an imaginary place. I would go there in my mind. I made up all kinds of make-believe stories about myself in this imaginary place. One time I told my big brother about my imaginary place. He laughed at me and told me I was silly. But it didn't bother me because nobody can stop me from thinking what I want.
Chapter 15 Still they could see the shape of the great lion lying dead in his bonds. They're nibbling at the cords.	When Aslan died I thought about when my Uncle Carl died. This reminds me of the story where the lion lets the mouse go and the mouse helps the lion.

with a reading buddy or in a **grand conversation** before they write comments or reflections in the right column.

Double-entry journals can be used in several other ways, too. Instead of recording quotes from the story, students can write "Reading Notes" in the left column and then add "Reactions" in the right column. In the left column students write about the events they read about in the chapter. Then in the right column they make personal connections to the events.

As an alternative, students can use the heading "Reading Notes" for one column and "Discussion Notes" for the second column. Students write reading notes as they read or immediately after reading. Later, after discussing the story or a chapter of a longer book, students add discussion notes. As with other types of double-entry journals, it is in the second column that students make more interpretive comments.

Younger students can use the double-entry format for a prediction journal (Macon, Bewell, & Vogt, 1991). They label the left column "Predictions" and the right column "What Happened." In the left column they write or draw a picture of what they predict will happen in the story or chapter before reading it. Then after reading, they draw or write what actually happened in the right column.

GRAND CONVERSA-TIONS

A grand conversation is a book discussion in which students explore interpretations and reflect on their feelings (Eeds & Wells, 1989; Peterson & Eeds, 1990). Students sit in a circle so that they can see each other. The teacher serves as a facilitator, but the talk is primarily among the students. Traditionally, literature discussions have been "gentle inquisitions"; here the talk changes to dialoguing among students. The steps are:

1. Have students read the book, or part of the book, or listen to the teacher read it aloud.

2. Have students respond to the book in a **quickwrite** (or quickdraw for younger students) or in a **reading log.** This step is optional.

3. Bring students together as a class or in a smaller group to discuss the book.

4. Have students take turns sharing their ideas about the book (the story, the language, the illustrations, the author/illustrator, etc.). To start the grand conversation, the teacher asks students what they think and allows them to share their personal responses. Possible openers are "Who would like to begin?" "What did you think?" and "Who would like to share?" Students may read from their quickwrites or reading log entries. They all participate and may build on classmates' comments and ask for clarifications. In order that everyone may participate, ask students to not make more than two or three comments until everyone has spoken once. Students may refer back to the book or read a short piece to make a point, but there is no round-robin reading. Pauses may occur, and when students indicate that they have run out of things to say, the grand conversation may end or continue with a second part.

5. Ask open-ended questions after students have had a chance to share their reflections. These questions should focus students' attention on one or two aspects of the book or story that have been missed. Teachers might:

   ■ *Focus on illustrations.*   "What about the illustrations in *El Chino*? Did you like them? Did you notice how the illustrations changed during the book? Why do you think Allen Say did that?"

Students often sit in a circle to talk about a book in a grand conversation.

- *Focus on authors.* "This is the third book we've read by Chris Van Allsburg. What is so special about his books? Why is it that we like his books so much? Is there something they all share?"

- *Focus on comparison.* "How did this book compare with . . . ?" "Did you like the book or the film version better? Why?" "Which of Beverly Cleary's characters is your favorite? Which is most like you?"

- *Focus on literary elements/stylistic devices/genre.* "Is *Johnny Appleseed* a legend? What are the characteristics of legends? Which of these characteristics did you notice in the book?" "What was the theme of the book? How did the author tell us the theme?"

6. Have students write (or write again) in a reading log or a quickwrite. This step is optional.

Grand conversations take only 10 to 20 minutes and can be done after a book or after every chapter (or section) of a longer book. It is not necessary to grade students' participation in grand conversations, but students are expected to make comments and be supportive of classmates' comments. Also, students can write a brief entry in reading logs before the grand conversation and then write a second entry describing what they have learned during the grand conversation.

INDIVIDUAL BOOKS AND REPORTS

Students write individual reports and informational books much like they write **collaborative books and reports.** They design research questions, gather information to answer the questions, and compile what they have learned in a report. Writing individual reports demands two significant changes: first, students narrow their topics, and second, they assume the entire responsibility for writing the report (Tompkins, 1994). The steps are:

1. Have students choose and narrow a topic. Students choose topics for informational books and reports from a content area, hobbies, or other interests. After choosing a general topic, such as cats or the solar system, they need to narrow the topic so that it is manageable. The broad topic of cats might be narrowed to pet cats or tigers, and the solar system to one planet.

2. Have students design research questions by brainstorming a list of questions in a **learning log.** They review the list, combine some questions, delete others, and finally arrive at four to six questions that are worthy of answering. Once they begin their research, they may add new questions and delete others if they reach a dead end.

3. Assist students as they gather and organize information. As in collaborative books and reports, students use **clusters** or **data charts** to gather and organize information. Data charts, with their rectangular spaces for writing information, serve as a transition for upper-grade students between clusters and note cards.

4. Have students draft their reports. Students write a rough draft from the information they have gathered. Each research question can provide the basis for a paragraph, a page, or a chapter in the report.

5. Work with students to revise and edit their books or reports. Students meet in **writing groups** to share their rough drafts and make revisions based on the feedback they receive from their classmates. After they revise, students use an editing checklist to proofread their reports and identify and correct mechanical errors.

6. Publish the books or reports. Students recopy their reports in books and add covers, a title page, a table of contents, and bibliographic information. Research reports can also be published in several other ways; for example, as a filmstrip or video presentation, as a series of illustrated charts or dioramas, or as a dramatization.

Students often write informational books and reports as projects during literature focus units, writing workshop, and across-the-curriculum themes. Through these activities, students have opportunities to extend and personalize their learning and to use the writing process.

K-W-L CHARTS

Teachers use K-W-L charts during across-the-curriculum themes (Ogle, 1986, 1989). The letters *K, W,* and *L* stand for What We *K*now, What We *W*ant to Learn, and What We *L*earned. Teachers introduce a K-W-L chart at the beginning of a theme and use the chart to identify what students already know about the topic and what they want to learn. Toward the end of the theme, students complete the last section of the chart, what they have learned. This instructional procedure helps students to combine new information with prior knowledge and to develop their vocabularies. The steps are:

1. Create a large chart as shown in Figure 4, dividing the chart into three columns and labeling the columns K (What We Know), W (What We Want to Learn), and L (What We Learned).

FIGURE 4   A K-W-L Chart

K What We Know	W What We Want to Learn	L What We Learned

Categories of information we expect to use:
A.
B.
C.
D.

Note. From "K-W-L: A Teaching Model That Develops Active Reading of Expository Text," by D. M. Ogle, 1986, *The Reading Teacher, 39,* p. 565. Reprinted with permission.

2. On the first day of the theme study, ask students to brainstorm what they know about the topic. Write this information down in the K (What We Know) column. Students also suggest questions they would like to explore during the theme.

3. Write the questions that students suggest in the W (What We Want to Learn) column.

4. Ask students to look for ways to "chunk" or categorize the information and questions they brainstormed. Write these categories in the section at the bottom of the

chart. If the topic is penguins, for example, the categories might include appearance, habitat, enemies, life cycle, and food.

5. Continue to add questions to the W column, and begin to write information that students learn in the L (What We Learned) column.

6. At the end of the theme, complete the L column of the chart and have students reflect on what they have learned during the theme.

Older students can make K-W-L charts in small groups or create individual charts to organize and document their learning. Class charts, however, are more effective for younger children, and for older students who have not made K-W-L charts before.

LANGUAGE EXPERIENCE APPROACH

The language experience approach (LEA) is based on children's language and experiences (Ashton-Warner, 1965; Lee & Allen, 1963; Stauffer, 1970). In this approach, children dictate words and sentences about their experiences, and the teacher writes the dictation for the children. The text they develop together becomes the reading material. Because the language comes from the children themselves and the content is based on their experiences, children are usually able to read the text easily. Reading and writing are connected, since students are actively involved in reading what they have written. The steps are:

1. Provide an experience to serve as the stimulus for the writing. For group writing, it can be an experience shared in school, a book read aloud, a field trip, or some other experience, such as having a pet or playing in the snow, that all children are familiar with. For individual writing, the stimulus can be any experience that is important for the particular child.

2. Talk about the experience to generate words, and review the experience so that the children's dictation will be more interesting and complete. Teachers often begin with an open-ended question, such as "What are you going to write about?" As children talk about their experiences, they clarify and organize ideas, use more specific vocabulary, and extend their understanding.

3. Record the child's dictation. Texts for individual children are written on sheets of writing paper or in small booklets, while group texts are written on chart paper. Teachers print neatly, spell words correctly, and preserve students' language as much as possible. It is a great temptation to change the child's language to the teacher's own, in either word choice or grammar, but editing should be kept to a minimum so that children do not get the impression that their language is inferior or inadequate.

For individual texts, teachers continue to take the child's dictation and write until the child finishes or hesitates. If the child hesitates, the teacher rereads what has been written and encourages the child to continue. For group texts, children take turns dictating sentences, and the teacher rereads each sentence after writing it down.

4. Read the text aloud, pointing to each word. This reading reminds children of the content of the text and demonstrates how to read it aloud with appropriate intonation. Then children join in the reading. After reading group texts together, individual children can take turns rereading. Group texts can also be copied so each child has a copy to read independently.

5. Help children extend the experience in several ways. These are possibilities:

- Add illustrations to their writing.
- Read their texts to classmates from the author's chair.
- Take their texts home to share with family members.
- Add this text to a collection of their writings.
- Pick out words from their texts that they would like to learn to read.

The language experience approach is an effective way to help children emerge into reading. Even students who have not been successful with other types of reading activities can read what they have dictated. There is a drawback, however; teachers provide a "perfect" model when they take children's dictation—they write neatly and spell words correctly. After language experience activities, some young children are not eager to do their own writing. They prefer their teacher's "perfect" writing to their own childlike writing. To avoid this problem, young children should be doing their own writing in personal journals and responding to literature activities at the same time they are participating in language experience activities. This way they will learn that sometimes they do their own writing, while at other times the teacher takes their dictation.

LEARNING LOGS

Students write in learning logs as part of across-the-curriculum theme studies. Learning logs, like other types of journals, are notebooks or booklets of paper in which students record information they are learning, write questions and reflections about their learning, and make charts, diagrams, and **clusters.** The steps are:

1. Have students make learning logs at the beginning of a theme study.
2. Plan activities for students to use their learning logs, such as taking notes, drawing diagrams, **quickwriting,** and clustering. Students' writing is impromptu in learning logs, and the emphasis is on using writing as a learning tool rather than creating polished products. Even so, students should be encouraged to work carefully and spell words on the **word wall** correctly.
3. Monitor students' entries. Teachers answer students' questions and clarify confusions.

Students also use learning logs to write about what they are learning in math. They record explanations and examples of concepts presented in class, and they react to mathematical concepts they are learning and any problems they may be having. Some upper-grade teachers allow students to use the last five minutes of math class to summarize and react to the day's lesson in their learning logs.

LITERATURE LOGS

See **Reading Logs.**

MINILESSONS

Teachers teach minilessons on literacy procedures, concepts, strategies, and skills (Atwell, 1987). These lessons are brief, often lasting only 10 to 20 minutes. Minilessons are usually taught as part of the reading process during the exploring step, or as part of the writing process during the editing step. The steps in conducting a mini-lesson are:

1. Introduce the procedure, concept, strategy, or skill.
2. Share examples of the topic using books students are reading or students' own writing projects.
3. Provide information about the topic and make connections to students' reading or writing.
4. Involve students in opportunities to practice the procedure, concept, strategy, or skill. Through practice activities, students bring together the information and the examples introduced earlier.
5. Have students make notes about the topic in their notebooks or on a poster to be displayed in the classroom.
6. Ask students to reflect or speculate on how they can use this information in their reading and writing.
7. Provide additional opportunities for students to use the procedures, concepts, strategies, or skills they are learning in meaningful ways.

Teachers present minilessons to the whole class, small groups, or individual students. The best time to teach a minilesson is when students will have immediate opportunities to apply what they are learning.

Teachers and students make charts about skills and strategies they are learning during mini-lessons.

To help students think more deeply about a character and reflect on story events from the character's viewpoint, students draw an open-mind portrait of the character. These portraits have two parts: the face of the character is on one page, and the mind of the character is on the second page. A fourth grader's open-mind portrait of Sarah, the mail-order bride in *Sarah, Plain and Tall* (MacLachlan, 1983), is shown in Figure 5. The steps are:

OPEN-MIND PORTRAITS

1. Have students draw and color a large portrait of the head and neck of a character in a book they are reading.
2. Have students cut out the portrait and attach it with a brad or staple to another sheet of drawing paper. It is important that students place the brad or staple at the top of the portrait.
3. Have students trace around the character's head on the second page.
4. Have students lift the portrait and draw and write about the character's thoughts on the second page.
5. Have students share their portraits with classmates and talk about the words and pictures they chose to include in the mind of the character.

FIGURE 5   An Open-Mind Portrait of Sarah of *Sarah, Plain and Tall*

PREREADING PLAN (PReP)

The prereading plan (PReP) is a diagnostic and instructional procedure used when students are reading informational books and content-area textbooks (Tierney, Readence, & Dishner, 1995). Teachers use this strategy to diagnose students' prior knowledge and provide necessary background knowledge so that students will be prepared to understand what they will be reading. The steps are:

1. Introduce a key concept to students using a word, phrase, or picture to initiate a discussion.
2. Have students brainstorm words about the topic, and record their ideas on a chart. Help students make connections among the brainstormed ideas.
3. Present additional vocabulary and clarify any misconceptions.
4. Have students draw pictures and/or write a **quickwrite** about the topic using words from the brainstormed list.
5. Have students share their quickwrites with the class, and ask questions to help students clarify and elaborate their quickwrites.

This activity is especially important when students have little technical vocabulary or background knowledge about a topic, and for students who are learning English as a second language.

QUICKWRITES AND QUICKDRAWS

Students use quickwriting as they write in response to literature and for other types of impromptu writing. Students reflect on what they know about a topic, ramble on paper, generate words and ideas, and make connections among the ideas. Quickdraws are a variation of quickwrites in which students draw instead of write. Young children often do quickdraws in which they draw pictures and add labels. Some students do a mixture of writing and drawing. Figure 6 presents a first grader's combination quickwrite and quickdraw made after reading *Sam, Bangs, and Moonshine* (Ness, 1966). In this Caldecott Medal story, a girl named Sam tells "moonshine" about a make-believe

FIGURE 6   A First Grader's Quickdraw After Reading *Sam, Bangs, and Moonshine*

baby kangaroo to her friend Thomas. The results are almost disastrous. In the quick-write/quickdraw, the child writes, "If you lie, you will get in big trouble and you will hurt your friends."

There are two steps in quickwrites and quickdraws:

1. Ask students to write or draw on a topic for 5 to 10 minutes. Encourage them to focus on interesting ideas, make connections between the topic and their own lives, and reflect on their reading or learning.

2. After students write, they usually share their quickwrites or quickdraws in small groups or during **grand conversations,** and then one student in each group shares with the class. Sharing also takes about 10 minutes, and the entire activity can be completed in approximately 20 minutes.

Students do quickwrites and quickdraws for a variety of purposes in literature-based reading classrooms, including:

■ as an entry for **reading logs**
■ to define or explain a word on the **word wall**
■ on the theme of story
■ about a favorite character
■ comparing book and film versions of a story
■ about a favorite book during an author study
■ about the characteristics of a literary genre
■ about the project the student is creating

Students also do similar quickwrites and quickdraws during theme studies.

Quickwriting, originally called "freewriting" and popularized by Peter Elbow (1973), is a way to help students focus on content rather than mechanics. Even by second or third grade, students have learned that many teachers emphasize correct spelling and careful handwriting more than the content of a composition. Elbow explains that focusing on mechanics makes writing "dead" because it does not allow students' natural voices to come through.

READ-AROUNDS

Read-arounds are celebrations of stories and other books, usually performed at the end of literature focus units. Students choose favorite passages from a book the class is reading to read aloud. The steps are:

1. Have students skim a book to locate one or more favorite passages (a sentence or paragraph) and mark the passages with bookmarks.

2. Have students rehearse reading the passages so that they can read them fluently.

3. Begin the read-around by asking a student to read a favorite passage aloud to the class. Then there is a pause and another student begins to read. Teachers don't call on students; any student may begin reading when no one else is reading. The passages can be read in any order, and more than one student can read the same passage. Teachers, too, read their favorite passages. The read-around continues until everyone who wants to has read.

Students like participating in a read-around because the featured book is like a good friend. Students enjoy listening to classmates read favorite passages and noticing literary language. They seem to move back and forth through the story, remembering events and reliving the story.

READING LOGS

Students keep reading logs or notebooks to write their reactions and opinions about books they are reading or listening to the teacher read aloud. Students also add lists of words from the **word wall,** diagrams about story elements, and information about authors and genres (Tompkins, 1994). For a chapter book, students write after reading every chapter or two. The steps are:

1. Have students make reading logs by stapling paper into booklets.

2. After reading a story or other book or listening to it read aloud, students write the name of the book on a page in their reading logs. Sometimes they also write the name of the author. For a chapter book, students write the name of the chapter and the chapter number.

3. Have students write their reactions and reflections about the book or chapter. Instead of summarizing the book, students relate the book to their own lives or to other literature they have read. Students may also list interesting or unfamiliar words, jot down quotable quotes, and take notes about characters, plot, or other story elements; but the primary purpose of reading logs is for students to think about the book, connect literature to their lives, and develop their understanding of the story or other book.

4. Monitor students' entries, checking that students have completed assignments. Teachers also write comments back to students about their interpretations and reflections. Because students' writing in reading logs is informal, teachers do not expect students to spell every word correctly, but it is not unreasonable to expect students to spell characters' names and other words on the word wall correctly.

READERS THEATRE

Readers theatre is a dramatic production of a script by a group of readers. Each student assumes a role and reads the character's lines in the script. Readers interpret a story without using much action. They may stand or sit, but they must carry the whole communication of the plot, characterization, mood, and theme by using their voices, gestures, and facial expressions.

Readers theatre avoids many of the restrictions inherent in theatrical productions: students do not memorize their parts; elaborate props, costumes, and backdrops are not needed; and long, tedious hours are not spent rehearsing. For readers theatre presentations, students can read scripts in trade books and textbooks, or they can create their own scripts. The steps are:

1. *Select a script.*   Students and the teacher select a script and then read and discuss it as they would any story. Then students volunteer to read each part.

2. *Rehearse the production.*   Students decide how to use their voice, gestures, and facial expressions to interpret the character they are reading. They read the script several times, striving for accurate pronunciation, voice projection, and appropriate inflections. Less rehearsal is needed for an informal, in-class presentation than

for a more formal production; nevertheless, interpretations should always be developed as fully as possible.

3. **Stage the production.**   Readers theatre can be presented on a stage or in a corner of the classroom. Students stand or sit in a row and read their lines in the script. They stay in position through the production or enter and leave according to the characters' appearances "onstage." If readers are sitting, they may stand to read their lines; if they are standing, they may step forward to read. The emphasis is not on production quality; rather, it is on the interpretive quality of the readers' voices and expressions. Costumes and props are unnecessary; however, adding a few small props enhances interest and enjoyment, as long as they do not interfere with the interpretive quality of the reading.

REPEATED READINGS

Teachers often encourage students to reread the featured book several times during literature focus units and to reread favorite books during reading workshop. Students become more fluent readers when they reread books, and each time they reread a book their comprehension deepens. Jay Samuels (1979) has developed an instructional procedure to help students increase their reading fluency and accuracy through rereading. The steps in the individualized procedure are:

1. Have the student choose a textbook or trade book and read a passage from the book aloud while the teacher records the reading time and any miscues.
2. Have the student practice rereading the passage orally or silently several times.
3. Then have the student reread the passage while the teacher again records the reading time and notes any miscues.
4. Have the student compare his or her reading time and accuracy between the first and last readings. Then the student prepares a graph to show his or her growth between the first and last readings.

This procedure is useful for students who are slow and inaccurate readers. When teachers monitor students' readings on a regular basis, students will become more careful readers. Making a graph to document growth is an important component of the procedure. The graph is concrete evidence of the student's growth.

RUNNING RECORDS

Teachers observe individual students as they read aloud and take running records of students' reading to assess their reading fluency (Clay, 1985). Through a running record, teachers calculate the percentage of words the student reads correctly and then analyze the miscues or errors. Running records are easy for teachers to take, although teachers need some practice before they are comfortable with the procedure. Teachers make a check mark on a sheet of paper as the child reads each word correctly. Teachers use other marks to indicate words that the student doesn't know or pronounces incorrectly. The steps in conducting a reading record are:

1. **Choose a book.**   Teachers have the student choose an excerpt 100 to 200 words in length from a book he or she is reading. For beginning readers, the text may be shorter.

2. ***Take the running record.***   As the student reads the excerpt aloud, the teacher makes a record of the words read correctly as well as those read incorrectly. The teacher makes check marks on a sheet of blank paper for each word read correctly. Errors are marked this way:

■ If the student read a word incorrectly, the teacher writes the incorrect word and the correct word under it:

$$\frac{\text{gentle}}{\text{generally}}$$

■ If the student self-corrects an error, the teacher writes *SC* (for self-correction) following the incorrect word:

$$\frac{\text{bath SC}}{\text{bathe}}$$

■ If the student attempts to pronounce a word, the teacher records each attempt and adds the correct text underneath:

$$\frac{\text{com- com- company}}{\text{companion}}$$

■ If the student skips a word, the teacher marks the error with a dash:

$$\frac{\text{—}}{\text{own}}$$

■ If the student adds words that are not in the text, the teacher writes an insertion symbol (caret) and records the inserted words:

$$\frac{\text{where he}}{\char`\^}$$

■ If the student can't identify a word and the teacher pronounces the word for the student, the teacher writes *T*:

$$\frac{\text{T}}{\text{routine}}$$

■ If the student repeats a word or phrase, the repetition is not scored as an error, but the teacher notes the repetition by drawing a line under the word or phrase (marked in the running record with check marks) that was repeated:

$$\underline{✓ ✓ ✓}$$

A sample running record was shown in Figure 12–6.

3. ***Calculate the percentage of miscues.***   Teachers calculate the percentage of miscues or oral reading errors. When the student makes 5% or fewer errors, the book is considered to be at the independent level for that child. When there are 6–10% errors, the book is at the instructional level, and when there are more than 10% errors, the book is too difficult—the frustration level.

4. ***Analyze the miscues.***   Teachers looks for patterns in the miscues in order to determine how the student is growing as a reader and to determine what skills and strategies the student should be taught. A miscue analysis of a running record was shown in Figure 12–7.

Many teachers conduct running records with all students in their classrooms at the beginning of the school year and at the end of grading periods. In addition, teachers do running records more often with students who are not making expected progress in reading in order to track their growth as readers and make instructional decisions.

In the SQ3R study strategy (Anderson & Armbruster, 1984), students use five steps—survey, question, read, recite, and review—to read and remember information in content-area reading assignments. This strategy is very effective when students know how to apply it correctly. The five steps are:

SQ3R STUDY STRATEGY

1. *Survey.* Students preview the reading assignment, noting headings and skimming (rapidly reading) the introduction and summary. They note the main ideas that are presented. This step helps students activate prior knowledge and organize what they will read.
2. *Question.* Students turn each heading into a question before reading the section. Reading to find the answer to the question give students a purpose for reading.
3. *Read.* Students read the section to find the answer to the question they have formulated. They read each section separately.
4. *Recite.* Immediately after reading each section, students recite from memory the answer to the question they formulated and other important information they have read. Students can answer the questions orally or in writing.
5. *Review.* After finishing the entire reading assignment, students take a few minutes to review what they have read. They ask themselves the questions they developed from each heading and try to recall the answers they learned by reading. If students took notes or wrote answers to the questions in the fourth step, they should try to review without referring to the written notes.

Story boards are cards to which the illustrations and text (or only the illustrations) from a picture book have been attached. Teachers make story boards by cutting apart two copies of a picture book. Students use story boards to sequence the events of a story, to examine a picture book's illustrations, and for other exploring-stage activities. The steps in making story boards are:

STORY BOARDS

1. Collect two copies of a book. It is preferable to use paperback copies of the books because they are less expensive to purchase. In a few picture books, all the illustrations are on either the right-hand or left-hand page, and only one copy of these books is needed for illustration-only story boards. In Chris Van Allsburg's *The Mysteries of Harris Burdick* (1984), for example, all illustrations are on the right-hand pages.
2. Cut the books apart. Teachers remove the covers and separate the pages. Next, they trim the edges of the cut-apart sides.
3. Glue each page or double-page spread to a piece of cardboard, making sure that each page in the story will be included.
4. Laminate the cards so that they can withstand use by students.

5. Use the cards in sequencing activities. Pass out the cards in random order to students. Have students line up around the classroom to sequence the story events.

Story boards can also be used when there are only a few copies of a picture book so that students can identify words for the **word wall,** notice literary language, and examine the illustrations.

For chapter books, students can create their own story boards, one for each chapter. Students can divide into small groups, and each group works on a different chapter. Students make a poster with a picture illustrating the chapter and a written paragraph-length summary of the chapter.

STORY MAPS

Teachers and students make a variety of diagrams and charts to examine the structure of stories they are reading (Bromley, 1991; Claggett, 1992; Macon et al., 1991). Six types of story maps are:

■ beginning-middle-end diagrams to examine the plot of a story
■ character **clusters** to examine the traits of a main character (Macon et al., 1991)
■ Venn diagrams to compare book and film versions of a story or for other comparisons
■ plot profiles to chart the tension in each chapter of a chapter book (Johnson & Louis, 1987)
■ sociograms to explore the relationships among characters (Johnson & Louis, 1987)
■ clusters to probe the theme, setting, genre, author's style, or other dimensions of the story

"Skeleton" diagrams for these six types of story maps are presented in Figure 7. Students use information from the story they are reading and add words, sentences, and illustrations to complete the story maps.

The steps in using story maps are:

1. Choose the type of story map that is appropriate for the story and the purpose of the lesson.
2. Draw the "skeleton" diagram on the chalkboard or on a chart.
3. Have students complete the diagram. Students usually work together as a class the first time they do a story map. The next few times they do the story map, they work in small groups. After this experience, students make maps individually. Students use a combination of words and pictures for most story maps.
4. Have students share their completed story maps and explain what they learned about the story by making the map.

Students often make story maps as an exploring activity, but they can also choose to make a story map as a project. There are many other types of story maps students can make, and teachers can invent their own maps to help students visualize other structures and relationships in stories.

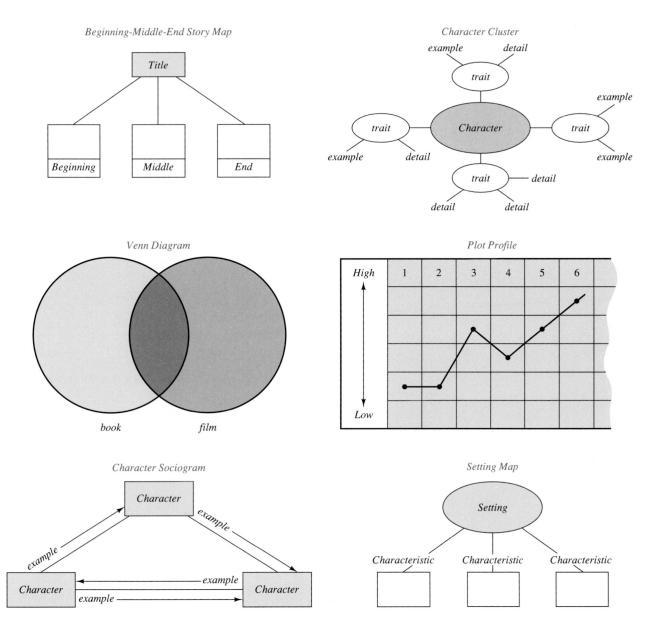

FIGURE 7   Six Types of Story Maps

Students make squares out of construction paper and arrange them to make a story quilt. These quilts are designed to highlight the theme and to celebrate a story that students have read during a literature focus unit. A square from a story quilt about *Fly Away Home* (Bunting, 1991), a story about a homeless boy and his dad who live at an airport, is shown in Figure 8. The third graders created a modified "wedding ring" quilt pattern for their story quilt. The steps in making a story quilt are:

STORY QUILTS

1. Choose a design for the quilt square that is appropriate for the story—its theme, characters, or setting. Students can choose a quilt design or create their own de-

FIGURE 8   A Quilt
Square From a Story Quilt
About *Fly Away Home*

sign that captures an important dimension of the story. They also choose colors for each shape in the quilt square.

2. Have each student make a square and add a favorite sentence from the story or a comment about the story around the outside of the quilt square or in a designated section of the square.

3. Tape the squares together and back the quilt with butcher paper, or staple the squares side by side on a large bulletin board.

Story quilts can be made of cloth, too. As an end-of-the-year project or to celebrate Book Week, teachers cut out squares of light-colored cloth and have students use fabric markers to draw pictures of their favorite stories and add the titles and authors. Then teachers or other adults sew the squares together, add a border, and complete the quilt.

WORD SORTS

Word sorts is a strategy for examining words and their meanings, sound-symbol correspondences, or spelling patterns (Morris, 1982; Schlagal & Schlagal, 1992). The purpose of word sorts is to help students focus on conceptual and phonological features of words and identify recurring patterns. Students sort a group of words (or objects or pictures) according to one of these characteristics:

■ conceptual relationships, such as words related to one of several character in a story or words related to the inner or outer planets in the solar system

■ rhyming words, such as words that rhyme with *ball, cat, car,* or *rake*

■ consonant sounds, such as pictures and objects of words beginning with *r* or *l*

■ sound-symbol relationships, such as words in which the final *y* sounds like long *i* (*cry*) and words in which the final *y* sounds like long *e* (*baby*)

FIGURE 9   A First-Grade Word Sort Using Words From Nancy Shaw's "Sheep" Books

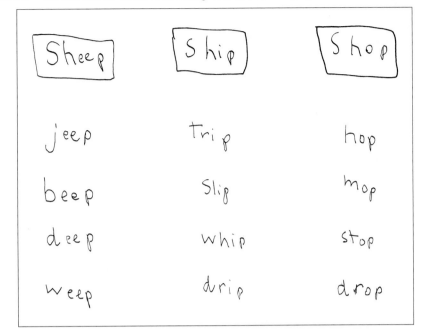

- spelling patterns and rules, such as long-*e* words with various spelling patterns *(sea, greet, be, Pete)*
- number of syllables, such as *pig, happy, afternoon,* and *television*
- root words and affixes

Many of the words chosen for word sorts should come from **word walls,** books students are reading, or across-the-curriculum theme studies. Figure 9 shows a first-grade word sort using words from Nancy Shaw's *Sheep in a Jeep* (1986), *Sheep on a Ship* (1989), and *Sheep in a Shop* (1991) books. Students sorted the words according to three rimes—*eep, ip,* and *op.*

The steps in this instructional strategy are:

1. The teacher compiles a list of 10 to 20 words that exemplify a particular pattern and writes the words on small cards. With younger children, small objects or picture cards can be used.
2. Students read the words and determine the categories for the sort. They may work individually or together in small groups or as a class.
3. Then students sort the words into two or more categories and write the sorted words on a chart or glue the sorted word cards onto a piece of chart paper.
4. Students share their word sort with classmates, emphasizing the categories they used for their sort.

WORD WALLS

Word walls are large sheets of butcher paper on which students and the teacher write interesting, confusing, and important words from stories, informational books, and textbooks they are reading. Students refer to the words on the word wall for writing activities and for word-study activities. A word wall for *Sarah, Plain and Tall* (MacLachlan, 1983) might include these words:

Papa	Anna	Caleb	prairie
hearthstones	hollow	slab	dough
troublesome	homely	holler	horrid
wretched	patches	cruel	widened
feisty	rascal	crowding	harshly
eagerly	housekeeper	shuffling	energetic
mild mannered	pesky	offshore	dunes
fogbound	preacher	blue flax	pitchfork
Indian paintbrush	suspenders	wild-eyed	nip
gophers	woodchuck	chores	shoveled
stalls	bonnet	windbreak	smoothing
roamer	conch shell	oyster	Sarah
paddock	wooly ragwort	whooped	slippery
coarse	shovel	mica	carpenter
biscuits	tumbleweeds	collapsed	squall
treaded (water)	longing	ayuh	colored pencils

Other word walls can be developed for social studies and science themes. Words from different themes should not be mixed on one word wall. Prepare separate word walls for different curricular areas so that students will categorize the words more easily. If words related to a literature focus unit on *Sarah, Plain and Tall* and words related to a theme study on machines are mixed together, for example, students may have trouble keeping track.

The steps in using a word wall are:

1. Hang a long sheet of butcher paper on a blank wall in the classroom and title it "Word Wall."

2. Introduce the word wall and write several key words on it during preparing activities before reading.

3. After reading a picture book or after reading each chapter of a chapter book, have students suggest other "important" words for the word wall. Students and the teacher write the words on the butcher paper, making sure to write large enough so that most students can see the words.

4. Use the words for a variety of vocabulary activities, such as **word sorts** and **story maps.** During literature focus units, students refer to the word wall when they are writing in **reading logs** or working on projects. During across-the-curriculum themes, students use the word wall in similar ways.

5. Refer to the word wall often, expect students to spell these words correctly in their writing, and use words in a variety of activities, including word posters, word chains, and word sorts.

For kindergartners and other emergent readers, teachers often write key words on small cards and place them in a pocket chart instead of writing the words on a word wall. When the words are written on cards, students can match the words to objects and pictures and use them for other activities. For a literature focus unit on *Rosie's Walk* (Hutchins, 1968), for example, key words might include *Rosie, hen, fox, rake, bees, wagon, mill,* and *flour.*

During the revising stage of the writing process, students meet in writing groups to share their rough drafts and get feedback on how well they are communicating (Tompkins, 1994). Revising is probably the most difficult part of the writing process because it is difficult for students to stand back and evaluate their writing objectively. Students need to learn how to work together in writing groups and provide useful feedback to classmates. The steps are:

1. Have students take turns reading their rough drafts aloud to the group. Everyone listens politely, thinking about compliments and suggestions they will make after the writer finishes reading. Only the writer looks at the composition, because when classmates and teacher look at it they quickly notice and comment on mechanical errors, even though the emphasis during revising is on content. Listening as the writing is read aloud keeps the focus on content.

2. Have classmates offer compliments. After listening to the rough draft read aloud, classmates in the writing group tell the writer what they liked about the composition. These positive comments should be specific, focusing on strengths, rather than the often-heard "I liked it" or "It was good." Even though these are positive comments, they do not provide effective feedback. When teachers introduce revision, they should model appropriate responses because students may not know how to of-

WRITING GROUPS

Students share their rough drafts and get feedback from classmates and the teacher during writing groups.

fer specific and meaningful comments. Teachers and students can brainstorm a list of appropriate comments and post it in the classroom for students to refer to. Comments may focus on organization, introductions, word choice, voice, sequence, dialogue, theme, and so on. Possible comments are:

> I like the part where . . .
> I'd like to know more about . . .
> I like the way you described . . .
> Your writing made me feel . . .
> I like the order you used in your writing because . . .

3. Have the writer ask clarifying questions. After a round of positive comments, writers ask for assistance with trouble spots they identified earlier when rereading their writing, or they may ask questions that reflect more general concerns about how well they are communicating. Admitting the need for help from one's classmates is a major step in learning to revise. Possible questions to ask classmates are:

> What do you want to know more about?
> Is there a part I should throw away?
> What details can I add?
> What do you think the best part of my writing is?
> Are there some words I need to change?

4. Have classmates offer other revision suggestions. Members of the writing group ask questions about things that were unclear to them and make suggestions about how to revise the composition. Almost any writer resists constructive criticism, and it is especially difficult for elementary students to appreciate suggestions. It is important to teach students what kinds of comments and suggestions are acceptable so that they will word what they say in helpful rather than hurtful ways. Possible comments and suggestions that students can offer are:

> I got confused in the part about . . .
> Do you need a closing?
> Could you add more about . . .
> I wonder if your paragraphs are in the right order because . . .
> Could you combine some sentences?

5. Have the writing group repeat the process so that all students can share their rough drafts. The first four steps are repeated for each student's composition. This is the appropriate time for teachers to provide input as well.

6. Have writers make plans for revision. At the end of the writing group session, each student makes a commitment to revise his or her writing based on the comments and suggestions of the group members. The final decision on what to revise always rests with the writers themselves, but with the understanding that their rough drafts are not perfect comes the realization that some revision will be necessary. When students verbalize their planned revisions, they are more likely to complete the revision stage. Some students also make notes for themselves about their revision plans. After the group disbands, students make the revisions.

References

Anderson, T. H., & Armbruster, B. B. (1984). Studying. In P. D. Pearson, R. Barr, M. L. Kamil, & P. Mosenthal (Eds.), *Handbook of reading research* (pp. 657–679). New York: Longman.

Ashton-Warner, S. (1965). *Teacher*. New York: Simon & Schuster.

Atwell, N. (1987). *In the middle: Writing, reading, and learning with adolescents*. Portsmouth, NH: Heinemann.

Barone, D. (1990). The written responses of young children: Beyond comprehension to story understanding. *The New Advocate, 3,* 49–56.

Berthoff, A. E. (1981). *The making of meaning*. Montclair, NJ: Boynton/Cook.

Bromley, K. D. (1991). *Webbing with literature: Creating story maps with children's books*. Boston: Allyn and Bacon.

Clagett, F. (1992). *Drawing your own conclusions: Graphic strategies for reading, writing, and thinking*. Portsmouth, NH: Heinemann.

Clay, M. M. (1985). *The early detection of reading difficulties* (3rd ed.). Portsmouth, NH: Heinemann.

Eeds, M., & Wells, D. (1989). Grand conversations: An exploration of meaning construction in literature study groups. *Research in the Teaching of English, 23,* 4–29.

Elbow, P. (1973). *Writing without teachers*. London: Oxford University Press.

Graves, D. H., & Hansen, J. (1983). The author's chair. *Language Arts, 60,* 176–183.

Head, M. H., & Readence, J. E. (1986). Anticipation guides: Meaning through prediction. In E. K. Dishner, T. W. Bean, J. E. Readence, & D. W. Moore (Eds.), *Reading in the content areas* (2nd ed.) (pp. 229–234). Dubuque, IA: Kendall/Hunt.

Hoskisson, K. (1975). The many facets of assisted reading. *Elementary English, 52,* 312–315.

Johnson, T. D., & Louis, D. R. (1987). *Literacy through literature*. Portsmouth, NH: Heinemann.

Lee, D. M., & Allen, R. V. (1963). *Learning to read through experience* (2nd ed.). New York: Meredith.

Macon, J. M., Bewell, D., & Vogt, M. E. (1991). *Responses to literature, grades K–8*. Newark, DE: International Reading Association.

Morris, D. (1982). "Word sort": A categorization strategy for improving word recognition. *Reading Psychology, 3,* 247–259.

Neeld, E. C. (1986). *Writing* (2nd ed.). Glenview, IL: Scott Foresman.

Ogle, D. M. (1986). K-W-L: A teaching model that develops active reading of expository text. *The Reading Teacher, 39,* 564–570.

Ogle, D. M. (1989). The know, want to know, learn strategy. In K. D. Muth (Ed.), *Children's comprehension of text: Research into practice* (pp. 205–223). Newark, DE: International Reading Association.

Peterson, R., & Eeds, M. (1990). *Grand conversations: Literature groups in action*. New York: Scholastic.

Reutzel, D. R., & Cooter, R. B., Jr. (1996). *Teaching children to read: From basals to books* (2nd ed.). Englewood Cliffs, NJ: Merrill/Prentice Hall.

Rico, G. L. (1983). *Writing the natural way*. Los Angeles: Tarcher.

Samuels, S. J. (1979). The method of repeated readings. *The Reading Teacher, 32,* 403–408.

Schlagal, R. C., & Schlagal, J. H. (1992). The integral character of spelling: Teaching strategies for multiple purposes. *Language Arts, 69,* 418–424.

Stauffer, R. G. (1970). *The language experience approach to the teaching of reading*. New York: Harper & Row.

Stauffer, R. G. (1975). *Directing the reading-thinking process*. New York: Harper & Row.

Tierney, R. J., Readence, J. E., & Dishner, E. K. (1995). *Reading strategies and practices: A compendium* (4th ed.). Boston: Allyn & Bacon.

Tompkins, G. E. (1994). *Teaching writing: Balancing process and product* (2nd ed.). New York: Merrill/Macmillan.

Children's Book References

Bunting, E. (1991). *Fly away home*. New York: Clarion.

Ehlert, L. (1989). *Eating the alphabet: Fruits and vegetables from A to Z*. Orlando, FL: Harcourt Brace Jovanovich.

Hunt, J. (1989). *Illuminations*. New York: Bradbury Press.

Hutchins, P. (1968). *Rosie's walk*. New York: Macmillan.

Lewis, C. S. (1950). *The lion, the witch and the wardrobe*. New York: Macmillan.

MacLachlan, P. (1983). *Sarah, plain and tall*. New York: Harper & Row.

Ness, E. (1966). *Sam, Bangs, and moonshine*. New York: Holt, Rinehart & Winston.

Shaw, N. (1986). *Sheep in a jeep*. Boston: Houghton Mifflin.

Shaw, N. (1989). *Sheep in a ship*. Boston: Houghton Mifflin.

Shaw, N. (1991). *Sheep in a shop*. Boston: Houghton Mifflin.

Van Allsburg, C. (1984). *The mysteries of Harris Burdick*. Boston: Houghton Mifflin.

APPENDIX A

Award-Winning Books for Children

Caldecott Medal Books

The Caldecott Medal is named in honor of Randolph Caldecott (1846–86), a British illustrator of children's books. The award is presented by the American Library Association each year to "the artist of the most distinguished American picture book for children" published during the preceding year. The award was first given in 1938 and is awarded annually. The winning book receives the Caldecott Medal, and one or more runners-up are also recognized as "Honor" books.

1996 *Officer Buckle and Gloria*, Peggy Rathmann (Putnam). **Honor books:** *Alphabet city*, Stephen T. Johnson (Viking); *Zin! Zin! Zin! A violin*, Lloyd Moss, illustrated by Marjorie Priceman (Simon & Schuster); *The faithful friend*, Robert D. San Souci, illustrated by Brian Pinkney (Simon & Schuster); *Tops and bottoms*, Janet Stevens (Harcourt & Brace).

1995 *Smoky night*, Eve Bunting, illustrated by David Diaz (Harcourt & Brace). **Honor books:** *Swamp angel*, Anne Isaacs, illustrated by Paul O. Zelinsky (Dutton); *John Henry*, Julius Lester (Dial); *Time flies*, Eric Rohmann (Crown).

1994 *Grandfather's journey*, Allen Say (Houghton Mifflin). **Honor books:** *Peppe the lamplighter*, Elisa Bartone (Lothrop); *In the small, small pond*, Denis Fleming (Holt); *Owen*, Kevin Henkes (Greenwillow); *Raven: A trickster tale from the Pacific northwest*, Gerald McDermott (Harcourt Brace Jovanovich); *Yo! Yes?* Chris Raschak (Orchard).

1993 *Mirette on the high wire*, Emily McCully (Putnam). **Honor books:** *Seven blind mice*, Ed Young (Philomel); *The stinky cheese man and other fairly stupid tales*, Jon Scieszka, illustrated by Lane Smith (Viking); *Working cotton*, Sherley Anne Williams, illustrated by Carole Byard (Harcourt Brace Jovanovich).

1992 *Tuesday*, David Wiesner (Clarion). **Honor book:** *Tar beach*, Faith Ringgold (Crown).

1991 *Black and white*, David Macaulay (Houghton Mifflin). **Honor books:** *Puss in boots*, Charles Perrault, illustrated by Fred Marcellino (Farrar, Straus & Giroux); *"More, more, more" said the baby*, Vera B. Williams (Morrow).

1990 *Lon Po Po, A Red Riding Hood story from China*, Ed Young (Philomel). **Honor books:** *Bill Peet: An autobiography*, William Peet (Houghton Mifflin); *Color zoo*, Lois Ehlert (Lippincott); *Herschel and the Hanukkah goblins*, Eric A. Kimmel, illustrated by Trina Schart Hyman (Holiday House); *The talking eggs*, Robert D. San Souci, illustrated by Jerry Pickney (Dial).

1989 *Song and dance man*, Jane Ackerman, illustrated by Stephen Gammel (Knopf). **Honor books:** *Goldilocks*, James Marshall (Dial); *The boy of the three-year nap*, Diane Snyder, illustrated by Allen Say (Houghton Mifflin); *Mirandy and Brother Wind*, Patricia McKissack, illustrated by Jerry Pickney (Knopf); *Free Fall*, David Wiesner (Lothrop).

1988 *Owl moon*, Jane Yolen, illustrated by John Schoenherr (Philomel). **Honor book:** *Mufaro's beautiful daughters: An African tale*, John Steptoe (Morrow).

1987 *Hey, Al*, Arthur Yorinks, illustrated by Richard Egielski (Farrah, Straus & Giroux). **Honor books:** *Alphabatics*, Suse MacDonald (Bradbury); *Rumplestiltskin*, Paul O. Zelinsky (E. P. Dutton); *The village of round and square houses*, Ann Grifalconi (Little, Brown).

1986 *The polar express*, Chris Van Allsburg (Houghton Mifflin). **Honor books:** *King Bidgood's in the bathtub*, Audrey Wood (Harcourt Brace Jovanovich); *The relatives came*, Cynthia Rylant (Bradbury).

1985 *Saint George and the dragon*, Margaret Hodges, illustrated by Trina Schart Hyman (Little, Brown). **Honor books:** *Hansel and Gretel*, Rika Lesser, illustrated by Paul O. Zelinsky (Dodd, Mead); *Have you seen my duckling?* Nancy Tafuri (Greenwillow); *The story of jumping mouse*, John Steptoe (Lothrop, Lee & Shepard).

1984   *The glorious flight: Across the channel with Louis Bleriot*, Alice and Martin Provensen (Viking). **Honor books:** *Little red riding hood*, Trina Schart Hyman (Holiday); *Ten, nine, eight*, Molly Bang (Greenwillow).

1983   *Shadow*, Blaise Cendrars, translated and illustrated by Marcia Brown (Scribner). **Honor books:** *A chair for my mother*, Vera B. Williams (Greenwillow); *When I was young in the mountains*, Cynthia Rylant, illustrated by Diane Goode (E. P. Dutton).

1982   *Jumanji*, Chris Van Allsburg (Houghton Mifflin). **Honor books:** *On Market Street*, Arnold Lobel, illustrated by Anita Lobel (Greenwillow); *Outside over there*, Maurice Sendak (Harper & Row); *A visit to William Blake's inn: Poems for innocent and experienced travelers*, Nancy Willard, illustrated by Alice and Martin Provensen (Harcourt Brace Jovanovich); *Where the buffaloes begin*, Olaf Baker, illustrated by Stephen Gammell (Warne).

1981   *Fables*, Arnold Lobel (Harper & Row). **Honor books:** *The Bremen-Town musicians*, Ilse Plume (Doubleday); *The gray lady and the strawberry snatcher*, Molly Bang (Four Winds); *Mice twice*, Joseph Low (Atheneum); *Truck*, Donald Crews (Greenwillow).

1980   *Ox-cart man*, Donald Hall, illustrated by Barbara Cooney (Viking); **Honor books:** *Ben's trumpet*, Rachel Isadora (Greenwillow); *The garden of Abdul Gasazi*, Chris Van Allsburg (Houghton Mifflin); *The treasure*, Uri Shulevitz (Farrar, Straus & Giroux).

1979   *The girl who loved wild horses*, Paul Goble (Bradbury). **Honor books:** *Freight train*, Donald Crews (Greenwillow); *The way to start a day*, Byrd Baylor, illustrated by Peter Parnall (Scribner).

1978   *Noah's ark: The story of the flood*, Peter Spier (Doubleday), **Honor books:** *Castle*, David Macaulay (Houghton Mifflin); *It could always be worse*, Margot Zemach (Farrar, Straus & Giroux).

1977   *Ashanti to Zulu*, Margaret Musgrove, illustrated by Leo and Diane Dillon (Dial). **Honor books:** *The amazing bone*, William Steig (Farrar, Straus & Giroux); *The contest*, Nonny Hogrogian (Greenwillow); *Fish for supper*, M. B. Goffstein (Dial); *The Golem: A Jewish legend*, Beverly Brodsky McDermott (J. B. Lippincott); *Hawk, I'm your brother*, Byrd Baylor, illustrated by Peter Parnall (Scribner).

1976   *Why mosquitoes buzz in people's ears*, Verna Aardema, illustrated by Leo and Diane Dillon (Dial). **Honor books:** *The desert is theirs*, Byrd Baylor (Scribner), illustrated by Peter Parnall; *Strega Nona*, Tomie de Paola (Prentice-Hall).

1975   *Arrow to the sun*, Gerald McDermott (Viking). **Honor book:** *Jambo means hello: A Swahili alphabet book*, Muriel Feelings, illustrated by Tom Feelings (Dial).

1974   *Duffy and the devil*, Harve and Margo Zemach (Farrar, Straus & Giroux). **Honor books:** *Cathedral:*

The story of its construction, David Macaulay (Houghton Mifflin); *The three jovial huntsmen*, Susan Jeffers (Bradbury).

1973   *The funny little woman*, Arlen Mosel, illustrated by Blair Lent (E. P. Dutton). **Honor books:** *Hosie's alphabet*, Hosea, Tobias, and Lisa Baskin, illustrated by Leonard Baskin (Viking); *Snow-White and the seven dwarfs*, translated by Randall Jarrell from the Brothers Grimm, illustrated by Nancy Ekholm Burkert (Farrar, Straus & Giroux); *When clay sings*, Byrd Baylor, illustrated by Tom Bahti (Scribner).

1972   *One fine day*, Nonny A. Hogrogian (Macmillan). **Honor books:** *Hildilid's night*, Cheli Duran Ryan, illustrated by Arnold Lobel (Macmillan); *If all the seas were one sea*, Janina Domanska (Macmillan); *Moja means one: Swahili counting book*, Muriel Feelings, illustrated by Tom Feelings (Dial).

1971   *A story, a story*. Gail E. Haley (Atheneum). **Honor books:** *The angry moon*, William Sleator, illustrated by Blair Lent (Atlantic-Little); *Frog and Toad are friends*, Arnold Lobel (Harper & Row); *In the night kitchen*, Maurice Sendak (Harper & Row).

1970   *Sylvester and the magic pebble*, William Steig (Windmill/Simon & Schuster). **Honor books:** *Alexander and the wind-up mouse*, Leo Lionni (Pantheon); *Goggles!* Ezra Jack Keats (Macmillan); *The judge: An untrue tale*, Harve Zemach, illustrated by Margot Zemach (Farrar, Straus & Giroux); *Pop Corn and Ma Goodness*, Edna Mitchell Preston, illustrated by Robert Andrew Parker (Viking); *Thy friend, Obadiah*, Brinton Turkle (Viking).

1969   *The fool of the world and the flying ship*, Arthur Ransome, illustrated by Uri Shulevitz (Farrar, Straus & Giroux). **Honor book:** *Why the sun and the moon live in the sky: An African folktale*, Elphinstone Dayrell, illustrated by Blair Lent (Houghton Mifflin).

1968   *Drummer Hoff*, Barbara Emberley, illustrated by Ed Emberley (Prentice-Hall). **Honor books:** *Frederick*, Leo Lionni (Pantheon); *Seashore story*, Taro Yashima (Viking); *The emperor and the kite*, Jane Yolen, illustrated by Ed Young (Harcourt Brace Jovanovich).

1967   *Sam, Bangs & Moonshine*, Evaline Ness (Holt, Rinehart & Winston). **Honor book:** *One wide river to cross*, Barbara Emberley, illustrated by Ed Emberley (Prentice-Hall).

1966   *Always room for one more*, Sorche Nic Leodhas, illustrated by Nonny Hogrogian (Holt). **Honor books:** *Hide and seek fog*, Alvin Tresselt, illustrated by Roger Duvoisin (Lothrop); *Just me*, Marie Hall Ets (Viking); *Tom tit tot*, Evaline Ness (Scribner).

1965   *May I bring a friend?* Beatrice Schenk de Regniers, illustrated by Beni Montresor (Atheneum). **Honor books:** *Rain makes applesauce*, Julian Scheer, illustrated by Marvin Bileck (Holiday House; *The wave*, Margaret

Hodges, illustrated by Blair Lent (Houghton Mifflin); *A pocketful of cricket*, Rebecca Caudill, illustrated by Evaline Ness (Holt).

1964 *Where the wild things are*, Maurice Sendak (Harper & Row). **Honor books:** *Swimmy*, Leo Lionni (Pantheon); *All in the morning early*, Sorche Nic Leodhas, illustrated by Evaline Ness (Holt); *Mother Goose and nursery rhymes*, illustrated by Philip Reed (Atheneum).

1963 *The snow day*, Ezra Jack Keats (Viking). **Honor books:** *The sun is a golden earring*, Natalia M. Belting, illustrated by Bernarda Bryson (Holt); *Mr. Rabbit and the lovely present*, Charlotte Zolotow, illustrated by Maurice Sendak (Harper & Row).

1962 *Once a mouse . . .* , Marcia Brown (Scribner). **Honor books:** *The fox went out on a chilly night: An old song*, Peter Spier (Doubleday); *Little bear's visit*, Else Holmelund Minarik, illustrated by Maurice Sendak (Harper & Row); *The day we saw the sun come up*, Alice E. Goudey, illustrated by Adrienne Adams (Scribner).

1961 *Baboushka and the three kings*, Ruth Robbins, illustrated by Nicolas Sidjakov (Parnassus). **Honor book:** *Inch by inch*, Leo Lionni (Obolensky).

1960 *Nine days to Christmas*, Marie Hall Ets & Aurora Labastida, illustrated by Marie Hall Ets (Viking). **Honor books:** *Houses from the sea*, Alice E. Goudey, illustrated by Adrienne Adams (Scribner); *The moon jumpers*, Janice May Udry, illustrated by Maurice Sendak (Harper & Row).

Newbery Medal Books

The Newbery Medal is named in honor of John Newbery (1713–67), a British publisher and bookseller in the 1700s. Newbery is known as the "father of children's literature" because he was the first to propose publishing books specifically for children. The award is presented each year by the American Library Association to "the author of the most distinguished contribution to American literature for children" published during the preceding year. The award was first given in 1922 and is awarded annually. The winning book receives the Newbery Medal, and one or more runners-up are also recognized as "Honor" books.

1996 *The midwife's apprentice*, Karen Cushman (Clarion). **Honor books:** *What Jamie saw*, Carolyn Coman (Front Street); *The Watsons go to Birmingham—1963*, Christopher Paul Curtis (Delacorte); *Yolanda's genius*, Carol Fenner (McElderry); *The great fire*, Jim Murphy (Scholastic).

1995 *Walk two moons*, Sharon Creech (HarperCollins). **Honor books:** *Catherine called Birdy*, Karen Cushman (Clarion); *The ear, the eye and the arm*, Nancy Farmer (Orchard).

1994 *The giver*, Lois Lowry (Houghton Mifflin). **Honor books:** *Crazy Lady!*, Jane Leslie Conly (HarperCollins); *Dragon's gate*, Laurence Yep (HarperCollins); *Eleanor Roosevelt: A life of discovery*, Russell Freedman (Clarion).

1993 *Missing May*, Cynthia Rylant (Orchard). **Honor books:** *The dark-thirty: Southern tales of the supernatural*, Patricia McKissack (Knopf); *Somewhere in the darkness*, Walter Dean Myers (Scholastic); *What hearts*, Bruce Books (HarperCollins).

1992 *Shiloh*, Phyllis Reynolds Naylor (Atheneum). **Honor books:** *Nothing but the truth*, Avi (Orchard); *The Wright brothers: How they invented the airplane*, Russell Freedman (Holiday).

1991 *Maniac Magee*, Jerry Spinelli (Little, Brown). **Honor book:** *The true confessions of Charlotte Doyle*, Avi (Orchard).

1990 *Number the stars*, Lois Lowry (Houghton Mifflin). **Honor books:** *Afternoon of the elves*, Janet Taylor Lisel (Orchard); *Shabanu, daughter of the wind*, Susan Fisher Staples (Knopf); *The winter room*, Gary Paulsen (Orchard).

1989 *Joyful noise: Poems for two voices*, Paul Fleishman (Harper & Row). **Honor books:** *In the beginning*, Virginia Hamilton (Harcourt Brace Jovanovich); *Scorpions*, Walter Dean Myers (Harper & Row).

1988 *Lincoln: A photobiography*, Russell Freedman (Clarion). **Honor books:** *After the rain*, Norma Fox Mazer (Morrow); *Hatchet*, Gary Paulsen (Bradbury).

1987 *The whipping boy*, Sid Fleischman (Greenwillow). **Honor books:** *A fine white dust*, Cynthia Rylant (Bradbury); *On my honor*, Marion Dane Bauer (Clarion); *Volcano: The eruption and healing of Mount St. Helen's*, Patricia Lauber (Bradbury).

1986 *Sarah, plain and tall*, Patricia MacLachlan (Harper & Row). **Honor books:** *Commodore Perry in the land of the Shogun*, Rhoda Blumberg (Lothrop, Lee & Shepard); *Dog song*, Gary Paulsen (Bradbury).

1985 *The hero and the crown*, Robin McKinley (Greenwillow). **Honor books:** *Like Jake and me*, Mavis Jukes (Alfred A. Knopf); *The moves make the man*, Bruce Brooks (Harper & Row); *One-eyed cat*, Paula Fox (Bradbury).

1984 *Dear Mr. Henshaw*, Beverly Clearly (Morrow). **Honor books:** *The sign of the beaver*, Elizabeth George Speare (Houghton Mifflin); *A solitary blue*, Cynthia Voigt (Atheneum); *Sugaring time*, Kathryn Lasky (Macmillan); *The wish giver*, Bill Brittain (Harper & Row).

1983 *Dicey's song*, Cynthia Voigt (Atheneum). **Honor books:** *The blue sword*, Robin McKinley (Greenwillow); *Doctor DeSoto*, William Steig (Farrar, Straus & Giroux); *Graven images*, Paul Fleischman (Harper & Row); *Homesick: My own story*, Jean Fritz (Putnam); *Sweet Whispers, Brother Rush*, Virginia Hamilton (Philomel).

1982 *A visit to William Blake's inn: Poems for innocent and experienced travelers*, Nancy Willard (Harcourt

Brace Jovanovich). **Honor books:** *Ramona Quimby, age 8,* Beverly Clearly (Morrow); *Upon the head of the goat: A childhood in Hungary, 1939–1944,* Aranka Siegal (Farrar, Straus & Giroux).

1981 *Jacob have I loved,* Katherine Paterson (Crowell). **Honor books:** *The fledgling,* Jane Langton (Harper & Row); *A ring of endless light,* Madeleine L'Engle (Farrar, Straus & Giroux).

1980 *A gathering of days: A New England girl's journal, 1830–1832,* Joan W. Blos (Scribner). **Honor book:** *The road from home: The story of an Armenian girl,* David Kerdian (Greenwillow).

1979 *The westing game,* Ellen Raskin (Dutton). **Honor book:** *The great Gilly Hopkins,* Katherine Paterson (Crowell).

1978 *Bridge to Terabithia,* Katherine Paterson (Crowell). **Honor books:** *Anpao: An American Indian odyssey,* Jamake Highwater (Lippincott); *Ramona and her father,* Beverly Clearly (Morrow).

1977 *Roll of thunder, hear my cry,* Mildred Taylor (Dial). **Honor books:** *Abel's Island,* William Steig (Farrar, Straus & Giroux); *A string in the harp,* Nancy Bond (Atheneum).

1976 *The grey king,* Susan Cooper (Atheneum). **Honor books:** *Dragonwings,* Laurence Yep (Harper & Row); *The hundred penny box,* Sharon Bell Mathis (Viking).

1975 *M. C. Higgins, the great,* Virginia Hamilton (Macmillan). **Honor books:** *Figgs and phantoms,* Ellen Raskin (E. P. Dutton); *My brother Sam is dead,* James Lincoln Collier and Christopher Collier (Four Winds); *The perilous guard,* Elizabeth Marie Pope (Houghton Mifflin); *Philip Hall likes me, I reckon maybe,* Bette Green (Dial).

1974 *The slave dancer,* Paula Fox (Bradbury). **Honor book:** *The dark is rising,* Susan Cooper (Atheneum).

1973 *Julie of the wolves,* Jean C. George (Harper & Row). **Honor books:** *Frog and Toad together,* Arnold Lobel (Harper & Row); *The upstairs room,* Johanna Reiss (Crowell); *The witches of worm,* Zilpha Keatley Snyder (Atheneum).

1972 *Mrs. Frisby and the rats of NIMH,* Robert C. O'Brien (Atheneum). **Honor books:** *Annie and the old one,* Miska Miles (Atlantic-Little); *The headless cupid,* Zilpha Keatley Snyder (Atheneum); *Incident at Hawk's Hill,* Allan W. Eckert (Little, Brown); *The planet of Junior Brown,* Virginia Hamilton (Macmillan); *The tombs of Atuan,* Ursula K. LeGuin (Atheneum).

1971 *The summer of the swans,* Betsy Byars (Viking). **Honor books:** *Enchantress from the stars,* Sylvia Louise Engdahl (Atheneum); *Kneeknock rise,* Natalie Babbitt (Farrar, Straus & Giroux); *Sing down the moon,* Scott O'Dell (Houghton Mifflin).

1970 *Sounder,* William Armstrong (Harper & Row). **Honor books:** *Journey outside,* Mary Q. Steele (Viking); *Our Eddie,* Sulamith Ish-Kishor (Pantheon); *The many ways of seeing, An introduction to the pleasures of art,* Janet Gaylord Moore (Harcourt Brace Jovanovich).

1969 *The high king,* Lloyd Alexander (Holt, Rinehart & Winston). **Honor books:** *To be a slave,* Julius Lester (Dial); *When Shlemiel went to Warsaw and other stories,* Isaac Bashevis Singer (Farrar, Straus & Giroux).

1968 *From the mixed-up files of Mrs. Basil E. Frankweiler,* E. L. Konigsburg (Atheneum). **Honor books:** *The black pearl,* Scott O'Dell (Houghton Mifflin); *The Egypt game,* Zilpha Keatley Snyder (Atheneum); *The fearsome inn,* Isaac Bashevis Singer (Scribner); *Jennifer, Hecate, Macbeth, William McKinley, and me, Elizabeth,* E. L. Konigsburg (Atheneum).

1967 *Up a road slowly,* Irene Hunt (Follett). **Honor books:** *The jazz man,* Mary Hays Weik (Atheneum); *The King's Fifth,* Scott O'Dell (Houghton Mifflin); *Zlateh the goat and other stories,* Isaac Bashevis Singer (Harper & Row).

1966 *I, Juan de Pareja,* Elizabeth Borton de Trevino (Farrar, Straus & Giroux). **Honor books:** *The animal family,* Randall Jarrell (Pantheon); *The black cauldron,* Lloyd Alexander (Holt, Rinehart & Winston); *The noonday friends,* Mary Stolz (Harper & Row).

1965 *Shadow of a bull,* Maia Wojciechowska (Atheneum). **Honor book:** *Across five Aprils,* Irene Hunt (Follett).

1964 *It's like this, cat,* Emily Neville (Harper & Row). **Honor books:** *The loner,* Ester Wier (McKay); *Rascal,* Sterling North (E. P. Dutton).

1963 *A wrinkle in time,* Madeleine L'Engle (Farrar, Straus & Giroux). **Honor books:** *Thistle and thyme: Tales and Legends from Scotland,* Sorche Nic Leodhas (Holt); *Men of Athens,* Olivia Coolidge (Houghton Mifflin).

1962 *The bronze bow,* Elizabeth George Speare (Houghton Mifflin). **Honor books:** *Frontier living,* Edwin Tunis (World); *The golden goblet,* Eloise McCraw (Coward); *Belling the tiger,* Mary Stolz (Harper & Row).

1961 *Island of the blue dolphins,* Scott O'Dell (Houghton Mifflin). **Honor books:** *America moves forward,* Gerald W. Johnson (Morrow); *Old Ramon,* Jack Schaefer (Houghton Mifflin); *The cricket in Times Square,* George Selden (Farrar, Straus & Giroux).

1960 *Onion John,* Joseph Krumgold (Crowell). **Honor books:** *My side of the mountain,* Jean Craighead George (Dutton); *America is born,* Gerald W. Johnson (Morrow); *The gammage cup,* Carol Kendall (Harcourt Brace Jovanovich).

APPENDIX B
Resources About Authors and Illustrators

Books About Authors and Illustrators

Aardema, Verna Aardema, V. (1992). *A bookworm who hatched.* Katonah, NY: Richard C. Owen (P–M)*

Andersen, Hans Christian Greene, C. (1991). *Hans Christian Andersen: Prince of storytellers.* Chicago: Childrens Press. (P–M)

Blegvad, Erik Blegvad, E. (1979). *Self-portrait: Erik Blegvad.* Reading, MA: Addison-Wesley, (P–M–U)

Brown, Margaret Wise Brown, M. W. (1994). *The days before now.* New York: Simon & Schuster. (P–M)

Bunting, Eve Bunting, E. (1995). *Once upon a time.* Katonah, NY: Richard C. Owen. (P–M)

Burnett, Frances Hodgson Carpenter, A. S., & Shirley, J. (1990). *Frances Hodgson Burnett: Beyond the secret garden.* Minneapolis: Lerner Books. (U)

Byars, Betsy Byars, B. (1991). *The moon and I.* New York: Messner. (M–U)

Carson, Rachel Wadsworth, G. (1991). *Rachel Carson: Voice for the earth.* Minneapolis: Lerner Books. (U)

Cleary, Beverly Cleary, B. (1988). *A girl from Yamhill: A memoir.* New York: Morrow (M–U)

Cole, Joanna Cole, J. (1996). *On the bus with Joanna Cole.* Portsmouth, NH: Heinemann. (M–U)

Cowley, Joy Cowley, J. (1988). *Seventy kilometres from ice cream: A letter from Joy Cowley.* Katonah, NY: Richard C. Owen. (P)

Dahl, Roald Dahl, R. (1984). *Boy: Tales of childhood.* New York: Farrar, Straus & Giroux. (M–U)

de Paola, Tomie de Paola, T. (1989). *The art lesson.* New York: Putnam. (P)

Dillon, Leo and Diane Preiss, B. (1981). *The art of Leo and Diane Dillon.* New York: Ballantine. (M–U)

Dr. Seuss Weidt, M. N. (1994). *Oh, the places he went: A story about Dr. Seuss—Theodor Seuss Geisel.* Minneapolis: Carolrhoda. (M)

Duncan, Lois Duncan, L. (1982). *Chapters: My growth as a writer.* Boston: Little, Brown. (U)

Fritz, Jean Fritz, J. (1982). *Homesick: My own story.* New York: Putnam (M–U); Fritz, J. (1992). *Surprising myself.* Katonah, NY: Richard C. Owen. (M)

Goble, Paul Goble, P. (1994). *Hau kola/ Hello friend.* Katonah, NY: Richard C. Owen. (M)

Goodall, John Goodall, J. S. (1981). *Before the war, 1908–1939. An autobiography in pictures.* New York: Atheneum. (M–U)

Henry, Marguerite Henry, M. (1980). *The illustrated Marguerite Henry.* Chicago: Rand McNally. (M–U)

Hinton, S. E. Daly, J. (1989). *Presenting S. E. Hinton.* Boston: Twayne. (U)

Hopkins, Lee Bennett Hopkins, L. B. (1992). *The writing bug.* Katonah, NY: Richard C. Owen. (M)

Howe, James Howe, J. (1994). *Playing with words.* Katonah, NY: Richard C. Owen. (M)

Hughes, Langston Cooper, F. (1994). *Coming home: From the life of Langston Hughes.* New York: Philomel. (M–U)

Hyman, Trina Schart Hyman, T. S. (1981). *Self-portrait: Trina Schart Hyman.* Reading, MA: Addison-Wesley. (P–M–U).

Kuskin, Karla Kuskin, K. (1995). *Thoughts, pictures, and words.* Katonah, NY: Richard C. Owen. (M)

Lewis, C. S. Lewis, C. S. (1985). *Letters to children.* New York: Macmillan. (M–U)

Mahy, Margaret Mahy, M. (1995). *My mysterious world.* Katonah, NY: Richard C. Owen. (M)

McPhail, David McPhail, D. (1996). *In flight with David McPhail.* Portsmouth, NH: Heinemann. (P–M)

Meltzer, Milton Meltzer, M. (1988). *Starting from home: A writer's beginnings.* NY: Viking. (U)

Mohr, Nicholasa   Mohr, N. (1994). *Nicholasa Mohr: Growing up inside the sanctuary of my imagination.* New York: Messner. (U)

Naylor, Phyllis   Naylor, P. R. (1978). *How I came to be a writer.* New York: Atheneum. (U)

Peck, Richard   Peck, R. (1991). *Anonymously yours.* New York: Messner. (U)

Peet, Bill   Peet, B. (1989). *Bill Peet: An autobiography.* Boston: Houghton Mifflin. (M–U)

Polacco, Patricia   Polacco, P. (1994). *Fire talking.* Katonah, NY: Richard C. Owen. (M)

Potter, Beatrix   Aldis, D. (1969). *Nothing is impossible: The story of Beatrix Potter.* New York: Atheneum. (M); Collins, D. R. (1989). *The country artist: A story about Beatrix Potter.* Minneapolis: Carolrhoda. (M)

Rylant, Cynthia   Rylant, C. (1992). *Best wishes.* Katonah, NY: Richard C. Owen. (P–M)

Singer, Isaac Bashevis   Singer, I. B. (1969). *A day of pleasure: Stories of a boy growing up in Warsaw.* New York: Farrar, Straus & Giroux. (U)

Uchida, Yoshiko   Uchida, U. (1991). *The invisible thread.* New York: Messner. (U)

Wilder, Laura Ingalls   Blair, G. (1981). *Laura Ingalls Wilder.* New York: Putnam. (P–M); Greene, C. (1990). *Laura Ingalls Wilder: Author of the Little House books.* Chicago: Childrens Press. (P–M)

Yep, Laurence   Yep, L. (1991). *The lost garden: A memoir.* New York: Messner. (U)

Yolen, Jane   Yolen, J. (1992). *A letter from Phoenix Farm.* Katonah, NY: Richard C. Owen. (P–M–U)

Zemach, Margot   Zemach, M. (1978). *Self-portrait: Margot Zemach.* Reading, MA: Addison-Wesley. (P–M–U)

Individual Articles Profiling Authors and Illustrators

Adoff, Arnold   White, M. L. (1988). Profile: Arnold Adoff. *Language Arts, 65,* 584–591.

Alexander, Lloyd   Greenlaw, M. J. (1984). Profile: Lloyd Alexander. *Language Arts, 61,* 406–413; Tunnell, M. O. (1989). An interview with Lloyd Alexander. *The New Advocate, 2,* 83–96.

Anno, Mitsumasa   Aoki, H. (1983). A conversation with Mitsumasa Anno. *Horn Book Magazine, 59,* 132–145; Swinger, A. K. (1987). Profile: Mitsumasa Anno's journey. *Language Arts, 64,* 762–766.

Baker, Keith   Baker, K. (1993). "Have you ever been dead?" Questions and letters from children. *The Reading Teacher, 46,* 372–375.

Baylor, Byrd   Bosma, B. (1987). Profile: Byrd Baylor. *Language Arts, 64,* 315–318.

Brett, Jan   Raymond, A. (April, 1992). Jan Brett: Making it look easy. *Teaching PreK–8, 22,* 38–40.

Brown, Marcia   Brown, M. (1983). Caldecott Medal Acceptance. *Horn Book Magazine, 59,* 414–422.

Brown, Margaret Wise   Hurd, C. (1983). Remembering Margaret Wise Brown. *Horn Book Magazine, 59,* 553–560.

Browne, Anthony   Marantz, S., & Marantz, K. (1985). An interview with Anthony Browne. *Horn Book Magazine, 61,* 696–704.

Bryan, Ashley   Marantz, S., & Marantz, K. (1988). Interview with Ashley Bryan. *Horn Book Magazine, 64,* 173–179; Swinger, A. K. (1984). Profile: Ashley Bryan. *Language Arts, 61,* 305–311.

Bunting, Eve   Raymond, A. (October, 1986). Eve Bunting: From Ireland with love. *Teaching PreK–8, 17,* 38–40.

Byars, Betsy   Robertson, I. (1980). Profile: Betsy Byars—Writer for today's child. *Language Arts, 57,* 328–334.

Carle, Eric   Yolen, J. (1988). In the artist's studio: Eric Carle. *The New Advocate, 1,* 148–154.

Ciardi, John   Odland, N. (1982). Profile: John Ciardi. *Language Arts, 59,* 872–876.

Cleary, Beverly   Cleary, B. (1984). Newbery Medal acceptance. *Horn Book Magazine, 50,* 429–438; Reuter, D. (1984). Beverly Cleary, *Horn Book Magazine, 50,* 439–443.

Clifton, Lucille   Sims, R. (1982). Profile: Lucille Clifton. *Language Arts, 59,* 160–167.

Collier, James and Christopher   Raymond, A. (January, 1988). Meet James and Christopher Collier. *Teaching PreK–8, 18,* 35–38.

Conrad, Pam   Raymond, A. (November/December, 1990). Pam Conrad: She said to herself, "Now what?" *Teaching PreK–8, 21,* 38–40.

Creech, Sharon   An interview with Sharon Creech, 1995 Newbery Medal winner. (1996). *The Reading Teacher, 49,* 380–382.

Degan, Bruce   Elliot, I. (October, 1991). Bruce Degan: Doing what he likes best. *Teaching PreK–8, 21,* 44–47.

Diaz, David   Conversation with a winner—David Diaz talks about *Smoky Night.* (1996). *The Reading Teacher, 49,* 386–388.

Dillon, Leo and Diane   Cummings, P. (1992). *Talking with artists* (pp. 22–29). New York: Bradbury Press.

Dr. Seuss   Roth, R. (1989). On beyond zebra with Dr. Seuss. *The New Advocate, 2,* 213–226.

Egielski, Richard   Cummings, P. (1992). *Talking with artists* (pp. 30–35). New York: Bradbury Press; Egielski, R. (1987). Caldecott Medal acceptance. *Horn Book Magazine, 63,* 433–435; Yorinks, A. (1987). Richard Egielski. *Horn Book Magazine, 63,* 436–438.

Ehlert, Lois   Cummings, P. (1992). *Talking with artists* (pp. 36–41). New York: Bradbury Press.

Feelings, Tom   Feelings, T. (1985). The artist at work: Technique and the artist's vision. *Horn Book Magazine, 61,* 685–695.

Fleischman, Sid   Fleischman, P. (1987). Sid Fleischman. *Horn Book Magazine, 63,* 429–432; Fleischman, S. (1987). Newbery Medal acceptance. *Horn Book Magazine, 63,* 423–438; Johnson, E. R. (1982). Profile: Sid Fleischman. *Language Arts, 59,* 754–759.

Fox, Mem   Manning, M., & Manning, G. (March, 1990). Mem Fox: Mem's the word in down under? *Teaching PreK–8, 20,* 29–31; Phelan, C. (1993, May). Talking with Mem Fox, *Book Links,* 29–32.

Freedman, Russell   Dempsey, F. J. (1988). Russell Freedman. *Horn Book Magazine, 64,* 452–456; Freedman, R. (1988). Newbery Medal acceptance. *Horn Book Magazine, 64,* 444–451.

Fritz, Jean   Ammon, R. (1983). Profile: Jean Fritz, *Language Arts, 60,* 365–369; Fritz, J. (1985). Turning history inside out. *Horn Book Magazine, 61,* 29–34; Heins, E. L. (1986). Presentation of the Laura Ingalls Wilder Medal. *Horn Book Magazine, 62,* 430–431.

Gerstein, Mordicai   Yolen, J. (1990). In the artist's studio: Mordicai Gerstein. *The New Advocate, 3,* 25–28.

Giff, Patricia Reilly   Raymond, A. (April, 1987). Patricia Reilly Giff: A writer who believes in reading. *Teaching PreK–8, 17,* 34–37.

Gilson, Jamie   Johnson, R. (1983). Profile: Jamie Gilson. *Language Arts, 60,* 661–667.

Goble, Paul   Stott, J. C. (1984). Profile: Paul Goble. *Language Arts, 61,* 867–873.

Goffstein, M. B.   Marantz, S., & Marantz, K. (1986). M. B. Goffstein: An interview. *Horn Book Magazine, 62,* 688–694; Shannon, G. (1983). Goffstein and friends. *Horn Book Magazine, 59,* 88–95.

Greenfield, Eloise   Kiah, R. B. (1980). Profile: Eloise Greenfield. *Language Arts, 57,* 653–659.

Haley, Gail E.   Haley, G. E. (1990). Of mermaids, myths, and meaning: A sea tale. *The New Advocate, 3,* 1–12.

Hamilton, Virginia   Hamilton, V. (1986). Coretta Scott King Award acceptance. *Horn Book Magazine, 62,* 683–687; Garret J. (1993, January). Virginia Hamilton: 1992 Andersen winner, *Book Links,* 22–25.

Henkes, Kevin   Elliot, I. (January, 1989). Meet Kevin Henkes: Young man on a roll. *Teaching PreK–8, 19,* 43–45.

Hoover, H. M.   Porter, E. J. (1982). Provile: H. M. Hoover. *Language Arts, 59,* 609–613.

Howe, James   Raymond, A. (February, 1987). James Howe: Corn, ham and punster cheese. *Teaching PreK–8, 17,* 32–34.

Hyman, Trina Schart   Hyman, K. (1985). Trina Schart Hyman. *Horn Book Magazine, 61,* 422–425; Hyman, T. S. (1985). Caldecott Medal acceptance. *Horn Book Magazine, 61,* 410–421; Saul, W. (1988). Once-upon-a-time artist in the land of now: An interview with Trina Schart Hyman. *The New Advocate, 1,* 8–17; White,

D. E. (1983). Profile: Trina Schart Hyman. *Language Arts, 60,* 782–792.

Jonas, Ann   Marantz, S., & Marantz, K. (1987). Interview with Ann Jonas. *Horn Book Magazine, 63,* 308–313; Raymond, A. (December, 1987). Ann Jonas: Reflections 1987. *Teaching PreK–8, 18,* 44–46.

Keats, Ezra Jack   Lanes, S. G. (1984). Ezra Jack Keats: In memoriam. *Horn Book Magazine, 60,* 551–558; Pope, M., & Pope, L. (1990). Ezra Jack Keats: A childhood revisited. *The New Advocate, 3,* 13–24.

Kellogg, Steven   Cummings, P. (1992). *Talking with artists* (pp. 54–59). New York: Bradbury Press.

Konigsburg, E. L.   Jones, L. T. (1986). Profile: Elaine Konigsburg. *Language Arts, 63,* 177–184.

Lasky, Kathryn   Lasky, K. (1990). The fiction of history: Or, what did Miss Kitty really do? *The New Advocate, 3,* 157–166.

L'Engle, Madeleine   Raymond, A. (May, 1991). Madeleine L'Engle: Getting the last laugh. *Teaching PreK–8, 21,* 34–36; Samuels, L. A. (1981). Profile: Madeleine L'Engle. *Language Arts, 58,* 704–712.

Lester, Julius   Lester, J. (1988). The storyteller's voice: Reflections on the rewriting of Uncle Remus. *The New Advocate, 1,* 137–142.

Livingston, Myra Cohn   Porter, E. J. (1980). Profile: Myra Cohn Livingston. *Language Arts, 57,* 901–905.

Lobel, Anita   Raymond, A. (November/December, 1989). Anita Lobel: Up from the crossroad. *Teaching PreK–8, 20,* 52–55.

Lobel, Arnold   Lobel, A. (1981). Caldecott Medal acceptance. *Horn Book Magazine, 57,* 400–404; Lobel, A. (1981). Arnold at home. *Horn Book Magazine, 57,* 405–410; White, D. E. (1988). Profile: Arnold Lobel. *Language Arts, 65,* 489–494.

Lowry, Lois   Lowry, L. (1988). Rabble Starkey. *Horn Book Magazine, 64,* 29–31; Lowry, L. (1990). *Number the stars:* Lois Lowry's journey to the Newbery Award. *The Reading Teacher, 44,* 98–101; Raymond, A. (October, 1987). "Anastasia, " and then some. *Teaching PreK–8, 18,* 44–46; An interview with Lois Lowry, 1994 Newbery Medal winner. (1994–1995). *The Reading Teacher, 48,* 308–309.

Macaulay, David   Ammon, R. (1982). Profile: David Macaulay. *Language Arts, 59,* 374–378.

MacLachlan, Patricia   Babbitt, N. (1986). Patricia MacLachlan: The biography. *Horn Book Magazine, 62,* 414–416; Courtney, A. (1985). Profile: Patricia MacLachlan. *Language Arts, 62,* 783–787; MacLachlan, P. (1986). Newbery Medal acceptance. *Horn Book Magazine, 62,* 407–413; MacLachlan, R. (1986). A hypothetical dilemma. *Horn Book Magazine, 62,* 416–419; Raymond, A. (May, 1989). Patricia MacLachlan: An advocate of "Bare boning." *Teaching PreK–8, 19,* 46–48.

Martin, Bill, Jr. Larrick, N. (1982). Profile: Bill Martin, Jr. *Language Arts, 59,* 490–494.

Mayer, Marianna Raymond, A. (January, 1991). Marianna Mayer: Myths, legends, and folklore. *Teaching PreK–8, 21,* 42–44.

McCloskey, Robert Mandel, E. (1991, May). *Make way for ducklings* by Robert McCloskey. *Book Links,* 38–42.

McDermott, Gerald McDermott, G. (1988). Sky father, earth mother: An artist interprets myth. *The New Advocate, 1,* 1–7; White D. E. (1982). Profile: Gerald McDermott. *Language Arts, 59,* 273–279.

McKinley, Robin McKinley, R. (1985). Newbery Medal acceptance. *Horn Book Magazine, 61,* 395–405; Winding, T. (1985). Robin McKinley. *Horn Book Magazine, 61,* 406–409.

McKissack, Patricia Bishop, R. S. (1992). A conversation with Patricia McKissack. *Language Arts, 69,* 69–74.

Merriam, Eve Cox, S. T. (1989). A word or two with Eve Merriam: Talking about poetry. *The New Advocate, 2,* 139–150; Sloan, G. (1981). Profile: Eve Merriam. *Language Arts, 58,* 957–964.

Mikolaycak, Charles White, D. E. (1981). Profile: Charles Mikolaycak. *Language Arts, 58,* 850–857.

Mohr, Nicholasa Zarnowski, M. (1991). An interview with author Nicholasa Mohr. *The Reading Teacher, 45,* 100–107.

Montresor, Beni Raymond, A. (April, 1990). Beni Montresor: Carmen, Cannes and Caldecott. *Teaching PreK–8, 20,* 31–33.

Moser, Barry Moser, B. (1987). Artist at work: Illustrating the classics. *Horn Book Magazine, 63,* 703–709; Moser, B. (1991). Family photographs, gathered fragments. *The New Advocate, 4,* 1–10.

Munsch, Robert Jenkinson, D. (1989). Profile: Robert Munsch, *Language Arts, 66,* 665–675.

Myers, Walter Dean Bishop, R. S. (1990). Profile: Walter Dean Myers. *Language Arts, 67,* 862–866.

Naylor, Phyllis Reynolds Naylor, P. R. (1992). The writing of *Shiloh. The Reading Teacher, 46,* 10–13.

O'Dell, Scott Roop, P. (1984). Profile: Scott O'Dell. *Language Arts, 61,* 750–752.

Parker, Nancy Winslow Raymond, A. (May, 1990). Nancy Winslow Parker: "I knew it would happen." *Teaching PreK–8, 20,* 34–36.

Paterson, Katherine Jones, L. T. (1981). Profile: Katherine Paterson. *Language Arts, 58,* 189–196; Namovic, G. I. (1981). Katherine Paterson. *Horn Book Magazine, 57,* 394–399; Paterson, K. (1981). Newbery Medal acceptance. *Horn Book Magazine, 57,* 385–393.

Pinkney, Jerry Cummings, P. (1992). *Talking with artists* (pp. 60–65). New York: Bradbury Press.

Prelutsky, Jack Raymond, A. (November/December, 1986). Jack Prelutsky . . . Man of many talents. *Teach-* *ing PreK–8, 17,* 38–42; Vardell, S. (1991). An interview with Jack Prelutsky. *The New Advocate, 4,* 101–112.

Provensen, Alice and Martin Provensen, A., & Provensen, M. (1984). Caldecott Medal acceptance. *Horn Book Magazine, 50,* 444–448; Willard, N. (1984). Alice and Martin Provensen. *Horn Book Magazine, 50,* 449–452.

Rice, Eve Raymond, A. (April, 1989). Meet Eve Rice: Author/artist/doctor (doctor?). *Teaching PreK–8, 19,* 40–42.

Rylant, Cynthia Silvey, A. (1987). An interview with Cynthia Rylant. *Horn Book Magazine, 63,* 695–702.

Say, Allen An interview with Allen Say, 1994 Caldecott Award winner. (1994–1995). *The Reading Teacher, 48,* 304–306.

Schoenherr, John Gauch, P. L. (1988). John Schoenherr. *Horn Book Magazine, 64,* 460–463; Schoenherr, J. (1988). Caldecott Medal acceptance. *Horn Book Magazine, 64,* 457–459.

Schwartz, Alvin Vardell, S. M. (1987). Profile: Alvin Schwartz. *Language Arts, 64,* 426–432.

Schwartz, Amy Cummings, P. (1992). *Talking with artists* (pp. 66–71). New York: Bradbury Press.

Scieszka, Jon Raymond, A. (1992, May). Jon Scieszka: Telling the *true story. Teaching PreK–8, 22,* 38–40.

Sendak, Maurice Sendak, M. (1983). Laura Ingalls Wilder Award acceptance. *Horn Book Magazine, 59,* 474–477.

Sewall, Marcia Sewall, M. (1988). *The pilgrims of Plimoth, Horn Book Magazine, 64,* 32–34.

Shulevitz, Uri Raymond, A. (January, 1992). Uri Shulevitz: For children of all ages. *Teaching PreK–8, 21,* 38–40.

Smith, Lane Cummings, P. (1992). *Talking with artists* (pp. 72–77). New York: Bradbury Press.

Soto, Gary Soto, G. (1992). Author for a day: Glitter and rainbows. *The Reading Teacher, 46,* 200–203.

Speare, Elizabeth George Hassler, P. J. (1993, May). The books of Elizabeth George Speare. *Book Links,* 14–20.

Spinelli, Jerry Spinelli, J. (1991). Capturing Maniac Magee. *The Reading Teacher, 45,* 174–177.

Steig, Bill Raymond, A. (August/September, 1991). Jeanne and Bill Steig: It adds up to magic. *Teaching PreK–8, 21,* 52–54.

Steptoe, John Bradley, D. H. (1991). John Steptoe: Retrospective of an imagemaker. *The New Advocate, 4,* 11–24.

Tafuri, Nancy Raymond, A. (January, 1987). Nancy Tafuri . . . Nature, picturebooks, and joy. *Teaching PreK–8, 17,* 34–36.

Taylor, Mildred D. Dussel, S. L. (1981). Profile: Mildred D. Taylor. *Language Arts, 58,* 599–604.

Taylor, Theodore Bagnall, N. (1980). Profile: Theodore Taylor: His models of self-reliance. *Language Arts, 57,* 86–91.

Uchida, Yoshiko Chang, C. E. S. (1984). Profile: Yoshiko Uchida. *Language Arts, 61,* 189–194.

Van Allsburg, Chris Cummings, P. (1992). *Talking with artists* (pp. 78–83). New York: Bradbury Press; Keifer, B. (1987). Profile: Chris Van Allsburg in three dimensions. *Language Arts, 64,* 664–671; Macaulay, D. (1986). Chris Van Allsburg. *Horn Book Magazine, 62,* 424–426; McKee, B. (1986). Van Allsburg: From a different perspective. *Horn Book Magazine, 62,* 556–571; Van Allsburg, C. (1982). Caldecott Medal acceptance. *Horn Book Magazine, 58,* 380–383; Van Allsburg, C. (1986). Caldecott Medal acceptance, *Horn Book Magazine, 62,* 420–424.

Voigt, Cynthia Kauffman, D. (1985). Profile: Cynthia Voigt. *Language Arts, 62,* 876–880; Voigt, C. (1983). Newbery Medal acceptance. *Horn Book Magazine, 59,* 401–409.

Weisner, David Cummings, P. (1992). *Talking with artists* (pp. 84–89). New York: Bradbury Press.

White, E. B. Hopkins, L. B. (1986). Profile: In memoriam: E. B. White. *Language Arts, 63,* 491–494; Newmeyer, P. F. (1985). The creation of E. B. White's *The Trumpet of the Swans:* The manuscripts. *Horn Book Magazine, 61,* 17–28; Newmeyer, P. F. (1987). E. B. White: Aspects of style. *Horn Book Magazine, 63,* 586–591.

Wiesner, David Caroff, S. F., & Moje, E. B. (1992–1993). A conversation with David Wiesner: 1992 Caldecott Medal winner. *The Reading Teacher, 46,* 284–289.

Willard, Nancy Lucas, B. (1982). Nancy Willard. *Horn Book Magazine, 58,* 374–379; Willard, N. (1982). Newbery Medal acceptance. *Horn Book Magazine, 58,* 369–373.

Williams, Vera B. Raymond A. (October, 1988). Vera B. Williams: Postcards and peace vigils. *Teaching PreK–8, 19,* 40–42.

Worth, Valerie Hopkins, L. B. (1991). Profile: Valerie Worth. *Language Arts, 68,* 499–501.

Yolen, Jane White, D. E. (1983). Profile: Jane Yolen. *Language Arts, 60,* 652–660; Yolen, J. (1989). On silent wings: The making of *Owl moon. The New Advocate, 2,* 199–212; Yolen, J. (1991). The route to story. *The New Advocate, 4,* 143–149; Yolen J. (1992). Past time: The writing of the picture book *Encounter. The New Advocate, 5,* 235–239.

Yorinks, Arthur Raymond, A. (November/December, 1991). Arthur Yorinks: Talent in abundance. *Teaching PreK–8, 21,* 51–53.

Zalben, Jane Breskin Yolen, J. (1990). In the artist's studio: Jane Breskin Zalben. *The New Advocate, 3,* 175–178.

Audiovisual Materials Profiling Authors and Illustrators

Alexander, Lloyd "Meet the Newbery author: Lloyd Alexander," American School Publishers (sound filmstrip). (U)

Andersen, Hans Christian "Meet the author: Hans Christian Andersen," American School Publishers (sound filmstrip or video). (M)

Armstrong, William H. "Meet the Newbery author: William H. Armstrong," American School Publishers (sound filmstrip). (M–U)

Babbitt, Natalie "Meet the Newbery author: Natalie Babbitt," American School Publishers (sound filmstrip). (U)

Berenstain, Stan and Jan "Meet Stan and Jan Berenstain," American School Publishers (sound filmstrip). (P)

Blume, Judy "First choice: Authors and books—Judy Blume," Pied Piper (sound filmstrip). (M–U)

Brown, Marc "Meet Marc Brown," American School Publishers (video). (P–M)

Byars, Betsy "Meet the Newbery author: Betsy Byars," American School Publishers (sound filmstrip). (M–U)

Carle, Eric "Eric Carle: Picture writer," Philomel (video). (P–M)

Cherry, Lynne "Get to know Lynne Cherry," Harcourt Brace (video). (M)

Cleary, Beverly "First choice: Authors and books—Beverly Cleary," Pied Piper (sound filmstrip). (M); "Meet the Newbery author: Beverly Cleary," American School Publishers (sound filmstrip). (M)

Collier, James Lincoln and Christopher "Meet the Newbery authors: James Lincoln Collier and Christopher Collier," American School Publishers (sound filmstrip). (U)

Cooper, Susan "Meet the Newbery author: Susan Cooper," American School Publishers (sound filmstrip). (U)

Crews, Donald "Trumpet video visits Donald Crews," Trumpet Book Club (video). (P–M)

Dahl, Roald "The author's eye: Roald Dahl," American School Publishers (kit with video). (M–U)

Fleischman, Sid "First choice: Authors and books—Sid Fleischman," Pied Piper (sound filmstrip). (M–U)

Fritz, Jean "Homesick: My own story," American School Publishers (sound filmstrip). (M–U)

George, Jean Craighead "Meet the Newbery author: Jean Craighead George," American School Publishers (sound filmstrip). (U)

Giovanni, Nikki "First choice: Poets and poetry—Nikki Giovanni," Pied Piper (sound filmstrip). (M–U)

Greene, Bette "Meet the Newbery author: Bette Greene," American School Publishers (sound filmstrip). (M–U)

Haley, Gail E.   "Tracing a legend: The story of the green man by Gail E. Haley," Weston Woods (sound filmstrip). (M); "Creating Jack and the bean tree: Tradition and technique," Weston Woods (sound filmstrip). (M)

Hamilton, Virginia   "First choice: Authors and books—Virginia Hamilton," Pied Piper (sound filmstrip). (U); "Meet the Newbery author: Virginia Hamilton," American School Publishers (sound filmstrip). (U)

Henry, Marguerite   "First choice: Authors and books—Marguerite Henry," Pied Piper (sound filmstrip). (M–U); "Meet the Newbery author: Marguerite Henry," American School Publishers (sound filmstrip). (M)

Highwater, Jamake   "Meet the Newbery author: Jamake Highwater," American School Publishers (sound filmstrip). (M–U)

Keats, Ezra Jack   "Ezra Jack Keats," Weston Woods (film). (P)

Kellogg, Steven   "How a picture book is made," Weston Woods (video). (P–M); "Trumpet video visits Steven Kellogg," Trumpet Book Club (video). (P–M)

Konigsburg, E. L.   "First choice: Authors and books—E. L. Konigsburg," Pied Piper (sound filmstrip). (M–U)

Kuskin, Karla   "First choice: Poets and poetry—Karla Kuskin," Pied Piper (sound filmstrip). (M–U); "Poetry explained by Karla Kuskin," Weston Woods (sound filmstrip). (M–U)

L'Engle, Madeleine   "Meet the Newbery author: Madeleine L'Engle," American School Publishers (sound filmstrip). (U)

Livingston, Myra Cohn   "First choice: Poets and poetry—Myra Cohn Livingston," Pied Piper (sound filmstrip). (M–U)

Lobel, Arnold   "Meet the Newbery author: Arnold Lobel," American School Publishers (sound filmstrip). (P–M)

Macaulay, David   "David Macaulay in his studio," Houghton Mifflin (video). (M–U)

McCloskey, Robert   "Robert McCloskey," Weston Woods (film). (P–M)

McCord, David   "First choice: Poets and poetry—David McCord," Pied Piper (sound filmstrip). (M–U)

McDermott, Gerald   "Evolution of a graphic concept: The stonecutter," Weston Woods (sound filmstrip). (P–M)

Merriam, Eve   "First choice: Poets and poetry—Eve Merriam," Pied Piper (sound filmstrip). (M–U)

Milne, A. A.   "Meet the author: A. A. Milne (and Pooh)," American School Publishers (sound filmstrip or video). (P)

Most, B.   "Get to know Bernard Most," Harcourt Brace (video). (P–M)

O'Dell, Scott   "Meet the Newbery author: Scott O'Dell," American School Publishers (sound filmstrip). (U); "A visit with Scott O'Dell," Houghton Mifflin (video). (U)

Paterson, Katherine   "The author's eye: Katherine Paterson," American School Publishers (kit with video). (M–U); "Meet the Newbery author: Katherine Paterson," American School Publishers (sound filmstrip). (M–U)

Paulsen, Gary   "Trumpet video visits Gary Paulsen," Trumpet Book Club (video). (U)

Peet, Bill   "Bill Peet in his studio," Houghton Mifflin (video). (M)

Pinkney, Jerry   "Meet the Caldecott illustrator: Jerry Pinkney," American School Publishers (video). (P–M)

Potter, Beatrix   "Beatrix Potter had a pet named Peter," American School Publishers (sound filmstrip or video). (P)

Rylant, Cynthia   "Meet the Newbery author: Cynthia Rylant," American School Publishers (sound filmstrip or video). (M–U); "Meet the picture book author: Cynthia Rylant," American School Publishers (video). (P–M)

Sendak, Maurice   "Sendak," Weston Woods (film). (P–M)

Seuss, Dr.   "Who's Dr. Seuss?: Meet Ted Geisel," American School Publishers (sound filmstrip). (P–M)

Singer, Issac Bashevis   "Meet the Newbery author: Isaac Bashevis Singer," American School Publishers (sound filmstrip). (U)

Sobol, Donald J.   "The case of the Model-A Ford and the man in the snorkel under the hood: Donald J. Sobol," American School Publishers (sound filmstrip). (M)

White, E. B.   "Meet the Newbery author: E. B. White," American School Publishers (sound filmstrip). (M–U)

Wilder, Laura Ingalls   "Meet the Newbery author: Laura Ingalls Wilder," American School Publishers (sound filmstrip). (M–U)

Willard, Nancy   "Meet the Newbery author: Nancy Willard," American School Publishers (sound filmstrip). (M–U)

Yep, Laurence   "Meet the Newbery author: Laurence Yep," American School Publishers (sound filmstrip). (U)

Zolotow, Charlotte   "Charlotte Zolotow: The grower," American School Publishers (sound filmstrip). (P–M)

Addresses for Audiovisual Manufacturers

American School
  Publishers
P.O. Box 408
Hightstown, NJ 08520

Houghton Mifflin
2 Park Street
Boston, MA 02108

Pied Piper
P.O. Box 320
Verdugo City, CA 91046

Trumpet Book Club
P.O. Box 604
Holmes, PA 19043

Weston Woods
Weston, CT 06883

AUTHOR AND TITLE INDEX

SUBJECT INDEX